THE RULING ELITE

THE RULING ELITE

THE ZIONIST SEIZURE OF WORLD POWER

Deanna Spingola

Order this book online at www.trafford.com
or email orders@trafford.com

Most Trafford titles are also available at major online book retailers.

Printed in the United States of America.

ISBN: 978-1-4669-1857-3 (sc)
ISBN: 978-1-4669-1858-0 (hc)
ISBN: 978-1-4669-1859-7 (e)

Library of Congress Control Number: 2012904431

Trafford rev. 06/08/2012

Trafford
PUBLISHING® www.trafford.com

North America & international
toll-free: 1 888 232 4444 (USA & Canada)
phone: 250 383 6864 ♦ fax: 812 355 4082

CONTENTS

INTRODUCTION

When I was a student, my favorite history teacher reiterated that the reason we study history is to avoid the mistakes that people have collectively made in the past. This, at the time, made logical sense. However, organizations like the American Historical Association, either directly or indirectly, influence most historians or history teachers and what they believe. Years ago, the tax-exempt Rockefeller Foundation resolved to regulate domestic education, while the Carnegie Foundation would dominate international education. Their first objective was to alter the way that instructors teach history. The Guggenheim Foundation, like the Rhodes scholarship program, granted fellowships, agreeing to fund twenty United States history students who were seeking doctoral degrees. These students, after indoctrination, formed the nucleus of the American Historical Association, which was founded by Andrew D. White, a member of the Order of Skull and Bones—(S&B) also known as the Brotherhood of Death. Such an organization manufactures a history commiserate with government and corporate objectives while concealing the hideous details of some of the most horrendous historical events.

Therefore, individuals need to evaluate what they believe about every historical event, consider where they obtained that information, and compare it to what is occurring now. Accurate history is prologue, whereas false history legitimizes the activities that many government officials are perpetrating against the citizens of their nations. Do those citizens, under deceptive circumstances, enjoy freedom, or are their governments incrementally imposing tyranny at home while engaging in terrorism abroad? If governments can lie about or conceal their past, then they can certainly engage in deception regarding contemporary circumstances.

Using the concept of herd mentality in government-provided public schools as mandated by Karl Marx's *Communist Manifesto*, teachers authoritatively instruct students on what to believe. They do not encourage or teach critical-thinking skills, but rather disseminate "facts" that correspond to the needs of corporations and federal guidelines to an obedience-trained group of mostly non-questioning students. High-priced education beyond taxpayer-funded government schools is only available to the wealthier members of society. They are those who, either knowledgeable or functioning as useless idiots, are willing to implement the corporate or government program. Others, without adequate funds, in order to obtain a piece of paper to qualify for a job, willingly burden themselves with massive debt they may be unable to pay after graduation in a deliberate decreasing marketplace.

Meanwhile, the American government, complicit with the well-connected corporations, since the so-called Civil War, the first modern example of a total war, with the slaughter of unarmed civilians, continues to wage war and destruction. Lincoln's revolutionary war, supported by Marx and Engels, caused the deaths of at least 618,222 and perhaps as many as 700,000 people, including about 50,000 Confederate civilians. Soldiers who were fighting, dying and killing during that war were in training for future wars. If Americans could kill fellow noncombatant citizens, then they would use force against foreign citizens on behalf of the government to coerce submission and change.

That total war was a foreshadowing of the devastating global warfare that followed with the Spanish American War, two World Wars, Korea, Vietnam, the First Gulf War, and the current wars in the Middle East. These wars do not include the bombings in the Baltic and elsewhere or the CIA's covert warfare wherein millions of people died. In the First World War, soldiers killed 9,911,000 people in action and wounded 21,219,500 people, while 7,750,000 people were missing in action for a total of 38,880,500. In the Second World War, there were over 24,000,000 military deaths and 49,000,000 civilian deaths, totaling 73,000,000 deaths, not including the number of wounded or missing. That is 82,911,000 deaths in two world wars, not including the 28,965,500 wounded or missing from World War I.

In the book, I raise the issue of the Holocaust and the fact that prominent Jews living in America before and during World War I introduced and advanced the idea that 6,000,000 Jews living in Europe were especially vulnerable. That number is incredibly significant, as it is the number of Jews who, according to their religious dogma, must "vanish" before the Jews may "return" to Palestine. If 6,000,000 Jews did perish during World War I or even during World War II, how does that warrant taxpayer funded museums in America? As early as World War I, an influential, predominantly Jewish faction controlled the majority of the press and exercised increasing political power in Washington. That faction has promoted United States participation in constant warfare.

Currently, as part of the formal educational program of the Congress-initiated United States Holocaust Memorial Museum, teachers in public schools teach susceptible students about these alleged events at the exclusion of other equally devastating occurrences, including America's ethnic cleansing of its indigenous population. Meanwhile, in those same government schools, teachers, using National Education Association-approved textbooks, conceal America's horrific warfare history, both overt and covert, over several decades in numerous countries. Obviously, the government must hide such facts to justify and even glorify further wars in order to successfully recruit the youth who will fight and die in them.

Several commonalities exist between genocide and total war—1) total war functions as a catalyst for premeditated genocide; 2) genocide and total war target innocent civilians for massacre; 3) nations instigate total war under false pretenses; 4) both are hostile to all humanitarian and Christian principle; and 5) officials appeal to our emotions to initiate both activities, using deceptive information based on scientific or technological factors.[1]

The civilian deaths during World War II were almost double the military deaths, which constitutes a deliberate mass genocide. Anglo—American alliances, with the support of international bankers, instigated these wars for imperialistic dominance. World War I, though planned well in advance, seemingly erupted over the

---

[1]   Eric Markusen and David Kopf, The Holocaust and Strategic Bombing: Genocide and Total War in the Twentieth Century, Westview Press, Boulder, Colorado, 1995, p. 55

deaths of two people in Sarajevo with the United States ultimately entering the war belatedly, over the Lusitania incident.

Carl von Clausewitz, in his book *On War,* evaluated the influences necessary for integrating a nation of diverse ethnicities and mobilizing those different factions into a cohesive fierce fighting machine.[2] Sun Tzu, the Chinese military strategist, in his book entitled *The Art of War,* advocated winning through logistical strategy rather than actually fighting and killing the enemy, which generates "bitterness and animosity."[3] Even in von Clausewitz's theory of absolute war, he envisioned the slaughter confined to a battlefield. Yet, today, with technology, the actualization of total war amounts to indiscriminate genocide.[4]

The homes, farms, workplaces, essential infrastructure, villages, and cities of today have replaced the battlefields of yesteryear. Civilians, ostensibly unavoidable collateral damage, now constitute a military target, armed or not—any age, any gender. The key characteristics of total war are an appalling number of battle casualties and the deliberate extermination of civilians. Military men have implemented the successful ideas, phrases, and strategies of past military theorists into modern military situations. The United States has deceptively described its intervention in Southeast Asia as a "limited war." However, it probably did not feel limited to the tens of thousands of unfortunate victims of indiscriminate bombing, napalm and the after effects of Agent Orange.[5]

The 1961 US Air force ROTC manual, *Fundamentals of Aerospace Weapons Systems,* formalized a military target as, "any person,

2   Biographical dictionary of literary influences By John Powell, Derek W. Blakeley, Greenwood Publishing Group, Westport, Connecticut, 2001, pp. 92-93
3   Walter S. Zapotoczny, Sun Tzu Compared to Clausewitz http://www. wzaponline.com/SunTzuClausewitz.pdf as of May 2012
4   On War By Carl von Clausewitz, Anatol Rapoport, Penguin Books, London, England, 1968, p. 62
5   Carl von Clausewitz, On War, Anatol Rapoport, Penguin Books, London, England, 1968, pp. 76-77

thing, idea, entity, or location selected for destruction, inactivation, or rendering nonusable with weapons which will reduce or destroy the will or ability of the enemy to resist." Political leaders determine the inevitable clashes between opposing states "by the imposition of the will of one state upon that of another."[6]

An increased scale of warfare requires the commitment of the economic resources of any warring nation. Temporarily relinquishing industrial production to government needs sets a precedent for institutionalizing communism in a country. The government assuming control over the means of production and distribution for the collective benefit of the population—those who support or fight in a war—is too significant to dismiss. It is most problematic when that government abandons that temporary requirement and adopts a permanent militarization mentality as a necessity, and when a large percentage of the population benefits from war production, military participation, or dependence on a nearby military base for business. War has the capacity to connect people emotionally, even those who adamantly claim to be peace-loving citizens. Antiwar rhetoric immediately draws criticism—"patriots" characterize dissidents as anti-American or unpatriotic.

Total-war ideologically requires the widespread use of propaganda to maintain soldier morale and civilian support through the vilification of the enemy. This denigration removes all restraint—no weapon is too atrocious, and the media does not dismiss anyone as too young or too old to kill. An offensive nation is unconstrained in their dissemination of Agent Orange, smallpox-contaminated blankets, depleted uranium, or other biological agents, as well as the indiscriminate use of cluster bombs, atom bombs, or bullets fired when one is sufficiently close to the embattled enemy to see his or her look of desperation.

Countries employ total war when the objective is to remove an enemy government or exterminate the people as a viable nation. Nations that engage in total warfare abandon their civility as they gradually adopt a totalitarian order at home. Citizens, who rarely, if

---

[6]   Ibid. 62-63

ever, clamor for war, distort the distinction between the morality of a tyrannical dictatorship and a democracy when they acquiesce to the questionable demands of their government with regard to alleged enemies. The essential component for executing total warfare is the excessive concentration of government power.[7]

The winners sanction the plunder of land and resources on behalf of multinational corporations and international banks. Nations wage total warfare to impose policy, eliminate local leaders who are unwilling to forfeit the country's resources, and exterminate the population. Governments initiate total warfare and accomplish their objectives using false pretenses to silence potential dissent from the taxpayers—the people who pay in money and blood. During the so-called peace process, which lawyers and bankers direct, the victorious rearrange borders, inevitably combining unrelated, dissimilar, divergent populations that consistently create havoc and dissension that requires military occupation.

Warfare—the ethnic cleansing of indigenous populations—eliminates vast amounts of people of competitive cultures. It creates famine due to the cessation of transportation and agricultural production. The victorious nations are those who have superior weaponry purchased by the unwitting taxpayers from the banker-controlled corporations. The lawyers, during the peace process, reward the victorious nations with spoils, reparations payments, and the right to occupy the vanquished nation with military bases and troops. Wars cause unnecessary long-term resentment among populations.

Warfare—repeatedly the results of false-flag events—does not always include shock-and-awe bombing raids, but can take the form of retributive sanctions prohibiting access to basic essentials. It is just as deadly over time, particularly for the most vulnerable—women, children and the elderly. Subtle assaults, perpetrated against the citizens of a nation by their own government and complicit profit-seeking corporations, include biological, environmental, medicinal,

7   Eric Markusen and David Kopf, The Holocaust and Strategic Bombing: Genocide and Total War in the Twentieth Century, Westview Press, Boulder, Colorado, 1995, pp. 35-40

and/or corporate sabotage, during which people perish while survivors naively blame natural occurrences—as such a catastrophic event frequently leaves no viable evidence pointing to a perpetrator, except for poor old Mother Nature. With this bloody, continuing quest, one must question who or what is behind it and what motivates such death and destruction.

I wish to thank my family and friends who supported me in this effort. Thanks to David Dees for his fabulous cover artwork. The politicians on the cover are, clockwise from Winston Churchill, Vladimir Lenin, Herbert Hoover, Arthur J. Balfour, Louis D. Brandeis, Woodrow Wilson, and Bernard Baruch. I have created a timeline connecting the most significant dates and events. One may view this timeline at www.spingola.com/timeline.html

SECTION 1

ZIONISM

The Non-Semitic Khazars

Many Eastern European Jews are not Semitic and have no genetic connection to Palestine or to Abraham. Numerous revisionist studies (a revised opinion because of further investigation) provide adequate evidence in *The Thirteenth Tribe* by Arthur Koestler, *The Ashkenazic Jews: A Slavo-Turkic People in Search of a Jewish Identity* by Paul Wexler, *The Jews of Khazaria* by Kevin A. Brook, and more recently, *The Invention of the Jewish People* by Shlomo Sand. Brook presents a logical online essay regarding the origination of the Eastern European Jews, including scholarly opinions from historians, in favor of the Khazar theory.[8] It is not about anti-Semitism, an accusatory political weapon utilized to silence unwanted queries and opposition to detrimental Zionist policies. Truth can withstand the most intense scrutiny and does not fear investigation but rather invites exploration. Governments and others habitually employ suppression, under the guise of anti-Semitism accusations, to silence truth and conceal mass criminality.

People use the term *anti-Semite* to silence dissent against US government policies as they relate to Israel. Accordingly, criticism of Israeli policies against the Palestinians becomes an attack on all Jews. Shulamit Aloni, minister of Education (1992-1993) and peace activist, says that calling people dissidents is a defamation tactic used to silence all criticism. If Europeans criticize Israeli policies, people remind them of the Holocaust. If people oppose Israeli policies toward the Palestinians, then people accuse them of anti-Semitism.

---

[8]   Are Russian Jews Descended from the Khazars? By Kevin Alan Brook, http://www.khazaria.com/khazar-diaspora.html as of May 2012

1

According to Aloni, Jews habitually remind others of their suffering to justify what they are doing to the Palestinians.[9]

The Khazars, classified by anthropologists as Turco-Finns, are not descendants of Judah, one of the twelve sons of Israel, but were warlike, violent people who originated in Asia, from where other nations drove them out. In the first century, using the route between the north end of the Caspian Sea and the south end of the Ural Mountains, they invaded several agricultural nations in Eastern Europe and occupied about one million square miles until about the seventh century. They worshipped the phallic symbol and engaged in sexual excess, until King Bulan, because of their moral degeneracy, abolished their idolatry and compelled them to adopt one of the three monotheistic religions, Islam, Christianity, or Talmudism (Judaism). They chose the latter as their new state religion. The king then imported rabbis from Babylon, who opened synagogues and instructed four thousand feudal nobles.[10]

The converted Khazars remained in Khazaria, and their descendants embraced Judaism, a theocratic religion where leaders functioned as civil administrators. The Talmud, with civil and religious tenets, functioned as a behavior manual in every aspect of their lives. The 1954 Jewish Encyclopedia, Volume IV, states, "Chazars: A people of Turkish origin whose life and history are interwoven with the very beginnings of the history of the Jews of Russia . . . driven on by the nomadic tribes of the steppes and by their own desire for plunder and revenge . . . In the second half of the sixth century, the Chazars moved westward . . . The kingdom of the Chazars was firmly established in most of south Russia long before the foundations of the Russian monarchy (855) . . . At this time the kingdom of the Chazars stood at the height of its power and was constantly at war . . . At the end of the eighth century . . . the king of the Chazars and his grandees,

---

9   "It's a Trick, We Always Use It." (calling people "anti-Semitic"), http://www. youtube.com/watch?v=jUGVPBO9_cA as of May 2012

10   Benjamin H. Freedman, The Truth about Khazars, a letter written to Dr. David Goldstein, 960 Park Avenue, New York City, October 10, 1954, pp. 30-34

together with a large number of his heathen people, embraced the Jewish religion."[11]

By 1016, the Slavs vanquished the Khazars and seized a major portion of their land, which became Poland, Lithuania, the Grand Duchy of Moscow, and other Slavic states. Most of the Khazars remained while others relocated to Kiev and other areas of Russia. The Khazars went northwest into Lithuanian, Polish territory, Russia, and Ukraine and became broadly dispersed in Western Russia. The people in Kiev did not want additional Jews in their territory, while the rulers of the Grand Duchy of Moscow pursued and maintained policies to restrict and exclude them from certain areas and prohibited Jewish merchants from traveling within Russia.[12]

They constructed thousands of synagogues, and the rabbis and their successors maintained absolute domination of the political, social, and religious thinking of their people. The multivolume Babylonian Talmud was the main reason the Khazars resisted Russian attempts to end separatism, a factor that still dictates their separatism elsewhere. The Babylonian Talmud, different from the Jerusalem or Palestine Talmud contains centuries of fundamental religious and cultural dogma. While many Jews in Mesopotamia assimilated, the Khazars refused to surrender their identity through Russianization or by becoming Christian. The rabbis instituted the ghettoization of the people, not the Russians or other host countries.[13]

The majority of the ethnic Jews in modern-day Iraq, parts of Syria, Turkey, and southwestern Iran, long ago embraced Islam, making many of today's Muslims and Christian Arabs ethnic Jews. The Khazars adamantly rejected assimilation in order to retain their unique identity. The rabbis realized that they would lose their power over their people if they accepted other authorities. They dictated fundamental traditions, daily practices, rules, and beliefs about God, man, and the universe, what to wear, what to eat or not eat, how

---

[11]   Ibid. 30-34
[12]   John Beaty, The Iron Curtain Over America, Chestnut Mountain Book, Barboursville, Virginia, 1968, pp. 18-19
[13]   Ibid. 19-20

to conduct business, who one may marry, and how to observe the holidays and Sabbaths. They refer to these practices as halakhah. The Khazars lived under the Babylonian Talmudic law as a population living in Russia—a state within a state. After the fall of Kiev in 1240, Moscow became the capital. The Khazars, through time, hated the Russians, whose country they lived in, and became known as Russian Jews.[14]

In 1613, Russian nobles, to establish a durable government, elected Mikhail Romanov as their czar. The Romanovs ruled through the seventeenth and eighteenth centuries and retained their attitude toward the Khazars. Peter the Great (1682-1725) referred to them as "rogues and cheats." The Romanov dynasty (1613-1917), included Catherine the Great's grandson, Alexander I (1801-1825), his brother, Nicholas I (1825-1855), his son Alexander II (1855-1881), his son Alexander III (1881-1894), and his son, Nicholas II (1894-1917) who the Bolsheviks, predominantly Jewish, would murder, along with his family, on July 17, 1918, after they seized power in Russia.[15]

Many Khazars of Russia moved into Germany, the home of a Jewish philosopher, Moses Mendelssohn (1729-1786), who appealed to many non-Jews as well as Jews. He believed that the "Jews had erected about themselves a mental ghetto to balance the physical ghetto around them." His goal was to guide the Jews "out of this mental ghetto into the wide world of general culture—without, however, doing harm to their culture." People refer to this movement as *Haskalah*, or *enlightenment*. He encouraged the Jews in Germany to learn the language instead of using an altered form of the vernacular. He translated the *Torah, Genesis, Exodus, Leviticus, Numbers,* and *Deuteronomy,* into German.[16]

In Russia, Isaac B. Levinsohn, an advocate of Mendelssohn's views, along with Abraham Harkavy, researched Jewish history and their settlement in Russia and discovered that they were not from Germany,

[14]   Ibid, 19-20
[15]   Ibid, 19-20
[16]   John Beaty, The Iron Curtain Over America, Chestnut Mountain Book, Barboursville, Virginia, 1968, pp. 23-24

as previously believed, but from the banks of the Volga. During the nineteenth century, czars vacillated on their attitudes regarding the Jewish "state within a state." Nicholas I was less lenient than Alexander I toward the Jews, but showed interest in Levinshohn's Haskalah movement, because he saw it as a way of eradicating Jewish separatism. However, Jews in Germany, including Moses Hess, opposed the movement, as many did in Russia, and evolved into radical nationalists. Nicholas I appointed Dr. Max Lilienthal to educate the Jews, with the opening of hundreds of schools to help eradicate their fanaticism and superstitions. Their leaders opposed it, because it would diminish the Talmud's authority and correct morals, and the rabbis would lose their control. The Jews, who viewed Lilienthal as a "traitor and informer," opposed the government intrusion into their spiritual lives. In 1845, he had second thoughts about the project, thus ending the Haskalah movement and Russia's efforts to defeat the Khazars' separatism.[17]

There have always been Jews in Jerusalem, Safed, Nablus, and Hebron. Individual immigration to the area has never ceased. Thousands of Jews had settled peacefully and assimilated in Palestine before others ever viewed the area as an exclusive, designated Jewish homeland.[18] Professor Heinrich Graetz, a Jewish historian, writes in his *History of the Jews* that, when Jews in other countries heard a rumor about the Jews in Khazaria, they believed them to be the "lost ten tribes," possibly the foundation for the belief that Palestine was the homeland of these converted Khazars. In 1948, Benjamin H. Freedman addressed a large audience at the Pentagon, including high ranking army and military intelligence officers regarding the developing situation in the Middle East. He explained the origin of the Khazars so they would have a comprehensive understanding and be able to evaluate the events that had occurred since 1917, starting with the Bolsheviks in Russia and ultimately culminating in Palestine.[19]

[17]   Ibid, 23-24
[18]   Walter Laqueur, A History of Zionism, From the French Revolution to the Establishment of the State of Israel, MJF Books, New York, 1972, p. 40
[19]   Benjamin H. Freedman, The Truth about Khazars, a letter written to Dr. David Goldstein, 960 Park Avenue, New York City, October 10, 1954, pp. 30-34

British Zionism, the Genesis of the Movement

For centuries, the Christian world opposed any kind of Jewish settlement in the Holy Land, as it would certainly place the control of the traditional Christian holy sites under Jewish jurisdiction. With the establishment of the enlightenment philosophy, Napoleon Bonaparte, a freemason (initiated into the Army Philadelphe Lodge in 1798), while camped near Acre, announced in a written proclamation to the Jews, dated April 20, 1799, that he was going to restore Palestine to them.[20] He ascended the throne as Emperor of France (1804-1815).

On October 6, 1806, the Assembly of Notables, a group of people who consulted with the French Emperor on state matters, issued a proclamation to Europe's Jewish communities, inviting them to send delegates to the Sanhedrin, scheduled for October 20 in Paris. However, the meeting did not take place until February 9, 1807, when a hundred rabbis and twenty-five laypeople from various parts of Europe met to authorize, on behalf of world Jewry, any compact made with Napoleon or presumably other government leaders who would support them. Joseph David Sinzheim, the chief rabbi of Strasbourg and a prominent member of the Assembly of Notables, presided at the meeting. Once assembled, like the ancient Sanhedrin, it became "a legal assembly vested with power of passing ordinances in order to promote the welfare of Israel." Despite the diaspora, the Sanhedrin exercises authority over Jews worldwide. The Jewish Sanhedrin functions today, with judges, financiers, intellectuals, orators, and politicians, who hold meetings where they devise essential requirements for the "welfare of Israel."[21]

In 1798, for economic advancement, Nathan M. Rothschild, son of the Rothschild banking family living in Frankfurt, relocated to Manchester, England, where he soon operated a large textile and

---

[20]   Stephen Sizer, Christian Zionism and the Roadmap to Armageddon, InterVarsity Press, Downers Grove, Illinois, 2005, pp. 68-69

[21]   Isidore Singer and Cyrus Adler, The Jewish Encyclopedia, a Descriptive Record of the History, Religion, Literature, and Customs of the Jewish People from the Earliest Times to the Present Day, Funk and Wagnalls Company, England, 1905, pp. 46-47

export firm. At the same time, Joseph Frey, an Orthodox Polish Jew and a student of Johannes Jänicke of the Berlin Missionary Society (BMS), had converted to Christianity by receiving baptism in New Brandenburg on May 8, 1798. Frey moved to England in 1801.

Rothschild also moved to London, where he became a freemason in the Lodge of Emulation on October 4, 1802.[22] In 1805, Frey created the Missionary Society and asked to be a missionary to the Jews.[23] He claimed that Christianity fulfilled the prophecies recorded in the Old and New Testaments. The local synagogues prohibited the activities of their former religionists, and Frey only baptized three Jews in 1806. The synagogue issued another prohibition in 1807, and thereafter, about a dozen Jewish children stopped attending the nondenominational Free School that the missionaries had opened. By August 17, 1808, Rothschild had become a financial advisor to the British government, and, in 1811, he sold his Manchester textile concerns. The Rothschilds frequently fund organizations, even "Christian" groups, and maintain their typical anonymity behind a non-Jew founder.

In 1809, Frey organized the London Society for Promoting Christianity among the Jews, which he later shortened to the Jews Society. This new, apparently well-financed organization, possibly supported by Rothschild funds, advocated the concept of Jewish settlement in Palestine. The Jews in England, many of whom had arrived there from Holland, had relative freedom beginning in the eighteenth century. The Society focused its efforts primarily on the Ashkenazim (Jews of German or Eastern European origin) while largely ignoring the Sephardim (Jews of Spanish or Portuguese origin), many of whom readily embraced Christianity. The Ashkenazi Jews resisted the

---

[22] William R. Denslow, 10,000 Famous Freemasons, Volume 4, Q-Z, Foreword by Harry S. Truman, Past Master, Missouri Lodge of Research, Macoy Publishing & Masonic Supply Co., Inc., Richmond, Virginia, 1957, p. 74; See also Two Faces of Freemasonry by John Daniel, Day Publishing, Longview, Texas, 2007, p. 131

[23] Robert Michael Smith, The London Jews' Society and Patterns of Jewish Conversion in England, 1801-1859, Jewish Social Studies, Indiana University Press, Volume 43, No. 3-4, Summer—Autumn, 1981, pp. 275-289

Society's efforts. Others energetically advanced the new evangelical movement, which quickly spread to America.[24]

The Jews Society became the Church's Ministry among Jewish People (CMJ). The society, with as many as 250 missionaries, began proselytizing to the Jews in the East End of London, and soon spread to Europe, South America, Africa, and Palestine. The CMJ promoted the opinion that Jewish people should have their own independent state in the Holy Land, long before certain Jews established the Zionist Movement.

Even before the fatal Battle of Waterloo on June 18, 1815, several individuals in Britain had already adopted Napoleon's idea of "restoring" Palestine to the Jews.[25] Rothschild allegedly provided the funds that guaranteed the victory at Waterloo. He had established a courier service that allowed the brothers to have daily communication, which gave them major advantages over their competitors.[26] Napoleon lost the war and had to rescind his promise to restore the Jews to Palestine. Thereafter, apparently with a change of heart, he tried to eliminate Jacobinism, a belief in a nationally uniform and centralized government, in France and its plan for world government and acquired other benefactors. Rothschild, by 1815, opposed him and funded the opposition.

There were other conversionist charitable organizations including the National School Society charity schools of the Established Church, the Episcopal Jews' Chapel (1813) and the school at Palestine Place, in Bethnal Green.[27] Lewis Way was the most prominent exponent of nineteenth century Restorationism and Christian Zionism. He rescued the Jews Society from a £20,000 debt. After the Napoleonic Wars,

24   Robert Michael Smith, The London Jews' Society and Patterns of Jewish Conversion in England, 1801-1859, Jewish Social Studies, Indiana University Press, Volume 43, No. 3-4, Summer—Autumn, 1981, pp. 275-289
25   Ibid, 275-289
26   Denise Sivester-Carr, The Rise of Rothschild, History Today, Volume: 48, Issue: 3, March 1998, p. 33+
27   David S. Katz, The Jews in the History of England, 1485 to 1850, Oxford University Press, New York, 1996, pp. 370-371

he advocated Jewish emancipation and their relocation to Palestine. He promoted his idea to European political leaders and attempted to gain their support for a Jewish homeland. Czar Alexander I of Russia agreed with him.[28]

In 1817, Way persuaded the czar to issue two documents—one that guaranteed protection to all baptized Jews and one that gave them land they could farm. Further, Way wrote *Mémoires sur l'Etat des Israélites Dédiés et Présentés à Leurs Majestés Impériales et Royales, Réunies au Congrès d' Aix-la-Chapelle* (1819), in which he stressed the Messianic significance of the Jews. Way asserted their importance to scriptural promises and the eventual realization of prophecy. He pleaded for their emancipation in Europe. In October 1818, Way presented his ideas to the Congress of Aix-la-Chapelle and to the czar, who gave the documents to his representatives, including Ioannis Kapodistrias; but nothing ever came of it.

British banker Henry Drummond Jr., a member of Parliament (1810), was reputedly Mayer Amschel Rothschild's connection through Drummond's father, Henry Sr., a Rothschild colleague and fabric contractor who made money selling military uniforms and financing the rental of Hessian soldiers for the Revolutionary War through Frederick II. Drummond bankers were then working with the British Treasury to oversee payments to British soldiers in America. Drummond, possibly a Rosicrucian, which was akin to freemasonry, had Zionist interests.

Between 1821 and 1823, Drummond sent Bavarian-born Joseph Wolff, the son of a rabbi and a Christian convert, to Jerusalem. In 1822, the Rothschilds unveiled the Star of David, the hexagram symbol of Zionism, now the flag of the Israeli State, as their family emblem.[29] There is no evidence in the Bible that shows any connection between this ancient occult image and King David. However, King Solomon, when he later adopted pagan gods and occult practices, used the

---

[28] Stephen Sizer, Christian Zionism and the Roadmap to Armageddon, InterVarsity Press, Downers Grove, Illinois, 2005, p. 37

[29] Simon Downing, World Empire and the Return of Jesus Christ, Xulon Press, 2011, p. 154

image. Wolff prophesied that Jesus would return to Jerusalem in 1847 in conjunction with the beginning of the millennium and the restoration of Israel.

In 1823, as recommended by Wolff, the Jews Society recruited John Nicolayson and sent him to Berlin for training before sending him to Jerusalem to work with George Dalton, a missionary to the Jews, who unexpectedly died on January 25, 1826, just before Nicolayson arrived.[30] Some people suspect that foul play was involved in Dalton's death so that Nicolayson could more effectively manage the Jews Society operations in Jerusalem. The Society moved Nicolayson to Jerusalem permanently, where he took over its operations. Assisted by Lord Shaftesbury, Anthony A. Cooper, the Society constructed Christ Church, completed in 1849, in Old Jerusalem, on land purchased by Nicolayson a short distance from the temple site. It is the Middle East's oldest Protestant church. Although Nicolayson stayed in Palestine to manage the resettlement of the Jews, the sultan would not allow it, and the Zionist plan collapsed.

Pastor Johannes Jänicke of the Berlin Missionary Society, who had trained Frey, also trained Nicolayson. This suggests that Pastor Jänicke was a principle in the Illuminati operations in Germany to train men in pseudo-Christianity. It is particularly significant that Frey supposedly converted to Christianity the same year that Rothschild relocated to England as directed by his father. While many people claim that Jews currently exploit Christian Zionists to further Zionism, its beginnings started much earlier.

In 1830, Drummond founded the Apostolic Church, and nurtured the Jews Society (CMJ), which probably had little to do with converting Jews to Christ. Rather, it appears to have been a vehicle for the implementation of a counterfeit millennium. Jews detest the idea of Christian conversion, but Zionism rather than Jewish evangelism was the Society's priority.

---

[30] Malta Family History, Index of Protestant Cemetery—Jerusalem, http://website.lineone.net/~stephaniebidmead/jerusalem.htm as of May 2012

On February 5, 1840, Father Thomas, a French citizen and the superior of a Franciscan convent in Damascus, and his servant disappeared. The French consul there began an investigation in the Jewish quarter, during which officials extorted confessions through torture. People refer to this event as the Damascus Affair. Some of the Jewish victims, to escape further torture, confessed to murdering the two individuals. Meanwhile, angry residents destroyed the local synagogue.

Lionel Rothschild, Moses Montefiore's nephew, convinced the British government that it should respond to the Damascus Affair in order to assist the persecuted Jews and the missionaries of the Jews Society in Muslim countries. Montefiore and the Rothschilds initiated a campaign to defend Jews in Syria, wherein Jews from around the world participated to aid their brethren. Eventually, wealthy Jews utilized this tragic event to unite the Jews and target attention on the minority Jewish populations in Palestine, Russia, Rumania, and other places. Apparently, for the first time in history, wealthy Jews, such as the Rothschilds and the Montefiores, could lend support.

Albert Cohn first settled in Paris in 1836, and instructed three of Baron James de Rothschild's children in Hebrew and Jewish history. By 1839, Rothschild had placed Cohn, a dedicated Zionist, in charge of his extensive charities, a position he retained until his death in 1877. Lionel Rothschild, Nathan's son, sent Joseph Wolff, already in the area, and Cohn with a delegation to Israel to give assistance to the Jews in the area because of the Damascus Affair. Cohn developed a lifelong association with the Rothschilds.

Lord Palmerston, Henry J. Temple, sent British troops to Palestine soon after Shaftesbury persuaded the British government to open a consulate in Jerusalem (1838-1839).[31] Given the Rothschilds' influence in the government, they might have suggested that the queen appoint a Protestant bishop in Jerusalem. The freemasons also supported the proposal. Both Palmerston and Shaftesbury were involved in freemasonry. Lord Palmerston, urged by Lord Shaftesbury, asked the

---

[31] M. Vereté, Why Was a British Consulate Established in Jerusalem?, The English Historical Review Volume 85, No. 335 (April 1970), pp. 316-345

Ottoman Sultan Abdülmecid I (1839-1861) if the British Jews could relocate to Ottoman Palestine.

On August 11, 1840, Lord Palmerston wrote to the British ambassador at Constantinople regarding the Jews. He wrote, "There exists at the present time among the Jews dispersed over Europe, a strong notion that the time is approaching when their nation is to return to Palestine . . . It would be of manifest importance to the Sultan to encourage the Jews to return and to settle in Palestine because the wealth which they would bring with them would increase the resources of the Sultan's dominions . . . I have to instruct Your Excellency strongly to recommend to (the Turkish government) hold out every just encouragement to the Jews of Europe to return to Palestine."[32] The sultan rejected the request.

On August 17, 1840, a newspaper published a report saying that the British government was considering a restoration of Jews to Palestine. Apparently, Lord Shaftesbury, who had religious motivations, persuaded Lord Palmerston to intercede, along with newspaper support. Shaftesbury, related to two Prime Ministers, had visions of Britain restoring Israel and redeeming humanity according to his interpretation of ancient biblical prophecy.[33] Clergyman Alexander Keith of the Church of Scotland, in his 1843 book *The Land of Israel According to the Covenant with Abraham, with Isaac, and with Jacob*, implied that the Holy Land was unpopulated, despite the fact that he had been there in 1839 and must have noticed the inhabitants.

In 1841, Queen Victoria appointed Michael Alexander as the Protestant bishop in Jerusalem, as suggested by King Frederick William IV of Prussia. Reportedly, the Jews Society and the German Rothschilds persuaded King Frederick and the Lutherans to establish Protestant representation in Jerusalem, akin to the Vatican. The Earl of Shaftesbury, the president of the Jews Society, "brought the support of numerous friends" to achieve this Jerusalem appointment.

---

[32] Barbara W. Tuchman, Bible and Sword, England and Palestine from the Bronze Age to Balfour, Ballantine Books, a division of Random House, 1956, reprinted in 1984, pp. 175-176
[33] Ibid, 175-176

His father-in-law, Lord Palmerston, avidly supported Zionism and Jewish settlement.

The Damascus Affair, a terrible but not necessarily isolated incident against minorities, laid the indispensable foundation for the creation of a Jewish state. England, a historically imperialistic country, in addition to its religious interest in the Holy Land, saw economic, political, and colonial opportunities as early as 1840. Cohn made numerous visits to Jerusalem. In 1854, rich European Jews and the Rothschilds would send him to Jerusalem to evaluate missionary activities, financially assist the Christian missionaries, and establish a hospital, a society of manual workers, a girls' school, and a loan society.

Lord Palmerston was the Prime Minister of the United Kingdom twice (1855-1858; 1859-1865) and the secretary of state for Foreign Affairs three times (1830-1834; 1835-1841; 1846-1851). On July 13, 1841, he signed the Straits Convention, wherein five countries agreed to the permanent closure of the straits to all warships. This superseded the Treaty of Unkiar Skelessi, signed on July 8, 1833, between Russia and the Ottoman Empire, through which Czar Nicholas I sought to preserve the authority and territorial integrity of the existing states in Europe and the Near East. The treaty also initiated an eight-year alliance between Russia and the Ottoman Empire, calling for Russian aid if another country attacked the sultan. The czar hoped that this alliance would keep the straits in the hands of the Ottomans and French and English warships out of the straits. They did not renew the treaty, which paved the way for the Crimean War.

Samuel Morse, an American counterintelligence officer, admitted that an extensive British espionage network functioned in America before the Civil War, with B'nai B'rith as its center. It incorporated the leading figures in the Democrat Party, Southern secessionists, abolitionists, and others, all attempting to destroy America. Palmerston, then foreign minister, with B'nai B'rith's help created the International Zionist Movement by 1860. He allegedly helped create Zionism, only one of numerous Masonic-based cults, some Jewish and some Christian, which agents disseminated throughout Europe and America. freemasons created B'nai B'rith as an extension of the Jewish Rite of freemasonry in America.[34]

The British and their collaborators, who refuted the idea of assimilation, were determined to retain exclusivity and distinctness, by design and by institutionalization, through numerous Jewish organizations, based on the Zionist notion of the "promised land of Palestine" as the only way for Jews to attain true salvation. To implement the concept, Jews in America established "benevolent societies" to indoctrinate newly arriving Jewish immigrants from the pogroms and ghettos of Europe, the same scheme that the Montefiores and others carried out, with the aid of British politicians, in England. However, Jews already living in America demonstrated intense animosity toward the new immigrants who realized there was more opportunity in America than in Europe. Therefore, the schemers had to devise a subversive program, using the B'nai B'rith, to counter the natural desire of the immigrants to assimilate and achieve.[35] B'nai B'rith International's current president is Allan J. Jacobs, a resident of Lake Forest, Illinois.[36] Its headquarters are in Chicago. It has had a voice in the UN since its inception.[37]

In July 1853, Lord Shaftesbury had written to Foreign Minister George H. Gordon, telling him that Greater Syria was "a country without a nation" that needed "a nation without a country," meaning the Jews. A year later, an individual writing in a Presbyterian magazine said, "Surely the land without a people, and the people without a land, are intended soon to meet and mutually possess each other." In 1858, Horatius Bonar, a Scottish churchman and poet, promoted the "Repatriation of Israel . . . we have a people without a country, as well

---

[34] Jennifer Golub, Japanese Attitudes Toward Jews, The Pacific Rim Institute of the American Jewish Committee, p. 1

[35] Paul Goldstein, B'nai B'rith, British Weapon Against America, http://www.campaigner-unbound.0catch.com/bnai_brith_british_weapon_against_america.htm as of May 2012

[36] B'nai B'rith International Elects New President; Allan J. Jacobs, Long-time Leader, Now Assumes Top Position, http://www.bnaibrith.org/latest_news/PresidentElected052311.cfm

[37] Jüri Lina, Architects of Deception, Referent Publishing, Stockholm, Sweden, 2004, pp. 343-344

as a country without a people." In 1881, American William Blackstone advocated the restoration of Palestine to the Jewish population while deploring the persecution of the Jews in Russia. He wrote about "a land without a people, and a people without a land." In 1884, George S. Bowes, author and Cambridge University clergyman, referred to "a land without a people . . . a people without a land" while advocating the restoration of the Jews to Palestine.[38]

Others in America and Britain, mostly from privileged backgrounds, used the phrase, and it became common by the late nineteenth century, especially among Christians. In 1901, American missionary Harlan P. Beach, a graduate of Phillips Academy, Yale, and Andover Theological Seminary, wrote that the Jews will, "In God's good time, inhabit the land of their forefathers; otherwise we can offer no valid explanation of a people without a land and a land without a people." In 1902, Winifred Graham penned a novel, *The Zionist*, in which her Jewish hero addresses the Zionist Congress and requests the return of "the people without a country to the country without a people." The first Zionist to use the phrase, "Palestine is a country without a people; the Jews are a people without a country" was Israel Zangwill, a British humorist and writer, in 1901, in the *New Liberal Review.*[39]

Augustus H. Strong, head of the Rochester Theological Seminary, was a friend and beneficiary of John D. Rockefeller, who donated thousands of dollars to that institution.[40] [41] In 1912, Strong utilized the phrase, "A land without a people for a people without a land," which a Christian journalist repeated in a prominent article in *The Washington Post* on December 12, 1917.[42]

---

[38] Diana Muir, "A Land without a People for a People without a Land," Middle East Quarterly, Spring 2008, pp. 55-62
[39] Ibid, 55-62
[40] Rockefeller Gives $150,000, Rochester Theological Seminary Must Raise an Equal Amount, The New York Times, November 15, 1899, p. 3
[41] Rockefeller Gives $90,000, Offered to Duplicate Any Amount Raised by Rochester Seminary, The New York Times. January 2, 1901, p. 1
[42] Diana Muir, "A Land without a People for a People without a Land," Middle East Quarterly, Spring 2008, pp. 55-62

Barbara W. Tuchman wrote *Bible and Sword: England and Palestine from the Bronze Age to Balfour*, published in 1956, which portrays Britain's centuries-old involvement with the people known as the Israelites. Whether she depicts history accurately or not, she certainly promoted the "prophesied" acquisition of Palestine, previously under Ottoman control, by just one of the Israelite tribes, the "returning" Jews. Her grandfather, Henry Morgenthau Sr., a member of the infamous Pilgrims Society, was in the unique position as ambassador to the Ottoman Empire (1913-1916) and certainly influenced its domestic and foreign policies. Individuals typically underestimate or fail to understand the impact that ambassadors, persuasive high-ranking diplomats, have in their host countries.

Tuchman wrote that Shaftesbury, part of the "ruling aristocracy," really believed that he was his "brother's keeper." While that seems incredibly noble and seemingly justified by Cain's question, "Am I my brother's keeper?"; most people recognize that Cain was a murderer and therefore assume that he was in error regarding the stewardship concept. The word "keeper" implies total control—the custodial care that one exercises over zoo animals or jail prisoners. While we, as individuals, should lift one another's burdens, government officials should never assume dominion or control over other people's lives. The role of a benefactor appears magnanimous, but always places growing obligations upon the recipients who gradually become dependent rather than free and self-governing.

Christian Zionism became a principal factor in American Evangelicalism because of five factors: 1) John Nelson Darby, an Anglo-Irish evangelist, visited the United States, where he disseminated radical dispensational ideas and a restoration of Israel; 2) James Brookes, Dwight L. Moody, Cyrus Scofield, and Blackstone had prophecy conferences and Bible schools and founded Christian Zionism, which merged with the evangelical establishment; 3) Christian Zionists adopted Scofield's reference Bible, which promoted Dispensationalism; 4) Lewis S. Chafer, Charles Ryrie, John Walvoord, and others justified Christian Zionism through schools like the Dallas Theological Seminary and the Moody Bible Institute; 5) Contemporary Christian Zionism evolved through the writings of

Hal Lindsey and Tim LaHaye and a multitude of agencies, such as Jews for Jesus.[43]

Organizing Circumstances Behind the Scenes

On October 13, 1843, in Sinsheimer's Café in New York City, twelve German Jewish freemasons, representing the twelve tribes of Israel, founded B'nai B'rith International, an order exclusively for Jews and half-Jews. They were Henry Jones, Isaac Rosenbourg, William Renau, Reuben Rodacher, Henry Kling, Isaac Dittenhoefer, Jonas Hecht, and a few other German-Jewish immigrants. They intended to introduce a program of cultural, philanthropic, and mutual-aid activities and to halt ethnic criticism. By 1855, they had twenty lodges in different parts of the country. They stopped using German as their official language during the meetings, anticipating an Americanized membership and agenda.[44]

Even before they established B'nai B'rith, Solomon Etting, of Baltimore, sent Senator Henry Clay a letter, dated July 15, 1832, saying, "You know that I am your friend, and therefore I write to you freely. Several of the religious Society to which I belong, myself included, feel both surprised and hurt by the manner in which you introduce the expression 'the Jew' on debate in the Senate of the United States, evidently applying it as a reproachful designation of a man whom you considered obnoxious in character and conduct. I do not know the person you allude to, the term 'the Jew' as used by you, is considered illiberal. If therefore you have no antipathy to the people of that religious Society, I can readily believe you will have no objection to explain to me by a line, what induced the expression."[45]

---

[43] Stephen Sizer, Christian Zionism and the Roadmap to Armageddon, InterVarsity Press, Downers Grove, Illinois, 2005, pp. 132-133

[44] American Jewry and the Civil War by Bertram Wallace Korn, Jewish Publication Society of America, Philadelphia, 1951, p. 4

[45] The Jews of the United States, 1790-1840: A Documentary History edited by Joseph L. Blau, Salo W. Baron, Columbia University Press, New York, 1963, p. 58

In Benjamin Disraeli's 1852 novel, *Coningsby*, the character Sidonia mentions the dozens of Jews involved in the intellectual movement, those acting as financiers behind the European thrones and in multiple commercial and investment interests. He speaks of those involved in the recent revolutions and in an imminent revolution in Germany. He refers to the Jews who monopolize the professorial positions in Germany and even the foundations of Spiritual Christianity. Sidonia says that when he reads of peace and war in the newspapers, and that sovereigns want treasure, it is the Jews that always provide the loans. He elaborates on the Jewish diplomats and their connections between belligerent countries that always favor Jewish interests. He lists numerous countries, Russia, Spain, Prussia or Holland, which, in every case, a Jew or a Nuevo Christiano is usually the influential decision-maker. After this account, he says, "So you see, my dear Coningsby, that the world is governed by very different personages from what is imagined by those who are not behind the scenes."[46] People often fail to cite the circumstances of that last sentence, but leave it to the reader's imagination to determine the identity of those people "behind the scenes."

An aggressive minority population needs a well-managed worldwide organization to facilitate their internationalist agenda and manipulate circumstances "behind the scenes." In 1827, Adolphe I. Crémieux (born Isaac Moise), a Jewish lawyer and diplomat, had advocated the repeal of the *More Judaico*, legislation that had stigmatized, perhaps justifiably, the Jews following the 1789 revolution. James Rothschild funded Crémieux, a thirty-third-degree Grand Orient freemason, the perfect organizer for any task. On May 17, 1860, in Paris, Crémieux created the Alliance Israélite Universelle, together with Rabbi Aristide Astruc, Narcisse Levon, Jules Carvallo, Isidore Cohen and many others.[47] [48] They, and seventeen young Jewish professionals, assembled at the home of Charles Netter. They endorsed a program

[46] Benjamin Disraeli (Earl of Beaconsfield), Coningsby or the New Generation, 1844, p. 176
[47] Arnold Leese, Gentile Folly: the Rothschilds, Reception, February 17, 1937, pp. 19, 23
[48] Alliance Israélite Universelle, http://www.kiah.org.il/eng/about/history/ as of May 2012

of enlightenment and emancipation, and espoused the worldwide protection of Jews from anti-Semitism. They formulated an official pact for widespread public distribution. The founders integrated the ideas from the revolution of 1789-1799, equality, justice, and human rights, together with the principals of Judaism.[49]

"If you believe that a large number of our fellow Jews, still overwhelmed by centuries of oppression, poverty, distress, humiliation, and cruel edicts, can recover their human and civil dignity; if you believe that the ways of the corrupt should be proven and corrected, and not merely discussed; in opening the eyes of the blind, and not forsaking them; relieving those who are beaten and supporting them, and not being satisfied with expressing condolences; defending those who are slandered, and not remaining silent . . . Jews of the world, come, listen to our call, join us, lend us your support and assistance."[50]

In the 1830s, Jacob I. Cohen, a friend of the Rothschilds, had financed the Baltimore branch of the slave trade for the British East India Company.[51] He opened a branch bank in New York City to accommodate that trade, and his brother married Solomon Etting's daughter. Etting and Cohen partnered in B&O Railroad. Later, the Cohens, with others, including Dr. Aaron Friedenwald, Dr. Cyrus Alder, and Rabbi Benjamin Szold of the Congregation Ohev Shalom in Baltimore, founded the Baltimore chapter of the Alliance Israélite Universelle.[52]

In 1862, the Alliance Israélite Universelle created a network of schools in order to disseminate a multicultural, humanistic education to over a million children. The organization, in its schools, promotes the significance of maintaining a special bond among Jews. The schools teach students how to create a liberal atmosphere, encourage

---

[49]   Ibid

[50]   Alliance Israélite Universelle, http://www.kiah.org.il/eng/about/history/ as of May 2012

[51]   Campaigner Special Report No. 24: The US Labor Party's Freeman Goes to Congress, Campaigner Special Report, Campaigner Publications Inc., New York, p. 7

[52]   Ibid. 7

community consensus, and how to engage in Jewish activism in their own communities. The organization builds the essential skills such as a "sense of criticism," a necessary condition for the continuity, development, and cultural and spiritual prosperity of the Jewish people in general and of every individual Jew." Currently, there are about fifty such institutes and branch schools, attended by tens of thousands of students who learn about their "Jewish heritage" and "loyalty to the Jewish tradition."[53] This network is in addition to the ORT schools.

Initially, the Masonic Alliance Israélite Universelle functioned as a powerful organization for the extension of Jewish power over gentile nations, by whatever means possible, and it used the B'nai B'rith as its executive organ. They largely developed an institutional network in the bigger urban communities. By the twentieth century, every major urban community in Germany would have Jewish hospitals, orphanages, old-age homes, and other institutions dealing with social problems. The main organizations were the B'nai B'rith lodges and the Jüdische Frauenbund. In Berlin, a network, the Landsmannschaften, served migrants from the province of Posen. Political and ideological groups (except for Orthodox groups) functioned primarily in the large cities, especially the Zionist groups.[54]

In 1863, Crémieux became president of the movement's central committee. The organization's motto was, "All Israelites are comrades." In 1866, he went to St. Petersburg to help defend the Jews of Saratov, who people accused of blood libel. Crémieux, a member of the Supreme Council, called the Rite of Mizraim, became Grand Master in 1869. He secured full citizenship for the Jews in French-ruled Algeria, via the 1870 Décret Crémieux. During the Franco-Prussian War, Jules Simon and Crémieux dictated policy, during which thousands of Frenchmen needlessly died. People sought peace, and Bismarck could have withstood the rhetoric of Jules Favre, another leader of the Opportunist Republicans faction, if not for the

---

[53] Alliance Israélite Universelle, http://www.kiah.org.il/eng/about/history/ as of May 2012

[54] Ezra Mendelsohn (editor) People of the City: Jews and the Urban Challenge, Oxford University Press, New York, 1999, p. 91

fanaticism of Simon and Crémieux, who apparently wanted further warfare. Wilhelm Marr claimed that these diplomats Judaized France. He claims that the Jews were the only people who benefitted from the bloodshed and the subsequent Congress of Berlin.[55]

In 1871, the elites utilized the Anglo-Jewish association to mastermind Jewish interests in Britain to work with the Alliance Israélite Universelle. The Sassoons, Rothschilds, Montefiores, and Goldsmids have always been the most prominent members. The Anglo-Jewish association later initiated daily communication with the central committee of the Alliance Israélite Universelle, an organization that often intercedes for Jewish criminals so they may escape justice. In 1878, leaders at the Congress of Berlin officially recognized the organization, whose goal was to enhance Jewish political power. The first objective was to infiltrate the governments of Rumania, Serbia, and Bulgaria to force the emancipation of the Jews in those countries. Rumania reneged on their obligation.[56]

On June 4, 1878, just prior to the Congress of Berlin, Disraeli, the British Prime Minister (1874-1880), established a secret alliance with the Ottoman Empire against Russia. This agreement permitted Britain to occupy the strategic island of Cyprus and enabled Disraeli to make demands and threaten warfare against Russia if that nation failed to accommodate Turkish demands. British and Austrian officials managed to find common ground—Britain agreed to support Austrian demands, while Austria would support British demands, particularly relative to any proposals about Bosnia and Herzegovina. All of these events set the stage for more warfare within the next three to four decades.

Jean Izoulet (1854-1929), a prominent freemason in the Grand Orient and member of the Alliance Israélite Universelle, wrote, "The meaning of the history of the last century has been that three hundred Jewish

---

Wilhelm Marr, The Victory of Judaism over Germanism, Viewed from a Nonreligious Point of View, Rudolph Costenoble, Bern, Switzerland, 1879, pp. 22-23

[56]   Arnold Leese, Gentile Folly: the Rothschilds, Reception, February 17, 1937, pp. 19, 23

financiers, all masters of the chair, will rule the world." Crémieux, grand master of the Alliance, collaborating with the Grand Orient in England, created a union to plan for the Masonic world revolution. Crémieux proclaimed the goals of the freemasons: "Nations must disappear. Religions must cease to exist. Israel alone will continue to exist, since its people have been chosen by God."[57] Crémieux spoke openly in his manifesto to the Alliance, "The union which we shall create will not be French, English, Irish or German, but a Jewish World Union . . . Under no circumstances shall a Jew befriend a Christian or a Muslim; not before the moment comes when Judaism, the only true religion, shines over the entire World."[58]

The Early Zionists

Biologically, the Jews are not a "race," and one can certainly abandon Zionism if he or she decides. If we really evaluate the racial or ethnic claims, we would probably conclude that race is not really the problem. Rather, the difficulty has always been their peculiar ideology. If it were simply a matter of race, a question of parentage, it might actually be easier. The challenge we confront, as individuals and as a nation, is their ability to disseminate that ideology and the population's willingness to accept it without question and at the expense of a preponderance of its own interests and values.

Moses (Moshe) Hess (1812-1875), a Jewish philosopher, was the author of *Holy History of Mankind* (1837), *European Triarchy* (1841) and *Rome and Jerusalem the Last National Question* (1862). Karl Marx, Hess's protégé, became a freemason and an agitator who edited the *Rheinische Zeitung* (1842-1843). Initially, Marx, who did "not actually originate anything but merely streamlined Talmudism for Gentile Consumption,"[59] opposed mass demonstrations, but,

[57] Jüri Lina, Architects of Deception, Referent Publishing, Stockholm, Sweden, 2004, pp. 350-351
[58] Jüri Lina, Under the Sign of the Scorpion: The Rise and Fall of the Soviet Empire, Referent Publishing, Stockholm, Sweden, 2002, p. 80
[59] Elizabeth Dilling, The Jewish Religion: Its Influence Today, formerly titled The Plot Against Christianity, Noontide Press, Newport Beach, California, 1983, p. 121

through his mentor's guidance, he soon adapted. In the fall of 1844, in Paris, Hess introduced Marx to Friedrich Engels, which began a lengthy collaboration. Hess formulated the communist ideology, including the abolition of all personal property. He advocated class warfare as a method of preventing mutual cooperation. He hoped to use Judaism, racism, and the class struggle to initiate a revolution and maintained that socialism was akin to internationalism, as socialists have no homeland and do not acknowledge nationality. However, he stated, this did not apply to Jews, as he believed that internationalism operated in the best interests of Judaism. He wrote, "Whoever denies Jewish nationalism is not only an apostate, a renegade in the religious sense, but also a traitor to his people and to his family."[60]

Moses Hess, in *Red Catechism for the German People*, wrote, "The socialist revolution is my religion." He felt that the Rothschild's red-family banner should signal the struggle of the revolution or, as he implied elsewhere, the struggle of the Judaists. Hess maintained that Judaism would evolve into a godless socialist, revolutionary ideology. In an 1845 article, *"About the Monetary System,"* He said that the Jews' function was to change mankind into a savage animal. Marx and Engels advocated many of his ideas, and Theodor Herzl endorsed and advanced Hess's Zionist dogma in the 1890s. Levi Baruch stressed that the Jews should retain Judaism so that other Jews would not view them as traitors. In earlier centuries, in Spain, some Jews pretended to convert to Christianity to gain access to important government and church positions. Baruch promoted this as a way for "revolutionary Jews" to conceal their Judaism. When ensconced in these administrative positions, they could enact laws prohibiting private property, thus allowing vast riches to fall into their hands and fulfilling the Talmud mandate that they would control the world's riches. According to Baruch, Jews would control the world, merge the races, abolish borders, eliminate the royal families, and establish the Zionist state.[61]

---

[60] Jüri Lina, Under the Sign of the Scorpion: The Rise and Fall of the Soviet Empire, Referent Publishing, Stockholm, Sweden, 2002, pp. 68-70
[61] Ibid. 68-70

Hess, an early advocate of socialism, helped found Zionism. He lived in Paris when the revolution began in 1848, and then fled to Belgium, and then Switzerland. He was a correspondent for the *Rheinische Zeitung*, an extremist newspaper for which Marx also worked. He was friends with both Marx and Engels who he converted to communism. Hess promoted Jewish assimilation into the Universalist Socialist movement and helped to transform Hegelian dialectical idealism into the dialectical materialism of Marxism and provided the basis for many of Marx's ideas, such as religion functioning as the "opiate of the people."

Hess was also close to Fritz Anneke, Carl Schurz and his wife, Mathilde F. Anneke, Andreas Gottschalk, and others associated with the Communist Club in Cologne. Some of his friends, Anneke, Schurz, and his wife, Mathilde, and Gottschalk, immigrated to America, but Hess remained in Europe and lived in Germany (1861-1863), where he experienced anti-Semitism. While in Germany, he reverted to Judaism and published *Rome and Jerusalem*. He acknowledged the surge of Italian nationalism, considered the idea of Jewish nationalism, and advocated the formation of a socialist state in Palestine as a response to the anti-Semitism prevailing in some Europe countries. Most German Jews were open to assimilation and ignored his ideas.

Dr. Leon Pinsker (Judah L. Pinsker) popularized nationalism when he wrote *Auto-Emancipation, an Appeal to His People by a Russian Jew*, a nonpassive strategy for future Jewish action. He wrote it in German and published it anonymously on January 1, 1882. The Zionist movement began to take shape in the late nineteenth century. Theodor Herzl read *Rome and Jerusalem* and later admitted that he would not have written *The Jewish State* if he had known about that book earlier. Vladimir Jabotinsky claimed that Hess was one of the individuals responsible for the Balfour Declaration, along with Herzl, Rothschild, and Pinsker. In 1961, officials reinterred Hess's body from the Jewish cemetery in Cologne to the Kinneret Cemetery in Israel.

In addition to emigration, the pogroms in southern Russia generated the idea of Jewish nationalism and an abandonment of the assimilation ideology that most Eastern European Jews had always accepted. The pogroms (1881-1884) prompted the consolidation of other methods of Jewish nationalism, which increased the Zionist Movement. Moshe L. Lilienblum, of Odessa, wrote an article, *Obshcheyevreiski Vopros I Palestina*, encouraging Jewish settlement in Palestine as the only solution of the Jewish problem.

In his pamphlet, a response to the pogroms, Dr. Pinsker wrote, "Of course, the establishment of a Jewish refuge cannot come about without the support of the respective governments. In order to obtain the latter and to insure the perpetual existence of a refuge, the molders of our national regeneration must proceed with caution and perseverance. What we seek is at bottom neither new nor dangerous to anyone. Instead of the many refuges which we have always been accustomed to seek, we would fain have one single refuge, the existence of which, however, would have to be politically assured. Let 'Now or never' be our watchword."[62]

In 1882, Anglican clergyman, William H. Hechler, whose father worked for the Jews Society, traveled to Germany, France, and Russia to investigate the Jews' circumstances in those locations. While in Russia, he heard about the pogroms against the Jews. In Odessa, he met Dr. Pinsker and saw the developing Zionist movement. He stopped in Constantinople to deliver a letter from Queen Victoria, via British Ambassador, Frederick Hamilton, to Abdülhamid. It suggested a restorationist solution to anti-Semitism and requested that the Sultan allow the Jews to return to Palestine. Hamilton refused to deliver the letter. In 1884, Hechler, then a chaplain at the British Embassy in Vienna, wrote *The Restoration of the Jews to Palestine According to the Prophets*.[63]

---

[62] Leon Pinsker, Auto-Emancipation, 1882, http://www.jewishvirtuallibrary. org/jsource/Zionism/pinsker.html

[63] Hershel Edelheit and Abfaham J. Edelheit, History of Zionism: A Handbook and Dictionary, Westview Press, Boulder, Colorado, 2000, p. 42

Turkey, an Economic Vassal State

Christopher Walker wrote, "The Armenian dispersion, or ëspiurk, is an ancient phenomenon. Enterprising Armenians have for centuries sought their fortunes in lands other than their own—although they have seldom lost their connections with and affection for their mother country."[64] Jews and Armenians have much in common, as they both experienced a diaspora and, as a consequence, learned to function quite effectively in their host countries. The Greeks, another minority, along with the predominantly Christian Armenians, became Ottoman Empire subjects. The flexible Armenians acquired confidence and skill in conducting business in Muslim countries. They, like the Sephardim, successfully bridged the gap between the Christian and Islamic worlds."[65]

Historians and others applied the classical term "diaspora" to three groups—the Jews, the Armenians, and the Greeks. By the twentieth century, the term took on great importance with the abundance of international migration, the advent of globalization, and the imminent demise of the nation-state. One should not dismiss the importance of the trade network or trade diaspora (Philip Curtin uses these terms interchangeably) and the tradesmen's natural and justifiable exemption from political participation in their host countries. Curtin says these groups were "only cross-cultural brokers helping to encourage trade between the host society and their own." Citizens typically view the nation-state as "natural," while diaspora minorities engage in "cross-cultural trade" and become specialists in a "single kind of economic enterprise" as opposed to the composite "host society," with cohesive multioccupational circumstances.[66]

In the Middle East and, presumably, elsewhere, the richest merchants were also the richest landowners. In Iran, where many Armenians

---

[64] Christopher J. Walker, Armenia, the Survival of a Nation, Routledge, London, 1980, p. 11
[65] Ina Baghdiantz McCabe, Gelina Harlaftis, and Ioanna Pepelasis Minoglou (editors) Diaspora Entrepreneurial Networks, Four Centuries of History, Berg Publishers, Oxford, UK, 2005, p. 4
[66] Ibid, 30-31

settled, they traded in gems, silk, wool, and cotton and became part of the bourgeoisie, but were still distinct from the local landowners.[67] Both Jews and Armenians were heavily involved in the opium trade in Singapore.[68] Diaspora minorities of Levantine origin have always conducted international business, without which European maritime trade would not have existed. Jews, Armenians, and Greeks actively traded in such ports as Antwerp, Amsterdam, London, Seville, Marseilles, Livorno, and Venice, where the merchant community and the community of foreign merchants were synonymous. From the sixteenth century, Jews, Armenians, and Greeks coexisted in the Ottoman Empire after its government restricted European traders.[69]

Prior to 1854, Turkey could have raised cheaper funds internally by borrowing from the Armenian bankers in Galata. However, by 1854, the nation needed to finance its participation in the Crimean War, so they acquired a loan via the British and French money markets for £3 million sterling, at 6 percent interest, even though the Quran condemned usury. In 1855, it borrowed £5 million, at 4 percent. By 1874, perhaps to gratify its indulgences, the Ottoman government burdened itself with £191 million through thirteen additional loans, with interest rates between 10 and 21 percent. It used only 10 percent of that money to increase its economic strength and squandered much of the rest. During that same period, Europe expanded economically, while its investments in Turkey functioned to keep the "Muslim empire backward and at the mercy of Europe." The Ottoman government discovered it was easier to borrow money than to raise taxes. To restore confidence, the government established the foreign-controlled Ottoman Bank in the capital. The Armenian bankers in Constantinople, without national loyalties, supported the pashas, who extorted taxes throughout the countryside.[70]

As a result of the Crimean War, between the Russian Empire on one side and an alliance of France, Britain, the Kingdom of Sardinia

---

[67] Ibid, 30-31
[68] Ibid, 221
[69] Ibid, 161-162
[70] Christopher J. Walker, Armenia, the Survival of a Nation, Routledge, London, 1980, pp. 92-93

(absorbed by Italy in 1861), and the Ottoman Empire on the other, the Turks had major debt obligations to the Europeans. The economic panic (1873), initiated in New York, had catastrophic world consequences, especially for the financially strapped Ottoman Empire. Competition of the major European powers for territorial influence in the declining empire led to war. On October 6, 1875, the Turkish government had defaulted on its interest payment. Abdülhamid II, who became the Sultan on August 31, 1876, was attempting to gradually extricate the economy from European debt slavery, which prevented modern infrastructure development and jeopardized Turkish sovereignty. He was trying to avoid the fate that Egypt experienced—virtual British occupation of the country following its inability to pay its debts. Therefore, the Zionists' plan appeared to be the solution to salvage the Turkish economy from the Europeans. However, the sultan would not accept the consolidation and colonization arrangement together but would consider consolidation alone.[71]

In 1876, investors in London and Paris heaped criticism on Turkey regarding their alleged atrocities against the Bulgarians. The Russo-Turkish War (1877-1878), which cost Turkey 250,000 dead and an influx of over 500,000 refugees into the empire, impeded the lenders' desire for an immediate debt settlement. Through their claims of atrocities and war debts, they evidently compelled the sultan to issue the Decree of Muharram on October 20, 1881, which immediately decreased the empire's indebtedness from £191 million to £106 million. However, this decree transferred a large proportion of the Ottoman Empire's total revenue to the Public Debt Administration (PDA) for the repayment of foreign creditors, practically bankrupting the Ottoman Empire after the war. The PDA was comprised of seven members, six of whom represented European bondholders. It collected revenues on certain products, such as salt and tobacco, to pay the foreign debt, which reduced Turkey to an economic vassal state and stripped it of sovereignty. The PDA could, if necessary, use military force to guarantee government compliance. Abdülhamid could not even reform the tax system because of the indebtedness created by

---

[71] Mim Kemal Oke, The Ottoman Empire, Zionism, and the Question of Palestine (1880-1908), International Journal of Middle East Studies, Published by: Cambridge University Press, Volume 14, No. 3 (August 1982), pp. 329-341

the two previous sultans, Abdülaziz (1861-1876) and Murad V (May-August 1876)—the first being financially incompetent and the last mentally incompetent.[72]

Resident non-Muslim minorities controlled the foreign branch banks in the Ottoman Empire until 1878. During the Balkan Wars (1912-1913), the government could not obtain credit from the Imperial Ottoman Bank, even though it was a state bank. The Committee of Union and Progress (CUP) government tried to institute a central bank using national capital, but it failed when World War I erupted. Following the war, they established the National Credit Bank as a central bank, conceived to undertake the duties of the Imperial Ottoman Bank. The National Credit Bank became the central bank when the Ottoman Empire fell in 1923.[73]

Seeking Government Sponsorship

William H. Hechler, an avowed Zionist, had tutored the children of Friedrich I, the Grand Duke of Baden. During this time, he had the opportunity to develop a relationship with Friedrich's nephew, the young Hohenzollern prince, who would later became Kaiser Wilhelm II (1888-1918). Through Hechler's instrumentality, Herzl first contacted Friedrich I, which led to Herzl's meeting with Wilhelm II in Eretz Israel in 1898.[74] Wilhelm, of Germany, very sympathetic to Turkey, had previously offered to intervene with the sultan in behalf of the Zionists.[75]

---

[72]   Christopher J. Walker, Armenia, the Survival of a Nation, Routledge, London, 1980, pp. 92-94

[73]   Gábor Ágoston and Bruce Alan Masters, Encyclopedia of the Ottoman Empire, InfoBase Publishing, New York, 2009, p. 77

[74]   Hershel Edelheit and Abfaham J. Edelheit, History of Zionism: A Handbook and Dictionary, Westview Press, Boulder, Colorado, 2000, p. 42

[75]   Mim Kemal Oke, The Ottoman Empire, Zionism, and the Question of Palestine (1880-1908), International Journal of Middle East Studies, Published by: Cambridge University Press, Volume 14, No. 3 (August 1982), pp. 329-341

Dr. Max Bodenheimer, the attorney for the Zionist Congress, and others accompanied Herzl on his journey to meet Kaiser Wilhelm in Constantinople. Wilhelm journeyed in the Near East (October 13-November 24, 1898), after the policy-setting Second Zionist Congress, when he visited Constantinople, Syria, and Palestine. The Zionists viewed this as an unprecedented opportunity to acquire German support, and Herzl attributed undue significance to a meeting between Sultan Abdülhamid II and Kaiser Wilhelm.[76] Theodor Herzl, searching for a strong country to support a Jewish homeland, proudly showed the Kaiser a Jewish settlement in Palestine. However, the Kaiser rejected the idea of sponsoring a Jewish homeland.

In 1899, Ahmed Tevfik Pasha had told Wilhelm, "The Sultan would have nothing to do with Zionism and an independent Jewish Kingdom." Further, he said that Zionism threatened Turkish sovereignty and "the Germans should renounce the idea of introducing the Jewish people into the international community as a state, because this project, by creating a state at the center of the Ottoman Empire, would assure the ruin of Turkey."[77] Wilhelm withdrew whatever support he ever had for Zionism. His attitude influenced some of the leaders of other countries regarding their potential support. One of those countries was Russia.

Herzl heard that Vyacheslav von Plehve, Russia's minister of the Interior, planned to prohibit the Zionist Movement. He helped fund the Kishinev newspaper, *Bessarabets*, which regularly published

---

[76] Klaus Polkehn, Zionism and the Kaiser's Germany: Zionist Diplomacy with the Empire of Kaiser Wilhelm, Journal of Palestine Studies, Volume 4, no. 2, 1975, pp. 78-79

[77] Mim Kemal Oke, The Ottoman Empire, Zionism, and the Question of Palestine (1880-1908), International Journal of Middle East Studies, Published by: Cambridge University Press, Volume 14, No. 3 (August 1982), pp. 329-341

anti-Jewish materials, a factor that may have fueled the pogrom there (April 6-7, 1903). Through a friend, Herzl made an appointment with him to appeal for three provisions. He wanted the following: 1) the government's authorization for the creation of Zionist societies modeled after the Basel plan; 2) the Russian government to obtain the sultan's charter for the Jewish colonization of Palestine; and 3) the subsidizing of Jewish emigration to Palestine out of Jewish sources. Von Plehve agreed to present Herzl's proposals to the czar on the condition that the Jews, during their Sixth Zionist Congress, slated for August 23, 1903, would withhold their criticism of the Russian government. Within three days, von Plehve reported that the czar approved of all three provisions. However, he never requested a charter from Abdülhamid.[78]

In August 1903, von Plehve wrote to Herzl and told him that Russia would support an independent state in Palestine. However, when Germany withdrew support, the Russians also withdrew support. France had always opposed Herzl's project, as it had interests in Syria and Palestine.[79] That same month, von Plehve met with Herzl in St. Petersburg to discuss the creation of Zionist societies. Because he apparently could not prevent anti-Jewish violence, revolutionaries targeted von Plehve. Yevno Azef, a double agent, a spy for the Okhrana, and terrorist, planned von Plehve's assassination; he had already survived three previous attempts. On July 28, 1904, Yegor Sozonov threw a bomb into his carriage killing him. Nicholas II then appointed Peter D. Sviatopolk-Mirskii as minister of the Interior. Shortly, the Bolsheviks initiated their first revolution in Russia.

Target Palestine, a Jewish Homeland

Some Eastern European-Jews considered Palestine, though smaller than Vermont and already overpopulated, as the origin of their "sages." They intended to use aggression, particularly in Iraq and

---

[78] Leslie Stein, The hope fulfilled: the rise of modern Israel, Praeger Publishers, Westport, Connecticut, 2003, pp. 76-77
[79] Mim Kemal Oke, The Ottoman Empire, Zionism, and the Question of Palestine (1880-1908), International Journal of Middle East Studies, Published by: Cambridge University Press, Volume 14, No. 3 (August 1982), pp. 329-341

Iran, even at the expense of the native Jewish population, many of whom had embraced Islam.[80] The First Aliyah (1881-1903) was the first modern wave of Zionist Jews who migrated to Palestine, mostly from Eastern Europe and Yemen. About 25,000 Jews immigrated to Ottoman Syria during that period. Throughout history, Jews that were typically religious rather than secular or political migrated to Palestine.

In November 1881, the Ottoman government in Constantinople, cognizant of the Jewish immigration situation, decided to impede migration before it increased. The sultan recognized that pogroms against the Jews followed their assassination of Czar Alexander II. On May 15, 1882, the Russian government imposed the May Laws, which caused many Jews to immigrate, mainly to America. Many Jews in Russia, Austro-Hungary, and Rumania began considering Jewish nationalism. Ottoman diplomats in St. Petersburg and Vienna regularly transmitted the details regarding Jewish affairs in Russia and Austria-Hungary to Constantinople. One report, *Situation of the Jews; Question of their immigration into Turkey: 1881*, described their settlement in the Ottoman Empire.[81]

Baron Edmond de Rothschild, the youngest child of James Mayer Rothschild, initially rejected colonization in Eretz Israel, but eventually accepted the idea. He financed the first settlement, Rishon LeZion, founded on July 31, 1882, by Hibbat Zion pioneers from Kharkov, Ukraine. By 1884, he financed four out of seven settlements. He employed heavy-handed bureaucracy, especially when it came to disseminating funds. By 1887, residents were prepared to mutiny against Baron Rothschild and his managers. Rothschild ended the Ekron mutiny (1888-1892) when he declared that he owned the settlement and the land and threatened to deport the settlers.[82]

[80] John Beaty, The Iron Curtain Over America, Chestnut Mountain Book, Barboursville, Virginia, 1968, p. 31
[81] Neville J. Mandel, The Arabs and Zionism before World War I, University of California Press, Berkeley and Los Angeles, California, 1976, pp. 1-2
[82] Hershel Edelheit and Abfaham J. Edelheit, History of Zionism: A Handbook and Dictionary, Westview Press, Boulder, Colorado, 2000, pp. 30-31

Beginning in 1882, the Ottoman authorities prohibited all foreign Jews, except pilgrims, to visit Palestine. Yet, some pilgrims never left. On March 5, 1883, the government, in an attempt to block Jewish land purchases in Palestine, passed a law to prevent them from acquiring any land there. However, this law failed to restrict Jewish residents from buying land on behalf of Zionist colonizers. They simply purchased and registered the land in their names. The Ottoman Land Code allowed property ownership in other parts of the Empire, except Arabia.[83]

Dr. Leon Pinsker, a physician, one of the first Jews to attend Odessa University, had always encouraged assimilation as the solution to the challenges that Jews had experienced prior to the pogroms. He organized an international conference of Hovevei Zion, also known as Hibbat Zion (Lovers of Zion), in Kattowitz (then part of Prussia), which thirty-four delegates attended, including Moshe L. Lilienblum, who acted as secretary. The delegates elected Rabbi Samuel Mohilever as the president and selected Pinsker, the ideological source behind Hibbat Zion, a pre-Zionist movement, as the chairman.[84]

On November 6, 1884, representatives from various countries gathered at an international Jewish assembly at Kattowitz. They were from diverse backgrounds and social classes and were determined to colonize Palestine. From the conference forward, the organization Haskalah in Russia became very nationalistic and advocated for Palestinian colonization. Those who initially opposed Palestinian colonization gradually became Hobebe Zion (Lovers of Zion). Perez Smolenskin, a militant Zionist Russo-Jewish student in Vienna, organized an academic society, Kadimah, a response to anti-Semitism, which comprised the Zionist philosophy.[85]

---

[83] Martin Sicker, Reshaping Palestine: from Muhammad Ali to the British Mandate, 1831-1922, Praeger Publishers, Westport, Connecticut, 1999, p. 59

[84] Hershel Edelheit and Abfaham J. Edelheit, History of Zionism: A Handbook and Dictionary, Westview Press, Boulder, Colorado, 2000, p. 28

[85] Jacob Salmon Raisin, The Haskalah Movement in Russia, The Jewish Publication Society of America, Philadelphia, Pennsylvania, 1913, pp. 285-288

Hibbat Zion groups emerged in various Eastern European countries, all promoting immigration to Palestine. In 1890, the Russian government approved of the group and officially sanctioned it as "The Society for the Support of Jewish Farmers and Artisans in Syria and Eretz Israel," otherwise known as the Odessa Committee. In September 1891, Dr. Max I. Bodenheimer, a German Jew, invited the Hovevei Zion societies to create a worldwide agency—"Zionists of all countries, unite!" He had contacts with Hovevei Zion groups in major European cities. In February 1892, he met David Wolffsohn, and they founded the National Jewish club, Zion of Cologne in 1893, a branch of Hovevei Zion, which became the National Jewish Association in 1894, the foundation of the German Zionist movement.

In 1899, because of health issues, Baron Rothschild withdrew from direct involvement in the settlements. Regardless of the continuing controversies, the settlements and Zionism would have totally collapsed without the assistance of Rothschild's specialists, who helped to establish Israel's agricultural economy. He transferred the stewardship of the settlements to the Jewish Colonization Association, which spawned the Palestine Jewish Colonization Association. Hibbat Zion no longer existed after he relinquished his control.[86]

In 1899, anti-Semitic outbreaks occurred in Rumania, leading to a new incursion of Jews into Palestine. On November 21, 1900, the Ottomans published regulations allowing the Jews to receive a three-month residence permit in Palestine, which they had to relinquish when they left. Officials were very strict and kept detailed records. During this time, the authorities did their best to protect the Jews who suffered no ill treatment.[87] In November 1892 the Department of Land Registration stopped the sale of land to all Jews, including Ottoman subjects.[88] Other countries welcomed Jewish immigration.

---

[86]   Hershel Edelheit and Abfaham J. Edelheit, History of Zionism: A Handbook and Dictionary, Westview Press, Boulder, Colorado, 2000, pp. 30-31

[87]   Mim Kemal Oke, The Ottoman Empire, Zionism, and the Question of Palestine (1880-1908), International Journal of Middle East Studies, Published by: Cambridge University Press, Volume 14, No. 3 (August 1982), pp. 329-341

[88]   Ibid, 329-341

Manipulating Jewish Colonization, a History

Most devout Jews attempted to assimilate in their respective countries and felt they had obligations to their host nations. Religious Jews, without the political influence enjoyed by the Zionists, viewed Zionism as a secular distortion of their religion. Many opposed Theodor Herzl, including Rabbis Moritz Giidemann and Hermann Adler, the principal rabbis of Vienna and Britain. Others condemned his scheme as false Messianism or heresy and insisted that it would increase anti-Semitism. Herzl was adamant, and ultimately implemented his goals through the European powers.

In February 1896, copies of Theodor Herzl's book, *Der Judenstaat (The Jewish State: An Attempt at a Modern Solution of the Jewish Question,* originally called *Address to the Rothschilds)* arrived at the local booksellers. Herzl, born in Budapest, was fully assimilated and living in Vienna. He advocated a Jewish territory with a socialist government.[89] He had studied law and was a correspondent with the very influential Jewish-owned *Neue Freie Presse,* a popular newspaper among middle-class Jews.[90] He wrote, "Palestine is our ever-memorable historic home. The very name of Palestine would attract our people with a force of marvelous potency. If His Majesty the Sultan were to give us Palestine, we could in return undertake to regulate the whole finances of Turkey. We should there form a portion of a rampart of Europe against Asia, an outpost of civilization as opposed to barbarism. We should, as a neutral state, remain in contact with all Europe, which would have

---

[89] Walter Laqueur, A History of Zionism, From the French Revolution to the Establishment of the State of Israel, MJF Books, New York, 1972, p. 84

[90] Amos Elon, Herzl, Holt, Rinehart and Winston, New York, Chicago, San Francisco, 1975, pp. 170-172

to guarantee our existence."[91] In May 1896, Dr. Max I. Bodenheimer wrote to Herzl and soon joined him to create the Zionist movement.

In his book, Herzl wrote, "I referred previously to our 'assimilation.' I do not for a moment wish to imply that I desire such an end. Our national character is too historically famous, and, in spite of every degradation, too fine to make its annihilation desirable." Moreover, "Thus, whether we like it or not, we are now, and shall henceforth remain, a historic group with unmistakable characteristics common to us all. We are one people, our enemies have made us one without our consent, as repeatedly happens in history. Distress binds us together, and, thus united, we suddenly discover our strength. Yes, we are strong enough to form a state, and, indeed, a model state. We possess all human and material resources necessary for the purpose."[92]

On May 3, 1896, Dionys Rosenfeld, editor of the *Osmanische Post* in Constantinople, told Herzl that, despite the nation's financial insolvency and diplomatic disadvantages, Turkey would not surrender sovereignty of any of its provinces. Philip M. Newleński, Herzl's newly hired diplomat in Constantinople and the Balkan countries, concurred. Abdülhamid II, the sultan of the Ottoman Empire would never relinquish Jerusalem.[93]

---

[91]   Theodor Herzl, The Jewish State: An Attempt at a Modern Solution of the Jewish Question, M. Breitenstein's Verlags-Buchhandlung, Leipzig and Vienna, 1896, p. 38

[92]   Theodor Herzl, The Jewish State, Dover Publications, Inc., New York, 1988, an unabridged republication of the work originally published in 1946 by the American Zionist Emergency Council, New York p. 36

[93]   Isaiah Friedman, Germany, Turkey, and Zionism 1897-1918, 1998, Transaction Publishers, New Brunswick, New Jersey, p. 92

In June 1896, despite those opinions, Herzl visited Constantinople, accompanied by Newleński and David Wolffsohn, to meet with Abdülhamid II, whose agent informed him that a meeting was impossible, because Herzl worked for a newspaper that published negative reports about the Sultan's treatment of the Armenians. Herzl wrote in his diary, "He could and would receive me as a friend—after I had rendered him a service." Herzl, according to his diary, would try to influence the Jewish-owned European press "to handle the Armenian question in spirit more friendly to the Turks." Additionally, he would "induce the Armenian leaders" by offering them "all sorts of concessions" and perhaps even suspend their demands. He then told Newleński that he was ready to start his campaign.[94]

Herzl asked the sultan to issue a charter for Jewish colonization of Palestine, in exchange for £20 million. Newleński urged Abdülhamid to accept the offer by saying, "Without the help of the Zionists, the Turkish economy would not stand a chance of recovery." The sultan responded, "If Herr Herzl is as much your friend as you are mine, advise him not to take another step in this matter. I cannot relinquish a square foot of land, for it does not belong to me, but to my people. My people have conquered and fortified this empire with their blood . . . The Jews should save their billions. When my empire is partitioned, perhaps they will get Palestine for nothing. But only our dead body will be divided. (As long as we are alive) I will not permit a vivisection."[95] [96]

Despite the lack of financial backing, Herzl pursued his objectives. Mehmet Nuri Bey, secretary general of the Foreign Ministry, Grand Vizier, was enthused about Herzl's plan to free Turkey from the foreign debt-control commission.[97] He and Mehmed Djavid Bey, his

---

[94] Lenni Brenner, The Iron Wall, Zionist Revisionism from Jabotinsky to Shamir, AAARGH Publisher, 1984, p. 30
[95] Amos Elon, Herzl, Holt, Rinehart and Winston, New York, Chicago, San Francisco, 1975, pp. 199-200
[96] Neville J. Mandel, The Arabs and Zionism before World War I, University of California Press, Berkeley and Los Angeles, California, 1976, pp. 9-11
[97] Amos Elon, Herzl, Holt, Rinehart and Winston, New York, Chicago, San Francisco, 1975, pp. 199-200

son and a member of the Council of State, favored the plan. In 1882, the Sultan had allowed a large contingency of Romanian Jews, and, by 1891, he was unhappy about having granted Ottoman nationality to them, as he feared that "it may in the future result in the creation of a Jewish government in Jerusalem." He ordered the deportation of other Jewish immigrants to America.[98]

While working in Paris as a correspondent, Herzl visited with Max Nordau, a man about ten years his senior, and with whom he had commonality. He soon became Herzl's "chief lieutenant" for Zionism.[99] Nordau, in discussing how long it would take to create a nation, said, "It might take three hundred years." He furnished an introduction and suggested that Herzl try to enlist supporters in London. Upon his arrival there, Herzl went to the home of Israel Zangwill, the well-known Jewish writer. His book, *Children of the Ghetto*, about the East End of London, aroused mass sympathy for Jewish refugees from czarist Russia.[100]

Zangwill introduced Herzl to numerous influential men and arranged for him to address a banquet at the Maccabeans, a club for Anglo-Jewish intellectuals and civil servants. He made certain that Herzl met the most prominent individuals in London's Jewish community. Herzl, attempting to evoke sympathy for the Jews, met Lord Shaftesbury, Viscount Palmerston, the men of the Palestine Exploration Society, biblical scholars, and the novelist George Eliot, the author who wrote *Daniel Deronda,* about a Jew who worked for the creation of a national home for Jews. English Fundamentalists encouraged the "restoration" of the Jews to Palestine, believing that it would generate the second coming of Christ.[101]

Herzl had lunch with Sir Samuel Montagu, an Orthodox Jew, leading banker, and a Member of Parliament. He initially gained Montagu's

---

[98]   Neville J. Mandel, The Arabs and Zionism before World War I, University of California Press, Berkeley and Los Angeles, California, 1976, pp. 9-11
[99]   Amos Elon, Herzl, Holt, Rinehart and Winston, New York, Chicago, San Francisco, 1975, p. 99
[100]   Ibid, 170-172
[101]   Ibid, 170-172

support and told him he would appeal to the Turkish Sultan for an award of 250,000 acres east of the Jordan River. Prime Minister William E. Gladstone approved of the plan, but Lord Walter Rothschild rejected it. Although a few Jewish millionaires supported him, he was unable to attract the interest of the Jewish money power in his attempt to acquire at least £100 million pounds. The Rothschilds refused to speak to him.[102] Zangwill sent him to see Colonel Albert E. W. Goldsmid, an army officer who had supported Baron Maurice de Hirsh's project to settle Jews in Argentina, which was really just a "nursing ground for Palestine." Goldsmid, who was born a Christian, was ready after hearing his plan to leave the British army and enter the Jewish service. His parents, perhaps for assimilation purposes, had accepted baptism, but he returned to Judaism, married in a synagogue, and was now an Orthodox Jew.[103]

While in London, on July 13, 1896, Herzl met with Avetis Nazarbekian, the leader of the Hunchak Party. Herzl told their intermediary, "I want to make it clear to this revolutionary that the Armenians should now make their peace with the sultan, without prejudice to their later claims when the Great Powers divide Turkey." He told Nazarbekian that he would try to persuade the sultan to discontinue the arrests and massacres. He explained how they could engage in peace negotiations without disarming, with their "guns at their feet." Nazarbekian ignored Herzl's pleading.[104]

The minute Turkey declared war on Greece on April 17, 1897, German Zionists began collecting funds for the Turkish Red Crescent, a faction of the International Red Cross, founded June 11, 1868. During that short war, those Zionists wanted to impress the Sultan by their show of humanitarianism. Dr. Max I. Bodenheimer, a key Zionist and a lawyer, corroborated this in his memoirs. He admitted that they organized their efforts "in order to show the sultan what valuable services we could offer to him." Herzl created a committee

---

[102] Amos Elon, Herzl, Holt, Rinehart and Winston, New York, Chicago, San Francisco, 1975, pp. 199-200
[103] Ibid, 170-172
[104] Lenni Brenner, The Iron Wall, Zionist Revisionism from Jabotinsky to Shamir, AAARGH Publisher, 1984, p. 30

exclusively for humanitarianism and appealed to the Zionist clubs for funds. With those donations, he dispatched a group of well-equipped doctors to the war zone.[105]

In February 1900, Herzl began developing a relationship with Ernest von Koerber, the new Austro-Hungarian Prime Minister. Koerber intervened with the Austrian treasury to remove its injunction on the sale of shares in the Jewish Colonial Bank. Herzl then fully described the dilemmas surrounding his lengthy yet unsuccessful project, and Koerber offered his support. Herzl awaited word from the sultan, and there were still difficulties with the Jewish Colonial Bank. Nordau and Wolffsohn attempted, once again, to contact Edmond de Rothschild, who was dead-set against the Zionist project, and had been since Herzl initially approached him over four years before. Rothschild would support it, and even sell the Zionists his Palestinian colonies, but only after they had officially established their bank.[106]

On June 17, 1900, after Nordau arranged an introduction, Herzl visited Arminius Vámbéry (born Hermann Wamberger), a double agent in Britain and Turkey, in the Tyrolean Alps to seek his assistance and influence. Vámbéry offered to write the sultan to urge him to see Herzl again. He asked Vámbéry to tell the sultan that he could help him in the world press and give him credibility following the Armenian massacres (1894-1896) and the response by the Western powers. The sultan told Vámbéry that they did not want a recreation of the Kingdom of Judea and that, henceforth, they would no longer allow Jews to enter Palestine. Vámbéry, through repeated appeals, finally arranged to have Abdülhamid see Herzl on May 19, 1901. However, Herzl could not speak about Zionism, especially regarding Jerusalem, as sacred to the Turks as Mecca. The sultan, who expected the promised financial assistance, wanted only to talk about the regime's indebtedness.[107]

---

[105] Klaus Polkehn, Zionism and the Kaiser's Germany: Zionist Diplomacy with the Empire of Kaiser Wilhelm, Journal of Palestine Studies, Volume 4, no. 2, 1975, pp. 78-79
[106] Amos Elon, Herzl, Holt, Rinehart and Winston, New York, Chicago, San Francisco, 1975, pp. 318-319
[107] Amos Elon, Herzl, Holt, Rinehart and Winston, New York, Chicago, San Francisco, 1975, pp. 322-327

The leaders of the multinational Ottoman Empire were cognizant of Zionist ambitions, as they had read Herzl's *Der Judenstaat*. Ahmed Tevfik Pasha, the Ottoman ambassador in Berlin, had agents at their conferences and was aware of their tactics and objectives. The colonists, temporarily content, would soon find living under Ottoman law unsatisfactory. They would inevitably demand recognition as an independent state. On August 17, 1900, the Pasha wrote, "We must have no illusions about Zionism. Although the speakers at the congress dwelled upon vague generalities, such as the future of the Jewish people, the Zionists, in effect, aim at the formation of a great Jewish state in Palestine, which would also spread toward the neighboring countries." Palestine was too small to accommodate all the world's Jews, then about 10,000,000.[108]

The sultan expressed his anxiety about Turkey's financial woes—the foreign creditors had declared Turkey bankrupt and had seized the country's public revenues via the Ottoman Public Debt Administration. Ibrahim Bey, the interpreter, said, "Ever since the beginning of his glorious reign, His Majesty has sought in vain to remove this thorn," an impossible burden acquired under his predecessors. Herzl thought he could help, but only under conditions of absolute secrecy. Herzl figured that he and his Jewish friends could purchase the debt, but the sultan had to reciprocate by adopting a friendly policy toward the Jews. The Sultan needed £1.5 million immediately to satisfy the previous year's deficit.[109] The desperate sultan gave Herzl four weeks to accomplish the task.

Herzl attempted to find the necessary money in Paris and London. Rothschild remained unapproachable, as did Baron Maurice de Hirsch's Jewish Colonization Association. Other offers were insufficient. In London, Herzl appealed to the bankers who had previously appeared supportive. They could not help without Lord Nathaniel Rothschild's approval. A few of these bankers urged Rothschild to receive Herzl,

---

[108] Mim Kemal Oke, The Ottoman Empire, Zionism, and the Question of Palestine (1880-1908), International Journal of Middle East Studies, Published by: Cambridge University Press, Volume 14, No. 3 (August 1982), pp. 329-341

[109] Amos Elon, Herzl, Holt, Rinehart and Winston, New York, Chicago, San Francisco, 1975, pp. 333-336

but he refused. Herzl appealed to Vámbéry, who said that he was about ready to "stage a coup d'état" in Constantinople and overthrow Izzet Bey and the sultan by calling in the Young Turks. Herzl asked Vámbéry to negotiate with the sultan and induce him to allow the establishment of an Ottoman-Jewish company in exchange for solving Turkey's financial problems within five years.[110]

On February 4, 1902, Herzl received a telegram from Ibrahim Bey, asking him to furnish "certain explanations of your scheme." Herzl left for Constantinople, accompanied by Joe Cowen. Negotiations began the next day with Izzet Bey and Ibrahim Bey. He wanted to free them from their foreign debt in exchange for allowing the Jews to colonize Palestine. The Turks wanted Herzl to turn the *Neue Freie Presse* into an unofficial Turkish mouthpiece. The sultan would allow the refugees to settle on two conditions—they could not settle in Palestine but could reside in other areas of the empire, and they had to accept Ottoman citizenship.[111]

In return for this, the sultan asked Herzl to "form a syndicate for the consolidation of the public debt on terms better than those currently offered by other financiers." Moreover, they wanted Herzl to develop the entire "present and future mining resources of the empire, under an imperial concession." Herzl was puzzled and asked what mines. Izzet responded, "All the mines . . . gold and silver, coal and oil." The Turks recognized that, inasmuch as he wanted something, they could entrust the mines to him. Herzl, after some consideration, rejected Izzet's demand of restricted colonization. The sultan refused to open Palestine, but offered the Jews Mesopotamia, Syria, and Anatolia. Herzl, with additional leverage, rejected the offer.[112] Negotiations ended in 1902, without resolution. Abdülhamid hoped that Herzl would mediate between the Ottomans and the Jewish financial houses.

---

[110] Ibid, 339-341
[111] Amos Elon, Herzl, Holt, Rinehart and Winston, New York, Chicago, San Francisco, 1975, pp. 344-345
[112] Ibid, 344-345

Abdülhamid, according to his memoirs, recognized that the Zionists intended to establish their own government in Palestine. He viewed additional Jewish immigration and settlement in Palestine as harmful, but continued to protect the Jewish subjects already there. He imagined that this situation would ultimately lead to "the emergence of a Jewish Question," similar to the Armenian Question. Officials in Europe sent what they referred to as "protégés" to Turkey to establish connections with non-Muslim groups in order to develop the natural resources. Through their investments, they hoped to intervene in the empire's internal concerns, especially the purported rights of "Ottoman minorities." British, French, and Russian agents exploited the religious differences in Palestine to set up potential political interventions to render aid to the persecuted victims.[113]

Although the Zionists did not get a charter for a Jewish state, they managed to settle thousands in Palestine. Chaim Weizmann, by 1901, along with Martin Buber and Berthold Feiwel, lobbied for the founding of a Jewish institution of higher learning in Palestine. They presented their ideas at the Fifth Zionist Congress, describing the need to teach science and engineering. Their ideas led to laying the cornerstone for the Technion, the Israel Institute of Technology in 1912. In 1907, Weizmann first visited Palestine and, while there, helped organize the Palestine Land Development Company to assist Jews to obtain land. He persuaded many Jews not to wait for legalities regarding the land. He said, "A state cannot be created by decree, but by the forces of a people and in the course of generations."

Those immigrants who became Ottoman subjects sought foreign protection. British officials promised to defend them. The other European countries accused Britain of using the Jews to increase their control in Palestine. Therefore, other countries began issuing "certificates of protection" to them. The Ottomans viewed them as "another advance guard of further political European influence in the Ottoman Empire." The sultan said, "We cannot view Jewish immigration favorably. We could only open our borders to those who

[113] Mim Kemal Oke, The Ottoman Empire, Zionism, and the Question of Palestine (1880-1908), International Journal of Middle East Studies, Published by: Cambridge University Press, Volume 14, No. 3 (August 1982), pp. 329-341

belong to the same religion as we do." He set the precedent for the Ottoman's policy regarding the Zionists and decided that the Turkish government should thwart all attempts of Jewish immigration and settlement in Palestine.[114]

The final government program, conveyed by the council of ministers with the sultan's approval, established four main criteria. The Ministry for Foreign Affairs was responsible for persuading the European Powers to disavow the Zionist movement. The Ministry of the Interior sought methods to halt Jewish immigration. Some Jews, despite all efforts, managed to enter the country. The Department of Land Registration was responsible for preventing Jews from obtaining land in Palestine.[115]

By 1908, the Jewish population of Palestine was 80,000, three times its number in 1882, when the country first imposed entry restrictions. By 1908, the Jews owned 156 square miles of land, and they had established twenty-six colonies. Despite the efforts of the local authorities, certain European countries promoted Zionist policies. As Herzl told Wilhelm II and Vyacheslav von Plehve, the exodus of the Jews from these countries would diminish the socialist movement, as they were its leaders. It would also minimize anti-Semitism. German and Russian officials perhaps thought that the Jews would bring added prosperity to their respective areas of interest in the Ottoman Empire. Wilhelm was convinced that the "settlement of the Holy Land by the wealthy and industrious people of Israel will bring unexampled prosperity and blessing to the Holy Land, which will do much to revive and develop Asia Minor."[116]

Ultimately, the European powers intimidated the Ottoman government into only applying restrictions to Jews coming to Palestine en masse. Single families could immigrate and could purchase land. In 1911, Abdülhamid II, then in exile, told his physician, "I am sure that

---

[114] Mim Kemal Oke, The Ottoman Empire, Zionism, and the Question of Palestine (1880-1908), International Journal of Middle East Studies, Published by: Cambridge University Press, Volume 14, No. 3 (August 1982), pp. 329-341

[115] Ibid, 329-341

[116] Ibid, 329-341

with time they can and will be successful in establishing their own state in Palestine."[117] In 1915, Louis D. Brandeis wrote, "It is not a movement to remove all the Jews of the world compulsorily to Palestine. In the first place, there are 14,000,000 Jews, and Palestine would not accommodate more than one-third of that number."[118] Most immigrants to Palestine following World War I were predominantly Eastern European Jews of Soviet and satellite origin. Therefore, the Soviets and Soviet-controlled Czechoslovakia supplied them with weapons. Political Zionists encouraged the use of violence, especially after the discovery of the vast mineral wealth of Palestine.[119]

There were numerous reasons for wanting Palestine. Interest in the potential resources in the Dead Sea began before World War I. Moise A. Novomeysky was a Russian engineer and political Zionist who became interested in the Dead Sea's possibilities when fellow scientist, Otto Warburg, mentioned them to him in 1906. Warburg had read a report by German geologist Dr. Max Blankenhorn, of the University of Erlangen, about Sodom and Gomorrah and the Dead Sea that appeared in the *Zeitschrift* of the German Palestine Society.[120] Novomeysky made the first survey of the area in 1911, and recognized its potential wealth. Winston Churchill, secretary of state for the colonies (1921-1922), gave Novomeysky a grant for the exploitation of the Dead Sea.[121] Novomeysky then established the Palestine Potash Company in 1929, the company that would supply 50 percent of Britain's potash during World War II.

In February 1924, in 1925, and in 1928, Weizmann and Marshall conferred with potential investors willing to further their interests in Palestine. In 1926, the Brandeis-Mack Group, headed by Louis

---

[117] Ibid, 329-341

[118] Louis Dembitz Brandeis, The Jewish Problem, How to Solve it, Zionist Essays Publishing Committee, New York, 1915, p. 7

[119] John Beaty, The Iron Curtain Over America, Chestnut Mountain Book, Barboursville, Virginia, 1968, pp. 30-31

[120] William Rainey Harper, Ernest De Witt Burton, and Shailer Mathews (editors), The Biblical world, Volume 13, January-June 1899, The University of Chicago Press, 1899, pp. 212-213

[121] Francis Neilson, The Makers of War, C. C. Nelson Publishing Company, Appleton, Wisconsin, 1950, p. 99

D. Brandeis and Julian W. Mack, both members of the American Jewish Congress, founded the Palestine Economic Corporation (PEC) to develop enterprises in Palestine. By 1946, PEC funded more than ninety operations and launched or enhanced industries such as chemicals, citrus products, paper, plastics, and tires. In 1967, PEC had 11,000 stockholders, primarily in the United States, with millions invested in Israel's industries.[122] Investors included Leon Blum, Albert Einstein, Herbert Samuel, Felix M. Warburg, Cyrus Adler, and Lee K. Frankel. Suddenly, Weizmann had support from American Jews. Marshall and Warburg assured him that his financial troubles were over, and he would no longer have to travel to make appeals to save his movement from bankruptcy.[123]

In Palestine, PEC invested funds in their subsidiary, the Mortgage and Credit Bank, which financed the construction of the majority of modern Jerusalem and northern Tel Aviv. In 1932, with PEC support, the bank participated in establishing the Kiryat Haim area in Haifa and several other settlements. PEC, with others, helped the Palestine Water Company to acquire modern drilling machinery. PEC's Haifa Bay Land Company purchased land in Haifa Bay to provide settlers with land. PEC purchased it from Arab owners. The Palestinians had been farming the land for decades, but the new residents subsequently forced them to relocate.[124]

Warburg, Abraham Flexner, and Robert Szold represented PEC on the board of the Palestine Potash Company, the firm that was exploiting the Dead Sea's resources. PEC had acquired $262,631 worth of the

---

[122] Yakir Plessner, The Political Economy of Israel: From Ideology to Stagnation, State University of New York, Albany, New York, 1994, p. 72

[123] Walter Laqueur, A History of Zionism, From the French Revolution to the Establishment of the State of Israel, MJF Books, New York, 1972, p. 468

[124] Yehuda Bauer: My Brother's Keeper, A History of the American Jewish Joint Distribution Committee 1929-1939, Holocaust preparations in Europe and resistance without solution of the situation, The Jewish Publication Society of America, Philadelphia 1974, http://www.geschichteinchronologie. ch/judentum-aktenlage/hol/joint/Bauer_joint04-10-work-in-Palestine-Emergency-Fund-1929-ENGL.html as of May 2012

company's shares. Theodor Herzl had promised that Palestine had the same kind of massive treasures as South Africa.[125]

On January 14, 1947, in *The New York Herald Tribune*, Zionist opponents inserted a full-page article, entitled *According to Zionists: Misleading World with Untruths for Palestine Conquest,* as an advertisement. Experts estimated the chemical and mineral wealth of the Dead Sea to have a proven value of $5 trillion (1947 money). In order for bankers and Zionists to acquire the resources, it was necessary to establish a Jewish state there. Rose M. Schoendorf, of the Cooperating Americans of the Christian Faiths, signed the article, along with Habib I. Katibah, of the Cooperating Americans of Arab Ancestry, and by Benjamin H. Freedman of the Cooperating Americans of the Jewish Faith. Apart from the Dead Sea minerals, people discovered oil in the Negev Desert in 1951, in addition to the rest of the oil resources in the Middle East.[126]

On November 29, 1947, the UN General Assembly resolved to divide Palestine into three parts—as proclaimed, "Independent Arab and Jewish States and the Special International Regime for the City of Jerusalem . . . shall come into existence in Palestine." On May 14, 1948, in the Provisional State Council in Tel Aviv, David Ben-Gurion, the first Prime Minister of Israel, standing below a portrait of Theodor Herzl, proclaimed the State of Israel.

Formalizing a Platform, the Zionist Congress

In July 1897, the Zionists created a German branch, which Dr. Max I. Bodenheimer directed until 1910. Theodor Herzl, acting as chair, planned to convene the conference in Munich, but opposition by the

---

[125] Yehuda Bauer: My Brother's Keeper, A History of the American Jewish Joint Distribution Committee 1929-1939, Holocaust preparations in Europe and resistance without solution of the situation, The Jewish Publication Society of America, Philadelphia 1974, http://www.geschichteinchronologie. ch/judentum-aktenlage/hol/joint/Bauer_joint04-10-work-in-Palestine-Emergency-Fund-1929-ENGL.html as of May 2012

[126] John Beaty, The Iron Curtain Over America, Chestnut Mountain Book, Barboursville, Virginia, 1968, pp. 30-31

leadership of both the Orthodox and Reform communities compelled him to change the location to Basel. By 1897, the Odessa Committee had more than four thousand members, who then joined the Zionist Organization, established during that First Zionist Congress (August 29-August 31, 1897). Herzl officiated with over two hundred delegates from seventeen countries around the world. Dr. Karpel Lippe opened the congress with the words, "Today is a great day in the history of the Jewish people. This congress represents all of Jewry. The question that we must discuss here is nothing less than enabling the Jews to return to the country of our ancestors. It is the first assembly that expresses the will of the different sectors concerning a national idea that has throbbed in every heart during the prolonged exile." He then introduced Herzl. On August 30, 1897, Dr. Bodenheimer addressed the congress, and delegates elected him as a member of the Action Committee, which drafted the Basle Program as follows:

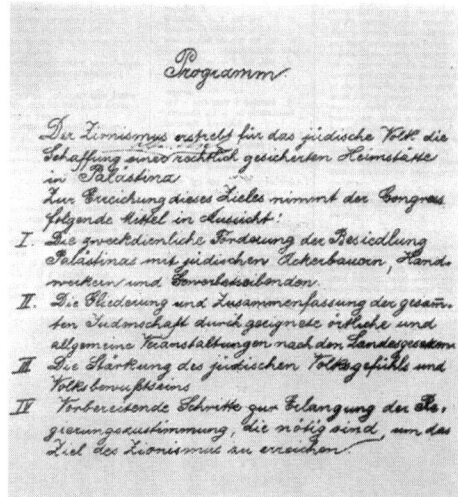

Zionism seeks to secure for the Jewish people a publicly recognized legally secured home in Palestine for the Jewish people. For the achievement of its purpose the congress envisages the following methods:

1) The programmatic encouragement of the settlement of Palestine with Jewish agricultural workers, laborers and those pursuing other trades;

2) The unification and organization of all Jewry into local and wider groups in accordance with the laws of their respective countries;

3) The strengthening of Jewish self-awareness and national consciousness;

4) Preparatory steps to obtain the consent of the various governments necessary for the fulfillment of the aims of Zionism.[127]

During this symposium, the Zionists devised a course outlining their ultimate objectives. They carefully avoided using the phraseology "founding a state," but rather emphasized that they merely wanted to "establish a home in Palestine." The Zionists designated the operations of their movement to the Actions Committee, under the presidency of Herzl. This committee took the responsibility of fulfilling the proposals of the Zionist Organization.[128]

According to Herzl, two agencies would execute the Basel Program— The Society of Jews and the Jewish Company.

Zionism seeks to establish a home for the Jewish people in Palestine, secured under public law. The congress contemplates the following means to the attainment of this end:

1) The promotion by appropriate means of the settlement in Palestine of Jewish farmers, artisans, and tradesmen.
2) The organization and uniting of the whole of Jewry by means of appropriate local and overall events, in accordance with the country's laws.
3) The strengthening and fostering of Jewish national sentiment and national consciousness.
4) Preparatory steps toward obtaining the consent of the government, where necessary, in order to reach the goals of Zionism.

---

[127] Walter Laqueur, A History of Zionism, From the French Revolution to the Establishment of the State of Israel, MJF Books, New York, 1972, p. 106

[128] The Ottoman Empire, Zionism, and the Question of Palestine (1880-1908) Author(s): Mim Kemal Oke Source: International Journal of Middle East Studies, Published by: Cambridge University Press, Volume 14, No. 3 (August 1982), pp. 329-341

In 1903, Joseph Chamberlain, secretary for the colonies, and others devised the British Uganda Program, located in modern-day Kenya, as the location for the Jewish state. Herzl initially declined this proposal, as he preferred Palestine. Following the Kishinev pogrom in April 1903, he proposed, at the Sixth Zionist Congress, that Uganda might serve as a temporary sanctuary for the Russian Jews. His emergency proposal incensed the Russian Jewish delegation, and it left the meeting. The British Uganda scheme was unpopular with possible immigrants, with the Jewish financiers and with politicians in the United States and elsewhere. Still, some of the Zionists supported the Uganda Program, until the Zionist leadership voted against it during the Seventh Zionist Congress in 1905. Herzl favored Uganda—not instead of Palestine, but as progress toward that destination. When Herzl and Litman Rosenthal discussed it afterward, he told Rosenthal, "There is a difference between the final aim and the ways we have to go to achieve this aim."

In August 1903, Max Nordau (Suedfeld), an atheist[129] Hungarian doctor and author, in his address to the Sixth Zionist Congress in Basel, revealed the Basel Program for even greater conflagrations— the coming world wars. Herzl's intimate associate apparently perceived the future, for he explained with clarity in his speech, actually a prognosis of "momentous occurrences." He said, "Let me tell you the following words as if I were showing you the rungs of a ladder leading upward and upward: 1) Herzl, the Zionist congress; 2) the English Uganda proposition; 3) the future world war; 4) the peace conference where; 5) with the help of England; 6) a free Jewish Palestine will be created." Dr. Nahum Sokoloff then elaborated on that speech, saying, "Jerusalem will one day become the capital of world peace."[130]

Litman Rosenthal, an American citizen, attended the World Jewish Congress at Basel in 1903. He later published Dr. Nordau's "ladder revelation" speech in the *American Jewish News* on September 19,

---

[129] Amos Elon, Herzl, Holt, Rinehart and Winston, New York, Chicago, San Francisco, 1975, p. 9
[130] Douglas Reed, The Controversy of Zion, Dolphin Press, Durban, 1978, p. 150

1919. Additional ascending rungs on the ladder leading to a "free and Jewish Palestine" were still required.[131]

To implement their objectives, the Zionists established the Jewish Colonial Trust (JCT), their financial apparatus, with a target figure of £8 million, following their Second Zionist Congress at Basle in August 1898.[132] They planned to use the funds to obtain a charter for Palestine. They also founded the first Zionist bank during that congress and incorporated it in London as the Anglo-Palestine Company on February 27, 1902. The JCT established the Anglo-Palestine Bank, with a start-up capital of £40,000, to carry out their objectives in Palestine. In 1903, the bank opened a Jaffa branch, under the management of Zalman D. Levontin, for purchasing land. After the success of the first branch, they opened offices in Jerusalem, Beirut (then the main commercial center), Hebron, Safed, Haifa, Tiberius, and Gaza.

At the Seventh Zionist Congress in Basle in 1905, Nordau opened the meeting with a eulogy for Herzl. Earlier, the congress appointed a commission to determine the suitability of Uganda, and the majority voted against it in favor of Palestine. Israel Zangwill led the territorialists, who left the congress in protest and later established the Jewish Territorial Association. Nordau declined the presidency of the organization, and Lithuanian-born David Wolffsohn became the new president. The organization moved its headquarters from Vienna to Cologne. In 1907, at the Eighth Zionist Congress, delegates set their sights on Palestine and discussed their strategy which included inciting chaos, such as the Young Turk Revolution against the Ottoman Empire. Wolffsohn sent Arthur Ruppin, of Berlin's Bureau for Jewish Statistics and Demography, (1902-1907) to establish a World Zionist Organization (WZO) branch in Palestine; he opened the Eretz Yisrael Office in Jaffa. In the Ninth Zionist Congress, 1909, in Hamburg, he

---

[131] Donn de Grand Pré, Barbarians Inside the Gates: The Black Book of Bolshevism, Book 1, The Serpent's Sting, G S G & Associates Publishers, San Pedro, California, 2000, pp. 130-131
[132] Mim Kemal Oke, The Ottoman Empire, Zionism, and the Question of Palestine (1880-1908), International Journal of Middle East Studies, Published by: Cambridge University Press, Volume 14, No. 3 (August 1982), pp. 329-341

and Nordau both anticipated that the Young Turk Revolution would drastically enhance their expectations in Palestine.

Wolffsohn died on September 15, 1914. According to his obituary in *The New York Times*, he gave the opening and closing remarks at the Eighth International Zionist Congress held at The Hague in 1907. In his closing remarks, he pleaded for "greater unity among the Jews" and said that eventually "they must conquer the world."[133] After his death, Otto Warburg assumed the presidency, and the WZO moved its headquarters from Cologne to Berlin.

The Anglo-Palestine Bank created a network of credit unions to give individual farmers, rather than the communal kibbutz, long-term loans, and he then helped to construct the first sixty houses in Tel Aviv. During World War I, the Turkish government viewed the bank as hostile, as the Zionists had originally registered it in Britain. The government closed the branches and confiscated the cash, but the Zionists managed to transfer the majority of its assets before the government liquidation. Following the war, the Zionists expanded their bank operations by establishing additional branches. In 1932, the Anglo-Palestine Bank relocated its main office from Jaffa to Jerusalem. In 1934, the JCT ended its financial endeavors, and thereafter functioned as a holding company for Anglo-Palestine Bank shares.

The Society of Jews would implement the "preparatory work in the domains of science and politics, which the Jewish Company will afterwards apply practically." The Jewish Company would function as "the liquidating agent of the business interests of departing Jews and will organize commerce and trade in the new country." Herzl had acknowledged that the "departure of the Jews" would be "gradual, continuous, and will cover many decades." The Jewish Company would send the poorest Jews to "cultivate the soil, construct roads, bridges, railways, and telegraph installations; regulate rivers; and build their own dwellings; their labor will create trade, trade will

---

[133] The New York Times, September 17, 1914

create markets, and markets will attract new settlers, for every man will go voluntarily, at his own expense and his own risk."[134]

Zionist Organization of America

In 1897, Zionists officially founded the Zionist Organization of America (ZOA), which evolved from the Federation of American Zionists (FAZ), founded the year before in Baltimore—an amalgamation of several Hebrew societies that would all endorse the Basle Program. Delegates to FAZ's first conference included Richard Gottheil, whom the delegates elected as president (1898-1904), and Stephen S. Wise as honorary secretary. Jacob de Haas succeeded Wise as secretary. They found the ZOA to support the establishment of the Jewish National Home in Palestine. Its sister organization was Hadassah, the Women's Zionist Organization of America, the Labor Zionist Po'ale Zion parties, and the Mizrachi (religious Zionism). Currently, the ZOA has a national membership of many thousands, with active chapters throughout America. It attempts to strengthen US-Israel relations via educational activities, public affairs programs, advocacy for pro-Israel legislation, and by contesting anti-Semitism and anti-Israel bias in the media, textbooks, travel guides, and on school campuses through the ZOA's Law and Justice Department.

De Haas was the secretary of the First Zionist Congress and, as the editor of the newspaper the *Jewish World* (1892-1900), in London, introduced Theodor Herzl to Britain. In 1899, the Third Zionist Congress elected Leopold J. Greenberg, a British journalist, and De Haas to the Propaganda Committee. Greenberg, a friend of David Lloyd George, invited Herzl to his home and introduced him to some prominent British Jews to persuade them to accept Zionism. De Haas moved to the United States in 1902, and, as a propagandist, he became editor of *The Boston Jewish Advocate* (1908-1918). Herzl recommended that Gottheil hire de Haas as the new ZOA secretary to replace Wise. De Haas soon befriended Louis D. Brandeis, a lawyer, and, by 1908, Brandeis was committed to Zionism.

---

[134] Theodor Herzl, The Jewish State, Dover Publications, Inc., New York, 1988, an unabridged republication of the work originally published in 1946 by the American Zionist Emergency Council, New York p. 37

In 1903, the Union of American Hebrew Congregations, founded July 8, 1873, suggested the establishment of a permanent American Jewish Congress to manage Jewish issues. Following the Kishinev pogroms, outraged Jews again proposed the creation of an American Jewish Congress and other agencies, as they felt that, with increased Jewish immigration, there was no representation of their views in the existing establishments. Soon, the Jewish press began agitating for a union of all Jewish forces, modeled on democratic principles. In 1908, officials appointed Louis Marshall as chairman of the New York State Immigration Commission. In 1890, Marshall had helped revise the judiciary article in New York's constitution and, in 1894, he was a delegate to the New York State Constitutional Convention. In 1902, he was chairman of a commission investigating the slum conditions on New York City's Lower East Side, where hundreds of Jewish immigrants resided.

Meanwhile, in London, prior to 1914, the year that war erupted, Greenberg, the editor of *Jewish Chronicle* (JC) (1907-1931), criticized czarist Russia over that country's alleged ill-treatment of the Jews. In his editorials, he advised Britain to join Austria and Germany in a war against Russia. After Germany entered Belgium, he maintained that Britain should join Russia and fight against Austria/Germany. On September 4, 1914, he wrote, "From the Russian people, Jews have never experienced anything but the deepest sympathy, and with the Russian people, they have ever felt on mutually agreeable terms."

Bernard G. Richards, the executive secretary of the Executive Committee for an American Jewish Congress wrote, "The outbreak of the great world war in August 1914, which at once hurled millions of our brethren into the cataclysm of ruin, devastation, and death, brought American Jewry to a sudden sense of its responsibility, as the only large Jewish center which had escaped the catastrophe and was living in freedom and prosperity."[135]

---

[135] Samuel Margoshes, The Jewish communal register of New York city, 1917-1918 By Jewish Community of New York City, pp. 1429-1435

American Zionists assumed the major responsibility for the Zionist organization when World War I broke out in Europe. They established the Provisional Executive Committee for Zionist Affairs in New York on August 20, 1914, and elected Brandeis to lead the organization (1914-1918). He, as the head of American Zionism, conducted a speaking tour in the fall and winter (1914-1915) to gain support for Zionism and the development of a Jewish homeland. He said that it would solve anti-Semitism and the Jewish problem in Europe and Russia. He was always coaxing the Jews to unite; organization is essential, especially for a minority ideological group.

The Zionists held a conference in New York on August 30, 1914, and adopted a resolution submitted by Dr. Nachman Syrkin, a founder of the Zionist Laborite movement, Baruch Zuckerman, and Richards.[136]

On October 21, 1914, Brandeis, as a representative of the Provisional Executive Committee for General Zionist Affairs (created August 30, 1914), wrote to Louis Marshall, the president and cofounder, with Jacob H. Schiff and Dr. Cyrus Adler, of the American Jewish Committee. It was an agency to monitor legislation and diplomacy pertinent to American Jews and to communicate their requests and information to US government officials. Brandeis invited Marshall to join him "in calling a conference of representatives of all important Jewish organizations and groups in the country." Brandeis, Marshall and Adler headed this conference to seek methods on creating more efficient organizations.[137]

On October 25, 1914, Marshall, Schiff and Felix M. Warburg organized and headed the American Jewish Relief Committee. Another organization, the Central Committee for the Relief of Jews Suffering through the War (Central Relief Committee), chaired by Leon Kamaiky, organized on October 4, 1914, funded the activities of the Joint Distribution Committee of (the American) Funds for Jewish War Sufferers (JDC), founded on November 27, 1914. The agency

---

[136] Ibid
[137] Ibid

centralized allocations of aid to Jews adversely affected by World War I. The socialist People's Relief Committee, chaired by Meyer London, joined these other groups in August 1915. Warburg was the JDC's first chairman.[138]

Brandeis, Rabbi Stephen S. Wise, and Judge Julian W. Mack directed the Jewish Congress Organization Committee, established in March 1915. They attempted to introduce American Jewry to the Jewish problem in Europe. Brandeis wanted to unite the American Jewish Committee, created in 1906, and other Jewish organizations. In 1916, before the conclusion of the war, delegates representing more than one million Jews convened in Philadelphia and prepared a list of Jewish demands to submit to the Paris Peace Conference. They elected a National Executive Committee and made Brandeis the honorary chairman.

Brandeis spoke about the importance of Zionism at a conference of Reform Rabbis in April 1915. In that speech he said, "They believe that only in Palestine can Jewish life be fully protected from the forces of disintegration . . . and that by securing for those Jews who wish to settle there the opportunity to do so, not only those Jews, but all other Jews will be benefited, and that the long perplexing Jewish Problem will, at last, find solution." He also explained, "Let no American imagine that Zionism is inconsistent with patriotism. Multiple loyalties are objectionable only if they are inconsistent . . . Every American Jew who aids in advancing the Jewish settlement in Palestine, though he feels that neither he nor his descendants will ever live there, will likewise be a better man and a better American for doing so. There is no inconsistency between loyalty to America and loyalty to Jewry."

On April 6, 1917, the United States entered the war. On June 10, 1917, at least 335,000 Jews living in America elected delegates who, along with representatives of thirty national organizations, established the American Jewish Congress (AJC). It elected Rabbi Stephen S. Wise, Judge Louis D. Brandeis, Judge Felix Frankfurter, Golda Meier

---

[138] American Jewish Joint Distribution Committee, The Yivo Encyclopedia of Jews in Eastern Europe, http://www.yivoencyclopedia.org/default.aspx as of May 2012

Meyerson, and others. Wise established policies stating that Jews are entitled to more than mere charity, but to justice.[139] The AJC elected Schiff, Marshall, Wise, Julian W. Mack, and Abram I. Elkus, US ambassador to Turkey (1916-1917), to its executive committee, with an aim toward convening a world tribunal.[140] Following World War I, the AJC and their associates partially failed to establish this tribunal, but succeeded in instituting one after World War II at Nuremburg, establishing the precedent of a world court dominated by the ruling elite.

After the United States entered the war, Frankfurter was a special assistant to the Secretary of War. During that time, he associated with Santeri Nuorteva (alias for Alexander Nyberg), a Bolshevik agent in the United States. On May 9, 1918, Frankfurter wrote to Nuorteva about "interests that mean much for the whole world."[141]

An administrative committee, in conjunction with the executive committee, decided to hold a congress with invited delegates. Professor Isaac A. Hourwitch and Solomon Sufrin received the 133,000 votes for likely delegates from all over the country. Out of that number, they would select 300 delegates to attend the congress, scheduled for November 18, 1918, after peace negotiations began.[142]

While they did not create the AJC until 1917, the influence of American Zionists, like Brandeis, was evident before then. He considered the United States an amalgamation of various ethnicities who would "spiritually enrich the United States and would make it a democracy *par excellence.*" American Zionists, both religious and secular,

---

[139] American Jewish Congress, http://www.ajcongress.org/site/PageServer as of May 2012

[140] The Jewish Congress elected Schiff, Marshall, Wise, Elkus and Mack to its Executive Committee with an aim toward convening a World Tribunal, The New York Times, June 1, 1920

[141] Selected Documents from Government Files of the United States and Great Britain, http://www.reformation.org/wall-st-bolshevik-app3.html as of May 2012

[142] Samuel Margoshes, The Jewish communal register of New York city, 1917-1918 By Jewish Community of New York City, pp. 1440-1441

adopted, promoted, and popularized these viewpoints.[143] Marshall, former chairman of the board of directors of the Jewish Theological Seminary of America, was the president of Congregation Emanu-El of New York City. He functioned as the AJC's chief policymaker and lobbyist. As its president until 1929, he strenuously opposed congressional bills that would prohibit illiterate Jews from entering the United States. He also wanted Congress to abolish the literacy test and led the movement that ultimately abrogated the US-Russian Commercial Treaty of 1832 in 1911.

In 1919, Marshall attended the Paris Peace Conference at Versailles, where he assisted in the formulation of the clauses for the "full and equal civil, religious, political, and national rights" of Jews in the constitutions of the newly created nations in Eastern Europe. He opposed the Census Bureau's proposal of enumerating Jews as a race. While he disagreed with some Zionist policies, he advocated the establishment of a Jewish homeland in Palestine. He helped organize the American Jewish Relief Committee to facilitate those colonization efforts.

In the 1920s and 1930s, the AJC promoted economic and political rights for the Jews living in Eastern Europe because of their reported persecution. AJC activism and demands might have actually increased ethnic tensions. The AJC, an influential, well-financed group, led by such people as Rabbi Stephen S. Wise and others, insisted that Jews have political representation, be able to establish separate communities, and maintain an independent Jewish national culture. When political leaders in European countries devised treaties with Turkey, they incorporated stipulations that required the state to furnish instructions in minority languages. Furthermore, per the treaty, authorities could not require Jews to attend court or other public events occurring on their Sabbath.[144]

---

[143] Kevin MacDonald, Jewish Involvement in Shaping American, Immigration Policy, 1881-1965: A Historical Review, Population and Environment: A Journal of Interdisciplinary Studies, Volume 19, Number 4, March 1998, pp. 295-297

[144] Kevin MacDonald, Jewish Involvement in Shaping American, Immigration Policy, 1881-1965: A Historical Review, Population and Environment: A

In 1924, Maurice Samuel wrote, "We Jews, we, the destroyers, will remain the destroyers forever. Nothing that you do will meet our needs and demands. We will forever destroy because we need a world of our own, a God-world, which it is not in your nature to build. Beyond all temporary alliances with this or that faction lies the ultimate split in nature and destiny, the enmity between the Game and God. But those of us who fail to understand that truth will always be found in alliance with your rebellious factions, until disillusionment comes. The wretched fate which scattered us through your midst has thrust this unwelcome role upon us."[145] In 1931, Ben Hecht, a Hollywood screenwriter, in his book, *A Jew in Love*, wrote, "One of the finest things ever done by the mob was the crucifixion of Christ. Intellectually it was a splendid gesture. But trust the mob to bungle. If I had charge of executing Christ, I'd have handled it differently. You see, what I would have done was had him shipped to Rome and fed to the lions. They never could have made a savior out of mincemeat."[146]

Journal of Interdisciplinary Studies, Volume 19, Number 4, March 1998, pp. 295-297

[145] Maurice Samuel, You Gentiles, New York, 1924, re-print, CPA Books, Boring, Oregon, 1995, p. 155

[146] Ben Hecht, A Jew in love, Covici Friede, New York, 1931, pp. 120-121

SECTION 2

SOCIAL ENGINEERING—MILITARIZATION, SOCIALIZATION, AND COMMUNISM

The Corporatization of Christianity, Worshipping another God

In his book, *Capitalism and Slavery*, Eric Williams concluded that the massive slave trade in the Atlantic helped fuel the Industrial Revolution, especially in Protestant countries, where governments allowed Jewish financiers to reside. Officials borrowed vast amounts of money from them for warfare and to construct and equip slave ships, which used various iron contraptions to restrain the slaves. Opportunists always use industry, technology, and warfare to profit. Andrew Carnegie exploited his position in the War Department and invested in iron manufacturing and coal mining and, by 1863, had an annual income over $40,000. In 1861, John D. Rockefeller's Cleveland merchandising business received "war orders," and, as prices increased, so did his profits. Two years later, he opened an oil-refining business. By 1880, he was refining 95 percent of the nation's oil.

People like Carnegie and Rockefeller set a new Darwinist-style, survival-of-the-fittest, love-of-money, dog-eat-dog standard, which some people adopted. Many people abandoned personal virtues, such as thrift, diligence, and honesty in their efforts to secure personal wealth while fostering the characteristics of shrewdness, mendacity, sophistication, and specialization. Darwinism transformed traditional values and beliefs.[147]

The gospel, as originally preached, focused on the internal soul, fixing oneself, not on altering society. When individuals or groups,

---

[147] Heather A. Warren, Theologians of a New World Order: Rheinhold Niebuhr and the Christian Realists, 1920-1948, Oxford University Press, 1997, p. 8

like socialists, assume the task of fixing others, they frequently adopt an egotistical stance of self-serving superiority. After all, to lift others, one must believe he/she is in a higher, loftier, morally-managerial position. While it is meritorious to help others, contrary to popular theological thought, we are not our brother's *keeper*, as the word itself implies control. People have distorted the verse's application. Because of free will, one cannot force others to change, unless they requisition the law to act in his/her behalf. A person only has power to change themselves. Socialists, posturing as noble, caring humanitarians, unify and vociferously demand change, even if it negatively impacts others, saying that free choice or spreading democracy often represents death and destruction for people. Many churches have abandoned traditional peaceful Christianity and use their money and power to influence government to impose their views on society through the force of law. Instead of traditional theology, churches veered toward a communal, socialistic approach to humanity's challenges, which actually serve a small, profit-seeking minority who exploit the people's naivety and ignorance for their own objectives. In order to affect such a theological shift, the money powers had to control the theological seminaries.

Before the Civil War, foreign-trained American theologians introduced socialism into the Protestant seminaries. In 1829, industrialist Cyrus H. McCormick established and funded the McCormick Theological Seminary, one of the eleven theological schools of the Presbyterian Church (US). It shares a campus with the Lutheran School of Theology, bordering the campus of the University of Chicago, possibly the American version of the University of Göttingen, a school where teachers regularly recruited students into secret societies. John D. Rockefeller financially supported the University of Chicago Divinity School, a seminary that they integrated into the host university, which he also funded. Rockefeller, through his tax-exempt foundations, bankrolled the Union Theological Seminary and later, the Federal Council of Churches.[148]

---

[148] Peter Collier and David Horowitz, The Rockefellers: An American Dynasty, Holt, Rinehart and Winston, Austin, Texas, 1976, p. 155

George Williams founded the original quasi-Masonic Young Men's Christian Association (YMCA) on June 6, 1844, in London, after witnessing the unhealthy social conditions due to the industrial revolution. He did for the YMCA what Lord Robert Baden-Powell had done for scouting. The Order of the Rag is a secret society within the YMCA, allegedly a Christian organization. The first YMCA American chapter was in Boston on December 29, 1844. Within eleven years, the YMCA had become an international movement. On November 14, 1861, Morris K. Jessup, later a Pilgrims Society member, a banker and philanthropist, assisted in the creation of the United States Christian Commission. He cofounded the New York City chapter of the YMCA and served as its president in 1872.

Jessup presided over the New York Chamber of Commerce (1899-1907) and was president of the American Sunday School Union and the American Museum of Natural History. He was a trustee of the Union Theological Seminary and the Peabody Education Fund and was the treasurer of the Slater Fund, which later became the Rockefeller Foundation. He sat on Rockefeller's General Education Board (GEB).[149]

By 1890, all of the major seminaries promoted theories about social justice, ideas that John Ruskin expounded on in his book, *Unto This Last* (1860). August Rauschenbusch, a Baptist minister, an ardent abolitionist, and a German immigrant (1846) who came from a long line of Lutheran preachers, taught at the Rochester Theological Seminary.[150] In 1885, his son, Walter, graduated from Rochester, fully indoctrinated in the tenets of Illuminism, a philosophy that encourages faith in man instead of in God. In December 1892, Walter Rauschenbusch, with others, organized the Brotherhood of the Kingdom to inculcate socialism into the nation's churches.[151]

[149] Charles Savoie, Pilgrims, Silver Investor, May 2005, www.silver-investor.com/charlessavoie/cs_may05_pilgrims.htm as of May 2012
[150] Christopher Hodge Evans, The kingdom is always but coming: a life of Walter Rauschenbusch, Wm. B. Eerdmans Publishing, Grand Rapids, Michigan, 2004, pp. 10-11
[151] Ibid, 103-104, 106, 121

He said, "If ever socialism is to succeed, it cannot succeed in an irreligious country. It must start in the churches."[152]

In 1893, Bishop Frederic D. Huntington, a graduate of Amherst College and Harvard Divinity School and an Anglican monk of the Order of the Holy Cross, founded the American branch of the Christian Socialist Movement, a faction of London's Fabian Society and the British Labour Party. Huntington, a dedicated socialist and a central New York Episcopalian bishop, was president of the Church Social Union and sympathized with his parishioners because of their working conditions. He and his son James established the Church Association in the Interests of Labor (CAIL). Huntington was the CAIL president (1887-1904).[153]

The dissemination of socialism in the churches coincided with the spread of socialism elsewhere. In 1902, delegates and lay officials of numerous churches had attended the national convention of the Socialist Party in Chicago. "Christians" then created two Christian Socialist organizations "with the avowed purpose of extending the principles of socialism among church people of America." The first and largest organization, created in June 1906, was the Christian Socialist Fellowship, an interdenominational group, headquartered in Chicago. Its general secretary was Rev. Edward Ellis Carr, Ph.D. It published *The Christian Socialist* and had over fifty branches; many of its members allied with the Socialist Party. Its officials delivered socialist sermons in thousands of churches and circulated millions of copies of its paper to preachers, teachers, and social workers. Many churches, YMCAs, and colleges were receptive to the socialist message.[154]

---

[152] David Emerson Gumaer, Apostasy, The National Council Of Churches, http://reformed-theology.org/html/issue07/apostasy.htm as of May 2012

[153] Robert E. Weir, Beyond Labor's Veil: The Culture of the Knights of Labor, Pennsylvania State University Press, University Park, Pennsylvania, 1996, pp. 81-82

[154] Alexander Trachtenberg (editor) The American labor year book, 1917-18, Volume 2, Rand School of Social Science. Dept. of Labor Research, New York, 1918, pp. 359-360

In 1906, a few clergy and lay people of the Episcopal Church organized the America Church Socialist League, which became more powerful as the influence of the Episcopal Church increased. Many leading American industrialists belonged to the Episcopal Church, an ecclesiastical body that officially adopted radical and even revolutionary policies. Out of six thousand clergy, several hundred advocated socialism, and nearly one hundred clerics were members of the Socialist Party.[155]

On November 15, 1905, theologians had created the Federal Council of Churches in New York City. Later it would become the National Council of Churches.[156] On December 4, 1908, this council adopted the Social Creed of the Churches, written by a protégé of Walter Rauschenbusch, London-born Harry F. Ward, American Methodist minister, left-wing activist, and the first chairman of the ACLU, an organization founded in 1920. Felix Frankfurter was one of its founding members. Ward taught ethics at the Union Theological Seminary (1918-1941), helped found the Methodist Federation for Social Action, and was the chairman of the American League against War and Fascism, a communist front. Ward met with Stalin in 1924 and again in 1929. He went to China in 1925, and taught Christian clergymen there. Korea's prominent religious leaders received training at Union Theological under the tutelage of Henry S. Coffin (S&B) who was president of the seminary (1926-1945).[157]

Leading Pilgrim Society members traditionally invite the Archbishop of Canterbury, the head of the Church of England, and the Episcopal Bishops of New York to senior positions within the Pilgrims Society. Bishop Henry C. Potter of the Episcopal Diocese of New York (1887-1908), president of the Pilgrims Society (1903-1907), advocated social reform and regularly went to London to preach at Canterbury

---

[155] Ibid
[156] John Frederick Woolverton, Robert H. Gardiner and the Reunification of worldwide Christianity in the Progressive Era, University of Missouri Press, Columbia, Missouri, 2005, p. 47
[157] Skull & Bones—The Bush's China Connection, From an article in the New Federalist, January 26, 1990, http://www.illuminati-news.com/S&B-China. htm as of May 2012

Cathedral, at Westminster Abbey, and at St. Paul's Cathedral. Members of the society allegedly staff St. Paul's Church.[158] St. Paul's is at the top of Ludgate Hill, the highest point in the City of London, and functions as the mother church of the Diocese of London.

The Pilgrims Society and organizations like the YMCA, Elks, and Rotary Clubs are philosophically integrated sects within the freemason framework. Though they differ, some of the rituals, objectives, and idiosyncrasies have commonality. Many are even identical to freemasonry. Pope Leo XIII wrote, "Let us remember that Christianity and freemasonry are essentially incompatible, to such an extent, that to become united with one means being divorced from the other."[159] Pope Benedict, on November 5, 1920, warned against such groups as the YMCA and similar sects, while unalike in name, apply similar Masonic principles. Pope Benedict XV (1914-1922) stated, "The YMCA intends to purify and spread a more perfect knowledge of real life, placing itself above all churches and outside of any religious jurisdiction." On November 5, 1920, in a letter, he wrote that the YMCA is fundamentally Masonic in nature.[160]

Leading theologians and prestigious seminaries promote an agenda of progressive reform and international expansion. John D. Rockefeller and J. Pierpont Morgan wholly supported their efforts in setting America's moral course at home and abroad, compatible with Woodrow Wilson's vision of building a new world order. Their support increased the membership of the Student Volunteer Movement for Foreign Missions, an organization founded in 1886 to recruit college and university students for missionary service abroad.[161] Arthur T.

[158] Joël van der Reijden, The Pilgrim Society: a Study of the Anglo-American Establishment, Institute for the Study of Globalization & Covert Politics, July 2008, p. 14

[159] Papacy and Freemasonry, Speech by Monseigneur Jouin, December 8, 1930, http://www.upholdingtradition.com/modernproblems/freemasonry/pmasnry.htm as of May 2012

[160] Papal Condemnations of Freemasonry, http://www.destroyfreemasonry.com/chapter12.htm as of May 2012

[161] Heather A. Warren, Theologians of a New World Order: Rheinhold Niebuhr and the Christian Realists, 1920-1948, Oxford University Press, 1997, pp. 17-18

Pierson, who was determined to evangelize the world, initiated the movement. Librarians categorized the records of the organization in the Yale Divinity School Library.

Pastor Harry E. Fosdick, a graduate of Union Theological Seminary, was, by 1922, the pastor of the Riverside Church. With financing from John D. Rockefeller Jr., he, with the congregation's support, decided to build a gigantic, Gothic-style interdenominational cathedral, modeled after France's Cathédrale Notre-Dame de Chartres, to characterize New York City values. It is now a UNESCO World Heritage Site. Fosdick remained senior minister at the Park Avenue Baptist Church until 1946 where he established diversity and progressivism.

J. Pierpont Morgan managed the financial resources of the Trinity Church, at the intersection of Broadway and Wall Street, in the Episcopal Diocese of New York. The church currently owns about forty commercial properties in Manhattan and sports a stock portfolio of about $50 million, which together produces a healthy yearly return of $25 million, of which officials expend $2.6 million for benevolent causes. Officials pay the rector a salary of $100,000 a year, and he resides on the Upper East Side. St. Bartholomew, located on Fifth Avenue, spends about $100,000 a year out of its annual budget of $3.2 million.[162]

On February 10, 1914, Carnegie, with leaders from the Federal Council of Churches, created the Church Peace Union, a council affiliate which hoped to appeal to both Protestants and Catholics. He pledged $2 million to the group. The Fabian Socialists established the International Fellowship of Reconciliation. On November 11, 1915, socialists organized an American branch of the fellowship.

That council spearheaded many interdenominational projects when the United States entered World War I, which gave "Christian" credibility to warfare. It coordinated the efforts of many denominations and other groups like the YMCA and YWCA. It created the general committee

---

[162] Eustace Mullins, Murder by Injection, the Story of the Medical Conspiracy Against America, the National—Council for Medical Research, Staunton, Virginia, 1988, pp. 339-348

66

on Army and Navy Chaplains and the General Wartime Commission of the Churches. The rigors of war convinced many people that worldwide cooperation was preferable to competition with each other for men's souls. Some theologians suggested the creation of an international Christian council comparable to the League of Nations, but without doctrinal divisions. Their motto "Doctrine divides, but service unites," sounded deceptively appealing.[163]

Eldon G. Ernst produced propaganda under the direction of Raymond B. Fosdick, Rockefeller's lawyer and brother of Pastor Harry E. Fosdick. Ernst, a graduate of Rochester Divinity School and Yale University, wrote *Moment of Truth for Protestant America: Interchurch Campaigns Following World War I*. It provided the standard interpretation of the Interchurch World Movement (IWM) of 1919-1920. It was a convoluted fabrication of the historical record based on a document entitled *History of the Interchurch World Movement*. Editors compiled that history to conceal Rockefeller's heavy financial role in the IWM, which began functioning immediately after the armistice, using big business promotional methods.[164]

The IWM sought to merge Protestant resources in an attempt to "Christianize the world" with their faux style of the gospels. Raymond B. Fosdick found the perfect deep pocket to help fund his internationalist ideology. Rockefeller also began funding the Eastern Establishment's Council on Foreign Relations (CFR).[165] Fosdick, a New World Order proponent, was one of Rockefeller's most confidential associates and a trustee (1921-1948) and president (1936-1948) of the Rockefeller Foundation. He had long supported Wilson, who he had known since 1903 when he studied at Princeton

---

[163] Heather A. Warren, Theologians of a New World Order: Rheinhold Niebuhr and the Christian Realists, 1920-1948, Oxford University Press, 1997, pp. 17-18

[164] Charles E. Harvey, John D. Rockefeller, Jr., and the Interchurch World Movement of 1919-1920: a Different Angle on the Ecumenical Movement, Church History, Volume: 51, Issue: 2, 1982, pp. 198-201

[165] Will Banyan, Rockefeller Internationalism, Part 1, Nexus Magazine Volume 10-Number 3, (April-May 2003)

University.[166] Fosdick was a civilian aide to General John J. Pershing and accompanied Wilson to the Paris Peace Conference (1919). He had a good relationship with Edward M. House, Wilson's adviser.[167]

In January 1920, during the IWM World Survey Conference in Atlantic City, Rockefeller, serving on the budget-review committee, endorsed IWM Industrial Relations Department's pro-union investigation of the steel strike. He reiterated that the church needed to be more socially concerned in the future. He became a member of the IWM executive committee soon after the conference and secretly promised to underwrite any IWM bank loans. Rockefeller, at his son's urging, endowed the IWM with at least $50 million or more. He made certain there was sufficient money to finance a huge campaign to sell the unification concept of the IWM to bind ministers of participating churches in a common pension fund as well as in foreign and domestic issues.[168]

John D. Rockefeller Jr. persuaded his father that the IWM would have more extensive influence than the League of Nations in promoting worldwide peace, contentment, goodwill, and prosperity. He envisioned a powerful religious alliance that would function, under his father's skillful tactics, like a corporation. The whole underlying intention for the enormous amount of financing was the financial amalgamation of the churches in order to advance a practical Christianity based on voluntary social welfare designed to eliminate class conflict and theological disputes and denominational controversies to impose the younger Rockefeller's social liberalism, ideas he had embraced at Brown University.[169]

In 1923, Raymond B. Fosdick, lobbying for US participation in the League of Nations, created the League of Nations Association. In January 1924, he visited President Wilson, who decried the fact

---

[166]   Ibid
[167]   Ibid
[168]   Charles E. Harvey, John D. Rockefeller, Jr., and the Interchurch World Movement of 1919-1920: a Different Angle on the Ecumenical Movement, Church History, Volume: 51, Issue: 2, 1982, pp. 198-201
[169]   Ibid. 202-203

that the United States was restraining human progress. He said it "was unthinkable that America would remain aloof, for America would not thwart the hope of the race." Wilson died a month later, but Fosdick continued working toward Wilson's goal of world peace through world government. In 1928, he published *The Old Savage in the New Civilization* and maintained that we must have a centralized government and dissolution of state sovereignty.[170]

The Federal Council assaulted free enterprise and capitalism and promoted socialism. In its 1932 official report, it stated, "The Christian ideal calls for hearty support of a planned economic system . . . It demands that cooperation shall replace competition as a fundamental method." In December 1932, at a meeting in Indianapolis, the council unanimously espoused the socialist creed: "The churches should stand for social planning and control of the credit and monetary system and the economic processes." The council changed its name to the National Council of Churches to distance itself from its communistic image. Even with the name change, many astute people denounced the organization for its continued propagation of radical socialism and totalitarian authority. Through the Ford Foundation, the National Council of Churches has donated hundreds of thousands of dollars to militarize revolutionary communist groups in Africa, while thousands of Americans condemn the slaughter and violence there.[171]

Monopolizing Minds, the Government's Education System

Centralized banking devastates a nation's economy but exclusive control of education is considerably more dangerous but ultimately more effective in the management of the population. Author Gary Allen maintains, "Those who control education will over a period of several generations control a nation."[172]

---

[170] Will Banyan, Rockefeller Internationalism, Part 1, Nexus Magazine Volume 10-Number 3, (April-May 2003)

[171] Gary Allen, The Rockefeller File, the Untold Story of the Most Powerful Family in America by, 76 Press, Seal Beach, California, 1976, pp. 36-37

[172] Ibid, 47

On March 2, 1867, officials created the National Bureau of Education, under the jurisdiction of the Department of Interior, with Yale-educated Henry Barnard as the first Commissioner of Education.[173] Immediately following the Civil War, American-born George Peabody, a freemason and a British banker, funded the Southern Education Fund, reportedly to resuscitate Southern culture. It was the precedent for Rockefeller's General Education Board.[174] In April 1872, the US Bureau of Education, to accommodate the needs of top businessmen concerned about the availability of compliant workers, published a pamphlet addressing problematic schooling.[175] In 1875, they adopted the name the Office of Education and began gathering statistical information on US educational institutions under the auspices of the Interior Department. Educator John Eaton claimed that public education would reduce crime and increase one's earning power.[176]

Thomas W. Bicknell, a freemason and president of the New England Publishing Company, became president of the new National Council of Education, a group of Hegelian educators who ultimately imposed certain educational philosophies, standards, and principles. The council included William T. Harris, John Dewey, Calvin Stowe, Nicholas Murray Butler, G. Stanley Hall, Josiah Royce, Charles W. Eliot, and James Earl Russell.[177] This group became the basis for the National Education Association (NEA), a monopoly labor union, incorporated in 1886 in the District of Columbia. Congress chartered it in 1906, under Title 36 of the US Code. The NEA is of little value

---

[173] Paolo Lionni, The Leipzig Connection, the Systematic Destruction of American Education, Delphian Press, 1988, pp. 51-52

[174] E. Richard Brown, Rockefeller Medicine Men, Medicine and Capitalism in America and the World, University of California Press, Berkeley, Los Angeles, 1979, p. 44

[175] Paolo Lionni, The Leipzig Connection, the Systematic Destruction of American Education, Delphian Press, 1988, pp. 51-52

[176] Report of the Honorable John Eaton, US Commissioner of Education, for the year 1877, on crime and education, giving the views of Dr. Elisha Harris and Hon. John Hitz, Washington DC, 1879

[177] Samuel Blumenfeld, NEA: Trojan Horse in American Education, The Paradigm Company, 1984, pp. 43-44

to individual instructors, but benefits the principals, superintendents, publishers, and school suppliers, all NEA members.[178]

In 1887, John D. Rockefeller gave $600,000 to Frederick T. Gates, a graduate of Rochester Theological Seminary, to establish the University of Chicago. Gates, who previously managed the philanthropic affairs of the late George A. Pillsbury (S&B), became the chief architect of Rockefeller's philanthropic donations and other personal holdings in 1891. Sixteen months later, Rockefeller gave William R. Harper $1 million to make the college a university.[179] Rockefeller ultimately endowed the school with nearly $50 million. By 1888, the Senate Committee on Education produced a 1,382 page document to define the purpose of mass education—impose conformity and subordination and restrain natural curiosity through an "anti-intellectual shift in schooling" under compulsory, regulatory standards.[180]

In 1890, Rockefeller purchased the well-renowned *Encyclopedia Britannica*. By 1900, Northern businessmen and their Southern collaborators developed schools, especially in the South, where people still embraced militant populism which endangered the objectives of certain Southern liberals and Northern businessmen, like Rockefeller Jr. and Robert C. Ogden, and others who wished to renovate and industrialize the South.[181] On January 12, 1902, with congressional approval, Rockefeller established the General Education Board (GEB) to disperse funds to advance certain predetermined objectives, as defined in Andrew Carnegie's two-part essay, *Gospel of Wealth*

---

[178]   Ibid, 40-42, 44-45

[179]   W. Allen Wallis, University Of Rochester Library Bulletin, Volume XXIV · Fall 1968 · Number 1, Rochester and Chicago, remarks, president of the University of Rochester

[180]   John Taylor Gatto, The Underground History of American Education: A School Teacher's Intimate Investigation Into the Problem of Modern Schooling, Oxford Village Press, 2000, pp. 184-185

[181]   E. Richard Brown, Rockefeller Medicine Men, Medicine and Capitalism in America and the World, University of California Press, Berkeley, Los Angeles, 1979, p. 44

(1889). Rockefeller and Gates designed the philanthropic General Education Board as an agency to transform society.[182]

Part of Rockefeller's GEB Occasional Letter Number One (1906) states, "In our dreams . . . people yield themselves with perfect docility to our molding hands. The present educational conventions (intellectual and character education) fade from our minds, and, unhampered by tradition, we work our own good will upon a grateful and responsive folk. We shall not try to make these people or any of their children into philosophers or men of learning or men of science. We have not to raise up from among them authors, educators, poets, or men of letters. We shall not search for embryo great artists, painters, musicians, nor lawyers, doctors, preachers, politicians, statesmen, of whom we have ample supply."[183]

Indoctrinating the Teachers, Shaping Children's Minds

G. Stanley Hall, who had studied at the Union Theological Seminary, then at Harvard, returned from Leipzig in 1883, where he had studied at Wilhelm Wundt's laboratory and joined the staff at Boston's Johns Hopkins University (founded January 22, 1876), where he established a psychology laboratory. In 1887, he founded the *American Journal of Psychology*.[184] Woodrow Wilson, after Princeton, also entered Johns Hopkins in the fall of 1883, and earned his doctorate in history and political science. On October 2, 1889, Hall became president (1889-1920) of the new Clark University in Worcester, Massachusetts, founded by US businessman Jonas G. Clark. In July 1892, Hall, an advocate of Darwin's theory, and twenty-five other individuals at Clark founded the American Psychological Association (APA), and he became its first president. In 1909, he invited Carl Jung and Sigmund Freud, a member of B'nai B'rith, to deliver lectures at Clark. The school played a prominent role in the development of psychology

---

[182] Ibid. 44
[183] John Taylor Gatto, The Underground History of American Education: A School Teacher's Intimate Investigation Into the Problem of Modern Schooling, Oxford Village Press, 2000, pp. 67-68
[184] Paolo Lionni, The Leipzig Connection, the Systematic Destruction of American Education, Delphian Press, 1988, p. 15

as a discipline. In 1904, Hall, the father of the child psychology movement, published the two-volume masterpiece, *Adolescence: Its Psychology and Its Relations to Physiology, Anthropology, Sociology, Sex, Crime, Religion, and Education.* In 1921, he published *Aspects of Child Life and Education.*[185]

Johns Hopkins' first president and cofounder was Daniel C. Gilman, one of the three individuals who incorporated The Russell Trust, The Order of Skull and Bones. It was the first American university to apply the German university model developed by Wilhelm von Humboldt and Friedrich Schleiermacher. Gilman incorporated both the John F. Slater Fund, which later became the Rockefeller Foundation and Rockefeller's General Education Board, which took over US medical education.[186] Rockefeller gave his foundation $100 million in its first year of operation, 1913. The elite transfer their funds into tax-exempt foundations, similar to taking money from one pocket and putting it into another pocket to escape taxes and to further grind the face of the poor by controlling and directing domestic and foreign policy.

John Dewey, a graduate of Johns Hopkins, studied under Hall and received his doctorate in 1884. In 1894, he joined the staff of the University of Chicago (1894-1904). The university, organized as the center of the Fabian socialist program in America, established an education laboratory.[187] Beginning in late 1895, Dewey, the "Father of American Education," headed the combined departments of philosophy, psychology, and pedagogy. In 1886,

---

[185]   Ibid. 15

[186]   Eustace Mullins, Murder by Injection, the Story of the Medical Conspiracy Against America, the National—Council for Medical Research, Staunton, Virginia, 1988, p. 11

[187]   Paolo Lionni, The Leipzig Connection, the Systematic Destruction of American Education, Delphian Press, 1988, pp. 16-17

he authored *Psychology*, a textbook on the application of revised education, which instructors used in the schools of educational training throughout the country.[188] Dewey, a statist, believed that a child exists exclusively for the benefit of the state, which requires the suppression of individual interests, skills, and propensities. Thus, students receive only approved knowledge.[189]

In 1887, Dr. Nicholas Murray Butler cofounded the New York School for the Training of Teachers (now Teachers College, Columbia University). Butler also lectured at Johns Hopkins University in Baltimore. He was president of Columbia University for forty-three years, beginning in 1902. Author Elizabeth Dilling, in *The Roosevelt Red Record and His Background,* stated that Columbia spawned many of the New Deal "brain-trusters" and was the "center of radicalism."[190]

Butler, who chaired the American Pilgrims Society of International Finance, was a lifelong friend of Elihu Root and was later president of the Carnegie Endowment for International Peace. He convinced Carnegie to provide the initial $10 million to establish the foundation in 1910. In 1942, Butler published a book of essays entitled *Liberty Equality Fraternity.* The elite intend to socialize the masses by managing the law, elections, the press, and by controlling education. Butler did his share as president of Columbia University for decades.

Equality, except ideally before the law, is impossible and illogical, even in nature. Individuals have inherent appearances, genetic intelligence, and native skills. For instance, female birds are never going to have the brilliantly colored plumage of their male counterparts. However, for generations, agent provocateurs have successfully incited the

---

[188] Charlotte Thomson Iserbyt, The Deliberate Dumbing Down of America, Conscience Press, Ohio, 1999, p. 5

[189] Antony C. Sutton, America's Secret Establishment, an Introduction to the Order of Skull & Bones, Trine Day, Walterville, Oregon, 2002, pp. 56, 92, 102-103

[190] Elizabeth Dilling, The Roosevelt Red Record and His Background, self-published, 1938, p. 9

masses to parrot the term, "liberty, equality, fraternity," to provide bottom-up demands for popularity-vote-seeking politicians who exploit the enthusiastic masses who, in their naivety accommodate the elite agenda by using their irrational noble-sounding phrases. This ultimately leads to the destruction of all privileges and the existence of the very factors that protect the populace and their liberty and property from the elite.

In 1899, Dewey was the president of the American Psychological Association. From 1904 on, he taught at the Teachers College at Columbia University. In 1905, he became president of the American Philosophical Association and was a member of the American Federation of Teachers. He cofounded The New School for Social Research with historian Charles Beard and economists Thorstein Veblen and James H. Robinson. He changed traditional education from teaching mental skills to feeding data to mold young minds and stimulate nervous systems to react in a predictable manner. Teachers became guides in the socialization of every student. Students are to adapt and become well adjusted (conditioned) in order to function in society, not as an individual but as part of the herd. He promoted the leveling of individual differences into a common social order. He, like Wundt, viewed individuals as animals whose learning occurred through experience and the stimulus-response mechanism. At the University of Chicago and the Teachers College, Dewey inculcated educational theories with psychology.[191]

Professor Edward L. Thorndike equated children with rats, monkeys, and other animals. He applied his "science," which de-emphasized traditional educational basics, to the training of teachers, who then conveyed it to every part of the United States. Thorndike focused on three objectives for the six-year period of elementary education: experience for the students, testing of native skills and intellect, and exploration of vocational aptitudes. This would ultimately entail psychological testing of all students.[192] Big Pharma would be prepared with appropriate medications for those who displayed too much

---

[191] Paolo Lionni, The Leipzig Connection, the Systematic Destruction of American Education, Delphian Press, 1988, pp. 19-20

[192] Ibid. 32, 37-38, 39

individualism, expended too much natural energy, or demonstrated too much native curiosity or some other demeanor incompatible with developing the herd mentality.

David Wechsler, a Jewish Romanian immigrant and a graduate of Columbia University (1925) had worked during World War I with the US Army in developing psychological tests to screen draftees. In 1939, as chief psychologist at Bellevue Psychiatric Hospital, he discarded quotient scores, and assigned an arbitrary value of 100 to denote average intelligence. He developed the Wechsler Adult Intelligence Scale (WAIS). In 1949, he devised a similar test of children (WISC), followed, in 1967, by a test for preschoolers (WPPSI). He based these tests on his philosophy that intelligence is "the global capacity to act purposefully, to think rationally, and to deal effectively with (one's) environment."

J. Pierpont Morgan totally dominated the administrations of the Ivy League schools from the 1880s to the 1930s. Morgan, an Anglophile internationalist, made large endowments followed by continuous communication with the administrations at Harvard, Columbia, and Yale, to a lesser degree, in order to set educational policies. Whitney money influenced the policies at Yale, and the Prudential Insurance Company determined policies at Princeton. The presidents of the universities owed their jobs to the financial powers. Morgan positioned Butler as president of Columbia.[193] He was Morgan's chief representative at Columbia for decades until the Depression-ridden 1930s, when Morgan's power began to decrease. He retained Butler in that position long after he was physically unable to effectively manage the responsibilities of the office.[194]

Rockefeller buffered himself from criticism by pouring his millions into productive philanthropies, like education and medicine. Raymond B. Fosdick, Rockefeller Foundation president, admitted that the whole idea was about social control. The GEB granted unlimited funds to the Wundt-educated psychologists, whose goals were to radically alter

---

[193] Carroll Quigley, Tragedy and Hope, a History of the world in Our Time, The Macmillan Company, New York, 1966, p. 937
[194] Ibid. 980

US education.[195] Rockefeller, by 1909, had given $53 million, and, by 1921, he had personally donated over $129 million to the GEB.[196] In the 1921 annual GEB report, Rockefeller directed the removal of all restrictions on the board's ability "to dispose in any manner it sees fit of the principal (and interest) of all gifts which he has made." The sum total of educational grants through this board amounted to $126,788,094. He created the GEB to "accomplish certain ends" and expected the recipients to administer the funds accordingly.[197]

In collaboration, the Rockefeller Foundation would regulate domestic education, and the Carnegie Foundation would dominate international education. Their first objective was to alter the way that instructors taught history. They approached the Guggenheim Foundation, which, like the Rhodes scholarship program, granted fellowships. It agreed to fund twenty US history students who were seeking doctoral degrees. These students, after indoctrination in London, formed the nucleus of the American Historical Association. This association gave a $400,000 grant to create a seven-volume subjective history designed to promote a socialistic future. The objective in all US government schools and most private colleges is to alter history and discredit constitutional principles as outdated and impractical.[198]

On October 17, 1979, Trilateralist Jimmy Carter, a Rockefeller minion, signed the Department of Education Organization Act, which made the US Department of Education a cabinet-level department. It began operating on May 4, 1980, administered by the Secretary of Education. Several Republicans claim, while on the campaign trail, that they want to abolish this agency. George W. Bush expanded and energized it with his No Child Left Behind law, enacted on January

[195] Paolo Lionni, The Leipzig Connection, the Systematic Destruction of American Education, Delphian Press, 1988, pp. 58-59

[196] James D. Anderson, The Education of Blacks in the South, 1860-1935, University of North Carolina Press, Chapel Hill, North Carolina, 1988, p. 86

[197] Samuel Chapman Armstrong, The Southern Workman, Volume 51, Press of the Hampton Normal and Agricultural Institute, Hampton, Virginia, January 1922, pp. 206-207

[198] Transcript of Norman Dodd with G. Edward Griffin, 1982 available at www.realityzone.com/hiddenagenda2.html as of May 2012

8, 2002. According to this law, each school must provide a student's personal information to military recruiters and institutions of higher education. The student may choose not to have their information shared, but silence is consent. The agency's budget increased 69.6 percent between 2002 and 2004.

The elite have dominated the educational system since the Civil War. They wish to create a two-class economy with a master/slave subordinate society to coincide with the *Communist Manifesto*, which advocates a "free education for all children in public schools, abolition of children's factory labor in its present form, and a combination of education with industrial production." Public schools, regulated by the Department of Education, indoctrinate students to be patriotic and obedient and to pay their fair share of sales, income and numerous other taxes. Further, teachers instruct them that the majority rules, whether that majority is right or wrong.

Immigration, Facilitating Political Objectives

People, like pawns in the elite's global chess game, migrate for diverse reasons—natural disasters, warfare, famine, economics, and religious or ethnic persecution. Often, for political or cultural objectives, certain entities manage and fund persecution, a form of terrorism. The elites, under humanitarian auspices shift populations, through immigration, to designated areas to facilitate cultural-engineering goals. Economic depression, forcing emigration from one area, accommodates cheap labor requirements elsewhere. Governments shift "expendable" populations to camps, isolated reservations, or crowded inner-city neighborhoods. They attempt to alter the demographics in numerous countries in order to affect political change.

On September 16, 1788, the Continental Congress, operating under the Articles of Confederation, recommended that the states pass laws to prohibit the transportation of malefactors from foreign countries. Until the Act of March 2, 1819, laws regulating immigration were nonexistent. That act, the origination of immigration statistics, did not restrict admittance but required the government to maintain a list of all foreigners. From 1790 to 1819, about 200,000 to 300,000 aliens came to America, probably from the same part of Europe as previous settlers to America.[199]

Most of the original settlers arrived from Britain, Scotland, Wales, Holland, and Germany, bringing with them particular cultural and political propensities, such as self-reliance and the desire for a limited, nonintrusive government. Thus, they shaped a society where the people and not the state held the sovereign power. The country was English-speaking, and the government intentionally restricted and regulated immigration to maintain an ethnic balance. Between 1830 and 1880, a little over 10,000,000 immigrants came to America, about 9,000,000 from Northern Europe and over 600,000 from Canada and Newfoundland.

According to the official history of the Temple Emanu-El (founded 1845) in New York, there were about 10,000 mostly Sephardic Jews living in the United States during the American Revolution.[200] This figure appears incompatible with the 1790, census unless the Jews claimed another ethnicity, which seems incongruent with their tradition of remaining separate and distinct. According to the 1790 census, the ethnic composition of America was: Total white: 3,172,444-English: 2,605,699, 82.1 percent; Scotch: 221,562, 7.0 percent; Irish: 61,534, 1.9 percent; Dutch: 78,959, 2.5 percent; French: 17,619, 0.6 percent; German: 176,407, 5.6 percent; Hebrew: 1,243, all other: 9,421, 0. percent.[201] The total population in 1790 was 3,929,214, which indicates that there were 756,770 nonwhites represented in the census. They did not include Indians until 1850.

After the failure of the revolutions in Europe in 1848, socialists, many of who were the Jewish instigators of those revolts, emigrated from

---

[199] Drew L. Smith, The Legacy of the Melting Pot, a Sociological, Historical Study, The Christopher Publishing House, North Quincy, Massachusetts, 1971, pp. 132-134

[200] Temple Emanu-El, History, http://www.emanuelnyc.org/simple.php/about_ history as of May 2012

[201] Drew L. Smith, The Legacy of the Melting Pot, a Sociological, Historical Study, The Christopher Publishing House, North Quincy, Massachusetts, 1971, pp. 78-79

Prussia and Austria and other places to England, and, from there, they immigrated to America. From 1835 to 1855, about 250,000 Jews arrived in the United States, settling primarily in New York, Baltimore, Cincinnati, San Francisco, and other large, urban areas. The roots of the oldest Reform synagogues in America are in those communities.[202]

In 1854, following the gold rush, 13,100 Chinese arrived and began displacing white labor in California mines. The state, in 1858, prohibited all people of the Chinese or Mongolian race from entrance. Then, in July 1868, commercial greed for cheap Chinese labor produced the Burlingame Treaty with China, which allowed unrestricted residence to the Chinese in the United States in exchange for the same privilege in China. It benefitted the Chinese and the industrialists, but most Americans did not want to relocate to China. In 1875, the United States began restricting immigration when they enacted prohibitions against foreign criminals and prostitutes and a provision addressing Japanese and Chinese labor, a particular problem in California. In 1882, Chinese arrivals totaled 39,579, which generated anti-Chinese riots by infuriated white laborers on the Pacific coast, who now had to compete with cheaper labor.[203]

Between 1820 and 1880, at least 228,945 Chinese came to America. Congress passed the first Chinese Exclusion Act, effective on May 6, 1882. To circumvent the law, the Chinese forged identification certificates and used other tactics. The Supreme Court then handed down a judgment in the Chae Chan Ping vs. United States case. The court stated that the United States had "the absolute right to exclude aliens as an inherent and inalienable right of every sovereign and independent nation."[204]

---

[202] Temple Emanu-El, History, http://www.emanuelnyc.org/simple.php/about_ history as of May 2012
[203] Drew L. Smith, The Legacy of the Melting Pot, a Sociological, Historical Study, The Christopher Publishing House, North Quincy, Massachusetts, 1971, pp. 134-135
[204] Ibid. 137-138

After 1880, certain politicians altered the nation's immigration policies, and millions of people came from Southern and Eastern Europe. Most of them were non-Christian and held socialistic objectives hostile to the ideals and ethics that most of the population championed.[205] Most of the assimilated Jews living in America, about 280,000 by 1877, were Sephardic from Germany. Because they were a minority, they could not contribute culturally to the hordes of new arrivals. According to official US immigration records, 3,237,079 people, mostly Jews, arrived in the United States between 1881 and 1920. They came from the area of Russia that was formerly the kingdom of Poland before the "partitions" (1772-1795).[206] Poland, between the two world wars, was the Republic of Poland. Those immigrants make up most of New York City's 2,500,000 or more Jews.[207] Other records indicate that about 2,000,000 Jews immigrated to the United States between 1880 and 1914.[208]

The vast numbers of incoming Eastern European Jews were decidedly more aggressive than the assimilated, westernized Jews who had settled in America before 1880. While we usually associate socialism with the Bolshevik Revolution, we should understand that people promoted revolutionary socialistic ideas decades before that revolution. The new arrivals were more politically oriented than their coreligionists, many of whom had become successful merchants, an occupation in which they excelled. The Jews now arriving quickly entered into the professions and the industries, and participated in politics.[209] The assimilated Jews, primarily from Germany before 1880, were very dissimilar to the newcomers.[210]

---

[205]   John Beaty, The Iron Curtain Over America, Chestnut Mountain Book, Barboursville, Virginia, 1968, p. 36
[206]   Carl L. Becker, Modern history: Europe since 1600, Silver Burdett, New York, 1964, p. 138
[207]   John Beaty, The Iron Curtain Over America, Chestnut Mountain Book, Barboursville, Virginia, 1968, pp. 37-38
[208]   Avraham Barkai, Branching Out: German-Jewish Immigration to the United States, 1820-1914, Holmes & Meier, New York, 1994, p. 191
[209]   John Beaty, The Iron Curtain Over America, Chestnut Mountain Book, Barboursville, Virginia, 1968, p. 38
[210]   Ibid. 38

After 1880, and in the first two decades of the twentieth century, emigration from Eastern Europe increased dramatically. The new arrivals, many of them Zionists, influenced the previous policies of American Reform Judaism to the extent that its leaders finally capitulated to their demands and persistent pressure.[211] Many of these immigrants perceived themselves as a separate nationality, a peculiar, even a special people, and considered assimilation quite unacceptable. Author Henry P. Fairchild wrote, "In the first place, the Jews have always considered themselves a superior people. This is neither remarkable nor reprehensible. Every nationality considers itself superior. That is inherent in the nature of nationality. Perhaps the Jews have been a little more candid and outspoken than other peoples in professing their superiority."[212] John Beaty, in his book, *The Iron Curtain over America*, wrote, "America now has virtually a nation within the nation, and an aggressive culture-conscious nation at that."[213]

New immigration answered the demand for cheap white labor in the eastern industrial factories, just as the Asian immigration had met the demand for cheap labor in the West. In addition to the hordes of Italians, immigrants came from Spain, Turkey, Russia, Poland, Austria, Hungary, Greece, and the Balkans. Many furious citizens appealed to government officials, who apparently did not study the assimilability of culturally incompatible people. Congress finally reacted with the Act of March 3, 1891, imposing a tax on each immigrant and disqualifying people with contagious diseases and felons and indigents.[214]

---

[211] John Beaty, The Iron Curtain Over America, Chestnut Mountain Book, Barboursville, Virginia, 1968, pp. 38-39

[212] Henry Pratt Fairchild, Race and Nationality as Factors in American Life, Ronald Press Co., New York, 1947, p. 145

[213] John Beaty, The Iron Curtain Over America, Chestnut Mountain Book, Barboursville, Virginia, 1968, p. 39

[214] Drew L. Smith, The Legacy of the Melting Pot, a Sociological, Historical Study, The Christopher Publishing House, North Quincy, Massachusetts, 1971, pp. 145-146, 148

On September 11, 1891, Baron Maurice de Hirsch, a German-Jewish banker and philanthropist, who sponsored the educational work of the Alliance Israélite Universelle, created the Jewish Colonization Association as an English society, with a capital of £2,000,000 along with Baron Alfred de Rothschild. Hirsch's goal was to facilitate a mass emigration of Jews from Russia and other Eastern European countries. He planned to relocate them to fertile lands in North and South America owned by the association. It had large agricultural colonies in Canada, Palestine and Argentina. Moises Ville, the colony in Argentina (1,250,000 acres) was a home for many Yiddish-speaking Russian Jews. Each family received a 200-acre homestead, a manageable mortgage, a few cows, and some chickens.[215]

As the pogroms in Eastern Europe increased in frequency and violence, Jewish refugees fled to the United States, which had just adjusted their immigration policies. To help the arriving evacuees to acclimate, Jacob H. Schiff, closely associated with the Rothschilds, organized humanitarian committees, which systematically shifted a majority of the new refugees into large cities, like New York, Chicago, Boston, Philadelphia, Detroit, and Los Angeles. Schiff, Isidor Straus, Samuel Greenbaum, Myer Isaacs, and Isaac Seligman thought that New York's recent immigrants, needing a "transformative educational institution" and assisted them in their efforts to adjust. On May 4, 1893, they formalized the Educational Alliance, a consolidation of many other factions whose leaders focused on social, educational, and other activities for the new immigrants. It catered to both males and females of all ages.[216]

Schiff, along with lawyers, rabbis, publishers, and business leaders, had constant, close communication with each other and with the European Jewish social and political leaders via cable, traditional correspondence, and the Alliance Israélite Universelle. They knew

---

[215] Fiddler on the Hoof: The Jewish Gauchos of Argentina by Mark Freeman, ORT Reporter, 1990, http://www-rohan.sdsu.edu/~mfreeman/resources.php?content_id=17 as of May 2012

[216] Hasia R. Diner, The Jews of the United States, 1654 to 2000, University of California Press, Berkeley, California, 2004, p. 136

that superior organization and constant communication were essential to their objectives.[217]

On December 18, 1904, Carl Schurz, an early Jewish immigrant following the failed socialist revolutions in Europe in 1848, delivered an address before the Educational Alliance at the Temple Emanu-El in New York City at the request of his "highly valued friend," Isidor Straus, co-owner of Macy's department store with his brother Nathan, was also a member of the US House of Representatives (1894-1895). Schurz told the audience, "The importance of the task undertaken by your association cannot be overestimated. There is in this City of Greater New York the greatest aggregation in the whole world of people of the Jewish race and faith, some 600,000 to 700,000 of them . . . mostly newcomers."[218]

Steamship companies and other labor-intensive entities encouraged Japanese immigration, which brought an outcry from California citizens. Organized labor also took a stand against this immigration. On February 15, 1907, President Theodore Roosevelt made a "gentlemen's agreement" with Japanese officials, which stipulated that they would not indiscriminately issue passports to the United States, except under certain conditions. The Japanese then entered the United States through Mexico. Japanese men, living in the United States, often arranged to have "picture brides," a proxy marriage. They then sent for their wives. The gentlemen's agreement ended on March 1, 1920, but, by then, many thousands of Japanese children had been born, as the Japanese birth rate was three times greater than the birth rate for the whites in California.[219]

[217] Ibid. 178-179

[218] Educating Immigrants, Address delivered before the Educational Alliance in the vestry rooms of Temple Emanu-El, New York City, December 18, 1904 by Carl Schurz. A clipping found in the papers of Carl Schurz in the Library of Congress taken from the 12th annual report of the Alliance, pp. 73-77, http://www.trip.net/~bobwb/schurz/speech/educationalliance.html as of May 2012

[219] Drew L. Smith, The Legacy of the Melting Pot, a Sociological, Historical Study, The Christopher Publishing House, North Quincy, Massachusetts, 1971, pp. 141-142

In the 1880s, white immigrants had been entering from Southern and Eastern Europe. From 1880 to 1900, over 8,000,000 immigrants inundated the country, many from Italy. In the decade 1820-1830, 68 percent of the immigrants came from Northern and Western Europe, while only 2.2 percent came from Southern and Eastern Europe. By 1910-1920, it had changed considerably—17.4 percent came from Northern and Western Europe, while 59.0 percent came from Southern and Eastern Europe.[220]

Between 1901 and 1910, despite restrictive legislation, authorities admitted 8,795,386 immigrants to America. Congress overrode President Woodrow Wilson's veto and passed the Immigration Act of February 5, 1917, which restricted immigration from Asia. On May 19, 1921, Congress passed the Emergency Quota Act, restricting immigrants, based on the number of that nationality who lived in the country in 1910, according to the census. The Immigration Act of 1924, enacted May 26, 1924, after considerable debate, supplanted the act of 1921.[221] This act restricted the number of immigrants from any country to 2 percent of the number of people from that country who were already living in the United States in 1890.

Regarding immigration, Calvin Coolidge said in his first annual message, on December 6, 1923, "American institutions rest solely on good citizenship." People who had a background of self-government created them. He endorsed "restricted immigration," in keeping with America's capacity to absorb immigrants willing to practice good citizenship. He said, "Those who do not want to be partakers of the American spirit ought not to settle in America."[222]

---

[220] Ibid. 143-144

[221] Drew L. Smith, The Legacy of the Melting Pot, a Sociological, Historical Study, The Christopher Publishing House, North Quincy, Massachusetts, 1971, pp. 145-146, 148

[222] Calvin Coolidge, First Annual Message, December 6, 1923, http://www.presidency.ucsb.edu/ws/index.php?pid=29564#axzz1MnTYMkRz as of May 2012

Indiscriminant Immigration, Creating Crime and Chaos

Many Jewish immigrants to America engaged in numerous criminal activities, such as murder, racketeering, bootlegging, prostitution and narcotics. They also participated in New York's socialistic labor movement, activities that naturally generated anti-Semitism. The Jewish mobsters competed with the Italian and Irish gangs, but generally operated in the Jewish neighborhoods in New York's Lower East Side. Jacob Levinsky headed the Yiddish Black Hand, and, by the beginning of the twentieth century, the Jewish underworld was more influential in New York than the Italian or Irish gangs.

In 1901, Joseph Petrosino, a New York City police officer who fought against organized crime, especially the Black Hand, assigned his intelligence network to infiltrate the Italian-based anarchist organization, a member of which, Benedetto Cairoli, had assassinated King Umberto of Italy on July 29, 1900. Petrosino's men discovered that the group intended to kill President William McKinley when he attended the Pan-American Exposition in Buffalo in 1901. He alerted the Secret Service, but officials ignored his warning. Leon F. Czolgosz shot McKinley on September 6, 1901. Vice President Theodore Roosevelt, who had a close relationship with the B'nai B'rith, stepped into the presidency when McKinley died on September 14, 1901.[223] Simon Wolf, the Washington DC representative for the B'nai B'rith, and Roosevelt later organized Jewish American backing for the collapse of the Russian czar.[224]

Petrosino thought that the only way to eradicate the Black Hand was to eliminate ignorance. He said, "The gangsters who are holding Little Italy in the grip of terror come chiefly from Sicily and Southern Italy, and they are primitive country robbers transplanted into cities." They used brutal methods. He said that an American would never "think of stopping somebody and slashing his face with a knife just to take his wallet" or "blow up a man's house or kill his children because he refused to pay fifty or a hundred dollars." Apparently,

---

[223] Executive Intelligence Review, The Ugly Truth About the ADL, Washington DC, 1992, pp. 28-31

[224] Ibid. 26-28

the crimes that Italian immigrants committed in America were the same kind perpetrated by rural outlaws in Italy." He said, "In short we are dealing with banditry transplanted to the most modern city in the world."[225]

By the turn of the century, local police officers were disturbed over the incidence of increasing crime, especially in the large urban areas. In September 1908, Theodore A. Bingham, the New York City Police Commissioner (1905-1909), wrote an article for the *North American Review*, entitled *"Foreign Criminals in New York."* His article described the increase in gambling, prostitution and drugs on the Lower East Side, attributing it to Jewish, Italian, and Irish immigrants.[226] He used the Secret Service in an attempt to quash crime and eradicate the Black Hand in that area. When he became commissioner, he said, "From this moment on, the goal of my life shall be to crush the Black Hand and to destroy these vile foreign criminals who have come to disrupt the serenity of our peaceful land."[227]

The Anti-Defamation League (ADL), then known as the Publicity Committee of the B'nai B'rith, condemned Bingham, one of their first targets, and accused him of anti-Semitism and of "maligning Jews" even though he focused his efforts against all criminal activity. Ultimately, his enemies succeeded in toppling him as police commissioner. Arnold Rothstein, the son of a garment manufacturer, headed racketeering in New York after the ADL eliminated Bingham's influence.[228] They also got rid of Petrosino. Members of New York's Black Hand followed him to Palermo and, on March 12, 1909, shot and killed Bingham's chief detective. He had traveled to Italy to gain the cooperation of the police there to inhibit the anarchist activities

225 Lt. Joseph Petrosino Murder, http://www.gangrule.com/events/petrosino-murder-1909 as of May 2012
226 Executive Intelligence Review, The Ugly Truth About the ADL, Washington DC, 1992, pp. 26-28
227 Lt. Joseph Petrosino Murder, http://www.gangrule.com/events/petrosino-murder-1909 as of May 2012
228 Theodore Alfred Bingham, The Girl that Disappears: The Real Facts about the White Slave Traffic, The Gorham Press, Boston, 1911, pp. 6-10

of the Black Hand, working jointly in the United States and Italy. *The New York Herald* had published the story of Petrosino's mission on February 20, 1909, just before his departure.[229] Apparently, someone deliberately leaked the story to the newspaper.

Because of the human trafficking emanating from New York, key Jewish families in the United States, Germany, France, and Britain held a meeting, the Jewish International Convention on the Suppression of the Traffic in Girls and Women, in London in April 1910. Arthur R. Moro, the keynote speaker, presented an account describing the association of Jewish gangsters in the worldwide prostitution and white slave trade.[230] He described how Jewish prostitution, by 1901, existed in Johannesburg, Pretoria, Lourenco Marques, Beira, and Salisbury. In 1903, a Jewish teacher reported the scandalous traffic by Jews of Jewesses in Alexandria, Cairo, and Port Said. Jewish prostitutes were more numerous than Greek, Italian, and French prostitutes. Moses Levi, the Chief Rabbi, in Constantinople (1872-1908) revealed that agents openly trafficked prostitutes and had their own synagogue.[231]

In 1911, Bingham wrote *The Girl That Disappears, the Real Facts about the White Slave Traffic*. In this book, he related the sinister facts regarding the thousands of young girls that disappeared every year from their homes in the cities or those who left their homes on the farm or small town to go to the city. Often, their families never heard from them again.[232]

In 1909, Rabbi Judah P. Magnes led prominent families in New York to create their own Bureau of Social Morals. The bureau engaged Abe Schoenfeld, the same investigator that John D. Rockefeller Jr. used in order to penetrate the criminal network on the Lower East Side. In 1922, the rabbi moved to Jerusalem, taking all of Schoenfeld's files with him. He founded the Hebrew University, which is the current

---

[229] Executive Intelligence Review, The Ugly Truth About the ADL, Washington DC, 1992, pp. 28-31
[230] Ibid. 26-28
[231] Ibid. 28-31
[232]

repository of those voluminous files detailing organized crime in New York, in the university's carefully secured archives, part of the school's most guarded records.[233] The B'nai B'rith established the ADL, in large measure, to protect Jewish-surnamed gangsters and possibly to counter criticism of many of the individuals responsible for the Federal Reserve.[234] Presidents Truman, Eisenhower, Kennedy, Johnson, and Reagan lavished praise on the ADL's efforts.

In October 1913, through the instrumentality of Sigmund Livingston, a Jewish attorney from Chicago, the B'nai B'rith formally founded the ADL, headquartered in New York, as an international nongovernmental organization (NGO) to thwart criticism and discrimination on an international basis regarding organized crime and international anarchist networks. He not only founded but also directed the ADL's activities its first thirty years. Prior to that, he headed the powerful B'nai B'rith Midwest Lodge #6. He was a lawyer for the Chicago and Alton Railway, whose owner, William Moore, had ties to J. Pierpont Morgan since the 1890s.[235]

On February 23, 1905, Paul P. Harris, of B'nai B'rith, along with Silvester Schele, Gustavus Loehr, and Hiram Shorey, founded Rotary International in Chicago. There are Rotary Clubs throughout the world, including Russia, Sweden, France, Estonia, and other unexpected areas. Similar groups with freemason connections include Lions International, founded in 1917 by Melvin Jones, a freemason[236] and a member of B'nai B'rith. Lions Clubs are located in America and around the world, with a total of 17,441 clubs. freemasons infiltrated the Bohemian Club, founded in 1872 Sonoma County, north of

---

233 Gyeorgos C. Hatonn, Advanced Demolition Legion: The ADL in Action, Phoenix Source Distributors, Inc., Las Vegas, Nevada, 1994, pp. 81-83

234 Executive Intelligence Review, The Ugly Truth About the ADL, Washington DC, 1992, pp. 28-31

235 Ibid. 28-31

236 American Freemasons, http://freemasonry.bcy.ca/textfiles/famous.html as of May 2012

San Francisco. Currently, there are at least 2,700 male members, politicians, bankers, and businessmen.[237]

Baron Maurice de Hirsch, allied with the B'nai B'rith, financed the relocation, from Romania, of Yechiel Bronfman in 1889. Not wanting to work in agriculture, he entered the hotel and prostitution business. His sons, Sam and Abe, produced whiskey during the Canadian Prohibition (1915-1919). They owned the Pure Drug Company, founded with the assistance of the Hudson's Bay Company.[238]

Meanwhile, in America, manufacturers of altered, chemicalized cheaply made liquor forced the distillers of good, fine whiskey out of the business. Pure whiskey requires years to age, whereas chemically altered, highly intoxicating liquor takes only three to four hours. The Jewish firms, by appropriating the name "whiskey," attempted to deceive the public into believing that it was the same product. However, the public still preferred the standard, American-made brands, so the makers of adulterated products had to resort to trickery. Prohibition bootleggers were not the first who sidetracked or stole shipments of whiskey.[239]

The people who controlled the majority of the top brands of whiskey were Isaac Strauss and Solomon W. Pritz, Max Hirsch, J. and Sol H. and A. Freiburg, Angelo Meyer, Nathan Hofheimer, Morris S. Greenbaum, Joseph Wolf, Lee Levy, Dreyfuss-Weil Company, and Bluthenthal and Blickert. Yet, a few authentic distillers remained.[240]

Therefore, like the sugar-industry moguls, the whiskey manufacturers devised a way of gathering the "honest distillers" into a trust, through which they hoped to gain credibility by their connection with such name

---

[237]   Jüri Lina, Architects of Deception, Referent Publishing, Stockholm, Sweden, 2004, pp. 345-346

[238]   Executive Intelligence Review, The Ugly Truth About the ADL, Washington DC, 1992, pp. 23-25

[239]   Henry Ford, The International Jew, The Noontide Press, Newport Beach, California, pp. 502-503

[240]   John Benedict, Who Controls the Whiskey Trust?, American Mercury, December 1959, 3-18

brands. With all the producers under one management, they would manipulate the price, as Rockefeller had done with oil, to downgrade the quality of those brands. In 1898, the legitimate distillers tried to establish such a conglomerate, the Kentucky Distillers, to counter the onslaught of imitation whiskey. Unfortunately, the group was unable to acquire sufficient capital to finance its plan. Conversely, the makers of bogus liquor, with adequate Jewish capital and with initial investment of $32,000,000, hired lawyers, Levy D. Mayer and Alfred Austrian (Rothstein's attorney), to create The Kentucky Distilleries and Warehouse Company which soon controlled 90 percent of the product, including the standard brands. Mayer said, "It was true that the legitimate distillers had suffered from Depression, not because the American people were not consuming liquor, however, but because the American people had been turned from pure whisky to 'red eye.'"[241]

The "Jewish agents of Jewish capital" built a huge network for generating massive revenues, complete with a propaganda apparatus to shape public opinion. From the time they consolidated the distillers, whiskey became so rotten in the whiskey state, Kentucky, that there remained only four wet counties by 1908. The Jewish controllers focused on selling their debauched liquor in quantity, including selling the cheap barrel-house at cut-rate prices. Many Jews became saloon owners and the number of dives selling barrel-house increased. Soon, there was a widespread wave of vice in various parts of the country, which people could not explain. However, the people behind it knew the cause.[242]

In 1908, Norman Hapgood, the editor of *Collier's Weekly*, published the names of the Jews behind the nation's liquor debauchery. He referred to something called "nigger gin," an abhorrent potion which apparently influenced the "Negro" in a "most vicious manner." William H. Irwin, a muckraking journalist, called this gin "the king iniquity in the degenerated liquor traffic of these United States." Irwin named the people who made this gin and other concoctions

---

[241] Henry Ford, The International Jew, The Noontide Press, Newport Beach, California, pp. 502-503
[242] Ibid. 506-507

like it. Irwin implied that this "nigger gin" incited certain Negroes to commit crime. Irwin wrote about the makers of this vile drink and suggested that they should be behind bars. He cited Lee Levy's gin, Dreyfuss, Weil & Company's gin, Bluthenthal & Blickert's gin, and the Old Spring Distilling Company's gin. Irwin claimed that these provoked a "peculiar lawlessness," as its "labels bore lascivious suggestions and were decorated with highly indecent portraiture of white women." This gin was always available to the Negro, whether in Galveston, New Orleans or elsewhere.[243]

When liquor became legal in Canada, the Bronfman brothers started peddling their whiskey to underworld gangsters in America, who had instituted Prohibition in 1920. The US government, through its records, claim that over 34,000 Americans died from drinking their whiskey during that short era. Edgar Bronfman Sr., Sam's son, a longtime ADL director, is the former president of the World Jewish Congress (1981-2007). His deputy was Israel Singer.[244]

Congressman Emanuel Celler, whose father, Henry, owned a whiskey business, had financial interests in liquor. The Celler's basement had a 25,000-gallon whiskey tank filled with the family brand, Echo Spring. In 1922, Emanuel Celler ran for Congress. He enlisted others to canvass the neighborhoods, stressing "the evils of Prohibition and the virtues of the League of Nations." He won the election and took office in March of 1923, where he stayed for forty-nine years and ten months.[245] In 1951, he introduced a bill that decreased the tax on whiskey by two-fifths.

Benjamin Fein and Romanian-born Joe Rosenzweig, who dominated the garment district with their extortion and labor racketeering while Arnold Rothstein established a gambling casino in Manhattan, had financial interests in a horseracing track and numerous speakeasies

243 Ibid. 506-507
244 Executive Intelligence Review, The Ugly Truth About the ADL, Washington DC, 1992, pp. 23-25
245 American Jewish Historical Society, A Voice for the Displaced, Chapter 72, http://www.ajhs.org/scholarship/chapters/chapter.cfm?documentID=262 as of May 2012

and made millions during Prohibition (1920-1933), running his organization like a corporation. Jewish gangsters were prominent in the underworld and in the distribution of illegal alcohol and organized crime. They operated in large cities like Cleveland, Detroit, Minneapolis, Newark, New York City, Chicago, and Philadelphia. Meyer Lansky (Majer Suchowliński), whose family immigrated from Poland (1911), and Benjamin "Bugsy" Siegel headed the violent Bug and Meyer Mob, and Abe Bernstein directed the Purple Gang. Others who grew rich during prohibition included Dutch Schultz, Morris B. Dalitz, Charles Solomon and Abner Zwillman. By 1931, Charles "Lucky" Luciano (Salvatore Lucania) eliminated the Sicilian Mafia bosses and the Jewish mobsters seized control of the New York Mafia. Luciano worked with Lansky and Siegel. Dalitz, the crime boss of Cleveland, had gambling interests, labor racketeering, and money-laundering operations in Hollywood, Las Vegas, and Miami.[246]

On November 11, 1931, the gangsters held a conference at New York's Franconia Hotel. Jacob Shapiro, Louis Buchalter, Joseph Stacher, Hyman Holtz, Louis Kravitz, Harry Tietlebaum, Philip Kovolick, and Harry Greenberg attended the meeting, during which the "Yids" and the "dagos" would collaborate in what the press called the National Crime Syndicate. Lansky developed gambling interests in Cuba, Florida, New Orleans, and Las Vegas. Buchalter led Murder Incorporated, the syndicate's organization of hit men.

In the early 1930s, Meyer Lansky and his gang disrupted rallies held by Nazi sympathizers. Lansky and his gang threw supporters out of windows and beat people who supported Adolf Hitler. The underworld gangsters got away with these criminal activities because of the Anti-Defamation League's public-relations campaigns. Otherwise, Dalitz, Lansky, Siegel, and others would never have the capability of inundating the country with illegal drugs and alcohol. The authorities would have incarcerated gangsters such as Morris Kleinmah, Sam Tucker, and Louis Rothkopf, and their self-described

---

[246] Executive Intelligence Review, The Ugly Truth About the ADL, Washington DC, 1992, pp. 23-25

"Jewish Navy" which smuggled rotgut whiskey into the Midwest from the Bronfmans in Canada.[247]

Lansky and Dalitz teamed up in Cuba, a place where gambling and narcotics were permissible and popular. Dalitz took over Bugsy Siegel's business in Las Vegas after his business partners had Siegel assassinated.[248] Dalitz was part of the national commission of the crime syndicate and was an ADL philanthropist. By the 1980s, drug money replaced petro-dollars as the main foundation of liquidity in the stock market. Because of the strength of drug money, the political and financial influence of the ADL also grew. Consequently, Dalitz (1899-1989) poured millions of dollars into the ADL. In exchange, the ADL targeted anyone who defied organized crime as an anti-Semite.[249] If not for the ADL's public relations, the Jewish criminals might not have inundated America with illegal drugs. In 1985, the ADL gave Dalitz, a Las Vegas "businessman," a prestigious award for all of the generous philanthropic donations over the years.[250]

Currently, the ADL promotes the activities of the homosexual lobbies in Washington and in numerous state legislative bodies. It also supports pro-abortion groups and the gun-control lobby. They collaborate with the American Civil Liberties Union (ACLU) and the People for the American Way, groups that work to prohibit voluntary religious expression in schools and other public facilities. Instead of thwarting anti-Semitism, their policies and practices, which strip the majority of the population of basic freedoms, might in fact generate anger and resentment. Additionally, the ADL attempts to prevent the publication of books negative to Israeli policies or that divulge Jewish history. The ADL promotes hate-crime legislation in order to eliminate free speech for the majority of the population. It views the Bible as "hate speech" and wishes to proscribe words that imply dissent against abortion, homosexuality, or other behaviors or actions. Subtly, by transforming words and titles, this has already occurred

---

[247] Ibid. 23-25
[248] Ibid. 23-25
[249] Ibid. 26-28
[250] Gyeorgos C. Hatonn, Advanced Demolition Legion: The ADL in Action, Phoenix Source Distributors, Inc., Las Vegas, Nevada, 1994, pp. 78-79

with the use of such words as "homophobic," and "gay" instead of "homosexual" and "pro-choice" rather than "abortion." This began decades ago.

Abraham Foxman is currently the ADL's national director. Its mission statement says, "The immediate object of the League is to stop, by appeals to reason and conscience and, if necessary, by appeals to law, the defamation of the Jewish people. Its ultimate purpose is to secure justice and fair treatment to all citizens alike and to put an end forever to unjust and unfair discrimination against and ridicule of any sect or body of citizens." On July 27, 1935, in the *Jewish Daily Bulletin*, Vladimir Jabotinsky said, "There is only one power which really counts—the power of political pressure. We Jews are the most powerful people on earth, because we have this power, and we know how to apply it." The objectives of the ADL seem to be scrutinizing the population, censorship, infiltrating existing organizations, intimidation, and pushing an anti-Christian agenda.

Multiculturalism, United States Immigration Policy

Professor Kevin MacDonald wrote, "Jews have been at the forefront in supporting movements aimed at altering the ethnic status quo in the United States in favor of immigration of non-European peoples. These activities have involved leadership in Congress, organizing and funding anti-restrictionist groups composed of Jews and gentiles, and originating intellectual movements opposed to evolutionary and biological perspectives in the social sciences."[251]

Emma Lazarus, the daughter of Moshe Lazarus, a wealthy New York sugar merchant, was a descendant of early

---

[251] Kevin MacDonald, Jewish Involvement in Shaping American, Immigration Policy, 1881-1965: A Historical Review, Population and Environment: A Journal of Interdisciplinary Studies, Volume 19, Number 4, March 1998, pp. 295-297

Jewish settlers during the colonial period. She wrote articles about the pogroms in Russia and helped immigrants learn practical skills to enable them to secure employment. In 1882, hoards immigrated from the Russian Pale to New York. She began promoting the formation of a Jewish homeland in the mid-1880s, over a decade before Theodor Herzl assumed the leadership of the Zionist movement. In 1883, she wrote the poem, *"The New Colossus,"* which, in 1903, officials engraved on a bronze plaque and mounted inside the Statue of Liberty. Since then, people associate Lady Liberty with her poem as a symbol of welcome to immigrants. A portion of that poem states,

> *Give me your tired, your poor,*
> *Your huddled masses yearning to breathe free,*
> *The wretched refuse of your teeming shore.*
> *Send these, the homeless, tempest-tost to me,*
> *I lift my lamp beside the golden door!*

Communism's deceptive dogma, a tool of the wealthy, appeals to the "poor," the "wretched," and the "homeless." America opened its doors to some of the very people who promoted communism and to the oppressed peoples who would unhesitatingly accept it, even though they relocated to a "free" country. Jewish immigrants, mainly from Eastern Europe, advanced "an internationalist foreign policy" because an "internationally minded" America was more likely to be sensitive to the problems of foreign Jews. Now, politicians still advocate a liberal immigration policy to guarantee a pluralistic instead of a unified, homogeneous society, the kind formerly found in Europe. While Jews prosper in their host countries, pluralism serves multiple Jewish interests, yet they, a distinct minority, concurrently reject assimilation for themselves and survive nicely by practicing partial crypsis (sufficiently mingling with others to conceal their exclusivity). Promoting liberal immigration policies makes them appear magnanimous. Yet, ironically, this generosity often involves jeopardizing the rights and properties of the majority of the host population, whereas it hardly affects their wellbeing.[252]

---

[252] Ibid. 295-297

In 1894, two years after the avid socialist Francis Bellamy wrote the Pledge of Allegiance, many Americans began demanding immigration restraint, similar to today. Theodore Roosevelt, an internationalist, then a member of the US Civil Service Commission, declared, "It is a base outrage to oppose a man because of his religion or birthplace . . . A Scandinavian, a German, or an Irishman who has become an American has the right to stand on exactly the same footing as any native-born citizen in the land, and is just as much entitled to the friendship and support, social, and political, of his neighbors."[253]

According to author Gary Gerstle, Roosevelt, as US president, believed in "racial mixing" and limited "racial assimilation" as long as a "superior race" controlled that particular process. He appreciated the warrior class who waged war against the "savage Indians" who had the audacity to think they had a right to live on their ancestors' lands. He said the subjugation of the Indians was "the greatest epic feat in the history of our race." The annihilation, rather than the assimilation, of the Indians resulted in the creation of what he called the "Americans, the fittest English-speaking race yet to appear on earth." He disdained blacks, as, he explained, they were unfit for democracy, "a form of government that depended on the kind of self-control and mastery that only white races had attained."[254]

Israel Zangwill, a freemason and close friend of H. G. Wells, wrote *The Melting Pot*, a popular sensation in America (1908-1909). He used the metaphorical phrase, "melting pot," to depict or promote America's incorporation of immigrants and the ostensible contributions they made. The hero of the play, David Quixano, immigrated to America after the Kishinev pogrom, which occurred April 6-7, 1903, in the capital of the Bessarabia Province in Russia, during which the government had killed his entire family. David had musical talent and created a splendid symphony, *The Crucible*, conveying his optimism for a classless society devoid of ethnic distinction. In the play, he falls in love with a Russian Christian immigrant named Vera, only

---

[253]   Gary Gerstle, American Crucible; Race and Nation in the Twentieth Century, Princeton University Press, Princeton, New Jersey, 2001, p. 47
[254]   Ibid. 21-23

to later discover that her father was the Russian officer who ordered his family's deaths. Ultimately, when confronted, Vera's father sorrowfully confesses, the orchestra plays the emotionally-charged symphony, and David and Vera decide to marry.

President Roosevelt attended the play's opening in Washington DC on October 5, 1909. From his special theater box, he shouted, "That's a great play, Mr. Zangwill, that's a great play." Interestingly, Roosevelt used the example of the Kishinev Pogrom, in part, to justify *The Roosevelt Corollary* to the *Monroe Doctrine*, presented during his *Annual Message to Congress* on December 6, 1904.

Zangwill encouraged the concept of the merging of the races into an American nation. The hero of his popularized play proclaims, "America is God's Crucible, the great Melting Pot where all the races of Europe are melting and reforming . . . Germans and Frenchmen, Irishmen and Englishmen, Jews and Russians—into the crucible with you all! God is making the American." Roosevelt later wrote a letter to Zangwill in which he said, "I do not know when I have seen a play that stirred me as much."[255]

Zangwill, a Zionist, employed the phrase, "A land without a people for a people without a land," in referring to Palestine. Actually, in December 1901, he wrote, in the *New Liberal Review*, "Palestine is a country without a people; the Jews are a people without a country." When he visited Palestine, he must not have noticed all of the Arabs, Greeks, Circassians, and other peoples living there under the jurisdiction of the Ottoman Empire. He admitted that he derived the phrase from Lord Shaftesbury, Anthony A. Cooper, who had written that Greater Syria was "a country without a nation" in need of "a nation without a country . . . Is there such a thing? To be sure there is, the ancient and rightful lords of the soil, the Jews!"

Pluralism allows Jews, about 2 percent of the American population, to associate, conduct business, and participate in society as just one of the many groups with its unique religious tenets and political

---

[255] Ibid. 51

convictions. In a pluralistic, diverse society, it is almost impossible for non-Jews, with such diversities, to unite in opposition to Judaism's predatory activities. MacDonald wrote, "Historically, major anti-Semitic movements have tended to erupt in societies that have been, apart from the Jews, religiously and/or ethnically homogeneous." Anti-Semitism is almost nonexistent in America, as compared to some European nations, largely due to the pluralistic nature of the society. In America, with some notable exceptions, Jews were rather inconspicuous, both religiously and culturally, until the twentieth century, because of their prominent role in many highly influential fields.[256]

Decades later, during Lyndon B. Johnson's administration, elected officials further implemented globalization via unchecked immigration and amnesty. On October 3, 1965, he signed the Hart-Celler Immigration and Nationality Act of 1965 into law after he and Edward M. Kennedy railroaded it through Congress. Representative Emanuel Celler (Jewish) of New York cosponsored the bill with Senator Philip A. Hart of Michigan. This 1965 Immigration and Nationality Act destroyed the 1921 pro-American national origins quota system of 3 percent. The 1921 law had filled its allotted immigration slots according to the immigrant's country of origin, giving 70 percent of these immigration slots to residents of England, Ireland, and Germany. The 1965 bill abolished the nationality factor putting all nations, third-world and industrialized, on an equal status.

Proponents of the Immigration Act of 1924, including the National Origins Act, wanted to preserve a distinct American character and "maintain the racial preponderance of the basic strain on our people and thereby to stabilize the ethnic composition of the population." Senator David Reed reminded the Senate that immigrants from Southern and Eastern Europe arrive sick and starving.

---

[256] Kevin MacDonald, Jewish Involvement in Shaping American, Immigration Policy, 1881-1965: A Historical Review, Population and Environment: A Journal of Interdisciplinary Studies, Volume 19, Number 4, March 1998, pp. 295-297

Yet, over the next four decades, Representative Celler determinedly worked to repeal the 1924 Act. Many of the advocates of the law wanted to avoid competition with foreign workers. AFL founder, Samuel Gompers, a Jewish immigrant, supported the act, as he opposed the cheap foreign labor, although the act would severely reduce Jewish immigration. However, millions of Jews had already arrived in the United States by the time the act would take effect. In July 1939, Celler sent a letter to Secretary of State Cordell Hull demanding support. Hull helped set immigration reform in motion.

In the 1940s, Celler opposed the isolationists and the Roosevelt administration by advocating a change in immigration laws on an emergency basis to allow those leaving Germany entrance to the United States. In 1943, he accused Roosevelt, because of his immigration policy, of being "cold and cruel." Senator Estes Kefauver and Celler created what became the Celler-Kefauver Act, which eliminated major regulatory loopholes. In the early 1950s, Senator Joseph McCarthy targeted Celler for his legislation. Celler responded by accusing McCarthy of undermining people's faith in their government. Beginning in 1950, McCarthy claimed that there were many communists working within the government.

Celler, the chairman of the House Judiciary Committee (1949-1973) participated in the drafting and passing the Civil Rights Act of 1964, the Civil Rights Act of 1968, and the Voting Rights Act. In January 1965, he proposed the Twenty-Fifth Amendment, regarding succession to the presidency. In 1965, he also proposed the Hart-Celler Act, eliminating national origins as a consideration for immigration.

Edward M. Kennedy, the Senate Immigration Subcommittee chairman, assured the nation and his fellow congressmen that our cities would not be flooded with a million immigrants annually from any one country or area, and that the ethnic pattern of immigration would not change or upset the ethnic mix of our society. Referring to the 1965 Immigration Reform Bill, Johnson said, "This bill we sign today is not a revolutionary bill. It does not affect the lives of millions. It will not restructure the shape of our daily lives." Myra C. Hacker, vice president of the New Jersey Coalition, opposed the bill and testified at a Senate Immigration subcommittee hearing, saying in part, "In light of our 5 percent unemployment rate, our worries over the so-called population explosion and our menacingly mounting welfare costs, are we prepared to embrace so great a horde of the world's unfortunates? . . . We should remember that people accustomed to such marginal existence in their own land will tend to live fully here, to hoard our bounteous minimum wages and our humanitarian welfare handouts . . . lower our wage and living standards, disrupt our cultural patterns."[257]

Unlike individuals coming from Western Europe, individuals coming into the country after 1965 typically lacked the equivalent education level of the average American. In addition, they required more social services, paid for by the taxpayer through plundering politicians and their efforts to redistribute wealth. Furthermore, by then, Europeans were not motivated to emigrate because their countries were more modern and industrialized.

From 1901 to 1920, the percent of Latin American immigrants comprised about 3 percent. The percent of Europeans during that same period was 88 percent. Yet, from 1980 to 1993, Latin American immigrants had risen to 43 percent and Europeans were down to 13 percent. These Latin American immigrants were more than twice as likely not to have finished high school, compared to native-born Americans, which has obviously had economic consequences as well as political ramifications. The conspiring elite changed the economic and political culture through immigration policy reform while appearing sympathetic to the plight of the poverty-stricken. Essentially, they have restructured America into a third-world nation. The poor are easier to control and typically lend their support to the political party that promises the most entitlements.

Unchecked immigration undermines our customs, culture, language, and institutions. The enslaved should attempt to emulate America within their countries rather than invade and reshape America. The enemy is not the poverty-stricken hordes at the border—yes, they are

---

[257] Ibid. 681-687

trespassers and lawbreakers, but the politicians have manipulated their circumstances. Our government and their governments use them as political pawns in the game of globalization. Although the politicians and the media constantly expose the population to a brainwashing blitz of politically correct thinking, it is not bigotry that motivates our wise rejection of unrestrained immigration. It is self-preservation and the preservation of our lifestyle that drives this fight. The politicians who promote diversity or multiculturalism are largely untouched by the mass migration that changes America's neighborhoods and jeopardizes our ability to take care of our families.

Nationalism, a Nation's "Right to Exist"

Benn Steil wrote in *Foreign Affairs*, "The right course is not to return to a mythical past of monetary sovereignty, with governments controlling local interests and exchange rates in blissful ignorance of the rest of the world. Governments must let go of the fatal notion that nationhood requires them to make and control the money used in their territory. National currencies and global markets simply do not mix; together they make a deadly brew of currency crises and geopolitical tension and create ready pretexts for damaging protectionism. In order to globalize safely, countries should abandon monetary nationalism and abolish unwanted currencies, the source of much of today's instability."[258] Nationalism is anti-establishment, isolationist, neutral, and people once considered it "conservative." Nationalists, in contrast to internationalists, do not exploit or suppress the liberties of others.

Government schools and the corporate media have indoctrinated and betrayed the American population to abandon nationalism, loyalty to one's country, in exchange for internationalism. Soon after the creation of the Federal Reserve, Americans became involved in a needless, senseless foreign war that had nothing to do with the

---

[258] Benn Steil, The End of National Currency, Foreign Affairs, May/June 2007, http://www.foreignaffairs.org/20070501faessay86308-p0/benn-steil/the-end-of-national-currency.html as of May 2012

best interests of the nation, the soldiers, or the target countries.[259] Author Gian Trepp wrote, "War, a place where moneymen can gather, because money is stronger than nationalism. Even during the war, the moneymen of different nations needed to keep in touch because, when the war stops, you have to rebuild, and you need free trade."[260] One might also accuse the leaders of multinational corporations whose greed for profit is "stronger than nationalism."

Nationalists believe in reasonable tariffs that protect the nation's industry rather than free trade. So-called "conservatives," even Republican "nationalists," claim to put the United States first, but they have promoted and enacted all of the nation's free-trade agreements. One cannot claim to cherish both sovereignty and accept free trade, via "multinational trade organizations and global financial conglomerates." Karl Marx advocated both the income tax and free trade because, he said, "it breaks up old nationalities" and eliminates the "bourgeoisie."[261]

University professors and administrators like Jacob G. Schurman, the third president of Cornell University (1892-1920) and ambassador to Germany (1925-1929), promoted internationalism and supported Wilson's warfare in Europe during World War I. Globalists like Henry R. Luce, the founder and crusading editor and publisher of *Time*, *Fortune*, and *Life* magazines, was a very outspoken internationalist who urged the abandonment of borders. He wrote *The American Century*, and possibly, the neo-conservative's *Project for a New American Century* played off Luce's earlier efforts.[262]

---

[259] Norman K. Denzin, Performance Ethnography: Critical Pedagogy and the Politics of Culture, Sage Productions, Thousand Oaks, California, 2003, p. 231

[260] Adam LeBor, Hitler's Secret Bankers, the Myth of Swiss Neutrality During the Holocaust, Birch Lane Press, New York, 1997, p. 73

[261] Michael Collins Piper, The Judas Goats, the Enemy Within, American Free Press, Washington, DC, 2006, p. 30

[262] Jacob Gould Schurman Public Lecture at the University of Heidelberg: "The Idea of the American Century," http://www.uni-heidelberg.de/presse/news/2005schurman2.html as of May 2012

The 1934 yearbook of the Carnegie Endowment for International Peace defined their globalist aspirations by complaining about the "economic nationalism which is still running riot and which is the greatest obstacle to the reestablishment of prosperity and genuine peace." Further, writers refer to nationalism as "this violently reactionary movement." In the 1946 report of the Rockefeller Foundation, in promoting globalism, we read, "The challenge of the future is to make this world one world, a world truly free to engage in common and constructive intellectual efforts what will serve the welfare of mankind everywhere."[263] Internationally minded foundations, under the guise of promoting world peace, want collectivism, with the elimination of all national borders, traditions, and all sentiments about sovereignty.[264] Tax-exempt foundations have spent millions to indoctrinate the masses to subtly relinquish their sovereignty, and they even abhor the very concept of nationalism communicating this through education and the entertainment media. Albert Einstein, an ardent globalist, said, "Nationalism is an infantile disease. It is the measles of mankind."

Globalists thoroughly vilify the word "nationalist" in their battle to induce us to accept world governance. Willis A. Carto explained that nationalists are populists and patriots who do not blindly follow bureaucratic wishes. They believe in maintaining their own race and culture and in strengthening their own sovereign nations. They have no imperialistic designs, nor do they engage in aggressive warfare, but rather respect the nationalistic endeavors of other countries. Imperialists criticize nationalism because it obstructs their exploitative objectives to bring all nations into one "Global Plantation" under their rule.[265]

Nations whose citizens thoughtlessly relinquish their nationalism are destined for destruction. The internationalists use numerous successful tactics to shift a nationalistic movement away from its

---

[263] René A. Wormser, Foundations: Their Power and Influence, 1958, Devin-Adair, New York, pp. 206-207

[264] Ibid. 206-207

[265] Willis A. Carto (editor) Populism vs. Plutocracy, the Universal Struggle, Liberty Lobby, Washington, DC, p. 275

objectives. Michael Collins Piper claims that infiltrators have taken over what used to be this country's nationalistic movement and have transformed and popularized it into the "right-wing" neo-conservative movement, which is diametrically opposed to nationalism.[266]

The Republican Party has adopted the policies of the neo-conservative faction. The policies of the neo-conservatives originated from a few different sources, including Vladimir Jabotinsky, a mentor of Leo Strauss. Jabotinsky was a revisionist Zionist leader and founder of the Jewish Self-Defense Organization, a militant group, in Odessa. In 1923, he left the Zionist movement because of differences with Chaim Weizmann and established a new revisionist party called Alliance of Revisionists-Zionists and its youth movement, Betar. The new party's objective was the establishment of a Jewish state, with territory on both banks of the Jordan River. He intended to establish a Jewish state with the support of Britain. Benjamin Netanyahu's father was Jabotinsky's personal secretary.

Leo Strauss attended the University of Hamburg, where he joined a Jewish fraternity, worked for the Zionist movement, and received his doctorate in 1921. He associated with other intellectuals—Leo Löwenthal, Norbert Elias, Hannah Arendt, Walter Benjamin, Jacob Klein, Karl Löwith, Gerhard Krüger, Julius Guttman, Hans-Georg Gadamer, Franz Rosenzweig, Gershom Scholem, Alexander Altmann, and Paul Kraus. He also associated with Carl Schmitt, who helped him acquire a Rockefeller Fellowship.

In 1932, Strauss left his position at the Academy of Jewish Research in Berlin, and ultimately, with the help of a Rockefeller Fellowship, he and his family relocated to England. In 1937, he was a research fellow at Columbia University. In 1949, he joined the University of Chicago's faculty, where he taught his neo-conservative philosophy, a mix between the teachings of Trotsky and Lenin. He preached the necessity of using deceptive propaganda in politics and promoted the concept of a hierarchical society, in which the elite rules the subservient masses.

---

[266] Michael Collins Piper, The Judas Goats, the Enemy Within, American Free Press, Washington, DC, 2006, Introduction

Obviously, he was not the first persuasive professor to promote political deception as a general policy in order to involve a country in war or some other debilitating political activity to benefit the elite. He promoted it to a new generation of leaders, including Abram Shulsky, Justice Clarence Thomas, Supreme Court nominee Robert Bork, former Deputy Defense Secretary Paul Wolfowitz, former Assistant Secretary of State Alan Keyes, former Secretary of Education William Bennett, *Weekly Standard* editor and former Quayle Chief of Staff, William Kristol, Allan Bloom, author of *The Closing of the American Mind,* former *New York Post* editorials editor John Podhoretz, and former National Endowment for the Humanities Deputy Chairman John T. Agresto, all known as Straussians.[267] Irving Kristol (CFR), the acclaimed godfather of the neo-conservative movement and William Kristol's father, also advocated the Straussian philosophy.

From Emancipation to Eugenics

Officials did not emancipate the slaves out of humanitarian or benevolent ideals but because of economics. As industrial capitalism and wage labor expanded, it became advantageous to eliminate the competition from slavery. Freed blacks became the target of a far deadlier enslavement, often with the help of the very people they trusted the most. After emancipation, the whites feared retribution and worried about the financial implications of freed slaves, formerly considered assets or property. Their new freedom constituted a potential liability. Northern residents, including the most vocal abolitionists, did not want them to travel northward, and they passed laws to prevent migration and potential intermarriage with the whites. The elite, working with Congress, financed numerous colonization programs in order to deport the emancipated blacks to other countries.

W.E.B. Dubois, a liberal, black PhD and Harvard scholar, helped found the Niagara Movement, with others, in July 1905, as an organization conceived to end racial bias, oppose segregation, promote civil rights for blacks, and end the disfranchisement of blacks in the South, which

---

[267] Leo Strauss, Conservative Mastermind by Robert Locke, Front Page Magazine, May 31, 2002, http://97.74.65.51/readArticle.aspx?ARTID=24239

began in 1890. In 1908, the organization, very short on funding, admitted its first white member, Mary W. Ovington, a socialist. After reading an article by socialist William E. Walling, she met with him and Dr. Henry Moskowitz in New York. They launched a civil-rights campaign on the centennial of Abraham Lincoln's birthday, February 12, 1909.

This meeting led to the formation of the National Negro Committee, which held its first meetings on May 31 and June 1, 1909. On May 30, 1910, they named their organization the National Association for the Advancement of Colored People (NAACP), with headquarters in Baltimore, and appointed Ovington as its executive secretary. Other members included Josephine Ruffin, Mary Talbert, Mary C. Terrell, Inez Milholland, Jane Addams, George H. White, W.E.B. Du Bois, Charles E. Russell, John Dewey, Charles Darrow, Lincoln Steffens, Ray S. Baker, Fanny G. Villard, Oswald G. Villard, and Ida B. Wells-Barnett.

The NAACP leadership was predominantly Jewish. That community contributed to its founding and continued financing. Initially, Dubois was the only black on its executive board. Joel E. Spingarn, a Columbia University professor, was the chairman (1913-1919). He recruited other board members and cofounders, Julius Rosenwald, chairman of Sears Roebuck, Lillian Wald, Rabbi Emil G. Hirsch, and Rabbi Stephen S. Wise. Jacob H. Schiff and Jacob Billikopf also sat on the NAACP board.[268] While it seems to have humane objectives, the actual motives might have been to create a rift between the white and black populations. The NAACP currently addresses the rights guaranteed in the Thirteenth, Fourteenth, and Fifteenth Amendments, disparities in economics, health care, education, voter empowerment, and the criminal justice system. Moorfield Storey, former president of the American Bar Association, was the first president of the NAACP. It would not have a black executive director until Benjamin Hooks on November 6, 1976.

---

[268] Howard Morley Sachar, A History of the Jews in America, Knopf, New York, 1992, pp. 803-804

While the blacks were enslaved, white "owners," for economic exploitation, encouraged them to have an abundant number of children. Eugenics, a pseudoscience, appeared to resolve some of the whites' concerns regarding the black population. Sir Francis Galton, a cousin to Charles Darwin and a eugenics pioneer, along with others, surmised that darker-skinned races were mentally and physically inferior to whites. In 1910, Charles Davenport, a Harvard University Zoology professor, became director of the Cold Spring Harbor Laboratory, a research facility of the Brooklyn Institute of Arts and Sciences. In 1911, he wrote *Heredity in Relation to Eugenics* for use as a college textbook. In 1912, at Cold Spring, he founded the Eugenics Record Office, an agency to keep racial records. That same year, he became a member of the National Academy of Sciences.

On May 14, 1913, the New York State legislature chartered the Rockefeller Foundation, founded by John D. Rockefeller, his namesake son, and Frederick T. Gates. Mary Harriman, the wife of railroad magnate Edward H. Harriman, along with the Carnegie Institution and the Rockefeller Foundation, soon began funding eugenics research at Cold Spring. Harriman was an enthusiastic advocate of selective breeding and donated at least $15,000 a year to Cold Spring.[269] Louis Marshall functioned as the legal advisor to the laboratory. Inasmuch as it would have been inappropriate to promote the extermination of specific races, their real objective, they used code words to promote the sterilization of certain groups. These included *feeblemindedness, moron, immoral, insane, unfit, criminal,* and *imbecile*. This verbal camouflage amounted to medical apartheid. Some of the same slave-trading corporations who once exploited the blacks now viewed them as expendable and shifted their focus to the employment and financing of likeminded minions to push birth control.

Margaret Sanger (1879-1966), a visiting nurse on Manhattan's Lower East Side and a member of the Socialist party, worked with the Industrial Workers of the World and orchestrated several militant

---

[269] Edwin Black, War Against the Weak, Eugenics and America's Campaign to Create a Master Race, Four Walls Eight Windows, New York, 2003, pp. 46, 95

strikes. She promoted feminism and, with atheist and anarchist Emma Goldman, believed that women should have liberal access to birth control and freedom from all sexual inhibitions and restraints. In 1914, Sanger organized the Birth Control League, which evolved into the American Birth Control League (ABCL).[270]

In 1921, Sanger, a fervent eugenics advocate, organized the Birth Control League in her home, which soon evolved into the American Birth Control League (ABCL), incorporated in New York State on April 5, 1922. In 1922, interested parties founded the American Eugenics Society, the propaganda apparatus of the whole movement, with Davenport and Harry Laughlin as board members. On January 19, 1939, the ABCL merged with the Birth Control Clinical Research Bureau (BCCRB) to form the Birth Control Federation of America (BCFA).[271] On January 29, 1942, because the word "control" might be offensive to some people, the BCFA would adopt a more acceptable name, the Planned Parenthood Federation of America (PPFA). The program was the same, but they now promoted abortion under the guise of "quality of life," and "better health" through "family planning."[272] Poor people did not necessarily have what the elite thought of as "quality of life." Rather than eliminate poverty through adequate education and occupational opportunities, they simply planned to exterminate the poor.

After this merger, Sanger developed the Negro Project. According to the official records, "The Negro Project was supervised by a special committee that included Margaret Sanger, Mary Lasker, and Clarence Gamble (of Procter & Gamble). A national Negro Advisory Council guided the project, composed of representatives from twenty-five major black organizations and universities. It included many prominent black leaders. The Project, with the help of local community organizations, assembled clinical data in order to position

---

[270] Ibid. 137

[271] Ibid. 46, 95

[272] Tanya L. Green, The Negro Project: Margaret Sanger's Eugenic Plan for Black Americans, Companion Reader to the Documentary Film, Maafa 21, Black Genocide in 21st Century America, November 2009, p. 2

clinics and ready access to contraceptive techniques in predominantly black communities of the South."[273]

Sanger cleverly manipulated black religious to collaborate with her in an effort to reduce the black population. She said, "The most successful educational approach to the Negro is through religious appeal. We do not want word to go out that we want to exterminate the Negro population, and the minister is the man who can straighten out that idea if it ever occurs to any of their more rebellious members." She also worked with W. E.B. Dubois of the NAACP.

Even before the official Negro Project, Harlem, a chiefly black area of New York City, was the site of the first birth-control clinic, which opened on November 21, 1930 at the beginning of the international banker-orchestrated depression. The black population suffered even greater privations and desperation than the white population, in addition to racial prejudice and discrimination. People failed to recognize the eugenic objectives of this foundation-financed clinic, whose records show that officials segregated 224,760 of 330,000 of New York's municipal black population in Harlem during the late 1920s and 1930s. Harlem's unemployment, mortality and tuberculosis death rates were higher than in the rest of New York City. Sanger, in a letter to DuBois, wrote that people established the clinic especially for the blacks, even though whites also lived in Harlem. She was a persuasive eugenics proponent who convinced Harlem's black population, through their trusted ministers, doctors, and journalists, that their lives could be better if they simply reduced their birth rate. However, Sanger failed to manipulate some black religious leaders.[274]

In her book, Sanger wrote, "Eugenics seems to me to be valuable in its critical and diagnostic aspects, in emphasizing the danger of

---

[273] Margaret Sanger Papers Project, Birth Control Federation of America, http://www.nyu.edu/projects/sanger/secure/aboutms/organization_bcfa.html as of May 2012

[274] Tanya L. Green, The Negro Project: Margaret Sanger's Eugenic Plan for Black Americans Companion Reader to the Documentary Film, Maafa 21, Black Genocide in 21st Century America, November 2009, p. 5

irresponsible and uncontrolled fertility of the 'unfit' and the feeble-minded, establishing a progressive unbalance in human society, and lowering the birth rate among the 'unfit.' But in its so-called 'constructive' aspect, in seeking to reestablish the dominance of healthy strain over the unhealthy, by urging an increased birth rate among the fit, the Eugenists really offer nothing more farsighted than a 'cradle competition' between the fit and the unfit. They suggest, in very truth, that all intelligent and respectable parents should take as their example in this grave matter of child-bearing the most irresponsible elements in the community."[275]

In 1933, the Federation of Jewish Women's Organizations voiced their support of the legalization of birth control. Other groups that actively promoted birth control included the National Council of Jewish Women, the General Federation of Women's Clubs, and the Young Women's Christian Association (YWCA). Sanger, of the National Committee on Federal Legislation for Birth Control, spoke at the Annual Convention of the Federation of Jewish Women's Organizations on January 25, 1937.[276] She said, "Last month, several hundred physicians, scientists, and representatives from birth control clinics met in a two day Conference of Contraceptive Research . . . There was discussion at one interesting session as to what a birth control center should be called. Many thought it might better be called a Mother's Health Center or a Race Betterment Center, and these terms well describe what such a center is."[277]

What are the consequences of the eugenics movement today? Prior to Roe v. Wade in 1973, the majority of those seeking an illegal abortion were white. Times and circumstances have changed. Pastor Johnny Hunter, head of the African American evangelical pro-life ministry LEARN, Inc., said, "Abortion is the number-one killer of blacks in

[275] Margaret Sanger, The Pivot of Civilization, Brentano's, New York, 1922, p. 31, the book was dedicated to Alice Drysdale Vickery
[276] Margaret Higgins Sanger Papers, Manuscript Division, Library of Congress, Washington, DC., Speech given at the 17th Annual Convention of the Federation Of Jewish Women's Organizations—Hotel Astor, NY (Radio Broadcast Station WMCA, January 25, 1937
[277] Ibid

America. We're losing our people at the rate of 1,452 *a day*. That's just pure genocide. There's no other word for it. (Sanger's) influence and the whole mindset that Planned Parenthood has brought into the black community . . . say it's okay to destroy your people. We bought into the lie; we bought into the propaganda."[278] He also points out that "black people were once exploited by the slave industry and are now being exploited by the abortion industry, yet this time they're not fighting it."[279] Black women are more likely to have an abortion than white women, according to the Alan Guttmacher Institute.[280]

Communist Base in America

Before the czar's overthrow, Lenin announced, "After Russia we will take Eastern Europe, then the masses of Asia, then we will encircle the United States, which will be the last bastion of capitalism. We will not have to attack. It will fall like an overripe fruit into our hands"[281]

Aristotle said, "Poverty is the parent of revolution and crime." Communism opportunistically thrives on and exploits destitution without adherence to principles and ignores the direct or secondary consequences of all unethical practices. Unfortunately, a majority of the people apparently wants numerous benefits without expending any personal effort or proportionate payment. The state is an artificial entity that produces no product or wealth, but rather seizes and redistributes the assets resulting from the labor of its citizens to select residents or foreign countries. Such Marxist policies, disguised as charitable policies, function to centralize power into one entity. Previously, private charitable organizations cared for the chronically ill. Before

[278] Tanya L. Green, The Negro Project: Margaret Sanger's Eugenic Plan for Black Americans, Companion Reader to the Documentary Film, Maafa 21, Black Genocide in 21st Century America, November 2009, p. 12
[279] Pastor Charlie Butts, Abortion Industry Exploits Blacks, December 3, 2008, http://www.onenewsnow.com/Culture/Default.aspx?id=338580 as of May 2012
[280] Julia Duin, Pastor's Crusade Aims to Halt Wave of Black Abortions, 'It's killed more than Ku Klux Klan'; The Washington Times, January 10, 1997
[281] Robert Preston, Wake-Up America-It's Later Than You Think!, Hawkes Publishing, Salt Lake City, Utah, 1979, p. 16

deindustrialization, when employment was readily available, people considered able-bodied people who refused to work as irresponsible or lazy. Reliance on the state, for any reason, inevitably increases one's dependence upon the burgeoning bureaucracy.

The Civil War effectively established a political environment detrimental to the principles of freedom and self-reliance. Congress then enacted subtle legislation, yet socialists still failed to dominate the country. Another violent revolution was out of the question. Instead, the Marxists, using Trotsky's devious method of subterfuge and infiltration, rather than Lenin's brutal revolt, would incrementally and ultimately shift the nation far left, through a series of situational legislative maneuvers, acceptable to a propagandized population, into a communist tyranny.

David Hirsch fled Germany due to his revolutionary activities. He settled in New York and opened David Hirsch & Company. Hirsh employees all belonged to the International Workingmen's Association, which moved its headquarters to New York in 1873. In that same year, twenty-three year old Samuel Gompers learned about the Knights of Labor when he was working for Hirsch, the only union shop in the city. Gompers swore several oaths, as is the custom, in response to the Master Workman's questions. Afterward he went through an initiation ceremony, where he heard several speeches, and, once the others accepted him as a member, they taught him the secret signs, grips, passwords, and ritual answers.[282]

Gompers, a Talmudist, could read Hebrew, but not German. Ferdinand Laurrell, a coworker, gave him a copy of the *Communist Manifesto*, and he learned to read German. He wrote, "Then, I read all the German economic literature that I could lay my hands on, Marx, Engels, Lassalle and the others." Although Marx urged the conquest of political power, he always regarded the unions as very important. He discouraged self-employment and promoted corporatocracy, which required low-interest loans, available through government

---

[282]   Robert E. Weir, Beyond Labor's Veil: the Culture of the Knights of Labor, The Pennsylvania State University, University Park, Pennsylvania, 1996, pp. 33-34

intervention, which necessitated political action in order to capture the state. On December 8, 1886, Gompers helped found and was president (1886-1894, 1895-1924) of the American Federation of Labor (later AFL-CIO), an alliance of craft unions disaffected from the Knights of Labor. Supposedly it was hostile to the communists.[283]

On February 28, 1906, Doubleday, Page and Company (created 1897), co-owned by Walter H. Page, published Upton Sinclair's novel, *The Jungle*. Sinclair, an avid socialist, once a Columbia University student, wrote this emotionally charged muckraking saga about Jurgis Rudkus, the main character who works in the brutal Chicago Stockyards, and of the desperate struggles of his extended family, all Lithuanian immigrants. The novel depicts unsanitary, revolting conditions and the filth of the slaughterhouse, as well as the use of diseased tubercular beef, workers falling into the rendering vat, and the harsh, inhumane working environment. The public was not necessarily concerned about the workers, but alarmed about what it was eating. Inevitably, his novel and the public uproar it created led to Talmudic government regulations, the Pure Food and Drug Act, and the Federal Meat Inspection Act, all on June 30, 1906, leading to the creation of the Food and Drug Administration (FDA). Charlie Chaplin later recruited Sinclair to write and produce several films. In the 1920s, Sinclair and his wife moved to Monrovia, where he founded California's chapter of the American Civil Liberties Union.

The president-appointed (with the Senate's consent), FDA Commissioner directs the agency, currently located in the Federal Research Center at White Oak. It operates under the Department of Health and Human Services and has 223 field offices and thirteen laboratories throughout the country, in the Virgin Islands, and in Puerto Rico. In 2008, it opened offices in India, Costa Rica, Chile, Belgium, England, and China. Theoretically, it regulates and supervises food safety, tobacco products, dietary supplements, prescription and over-the-counter drugs, vaccines, biopharmaceuticals, blood transfusions, medical devices, electromagnetic-radiation emitting devices,

---

[283] Louis S. Reed, The Labor Philosophy of Samuel Gompers, Columbia University Press, New York, 1930, pp. 55-56, 63-64

veterinary products, and cosmetics. Given that live disease-causing viruses and mercury are in vaccines, that debilitating fluoride is in our water, and the neurotoxin, aspartame, is in our food, either the FDA is patently ignorant and grossly ineffective, or it is deceptively acquiescent to corporate interests at the expense of public health, or the FDA is subtly and deceptively implementing Henry Kissinger's 1974 Depopulation Program, NSSM 200.

On February 16, 2011, the US Department of Health and Human Services, via its National Vaccine Program Office (NVPO), unveiled the 2010 National Vaccine Plan, the nation's ten-year strategy to ensure that all Americans receive vaccines.[284]

Socialist Charles P. Steinmetz fled from Germany to Switzerland to escape arrest for his socialist activities. He immigrated to the United States, arriving on May 20, 1889. An electrical engineer, he went to work for General Electric in 1893 at its Lynn, Massachusetts, factory. In his employment, he recognized a symbiotic relationship between corporations and socialism, a dogma akin to capitalism. In late 1902, he became a part-time professor at Union College and then became professor of electro-physics (1913-1923). In 1911, while living in Schenectady, he rejuvenated his interest in politics and joined the Socialist Party, whose nationwide membership was over 88,000, with socialist mayors in seventy-four cities, including Schenectady. To alter society, Steinmetz advocated incremental government reforms.[285]

In 1912, George R. Lunn, Schenectady's mayor, appointed Steinmetz to the Board of Education, where the board members immediately elected him as president, who followed a socialist agenda, including medical care for students. In 1913, Steinmetz became president of the Schenectady's Board of Parks and City Planning, where he used bond issues to purchase properties for parks. While he was moderately successful, by 1922, Steinmetz decided that socialism would never be

---

[284]   National Vaccine Program Office (NVPO), US Department of Health and Human Services, http://www.hhs.gov/nvpo/ as of May 2012
[285]   Charles Steinmetz: Union's Electrical Wizard, Union College Magazine, November 1, 1998, http://www.union.edu/N/DS/s.php?s=1512 as of May 2012

effective in America without a "powerful, centralized government of competent men, remaining continuously in office" and because "only a small percentage of Americans accept this viewpoint today."[286]

Steinmetz lectured at the Economic Club of Boston on social insurance and provisions for the old, the sick, and the unemployed. He thought that industry should, out of their overhead, shoulder the expenses of social programs. Because of his rhetorical brilliance, and, despite his political left leanings, he was popular and spoke at many societies attended by electrical engineers, his profession. He had studied and adopted the ideas of Karl Marx, Friedrich Engels, and Ferdinand Lassalle, ideas that he promoted in his speeches.[287]

Mikhail Borodin, who would later train troops in China, joined Lenin in 1903 and had sixteen different aliases in a revolutionary career that took him to Europe, America, Turkey, Mexico, Scotland, and China. He lived, for a time, in Chicago.[288]

There were other liberal intellectuals from Eastern Europe, like the family of Louis D. Brandeis, from Prague. Woodrow Wilson appointed him to the Supreme Court, against substantial opposition due to his "radicalism." The Senate confirmed him on June 1, 1916 after a close vote. He interpreted the law, not from precedent or constitutionally, but according to his personal Judaic worldview. He felt that the "Constitution must be given liberal construction." He played a role in persuading Wilson to get the United States into the war. During World War I, he studied the political aspects of Jewish affairs in every country. He then adopted Zionism and visited Palestine in 1919. Since his time on the court, there has been a tendency to adjudicate, not by law, but like a legislative body. Wilson told Rabbi Stephen S. Wise, regarding Zionism, "Whenever the time

---

[286] Ibid

[287] Sender Garlin, Three American Radicals: John Swinton, Crusading Editor Charles P. Steinmetz, Scientist and Socialist: William Dean Howells and the Haymarket Era, Westview Press, Boulder, Colorado, 1991, p. 51

[288] Milly Bennett, On her own, Journalistic Adventures from San Francisco to the Chinese Revolution, 1917-1927, edited by A. Tom Grunfeld, M.E. Sharpe, Inc., New York, 1993, p. 224

comes, and you and Justice Brandeis feel that the time is ripe for me to speak and act, I shall be ready."[289]

Dedicated Bolsheviks established a branch of the Communist Party in America (CPA) during a convention, September 1-7, 1919, in Chicago, as the Moscow-directed American Section of the Third International. There were approximately 125 delegates. The leaders divided the group into three caucuses—the Russian Federation group (including the Jewish Federation) headed by Alexander Stoklitsky, Daniel Elbaum, George Ashkenudzie, and Nicholas Hourwich; the National Left Wing Council group, including Charles Ruthenberg, Isaac Ferguson, Louis Fraina, John Ballam, and Maximilian Cohen; and the Michigan group, including Dennis Batt and John Keracher.[290]

The CPA was the dominant underground policymaker of the legal Workers' Party, which focused on political activism, while William Z. Foster, of the Trade Union Educational League, concentrated on labor. There was also a short-lived organization called the Communist Labor Party of America (CLP) which they founded in Chicago, during a Founding Convention, August 31-September 5, 1919, with Alfred Wagenknecht as national executive secretary. He applied to Moscow for Comintern membership in a letter dated September 21, 1919.

Many of those who established the official Communist Party had emigrated from Russia, Poland, and other countries. Their initial objective was to overthrow the US government, not through revolution, but by deception and infiltration. The founders included Jay Lovestone, Earl Browder, John Reed, James Cannon, Bertram Wolfe, William B. Lloyd, Benjamin Gitlow, Charles Ruthenberg, William Dunne, Elizabeth G. Flynn, Louis Fraina, Ella R. Bloor, Rose P. Stokes, Claude McKay, Max Shachtman, Martin Abern, Michael Gold, and Robert Minor. They infiltrated the churches, where they disseminated socialist doctrine.

---

[289] John Beaty, The Iron Curtain Over America, Chestnut Mountain Book, Barboursville, Virginia, 1968, pp. 49-50
[290] The Communist Party of America, 1919-1946, http://www.marxists.org/history/usa/eam/cpa/communistparty.html as of May 2012

Just as in other countries, socialist infiltrators emerged in America, a productive nation of independent workers. Assuming control of the workers of America, part of the world's workers, was logical, particularly because many employers exploited and oppressed them, and they had very little recourse, had no legislative power, and lacked media influence. This was very problematic, and labor unions, like the National Textile Workers Union (1889), the Workers International Relief, created in Berlin on September 12, 1921, per Lenin's instructions, and the International Labor Defense (1925), headed by William L. Patterson, were all powerful groups founded and led by immigrants, who could conceivably provide ready solutions.[291] These Marxist immigrants, hawking socialism disguised as humanitarianism, like those editors and writers in the 1850s, began publishing numerous newspapers targeted at disgruntled workers, a group extremely vulnerable to communist exploitation, indubitably by design. Keep in mind that the House of Rothschild sought to control labor, through what he called the European plan, a characteristic that the capitalists have in common with the communists.

The *Izvestia*, the official newspaper of the Russian Central Executive Committee, published an article March 31, 1921, in which it stated, "a notice (was given) to all members of the Russian Communist Party in regard to the strict fulfillment of Article 13 of the constitution of the Russian Communist party, which compels all members to carry on antireligious propaganda." The party also has a "monopoly of legality" and would allow no other political associations under strict penalties. There was, according to the Soviets, only one legal party in the country. Since it ran the government, it had "a monopoly of legality." Grigory Zinoviev, in *Pravda*, April 2, 1922, said, "We do not grant our opponents political freedom. We do not give the possibility of legal existence to those who pretend to compete with us."[292]

---

[291]   Louis Marschalko, The World Conquerors, the Real War Criminals, Translated from the Hungarian by A. Suranyi, Joseph Sueli Publications, London, 1958, pp. 54-57

[292]   Richard Merrill Whitney, Reds in America; the present status of the revolutionary movement in the U. S. based on documents seized by the authorities in the raid upon the convention of the Communist party at

Senator Henry Cabot Lodge addressed the Senate on January 7, 1924, and presented evidence of the manipulations manufactured in Moscow for world revolution. The Senate's Subcommittee of the Committee on Foreign Relations convened hearings under the chairmanship of William Borah, during which its members issued a recommendation for the recognition of the Soviet Government in Russia. Robert F. Kelley and Alfred W. Kliefoth, a former attaché to the American Embassy in Russia, testified and provided numerous documents to support their conclusions. The Russian Communist Party never totaled over 700,000 members out of the nation's population of 120,000,000. At the time of that recommendation, there were about 387,000 members, mainly in the larger urban areas.[293]

Before the Bolsheviks overthrew Russia, between 1880 and 1914, waves of immigrants came to the United States. After the Bolsheviks seized control in 1917, there was a five-year period (1919-1924) where "communist-inclined immigrants" from Eastern Europe immigrated to the United States, until Congress passed a restrictive law in 1924. During that period, about 3,000,000 people came from Eastern Europe, many of whom were Soviet agents, among them—Sidney Hillman. Twenty-two years later, he was working with President Franklin D. Roosevelt. The immigrants were not all confirmed Marxists, but enough of them to influence national policy were. Most of those largely non-Christian Eastern European immigrants embraced the Democrat Party. They helped to elect Franklin D. Roosevelt. He won over Herbert Hoover (9,129,606 to 8,538,221). They were attracted to the Democratic Party, because it insiders had transformed it into a leftist collection of several groups. Previously, the party consisted of the rural Protestant Southerners and the northern Catholics, who both championed Christian fundamentals and traditions.[294]

Bridgman, Mich., Aug. 22, 1922, together with descriptions of numerous connections and associations of the Communists among the Radicals, Progressives, and Pinks, The Beckwith Press, Inc., New York City, 1924, pp. 8-9

[293] Ibid. 7-8
[294] John Beaty, The Iron Curtain Over America, Chestnut Mountain Book, Barboursville, Virginia, 1968, pp. 46-47

On May 1, 1932, the *Proletarian News*, the newspapers of the Communist International, reported, "The organization in America that is preparing the workers for the momentous act of self-emancipation is the Proletarian Party." On February 15, 1932, that paper reported, "We must spread the message of communism to all. Workers, Comrades, Friends support the *Proletarian News*. It is needed to instill class consciousness into the American workers, to organize them for the approaching conflict. Build for Communism in America!"[295] By 1933, Earl Browder, General Secretary of the Communist Party USA (1934-1945), estimated that there were 1,200,000 members in the party. By 1936, communists were editing about 600 newspapers and periodicals.[296]

According to the Fourth Report of the Senate Fact-Finding Committee on Un-American Activities of 1948, "The Communist Party of the United States is the agent of the Soviet Government and its totalitarian dictator, Joseph Stalin. The committee finds that the Communist Party is, in no sense, a domestic political party."[297]

[295] Elizabeth Kirkpatrick Dilling, The Red Network: a "who's who" and Handbook of Radicalism for Patriots, Ayer Publishing Company, 1935, p. 218

[296] Louis Marschalko, The World Conquerors, the Real War Criminals, Translated from the Hungarian by A. Suranyi, Joseph Sueli Publications, London, 1958, pp. 54-57

[297] Fourth Report of the Senate Fact—Finding Committee On Un-American Activities, 1948, Communist Front Organizations, p. 20

SECTION 3

IMPERIALISM AND WARFARE

The Sugar Trust

The Havemeyers were the sugar-kings of the East, as they had established their conglomerate long before Adolph Spreckels started his business. William and Frederick C. Havemeyer emigrated from Bückeburg, Germany, where they had learned the art of sugar refining. They established a business in New York City and, beginning in 1828, their sons ran the business under the name of W. F. & F. C. Havemeyer.[298] In 1857, they opened the Havemeyer, Townsend and Company in Williamsburg, Virginia, the site of a deep-water harbor. Henry O. Havemeyer's grandfather, the immigrant, made a fortune from his refining business and, upon his death in 1861, left Henry $3 million. Henry collaborated with his cousin William F. Havemeyer, the three-term mayor of New York, in the refining business. Union soldiers and the devastation of the Civil War destroyed the South's sugar industry, along with other industries.

The Civil War accelerated the growth of manufacturing and the power of the men who owned corporations. Afterward, corporations campaigned to eliminate the legal restrictions that prohibited industrial corruption. America's sugar consumption has drastically increased since then. America, according to William Dufty, consumes about one-fifth of the world's sugar every year. Mark Hanna and Henry O. Havemeyer instituted the continuing, systematic bribing of corrupt officials, like Senator Nelson W. Aldrich and his congressional and judicial cronies. Most Supreme Court judges were former corporate lawyers.[299]

---

[298] Albert Faust Bernhardt, The German Element in the United States with Special Reference to Its Political, Moral Social and Educational Influence, Volume: II, Houghton Mifflin Company, Boston, 1909, pp. 70-71

[299] Luzviminda Bartolome Francisco and Jonathan Shepard Fast, Conspiracy for Empire: Big Business, Corruption, and the Politics of Imperialism in

Manufacturers produce the majority of sugar, which is equally as addictive as cocaine, from sugar cane or sugar beets that they then reduce to sucrose. The process extracts all of the vitamins, minerals, proteins, enzymes, and nutrients, leaving an artificial, heroin-like substance. Sugar is more destructive than other poisons, drugs, or narcotics, in that people regard it as a food and consume it in enormous amounts. It is one of the first toxins innocently introduced to an infant, either through its formula or through sugar-contaminated breast milk. Producers process heroin and sugar the same way. Workers extract opium from the poppy plant, and then process the opium into heroin and refine it into morphine. With sugar, juice is extracted from the cane or beet, refined into molasses, and then into brown sugar, and then into white crystals (C12H22O). Both sugar and heroin are biologically unfamiliar to the body, which cannot naturally metabolize them.[300]

Manufacturers centered their sugar-refining in New York City, where it became the city's most profitable industry (1870-1920). In 1880, Henry O. Havemeyer retained attorney Elihu Root, an influential man with numerous powerful friends in Washington.[301] New York producers processed about 59 percent of the country's raw sugar in 1872, growing to about 68 percent by 1887.[302] The sugar-refining business focused on imported sugar and companies, like Havemeyer, who maintained large waterfront plants in Brooklyn. They began working to expand and consolidate their controlling interests by 1887. Havemeyer resided at Penataquit Point on Long Island, where his neighbors included Simon F. Rothschild, Edward Blum, both of A&S Department Stores, and August Belmont Jr., who built Belmont Park and Robert A. Pinkerton, the son of the Pinkerton Detective Agency founder.

America, 1897-1907, Foundation for Nationalist Studies, Quezon City, 1985, pp. 92-97

[300] Helen Cannington, Sugar, the Sweetest Poison, New Dawn Magazine, May-June 2003, pp. 41-43

[301] John R. Vile, Great American Lawyers, an Encyclopedia, ABC-Clio, 2001, pp. 616-618

[302] Kenneth T. Jackson, Encyclopedia of New York City, Edited, Yale University Press, New Haven and London, the New-York Historical Society, New York

Before August 1887, free competition existed throughout the sugar trade. Raw sugar producers throughout the world came to New York and other US ports to market their produce. Numerous buyers were prepared to purchase, according to the flexible price of supply and demand.[303] Havemeyer, like other industrialists, attempted to fix prices, control the market, and destroy his competition. In the fall of 1887, he formed the Sugar Refining Company, a holding company, or trustee device, comprised of twenty-one major Brooklyn sugar refineries. Havemeyer, the company's president, became something of a financial expert.[304]

Under President Grover Cleveland, US foreign policy, particularly toward Cuba, was dependent on the economic goals of America's leading business interests. According to Edwin F. Atkins, Richard Olney was "always willing to listen to what I had to say upon the Cuban situation." Atkins also maintained close connections to John D. Long, Mark A. Hanna, and Charles F. Adams. They were his conduit in William McKinley's administration when it came time to prevent recognition of the Cuban insurgents.[305] Havemeyer and Atkins were some of the first Americans to invest money in the Cuban sugar industry, and their joint investments were extremely profitable. Atkins had good political connections and aggressively pushed tariff legislation favorable to his investment interests. He worked with Olney, the Attorney General, on the tariff issues of the late 1890s.[306]

Senator John Sherman, chairman of the Senate Finance Committee and a Rockefeller associate, sponsored antitrust legislation. Congress enacted the Sherman Antitrust Act, and President Benjamin Harrison

---

[303] Richard Franklin Pettigrew, Imperial Washington, the Story of American Public Life From 1870 to 1920, Charles H. Kerr and Company, 1922, pp. 46-51

[304] The Sugar Trust Illegal; An Adverse Decision By The Court Of Appeals, The Corporations Forming The Trust Had No Right To Combine Under The Laws Of The State, *The New York Times,* June 25, 1890, p. 8

[305] Leland Hamilton Jenks, Our Cuban Colony: A Study in Sugar, Vanguard Press, New York, 1928, pp. 44-45

[306] Stephanie Rugoff, The Imperialist Role of the American Sugar Company, North American Congress of Latin America, 1970, Issue 4, Volume 4

signed it into law on July 2, 1890, the first federal statute to limit cartels and monopolies, declaring that trusts were illegal according to courts. Rather than limit trusts, it really functioned to restrict competition. On January 10, 1891, Havemeyer, with Elihu Root's legal advice, reorganized and incorporated the trust into the American Sugar Refining Company (ASRC) in New Jersey, a state that had altered their regulations regarding corporations although he kept the offices at 117 Wall Street.[307] Havemeyer reorganized and capitalized his company at $50 million.[308]

Roger Q. Mills, chairman of the US House Committee on Ways and Means (1887-1889), was a leading authority on tariffs in Congress. He was a tariff-for-revenue-only Democrat. He argued that a tax on raw sugar was one of the least obnoxious taxes that Congress could impose, which generated good steady revenue. Interestingly, William McKinley, supported by big money, replaced him as chairperson of the US House Committee on Ways and Means (1889-1891).[309]

McKinley then introduced his legislation. Essentially, the McKinley Bill of 1890, which became law on October 1, 1890, made raw sugar free and allowed one-half cent a pound for refined sugar, a huge benefit to the Sugar Trust. The economic panic temporarily depressed sugar-trust certificates and other securities on the New York Stock Exchange. Yet, under the McKinley Act, the sugar-trust certificates went above par and ultimately reached 134 or 135, from 85 points in January 1890, when McKinley introduced the bill. The sugar trust certificates, at 85 Points, or $42,500,000 advanced to $63,750,000 on the American Sugar Refining Company's Stock. In 1890, the Sugar Trust had 8,000,000 shares, worth $800,000,000. Havemeyer admitted on the witness stand in 1894, that the trust profited by about $25 million in three years. He stated, "as long as the McKinley Bill

---

[307] Ibid.

[308] Eliot Logan Jones, The Trust Problem in the United States, Macmillan, New York, 1921, p. 92

[309] Ida M. Tarbell, The Tariff in Our Times, Macmillan, New York, 1911, pp. 222-227

is there we will exact that profit." Without the McKinley Bill, this would have been impossible.[310]

Havemeyer contributed large amounts to both parties. He once claimed, "We get a good deal of protection for our contributions."[311] With donations, he manipulated congressional votes on tariffs and taxes placed on foreign goods. The larger, high-volume refineries secured the majority of their raw-sugar imports from Cuba, and preferential treatment guaranteed stable supplies at low prices. From 1891 on, tariffs excluded the importation of refined sugar, which would have competed with the domestic refiners.[312] During the 1892 congressional elections, the Sugar Trust made large contributions to certain Democrats. Reportedly, Matthew S. Quay received $100,000 from the same source as he had in the 1888 campaign. The sugar refiners got what they paid for, the rates in the William L. Wilson Bill. They had sufficient people in their pocket, like northern Senators Arthur P. Gorman and Calvin S. Brice, that they overpowered the senators from Louisiana, the home of many sugar producers.[313]

Havemeyer convinced Congress to lower the tariffs on imported raw sugar. He also wanted protection against competing imports of his product—refined sugar. He used price-cutting and price wars in the early 1890s against domestic refiners, especially against Adolph Spreckels, the West Coast's dominant sugar refiner. Spreckels even built a refining plant in Philadelphia. However, Havemeyer won this war by acquiring all sugar-refining firms in Philadelphia, including the Spreckels Sugar Refining Company. Within several years, the American Sugar Refining Company controlled about 90 percent of the industry.

Lenient New Jersey corporation laws enabled Senator Aldrich to expand his railway interests, resulting in the Union Traction and

---

[310]   Ibid. 222-227

[311]   Ferdinand Lundberg, America's 60 Families, The Citadel Press, 1937, p. 54

[312]   Stephanie Rugoff, The Imperialist Role of the American Sugar Company, North American Congress of Latin America, 1970, Issue 4, Volume 4

[313]   Ida M. Tarbell, The Tariff in Our Times, Macmillan, New York, 1911, pp. 222-227

Electric Company of New York. His company was a consolidation of smaller firms of which he was president, in addition to being president of the Pawtucket Street Railway Company, which was in the process of constructing eighteen miles of road, a source of potential profit. Aldrich needed cash and called on his friends to supply it. In 1892, the directors of the Union Traction and Electric Company, also members of the Sugar Trust, gave $1,500,000 cash to Aldrich's enterprise. One of those directors was John E. Searles, Secretary/Treasurer of the trust. The cash contribution helped Aldrich to complete his scheme and probably seemed insignificant to Searles. The citizens elected Aldrich for another six years. The Sugar Trust, over three years, according to Havemeyer, made about $35 million because of his legislation.[314] August Belmont, affiliated with the Tammany Society, also invested Rothschild money in New York traction companies.

The New York Times reported that the Sugar Trust, in the mid-1890s, had agents in Washington "seeking by every means in their power to defeat every attempt to deprive them of the benefits which the trust was enjoying under the operation of the McKinley Tariff." Some Democrats in Congress were trying to smash the Sugar Trust and introduced legislation early in 1894.[315] The directors of the Sugar Trust were Theodore A. Havemeyer, Francis O. Matthiessen, William Dick, and Washington B. Thomas, with Henry O. Havemeyer as president. Matthiessen was also the treasurer of the American Sugar Refining Company and a director of several other important companies. On March 9, 1902, when he died because of diabetes, he was worth between $10,000,000 and $20,000,000.[316]

In the spring of 1894, the House bill angered the Sugar Trust. Accordingly, one or more of its officers visited Washington, negotiating with members of the Senate and the administration. Havemeyer, Theodore A. Havemeyer, and Searles, with massive political influence, persuaded reluctant committee members to provide

---

[314] Senator Aldrich and Sugar, the Republican Tariff Leader Owned by the Trust, Indebted to it for Financial Aid, *New York Times*, June 20, 1894, p. 1

[315] Carlisle and the Sugar Trust, The New York Times August 25, 1894

[316] F. O. Matthiessen Dies in his Paris Home, The New York Times, March 10, 1901

a schedule that would give them as large a benefit as they had under the McKinley Bill. Henry O. Havemeyer approached Senator Mills repeatedly, but failed to win his support. Finally, he asked Treasury Secretary John G. Carlisle to intercede with a letter to Senator Roger Q. Mills. Carlisle gave him what he requested, and he was back at the senator's door, but Senator Mills refused to see him.[317]

The Sugar Trust opposed the House of Representatives' sugar schedule that the House had sent to the Senate on February 2, 1894. The Senate made alterations on the House bill by March 20, but the Sugar Trust wanted to retain the McKinley Tariff, which was impossible. Secretary Carlisle visited the Wall Street offices of the Sugar Trust, on March 29-30, 1894. The agents of the Sugar Trust then busily altered the sugar schedule to suit their purposes. On May 5, 1894, Senator James Jones visited with Secretary Carlisle, and, within a few days, Carlisle presented an amended sugar schedule, effective as of January 1, 1895. The new schedule maintained the reciprocity treaty between the United States and Hawaii.[318]

Rumors were abounding about the Sugar Trust, and, on March 20, 1894, Congress levied a rate of about one cent a pound on raw sugar and an additional one-eighth of a cent per pound on refined, which caused an immediate outcry from the Sugar Trust. Congress then made further changes, making it more intricate and more advantageous to the refiners. There were rumors about bribes, deals, and threats. A journalist for *The Philadelphia Press* claimed that the Sugar Trust had contributed $500,000 to the Democratic campaign fund in exchange for promises regarding the trust. When the House removed the duty, the trust reminded the administration of its promises. Secretary Carlisle, at the direction of President Cleveland, told the sub-committee that the party was financially obligated.[319]

---

[317] Ida M. Tarbell, The Tariff in Our Times, Macmillan, New York, 1911, pp. 222-227

[318] Carlisle and the Sugar Trust, The New York Times, August 25, 1894

[319] Ida M. Tarbell, The Tariff in Our Times, Macmillan, New York, 1911, pp. 222-227

Many senators took advantage of the congressional information regarding the sugar schedule and speculated in sugar stock. The media heard that numerous senators had invested in sugar, which compelled other congressmen to investigate. These speculators included Mills, Cushman K. Davis, George Gray, George F. Hoar, John M. Palmer, John Sherman, and John T. Morgan. Charges against Mills seemed doubtful, inasmuch as he had opposed Havemeyer. Additionally, Senators John R. McPherson and Matthew S. Quay admitted that they invested in sugar while the sugar schedule was in the Senate. Other equally guilty senators denied their participation in the sugar stock scandal. Senator Aldrich had been the sugar refiner's chief advocate in the Senate for years, was a friend of Searles, and had spent considerable time with him while the Senate worked on the schedule in 1894. Meanwhile, his fortunes expanded rapidly at this time.[320]

After an investigation in May 1894, Congress discredited many of the allegations and cleared Cleveland, Carlisle, and Mills, but the scandal remained. Havemeyer admitted that he contributed to both parties so that the Sugar Trust could look to both for favors. However, he made the biggest contributions to the majority party. During the investigation, he said that his firm had no politics of any kind, "only the politics of business."[321]

On June 4, 1894, *The New York Daily Commercial Bulletin* reported in an editorial column that the trust controlled the government. The newspaper estimated that the trust's profit, because of the protective tariff and duty on raw sugar, amounted to $34,620,000 during a six-month period.[322] *The New York Times* of June 20, 1894, also exposed the background of McKinley's Tariff Act of 1890. Senator Aldrich, of the Finance Committee, inserted changes into Representative McKinley's bill when he managed its passage in the Senate. The changes decreased duties on raw sugar and allowed the Sugar Trust to

---

[320] Ida M. Tarbell, The Tariff in Our Times, Macmillan, New York, 1911, pp. 222-227

[321] Ibid. 222-227

[322] Henry Demarest Lloyd, Wealth against Commonwealth, Harper & Brothers, New York, 1898, p. 450

acquire an unwarranted $35,000,000 in profits at the citizen's expense. Aldrich claimed that there was no trust, and that the decreased duty benefited everyone. The Finance Committee, composed of both parties, had passed the bill, which later became a law.[323]

The House Democrats initially proposed a duty of one-fourth cent a pound on refined sugar, half of what McKinley had given but the refiners opposed this. Representative William L. Wilson sponsored a bill in the House, proposing that both refined sugar and raw sugar be free. However, with free raw and refined sugar, the government's revenue stream would drastically suffer.[324] Mills told his colleagues, "We have got to have more money than the Wilson Bill makes, and we have to have a duty on sugar . . . I would not have taken sugar off the dutiable list and put it on the free list. It has been done, and I do not like to put anything back on the dutiable list . . . We have to have more money."[325]

On August 27, 1894, Congress passed the Revenue Act or Wilson-Gorman Tariff of 1894, which minimally decreased the US tariff rates. Both Wilson and Gorman were financially indebted to the Sugar Trust. Instead of imposing tariffs and making the industrialists responsible for appropriately providing money, through legitimate tariffs, for the government to function, they shifted the entire responsibility to the taxpayer by imposing a peacetime 2 percent tax on income over $4,000. Wilson was the chair of the House Ways and Means Committee, and Senator Arthur P. Gorman, both Democrats, supported the tariff-reform bill, along with other party members. This income-tax bill affected less than 10 percent of US households, but compensated for the lost government revenue because of the tariff reductions.[326] On April 8, 1895, the Supreme Court declared

---

[323] Senator Aldrich and Sugar, the Republican Tariff Leader Owned by the Trust, Indebted to it for Financial Aid, *New York Times*, June 20, 1894, p. 1

[324] Ida M. Tarbell, The Tariff in Our Times, Macmillan, New York, 1911, pp. 222-227

[325] Ibid. 222-227

[326] The Statutes at large of the United States from August 1893 to March 1895, Volume 28 by United States Department of State, by authority of Congress, Government Printing Office, Washington, 1895, p. 570

the tax law unconstitutional. The 1894 law required unapportioned income taxes, essentially direct taxes, which violated the provision that Congress should apportion direct taxes.

The State Department and the special interests of Edwin F. Atkins and others should not have involved the nation in a war with Spain in 1898, as it had nothing to do with intervening in behalf of the American-owned property seizures in 1896, or Spain's horrific concentration policies. Frankly, the government presented a very faulty case for war in April 1898.[327]

On July 18, 1899, Atkins told the industrial commission that the tariff had commercially ruined Cuba, especially if it became an independent nation. No one in the US government seriously thought that Cuba would become independent. There were too many Americans investing money in sugar mills, supported by the policies of the US government. Those investors ignorantly expected that American blacks would migrate to Cuba to work on the plantations, which would Americanize the country. Havemeyer was not worried about sugar refiners in Cuba competing with the Sugar Trust. Apparently, whether America legally annexed Cuba or not, it was immaterial to the them as long as Cuba provided sugar at the prices he wanted to pay.[328]

By 1900, Havemeyer had eliminated the remaining competition in the area by merging them into the National Sugar Refining Company of New Jersey, of which the most important company was the American Sugar Refining Company. By 1907, the Havemeyers controlled, directly or indirectly, about 98 percent of all national sugar production.[329] According to *The New York Times* of January 15, 1902, the board of National City Bank reelected Havemeyer to their

---

[327] Leland Hamilton Jenks, Our Cuban Colony: A Study in Sugar, Vanguard Press, New York, 1928, pp. 44-45
[328] Ibid. 129-131
[329] Kenneth T. Jackson, Encyclopedia of New York City, Edited, Yale University Press, New Haven and London, the New-York Historical Society, New York

board.[330] He also sat on the board of Kennecott Copper Company and participated as a board member with other corporations engaged in the sugar, coal, and railroad business and was a trustee with Solomon R. Guggenheim on the Guggenheim Foundation.[331] He, with his neighbor Simon F. Rothschild, was a director at the Williamsburgh Trust Company in Brooklyn.[332] He was on the board of the Colonial Trust Company, the Colonial Safe Deposit Company, the City Trust Company of New York, and the Central Realty Bond and Trust Company.[333]

In 1906, Havemeyer collaborated with others investors and bought into the Cuban American Sugar Company. In 1906, he refused to raise the wages of striking workers to eighteen cents per hour, though his company posted profits of $55 million. In 1907, the courts found the American Sugar Refining Company guilty of taking illegal railroad rebates. When he died on December 4, 1907, he left an estate of $17 million. The American Sugar Refining had only 49.3 percent of the US market, despite its twenty-five plants. After his death, his company sold off a number of holdings and developed its own brand of sugar for the marketplace, Domino.

Political Puppets for Corporate Interests

Wealthy industrialists and lawyers installed Democrat Grover Cleveland into the US Presidency twice (1884-1888, 1892-1896). Their management of Cleveland instituted an ongoing precedent for succeeding administrations of both parties—financial donations entail specific commitments and obligatory political appointments.

---

[330] Bank Board Elections, The New York Times, January 15, 1902, p. 7, http://query.nytimes.com/mem/archive-free/pdf?_r=1&res=9C0CE7D61430E733 A25756C1A9679C946397D6CF as of May 2012

[331] Richard B. K. McLanathan and Gene Brown, The Arts, Ayer Publishing and the New York Times Company, New York, 1978, p. 367

[332] Brooklyn Daily Eagle, Brooklyn Daily Eagle Almanac, a Book of Information, General of the World, and Special of New York City and Long Island, 1900, p. 623

[333] Documents of the Senate of the State of New York, Volume 4, Issues 11-24 By New York (State), James B. Lyon, State Printer, 1901, pp. 449, 454-455, 532, 625

Cleveland then appointed William C. Whitney (S&B), a corporate lawyer, as Navy Secretary in his first administration.[334] Whitney was married to Flora Payne, daughter of Ohio Senator Henry B. Payne and a sister of Whitney's Yale classmate, Oliver H. Payne, later Standard Oil's treasurer. Whitney, with counsel from industrialists, directed the navy's expansion, including building the *USS Maine* and the *USS Texas,* authorized by Congress on August 3, 1886, as part of the "New Navy." The *USS Maine* was the first steel warship that workers totally constructed in the United States. Whitney facilitated the domestic production of advanced weaponry and plate armor and reorganized the finances and logistics of the Navy Department and helped make the Naval War College a success.

William McKinley, a popular politician, caught the attention of Mark Hanna, a Cleveland industrialist who was anxious to install another obliging president. Hanna helped McKinley become Ohio's governor in 1891 and 1893. In 1893, McKinley, because of his assistance to a friend, had a staggering debt of $130,000. Hanna and his wealthy cronies, Myron T. Herrick, Samuel Mather, Charles Taft, Henry C. Frick, Andrew Carnegie, and others, paid this debt.

On August 15, 1896, after an informal meeting between Mark Hanna and James J. Hill, CEO of the Great Northern Railway, Hill offered to introduce Hanna to some of his close Wall Street connections. Within a week, the entire J. Pierpont Morgan clique transferred their allegiance to McKinley. Standard Oil donated $250,000 to the Republican Party, as did every Wall Street bank and most of the insurance companies. New York Life (Morgan), the Mutual Life (Rockefeller), and Equitable Life (Ryan-Harriman) all generously backed McKinley.[335] Taft, Harding and McKinley were all from Ohio,

---

[334] Ferdinand Lundberg, America's 60 Families, The Citadel Press, 1937, p. 55-57
[335] Ibid. 55-57, 59-64

the center of the Standard Oil Empire, a huge supporter of Hanna beginning in 1876.[336]

Hanna succeeded in getting the political support of Booker T. Washington, the director of the Tuskegee Institute, located in Georgia. The Republicans had strong Northern and Midwestern support, but needed to win in the South.[337] Hanna rented a cottage in Thomasville, Georgia, where he and McKinley scheduled daily visitors, among whom were journalists, publishers, and politicians. He soon had the support of numerous Southern delegates.[338] The 1896 election, a "realignment" election, was the last one in which a candidate attempted to capture the presidency with a majority of agrarian votes. Beginning with the election of 1800, presidential campaigns had been a competition between agrarian or mercantile interests. It was a struggle between the independent farmers and common people and the industrial interests, represented by Wall Street and later, after the Civil War, became corporate interests.[339]

Elites installed McKinley as president in 1896, and Hanna was elevated to the Rockefeller-controlled Senate, controlled by Nelson W. Aldrich of Rhode Island.[340] After a visit from J. Pierpont Morgan and an instructive letter from Andrew Carnegie, President McKinley, a freemason,[341] appointed Philander C. Knox as his Attorney General, despite strong opposition from the labor sector. An Attorney General is supposed to protect the general population, and he should have prosecuted numerous individuals for anti-trust-law violations. Knox

---

[336] Ibid. 55-57, 55-57
[337] Eric Rauchway, Murdering McKinley, the Making of Theodore Roosevelt's America, Hill and Wang, New York, 2003, pp. 66-68
[338] Ibid. 66-68
[339] The Authentic History Center, The Progressive Era: 1890s, The Election of 1896: William McKinley (R) v. William Jennings Bryan (D), http://www.authentichistory.com/1865-1897/progressive/mckinley/index.html as of May 2012
[340] Ferdinand Lundberg, America's 60 Families, The Citadel Press, 1937, pp. 59-64
[341] A. Ralph Epperson, The Unseen Hand, Publius Press, 1985, p. 127

did nothing to halt the predatory monopolists, most of whom were former clients.[342]

J. Pierpont Morgan financially backed McKinley's Assistant Navy Secretary Theodore Roosevelt, a freemason (Lodge #806, Oyster Bay, New York),[343] and Senator Henry Cabot Lodge, who were the nucleus of a jingoistic Washington cabal that promoted war and worked tirelessly to provoke it.[344] James D. Bulloch, the Confederate States main foreign agent in Britain, was the half-brother of Martha Bulloch Roosevelt, the mother of Roosevelt and the grandmother of Eleanor Roosevelt. In other words, Bulloch was Theodore Roosevelt's uncle.

Lodge, Roosevelt's professor at Harvard, was a member of the Senate Foreign Relations Committee's subcommittee on Cuba. The president appointed Roosevelt as Assistant Navy Secretary on April 19, 1897. He worked with Harvard-educated John D. Long, who the president appointed as Navy Secretary on March 5, 1897. Within a week of his appointment, Roosevelt began warning McKinley about potential trouble with Cuba and pushed for warfare preparation. Within two months, Roosevelt delivered a speech at the Naval War College, during which he promoted US supremacy and the need for the United States to become a world power. He also 1) advocated the importance of being adequately prepared for war; 2) the duty of Congress to fund better equipment; 3) the preeminence of offense rather than defense in naval tactics; 4) the ineffectiveness of diplomacy without force; 5) the delusion of "peace at any price," the clash of the races, and most importantly; 6) the virtues of war. His superiors never

---

[342] Who Was Philander Knox? Is It Credible That He Would Commit Fraud?, http://www.givemeliberty.org/features/taxes/philanderknox.htm as of May 2012

[343] Masonic Presidents, Theodore Roosevelt (1858-1919), Twenty-sixth President (1901-1909), http://www.pagrandlodge.org/mlam/presidents/troosevelt.html as of May 2012

[344] Ferdinand Lundberg, America's 60 Families, The Citadel Press, 1937, pp. 59-64

refuted his speech. He used the word "war" sixty-two times during his speech.[345]

McKinley's administration allegedly opposed war. For Roosevelt, who had no combat experience, war was a test of greatness. His book, *The Naval War of 1812*, published in 1882, was required reading at the War College. He intended to use public opportunities to push the government into a war.[346] He finished the book on his five-month European honeymoon, beginning in May 1881. In the first chapter, he talked about the Aryans' racial purity, and how the Norsemen were excellent fighters and seaman, as opposed to the Portuguese and Italians.[347] In a letter to a friend in 1897 he said, "In strict confidence . . . I should welcome almost any war, for I think this country needs one." During McKinley's presidency, the United States invaded Cuba, seized Manila in the Philippines, and occupied Puerto Rico.[348]

Roosevelt, in reviewing history, consistently justified the numerous government atrocities against the existing native population during the 1800s with three arguments—the land did not really belong to them, the whites would put the land to better use, and "it was our manifest destiny to swallow up the land of all adjoining nations who were too weak to withstand us."[349] He felt that war was "purifying and ennobling."[350]

[345] Warren Zimmerman, First Great Triumph, How Five Americans Made Their Country a World Power, Farrar, Straus and Giroux, New York, 2002, pp. 238-244
[346] Ibid. 238-244
[347] Theodore Roosevelt, The Naval War of 1812 or The History of the United States Navy during the Last War with Great Britain to Which Is Appended an Account of the Battle of New Orleans, Modern Library, New York, 1999, p. 26
[348] William McKinley, http://www.whitehouse.gov/history/presidents/wm25.html as of May 2012
[349] Warren Zimmerman, First Great Triumph, How Five Americans Made Their Country a World Power, Farrar, Straus and Giroux, New York, 2002, pp. 215-224
[350] Ibid. 146

War Secretary Elihu Root built up America's military machine. On November 27, 1901, US officials, through his plans and promptings, established, by General Order 155, the US War College in Washington, DC. He also reorganized the administrative system of the War Department and established US authority in the Philippines.[351] William C. Sanger (Pilgrims Society), related to the Dodge and Cleveland families, was assistant War Secretary. On February 21, 1903, Roosevelt, now president, after McKinley's assassination, attended the Masonic laying of the cornerstone of Roosevelt Hall, part of the War College. Samuel Young (Pilgrims Society), a veteran of the Civil and Spanish-American Wars, was the first president of that institution (1902-1903).[352] Roosevelt ordered the construction of new ships and by February 22, 1909, laborers had constructed sixteen US battleships.

By the time Roosevelt was ready to leave office on March 4, 1909, the navy had acquired the "Great White Fleet"—those sixteen first-class battleships. To appear more warlike, they would paint future ships battleship gray. Author Warren Zimmerman claims that John Hay, Alfred Thayer Mahan, Elihu Root, Henry Cabot Lodge, and Roosevelt could be called the "fathers of modern American imperialism and the men who set the United States on the road to becoming a great power."[353]

Annexing Hawaii for Its Own Good

In 1778, Captain James Cook and his men found a group of people who were much healthier and stronger than their European counterparts, with a much longer life expectancy. They had no major health issues, were vigorous, strong, and well nourished. Among other things, Cook's men brought tuberculosis to Hawaii. Like most

---

[351] John R. Vile, Great American Lawyers, an Encyclopedia, ABC-Clio, 2001, pp. 616-618

[352] Charles Savoie, Pilgrims, Silver Investor, May 2005, www.silver-investor. com/charlessavoie/cs_may05_pilgrims.htm as of May 2012

[353] Warren Zimmerman, First Great Triumph, How Five Americans Made Their Country a World Power, Farrar, Straus and Giroux, New York, 2002, pp. 8-9

ship captains, his crew was from the dregs of English society, which was chronically plagued with numerous diseases, such as typhus, smallpox, typhoid fever, measles, bronchitis, whooping cough, and venereal diseases.[354]

In 1846, Adolph Spreckels, born in Germany, immigrated to Charleston, South Carolina, where he worked in a grocery store. By 1856, he and his family relocated to San Francisco, where he established a brewery, a big source of wealth. In 1863, he opened the Bay Sugar Refining Company. He returned to Germany and spent two years studying the sugar industry, including eight months as a day laborer. Thereafter, with extensive notes and experience, he operated his newly established California Sugar Refinery to become the West Coast's major sugar refinery. He used raw cane sugar from US planters in the Hawaiian Kingdom. Planters began lobbying for tariff reductions as they competed with sugar growers in Java, Australia, Taiwan, and the Philippines. Those tariffs on sugar imported into the United States, at times, supplied one-fifth of the Treasury's total receipts.[355]

Senators Justin S. Morrill, the sponsor of the Morrill Land-Grant Colleges Act in 1857, and John Sherman, author of the Sherman Antitrust Act and brother of General William T. Sherman, sat on the Senate Finance Committee. They opposed any official trade agreements with Hawaii. Morrill represented the East Coast sugar refiners, who worried that an overabundance of sugar would reduce profits. Free trade would also affect Louisiana's cane-sugar growers. Kalākaua, the reigning king of the Hawaiian Kingdom, close to the sugar growers, sent representatives to the United States as early as October 1874, to negotiate a reciprocity treaty in an attempt to halt an economic depression in the islands because of excessive exploitation by the growers. In November, he went to Washington to meet with

---

[354] James Bradley, The Imperial Cruise, a Secret History of Empire and War, Little, Brown and Company, New York, 2009, pp. 148-149

[355] Luzviminda Bartolome Francisco and Jonathan Shepard Fast, Conspiracy for Empire, Big Business, Corruption and the Politics of Imperialism in America, 1876-1907, Foundation for Nationalist Studies, Quezon City, Philippines, 1985, pp. 1-2

President Ulysses S. Grant. The United States drafted a treaty on January 30, 1875, allowing the tax-free US importation of Hawaiian goods, mainly sugar and rice.

However, Spreckels opposed that treaty, as it contained no provisions for higher grades of raw sugar or refined sugar, offering no protection for his products. In addition, he feared that Hawaiian planters would refine and export sugar into the United States and bypass him. Congress passed another treaty in May 1876, about the same time that he visited Hawaii, to buy the bulk of the 1876 sugar crop, along with investing in the Waihee Plantation on Maui. While there, he loaned $50,000 to Kalākaua, among other gifts, and was able to purchase several thousand acres of Crown land on Maui. He diversified into banking and began loaning the Hawaiian government money. Soon, Kalākaua removed all government officials antagonistic to Spreckels. In 1878, Spreckels purchased additional land in Hawaii and formed the Hawaii Commercial Company. He also built a $250,000, thirty-mile-long irrigation ditch. In 1880, he acquired another 24,000 acres of choice Wailuku Crown land.[356]

In 1879, Spreckels bought controlling interest in W. G. Irwin & Company, Hawaii's leading brokerage firm, giving him control over a significant amount of the island's sugar crop. He purchased *The Pacific Commercial Advertiser* in 1880 and became its publisher. In 1881, he organized the Oceanic Steamship Company, giving him the ability to grow and ship the sugar to his West Coast refinery, where he marketed it under his own brand, Spreckels. He bragged that he owned Hawaii's government officials, who appointed Spreckels's personal attorney, John T. Dare, as Hawaii's Attorney General. By 1887, that government owed him $700,000.[357]

As early as 1854, Secretary of State James G. Blaine, a prominent Republican (1865-1900) and a huge fan of government expansion,

---

[356] Luzviminda Bartolome Francisco and Jonathan Shepard Fast, Conspiracy for Empire, Big Business, Corruption and the Politics of Imperialism in America, 1876-1907, Foundation for Nationalist Studies, Quezon City, Philippines, 1985, pp. 5-6

[357] Ibid. 5-6

promoted Hawaii annexation. Using the 1875 version of the reciprocity agreement, he extended the US security perimeter to Hawaii.[358] Anti-imperialist opposition had prevented Grant, and later Blaine, from further realizing their imperialistic plans. US officials took steps toward a formal empire during the immediate decades following the Civil War. In 1878, a treaty consolidated the US connection to Samoa and the rights to a coaling station at Pago Pago. In 1881, Blaine originated the reciprocity treaty with Hawaii, which allegedly put Hawaii within the US system. The United States renewed the treaty on January 20, 1887, with an amendment giving the United States exclusive rights to build a naval base at Pearl Harbor.[359]

Corporate greed, including passive and/or aggressive regime change, drives America's long-term foreign policy. Trade agreements or "reciprocity treaties" (tariff-free trade akin to economic annexation or the creation of US protectorates), always favor business. These obligatory contracts generally include the exclusive right to extract resources, sell products, and maintain commercial properties and military bases, despite the justifiable objections of the native populations.[360]

US sugar growers, eager to expand their Hawaiian production found a compliant Hawaiian monarch, Kalākaua, who signed the "Bayonet Constitution," on July 6, 1887, which was written by Hawaii's Interior Minister Lorrin A. Thurston, an elite resident who considered his white-supremacist mentality a form of patriotism. This document reduced the king's executive power and deprived native Hawaiians of their voting rights. The composition of the islands in 1890 was 40,612 native Hawaiians, 27,391 Chinese and Japanese laborers, and 6,220

---

[358] Edward S. Mihalkanin (editor) American Statesmen: Secretaries of State from John Jay to Colin Powell, Greenwood Press, Westport, Connecticut, 2004, pp. 61, 65

[359] Stuart Creighton Miller, "Benevolent Assimilation," the American Conquest of the Philippines, 1899-1903, Yale University Press, New Haven, Connecticut, 1982, pp. 3, 5, 7

[360] Treaty Of Reciprocity Between The United States Of America And The Hawaiian Kingdom, http://www.hawaii-nation.org/treaty1875.html as of May 2012

Americans, Britons, Germans, French, Norwegians, and Hawaii-born whites who were not the least bit interested in equality. Thurston set up a secret organization called the Hawaiian League to infiltrate and ultimately overthrow the monarchy. League members, who were fellow conspirators, controlled Kalākaua's administration.[361]

Kalākaua, much to his sister's horror, relinquished Pearl Harbor, the best natural port in the Pacific, to the United States. She regarded it as "a day of infamy in Hawaiian history." He died on January 20, 1891, and she soon became queen. Thurston, authorized by the Harrison administration, tried to bribe Queen Liliuokalani and each of her likeminded associates with the sum of $250,000. She refused and introduced a new constitution, restoring native political power and equal voting rights to every resident.[362] According to her detractors, democracy and decision-making were only suitable for the white elite.

William J. McGee, geologist for the US Geological Survey in 1881, was the vice president of the National Geological Society, and then president. He managed the Bureau of American Ethnology (1893-1903), established in 1879 by an act of Congress. He insisted that Hawaii's annexation was a "natural" step by an "enlightened" nation interested in "the elevation of humanity and the ultimate peace and welfare of the world." He further asserted that "enlightened," invincible Americans, on a higher moral plateau, could subjugate lower-level people. White-skinned men, he said, lead the world and Americans should "take up the White Man's Burden," to lift up the world's weaklings—white, yellow, red, or black.[363]

President Benjamin Harrison (1889-1893), a grandson of President William H. Harrison, and his administration attempted to annex Hawaii in 1893. They feared that the reciprocity agreements would

---

[361] Stephen Kinzer, Overthrow, America's Century of Regime Change From Hawaii to Iraq, Henry Holt and Company, New York, 2006, pp. 13-30

[362] Ibid. 13-30

[363] Julie A. Tuason, The Ideology of Empire in National Geographic Magazine's Coverage of the Philippines, 1898-1908, The Geographical Review, Volume: 89, Issue: 1, 1999

not protect Hawaii's white sugar growers from paying duties. Henry A. P. Carter, Hawaii's minister to Washington, and Blaine devised an agreement in 1889 to establish Hawaii as a US protectorate, which assured complete trade reciprocity between the United States and Hawaii.

Additionally, the United States guaranteed Hawaii's independence on the condition that Hawaii would not enter into agreements with other governments without US approval. Further, the agreement allowed the US military to enforce domestic peace and guard Hawaii from foreign takeovers. The Hawaiian monarch was justifiably suspicious that the United States would manipulate this provision to seize control of the island, so she rejected the agreement. Accordingly, Congress passed the McKinley Tariff in 1890, removing sugar from the tariff list, which placed Hawaii at a severe economic disadvantage, as industrialists could now import sugar from anywhere. The entire economy of Hawaii was based on sugar; this would destroy the islands. Blaine told Harrison that the United States could now easily annex the island.[364]

Blaine appointed John L. Stevens as US minister to Hawaii. He was a partner and coeditor of *The Kennebec Journal*, an Augusta, Maine, newspaper that had advocated for Hawaiian annexation since the 1850s. Stevens arrived in Honolulu in the summer of 1889.[365] Thurston and a group of sugar-stock-owning wealthy, immigrant collaborators, including Samuel Castle, the country's largest landowner, met to discuss the situation. In the dark of night, the conspirators visited Stevens, and they decided to overthrow Hawaii's queen. Within a couple of days, more white landowners rallied. The queen's supporters also rallied. The conspirators had leverage—the support of the 3,000-ton cruiser *USS Boston*, sitting in the harbor.

In January 1893, the conspirators, with Stevens' support, staged a coup d'état. On January 16, Stevens ordered armed sailors and marines

---

[364] Ibid. 30-31
[365] Edward S. Mihalkanin (editor), American Statesmen: Secretaries of State from John Jay to Colin Powell, Greenwood Press, Westport, Connecticut, 2004, pp. 68-70

from the ship to disembark and guard certain locations in Honolulu that were under the queen's control.[366] The unwary citizens assumed they had dispatched the military to protect the monarchy. The queen resisted, but Stevens had the support of the obedience-trained troops. Judge Sanford Dole, grandson of early missionaries, agreed, at the conspirator's request, to take control of a new provisional government which the US government recognized within forty-eight hours.[367] Dole facilitated the annexation with Congress. The Hawaiian general public made two attempts to restore their government, which resulted in numerous deaths and penalties for the insurgents.[368]

Ambassador Stevens went to Hawaii to do exactly what the president wanted him to do. The task of all US ambassadors is to protect US business interests. Official orders from Blaine or his successor, John W. Foster, grandfather of the John Foster Dulles and Allen Welsh Dulles, were unnecessary. Stevens alerted Washington officials of the impending coup. Thurston, an annexation advocate and leader of the Annexation Club, and Stevens devised the scheme to put Hawaii under US control. Stevens met with Blaine in 1892 to inform him of the political unrest in Hawaii, allegedly caused by the queen's rule. Thurston admitted later that Blaine told him that the United States would not oppose forced annexation.[369]

The Harrison administration disapproved of the protectorate, but approved of the coup. Secretary of State Foster and numerous members of Hawaii's provisional government convened to devise the terms of the annexation. They did not invite any Hawaiians. They submitted plans to Harrison the following day.[370] Secretary Foster had authorized an attempt to purchase the islands in 1892, cautioning

---

[366] Ibid. 68-70
[367] Stephen Kinzer, Overthrow, America's Century of Regime Change From Hawaii to Iraq, Henry Holt and Company, New York, 2006, pp. 13-30
[368] Leis and Lies: Why Hawaii and Iraq are Birds of a Feather By Matt Hutaff, April 5, 2004, http://www.thesimon.com/magazine/articles/canon_fodder/0590_leis_lies_why_hawaii_iraq_birds_feather.html as of May 2012
[369] Edward S. Mihalkanin (editor), American Statesmen: Secretaries of State from John Jay to Colin Powell, Greenwood Press, Westport, Connecticut, 2004, pp. 68-70
[370] Ibid. 68-70

the planters to be careful of any annexation attempts before Harrison left office. Yet the coup took place. Foster immediately recognized the new government and manipulated conditions in Washington to put the annexation treaty before the Senate, which they rejected due to the adverse publicity associated with US involvement and because of president-elect Grover Cleveland's position.[371]

Harrison conceded to the annexation, but Cleveland, the incoming president, did not. On January 19, 1895, Harvard-educated attorney, Henry Cabot Lodge, addressed the Senate and railed against Cleveland's anti-annexation policy. He claimed that Britain would be the chief benefactor, and that Britain had attempted to lay a telegraph cable on one of the islands to establish economic superiority. Lodge asserted that the United States should control the islands, and that they should be a part of the United States so that US interests could predominate. Three days later, in another speech, he claimed that Japan and Britain targeted the islands. He assured the Senate that he was not promoting US colonization, but the necessity of taking "all outlaying territory necessary for our own defense . . . the upbuilding of our trade and commerce, and to the maintenance of our military safety everywhere."[372]

On March 2, 1895, Lodge revisited the imperial idea and praised Alfred Thayer Mahan's writings regarding the influence of sea power. He was adamant about Hawaii's strategic and commercial importance. Regarding the islands, he said, "even if they were populated by a low race of savages, even if they were desert rock, (they) would still be important to this country from their position . . . The main thing is that those islands lie there in the heart of the Pacific, the controlling point in the commerce of that great ocean . . . Upon those islands rests a great part of the future commercial progress of the United States." The projected canal through the isthmus made Hawaii very significant, as the main routes would pass the islands.[373]

---

[371] Ibid. 217
[372] Warren Zimmerman, First Great Triumph, How Five Americans Made Their Country a World Power, Farrar, Straus and Giroux, New York, 2002, pp. 149-153
[373] Ibid. 149-153

Mahan, a US Navy flag officer, geostrategist, and historian, became friends with Theodore Roosevelt in the early 1890s because of their shared interest in naval history. Mahan, twice president of the Naval War College, also belonged to the Philolexian Society, whose members have exerted significant influence, as they included eight members of the House of Representatives, eight college presidents, five US ambassadors, four governors, two senators, and two New York City mayors. Like other members, journalist John L. O'Sullivan, who coined the phrase "manifest destiny," promoted US superiority and domination. Mahan influenced Roosevelt and advocated US militarism and imperialist expansion.

Lodge, a war hawk Republican, used every imaginable tactic to convince the Senate to seize Hawaii. He showed a map of Britain's bases throughout the world and suggested that Japan was a rival. He sought funding for more battleships and nine torpedo boats for a world-class navy. Roosevelt supported him, but was not yet in a position to promote expansionism. Lodge was the internationalist's point man. He wrote numerous magazine articles promoting expansion and "the advancement of the race." He claimed, "We must have a record of conquest, colonization, and territorial expansion unequalled by any people in the nineteenth century."[374]

Cleveland's Secretary of State, Richard Olney, a Boston attorney and board member of the Morgan-run Boston and Maine Railroad, pursued an aggressive policy of interventionism. He manipulated the Monroe Doctrine to extend it to Hawaii or anywhere else big business wanted to go. He informed the British that the United States was "practically sovereign" on the continent. He shifted the doctrine from a prohibition against foreign interference to a justification of unilateral US intervention and American imperialism.[375]

Lodge, armed with the Monroe Doctrine, an early claim for hemispheric dominance, railed against Britain's interest in the

---

[374] Ibid. 149-153
[375] Warren Zimmerman, First Great Triumph, How Five Americans Made Their Country a World Power, a Yale graduate and a Fulbright Scholar, Farrar, Straus and Giroux, New York, 2002, pp. 32-33

mineral-rich border between British Guiana and Venezuela. He asserted that Britain, America's adversary, could very easily take any country in South America, if allowed to occupy the ports of Nicaragua and claim Venezuela—"an absolute violation" of the Monroe Doctrine and an attempt to make the Caribbean Sea "little more than a British lake." He further claimed, "the supremacy of the Monroe Doctrine should be established and at once—peacefully if we can, forcibly if we must . . . because it is essential to our safety and defense . . . the Monroe Doctrine rest primarily on the great law of self-preservation."[376]

Politicians overturned the will of the Hawaiian people in the interests of profit and strategic military operations, despite anti-annexation petitions signed by 29,000 native Hawaiians. The US Senate never saw those petitions, and the Senate never put the issue to a popular vote. Queen Liliuokalani (January 29, 1891-January 17, 1893), then went to Washington and gave a written statement to then-Secretary of State Foster, stating that the rebellion in her country occurred because of the actions of the United States. She further stated that the new government did not have the moral or physical support of the Hawaiian people.[377]

Mahan's advocacy for Hawaiian seizure coincided with Hawaii's 1893 revolution and annexation. He wrote a letter to the editor of *The New York Times,* urging the islands' acquisition by "a great, civilized maritime power" instead of taking the chance of losing them to the control of barbaric nations like China or Japan. At their request, he wrote an article for *Forum Magazine,* entitled, *Hawaii and Our Future Sea Power*, in which he elaborated on the correlation between the islands and the proposed isthmian canal. He adamantly maintained that Hawaii was paramount to America's commercial and military hegemony of the Pacific, especially the northern Pacific.[378]

---

[376] Ibid. 149-153
[377] Stephen Kinzer, Overthrow, America's Century of Regime Change from Hawaii to Iraq, Henry Holt and Company, New York, 2006, pgs. 13-30
[378] Richard W. Turk, The Ambiguous Relationship: Theodore Roosevelt and Alfred Thayer Mahan, Greenwood Press, New York, 1987, pp. 25-26

In a letter, Mahan reiterated to Roosevelt that the Cleveland administration could have taken Hawaii easily, and the failure to do that led to a "present danger of war" with Japan. He wrote, "The decision not to bring under the authority of one's own government some external position, when just occasion offers, may by future generations be bewailed in tears of blood." Roosevelt responded, "as regards Hawaii I take your views absolutely, as indeed I do on foreign policy generally. If I had my way, we would annex those islands tomorrow. If that is impossible I would establish a protectorate over them . . ." He stated that Secretary of the Navy John D. Long held those same opinions. Roosevelt prompted Long to goad the administration to take immediate action before Japan became stronger. He wrote, "With Hawaii once in our hands, most of the danger of friction with Japan would disappear." He was also angry over Cleveland's mismanagement of the Hawaiian issue, and viewed the possession of the islands as vital to building an isthmian canal and the expansion of US naval strength.[379]

William McKinley, the new president, appointed Roosevelt as Assistant Secretary of the Navy (1897-1898), which delighted Mahan. Mahan expressed his concerns to Roosevelt about Japan's rising naval power, especially after the Sino-Japanese War (1894-1895), and urged the use of US naval forces in the Pacific. He, through his writings, criticized the Cleveland administration over its "crass blindness" and failure to take Hawaii in 1893. He said that the United States should have seized the islands and afterward resolved any accompanying problems after the fact. He wrote, "We stand at the opening of a period when the question is to be settled decisively, though the issue may be long delayed, whether Eastern or Western civilization is to dominate throughout the earth and to control its future."[380]

In June 1897, Mahan shared a letter with Roosevelt that he received from the Oriental Association of Tokyo. Apparently, members of the Club of Naval Officers of Japan had translated Mahan's book, *Influence of Sea Power upon History,* into Japanese and had sold several thousand

---

[379] Ibid. 26-27
[380] Ibid. 25-26

copies within a few days. Mahan said that this provided "further evidence" of Japan's objectives. Roosevelt immediately shared the "very remarkable" letter to Long, who advised President McKinley to take "immediate action" in Hawaii."[381]

Roosevelt then enlisted Mahan's assistance to persuade indecisive senators to favor annexation. Mahan, at Roosevelt's request, wrote to Senator George Frisbie Hoar, who questioned the wisdom of annexation. Mahan recommended that the senator read *Interest of America in Sea Power*, which Mahan had just published. Early in 1898, Roosevelt urged Senator James H. Kyle to write to Mahan, requesting his expert assessment of the "strategic importance of Hawaii to the United States." Mahan responded that possession of Hawaii would unquestionably enlarge the United States militarily. A naval base in Hawaii would impede any communication in the event that a potential enemy from East Asia ever decides to attack the Pacific Coast. However, if Hawaii fell to antagonistic or neutral control, the likelihood of an invasion would be more probable. Therefore, according to Mahan, the United States should maintain a superior force in the Pacific to defend the West Coast.[382]

The US Justice Department admitted that Congress had not sanctioned Hawaii's July 7, 1898, annexation, and it was technically illegitimate. In addition, the US government signed Public Law #103-150, acknowledging the illegality of the overthrow of the Hawaiian government. Hawaiians did not want annexation and never surrendered their sovereignty.[383]

Early Expansionism in the Caribbean

US commercial relations with Cuba go back to the days of smuggling and piracy and the old colonial system. By the early 1790s, Cubans welcomed neutral ships. Yankee traders exchanged lard, flour, and

---

[381] Ibid. 26-27
[382] Ibid. 26-27
[383] Matt Hutaff, Leis and Lies: Why Hawaii and Iraq are Birds of a Feather, April 5, 2004, http://www.thesimon.com/magazine/articles/canon_fodder/0590_leis_lies_why_hawaii_iraq_birds_feather.html as of May 2012

hardware for sugar, coffee, molasses, and rum. By 1818, many Americans moved to Cuba, as officials did not enforce laws against foreigners, allowing them to avoid taxation. In 1837, Americans, with British loans, finished the first railway connecting Havana and Güines. They introduced steam engine machinery to the sugar industry in Matanzas and Cárdenas. Spanish officials then imposed a duty on US flour, and US officials retaliated by levying a duty against Cuban coffee. By 1850, the United States was exporting about $8 million in goods to Cuba and importing about $12 million from Cuba. Between 1851 and 1855, half the ships entering Cuban ports were from America. Sugar comprised 84 percent of Cuba's exports to the United States, where sugar consumption quadrupled between 1840 and 1860.[384] Cuba was the world's largest exporter of sugar, man's first and most accessible mind-altering drug. It was the most profitable commodity in world trade at that time.

Hamilton Fish, named after Alexander Hamilton, was President Ulysses S. Grant's handler. Every president—a mere figurehead—as a mentor, especially since the Civil War. Fish, a Whig, graduated from Columbia College, where he belonged to the Philolexian Society and Sons of Liberty, a secret organization. Fish became a New York attorney and practiced law in New York with William B. Lawrence.[385] Fish and his family spent two years traveling in Europe, and he returned in order to campaign for Lincoln, who was running for US president.[386]

Fish was the vice-president general of the Society of the Cincinnati (1848-1854), and then was president general from 1854 until his death. The Society of the Cincinnati (founded May 13, 1783) sought the complete seizure of power in order to install a dictatorship in the United States, as proposed by the Federalists. The rich would

---

[384] Our Cuban Colony: A Study in Sugar by Leland Hamilton Jenks, Vanguard Press, New York, 1928, p. 18-21

[385] American Statesmen: Secretaries of State from John Jay to Colin Powell edited by Edward S. Mihalkanin, Greenwood Press, Westport, Connecticut, 2004, pp. 191-192

[386] Encyclopedia of the Reconstruction Era: A-L By Richard Zuczek, Greenwood Publishing, Westport, Connecticut, 2006, pp. 253-254

dominate this dictatorship, a highly centralized government. Fish was New York's sixteenth governor (1849-1850) and a member of the New York Historical Society, founded with the aid of Peter G. Stuyvesant, who donated the land that is now Stuyvesant Square in Manhattan.[387] Fish was a trustee at Columbia University (1840-1849, 1851-1893) and board chairman (1859-1893).

Fish befriended "war hero," General Grant, a potential president, and even provided money for Grant's family, for which he might prove acquiescent to Fish and his friends. The world traveler, Fish, apparently possessing very deep pockets, financed Grant's campaign and influenced others to support his candidacy, despite the scandalous rumors of Grant's corruption and alcoholism. Fish was Grant's Secretary of State for two terms (1869-1877), and, during that crucial time, he negotiated the Treaty of Washington on May 8, 1871, which settled many issues between Britain and the United States.[388]

President Grant and Secretary of State Fish, both ambitious expansionists, targeted Latin America and the Pacific, beginning a chain of expansionist efforts from Grant to Theodore Roosevelt and beyond. William H. Seward had attempted to sign a reciprocity treaty with Hawaiian officials, the first port beyond the continent, but was unsuccessful.[389] Fish presided over the Washington Peace Conference between Spain, Peru, Chile, Ecuador, and Bolivia and promoted a litmus test for job applicants in the State Department.

Fish wanted to annex several Caribbean islands and maintain them under US ownership.[390] He had visited Cuba, a Spanish colony, in 1855, and was impressed with its climate and beauty. Yet, he noted, "With its present population, the island of Cuba is anything other

---

[387] Hamilton Fish: The Inner History of the Grant Administration, Volume: 1 by Allan Nevins, F. Ungar Pub. Co., New York, 1957, p. 22
[388] Richard Zuczek, Encyclopedia of the Reconstruction Era: A-L, Greenwood Publishing, Westport, Connecticut, 2006, pp. 253-254
[389] Walter LaFeber, The New Empire, an Interpretation of American Expansion, 1860-1898, Cornell University Press, Ithaca, New York, 1963, pp. 32, 35
[390] Richard Zuczek, Encyclopedia of the Reconstruction Era: A-L, Greenwood Publishing, Westport, Connecticut, 2006, pp. 253-254

than a desirable acquisition to the United States, and I can see no means of getting rid of a population of some 450,000 called white, but really every shade and mixture of color, who own all the land on the island."[391] Like Grant, Fish was prejudiced against people with a darker skin.

After the Civil War, American industrialists targeted Cuba, 750 miles from west to east, an area equal to that of Pennsylvania, specifically for commercial interests. It was the industrialist's first ownership objective in the Caribbean. The Ten Years' War, the first of three wars for independence, erupted on October 10, 1868. Carlos Manuel de Céspedes, the owner of a sugar mill, La Demajagua, freed his slaves to fight with him for a free Cuba. On December 27, 1868, he publicly condemned slavery and declared that any slave master who would relinquish his slaves for military service should free them.

Grant and Fish proclaimed the nontransfer principle, a modification of the Monroe Doctrine, especially devised for the Caribbean, Hawaii, and Samoa. It mandated that the United States would not consider any territory on the North American continent or the designated islands subject to transfer to any European power. Modifications to the Monroe Doctrine were necessary in order to justify military interventions, especially in Latin America, in an attempt to create order and maintain stability, and therefore protect the commercial interests of numerous US industrialists. Roosevelt later enlarged this document as part of the Roosevelt Corollary.

The Cuban rebellion gave the US government an opportunity to intervene, due to the physical proximity to the island. Moreover, the United States would assist any revolt that eradicated European interests in the hemisphere. Individuals collaborated with a well-financed New York cabal that spent at least $1 million in its first year to provoke pro-rebel support. Fish wanted to pay $100 million to Spain for Cuba's independence to avoid a war, as he did not favor annexation predicated on his racial views. He also felt that the administration

---

[391]   Edward S. Mihalkanin, American Statesmen: Secretaries of State from John Jay to Colin Powell, Greenwood Press, Westport, Connecticut, 2004, pp. 196-197

of the island by locals might prove very ineffective. However, Grant and Congress disagreed; they wanted Cuba at whatever cost, a cash payment, a war, or both.[392]

Spain had lost most of their Latin American colonies earlier in the century. Now, US industrial interests, to accommodate their own agenda, supported the Cubans in their revolt against Spain, their colonial masters. The revolutionaries wanted the United States to annex Cuba, or at least to officially recognize them. Secretary of State Fish rejected this proposal, but Grant favored it.[393] Numerous sugar industrialists wanted the United States to recognize the belligerent Cubans, an act that would inevitably lead to war with Spain. Grant favored recognition, and, in August 1869, he signed a proclamation of neutrality and encouraged Spain to grant Cuban independence and free the slaves. He then provoked the situation by sending US expeditionary forces, which greatly displeased the Spanish colonial administration.[394]

Fish tried to persuade Grant to withhold the neutrality document until his annual message on December 6, 1869. By then, Grant had already decided that recognition was unwarranted. Some Rebel Cubans purchased a US steamer, *Virginius*, registered it in the United States, and deceptively flew the US flag while supplying contraband to the Cuban rebels, but Spain surprised them and seized the ship and forced it to Cuba. The Spanish colonial government executed the captain and fifty-three predominantly US crewmembers, which destroyed any negotiation possibilities with Spain. On November 14, 1870, Fish issued an ultimatum to Spain, giving the nation twelve days to release the survivors. He demanded punishment for the officials who had seized the ship and ordered them to officially salute the US flag,

---

[392] Walter LaFeber, The New Empire, an Interpretation of American Expansion, 1860-1898, Cornell University Press, Ithaca, New York, 1963, pp. 37-39

[393] Warren Zimmerman, First Great Triumph, How Five Americans Made Their Country a World Power, Farrar, Straus and Giroux, New York, 2002, pp. 246-257

[394] Edward S. Mihalkanin, American Statesmen: Secretaries of State from John Jay to Colin Powell, Greenwood Press, Westport, Connecticut, 2004, pp. 196-197

a demand that they would drop if they could prove that the ship was illegally registered, which it was. The Spanish dismissed the other demands, which added to the conflict between the two nations.[395]

The president appointed Caleb Cushing as US Minister to Spain in February 1874. He pressured Spanish officials for reforms, abolition of slavery, and self-government for Cuba. Instead, Spain reinforced their military presence on the island, which temporarily suppressed the rebel forces. The US conflict with Spain regarding Cuba continued for over two decades.[396]

The Ten Years' War ended with the Pact of Zanjón on February 10, 1878. After the war, the United States did not recognize the new Cuban government, while other European and Latin American nations did. The bloody ten-year battle devastated Cuba, apparently without it obtaining independence or any practicable resolutions, producing nothing but bitterness and resentment against the United States. About 208,000 Spanish soldiers died, while 50,000 Cubans lost their lives.[397] Spain promised greater autonomy to Cuba. In 1879-1880, Cuban patriot Calixto García attempted to initiate another rebellion against Spain, the Little War (1879-1880), but few people supported him.

Other planters, seeking protection against Spain, became US citizens as insurance against the economic consequences of future rebellions. At the same time, beet-sugar production, as opposed to cane-sugar production, coupled with the upheaval of the revolt, decreased sugar production and bankrupted many Cuban planters, who then relinquished their plantations to US bargain hunters. Certain US interests now had the best of both worlds—property and the control over the profitable production of natural resources without the challenge of political responsibilities.[398]

---

[395] Ibid. 196-197
[396] Ibid. 196-197
[397] Warren Zimmerman, First Great Triumph, How Five Americans Made Their Country a World Power, Farrar, Straus and Giroux, New York, 2002, pp. 246-257
[398] Walter LaFeber, The New Empire, an Interpretation of American Expansion, 1860-1898, Cornell University Press, Ithaca, New York, 1963, pp. 37-39

The Cuban's revolution destroyed numerous Spanish and Cuban planters, who were obligated to sell their properties to satisfy their debts. Elisha Atkins had invested in the Cuban sugar business as early as 1835, with E. Atkins & Company, headquartered in Boston. Atkins owned the Bay State Sugar Refinery before it became part of the American Sugar Refining Company. He sent his son, Edwin F. Atkins, to Cuba in the 1860s and in 1884.[399] Atkins's company also financed agents, Torriente Brothers of Cienfuegos, who worked with local planters, advancing them money and supplies. After the war, the Sarría family was unable to pay, so, in 1883, Atkins seized one of their estates, Soledad. He enlarged the property and brought in new equipment. By 1893, Soledad comprised 12,000 acres, of which Atkins planted cane on 5,000 acres. The firm also created twenty-three miles of private railway. The firm employed 1,200 men at harvest time and became one of the largest sugar mills in Cuba.[400] Soledad Plantation became the largest single US producer in Cuba. Edwin F. Atkins later became the chairman of the American Sugar Refining Company. In 1892, he and Havemeyer jointly owned the Trinidad Sugar Company on the land previously owned by the Iznaga family.[401]

In 1891, after the treaty with Spain, Cuban sugar was duty-free into the United States. A group of New York sugar merchants created the Tuinucüa Cane Sugar Company and began processing cane near Sancti Spiritus in 1893. The Sugar Trust did not invest in Cuba prior to 1898. Havemeyer merged the Atkins refinery to form the trust. Havemeyer and Edwin F. Atkins formed a partnership and invested in Cuban sugar near Trinidad and Tanamo.[402]

---

[399] Hugh Thomas, Cuba, or, The pursuit of freedom, First Da Capo Press, New York, 1998, p. 290

[400] Leland Hamilton Jenks, Our Cuban Colony: A Study in Sugar, Vanguard Press, New York, 1928, pp. 34-35

[401] Hugh Thomas, Cuba, or, The pursuit of freedom, First Da Capo Press, New York, 1998, p. 290

[402] Leland Hamilton Jenks, Our Cuban Colony: A Study in Sugar, Vanguard Press, New York, 1928, pp. 34-35

Cuba, Imperialism in the Neighborhood

In 1886, Spain abolished slavery in Cuba. Sugar plantations and mills disappeared, and wealthy Cubans forfeited their properties and became part of the middle class while the number of tenant farmers increased. Only the most powerful plantation owners retained their assets and status. US businessmen invested almost $50 million by 1895, mostly in sugar and tobacco. Cuba, still a Spanish colony, was economically dependent on the United States. On February 4, 1887, President Grover Cleveland (1885-1889; 1893-1897) signed an act creating the Interstate Commerce Commission, a shift in the powers of government from service to regulation, because of the increasing public concern over the expanding power and wealth of corporations, especially railroads.

Between 1890 and 1895, Alfred Thayer Mahan, a geostrategist and historian and author of *The Influence of Sea Power Upon History, 1660-1783* (1890), wrote articles for the *Atlantic Monthly*, the *Forum*, the *North American Review* and *Harper's New Monthly Magazine,* which they then published in book form as *The Interest of America in Sea Power, Present and Future.* He called attention to Cuba's size, over 600 miles long, which he deemed almost an extension of America's east coast. He felt that Cuba has key, "preeminent intrinsic advantages," like its strategic position in the Caribbean, which, under the control of the "world of civilized Christianity," was essential to military supremacy. He emphasized the military importance of Cuba's three natural harbors, Havana, Santiago, and Cienfuegos, perfect sites for naval operations and sources of supplies, especially coal, which was essential to warfare. He said that Cuba was unique among all of the Caribbean islands, all of which were to Spain's benefit. Mahan also extolled the attributes of Port Royal in Jamaica and Samaná Bay, at the northeast corner of Santo Domingo, as well as Panama.[403]

---

[403]   Alfred T. Mahan, The Interest of America in Sea Power, Present and Future, Little, Brown & Company, Boston, 1897, pp. 271-314

In 1895, Senator Henry Cabot Lodge said, "We have a record of conquest, colonization, and expansion unequalled by any people in the nineteenth century. We are not to be curbed now."[404] Senator Lodge and Theodore Roosevelt both encouraged US officials to expel the Spanish from the hemisphere by adopting Britain's tactics. However, humanitarian interventionists urged the government to retain what remained of our constitutional values and instead assist our neighbors to acquire freedom. The press, favoring business over principles, exaggerated Spain's tyrannical attitude toward the Cubans, which predictably provoked widespread outrage and a call for military action. Many US citizens renounced any kind of foreign military intervention as unconstitutional.[405]

Journalist Henry Adams, the grandson of John Quincy Adams, introduced Henry Cabot Lodge to two representatives of the Cuban insurrection who were attempting to gain US support. Lodge and the Cubans met secretly at the home of Senator James D. Cameron, and, behind President Cleveland's back, they proposed a nonbinding resolution recognizing Cuban independence. Several US businessmen opposed giving assistance to the Cuban dissidents, but rather favored a war against Cuba. The United States would certainly win, which would clearly enhance their business.[406]

In 1896, President Cleveland, cognizant of the bank and business interests that put him into power during a period of Republican domination (1860-1912), said about Cuba, "It is reasonably estimated that at least $30,000,000 to $50,000,000 of American capital is invested in the plantations and in railroads, mining, and other business enterprises on the island. The volume of trade between the United States and Cuba, which, in 1889, amounted to $64,000,000,

---

404   Time Magazine, Philippine Gold, March 26, 1934
405   Michael Mann, American Empires: Past and Present by, Department of Sociology, UCLA, The Canadian Review of Sociology and Anthropology, Volume 45, Issue 1, 2008
406   Warren Zimmerman, First Great Triumph, How Five Americans Made Their Country a World Power, Farrar, Straus and Giroux, New York, 2002, pp. 153-157

rose in 1893 to about $103,000,000.'⁴⁰⁷ He preferred to use diplomacy to protect his "friends" and their investments in Cuba and was not particularly interested in foreign affairs or intervention, but was inherently more of an isolationist.⁴⁰⁸

Havana native, José Martí, a prolific writer and Cuban patriot, had lived in New York (1881-1895), where he had joined General Calixto García's Cuban revolutionary committee, composed of exiled Cubans seeking independence. He gave speeches in numerous US cities in order to gain support for a Cuban revolutionary movement. Pro-independence Cubans quickly joined Martí's Cuban Revolutionary Party, created in early 1892. On February 24, 1895, the rebels, led by Máximo Gómez and inspired by Martí, demanded independence and rebelled against Spain, with uprisings all over the island. Within a month, Martí and Gómez issued the Manifesto de Montecristi, an explanation of the purposes of the revolution. On May 19, 1895, at the Battle of Dos Ríos, Spanish troops killed Martí, who had also opposed potential US expansionism. His death did not alter the passion of the rebels for independence.

Theodore Roosevelt, along with other war hawks, glorified war and advocated the theoretical nobleness of military conquest. He and his likeminded cohorts convinced others in Congress to assist Cuba, a vigorous trading partner, in their rebellion to protect sizable business investments there. Congressional leaders had previously approached President Cleveland about declaring war against Spain. He had rejected their petition and said that, if it declared war, then he, as commander in chief, would refuse to mobilize the troops.

Cleveland did not intend to seek reelection, so he did not respond to political pressure. He claimed he did not want to engage in a war, but he quietly maneuvered officials in Madrid to initiate diplomatic

---

⁴⁰⁷ Howard Zinn, A People's History of the United States, 1492 to Present, Harper Collins Publishers, 1999, New York, p. 305, Zinn definitely had socialist, if not Communist values, which does not discredit some of his statements.
⁴⁰⁸ Robert McElroy, Grover Cleveland, the Man and the Statesman: An Authorized Biography, Volume: 1, Harper & Brothers, New York, 1923, p. 242

reforms to staunch the rebellion that General Arsenio Martínez de Campos had failed to pacify.[409] In April 1895, Spain deployed about 80,000 Spanish forces, which far outnumbered the rebels. Landowners volunteered their workers to fight, but the local troops lacked military structure. In October 1895, Senator Lodge visited the Spanish Prime Minister, Antonio Cánovas del Castillo, who was very concerned over the Cuban insurrection and worried that the United States would interfere. Lodge encouraged him to quickly and forcefully end the revolt, because it might interrupt US business. Spain, already dispirited and weakened, was incapable of ruling their colony, and was thoroughly prepared to relinquish Cuba.[410]

By December 1895, Prime Minister Castillo again sent General Campos, with 98,412 troops, to halt the rebel forces, but he failed. On February 10, 1896, General Valeriano Weyler (of German and Spanish descent) replaced Campos. Weyler had studied General William T. Sherman's scorched-earth policies during the Civil War.[411] Sherman earlier vowed that "no earthly power" could keep the United States out of Cuba.[412]

General Weyler failed militarily, but immediately began rounding up civilians to isolate them from the rebels and eliminate potential sympathizers. He relocated the rural peasants to urban areas under the jurisdiction of the Spanish military. The relocation, or *reconcentrado*, of the population into crowded camps soon included the majority of the island's rural inhabitants. He intended to deprive the rebels of food, supplies, and potential information from noncombatants. He ended all sugar production and tobacco exports to prevent Cuban planters from using their funds to help the insurgents. Weyler, along

---

[409] Stuart Creighton Miller "Benevolent Assimilation," the American Conquest of the Philippines, 1899-1903, Yale University Press, New Haven and London, 1982, pp. 9-12

[410] Warren Zimmerman, First Great Triumph, How Five Americans Made Their Country a World Power, Farrar, Straus and Giroux, New York, 2002, pp. 153-157

[411] Ibid. 246-257

[412] Stuart Creighton Miller, "Benevolent Assimilation," the American Conquest of the Philippines, 1899-1903, Yale University Press, New Haven and London, 1982, p. 9

with General Gómez, quickly shut down the island's economy, which, within a short time, sent about 400,000 rural refugees, now unemployed, into the fortified towns, which, with limited resources, were unprepared. Housing, food, sanitation, and medical care were inadequate. Starvation and disease were soon rampant. By 1897, the concentration camps became death camps.[413]

Senator Jacob H. Gallinger, after returning from Cuba, spoke to the Senate about the war as one of "starvation and extermination, a war more cruel than the world has ever known." He referred to the scenes in Havana as "beyond description," with "walking skeletons, naked children, emaciated and ragged women, and diseased and starving men" thronging the streets. He reported, "Many have refused to believe that a great government was waging a war of extermination instead of a war of honor." Regarding the wretched people in the streets of Matanza, he said, "It occurred to me as I looked upon the scenes of suffering and horrors that the Cuban *reconcentrados* might well have adopted the words of Dante: who enters here leaves hope behind." The soldiers herded the people like cattle. Weyler, like Sherman during the Civil War, had conceived of a scheme of "human suffering and sorrow," wherein he transformed a "contented, prosperous people into a herd of suffering, starving unfortunates." Out of an estimated population of 800,000 people, about 225,000 died of starvation. Yet the Red Cross reported 425,000 Cuban deaths as a result of Spanish brutality. Because of the conditions, officials expected another 200,000 deaths.[414] One report said that 321,934 people died under the Reconcentration Policy.

President William McKinley (1897-1901) publicly maintained Cleveland's purported noninterventionist policy and refused to cater to the jingoistic presses' demands. He replaced Senator John Sherman with Mark Hanna and appointed Sherman as the Secretary of State. Hanna, from Cleveland, Ohio, was an industrialist, politician, and

---

[413] John L. Offner, An Unwanted War: The Diplomacy of the United States and Spain over Cuba, 1895-1898, University of North Carolina Press, Chapel Hill, North Carolina, 1992, p. 13

[414] Horrors of Cuban War, Senator Describes the Misery on the Unfortunate Island, the Victims of Starvation, The Baltimore Sun, March 24, 1898

skilled political mentor. Sherman, brother of the infamous General William T. Sherman, was anxious to involve the country in Cuba, and therefore began dispatching inflammatory messages to officials in Madrid. McKinley retained Fitzhugh Lee, a Cuban sympathizer, as Consul-General in Havana. McKinley sent William J. Calhoun to Cuba on a fact-finding mission, which alleviated him from taking any immediate actions other than a strongly worded ultimatum to Spain.[415] On August 8, 1897, Michele A. Lombardi, an Italian anarchist, assassinated Prime Minister Castillo, for which the state executed him on August 20, 1897. Spanish leaders, dissatisfied with Weyler's methods, recalled him to Spain and initiated new reforms for Cuban autonomy.

In mid-January 1898, Spain's insufficient reforms provoked rioting. Weyler's former soldiers and Spanish colonists destroyed the business and newspaper offices supportive of the reforms. Spain's emissary, Enriqué Dupuy de Lōme, told an intimate friend that McKinley was weak and ineffective, an opinion that some US politicians shared. The Cuban junta in Washington leaked these negative views to William Randolph Hearst, known for his yellow journalism—a pejorative phrase "associated with misconduct in newsgathering."[416] The *New York Journal* printed the headline "Worst Insult to the United States in its History." Fitzhugh Lee requested that McKinley send a battleship to provide an intimidating naval presence.[417]

Accordingly, on January 25, 1898, McKinley sent the *USS Maine*, a 300-foot-long, 6,682-ton armored cruiser with ten mounted guns to Havana, supposedly to protect Consul General Lee, US business interests, and the US citizens living there. On February 15, 1898,

---

[415] Stuart Creighton Miller, "Benevolent Assimilation," the American Conquest of the Philippines, 1899-1903, Yale University Press, New Haven and London, 1982, pp. 9-12

[416] Yellow Journalism, Puncturing the Myths, Defining the Legacies by W. Joseph Campbell, Praeger Publishers, Westport, Connecticut, 2007, p. 26

[417] Stuart Creighton Miller, "Benevolent Assimilation," the American Conquest of the Philippines, 1899-1903, Yale University Press, New Haven and London, 1982, p. 9

there was a deadly explosion, and the huge ship quickly sank to the bottom of Havana Harbor.

Hearst, a chief proponent of tabloid-like journalism, devoted more than fifty pages to cover the *USS Maine* disaster. The second day after the disaster, the *Journal* headlined—"*The Warship Maine was Split in Two by an Enemy's Secret Infernal Machine.*" He offered a $50,000 reward "for the conviction of the criminals" who had sent US sailors to their watery graves.[418] On February 17, 1898, his *New York Journal* ran the front-page headline—"Destruction of the Warship *Maine* was the Work of an Enemy! Assistant Secretary Roosevelt Convinced the Explosion of the Warship Was Not an Accident; Naval Officers Think the *Maine* was Destroyed by a Spanish Mine; and Who Destroyed the *Maine*—$50,000 Reward."[419]

By 1898, the US Navy and Army accepted black Americans. The Marine Corps did not accept them until World War II. Native Americans also participated in the Spanish-American War as volunteers, especially in the First Volunteer Cavalry and First Territorial Volunteer Infantry.[420] There were thirty black Americans out of 350 personnel on board the *USS Maine on* that dreadful day. Of the 260 who died, twenty-two were African Americans, as officers usually assigned them to work in the engine rooms as firemen, oilers, and coal passers, the area most affected by the explosion that day. There were more casualties on the *USS Maine, almost three months before the declaration of war, than all the casualties sustained during the war itself. Ninety people survived the* explosion. Eighty-five US personnel died during the war, of which only sixteen died in action.[421]

---

[418] Warren Zimmerman, First Great Triumph, How Five Americans Made Their Country a World Power, Farrar, Straus and Giroux, New York, 2002, pp. 236-241
[419] Daniel Cohen, Yellow Journalism, Scandal, Sensationalism, and Gossip in the News, Twenty-first Century books, Brookfield, Connecticut, 2000, p. 34
[420] Sailors, Soldiers, and Marines of the Spanish-American War: The Legacy of USS *Maine* by Rebecca Livingston, *Prologue Magazine, National Archives,* Spring 1998, Vol. 30, No. 1
[421] Ibid

The government reprinted a list of those who perished in the *Annual Reports of the Secretary of the Navy for 1898.* They treated the survivors at naval hospitals, and the navy compensated many of them for the personal items that they lost when the ship sank. Seven survivors later deserted, while two ultimately received treatment at the Government Hospital of the Insane in Washington, DC. The distress of witnessing the drowning, burning, and mutilation of their companions was evidently too difficult to withstand. Many survivors had multiple burns and injuries and spent lengthy periods in recovery.[422]

Captain Charles D. Sigsbee and Richard Wainwright, the Executive Officer of the *USS Maine,* survived the explosion and the sinking of the ship. Wainwright assumed command of the *USS Gloucester,* J. Pierpont Morgan's yacht which the government had purchased for $225,000 at the outbreak of the war. Sigsbee took command of the *USS St. Paul* and was later the chief intelligence officer for the navy before they appointed him to rear admiral.

On March 31, 1898, William Jennings Bryan said, "The time for intervention has arrived, humanity demands that we shall act." Bryan did not try to persuade others to wait and determine if arbitration would work. Representative Charles H. Grosvenor told the House on that same day, "Do you think that this great party in power today is going to be unfaithful to a trust which . . . will, if properly discharged, bring glory to the administration?"[423]

In June 1892, William T. Sampson, an intelligence officer specializing in chemistry and physics programs, accepted the office of the Inspector of Ordnance in the Washington Navy Yard. On January 28, 1893, officials appointed him as chief of the Bureau of Ordnance. He created smokeless gunpowder and promoted the use of telescopic sights and the application of electric energy on all new battleships.

---

[422] *Rebecca Livingston,* Sailors, Soldiers, and Marines of the Spanish-American War: The Legacy of USS *Maine, Prologue Magazine, National Archives,* Spring 1998, Vol. 30, No. 1

[423] Leland Hamilton Jenks, Our Cuban Colony: A Study in Sugar, Vanguard Press, New York, 1928, pp. 54-55

On June 15, 1897, he took command of the battleship *Iowa*. On February 17, 1898, officials appointed him as president of the Board of Inquiry to investigate the *USS Maine's* destruction. Apparently, his conclusions pleased his superiors, because, on March 26, 1898, they advanced him over several officers who had more seniority and appointed him as the head of the navy's North Atlantic Fleet, with the rank of rear admiral. On June 1, 1898, he would take command of the flagship *New York*, which blockaded the Santiago Harbor. He directed the design of about 95 percent of the guns used in the Battle for Santiago.

President McKinley claimed to be against a full-blown war, preferring diplomacy instead. On April 11, 1898, based on Sampson's findings, he reported to Congress that the cause was an external submarine mine. No one has ever accurately determined the exact reason for the explosion, after four investigations, in 1898, 1911, 1976, and 1999. Nevertheless, the media and US officials blamed Spain. Assistant Naval Secretary Roosevelt accused Spain of "an act of dirty treachery." Senator Redfield Proctor gave a three-hour discourse on the horrors of the *concentrados* and the accompanying widespread starvation in Cuba and called for an intervention. McKinley sent another ultimatum to officials in Madrid, demanding Cuban independence by April 15, 1898. On April 19, the Senate passed the Teller Amendment to disclaim any US intentions of taking permanent control of Cuba, but promised that the Cubans could govern the island after the Spanish left. Spanish troops vacated the island in 1898, and the United States occupied Cuba until 1902. However, the Platt Amendment of February 1901 allowed continued US intervention, allegedly to protect life, liberty, and property. Congress finally abrogated the Platt Amendment on May 29, 1934.

McKinley asked Congress for a $50 million military appropriation, obviously planning for a much larger military operation. Congress declared war on April 25, predated to April 21, despite papal offers to arbitrate. In a surge of patriotism, young men enlisted in the military, while veterans begged for a chance to go to war. Hearty cheers erupted from pulpits, a residual of socialist infiltration from the previous war. Editors endorsed warfare in the editorial pages of newspapers. John Hay, appointed as secretary of state on September 30, 1898, called the hundred-day war "a splendid little war." The US intervention consisted of two naval victories—one at Manila on May 1, 1898, those "darned islands" that forced McKinley to consult a map; and the other at Santiago Bay in Cuba in July 1898. The army campaigns consisted of Lawton's forces at El Caney and Colonel Roosevelt's escapade at San Juan Hill. More troops perished from the tropical diseases than from bullets.[424] After hearing reports of Spanish atrocities, the US "liberated" the Cubans. The conflict was over in a few months; the Spanish fleet left the harbor on July 1, 1898. Combat ensued with ground troops, which culminated on August 12, 1898.

The industrialists and bankers, like Morgan and Carnegie, publicly denounced war, while privately embracing the opportunity to exploit natural resources in Cuba. Lodge, a war hawk like Roosevelt, applauded the newspaper owners, Hearst and Pulitzer, who goaded their readers into war frenzy. Senator Joseph B. Foraker and Representative Joseph Bailey, both Standard Oil Company benefactors, demanded a declaration of war. Rockefeller-Stillman National City Bank set up branches in Cuba, the Philippines, and, ultimately, all over Latin America. National City handled Cuba's sugar-industry funds. McKinley failed to tell Congress that Spain, at the last moment, had capitulated on every single demand. They could have avoided war and the resulting deaths.[425] Wall Street had its greedy eyes on South America's mineral resources. Additionally, they wanted an isthmian canal built, one of the reasons for the seizure of Cuba and Puerto Rico.[426] On July 25, 1898, during the Spanish-American War, the United States invaded Puerto Rico by landing at Guánica. In 1917, the Jones-Shafroth Act granted US citizenship to all Puerto Rican inhabitants.

---

[424] Stuart Creighton Miller, "Benevolent Assimilation," the American Conquest of the Philippines, 1899-1903, Yale University Press, New Haven and London, 1982, pp. 9-12
[425] Ferdinand Lundberg, America's 60 Families, The Citadel Press, New York, 1937, pp. 61-62
[426] Ibid. 59-64

Elihu Root authored the Foraker Act; Congress passed it on December 22, 1899. It forbade the granting of franchises in Cuba during the period of the occupation, similar to the Teller Amendment, which prevented the United States from taking control of the island, following the occupation. Similarly, the Foraker Act was a measure to prevent US businessmen from seizing economic control of the Philippines. The law, though ostensibly designed to prevent the rush of US business interests, was ineffective. Industrialists simply had to find and install accommodating government officials during the occupation and then exercise patience.[427]

The Cuban revolutionaries aided the United States after the invasion by providing intelligence and guarding roads until the United States banished Spain. US officials no longer needed them and did not invite them to attend the surrender ceremonies, nor did they participate in the formation of a new Cuban government, which, for the first four years, was a military dictatorship. Coincidentally, at about the same time that the international bankers were promoting and funding Japan's war hawk behavior against Korea, China, and Manchuria, government and banker-backed US corporations were looking for ways to seize productive land and control in Cuba. They ultimately achieved this through the Platt Amendment on March 2, 1901.

Smedley D. Butler, author of *War is a Racket,* is distinguished for his courage against those, including military and government officials, who needlessly drag men into war for profit. Sixteen-year-old Butler, enamored by the dashing military uniforms, persuaded his mother to help him join the Marine Corps following the explosion of the *Maine.*[428] He arrived at Santiago, Cuba, on July 1, 1898, and boarded a ship for Guantánamo Bay (southern end of Cuba). His superiors commissioned him a first lieutenant on April 8, 1899, and he left four days later with 300 other marines for the Philippines. Next, he would go to another hot spot, northern China.[429]

---

[427] Philip C. Jessup, Elihu Root, Dodd Mead, New York, 1938, pp. 293-294
[428] Who's Who in Marine Corps History, http://www.tecom.usmc.mil/HD/Whos_Who/Butler_SD.htm as of May 2012
[429] Jules Archer, The Plot to Seize the White House, Hawthorne Books, Inc., New York 1973, p. 40-46

Cubans thought they were free of foreign domination, and Spanish expulsion served US business interests. However, that did not assuage the expansionists. The US government compelled the Cubans to adopt a US-friendly constitution, one that would make Cuba a protectorate and protect US business concerns from trade barriers and expropriation. This was part of the Platt Amendment attached to Cuba's new constitution. The United States would protect Cuba, requested or not, from invasion by other countries, which would require a perpetual lease for a military base, Guantánamo Bay Naval Station. This would allow US control of the Caribbean. John Hay, then ambassador to London, wrote President McKinley from London, "We have never in all our history had the standing in the world we have now."

In 1901, Andrew W. Preston, the president of the Boston-based United Fruit Company, and his syndicate purchased from 175,000 to 190,000 acres on Nipe Bay, on the northern coast of eastern Cuba, for $400,000. The company began planting cane and bananas after the war. The Rionda family revitalized its plantation at Tuinucú and merged with the Philadelphia-based McCahan sugar-refining firm to develop an 80,000-acre estate, Francisco, on the southern coast. Stuyvesant Fish, president of the Illinois Central Railroad, backed a company that bought the mill at Constancia and combined it with the Gramercy refinery in Louisiana. These projects were larger than the planters in Cuba had ever implemented.[430]

United Fruit transformed the perishable tropical banana into an item of importance in world trade. The company had 112 miles of railroad and 212,394 acres of land, with 61,263 acres in production and total capital of $11,230,000. It began expanding its potential supply sources and purchased more property in Santo Domingo, Honduras, Guatemala, and Panama, as well as more acreage in Colombia, Nicaragua, Cuba, and Jamaica. By 1930, the company had increased their capital to $215 million. Land was extremely inexpensive in these undeveloped countries, and their governments

---

[430] Leland Hamilton Jenks, Our Cuban Colony: A Study in Sugar, Vanguard Press, New York, 1928, p. 13o

were eager to sell large tracts of jungle in order to open them to lucrative development, especially to companies that would provide railroad and port facilities.[431]

Although United Fruit began with bananas, it quickly diversified into other products. It shipped sugar from Cuba and Jamaica, cocoa from Costa Rica, Ecuador, and Panama. It brought African palm oil from Costa Rica, Honduras, Guatemala, Nicaragua, and Colombia and functioned as an agent for the US government in the growing and processing of abaca (Manila hemp) in Guatemala and other areas. It planted and processed rubber, quinine, essential oils, and numerous hard and soft woods. Additionally, it produced and shipped bananas from six countries, including the Dominican Republic and the former British Cameroons in West Africa.[432]

United Fruit employed 82,000 tropical employees to maintain about 49,000 cattle, and 16,000 horses and mules on agricultural and pasture land. It operated a network of railways and tramways and had sixty-two ships. In 1904, it founded and managed the Tropical Radio Telegraph Company to facilitate the company's communication in order to coordinate its shipments. This radio network connected to offices in Boston, New York, San Francisco, New Orleans, Miami, Mexico, and the West Indies, through Central America to Bogotá, Quito, Rio de Janeiro, Asunción, Montevideo, and Buenos Aires to South America. It owned the Fruit Dispatch Company, their distribution agent for all the bananas it sold in America, Europe and Canada.[433]

US troops occupied Cuba until 1904, during which time that United Fruit was establishing their system. However, under the intervention provisions of the new Cuban constitution, the US government sent troops in 1906, 1912, 1917, and 1920 to halt the justifiable uprisings against US control over the Cuban economy. The Cubans rebelled

---

[431] Stacy May and Galo Plaza, The United Fruit Company in Latin America, National Planning Association, Washington, DC, 1958, 7, 104-108
[432] Ibid. 7, 104-108
[433] Ibid. 7, 104-108

against this injustice, and Congress finally repealed the Platt Amendment in 1934.

Santo Domingo, a Third-World County

John Quincy Adams had claimed that Cuba and Santo Domingo were "natural appendages" to the United States, which was then altered by others to mean "natural borders," which was then changed to include a "natural defense perimeter."[434] Santo Domingo is the capital and largest city in the Dominican Republic, located on the island of Hispaniola, which is part of the Greater Antilles archipelago in the Caribbean. Haiti comprises the western third of the island.

President Ulysses S. Grant believed that the acquisition of Santo Domingo was imperative for the establishment of a naval base, essential to US interests in the Caribbean and as a defense for a potential canal through the Isthmus of Panama. He had visited Panama and immediately recognized the incalculable commercial and strategic military benefits. Accordingly, he ordered at least a half-dozen survey expeditions and was determined to seize the Dominican Republic's Samaná Bay, viewing it as a possible colony for freed slaves, whom he, like previous presidents, secretly wanted to deport. However, when the opportunity came to seize the Dominican Republic, Secretary of State Hamilton Fish did not relish the idea of governing a bankrupt and politically unstable foreign territory.[435]

President Buenaventura Baez of the Dominican Republic tried to secure a loan from the United States in which he and his associates could receive a commission. When that plan failed, he offered to sell his country, unbeknown to its inhabitants, to the United States in exchange for military support against his rivals. Grant sent his private secretary, Orville E. Babcock, who was regularly involved in

---

434 Stuart Creighton Miller, "Benevolent Assimilation," the American Conquest of the Philippines, 1899-1903, Yale University Press, New Haven and London, 1982, pp. 3, 5, 7

435 Edward S. Mihalkanin (editor), American Statesmen: Secretaries of State from John Jay to Colin Powell, Greenwood Press, Westport, Connecticut, 2004, pp. 193-194

corruption and scandal, to Santo Domingo to evaluate the situation, as Grant wanted to annex the country. Babcock returned with an annexation treaty signed by Baez, who wanted $2 million for Samaná Bay and the assumption of the nation's $1.5 million debt. Fish reminded Babcock that he did not have the authority to negotiate US treaties or the power to promise the use of military force. Babcock returned to the Dominican Republic and signed a lease agreement for Samaná Bay on November 29, 1869. He left a supply of arms and a US naval force to defend the Baez government, along with an extra $100,000. Now Baez could oppose his enemies, led by Gregorio Luperón, a military and political leader who facilitated the restoration of the Dominican Republic after the Spanish annexation in 1863. Many people in Haiti supported Luperón. Grant started building Senate support for annexation.[436]

The same New York scavengers were intent on developing the resources of Santo Domingo, financed by people like Cyrus H. McCormick, Ben Holliday, and Thomas Spofford of Spofford & Tileston Company, who were New York bankers. Grant was interested in the military and strategic value of Samaná Bay, in the eastern part of the Dominican Republic. Still, Fish and some members of Congress objected to the annexation of Santo Domingo, as it might entail the future seizure of Haiti and create a volatile racial crisis, a possibility the expansionists refused to acknowledge. Senator Sumner, still bitter over the president not appointing him as secretary of state, opposed Grant. Other senators justifiably suspected that Grant and the New York financiers were collaborating. Grant had the military muscle, used previously against the South, and he would use it again to allow US industrialists to dominate the natural resources of any targeted area.[437]

In 1893, a group of New York bankers, the Santo Domingo Improvement Company (SDIC), incorporated in New Jersey, purchased the entire debt of Santo Domingo, and took over its railroad contracts and European bondholders, which enabled them to collect all customs

[436] Ibid. 193-194
[437] Walter LaFeber, The New Empire, an Interpretation of American Expansion, 1860-1898, Cornell University Press, Ithaca, New York, 1963, pp. 37-39

and revenues in payment of that debt. This created a dispute with the Dominican National Bank, which the French Crédit Mobilier had chartered. In 1892, a French warship arrived to protect the bank's interests. In 1895, three US Navy ships arrived. The SDIC purchased the national bank from Crédit Mobilier and resolved the issue. The SDIC was in Santo Domingo to exploit the sugar industry, and now they owned the national bank.[438]

In 1900, the Dominican Republic owed the SDIC, in addition to the bonds that the company had sold in France, Belgium, Germany, Italy, and England, a total of $23,957,078, increasing the internal debt. The company's presence in the country gave the United States more influence in the area. Smith M. Weed, a prominent New York Democrat, was the president of the SDIC and a close friend of Grover Cleveland.[439]

The company intended to move the country's peasant farmers toward a profitable, exportable cash crop for their financial benefit. The SDIC borrowed $30 million by selling Dominican bonds in Europe. These loans and their unrestricted printing of currency via the national bank ultimately pushed the republic into financial ruin. In 1901, the Dominicans finally expelled the SDIC, a parasitical pariah that justifiably reviled by its host nation. In retaliation, President Roosevelt, controlled by private interests, deployed the US Navy's Caribbean Squadron to Dominican waters. SDIC's private interests and Washington's Caribbean policy was instituted in 1904, supported by US warships.[440] People deceptively refer to that policy, still current, as "national interests."

By 1904, the Dominican Republic was desperate and bankrupt. President Theodore Roosevelt and Secretary of State John Hay intervened in the political and financial affairs of the Dominican

---

438   Eric Paul Roorda, The Dictator Next Door: The Good Neighbor Policy and The Trujillo Regime in the Dominican Republic, 1930-1945, Duke University Press, Durham, North Carolina, 2004, pp. 12-13
439   Cyrus Veeser, A World Safe for Capitalism: Dollar Diplomacy and America's Rise to Global Power, Columbia University Press, New York, 2002, pp. 3-5
440   Ibid. 3-5

Republic in favor of the SDIC's interests. This intervention was soon applicable to all of Latin America, with Roosevelt's Corollary to the Monroe Doctrine—US intervention anywhere that "wrongdoing or impotence" threatened "civilized society"[441] The US Marine-trained Rafael Trujillo, a brutal dictator, officially and unofficially ruled the Dominican Republic for thirty years, from 1930 to 1961, helping multinational corporations exploit the country's resources while impoverishing the citizens. Trujillo, backed by the United States, was responsible for atrocities, assassinations, and the kidnappings of his political adversaries. In 1937, he sent troops to the Haitian border, where they slaughtered between 19,000 and 20,000 Haitian squatters. An unknown assailant assassinated him on May 30, 1961.

The Panama Canal, Essential for National Defense?

Imperialism necessitates "international military commitments," including a substantial number of permanent military bases. At the beginning of the twentieth century, it also required an increase in military forces. Therefore, business-friendly Congress authorized a 300 percent increase in the Marine Corps to forcefully facilitate imperialist objectives.[442]

In May 1879, Ferdinand de Lesseps convened a geological congress in Paris composed of 136 delegates, forty-two of whom were engineers, the rest speculators, politicians, and de Lesseps's friends. They discussed the problems of building a sea-level canal, as opposed to a lock canal, across the Isthmus of Panama, a project he began in 1878 with a concession from the Colombian government. Adolphe G. de Lépinay, known as Baron de Brusly, an engineer, studied the isthmus and then strongly opposed the project, based on the surface characteristics at Panama, and instead proposed a practical plan for building a canal, calling for a dam at Gatún and another at Miraflores. Politicians then arranged a treaty with Columbia, as Panama was then part of Columbia.

---

[441] Ibid. 3-5
[442] Robin Kadison Berson, Marching to a Different Drummer: Unrecognized Heroes of American History, Publisher: Greenwood Press, Westport, CT. 1994, p. 22

Aniceto G. Menocal, a graduate of the Rensselaer Polytechnic Institute and the chief engineer in the Department of the Navy by 1872, completed a survey in Nicaragua, as directed by Navy Secretary George M. Robeson. The Provisional Society from the Executive of Nicaragua confirmed Menocal's survey, conducted in the summer of 1879, and approved of the construction of a proposed canal across their country. Menocal attended de Lesseps's meeting in Paris that same year. According to *The New York Times*, of October 25, 1880, the Executive Committee of the Provisional Interoceanic Canal Society prepared a report about a potential ship canal in Nicaragua.[443] [444]

On January 1, 1882, de Lesseps, founder of the privately owned Compagnie Universelle du Canal Interocéanique, began the project with 20,000 men, nine-tenths of whom were African-Caribbean laborers from the West Indies along the route of the 1855 Panama Railroad. De Lesseps was the president of the French committee of Leopold II of Belgium's International African Society, created in 1876. He facilitated Pierre Savorgnan de Brazza's explorations, which ultimately led France's Central African colonies, the French Congo. De Lesseps, head of the Franco-American Union, officially presented the Statue of Liberty to the United States.

In 1887, the US government dispatched Lieutenant Menocal and a regiment to resurvey Nicaragua for a canal site under the auspices of the Maritime Canal Company, a congressional-chartered firm headed by J. Pierpont Morgan. Menocal recommended Nicaragua, and construction began. Maritime lost its financial backing in the stock panic of 1893, and they stopped excavation. In 1897, Congress

---

[443] Panama Canal Schemes; Mr. Menocal's Resurvey Of The Nicaragua Route, The New York Times, October 25, 1880, http://query.nytimes.com/gst/abstract.html?res=F20A17F93E5B1B7A93C7AB178BD95F448884F9 as of May 2012

[444] A. G. Menocal Dead; Noted Engineer, Served with Great Distinction on Panama and Nicaragua Canal Surveys. Expert On Hydraulics Was the Representative of This Country at the Paris Canal Congress of 1879 The New York Times, July 21, 1908, http://query.nytimes.com/mem/archive-free/pdf?res=F60F16FC395A17738DDDA80A94DF405B888CF1D3 as of May 2012

would establish the Canal Commission, which recommended the Nicaraguan route.

De Lesseps had successfully directed the building of the Suez Canal (1869), which joined the Mediterranean and Red Seas, and thus he had public support. He sold public stock to countless small French investors, but failed to raise as much money as he had hoped—only 30 million of his requested 400 million francs. On May 15, 1889, the French Canal Company suspended operations, and de Lesseps liquidated the firm and reimbursed investors and banks, after spending $234,795,000 (1.5 billion francs). He suspended the venture as over 22,000 laborers had died since its inception from tropical diseases. Additionally, there were engineering problems and frequent floods and mudslides. In 1894, he formed the New Panama Canal Company to salvage the project, and he obtained a new concession from Colombia. By 1896, the firm began looking for a buyer with a sale price of $109,000,000.

In 1897, Theodore Roosevelt, then assistant navy secretary, and Senator Henry Cabot Lodge, backed by J. Pierpont Morgan and other international bankers, began promoting US supremacy and warfare.[445] In 1898, to facilitate the sale of its failed project and its assets, the New Panama Canal Company hired New York lawyer, William N. Cromwell of Sullivan and Cromwell, to lobby Congress, an activity he perfected, as no one in Congress even considered a canal in Panama until he arrived in Washington. He immediately ingratiated himself with President William McKinley and Mark Hanna through Hanna's banker, Edward Simmons, president of the Panama Railroad, which the New Panama Canal Company owned.[446]

In 1899, Congress created the Isthmian Canal Commission to evaluate the possibilities of a Central American canal, and it selected Nicaragua, with Senator John T. Morgan as its chief proponent.

---

[445] Ferdinand Lundberg, America's 60 Families, The Citadel Press, 1937, pp. 59-64

[446] Nancy Lisagor and Frank Lipsius, A Law Unto Itself, the Untold Story of the Law Firm Sullivan & Cromwell, 100 Years of Creating Power & Wealth, William Morrow and Company, Inc., New York, 1988, pp. 40-43

Cromwell planted news items, used scare tactics, claimed that a German consortium was considering assuming the Panama project, and then donated $60,000 of the New Panama Canal Company's money to the Republican Party, enough for it to abandon the Nicaragua option on its 1900 platform in favor of the Panama route.[447] Cromwell also represented Kuhn Loeb and Company, the Harriman interests, the Sugar Trust, and Standard Oil.

Senator Morgan, a secessionist and former Confederate general, an expansionist, a segregationist in favor of black colonization, a staunch advocate for the Cuban revolutionaries in the 1890s, and a strong supporter of the annexation of Hawaii, Cuba, and the Philippines, introduced a bill to secure funding for a Nicaraguan canal. Like many other Southerners, he never forgave those he perceived as enemies of his region's way of life, particularly the Republicans. Possibly, he thought a canal in Nicaragua would aid the post-Civil War economic development in the South and reverse the North's financial dominion.[448] An assassin's bullet prevented McKinley from signing that bill, and Roosevelt assumed the presidency.

Certain globalist politicians had long dreamed of a canal linking the Atlantic and the Pacific. Roosevelt, a pragmatist, felt that a canal was practical, vital, and indispensable to the globalist destiny of supremacy over US coastal waters. The globalist goal, even then, was US control of key islands in the Caribbean and the Pacific.[449] He was a proponent of a doctrine proposed by US naval officer and scholar, Alfred Thayer Mahan, in his 1890 book *Influence of Sea Power upon History*, where he claimed that supremacy at sea was an integral part of commercial and military prowess. Mahan's supremacy mentality also included the Indian Ocean and islands like Diego Garcia. Mahan

---

[447] Ibid. 40-43

[448] John Tyler Morgan by Thomas Adams Upchurch, the Encyclopedia of Alabama, http://www.encyclopediaofalabama.org/face/Article.jsp?id=h-1508 as of May 2012

[449] Panama Canal Authority Technical Resources Center and Corporate Communications Division, A History Of The Panama Canal, French and American Construction Efforts Prepared, The American Canal Construction, http://www.pancanal.com/eng/history/history/index.html as of May 2012

maintained that whoever seizes naval supremacy in the Indian Ocean, the third largest in the world, would be a prominent player on the international scene.[450]

Roosevelt's belief in the vital need for a canal and foreign affairs began with his trip on the USS *Oregon* around the Horn during the Spanish American War. He and Mahan promoted the canal as a method of "national defense." He, in the 1890s, strongly opposed any efforts that would allow foreigners a position in the building, operation, or defense of a canal because that would undermine US naval power and the veracity of the Monroe Doctrine.[451]

According to Roosevelt, the United States needed to fulfill certain requirements in order to enter the global schematic. Initially, the United States should control an isthmian canal to establish US dominance in the Caribbean and the Pacific. To protect and exploit the canal, the United States also required a militarized navy. Lastly, to dominate, the United States had to position naval bases in strategic areas adjacent to the canal. Using an Anglo American alliance and military power, the British would supervise the east while the United States dominated the west. Each power would secure the best interests of "civilization" against the "barbarians" in their designated sphere. Their respective navies, the best in the world, would enforce peace. He recapped the New World Order strategy in 1899, "Together . . . the two branches of the Anglo-Saxon race . . . can whip the world."[452]

Roosevelt wrote to Secretary of State John Hay in 1900 and reiterated Mahan's argument that a canal uncontrolled by US naval forces would be disastrous during warfare. Additionally, he argued that joint ownership or control of the canal would make the Monroe

---

[450] A. T. Mahan, The Influence of Sea Power upon History, 1660-1783, Little, Brown, Boston, 1918, pp. 242-243
[451] The Monroe Doctrine and the Roosevelt Corollary, http://www. theodoreroosevelt.org/life/RooseveltCorollary.htm
[452] The Panama Canal in American Politics: Domestic Advocacy and the Evolution of Policy by J. Michael Hogan, Southern Illinois University Press, Carbondale, Illinois, 1986, pp. 26-27

Doctrine insignificant.[453] Roosevelt, in his corollary to the Monroe Doctrine, claimed that America had a right to wield a "big stick" against any country in the western hemisphere that merited such intervention.[454]

At the suggestion of the Commission, US speculators formally decided, on June 28, 1902, to fund a canal through Nicaragua, evaluated as early as the 1850s, as it was close to the ports of Galveston, New Orleans, and Biloxi, a benefit to the Southern states. A canal in Nicaragua would make the French canal in Panama ineffectual, unless the French were willing to sell it for $40,000,000 or get nothing. The commission figured $27,474,033 for the excavation, $6,850,000 for the Panama Railroad stock, and $2 million for the maps, charts and records, and 10 percent for any contingencies. The French had already invested $260 million into the Panama project, while the owners capitalized the New Panama Canal Company at $12 million. If they accepted $40 million, it would represent a $4 million profit for Cromwell's French clients.[455]

William Cromwell and Philippe Bunau-Varilla, French engineer and soldier, both owned stock in the French holding company and would lose money unless Congress selected Panama over Nicaragua. Cromwell and Bunau-Varilla, both very wealthy, purchased publicity in newspapers, magazines, and pamphlets, pushing Panama. Soon, a few senators supported their efforts. In 1902, Senator William Hepburn introduced a bill for a Nicaraguan canal. Senator John Spooner attached an amendment to that bill that essentially invalidated it, allowing the president $40 million to purchase the New Panama Canal Company, and stipulated a canal in Panama. Bunau-Varilla sent fifty copies of a Nicaraguan stamp depicting a huge volcano twenty miles away from the canal site to each senator. The Senate then voted for Spooner's amendment, and Roosevelt signed the bill.

---

[453] Ibid. 26-27
[454] The Monroe Doctrine and the Roosevelt Corollary, http://www.theodoreroosevelt.org/life/RooseveltCorollary.htm
[455] Nancy Lisagor and Frank Lipsius, A Law Unto Itself, the Untold Story of the Law Firm Sullivan & Cromwell, 100 Years of Creating Power & Wealth, William Morrow and Company, Inc., New York, 1988, pp. 41-44, 49-50

José Santos Zelaya was president of Nicaragua (1893-1909), a pro-American country. US officials praised Zelaya, a progressive nationalist. However, he quickly fell into disfavor soon after the United States viewed Panama for the potential canal based on the possibility that the Paris-based company might be willing to sell it to the US government.[456] Cromwell billed the New Panama Canal Company a sizable $800,000 fee for his efforts, but the company rejected it and submitted the bill to a French attorney, an arbitrator that Cromwell picked, Raymond Poincaré. They settled it at $200,000. Cromwell, though underpaid for eight years of work, managed to purchase 22 percent of the electric company in Panama, which more than compensated.[457]

J. Pierpont Morgan and Company functioned as the fiscal agents for the transaction. Morgan directed the buyers to deposit a payment of $40 million in gold bullion and currency into the Bank of France for the New Panama Canal Company and the liquidator of the old de Lesseps company. Sullivan and Cromwell successfully completed liquidation, according to the price the commission had set in early 1900.[458]

There was, however, one problem—Panama was a province of Columbia. To gain unfettered access to Panama, Roosevelt and the State Department provoked and funded a rebellion against Columbia by some Panamanian "revolutionaries," and then used US forces to prevent the Columbian army from restoring control. Two US warships were nearby, the *Nashville* and the *Dixie,* to provide intimidation. Four hundred marines from the *Dixie* went ashore. Major John Lejeune landed his marine battalion on November 5, 1903. Within three days from the inception of the "brazen gunboat diplomacy,"

---

[456] Stephen Kinzer, Overthrow, America's Century of Regime Change From Hawaii to Iraq, Henry Holt and Company, New York, 2006, pp. 56-77
[457] Nancy Lisagor and Frank Lipsius, A Law Unto Itself, the Untold Story of the Law Firm Sullivan & Cromwell, 100 Years of Creating Power & Wealth, William Morrow and Company, Inc., New York, 1988, pp. 41-44, 49-50
[458] Ibid. 49-50

Washington officials recognized their handpicked rebels as leaders of a new Republic of Panama.[459]

Bunau-Varilla became Panama's ambassador to the United States on November 18, 1903. He and Hay signed the Hay-Bunau-Varilla Treaty, and the new Panamanian Government ratified it. The Senate ratified it in early 1904, and officials ultimately rescinded it in 1978. Cromwell negotiated a ninety-nine-year lease for a ten-mile wide canal zones "in perpetuity, as if it were the sovereign of the territory . . . to the entire exclusion of the exercise by the Republic of Panama of any such sovereign rights, power, or authority." In exchange, the United States guaranteed an initial payment of $10 million and $250,000 a year following the completion of the canal.[460]

The United States paid the French syndicate $40 million, reduced from $109 million, and paid $10 million to Panama. The United States officially took control of the French property on May 4, 1904, when Lieutenant Jatara Oneel of the US Army accepted the keys. Roosevelt appointed army engineer, Major George W. Goethals, as chief engineer in February 1907. The United States formally opened the canal on August 15, 1914. Military governors (1904-1914) temporarily directed the affairs of the area. In 1914, the civil governors were in place.

Although the French effort failed, the old and new companies excavated nineteen million cubic yards of material between them. The first company dredged a channel from Panama Bay to the port at Balboa. They also dredged the channel on the Atlantic side, known as the French canal, which was useful for transporting sand and stone for the locks and spillway concrete at Gatún. The French, with their $260 million investment also left roads, housing, and hospitals.[461]

---

[459]   Stephen Kinzer, Overthrow, America's Century of Regime Change From Hawaii to Iraq, Henry Holt and Company, New York, 2006, pp. 56-77

[460]   Nancy Lisagor and Frank Lipsius, A Law Unto Itself, the Untold Story of the Law Firm Sullivan & Cromwell, 100 Years of Creating Power & Wealth, William Morrow and Company, Inc., New York, 1988, pp. 48-49

[461]   Ibid. 41-43

The Panama Canal Company operated the canal (1903-1979), owned all the houses, and managed all the utilities. The head of the company was the governor of the Panama Canal Zone, actually an unincorporated US territory until 1979, with numerous townships and military installations. A joint US-Panamanian entity controlled the canal (1979-1999). On September 7, 1977, the Torrijos-Carter Treaties established the canal's neutrality. Currently, though China does not control the canal, a Chinese-controlled entity, Hutchison-Whampoa, has a subsidiary company, the Panama Ports Company, that operates Cristobal and Balboa, the ports situated at each end of the Panama Canal.

Liberating the Philippines, 1898

In the tenth century, Chinese merchants began trading in the Philippines (7,000 islands), a Spanish colony by 1575. In exchange for Chinese goods, Spanish traders received gold and silver from the New World and Mexico. These traders returned to Luzon's Manila Bay from Acapulco with ships laden with precious metals, making Manila an important financial center by the sixteenth century. Chinese middlemen made a reasonable profit and sent the majority of the gold and silver to China to pay for goods. The Spanish, intimidated by Chinese capabilities and economic access, denied them citizenship and prohibited them from owning land. Occasionally, they would massacre the ghetto-dwelling Chinese, sending a persuasive message while reducing the ethnic population. Inevitably, the Chinese cohabited with Malay girls to produce a large number of Chinese mestizo children. Parents raised these minority children as good Catholics, who often inherited their father's financial acuity, bought land, and acted as moneylenders and arbitrators.[462]

The Spanish mestizos, not as business-savvy as their Chinese counterparts, used the law to manipulate the native Malays into forfeiting their land. This ultimately resulted in a lengthy Katipunan Rebellion (1834-1897), with another uprising against Spanish

---

[462] Sterling Seagrave, The Marcos Dynasty, Harper and Row, New York, 1988, pp. 8-9

dominance beginning on August 23, 1896. Emilio Aguinaldo, a member of the Chinese-mestizo minority, led that rebellion.[463] It initially failed, and he fled to Hong Kong, where he purchased weapons to continue the struggle for Philippine independence.

When wealthy industrialists installed William McKinley as US president in 1896, Senator Henry Cabot Lodge visited the president-elect's home in Canton, Ohio, to persuade him to appoint Theodore Roosevelt, a member of the British Royal Society, as the assistant navy secretary, a position initially created on August 1, 1861. Lodge also approached John D. Long the new navy secretary, and Mark Hanna, McKinley's political mentor. It took Lodge four months of persistence until he received Roosevelt's cable on April 6, 1897- he got the job. Lodge spent thirty-seven years in Washington and had friends, enemies, and plenty of influence.[464] Lodge, a native Bostonian, was a former Harvard history professor who owed his political position to J. Pierpont Morgan, whose money dictated policy at Harvard. Roosevelt was a former student of the now-powerful politician.

McKinley, like most presidents, was really a front man for big business and the banks. Hanna, his campaign manager, thoroughly controlled him. Primarily, McKinley, during the honeymoon period of his presidency, had adopted many of President Cleveland's foreign and military policies. McKinley promised in his campaign speeches and reiterated in his inaugural address that "the United States cherished the policy of noninterference with affairs of foreign governments . . . we want no wars of conquest; we must avoid the temptation of territorial aggression."[465] McKinley's Treasury secretary, Lyman J. Gage, a National City Bank man and staunch proponent of the gold standard,

---

463 Emilio F. Aguinaldo (1869-1964), http://geocities.com/sinupan/AguiE.htm as of May 2012

464 Warren Zimmerman, First Great Triumph, How Five Americans Made Their Country a World Power, a Yale graduate and a Fulbright Scholar, Farrar, Straus and Giroux, New York, 2002, pp. 175-176

465 David J. Silbey, A War of Frontier and Empire, the Philippine-American War, 1899-1902, Hill and Wang, a Division of Farrar, Straus and Giroux, New York, 2007, pp. 30-31

chose Frank A. Vanderlip, financial editor of *The Chicago Times* as his assistant. Vanderlip ultimately became the president of National City Bank (1918-1919). James A. Stillman, president of National City Bank (1891-1909) selected Gage as president of the United State Trust Company (1902-1906) when he left the Treasury.[466]

Despite McKinley's campaign rhetoric, Long and Roosevelt were huge advocates of US naval superiority and expansionism. McKinley soon rescinded Cleveland's policy regarding Hawaii by signing the annexation treaty in June 1897, which still required congressional approval. However, the continuing Cuban revolution soon overshadowed annexation issues.[467] McKinley asked Elihu Root, a powerful corporate lawyer and millionaire, to go to Madrid in 1897 to participate in the negotiations over the Cuban controversy. However, Root declined McKinley's request. Root, always associated with the elite, would become the vice president of the Pilgrims Society after World War I. He had a numerous well-connected clients—Jay Gould (Pilgrims Society), Chester A. Arthur, Charles A. Dana, William C. Whitney, Thomas F. Ryan, and Edward H. Harriman (Pilgrims Society).

Roosevelt viewed George Dewey, president of the Board of Inspection and Survey, of the Navy Department, an avid expansionist, as just the kind of man he wanted to command the Asiatic Squadron. The biggest challenge was pulling the strings to get Dewey transferred to that auspicious position. He lacked the political, business, and familial connections, the actual routes to all high military appointments. Other politicos backed Commodore John A. Howell for the job; a person Roosevelt felt was altogether inadequate and entirely resistant to imperialism. Roosevelt referred Dewey to Senator Redfield Proctor, a lifetime politician, who maneuvered to get Dewey appointed as head of the Asiatic Squadron.[468]

---

[466] Ferdinand Lundberg, America's 60 Families, The Citadel Press, New York, 1937, pp. 61-62

[467] David J. Silbey, A War of Frontier and Empire, the Philippine-American War, 1899-1902, Hill and Wang, a Division of Farrar, Straus and Giroux, New York, 2007, pp. 30-31

[468] Nathan Miller, Theodore Roosevelt, Quill/William Morrow, 1994, pp. 260-261

On October 21, 1897, Dewey, now sufficiently appreciative and acquiescent, left the United States and went to Japan, where he would replace Admiral Frederick G. McNair as commander of the Asiatic Squadron, composed of the flagship *Olympia, Raleigh, Petrel, Concord, Boston,* and *McCulloch,* and later the *USS Baltimore.* On January 1, 1898, Commodore Dewey officially took command of the cruiser *Olympia,* at Nagasaki.

Soon, Roosevelt sent Dewey the cable, "ORDER THE SQUADRON, EXCEPT THE MONOCACY, TO HONG KONG. KEEP FULL OF COAL. IN THE EVENT OF DECLARATION WAR [against] SPAIN, YOUR DUTY WILL BE TO SEE THAT THE SPANISH SQUADRON DOES NOT LEAVE THE ASIATIC COAST AND THEN [begin] OFFENSIVE OPERATIONS IN PHILIPPINE ISLAND. KEEP OLYMPIA UNTIL FURTHER DETAILS. ROOSEVELT." Neither McKinley nor Long rescinded his message. The United States had no grievances with the Filipinos, but the vulnerable islands were a good place to defeat the Spanish.[469] Roosevelt's only challenge was to engineer the circumstances that would justify a US declaration of war against Spain.

On February 11, 1898, before the explosion on the *USS Maine,* the *Olympia* left Japan headed toward Hong Kong. US officials scheduled the Philippine invasion, but needed a pretext to justify their aggression, conveniently provided by the *USS Maine* operation, which the same collaborators planned. Following the timely incident in Havana Harbor on February 15, 1898, Dewey and the Asiatic Squadron waited in Hong Kong for the *USS Baltimore* on its way from Honolulu with adequate ammunition. Dewey could not remain in Hong Kong, as Britain was allegedly neutral, so the British governor ordered Dewey out of the area.

It took time and newspaper propaganda to provoke Congress and the masses to support military action. However, on April 21, 1898, before Congress approved of the war resolution on April 25, the US fleet began

---

[469]   Warren Zimmerman, First Great Triumph, How Five Americans Made Their Country a World Power, Farrar, Straus and Giroux, New York, 2002, p. 243-257

a blockade of Cuba. Dewey cabled Washington for instructions, and, with McKinley's approval, Secretary Long responded, "PROCEED AT ONCE TO THE PHILIPPINES, COMMENCE OPERATIONS AGAINST THE SPANISH SQUADRON, YOU MUST CAPTURE OR DESTROY, USE UTMOST ENDEAVORS."[470] On April 24, officials formally notified Dewey that the United States had declared war against Spain. The squadron proceeded thirty miles north to Mirs Bay, and then, on April 27, departed for the Philippines, arriving in Manila Bay on the night of April 30. They quickly defeated the Spanish fleet the next day. Dewey, known to be vain and arrogant, defeated and sank the entire Spanish fleet in six hours with the loss of one American life. On March 24, 1903, because of his performance, his superiors would promote Dewey to admiral of the navy, an office created by Congress.

On May 1, 1898, in America's first acknowledged overseas war of conquest, the United States claimed victory against Spain. Interestingly, Adam Weishaupt formalized the Illuminati on May 1. If assistance to the Filipinos had been the actual objective, they should have departed, satisfied and victorious. Instead, on May 2, Congress voted a war emergency credit of $34,625,725. Soon, the government replaced Dewey's fleet of seven ships with twenty ships.

On May 19, 1898, Aguinaldo, the popular leader in the Filipino's fight for independence, at the invitation of the United States, returned from his Hong Kong exile. On May 25, the Philippine Expeditionary Force of 8,500 men, Eighth Army Corps, left San Francisco and arrived at Cavite. Aguinaldo declared independence on June 12, established the First Philippine Republic, and proceeded to establish a fully functioning government.

Aguinaldo stated in his 1899 book, *True Version of the Philippine Revolution*, "On the fourth of July [1898] the first United States military expedition arrived, under command of General Anderson, and it was quartered in Cavite Arsenal . . . we were friends, of equal

---

[470] Stanley Karnow, In Our Image, America's Empire in the Philippines, Random House, New York, p. 102

rank, and allies . . . General Anderson solemnly and completely endorsed the promises made by Admiral Dewey to me, asserting on his word of honor that America had not come to the Philippines to wage war against the natives, nor to conquer and retain territory, but only to liberate the people from the oppression of the Spanish Government." Dewey had said, "Documents are useless when there is no sense of honor . . . have faith in my word, and I assure you that the United States will recognize the independence of the country."[471]

While the public's attention was riveted on the war, on May 4, 1898, the House, with McKinley's consent, approved the annexation of Hawaii. On June 11, McKinley said, "We must have Hawaii to help us get our share of China."[472] On June 21, the United States seized Guam, a small Spanish-held island. On July 7, the United States annexed Hawaii. In relation to the United States, the Philippines are 7,000 miles across the Pacific Ocean, 600 miles from the Asian continent, and more than 4,500 miles from Hawaii. On August 14, the United States seized Puerto Rico. On December 10, Spain ceded the Philippines, Puerto Rico, Guam, and Cuba. On January 17, 1899, the United States took Wake Island, an uninhabited island in the North Pacific Ocean, located about two-thirds of the way between Honolulu and Guam.

In September 1898, Rudyard Kipling, a colleague of Cecil Rhodes and Alfred Milner, wrote to his imperialist friend Roosevelt, urging the US seizure of the Philippines as the spoils from the Spanish-American War. "Now go in and put all the weight of your influence into hanging on permanently to the whole Philippines. America has gone and stuck a pickaxe into the foundations of a rotten house, and she is morally bound to build the house over again from the foundations or have it fall about her ears." The implications were that the United States should rule their new colony the way that Britain

---

[471] Don Emilio Aguinaldo y Famy, True Version of the Philippine Revolution, Chapter X. The Proclamation of Independence, Tarlak, 23rd September, 1899, http://www.authorama.com/true-version-of-the-philippine-revolution-11. html as of May 2012

[472] Chronology for the Philippine Islands and Guam in the Spanish-American War, http://www.loc.gov/rr/hispanic/1898/chronphil.html as of May 2012

ruled the nonwhite populations of India and Africa. In November, Kipling sent his poem *"The White Man's Burden"* to Roosevelt.[473]

President McKinley, regarding the Philippines, said, "I went down on my knees and prayed to Almighty God for light and guidance and one night late it came to me this way. We could not leave [the Filipinos] to themselves, they were unfit for self-government, and they would soon have anarchy and misrule over there worse than Spain's was. There was nothing left for us to do but take them all and educate the Filipinos, and uplift and Christianize them."[474] On December 21, 1898, McKinley, in his skillfully worded *Benevolent Assimilation Proclamation,* claimed that the United States did not come as "invaders or conquerors, but as friends, to protect the natives in their homes, in their employments, and in their personal and religious rights." However, the document extended US military control, with 75,000 troops by 1899 and, within a few years, 126,000 men. It arrogantly granted military dominion over the entire country in fulfillment of the rights of US sovereignty.[475]

In George F. Kennan's official version of the Spanish American War, the US population and the media forced the war upon "an unwilling President McKinley and a disapproving business and financial community." The historian and diplomat blamed US imperialism on the American people, who wanted to see the US flag flying on distant tropical isles and to bask in the "sunshine of recognition as a great imperial power." He did not mention the thousands of Americans who opposed both the war and a US empire. Somehow, he claimed, the leaders just could not resist the citizen's demands.[476]

---

[473] Patrick Brantlinger, Kipling's "The White Man's Burden" and Its Afterlives, English Literature in Transition 1880-1920, Volume: 50, Issue: 2, 2007, p. 172+

[474] Stanley Karnow, In Our Image, America's Empire in the Philippines, Random House, New York, p. 104

[475] Hazel M. McFerson, Mixed Blessing: The Impact of the American Colonial Experience on Politics and Society in the Philippines, Greenwood Press, Westport, Connecticut, 2002, p. 267

[476] Thomas A. Breslin, Mystifying the Past: Establishment Historians and the Origins of the Pacific War, Bulletin of Concerned Asian Scholars, Volume: 8. Issue: 4, 1976, pp. 18-35

US governors general over the islands were General Wesley Merritt, a West Point graduate, August 14 to August 28, 1898, General Elwell S. Otis, August 28 1898 to May 5, 1900, and General Arthur MacArthur Jr., May 25, 1900 to July 4, 1901. The United States then installed a civilian, William Howard Taft (1901-1903), whose father, Alphonso Taft, had cofounded Skull and Bones (S&B) at Yale University. Taft became secretary of war (1904-1908), US president (1909-1913) and then Chief Justice of the Supreme Court (1921-1930). Spain ceded the Philippines, Puerto Rico, and Guam to the United States for $20 million dollars per the Treaty of Paris, secretly signed on December 10, 1898, and ratified by the Senate on February 6, 1899. It became effective on April 11, 1899. Many US citizens disapproved of the US seizure of territory so far away.

However, there were other influences. Harvard-educated Gardiner Greene Hubbard, the National Geographic Society's (NGS) first president, was a lawyer, financier, philanthropist, and member of the Massachusetts Board of Education.[477] His wife was Gertrude McCurdy, the sister of Richard A. McCurdy, a Pilgrims Society member and a director of Guaranty Trust. Hubbard's daughter Mabel married Alexander Graham Bell.[478] The NGS had published the first issue of *National Geographic* in October 1888. The magazine soon became a propaganda tool for the government, especially during the war, by promoting territorial acquisition and economic exploitation. Geographers reinforced these ideologies in *National Geographic* during America's first ten years in the Philippines.[479]

The June 1898 issue of *National Geographic* was devoted to "the enormous possibilities of an extended commerce that now lie within

---

[477] Universities and Their Sons, History, Influence and Characteristics of American Universities With Biographical Sketches, Editor-in-Chief—General Joshua L. Chamberlain, LL.D, United State Commissioner of Education, R. Herndon Company, Boston, The University Press, Cambridge, 1900

[478] Charles Savoie, Pilgrims, Silver Investor, May 2005, www.silver-investor.com/charlessavoie/cs_may05_pilgrims.htm as of May 2012

[479] Julie A. Tuason, The Ideology of Empire in National Geographic Magazine's Coverage of the Philippines, 1898-1908, The Geographical Review, Volume: 89, Issue: 1, 1999

our reach as a nation." One article demanded that the United States "take its rightful position among the nations of the earth" through overseas expansion and commercial exploitation. By controlling the island's resources, Henry Gannett, Chief Geographer of the United States, unabashedly claimed that the United States "shall become the dominant power of the Pacific, both politically and commercially."[480]

In 1899, Gilbert H. Grosvenor, Taft's cousin, became the full-time editor of the magazine. In 1900, McKinley appointed Taft as the Philippines governor general, and also chair of the US-Philippine Commission, he began organizing a civilian government. Taft wrote articles for *National Geographic* (1901-1905) focusing on the civic and scientific progress in the Philippines, allegedly for the benefit of the Filipinos. He claimed that US motives in Cuba, Puerto Rico, and the Philippines were selfless but admitted that the United States had spent $170 million to suppress guerilla warfare, which Aguinaldo led. He failed to mention the Filipino death toll during this so-called selfless endeavor. The United States established American-directed education to indoctrinate future workers for the developing US commerce.[481]

Between 1898 and 1908, pro-imperialist authors, employees of federal and military agencies, such as the US Geological Survey, and the War and Navy Departments and university professors wrote at least thirty articles about the Philippines, the US "foothold in the development of the Orient." *National Geographic* articles claimed that the United States had a moral obligation to deliver progress, self-government, and material prosperity to the "weaker races of the earth." Authors elaborated that the political, naval, and industrial possibilities in the islands, located at "the very ideal center of all the land that face the Pacific," can all have "practical value to the US."[482] Gannett, a vice president of the American Statistical Association, became the president of the *National Geographic* in 1909, soon to be tax-exempt.

---

[480] Ibid
[481] Ibid
[482] Ibid

Theodore Roosevelt, a member of Britain's Royal Society, had resigned from the Navy Department. With the assistance of General Leonard Wood, a Harvard graduate and one of Milner's US cronies. Roosevelt then formed the Rough Riders, a volunteer regiment that fought in Cuba. After the Battle of San Juan Hill in July 1898, Roosevelt returned as a war hero, which successfully catapulted him into the office of governor of New York (January 1, 1899 to December 31, 1900). The government awarded Wood (Pilgrims Society),[483] the Medal of Honor in 1898 for his warfare against the Apache Indians. He was the military governor of Santiago (1898) and of Cuba (1899-1902). In 1902, he went to the Philippines, where he was governor of Moro Province (1903-1906). In December 1905, Roosevelt assured Congress that there was peace in the Muslim area of the islands—one of the numerous times that he had announced an end to the hostilities.[484] Wood directed numerous campaigns against Muslim Moro natives, including the Moro Crater massacre on March 10, 1906, wherein he gave the order, "Kill or capture the six hundred."

Mark Twain reported, "A tribe of Moros, dark-skinned savages, had fortified themselves in the bowl of an extinct crater not many miles from Jolo; and, as they were hostiles, and bitter against us because we have been trying for eight years to take their liberties away from them, their presence in that position was a menace. Our commander, General Leonard Wood, ordered a reconnaissance. It was found that the Moros numbered six hundred, counting women and children; that their crater bowl was in the summit of a peak or mountain twenty-two hundred feet above sea level, and very difficult of access for Christian troops and artillery. Then General Wood ordered a surprise, and went along himself to see the order carried out. Our troops climbed the heights by devious and difficult trails, and even took some artillery with them. The kind of artillery is not specified, but in one place it was hoisted up a sharp acclivity by tackle a distance of some three hundred feet. Arrived at the rim of the crater, the battle began. Our soldiers numbered five hundred and forty. They were assisted by

[483] Charles Savoie, Pilgrims, Silver Investor, May 2005, www.silver-investor.com/charlessavoie/cs_may05_pilgrims.htm as of May 2012

[484] James Bradley, The Imperial Cruise, a secret History of Empire and War, Little, Brown and company, New York, 2009, p. 322

auxiliaries consisting of a detachment of native constabulary in our pay—their numbers not given—and by a naval detachment, whose numbers are not stated. But, apparently, the contending parties were about equal as to number—six hundred men on our side, on the edge of the bowl; six hundred men, women, and children in the bottom of the bowl. Depth of the bowl, fifty feet."[485]

In Washington on March 10, 1906, President Roosevelt wrote a message to Wood, in Manila, which read, "I congratulate you and the officers and men of your command upon the brilliant feat of arms wherein you, and they so well upheld the honor of the American flag." The men had, from a safe, advantageous height, shot down into the crater and had massacred "six hundred helpless and weaponless savages." After they counted the dead, they discovered that there were actually nine hundred instead of six hundred.[486]

The Filipinos Fight Back

On February 4, 1899, General Elwell S. Otis ordered US military forces to encircle not just Manila, but to extend into the Philippines Army territory. He then ordered the sentries to fire on any Filipino intruders. Privates William Grayson and Orville Miller, on guard duty, saw four drunk and unarmed men. Grayson yelled, "Halt!" One of the Filipinos drunkenly responded "Halto!" Grayson recalled, "Well, I thought the best thing to do was to shoot him." Before it was over, the sentries killed four inebriated, unarmed Filipinos.[487] General Arthur MacArthur Jr., a freemason, used this incident, characterized as Filipino aggression, to initiate the Battle of Manila. Within

---

[485] Mark Twain, Comments on the Moro Massacre, March 12, 1906, http://www.is.wayne.edu/mnissani/cr/moro.htm as of May 2012

[486] Ibid

[487] James Bradley, The Imperial Cruise, a Secret History of Empire and War, Little, Brown and Company, New York, 2009, p. 102

twenty-four hours, US soldiers had slaughtered over 3,000 Filipinos, whose corpses lay in the streets. The Filipinos killed between fifty and sixty Americans in defense. Soldiers dug trenches and buried the Filipinos in a mass grave. McKinley announced, "Insurgents had attacked Manila" and Aguinaldo was now an "outlaw bandit."

US officials viewed the 3,000 dead Filipinos as insurgents because of the Treaty of Paris. Technically, the Senate did not ratify it until February 6, 1899, two days after the killing of the four unarmed people. Possibly, the Filipinos might not have dissented had it not been for the killings. The United States, after the treaty, considered all revolutionaries as insurgents. Once the United States legally established sovereignty, they would not tolerate the government at Malolos, just as the United States had forbade an independent government at Richmond, Virginia. The Senate had only one choice according to one newspaper—go to war against the insurgency, forcing the Filipinos to trade one imperial antagonist for another.[488]

On February 9, 1899, *The New York Times* ran an article entitled *"The Status of the Filipinos."* The Treaty of Paris imposed a military government, chosen by the president, in each of three countries, Puerto Rico, Guam, and the Philippines, all former Spanish colonies. Thinking they were free from their longtime oppressor, citizens had begun to set up independent governments. The indigenous peoples did not view the US military as liberators, especially in the Philippines, where they concluded that they had invaded and had "taken up arms against us."[489]

On August 1, 1899, McKinley appointed Elihu Root, a New York corporate attorney, as war secretary (1899-1904). He knew nothing about the military, so he logically assumed that McKinley was more interested in his legal skills—handling the legalities involved with manipulating foreign government officials to concede to the big-

---

[488] Paul A. Kramer, The Blood of Government, Race, Empire, the United States, and the Philippines, The University of North Carolina Press, 2006, pp. 87-88
[489] Ibid. 87-88

business demands made within their countries.[490] Root was the principal architect of US colonial policy. He directed Congress to create and enact practical legislation for Puerto Rico, the Philippines, and Cuba, all targeted for permanent resource seizure and colonization, while the United States professed to provide protection. A succession of military governors general ruled Puerto Rico, after dismantling the government established by Spain's Autonomic Charter.[491]

Attorney and Congressman Joseph Wheeler, a West Point graduate and a Confederate Army veteran, arrived in the Philippines in August 1899, where he commanded the First Brigade under General Arthur MacArthur until January 1900. On June 16, 1900, his superiors commissioned Wheeler, a volunteer, as a brigadier general in the regular army. After he left the Philippines, he moved to New York and authored numerous books on military strategy, including *A Revised System of Cavalry Tactics*. One book, *The Santiago Campaign in 1898*, detailed Major General William Shafter's assault on Santiago, Cuba, July 3-17, 1898. Wheeler said, "My plan would be to disarm the natives of the Philippine Islands, even if we have to kill half of them to do it."[492] He was at the organizational meeting of the Pilgrims Society in 1902 in London and became one of their US vice presidents.[493] He was also a Smithsonian Institution regent (1886-1900).[494]

Murat Halstead, lawyer, journalist, and editor of the *Cincinnati Commercial,* was a chief propaganda agent for the Ohio political machine and the US imperialistic agenda. On November 20, 1894, Halstead, in a speech entitled *"Our New Country,"* referred to Tennyson's *Locksley Hall* and the oft-quoted lines "In the Parliament

---

[490] Philip C. Jessup, Elihu Root, Dodd Mead, New York, 1938, p. 329

[491] Pedro A. Caban, Constructing a Colonial People: Puerto Rico and the United States, 1898-1932, Westview Press, Boulder, Colorado, 1999, pp. 41-42

[492] A Century Of Crimes Against The Filipino People, Presentation by Atty. Romeo T. Capulong Public Interest Law Center, World Tribunal for Iraq, Trial in New York City on August 25, 2004, p. 2

[493] Joël van der Reijden, The Pilgrim Society: a Study of the Anglo-American Establishment, Institute for the Study of Globalization & Covert Politics, July 2008

[494] Charles Savoie, Pilgrims, Silver Investor, May 2005, www.silver-investor. com/charlessavoie/cs_may05_pilgrims.htm as of May 2012

of man," the "Federation of the world." He claimed, "The ends of the earth are in our neighborhood" and "all the continents and the islands are a federation" and "the drift of human experience is to increased aggregations, to concentration and to centralization."[495] The US military authorized him as a war correspondent. He traveled with General Wesley Merritt, the military governor of the Philippines, which people referred to as "the El Dorado of the Orient." Halstead reported Admiral George Dewey's victory in *The Life and Achievements of Admiral Dewey*. He praised the actions of General Merritt, Major General Elwell S. Otis, and Major James F. Bell and vilified "Aguinaldo, the leader of the insurgents of his race in Luzon."[496] Bell estimated that the US military killed one-sixth of the population of the main island of Luzon, about 600,000 people.

For imperialist expansion, Britain and the United States officially formed an alliance in 1897. Britain also had prior alliances with France and Japan. Chauncey M. Depew, of the Pilgrims Society and a New York Senator supported war hawk Theodore Roosevelt as the US vice president in 1900. He said, "by the providence of God, by the statesmanship of William McKinley, and by the valor of Roosevelt and his associates, we have our market in the Philippines, and we stand in the presence of eight hundred millions of people, with the Pacific as an American lake."[497] The Democratic Party Platform of 1900 stated, "We are in favor of extending the Republic's influence among the nations, but we believe that that influence should be

---

[495] New York Chamber of Commerce, 126th Annual Banquet, November 20, 1894, New York City

[496] Murat Halstead, The Story of the Philippines and Our New Possessions, Including the Ladrones, Hawaii, Cuba and Porto Rico, The author inscribed it To the Soldiers and Sailors of the Army and Navy of the United States, With Admiration for their Achievements in the War With Spain; Gratitude for the Glory They Have Gained for the American Nation, and Congratulations That All the People of All the Country Rejoice in the Cloudless Splendor of Their Fame That is the Common and Everlasting Inheritance of Americans," Our Possessions Publishing Company, 1898, http://www.fullbooks.com/The-Story-of-the-Philippines-and-Our-New1.html as of May 2012

[497] E. C. Knuth, The Empire of the City, the Secret History of British Financial Power, The Book Tree, San Diego, California, Originally published 1944 by E. C. Knuth, Wisconsin, pp. 11-12

extended not by force and violence, but through the persuasive power of a high and honorable example." Further, it stated, "The Filipinos cannot be citizens without endangering our civilization; they cannot be subjects without imperiling our form of government."[498]

General Arthur MacArthur, a Union veteran, took charge on May 25, 1900. He had warred against America's native population for thirty years and was fighting in the Dakota Territory when the Spanish-American War began. On December 20, 1900, MacArthur declared that the Filipinos were an "inferior race" and further stated that guerrilla warfare was contrary to "the customs and usages of war. Further, he said that those who engaged in it automatically "divest themselves of the character of soldiers, and if captured, are not entitled to the privileges of prisoners of war" but were to be treated as criminals. According to official hearings, the United States frequently employed waterboarding, which often proved lethal to the recipient.[499] [500] [501] As early as 1556, in Antwerp, many countries banned that morally repugnant practice. By 1902, despite the deceptive language of liberation and freedom, US citizens were perplexed by the news that US soldiers were torturing Filipinos with water.

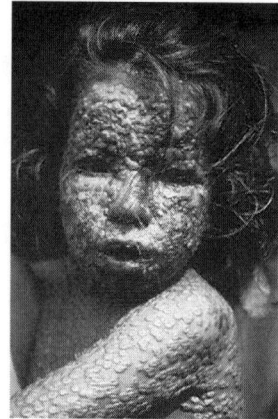

The US military also subjected the Filipinos to biological experimentation. In 1900, the US Army began conducting tests using biological weapons. As reported in the *US Philippine*

[498] Lars Schoultz, Beneath the United States: A History of US Policy Toward Latin America, Harvard University Press, Cambridge, Massachusetts, 1998, p. 142

[499] Nation Master Encyclopedia, Lodge Committee, January 1902, http://www.nationmaster.com/encyclopedia/Lodge-Committee as of May 2012

[500] The Lodge Committee, Testimonies, http://en.wikipedia.org/wiki/Lodge_committee

[501] Secretary Root's Record: "Marked Severities" in Philippine Warfare, Report of the Philippine Investigating Committee formed in April of 1902 to investigate and publicize US military atrocities in the Philippines, http://en.wikisource.org/wiki/Secretary_Root's_Record as of May 2012

Health Service Report, in 1903, the military dictatorship, despite the vibrant health of the native population, enacted a compulsory countrywide vaccination program. The residents, with access to clean air, water, and unadulterated food, were quite healthy. Smallpox was relatively unknown, but the military rounded up the unwilling Filipinos and herded them into vaccination centers. By 1905, there was a smallpox epidemic and numerous deaths, and, by 1910, vaccination was mandatory. Given the smallpox outbreak in a relatively virgin population, one would suppose that the countrywide would halt the program there and in the countrywide as well. However, they were intent on testing and marketing the vaccines rather than promoting health. They actually increased the vaccination program each year. This produced another horrific epidemic in 1907 and 1908.[502]

In February 1927, Dr. William W. Keen, the first brain surgeon in the United States, part of the propaganda apparatus, wrote an article for the *American Review of Reviews,* in which he praised the effectiveness of the vaccine program in the Philippines. He wrote that, by 1921, in the Philippines, there had been 130,264 cases of smallpox, resulting in 74,369 deaths, and then he praised the fact that, in 1921, General Wood reinstated the vaccination program. There had been one epidemic after another from 1905 to 1923, when Wood began suppressing reports to give the impression that he had "conquered smallpox." The mortality rate varied from 25 percent to 75 percent, depending on the location in the islands. There were fewer cases of smallpox in the more remote jungle areas, where people fled to avoid shots, but in the cities, where they vaccinated people, the epidemics were a critical calamity, the worst smallpox statistics in the world, along with the highest percentages of vaccinations.[503]

Many doctors, government statisticians, and others determined that the vaccine program increased the incidence of smallpox rather than decreasing it. Dissenters accused the government of deliberately attempting to kill off the Filipinos so that the United States could

---

[502] Dr. Eleanor Elben McBean, Vaccination Condemned by all Competent Doctors, Book One, Better Life Research, Los Angeles, California, 1981, pp. 190-193

[503] Ibid. 190-193

seize the islands. They also charged that the drug companies and US doctors were using the population, whom they apparently cared nothing about, as guinea pigs for their experimental vaccines and drugs. The military is one of the biggest vaccine and drug-company customers, not only in the United States but in other countries. Drug companies, with their vaccine racket, lobby the government to inoculate all military personnel at taxpayer expense, including the health consequences resulting from those vaccines. The vaccine manufacturers viewed 11,000,000 Filipinos, under military occupation, as a profitable market, especially for the overstocked or spoiled vaccines. Otherwise, they would have to foist them on senior citizens, institutionalized soldiers, orphans, or prisoners. Currently, the drug companies use children in the foster-care system as guinea pigs. The vaccines caused preventable diseases such as typhoid, malaria, beriberi, and tuberculosis.[504]

Given the consequences, scientific studies and historical facts resulting from vaccinations, it is delusional to believe the media propaganda and government lies claiming that vaccines are a "harmless" method of immunizing men, women, children, and infants against disease. Not only do they not protect an individual against the specific disease they claim to eradicate, the vaccines, with poisonous substances and other questionable ingredients—even disgusting animal and human byproducts—cannot help but cause harm and diminish the ability of the immune system to fight opportunistic diseases that would otherwise never be a problem.[505]

The biological experimentation in the Philippines, with its accompanying propaganda, government deception, and complicity with the drug companies, provided a shameful testing ground for introducing the beginnings of socialized medicine in America through the imposition of compulsory vaccination programs in the government schools. In 1981, Dr. Eleanor McBean wrote, "Medical practice is too haphazard, unscientific, unreliable, and dangerous to

[504] Dr. Eleanor Elben McBean, Vaccination Condemned by all Competent Doctors, Book One, Better Life Research, Los Angeles, California, 1981, pp. 190-193
[505] Ibid. 194-197

be trusted with the health and lives of the people. The United States is one of the sickest nations in the world at the present time." US health statistics, despite the claims that we have the best health system in the world, have greatly decreased since she wrote those words.[506]

Death by drugs was not the only manner in which the military assaulted the Filipinos. In writing about the battles of February 4-5, 1899, E. D. Furnam said, "We burned hundreds of houses and looted hundreds more. Some of the boys made good hauls of jewelry and clothing. Nearly every man has at least two suits of clothing, and our quarters are furnished in style; fine beds with silken drapery, mirrors, chairs, rockers, cushions, pianos, hanging-lamps, rugs, pictures, etc. We have horses and carriages, and bull-carts galore, and enough furniture and other plunder to load a steamer." Anthony Michea, of the Third Artillery, wrote, "We bombarded a place called Malabon, and then we went in and killed every native we met, men, women, and children. It was a dreadful sight, the killing of the poor creatures. The natives captured some of the Americans and literally hacked them to pieces, so we got orders to spare no one."[507]

H. L. Wells, a correspondent for the *New York Evening Post,* stated that there had been no widespread outrageous acts committed by US troops. He wrote, "There is no question that our men do 'shoot niggers' somewhat in the sporting spirit, but that is because war and their environments have rubbed off the thin veneer of civilization . . . Undoubtedly, they do not regard the shooting of Filipinos just as they would the shooting of white troops. This is partly because they are 'only niggers,' and partly because they despise them for their treacherous servility . . . The soldiers feel they are fighting

---

[506] Ibid. 194-197

[507] Philip S. Foner and Richard Winchester, Soldier's Letters, pamphlet, Anti-Imperialist League, 1899, The Anti-Imperialist Reader: A Documentary History of Anti-Imperialism in the United States, Volume 1, Holmes and Meier, New York, 1984, 316-323

with savages, not with soldiers . . .”[508] [509] The US recruiters had promised the troops, many of whom were mercenaries, good wages, in addition to war booty and confiscated land.[510]

US army and volunteer troops engaged in wide-scale looting. Wells claimed that the military had not killed prisoners, but readily admitted to pervasive looting in his article published on July 20, 1899, as follows, “As I said before, every house was entered, and if anything had been left by the former occupants, it was thoroughly overhauled. Clothing was snatched out of bureaus and scattered over the floor in search of valuables. Boxes were broken open. Suspicious mounds in backyards were dug into. Cisterns were probed, and bamboo thickets were inspected. Caches of clothing, crockery, books, etc., were discovered, and their contents scattered in the search for valuables, very few of which were found. Probably the two richest places, which were hastily abandoned, were the cities of Pasig and Malabon.”[511]

Military leaders applied Abraham Lincoln’s General Order Number 100 in the Philippines, which authorized the shooting, on sight, of all persons not in uniform or acting as soldiers and those committing, or seeking to commit, sabotage. The Seventh Calvary Regiment, originally organized on September 21, 1866, occupied the Philippines (1904-1907), and again (1911-1915). It employed the same scorched-earth policies against the Filipinos as it had against the vulnerable Plains Indians. They burned entire villages, and killed unarmed Filipinos, including women and children. The troops thought they

---

[508] The Balangiga Massacre: Getting Even by Victor Nebrida in Hector Santos, ed., Philippine Centennial Series, June 15, 1997, http://www.bibingka.com/phg/balangiga/default.htm as of May 2012

[509] Paul A. Kramer, The Blood of Government, Race, Empire, the United States, and the Philippines, The University of North Carolina Press, 2006, pp. 87-88

[510] A Century Of Crimes Against The Filipino People, Presentation by Atty. Romeo T. Capulong Public Interest Law Center, World Tribunal for Iraq, Trial in New York City on August 25, 2004, p. 1

[511] Herbert Welsh, The other man’s country: an appeal to conscience, J. B. Lippincott & Company, Philadelphia, 1900, pp. 134-135

all looked alike and similar to the "red savages." In fact, they called the Filipinos "Apaches" or "gooks."[512]

US military leadership in the Philippines consisted of men who had warred against the Apaches, Comanches, Kiowas, and Sioux. The Seventh Cavalry Regiment had taken part in the Wounded Knee massacre on December 29, 1890, where they slaughtered 370 unarmed women and children. One squad killed more than 1,000 "dark-skinned" Filipinos in just one village. General MacArthur defended his army's civilian massacres as "carrying out the civilizing mission of its Aryan ancestors."[513]

General MacArthur left the Philippines on July 5, 1901. He was the commander of the Department of the Pacific (1904-1907). The government sent him to Manchuria to observe the Japanese military from January to September 1905, toward the end of the Russo-Japanese War. He then did a short stint as military attaché to the US Embassy in Tokyo.[514] While in Japan, both the general and his son, Lieutenant Douglas MacArthur, met with Emperor Meiji, who had collaborated with the British bankers in Japan's assault against Korea, China, and Russia. The general, his wife, and his son then toured several Asian countries, from November 1905 through June 1906, to ascertain their military strength. They visited Shanghai, Hong Kong, Ceylon, India, Burma, Bangkok, Batavia, Singapore, Rangoon, Saigon, and Vietnam, making him possibly among the first US officers to visit Vietnam.[515]

For three years, US troops battled to "emancipate" the Filipinos from the influence of Aguinaldo, who had hoped that America, a

[512] Charles J. Hanley, The Bridge at No Gun Ri, A Hidden Nightmare from the Korean War, San-Hun Choe and Martha Mendoza, Reviewed by: Lee Wha Rang, http://www.korean-war.com/Archives/2001/09/msg00019.html as of May 2012

[513] Ibid

[514] Arlington National Cemetery, Arthur MacArthur, Jr., Lieutenant General, United States Army, http://www.arlingtoncemetery.net/amacart.htm as of May 2012

[515] Lt. Gen. Arthur MacArthur (1845-1912) by James M. Gallen, http://www.spanamwar.com/macarthur.htm as of May 2012

nation that had rebelled against England's imperial power, would not colonize another freedom-loving people. In the process, US troops killed hundreds of thousands of Filipinos, while about 4,000 US soldiers died for the imperialistic industrialists who coveted the resources in the Philippines. Beginning in the first year of the conflict, reports of US atrocities, the torching of villages, and the killing of prisoners, appeared in newspapers. Apparently, the military censors overlooked what reporters were writing or what soldiers revealed in the uncensored letters they sent home.[516]

Cuba, Puerto Rico, and the Philippines became America's first "colonies," though it was unacceptable to use that word. The Supreme Court claimed, "Constitutional freedoms must follow the flag." Therefore, the Justices referred to them as "nonincorporated territories," entities that were not allowed to fly the US flag.[517] The voters reelected McKinley in 1900. Leon F. Czolgosz shot him on September 6, 1901, at the Pan-American Exposition in Buffalo. Reportedly, Emma Goldman and Alexander Berkman, both immigrants from Russia in the 1880s, influenced Czolgosz, an emotionally demented anarchist. McKinley died from his wounds on September 14, 1901. Theodore Roosevelt, the vice president, succeeded McKinley.

Robert Todd Lincoln, President Lincoln's son, was with McKinley when Czolgosz shot him. He was also with President James Garfield when Charles J. Guiteau shot him on July 2, 1881. Robert T. Lincoln associated with the individuals who had escaped culpability in his father's death. Lincoln, upon later discovering documents that implicated his friends, destroyed the evidence.[518] Lincoln was President Garfield's war secretary (1881-1885) and US ambassador to Britain (1889-1893) under President Benjamin Harrison. He was general counsel to the Pullman Company and then president after

---

[516] Paul Kramer, The Water Cure, Debating torture and counterinsurgency—a century ago
[517] Lars Schoultz, Beneath the United States: A History of US Policy Toward Latin America, Harvard University Press, Cambridge, Massachusetts, 1998, p. 142
[518] Steven Sora, The Secret Societies of America's Elite, From the Knights Templar to Skull and Bones, Destiny Books, 2003, p. 236

George Pullman's death on October 19, 1897. He was Pullman's chairman until his death on July 26, 1926. Researcher Charles Savoie claims that Pullman Company investors included charter members of the Pilgrims Society, such as Marshall Field, John D. Rockefeller, Andrew Mellon, and the Vanderbilts.[519] Presumably, Lincoln was also a member, given his British ambassadorship and his business associations.

Some years after his death, family members discovered McKinley's handwritten note, scribbled right after his aides notified him of Dewey's victory over the Spanish. He wrote, "While we are conducting war, and, until its conclusion, we must keep all we can get. When the war is over, we must keep what we want."[520] A short time before, McKinley admitted to a friend that he "could not have told where those darned islands were within two thousand miles."[521] By an act of Congress, dated July 1, 1902, establishing the Philippine government, officials conducted a census that revealed a population of 7,572,199. According to Manuel Arellano Remondo's book, *General Geography of the Philippine Islands*, there were 9,000,000 people in the Philippines in 1895. The war officially ended on July 4, 1902, but hostilities and the work of death continued for almost a decade.

Historians disagree on the number of Filipinos killed during the US invasion. Individuals have repeated the figure, 250,000; often enough that people accepted it as fact, despite sufficient evidence that positively refutes that number. However, the United States did not maintain records. As Colin Powell, Donald Rumsfeld, and others have since reiterated, the United States does not do body counts. However, the United States was anxious to suppress the extent of the slaughter to avoid anti-imperialistic sentiments at home. In May 1901, General Bell estimated in a *New York Times* interview that the United States had killed over 600,000 Filipinos, or they had perished due to war-related diseases *just* in Luzon. The US military killed at least 100,000 just in the Panay Campaign, the Samar Campaign, and

[519] Charles Savoie, Meet the World Money Power, December 2004, p. 47
[520] Stanley Karnow, In Our Image, America's Empire in the Philippines, Random House, New York, 1989, p. 108
[521] Ibid. 104

199

the Batangas Campaign, which all occurred after Bell's interview with *The Times*. Further, it did not include the post-war period when the United States incarcerated 300,000 people in Albay. Nor did that figure include the slaughter in Mindanao and the high death rates in Bilibid Prison, all locations where wanton killing continued. One must conclude that the United States killed more than one million Filipinos in their effort to "liberate" and subdue them.[522]

Mark Twain later said the following about McKinley's Benevolent Assimilation, "We have pacified some thousands of the islanders and buried them; destroyed their fields; burned their villages and turned their widows and orphans out-of-doors; furnished heartbreak by exile to some dozens of disagreeable patriots; subjugated the remaining ten millions by Benevolent Assimilation, which is the pious new name of the musket; we have acquired property in the three hundred concubines and other slaves of our business partner, the Sultan of Sulu, and hoisted our protecting flag over that swag. And so, by the providences of God—and the phrase is the government's, not mine—we are a World Power."[523]

US Pacification and Concentration in the Philippines

About 50,000 people resided on Marinduque, the thirteenth-largest island in the Philippine archipelago, approximately eleven miles from Luzon, the largest island. Before the US invasion in 1898, the residents engaged in agriculture, growing hemp, rice, coconuts, raising cattle, and other stock. There were five towns on Marinduque, Boac, the capital, Santa Cruz, Mogpog, Torrijos, and Gazan, as well as ninety-six villages in the agricultural valleys in the interior. Lieutenant Colonel Máximo Abad, a schoolteacher from Luzon's Cavite province, led Marinduque's military resistance. He had a battalion of 250 full-

---

[522] The Philippines, End of an Illusion, Pambungad Sa Kasaysayan NG Pilipinas, Association for Radical East Asian Studies and Journal of Contemporary Asia, Volume 2, no.2, 1973, p. 49

[523] Howard Zinn, A People's History of the United States, 1492-Present, Harper Collins, 1999, p. 316

time, uniformed, armed men and a part-time militia of 1,000 to 2,000 farmers, armed with bolos, short machetes.[524]

The US Army concentrated its initial efforts around Manila and the northern half of Luzon in an attempt to crush Emilio Aguinaldo's main army. In early 1900, the army, under Major General John G. Bates, occupied the islands further south. On April 25, 1900, Colonel Edward E. Hardin sent eighty-eight inexperienced volunteers, who set up a control center in Boac's church. General Bates later reinforced Marinduque with seventy-two men from Major Charles H. Muir's command. He, a veteran of the Indian Wars, intended to quash the insurgency.[525]

Captain John L. Jordan was on Marinduque, where he wanted to use the same scorched earth-policies as the US government had used in the South during the Civil War. He wrote home that Filipinos "only understand and respect the law of force. If we should go out here and carry on a war as William T. Sherman did in his march to the sea we would bring every one of them to submission quickly." In June, Bates recalled Muir, Jordan, and their men to Luzon and replaced them with Captain Devereux Shields and his volunteers, who occupied Santa Cruz. There were fewer than a hundred men at each garrison, and they were unable to protect it and simultaneously carry out offensive warfare. Bates did not consider the garrison sufficiently important to merit more than periodic naval support.

In early October 1900, Major General Arthur MacArthur, the commander of US forces in the Philippines, sent Brigadier General Luther R. Hare and two battalions to Marinduque with orders to begin "the complete stamping out of the insurrection on that island." MacArthur told Hare to consider every male over fifteen as an enemy and to round up the male population, approximately 7,000 to 10,000, and treat them as prisoners of war, as hostages, until the US Army had killed or captured the insurgents and all weapons. Bates

---

[524]   Andrew J. Birtle, The US Army's Pacification of Marinduque, Philippine Islands, April 1900-April 1901, The Journal of Military History, Volume 61, No. 2, April 1997, pp. 255-282

[525]   Ibid

authorized the arrest of anyone suspected of aiding the insurgents, without proof of their guilt. Abad sent Hare a letter asking for a weeklong truce.[526]

Accordingly, on October 22, 1900, Hare, with 1,200 men, began a campaign to arrest the male population between fifteen and sixty and to destroy any village or house from which hostile fire emanated. The military was to shoot any male who ran or acted suspicious. Hare planned to ship the prisoners to Polo Island, 400 yards off the coast of Santa Cruz. Two ships would guard the island to prevent escapes. Out of over 600 captives, all were noncombatants. The military torched several villages and two rice storehouses. They shot several villagers who tried to escape. The soldiers moved most of the captives to Polo Island for internment.[527]

Captain William M. Wright, Bates's aide-de-camp, advocated the deportation of all suspected guerrillas throughout the Philippines. By November, the military had not captured a single guerrilla or confiscated any rifles. However, they incarcerated several hundred men. Hare received a promotion and soon left the island. Officials suspended all operations as they shuffled troops to other locations. In September, Abad had ambushed some of the men in transit. In retaliation, the US military went to Payi, an adjacent village, and torched all forty houses and over two tons of rice. Bates ordered Hare's successor, Lieutenant Colonel Augustus W. Corliss, to arrest all Filipino men of military age and to treat all natives with severity. Corliss, with MacArthur's approval, began destroying everything in the interior capable of sustaining any insurrection—rice, cattle, caribou, and ponies.[528]

By the end of 1900, many officers agreed with Jordan's analysis—the Filipinos deserved severe treatment, as they would not submit to US sovereignty. On December 20, the US military authorized General

---

[526] Ibid
[527] Andrew J. Birtle, The US Army's Pacification of Marinduque, Philippine Islands, April 1900-April 1901, The Journal of Military History, Volume 61, No. 2, April 1997, pp. 255-282
[528] Ibid

Order Number 100 from 1863. This law had a convenient loophole that allowed the US military to fine the residents, confiscate and destroy property, incarcerate, deport or relocate populations, and arbitrarily execute guerrillas. MacArthur sanctioned the arrest and detention of anyone based merely on "suspicion amounting to moral certainty" instead of absolute proof. Corliss began the operation in mid-December 1900.[529]

Over a five-day period in mid-December, Captain Francis E. Lacey Jr., and 127 men destroyed 364 houses, forty-five tons of palay (unmilled rice), 600 pounds of rice, thirty bushels of corn, 188 bales of hemp, 330 ponies, one hundred caribou, and 233 cattle, and killed one Filipino man who ran when he saw the military. However, Lacey could not link the destroyed property to the insurgents. Because circumstances were so horrific in the interior, people began returning to the coastal towns. Santa Cruz's population increased from one hundred individuals to 8,000 by the end of January. The army's destructiveness created severe food shortages, which generated chronic illness and malnutrition. Corliss amended his destruction order—they would not destroy supplies in private homes, just the supplies in general storehouses.[530]

On February 6, 1901, Major Frederick A. Smith, an Indian Wars veteran, assumed command of Marinduque. He halted the destruction of cattle and hemp, the island's most important commodities. On February 7, 1901, he started a concentration policy similar to that used against America's indigenous population. The military ordered all 50,000 citizens to move to the occupied towns of Boac, Santa Cruz, Mogpog, Gazan, Torrijos, or Buenavista. By separating the peaceful inhabitants from the insurgents, Smith hoped to break the link between the population and the guerrillas. The military would not allow any citizen, once inside the zone, to leave without a pass. They treated uncooperative people, who would not snitch on the members of the resistance, as enemies. Within a few weeks, war-weary Filipinos surrendered and entered the concentration camps.

---

[529] Ibid
[530] Ibid

By the end of February, 12,000 people were in Santa Cruz, and over 7,000 each were at Mogpog and Gazan. Thousands took the oath of allegiance. Smith enticed prominent Boac citizens to sign a statement saying that the insurrection was destroying the island.[531]

After touring the islands, Commissioner William Howard Taft wrote to the war secretary on February 24, 1901, regarding Smith's concentration campaign and destruction, the "work of pacification" on Marinduque. He said, "The severity with which the inhabitants have been dealt with would not look well if a complete history of it were written out."[532] Washington officials did not respond to Taft's letter. On March 19, Army Adjutant General Henry C. Corbin saw a press dispatch about Smith's concentration policy and wired MacArthur for verification. He defended the policy.[533]

On March 15, 1901, Taft visited Marinduque with other members of the Philippine Commission in order to establish civilian governments. The commission met with leading citizens, who were now docile and willing to accept the commission's dictates. It planned to install a provincial government by May if Marinduque remained peaceful. Taft manipulated the people by threatening to use the army's concentration tactics on those who even thought of resisting US sovereignty.[534]

US forces captured Emilio Aguinaldo on March 23, 1901, and some of his forces soon surrendered their weapons. General MacArthur convinced him to surrender and to swear allegiance to the US. Vice President Roosevelt thought Manila should become a US Hong Kong.[535] On April 29, 1901, Smith proclaimed the end of the insurrection on Marinduque. He terminated the concentration policy

---

[531] Andrew J. Birtle, The US Army's Pacification of Marinduque, Philippine Islands, April 1900-April 1901, The Journal of Military History, Volume 61, No. 2, April 1997, pp. 255-282

[532] Philip C. Jessup, Elihu Root, Dodd Mead, New York, 1938, pp. 340-341

[533] Andrew J. Birtle, The US Army's Pacification of Marinduque, Philippine Islands, April 1900-April 1901, The Journal of Military History, Volume 61, No. 2, April 1997, pp. 255-282

[534] Ibid

[535] Sterling Seagrave, The Marcos Dynasty, Harper and Row, New York, 1988, pp. 10-11

and allowed the citizens to return to their homes. He said, "That the misfortunes and desolations of war be soon forgotten under the new conditions of peace." The inhabitants left the filthy, overcrowded camps and returned to their homes to plant a new crop before the beginning of the rainy season. Marinduque's population never again took up arms against America.[536]

Between April 1900 and April 1901, the army had conducted 142 operations on Marinduque. US losses totaled eight dead, nineteen wounded, and forty-five captured. The army verified forty-eight Filipino deaths and sixteen wounded. The United States had captured about 1,800 Filipino men. Fatalities on Marinduque exceeded many more than those hit by bullets. The army had destroyed the majority of the homes outside of the six concentration zones. They had slaughtered about 3 percent of Marinduque's cattle, 4 percent of its caribou, and 17 percent of its ponies. By mid-1901, citizens had to import rice in order to survive. Before the US invasion, they had been a major rice exporter. The army reopened the ports in May 1901. Hemp sales supplied the cash needed to purchase rice to prevent starvation.[537]

In October 1900, two typhoons had destroyed the Philippines' coconut crop, and locusts damaged most of the 1901 rice crop, and rinderpest, a disease that accompanies warfare, killed most of the island's remaining cattle and caribou. Between 1901 and 1903, several thousand vulnerable people perished from typhoid, cholera, and malaria, diseases that often occur after relocation and war trauma, similar to the consequences the Native American populations experienced. By 1902, there was a 46 percent reduction of land under cultivation on Marinduque, compared to prewar levels. Benguet, Batangas, and Capiz experienced similar agricultural declines due to the invasion. Brigadier General J. Franklin Bell in Batangas and

---

[536] Andrew J. Birtle, The US Army's Pacification of Marinduque, Philippine Islands, April 1900-April 1901, The Journal of Military History, Volume 61, No. 2, April 1997, pp. 255-282
[537] Ibid

General Jacob H. Smith in Samar used concentration camps on a larger scale.[538]

On August 11, 1901, US troops arrived in Balangiga on Samar Island in order to close the port to obstruct food and other essentials from getting to the Filipino military forces in the islands interior under the jurisdiction of General Vicente Lukban. Captain Thomas W. Connell, a West Pointer and devout Catholic, instructed residents to clean up the town for the imminent visit of the army's inspector-general in preparation for a local fiesta. He told the young women to change their "seductive" sarongs for more modest clothing, and he demonstrated justifiable disdain for the cockfighting that the townspeople regularly enjoyed.

On September 18, 1901, almost 400 guerrilla fighters arrived in the Balangiga vicinity. Shortly, Connell ordered all of the town's males seized and detained. He also confiscated the men's bolos and their rice stores. On September 26, 1901, Connell received word of McKinley's assassination, and he ordered his troops to hold a mass at the town square in one of the large tents on Sunday, September 28, 1901.

The military's confiscation of the guerillas' weapons outraged them, as they planned to attack the Americans. The locals had no weapons, but they had plenty of palm wine (tuba) and used it to get the troops intoxicated on Saturday night. Just before the attack, the townspeople removed all the women and children to a secure place. Thirty-four guerillas dressed as women, each carrying a small casket with a bolo inside. They proceeded to the church at dawn. Sergeant Henry J. Scharer, a sentry in the town plaza, along with two others, challenged one of the "women" who opened the casket to reveal the body of a small child, purportedly a cholera victim. He let all of the "women" proceed to the church without examining the contents of any of their coffins.

On the morning of September 28, 1901, the local police chief seized one of the sentry's rifles and fired it, signaling the guerrillas to

---

[538] Ibid

attack. The church bells began ringing, and the locals rushed into the mess tent and the adjacent convent, which they used as a barracks. They attacked and killed forty-eight unsuspecting US soldiers. A few escaped to another island, and soon a fresh detachment of fifty-three volunteers was sent to the Balangiga and, with their ship's machine gun and cannon killed about 250 villagers, who they immediately cremated, despite protests from survivors.[539] General Smith instigated a reign of terror against the Filipinos because of the Balangiga massacre.[540] Writers for American textbooks focus on the forty-eight dead Americans of the Balangiga Massacre, but fail to mention the slaughter of tens of thousands of Filipino civilians.[541]

Word of the incident outraged the American public. President Roosevelt gave orders to Major General Adna R. Chaffee, military governor of the islands, to pacify Samar. He appointed General Smith to take charge of the situation. Smith ordered Major Littleton Waller, officer of a 315-man battalion of marines to reinforce his troops. He told Waller, "I want no prisoners. I wish you to kill and burn; the more you kill and burn, the better you will please me. I want all persons killed who are capable of bearing arms in actual hostilities against the United States." Waller asked if there was an age limit. Smith replied, "persons of ten years and older are those designated as being capable of bearing arms."[542] Smith ordered his soldiers to turn Samar into a "howling wilderness," so that even the birds could not live there. He boasted that what fire and water (waterboarding) had done in Panay, water and fire could do in Samar. Operations began at once. The United States ordered all residents (population 266,000) to present themselves to concentration camps in specific coastal towns. They shot anyone who disobeyed or who left the perimeter of

[539] Stanley Karnow, In Our Image, America's Empire in the Philippines, Random House, New York, 1989, pp. 190-191

[540] The Philippines, End of an Illusion, Pambungad Sa Kasaysayan NG Pilipinas, Association for Radical East Asian Studies and Journal of Contemporary Asia, Volume 2, no.2, 1973, p. 33

[541] Victor Nebrida, The Balangiga Massacre: Getting Even in Hector Santos, ed., Philippine Centennial Series, June 15, 1997, http://www.bibingka.com/phg/balangiga/default.htm as of May 2012

[542] Stanley Karnow, In Our Image, America's Empire in the Philippines, Random House, New York, 1989, pp. 190-191

the camp. One of the few reporters who covered the carnage wrote, "The truth is the struggle in Samar is one of extermination." The War Department claimed it had no records of the orders carried out at Samar.[543]

When people revealed Smith's barbarism, the War Department attempted to depict his Samar Campaign as a departure or irregularity from normal practices. Even the war secretary claimed to have made a thorough investigation and asserted, "That the army had scrupulous regard for the rules of civilized warfare with careful and genuine consideration for the prisoner and noncombatant, with self-restraint and with humanity never surpassed if ever equaled in any conflict, worthy only of praise, and reflecting credit upon the American people." Actually, the Samar Campaign was similar to the extermination policy imposed in Northern Luzon and in Panay. The Samar Campaign was not the end of the brutal policies. The Batangas Campaign, a few months later, employed the same practices. After all, Smith was simply following General Chaffee's explicit orders.[544]

Adna R. Chaffee, like many military men, belonged to the Pilgrims Society. Military men often ally with financiers to gain support for their wars. Chaffee was, according to the Combined Arms Research Library at Fort Leavenworth, Kansas, the first soldier in US history to enlist in the army as a private and become chief of the army general staff. He joined the Sixth Cavalry Regiment and participated in the Civil War and the Indian Wars. He was in the first unit to arrive in Cuba and became chief of staff of the US command during that war. He was in China during the Boxer Rebellion. He replaced MacArthur on July 4, 1901. He intended to crush the "insurrection," and he appointed General Bell to Batangas and Smith to Samar. He wanted an Indian-style campaign, instead of the previous "humanitarian warfare." His orders led to the massive atrocities in the later stages of the war.[545]

---

[543] The Philippines, End of an Illusion, Pambungad Sa Kasaysayan NG Pilipinas, Association for Radical East Asian Studies and Journal of Contemporary Asia, Volume 2, no.2, 1973, p. 33
[544] Ibid
[545] Charles Savoie, Pilgrims, Silver Investor, May 2005, www.silver-investor. com/charlessavoie/cs_may05_pilgrims.htm as of May 2012

Bell said, "All consideration and regard for the inhabitants of this place cease from the day I become commander. I have the force and authority to do whatever seems to me good, and especially to humiliate all those in this province who have any pride." On December 15, 1901, he announced that all "acts of hostility or sabotage" would result in the "starving of unarmed hostile belligerents." As Smith assaulted Samar, General Miguel Malvar and his men carried on their guerrilla campaign in Batangas, Tayabas, Laguna, and Cavite. In 1901, Smith told General Malvar, the commander of the Philippine forces following Aquinaldo's capture, that the detainees had to give up the struggle or face "mass starvation." On December 20, 1901, to illustrate his sincerity, Bell ordered all rice and other food outside of the concentration camps confiscated and destroyed. The United States poisoned all wells and slaughtered all farm animals.[546]

Beginning January 1, 1902, under Bell's direction, the US military rounded up Filipinos in Batangas, as in the previous extermination campaigns, and incarcerated them into the camps that soon became overcrowded. Lack of proper food and clothing predictably led to an eruption of infectious diseases like malaria, beriberi, and dengue fever. Outside the camp, the US military destroyed or torched all property and food and slaughtered all animals. By the time that Bell was finished, his soldiers had killed at least 100,000 people in Batangas alone. The US Civil Governor of Tayabas documented in his official records that killing, burning, torture, and other harsh treatment was "sowing the seeds for a perpetual revolution."[547] The Union had employed the same scorched-earth policy against the Confederate civilians. General Malvar surrendered, and President Roosevelt officially declared the war to be over on July 4, 1902. However, the fighting did not end.

General Smith, previously a speculator in whiskey, gold, and diamonds who had stolen enlistment money from "colored" recruits, vowed to turn Samar into "a howling wilderness." Major Chaffee

---

[546] The Philippines, End of an Illusion, Pambungad Sa Kasaysayan NG Pilipinas, Association for Radical East Asian Studies and Journal of Contemporary Asia, Volume 2, no.2, 1973, pp. 36-37
[547] Ibid. 38

advised reporters not to be sentimental over the deaths of "a few Goo-Goos." One soldier wrote home about the incident and said, "About one thousand men, women, and children were reported killed. I am probably growing hard-hearted, for I am in my glory when I can sight my gun on some darkskin and pull the trigger . . . Tell all my friends that I am doing everything I can for Old Glory and for America I love so well."[548]

Littleton also sought to avenge the deaths of his military comrades who had died in North China. *The Chicago Tribune* reported, "We are the trustees of civilization and peace throughout the islands." In an effort to persuade the Filipinos of US generosity and goodwill, the United States established a few schools, reorganized city governments, and improved sanitation conditions.[549] The Senate whitewashed the real war criminals, Smith and Waller. The Senate admonished them and then acquitted them during an investigation, headed by imperialist Senator Henry Cabot Lodge. Apparently, Waller was just following orders, a defense that US judges disallowed the German defendants at Nuremburg.[550]

In 1903, Governor Taft signed a law permitting the use of concentration camps. During the next four years, US authorities used concentration camps in almost a dozen provinces to stifle postwar disturbances. The residents of the Albay Province in 1903 and Samar in 1907-1908 experienced concentration at the hands of Marinduque veterans Harry H. Bandholtz and Frederick A. Smith. As a result of the effectiveness of concentration in the Philippines, the General Service and Staff College expanded its curriculum by adding guerrilla warfare and concentration.

Army generals William E. Birkhimer and George B. Davis, in their textbooks, endorsed population concentration and the pervasive

[548] Sterling Seagrave, The Marcos Dynasty, Harper and Row, New York, 1988, pp. 12-13
[549] Victor Nebrida, The Balangiga Massacre: Getting Even in Hector Santos, ed., Philippine Centennial Series, June 15, 1997, http://www.bibingka.com/phg/balangiga/default.htm as of May 2012
[550] Ibid

destruction of enemy territory. As late as 1926, military manuals used at the Infantry School mentioned the use of concentration for population control. This remained in effect past the end of World War II. War Secretary Root wrote, "It is evident that the insurrection has been brought to an end both by making a war distressing and hopeless on the one hand, and by making peace attractive. Once the army began to make the people feel the hard hand of war, however, they grasped at the hand of friendship."[551]

The Philippines, the Evolution of a Third World Country

By 1800, an indigenous ruling class had arisen in the Philippines, a Spanish colony. Spain, economically weak, had not developed agricultural products for the world market and could not prevent the plentiful British and US commercial interests from penetrating the islands in the second half of the nineteenth century. Britain's superior naval fleet had emasculated Spain, rendering it little more than a colonial administrator. Yet, Anglo-American corporations were reluctant to make major investments in the Philippines because Spain still maintained a modicum of power. By 1850, there were about a dozen merchant houses that influenced internal economics, a pittance compared to the investments that British and US industries had elsewhere.[552] Thus, the United States would have to expel Spain under some pretense so that American-based corporations could expand into the resource-rich Philippines.

Immediately after Admiral George Dewey defeated the Spanish, President William McKinley cabled him to compile an accurate account of the Philippines' natural resources, including mining, farming, and any industrial production. He also sent a State Department emissary to prepare a detailed directory for the economic exploitation of the area. US companies then quickly targeted the most fertile lands, but,

---

[551]   Andrew J. Birtle, The US Army's Pacification of Marinduque, Philippine Islands, April 1900-April 1901, The Journal of Military History, Volume 61, No. 2, April 1997, pp. 255-282

[552]   The Philippines, End of an Illusion, Pambungad Sa Kasaysayan NG Pilipinas, Association for Radical East Asian Studies and Journal of Contemporary Asia, Volume 2, no.2, 1973, p. 1

by law, foreign corporations were restricted to 1,024 hectares (2,530 acres). A Del Monte subsidiary asked the US governor to convert public land into a US navy preserve. Navy officials then subleased 20,000 hectares to Del Monte.[553] Obviously, there were methods of avoiding or subverting restrictions. The 1901 Spooner Bill and the Philippine Tariff Act of 1902 stipulated a 25 percent reduction in the tariff on products from the Philippines.[554]

Harvard-educated Henry Gannett, chief geographer of the United States, assisted the government in surveying domestic and international territory, organizing the 2,000 enumeration districts in preparation for the 1880 census. On July 1, 1902, Congress authorized a census of the Philippines, to occur after the "existing insurrection" ended, as certified by the president of the Philippine Commission. The census, taken by the commission, would verify the population, including name, age, sex, race, or tribe, whether native or foreign born, literacy, property, ownership and numerous other facts on all inhabitants.[555] Gannett was the assistant director of the Philippines census and the Cuba census (1907-08).

The government also ordered a census after the Civil War and the Reconstruction period (1865-1877) to assess population structure and, particularly, the area's resources. The census, ostensibly for taxing purposes only, began in 1790 and was restricted to the name of the head of household and the number of persons living in the household within specific age groups. However, by 1880, the census included extensive personal information that, frankly, was and is none of the government's business. Seen in the context of the wars in the Philippines and in Cuba, where the government wanted information

[553] Sterling Seagrave, The Marcos Dynasty, Harper and Row, New York, 1988, p. 30
[554] Patricio N. Abinales, Donna J. Amoroso, Paul Barclay, Vince Boudreau, Anne L. Foster, Julian Go, and Paul A. Kramer The American Colonial State in the Philippines: Global Perspectives, Duke University Press, Durham, North Carolina, 2003, pp. 195-197
[555] United States Bureau of the Census, Census of the Philippine Islands: taken under the direction of the Philippine Commission in the Year 1903, Joseph Prentiss Sanger, Henry Gannett, Victor Hugo, United States Bureau of the Census, Washington, 1905, p. 11

on personal resources and property ownership, the US census became highly significant.

President William McKinley, who portrayed himself as a prayerful Christian, encouraged the exploitation of the vast mineral reserves in the Philippines. First Lieutenant John W. Haussermann, an Ohio native and an attorney, who literally saw a golden opportunity, favored McKinley's approach. Haussermann had joined the military when the Spanish American War erupted and ultimately ended up in the Philippines. He received his discharge there on September 1, 1899, and soon became Manila's city attorney.[556] [557]

Since Philippine law did not recognize the artificial US entity known as a "corporation," the US Congress accommodated Haussermann and passed a law on July 1, 1902, enabling him to bypass local laws and create a corporation in June 1903. By 1906, he established the Benguet Consolidated Mining Company.[558] By 1904, over 10,000 Americans were living in the islands, where they initially wholly appreciated the Filipino laborers, especially the so-called wild tribes—the Igorot people in the mountainous Benguet Province. Gradually, US investors clamored for less-expensive, harder-working Chinese coolies.[559]

In 1927, Benguet bought Balatoc Mining, its competitor, giving Haussermann's company 80 percent of the nation's gold industry, a monopoly. Known as the "Gold King," he and his associates made a massive fortune, which his company would later selectively share with local influential political puppets and US military leaders like General Douglas MacArthur, who identified with the Philippine

---

[556] David Shavit, The United States in Asia: A Historical Dictionary, Greenwood Publishing Group, 1990, p. 223

[557] Kansas History, Kansas State Historical Society, February 1940 (Vol. 9, No. 1), pp. 106-109

[558] Republic of the Philippines, Supreme Court, Manila, G.R. #L-37331, March 18, 1933, http://www.lawphil.net/judjuris/juri1933/mar1933/gr_l-37331_1933.html as of May 2012

[559] Julie A. Tuason, The Ideology of Empire in National Geographic Magazine's Coverage of the Philippines, 1898-1908, The Geographical Review, Volume: 89, Issue: 1, 1999

oligarchy.[560] Haussermann was the richest man in the Philippines, and his family remained the biggest stockholders in the Benguet group of companies, which mined about $150 million worth of gold and paid over $35 million in cash dividends.[561]

The indigenous Igorot of the Benguet Province had always used "pocket mining" to extract gold from the earth. The men would excavate a small cave into the mountain and find gold-bearing rocks, and the women and children would hammer these rocks into small nuggets. It was an environmentally-friendly method of mining, but American-based companies rejected it as too time-consuming. Now, a few wealthy Filipinos, the Philippine government, and a few US investors own Benguet, which controls those ancestral lands. They value the substantial profits more than the local residents and the environment. Huge, open-pit mines have altered the once paradisiacal landscape, all to produce gold for export. Bulldozers cut deep wounds into the mountain. Contractors have ripped out trees and displaced fertile topsoil, and workers have dumped truckloads of toxic chemical waste into the riverbeds. The Igorot had merely used water to separate gold from the rock, whereas mining firms use toxic chemicals like cyanide, which destroys local water sources. Due to water toxicity, the Igorot are no longer able to grow rice and bananas and must carry all of their water from the other side of the mountain.[562]

Downstream, the cattle sickened and died from drinking the cyanide-laced water. Rice farmers in parts of the Pangasinan Province yearly lost about 250 million pesos, because Benguet's workers deposited debris wherever it was convenient, including adjacent rice fields, causing a dire decline in rice production. This spoliation of the land forced farmers, whose ancestors had worked the land for generations, to relocate in order to care for their families. American contractors irresponsibly disposed of mine debris, which has affected the entire

[560] Sterling Seagrave, The Marcos Dynasty, Harper & Row, New York, 1988, pp. 30-34

[561] Florence Horn, Orphans of the Pacific, the Philippines, Reynal & Hitchcock, New York, 1941, pp. 206-207

[562] David C. Korten, When Corporations Rule the World, Kumarian Press; Berrett-Koehler Publishers, 1995, pp. 43-44

ecosystem of the coral reef, creating a significant fish-population reduction and affecting the men who depended on the sea for their livelihood. By 1995, Benguet and other mining companies were earning 1.1 billion pesos a year, while the natives continued to suffer and live in poverty, because local politicians, who financially benefit, have relegated their citizens to destitution and hopelessness because of corporate exploitation.[563]

Timber companies have stripped the forests without concern for the needs of local residents. Prior to the loggers and their huge trucks, there was plenty of fish, corn, and rice. Logging has changed the flow of the rivers and during monsoon season, and rivers overflow their banks and strip the top soil from once-fertile fields. Corporate workers have obliterated the meandering creeks that farmers used for irrigation. This disrupted the forest's ecological balance with natural predators. For instance, rodents now ravage the farmers' fields instead of feasting in the forest. Their natural enemies, now gone, had previously restrained the rat population. Children, the most vulnerable citizens in every population, once lived in agriculturally rich communities and had plenty to eat. Now, the majority of children, except for the elite class, regularly experience pervasive hunger and systemic malnutrition.[564]

Citizens elected Manuel L. Quezon, leader of the Nacionalista Party to the first Philippine Assembly in 1907. In March 1909, with the rhetoric over the Payne bill in the House, numerous foreign diplomats made inquiries at the State Department regarding products from their countries. Under the Payne bill, the entire list of American maximum rates would negatively affect many countries, especially Germany. Brazil was concerned about the export duty on their coffee. Ecuadorian officials were concerned that the proposed duty on cocoa would be disastrous to that country. President William Howard Taft (S&B), Secretary of State Philander C. Knox, Treasury Secretary Franklin MacVeagh (S&B),[565] and Senator Nelson W. Aldrich had

[563] Ibid
[564] Ibid. 43-44
[565] Antony Sutton, America's Secret Establishment: An Introduction to the Order of Skull & Bones, Trine Day, Walterville, Oregon, 2002, p. 136

an extended conference at the White House in order to consider options to assist certain business interests, their friends, and their law clients.[566]

Immediately after his inauguration, March 4, 1909, President Taft convened a special session of Congress to discuss tariff reduction on Philippine products. Taft advocated reciprocal free trade, or preferential treatment, between the United States and the Philippines. US sugar and tobacco interests initially opposed free trade, but soon relented when Representative Sereno Payne offered to place those items on a free list with an extra-high quota. Rice growers fought to remove rice from the free list. The Payne bill went to the Senate, despite the complaints of Filipino leaders. In the Philippine Assembly, Quezon condemned free trade with the United States and pointed out that they would not benefit from the nonreciprocal quotas, because they only applied to items exported from the Philippines to America. Whereas, their treasury would have to forfeit needed revenues if US products were duty free. He argued that Payne's proposal would be disastrous for the Philippine economy and the nation's political future.[567]

Quezon said, "Free trade between the United States and the Philippines would attract powerful American companies to the Philippines and would make American capital the absolute owner of our market . . . That the coming of large American companies would bring as a result the monopoly of the wealth of the country by them is a fact that is beyond all doubt; they would first take possession of our market, through lack of competition, and then of our agriculture."[568] Free trade, for the middle and poorer classes, always proves harmful for any nation. Free trade, which sounds innocuous, only benefits big

[566] Payne Bill Arouses Opposition Abroad; Diplomats Point Out That It Would Provoke Retaliation—Taft Confers on Changes. Democrats Breaking Away Southern Men Want Duties on Lumber and Rice—Broussard Is Kept Out of Conference, The New York Times, March 21, 1909, p. 2
[567] H. W. Brands, Bound to Empire: The United States and the Philippines, Oxford University Press, New York, 1992, pp. 96-97
[568] Ibid. 96-97

business. The word *free* is a very deceptive misnomer—who but the educated would reject something labeled free?

Taft appointed William C. Forbes, a former investment banker, as governor general of the Philippines (1909-1913). He was the son of the president of the Bell Telephone Company. His wife, Edith Emerson, was a daughter of Ralph Waldo Emerson. The Forbes family, like other blue bloods, made their fortune trafficking in opium.[569] Forbes disregarded Quezon's objections to free trade. As head of the American-run Philippine government, he endorsed and encouraged free trade and investment and vetoed Quezon's resolution and commended Congress for the Payne bill, despite considerable Filipino opposition. He applauded the great Taft Administration for their efforts in getting this bill passed. Forbes falsely claimed that this was the route to Filipino prosperity. Referring to the men in the Philippine Assembly who voted against the bill, he said, "Those fool assemblymen who voted unanimously against free trade will have a chance to see practically what asses they have made of themselves in the eyes of the world." Quezon and the Nacionalistas worried about the consequences of US investments and so-called free trade.[570] Yet Congress passed the bill on April 9, 1909.

This legislative reduction gave the growers a small competitive advantage in the US market and helped win the loyalty of the mestizo elite. The Payne-Aldrich Tariff Act permitted 300,000 tons of Philippine sugar to enter the United States duty-free. However, the prerequisite was the free entry of all US products into the Philippine market. Without any tariff protections, the US politicians, deliberately or inadvertently, targeted the Philippine manufacturing industry for destruction, the exact same reason for the destruction in the US manufacturing.[571]

---

[569] Steven Sora, The Secret Societies of America's Elite, From the Knights Templar to Skull and Bones, Destiny Books, 2003, pp. 254-257

[570] H. W. Brands, Bound to Empire: The United States and the Philippines, Oxford University Press, New York, 1992, pp. 96-97

[571] The Philippines, End of an Illusion, Pambungad Sa Kasaysayan NG Pilipinas, Association for Radical East Asian Studies and Journal of Contemporary Asia, Volume 2, no.2, 1973, p. 3

Quezon went to Washington as a Resident Commissioner (per the Philippine Act of 1902) to the US House of Representatives (1909-1916). Quezon, one of the Philippines' two resident commissioners, lobbied for the Philippine Autonomy Act of 1916 to replace the Philippine Organic Act of 1902. Quezon drafted the bill, which Congress passed on August 29, 1916. It promised Philippine independence at some vague future date on condition of a "stable government"—in other words, compliant with US business interests.[572] Quezon left the decadence of Washington and returned to the Philippines in 1916.

Hemp and sugar were the leading exports in the late nineteenth and early twentieth centuries. Sugar was the key commercial cash crop while, small landowners grew hemp. The elite class produced labor-intensive sugar on a few hundred large-scale plantations, which generated huge fortunes. However, the successful introduction of beet sugar caused a decreasing need in the West for cane sugar. Farmers in the moderate climates of Europe and America could grow beets, which altered the world's sugar economy. Along with political ramifications, tariff policies, trade agreements, subsidies, and production costs, the European market reduced their importation of Filipino sugar.[573]

Both Puerto Rico and the Philippines were sugar-producing countries. Therefore, US sugar-beet farmers were interested in retaining high tariffs. They pressured Congress to impose limits on the quantity of land that US sugar corporations could lease in the US colonies to obstruct US corporations from organizing sugar plantations. The Beet Sugar Manufacturers Association and the League of Domestic Producers opposed free trade and wanted protectionist high tariffs on all goods coming in from the colonies. Elihu Root and other imperialists discouraged and eschewed this opposition.[574] Like-

---

[572] Sterling Seagrave, The Marcos Dynasty, Harper & Row, New York, 1988, pp. 30-34
[573] The Philippines, End of an Illusion, Pambungad Sa Kasaysayan NG Pilipinas, Association for Radical East Asian Studies and Journal of Contemporary Asia, Volume 2, no.2, 1973, p. 3
[574] Patricio N. Abinales, Donna J. Amoroso, Paul Barclay, Vince Boudreau, Anne L. Foster, Julian Go, and Paul A. Kramer, The American Colonial State

minded people joined Root in his attempts to attract investors. Sugar industrialists were particularly interested in investing in Puerto Rico and the Philippines. The Havemeyers, who had a sugar monopoly and therefore could manipulate the prices, pressured Congress to impose free trade.[575]

Congress determines tariffs, duties, and any other restraints or lack thereof on all trade. Root and his congressional cronies made many of those early trade decisions. They promoted a reduction in the existing Dingley tariffs relating to incoming foreign goods to induce investment in the new US colonies. This tariff reduction would motivate investors, especially if US industrialists could develop sizeable plantations. Because Congress was responsible for tariff activities, it was important to influence congressmen.[576] The Seventeenth Amendment, the direct, popular election of Senators, passed on April 8, 1913, made this much easier.

When Americans first went to the Philippines, they established relationships with the owners of the Philippine hacenderos and mill owners, the elite in island society. Naturally, inasmuch as they were making a nice profit while employing cheap labor, they did not favor independence, despite their nationalistic rhetoric. The elite, wealthy, landed oligarchy was quite comfortable with their alliance with the US colonial administrators. Elected representatives also maintained the fiction that they wanted to end US colonialism in favor of independence. As long as it was a remote possibility, keeping up the appearances with the right patriotic slogans to retain mass support worked well until about 1928, when independence appeared imminent, along with a curtailment of the protectionist prices.[577]

---

in the Philippines: Global Perspectives, Duke University Press, Durham, North Carolina, 2003, pp. 195-197

[575]   Ibid. 195-197

[576]   Ibid. 195-197

[577]   Patricio N. Abinales, Donna J. Amoroso, Paul Barclay, Vince Boudreau, Anne L. Foster, Julian Go, and Paul A. Kramer, The American Colonial State in the Philippines: Global Perspectives, Duke University Press, Durham, North Carolina, 2003, p. 5

After 1925, overproduction became problematic for the world's sugar producers. This was a particularly true for producers who lacked a political affiliation where there were guaranteed tariffs or trade agreements. Cuba, the main cane producer, was also the most economically efficient producer. Americans owned most of the sugar production companies in Cuba. However, Cuba's market shrunk because of the protectionist legislation supporting high cost producers in the Philippines. The indigenous owners received big tariff reductions because, essentially, they resided in a US colony.[578]

The elite Filipino class adamantly opposed ending their special trade agreements, which would dramatically alter their sugar exports to the United States. The US offered independence on the condition that the Filipinos accepted the one-sided trade provisions that benefitted US business interests. The Philippine oligarchy had to determine if they wanted political independence and nationalism or the continuation of a profitable US market. Filipino politicians, when dealing privately with the United States, attempted to prevent or delay independence. The high sugar profits were a direct result of the tariff, maintained at the expense of a balanced development of the Philippine economy; it was either the sugar growers, on corporate welfare, or the best interests of the country.[579]

The Philippines is a classic case of the development of underdevelopment. The export business depended on four crops—sugar, coconuts, hemp fiber, and tobacco. About 60 percent of their export earnings came from sugar, and 20 percent of their imports were foodstuffs—cocoa, coffee, eggs, fish, meat, and rice—all of which people could have produced locally, if the elite had not dominated the land for sugar production. Now, merchants imported huge quantities of rice, a staple, as well as cotton products, although the islands were quite capable of growing and processing their own cotton. The Filipinos could have manufactured other basic items instead of importing them. Exclusive production of sugar, a cash crop

---

[578]   Ibid. 4-5
[579]   Ibid. 6-7

like heroin, had created an unnecessary third-world environment because of a select greedy minority.[580]

A 1936 survey of the Philippine industrial manufacturing sector revealed that the ten leading products were coconut oil, cigars and cigarettes, sugar refining, desiccated coconut, embroideries, copra cake, cordage, pineapple canning, vegetable lard, and straw hats. The United States had inundated the country with duty-free products, so there was little motivation for Philippine industry to develop based on the country's actual interests and needs. The sugar barons, living in luxury, were satisfied to allow circumstances to remain at a primitive level for the masses.[581]

After almost four decades of US exploitation, Japan invaded the Philippines on December 8, 1941. US wartime sugar prices skyrocketed as the sugar supply from the islands decreased and the US sugar-beet industry could not meet the demand. Wartime made sugar even more profitable. Therefore, both factions, the US sugar-beet industry and the Philippine sugar industry, were amenable to continued sugar production in the Philippines.[582] After the war, in order to retain the same win/lose relationship, and to accommodate business interests, US officials returned the sugar oligarchy to power. The US military leaders, after they returned in 1944, restored Philippine's elite class, loyal to the United States, to its mutually beneficial prewar position. This entailed overlooking the demands of the militant peasantry, who still clamored for self-determination, and independence.[583]

Post-war economic planning included maintaining deliberate underdevelopment or the reestablishment of the colonial pattern and imperialistic trade patterns. The United States financed the restoration of the sugar industry, rebuilt the milling facilities, and reconstructed

---

580   Ibid. 7
581   Ibid. 7
582   Patricio N. Abinales, Donna J. Amoroso, Paul Barclay, Vince Boudreau, Anne L. Foster, Julian Go, and Paul A. Kramer, The American Colonial State in the Philippines: Global Perspectives, Duke University Press, Durham, North Carolina, 2003, pp. 10-11
583   Ibid. 9

the centrals, paid for with US war rehabilitation (taxpayer) funds. US officials then relinquished all of these facilities to the mill owners. US politicians gave the sugar producers quotas and tariff concessions for continued profitability. Politicians drafted the 1946 Philippine Trade Act to accommodate the interests of US exporters and US corporations with their investments in the Philippines. The law included a clause giving US citizens equal rights to exploit the Philippines' natural resources. Politicians amended their constitution to accommodate the clause. Filipino officials obediently pushed the amendment through the Philippine Congress, which essentially stripped the islands of their sovereignty. The Philippines, recognized as an independent country on July 4, 1946, had a flag, a national anthem, and a seat in the UN—the total extent of their freedom. The Pentagon created long-term lease contracts for army and navy bases in the islands. The elite accommodated those US bases, as it afforded them protection against internal agrarian revolts against the elite class.[584]

The Laurel-Langley Agreement, signed in 1955, between the Philippines and the United States, allowed for the subsidization of US sugar consumption supplied by the Philippines, while the United States guaranteed the continued support of the majority of the Philippine elite class. US investors subsidized light industry, but the country was never industrialized or developed. Bankers and their predatory agents marketed big, expensive, limited-use infrastructure projects just to create endless national indebtedness to keep the Philippines forever impoverished. The exploitive clause in the trade agreement allowed the full-scale harvesting of timber, which took the place of sugar as the major export. Cuba discontinued their sugar exportations to the United States in 1960, which actually benefited the Philippines.[585]

There is a mile-wide inequality gap between the insulated elite and the Filipino poor. The elite, who reside in comfort behind gated walls, travel in limousines from one exclusive area to another. Servants clean their homes, and nannies care for their children. The women,

---

[584]   Ibid. 10-11
[585]   Ibid. 13-16

free from menial household chores, spend their time socializing and shopping, often in Hong Kong. Husbands work in downtown Manila or in neighboring Makati in plush offices, where business and politics typically overlap. Frequently, there is a beautiful mestizo mistress stashed away in a luxury apartment. Chauffeurs drive the elite's sons and daughters to secure, exclusive private ecumenical school each morning. Chaperones accompany the children whenever they leave their homes.[586]

Meanwhile, the masses live in the old working-class neighborhoods or in the squatter zones of Manila. Large families crowd into makeshift two-room shacks without sanitation, often amid urban garbage and adjacent, putrid pools of water. Each family combines their sparse resources enough to stay alive, and every member contributes; parents leave their small children on a street corner for hours to pander. Children learn early how to avoid cars when they dart across the street, hoping for a more productive location. Their future, if there is one, might include menial labor with meager wages or prostitution and crime. However, there is always a steady surplus of this kind of labor.[587]

Unfortunately, this scenario is not limited to the Philippines. Third-world countries do not just happen; they evolve because of local elitism and external imperialism. The world's elite are determined and are in the process of making the United States a third-world country, as evidenced by the circumstances over the last few decades. American politicians, the elite class, while spewing the appropriate rhetoric, have the same incestuous-like relationship with banker-controlled big business as the elite in the Philippines. They are even using the same tactics, but on a much broader scale—decreased production, dependence on imports, exploitation of natural resources for the benefit of a few, loss of agricultural production, etc.

---

[586] Patricio N. Abinales, Donna J. Amoroso, Paul Barclay, Vince Boudreau, Anne L. Foster, Julian Go, and Paul A. Kramer, The American Colonial State in the Philippines: Global Perspectives, Duke University Press, Durham, North Carolina, 2003, p. 50

[587] Ibid. 50

SECTION 4

CAPITALISM AND CORPORATISM

The Secretive Pilgrims Society

Philanthropist Felix J. Slade, a lawyer, endowed the first Slade Professorships of Fine Art at Oxford University especially for John Ruskin, a freemason, who taught at Oxford (1869-1879) and ideologically influenced numerous students, some of whom were the most privileged members of society. He taught three main topics— art, the nation's prospective expansion as an Anglo-American empire, and the problems of Britain's struggling masses. His students included Arnold J. Toynbee, Alfred Milner, a freemason,[588] Arthur Glazebrook, George Parkin, Philip L. Gell, and Henry Birchenough, all of whom devoted their life's efforts to promoting Ruskin's imperialist ideas.[589]

Cecil Rhodes, a freemason, and his brother floundered in their efforts to develop a cotton plantation in Africa. Funded by Rothschild, they went into the diamond-mining business. Rhodes, with his exploitation of the resources of Rhodesia, later renamed Zimbabwe, soon amassed a huge fortune through his De Beers diamond conglomerate, with Rothschild as the biggest shareholder. Rhodes earned £5,000 in 1872. In 1873, he returned to England to attend Oxford, leaving his associate, Charles Rudd to manage the business. Rhodes met Ruskin at Oxford.[590]

William T. Stead, a journalist and social reformer, introduced Rhodes to Reginald B. Brett, Sir John B. Seeley, Albert Grey, and Edmund Garrett, who soon became Rhodes's disciples. On February

---

[588] Jüri Lina, Architects of Deception, Referent Publishing, Stockholm, Sweden, 2004, pp. 336-337
[589] Ibid. 130-131
[590] Pat Riott, The Greatest Story Never Told, Winston Churchill and the Crash of 1929, Nanoman Press, Oak Brook, Illinois, 1994, p. 4

5, 1891, Rhodes established the British Round Table, a Masonic organization, later formalized as the Pilgrims Society. He envisioned such a society for almost twenty years. Stead, Brett, and Milner made up the executive committee. Arthur J. Balfour, Harry Johnston, Nathan "Natty" Rothschild, and Albert Grey were the "Circle of Initiates." An outer circle was composed of associates.[591] Rhodes left the majority of his estate to Rothschild, a freemason and eldest son of Lionel de Rothschild, to manage a scholarship program.[592] Rhodes left about $150 million to the Rhodes Foundation, for the exclusive purpose of fulfilling his ideological objectives of bringing about a one-world government through the machinations of a network of secret societies.

Rhodes was intent on the "ultimate recovery" of the United States as an "integral part of the British Empire" to culminate in an Illuminati utopian global system with an Imperial Parliament. Rothschild appointed Milner to chair the group. Milner recruited Rudyard Kipling, Balfour, and other illuminated alumnae from Oxford to form the Round Table, after the Knights of the Round Table, known as Milner's Kindergarten.[593] In 1902, after Rhodes's death, Milner led the group. The Round Table created other organizations in the coming years.

The Round Table in the United States included early members George L. Beer, Walter Lippmann, Frank Aydelotte, Whitney H. Shepardson, Thomas W. Lamont, Jerome D. Green, Frederick Dixon, and others. Its network gathered information following the early nineteenth-century Rothschild banking model, provided by Nathan M. Rothschild, and made wise investments. Stead and others used financial information in psychological operations targeted at specific groups serviced by specific publishing houses and newspapers under the jurisdiction of Round Table members. Council members Beer, Edward M. House,

---

[591] Carroll Quigley, Tragedy And Hope, A History of the World in our Time, The Macmillan Company, New York, 1966, pp. 130-131

[592] Pat Riott, The Greatest Story Never Told, Winston Churchill and the Crash of 1929, Nanoman Press, Oak Brook, Illinois, 1994, pp. 6-8

[593] David Livingstone, Terrorism and the Illuminati, a Three Thousand Year History, Booksurge, LCC., Charleston, South Carolina, 2007, p. 158

Lippmann, Shepardson, James T. Shotwell, Charles Seymour, and Isaiah Bowman, later the president of Johns Hopkins University (1935-1948), became members of America's initial official intelligence organization, the Inquiry, as suggested to President Woodrow Wilson by Felix Frankfurter.

Lord Alfred Milner, educated at Tübingen, and then at London's King's College, was a scholar at Balliol College in Oxford. He studied under the classicist theologian Benjamin Jowett and was a protégé of Sir Evelyn Baring, the first Earl of Cromer and a Baring Brothers partner. He was active in the Royal Colonial Institute, financed by Barclays Bank, the Barings, the Sassoons and Jardine Matheson, the founders of the Hong Kong Shanghai Bank, who made a fortune from the Asiatic drug trade. Alfred Marshall, an economist associated with the Royal Colonial Society, originated the monetarist philosophy adopted by Milton Friedman, formerly of the Hoover Institution, a "right-wing" think-tank. Marshall, via his connection to the Oxford Group, mentored Wesley C. Mitchell, director of the National Bureau of Economic Research, who then instructed Arthur F. Burns (Burnseig) and Friedman.[594] Mitchell attended the University of Chicago, where he studied under John Dewey and earned a PhD in 1899.

Rothschild, as the Rhodes trustee, managed his estate according to one of the seven wills that Rhodes left. The Pilgrims Society would devote its efforts to "the extension of British rule throughout the world." Rhodes argued that the "British elite" were entitled to rule the world for the benefit of mankind. In the past, rule meant the seizure and exploitation of the world's raw materials, like gold and oil, through her military dominance overseas. An attachment to his will mandated the creation of the Rhodes scholarship. His will also directed "the furtherance of the British Empire, for the bringing of the whole uncivilized world under British rule, for the recovery of the United States, for the making the Anglo-Saxon race but one Empire."[595] In another will, he states, "To and for the establishment,

---

594 Eustace Mullins, The World Order, a Study in the Hegemony of Parasitism, Ezra Pound Institute of Civilization, Staunton, Virginia, 1985, p. 23
595 Alan B. Jones, How The World Really Works, ABJ Press, Paradise, California, 1997 p. 67; Cecil Rhodes by John Flint, Rhodes House, Oxford, 1974, book

promotion, and development of a secret society, the true aim of which and object whereof shall be the extension of British rule throughout the world . . . and finally the foundation of so great a power as to hereafter render wars impossible and promote the best interests of humanity."[596] The Pilgrims Society's major economic target was Germany, a country whose citizens were highly skilled.

Attorney Lindsay Russell, founder and president of the Japan Society and a junior partner with Carter, Hughes & Dwight of New York, visited London. In his quest to organize International Friendship Societies, he met with Lord Frederick Roberts, General Joseph Wheeler, and Sir Harry Brittain at the Carlton Hotel on July 11, 1902, along with forty other people.[597] General Wheeler presided. Two weeks later, members elected Roberts as president of the Pilgrims Society, with Lord Francis Grenfell and Admiral Hedworth Lambton as the British vice presidents and Senator Chauncey M. Depew (S&B) and Wheeler as the Society's US vice presidents.[598] Hugh Fisher, using Russell's suggestions, designed the Pilgrims Society emblem in 1902 which received the approval of Rider Haggard, author of *King Solomon's Mines*.[599]

Upon their return to New York, Russell and Depew approached the Bishop of New York, Henry C. Potter, J. Pierpont Morgan Sr., and former President Grover Cleveland to entice them to join the society,

pages are not numbered

[596] Frederick Franklin Schrader, "1683-1920" The Fourteen Points and What Became of them, Foreign Propaganda in the Public Schools, Rewriting the History of the United States, Concord Publishing Company, Incorporated, New York, 1920, p. 195

[597] Promoter Of International Amity; Lindsay Russell's Hobby Is the Encouragement of Better Feeling Between Our Country and Others, and He Applies Science to It by Hamilton Holt, New York Times, April 4, 1920, p. XX7

[598] Joël van der Reijden, The Pilgrim Society: a Study of the Anglo-American Establishment, Institute for the Study of Globalization & Covert Politics, July 2008, p. 5

[599] Anne Pimlott Baker, The Pilgrims of Great Britain, a Centennial History, Profile Books, London, England, the copyright is held by the Pilgrims of Great Britain, 2002, p. 10

which they organized on January 13, 1903. Cleveland became a member.[600] American surnames associated with the Pilgrims Society include Astor, Aldrich, Belmont, Baker, Carnegie, Dillon, Dodge, Drexel, Duke, DuPont, Gould, Harkness, Harriman, Lamont, Lodge, Loeb, Mellon, Meyer, Morgan, Peabody, Pyne, Reynolds, Rockefeller, Schiff, Stillman, Vanderbilt, Warburg, Watson, and Whitney. There are now about 1,500 members, most of them US citizens who manage huge corporations, banks, law firms, and insurance and media companies.[601]

Lord Frederick Roberts, president of the British Pilgrims, died on November 14, 1914, which prompted memorials in New York and London. Major General Leonard Wood, military governor of Cuba for four years, remarked in his eulogy that Roberts encouraged the "strengthening of the military and naval defenses of the country," a euphemism for militarizing a country for offensive warfare.[602]

Isaac Seligman, a Pilgrims Society member, married into the Loeb banking family. John L. Loeb Jr. was also a Pilgrims Society member. J. & W. Seligman & Company had offices in Manhattan by 1878. They later relocated to 54 Wall Street and interlocked with the Anglo-California Bank. Seligman was a London correspondent for the London Rothschilds and associated with Nathan Rothschild, a member of Parliament (1865-1885). The Rothschilds, the Morgans, and the Seligmans backed the Society's first transaction of $55 million.[603]

---

[600] Charles Savoie, Pilgrims, Silver Investor, May 2005, www.silver-investor. com/charlessavoie/cs_may05_pilgrims.htm as of May 2012

[601] Joël van der Reijden, The Pilgrim Society: a Study of the Anglo-American Establishment, Institute for the Study of Globalization & Covert Politics, July 2008, pp. 5-6

[602] Pilgrim Memorial For Lord Roberts, International Societies to Commemorate Field Marshal in England and America, May Be In Trinity Church Famous British Soldier Eulogized at Luncheon Here—Sympathy Sent to Widow, New York Times, January 28, 1915, p. 6

[603] Charles Savoie, Pilgrims, Silver Investor, May 2005, www.silver-investor. com/charlessavoie/cs_may05_pilgrims.htm as of May 2012

People referred to the Seligmans as the "American Rothschilds." Isaac Seligman was a trustee of Munich Reinsurance Company and the Russia Reinsurance Company. The banking conspiracy is not necessarily ethnic-based but centered on society membership, especially the Pilgrims Society. The Seligmans intermarried with the Guggenheims, who got wealthy through their South American mining efforts. The Guggenheims were also associated with the Pilgrims.[604]

Winston Churchill advocated total war and pushed for "victory at any price" during the Boer War (October 11, 1899-May 31, 1902). He supported Lord Herbert H. Kitchener's scorched-earth policies against the civilian population. In the early 1930s, Churchill wrote, "I have always urged fighting wars and other contentions with might and main till overwhelming victory, and then offering the hand of friendship to the vanquished."[605] Kitchener was a freemason, a fellowship whose upper echelon appears to support genocide. The whole point of the Boer War was to enable Britain to seize South Africa's mineral wealth. In 1886, explorers had discovered massive gold deposits in the South African Republic, which immediately drew British interests to that country.

Lord Frederick Roberts and Kitchener, during the Second Boer War, gained notoriety for incarcerating thousands of Boers and black Africans in concentration camps, where many of them starved to death. The pair orchestrated the burning of farms, which forced the inhabitants to flee. They also salted the fields to senselessly destroy productivity causing many farmers to abandon their farmlands. Kitchener was Roberts's chief-of-staff and earned a reputation for his utter ruthlessness.[606] Expansionists and soldiers, like Rhodes, Milner, Kitchener, and Roberts, became national heroes due to the "imperial propaganda" that saturated society. People then embraced the imperial dogma, because imperialism generated profits instead of

---

[604] Ibid
[605] Tuvia Ben-Moshe, Churchill, Strategy and History, Lynne Rienner, Boulder, Colorado, 1992, pp. 71-72
[606] Fred R. Van Hartesveldt, The Boer War: Historiography and Annotated Bibliography, Greenwood Press, Westport, Connecticut, 2000, pp. 30, 36

expenses.[607] Roberts's estate in 1915 was £77,304 (equivalent to £5.32 million today). Milner, the British High Commissioner of Southern Africa, was largely to blame for starting the war in the Union of South Africa.

Milner's Kindergarten supervised the postwar Reconstruction Administration in South Africa, which ultimately became the Union of South Africa. They installed unelected local officials, who restructured the economy and instituted the gold standard. Obedient civil servants reorganized ethnic groups in the interior of what were previously the Boer Republics to inculcate a new distinctiveness— British South Africans, who would later be white South Africans. Four years later, the Boer Rebellion erupted. The measures imposed at that time produced South Africa's current political and socioeconomic environment.

As the media grew in importance, secret alliances seized and dominated the flow of information. In 1920, Milner and Lord Robert Cecil, along with J. P. Morgan associates, created the Illuminati-based Royal Institute of International Affairs (RIIA), a Milner group subsidiary, based in St. James's Square, London, following a meeting at the previous year's Paris Peace Conference. On July 29, 1921, they incorporated the Council on Foreign Relations (CFR), a branch of Britain's RIIA, in New York. In 1925, they established the Institute of Pacific Relations (IPR). Lippmann, a Fabian, was a member of the American Round Table. On April 7, 1785, Professor Vitus Renner, had said, "The Illuminati fear nothing more than to be known under their right name. They hide under the cloak of freemasonry."[608]

There is a lengthy, close relationship between the Milner Group, J. P. Morgan, and the Carnegie Trust. Those directly involved included Thomas W. Lamont, a Morgan banker who focused on information

[607] Denis Judd, The British Imperial Experience from 1765 to the Present, Basic Books, New York, 1996, p. 9
[608] Jüri Lina, Architects of Deception, Referent Publishing, Stockholm, Sweden, 2004, pp. 338-339

control, and Jerome Greene of Lee, Higginson and Company.[609] The London Rothschilds established a business alliance with Lee, Higginson & Company of Boston in 1901.[610] Rockefeller's Standard Oil treasurer, Charles Pratt, bestowed his New York mansion to the CFR to use as its world headquarters.

Greene, with both Morgan and Rockefeller interests, chaired the Pacific Council of the Institute of Pacific Relations (1929-1932), a CFR spinoff. Lamont also had an influential position in that organization. J. P. Morgan immediately seized control of the CFR after its creation in New York. Carroll Quigley claimed that the US Eastern Establishment was a branch of the British Establishment.[611]

In 1919, after the first premeditated World War, to memorialize the clandestine alliance, Irving T. Bush, a US industrialist and Pilgrims Society member, built the London Bush house. In the portico high above, there is a magnificent statue of two muscular classic warriors, each with a shield. The inscription on the base of the statue reads, "To the friendship of English Speaking Peoples." The warriors symbolize the United States and Britain. Just as enlightening is the single flaming torch they jointly hold high in the air. People personify Lucifer, the morning star, as a male figure bearing a torch. Elitists use buildings, statues, obelisks, phallic symbols to reveal, in plain sight, their demonic intentions to govern the entire world.

Pilgrim Society members have filled prominent, influential positions. Harvard-educated C. Douglas Dillon, the grandson of Samuel Lapowski, a Jewish immigrant, and the son of Clarence Dillon, was ambassador to France (1953-1957) and a secretary of the Treasury (1961-1965) during the time that the government demonetized silver. Dillon was the vice president and director of Dillon, Read &

---

609 Donald Gibson, Communication, Power, and Media, Nova Science Publishers, Inc., New York, 2004, pp. 77-78
610 Rondo E. Cameron, International banking, 1870-1914, Valerii Ivanovich Bovykin, B. V. Anan□ich, Oxford University Press, New York, 1991, pp. 244-245
611 Donald Gibson, Communication, Power, and Media, Nova Science Publishers, Inc., New York, 2004, pp. 77-78

Company, and then became chairman of the firm in 1946. People refer to the negotiations (1960-1962) for the acceptance of the General Agreement on Tariffs and Trade (GATT) in Geneva, Switzerland, as the Dillon Round, because he suggested the meetings. These negotiations led to a huge decrease in tariffs. He was chairman of the Rockefeller Foundation (1972-1975) and a close associate of John D. Rockefeller, III. He participated, with Rockefeller, on the 1973 Commission on Private Philanthropy and Public Needs. He has been president of Harvard Board of Overseers, chairman of the Brookings Institution, and a CFR vice chairman.

C. Douglas Dillon and President Lyndon B. Johnson removed the use of silver coins during the time that William David Ormsby-Gore, Fifth Baron Harlech, also a Pilgrims Society member, was ambassador to Washington.[612] His father, William Ormsby-Gore, Fourth Baron Harlech, was also a Pilgrims Society member.

The Pilgrims Society awards an honorary membership to London's secretary of state for Foreign Affairs, the American minister in London, the British consul general in New York, the British ambassador to America, the US ambassador to England, the British ambassador to the United Nations, the US secretary of state, and the US president. The secretary of state manages all official state business with all foreign ambassadors.[613] Since 1903, the very secretive Pilgrims Society has granted an honorary membership to every US president and secretary of state.

Imperialism Abroad, Debt Enslavement at Home

The Metropolitan Club, the gathering place for military officers, officials and diplomats, opened in 1863 at Seventeenth and H Street, close to the State, War, and Navy Departments in Washington. By the 1890s, all the prominent US imperialists, civilian and military, gathered there—Henry Cabot Lodge, Theodore Roosevelt, Elihu Root, Senator James D. Cameron, Commodore George Dewey, Commodore

---

[612] Charles Savoie, Meet the World Money Power, December 2004, p. 14, http://freedom4um.com/cgi-bin/readart.cgi?ArtNum=20574 as of May 2012
[613] Ibid

Winfield Scott Schley, Captain R. Evans, and Lieutenant Colonel Arthur MacArthur, a freemason. Presidents and vice presidents were honorary members and were always welcome.[614]

John Hay, Lincoln's assistant private secretary, believed that the Civil War transformed the United States into a great nation. He said the military needed to protect the nation against any who should attempt to subvert its achievements, evidently, even if it meant killing the nation's citizens who favored states' rights over a centralized government. Secretary of State William H. Seward, former governor of New York and Hay's mentor, encouraged American imperialism.[615]

A cozy relationship between the government and industry materialized during the Civil War, with the alliance of the US Navy and the emerging steel industry. After the war, officials neglected the maintenance of the US Navy's powerful 700-ship fleet, specifically designed for defense and composed of shallow-draft monitors to repel invasions. Rather, government officials focused on reconstruction and other domestic issues. Meanwhile, England and France were competing in a naval arms race and were purchasing the best equipment offered by private industry. Shipyards in England and France were soon accepting foreign orders.[616]

By 1867, through Seward, Hay associated with some of the most powerful elected and appointed political figures in Washington, including Senator Charles Sumner and Justice Salmon P. Chase. Seward arranged Hay's diplomatic appointment to Vienna as chargé d'affaires (1868-1870). He was then back in New York, writing editorials about foreign affairs, national politics, and cultural issues for Horace Greeley's *Tribune*. Hay befriended Walt Whitman, Bret

---

[614] Warren Zimmerman, First Great Triumph, How Five Americans Made Their Country a World Power, Farrar, Straus and Giroux, New York, 2002, pp. 180-181

[615] Ibid. 52-60, 71

[616] Kurt Hackemer, The US Navy and the Late Nineteenth-Century Steel Industry, The Historian, Volume 57, Issue: 4, 1995, p. 703+

Harte, and Mark Twain; and financiers William Astor, Jay Gould, and William K. Vanderbilt.[617]

Since the Rockefeller Empire was in Ohio, it is not surprising that Ohio was the pinnacle of nineteenth-century politics. Between 1869 and 1901, five out of seven presidents, all Republicans, came from Ohio—Ulysses S. Grant, Rutherford B. Hayes, James A. Garfield, William H. Harrison, and William McKinley. All had been in the Union Army. William T. Sherman, Phil Sheridan, and John Sheridan, the Treasury secretary, a Senator, and secretary of state were also from Ohio, as was Senator Joseph B. Foraker, who played a key role in US policies in Cuba and Puerto Rico.[618]

During the 1870s and early 1880s, even Chile, with British-built ships, was better equipped than the United States. Therefore, Congress used the treasury surplus, derived from tariffs, to fund the building of the first steel ships in the navy's history. The United States, at that time, opposed dependency on foreign supplies and technology for their defense requirements.[619]

In 1882, military theorist Alfred Thayer Mahan, a Philolexian member, argued for a navy with larger, steam-driven, steel-hull battleships to protect a growing commercial empire and for offensive warfare. Sea power, he maintained, controlled the results of every major conflict. Britain's capacity to blockade errant countries into desperate starvation supported his argument. He prompted officials to acquire coal stations and establish bases, especially in Hawaii, on the way to Asia, a potential Mecca for commercialization, and in the Caribbean. Later, War Secretary Henry L. Stimson referred to him as the navy's prophet. In 1883, Congress allocated money to

---

[617] Warren Zimmerman, First Great Triumph, How Five Americans Made Their Country a World Power, Farrar, Straus and Giroux, New York, 2002, pp. 52-60

[618] Ibid. 25-28

[619] Kurt Hackemer, The US Navy and the Late Nineteenth-Century Steel Industry, The Historian, Volume 57, Issue: 4, 1995, p. 703+

restructure the navy.[620] Andrew Carnegie provided the steel for the navy's buildup.

On October 6, 1884, Commodore Stephen B. Luce, Mahan's mentor, established and became the first president of the US Naval War College at Newport, Rhode Island, to teach naval officers the latest in seaborne weaponry and to produce brighter, better-trained, highly skilled naval personnel. The college began teaching war-gaming tactics in 1887, ultimately becoming a war-plans development laboratory. Mahan began teaching at the naval college in 1886 after spending nine months of preparation in prominent libraries.[621]

Mahan became president of the college (1886-1889, 1892-1893), during which time he published his book, *The Influence of Sea Power upon History, 1660-1783*. The book, acclaimed by US policy makers, examined Britain's status as a world power—apparently, a strong navy is indispensable proof of a great nation. His book appealed to industrialists, especially those who had an imperialistic worldview without regard for national sovereignty. Six weeks after his death, Theodore Roosevelt wrote *A Great Public Servant*, an obituary. He said that Mahan stood alone in his greatest skill—educating the public to a "true understanding of naval needs" and the "only great naval writer who also possessed in international matters the mind of a statesman of the first class."[622]

In 1884, citizens elected Grover Cleveland as president. Morgan interests controlled both Cleveland administrations (1884-1888, 1892-1896). He accommodated certain individuals on Wall Street and allowed them to purchase US gold bonds at highly reduced rates while forcing taxpayers to bail out the government. Morgan, August Belmont, and their British backers continued to force prices

[620] Warren Zimmerman, First Great Triumph, How Five Americans Made Their Country a World Power, Farrar, Straus and Giroux, New York, 2002, p. 87
[621] Stuart Creighton Miller, "Benevolent Assimilation," the American Conquest of the Philippines, 1899-1903, Yale University Press, New Haven and London, 1982, pp. 3, 5, 7
[622] Richard W. Turk, The Ambiguous Relationship: Theodore Roosevelt and Alfred Thayer Mahan, Greenwood Press, New York, 1987, pp. 2-3

down between the dollar and US gold stocks, which accelerated the 1890s depression. The Rothschild-controlled British Empire was intent on maintaining its control of the world's capital while retaining dominance of the world's trade markets. Montagu Norman, who controlled the Bank of England, viewed the United States as a threat. Therefore, he executed economic warfare in an attempt to restore Britain's declining economic power, which had decreased because of the huge debt incurred by their numerous wars around the world.[623]

Both J. Pierpont Morgan, later a Pilgrims Society member, and Belmont regularly visited President Cleveland and maintained constant correspondence with him, persuading him to issue each of them government bonds in exchange for gold. Wall Street banks then immediately bought the gold from the Treasury, making it necessary to issue more bonds. Cleveland's former law partner, Francis L. Stetson, negotiated and bought the bargain bonds from the Treasury and sold the bonds to the bankers who resold them at higher prices, all in behalf of J. P. Morgan.[624]

After 1873, J. P. Morgan became the leading US investment firm and wielded the most influence in the Democrat Party. Belmont was the treasurer of that party for many years. The Treasury was almost bankrupt and faced imminent budget deficits when Cleveland, the only Democrat that Morgan had ever voted for, relinquished control of the US public debt to Morgan and Belmont, both Rothschild associates.[625] America had insufficient gold and was unable restore solvency in the Treasury. The government relied on the Rothschilds, who agreed to a European bond issue only if Morgan personally handled the US portion of the preparations with their New York representative, August Belmont Jr.[626]

---

[623] Charles Merlin Umpenhour, Freedom, a Fading Illusion, BookMakers Ink, West Virginia, 2005, pp. 134-136
[624] Ferdinand Lundberg, America's 60 Families, The Citadel Press, 1937, p. 55-57
[625] Charles Merlin Umpenhour, Freedom, a Fading Illusion, BookMakers Ink, West Virginia, 2005, pp. 134-136
[626] Peter L. Bernstein, The Power of Gold: The History of an Obsession, Wiley, New York, 2000, pp. 274-275

When Cleveland left the presidency, Morgan awarded him with an appointment as a trustee of the Harriman-Ryan Equitable Life Assurance Society, which was also good publicity for the company. Cleveland then dabbled in a stock-market pool with Oliver H. Payne, William C. Whitney (S&B), and Senator Calvin S. Brice.[627] Cleveland was also a Princeton University trustee and was a member of the Executive Committee of the National Civic Federation. He maintained his relationship with Morgan, whose banks, along with the other huge institutions, had waged war against the use of silver as money beginning in 1878.[628]

Cleveland, as a railroad lawyer, handled the Morgan-controlled New York Central Railroad. He was a partner (1888-1892) in Bangs, Stetson, Tracey and MacVeagh, a major Morgan law firm. Charles B. Tracey, one of the partners, was J. Pierpont Morgan's brother-in-law. Morgan men filled Cleveland's cabinet, especially in positions dealing with foreign policy. Belmont mentored Thomas F. Bayard (S&B), who was Cleveland's first secretary of state. Bayard, later a Pilgrims Society member, was US minister to Britain in 1893.[629]

Richard Olney, after attending Brown University and Harvard Law School, went to work for Judge Benjamin F. Thomas in his prominent law firm. He married Agnes, the judge's daughter, and inherited the lucrative law practice when the judge died in 1876. Olney was an attorney for Boston's corporate aristocracy. Olney dabbled in politics, in the state legislature, but the citizens did not reelect him for a second term. He then focused on corporate law, particularly railroad law, and, in the early 1880s, he manipulated the law in favor of the Eastern Railroad Company's monopoly in the northern part of the state. In 1893, Cleveland appointed him attorney general.[630] Cleveland also appointed Olney as secretary of state (1895-1897).

---

627 Ferdinand Lundberg, America's 60 Families, The Citadel Press, 1937, p. 55-57
628 Charles Savoie, Pilgrims, Silver Investor, May 2005, www.silver-investor. com/charlessavoie/cs_may05_pilgrims.htm as of May 2012
629 Ibid
630 Edward S. Mihalkanin (editor) American Statesmen: Secretaries of State from John Jay to Colin Powell, Greenwood Press, Westport, Connecticut, 2004, p. 393

Olney assisted Morgan in organizing the General Electric Company in 1902. He claimed that the United States, despite abundant resources, needed to develop greater commercial interests and larger markets elsewhere, while seizing a powerful position among the nations. The bankers governed the War and Navy departments during Cleveland's presidency. War Secretary William C. Endicott married into the wealthy Peabody family, which had a close relationship with J. P. Morgan.

New York financier William C. Whitney, close to Morgan, was Cleveland's Navy secretary. Whitney married Oliver H. Payne's daughter, and they were the parents of Harry Payne Whitney (S&B), Payne Whitney, Lady Almeric Paget, and Mrs. Willard D. Straight. Because of his ties to Richard Croker, he was the Rockefeller pipeline into the Cleveland cabinet. The president acknowledged that he owed his nomination to Whitney, his campaign financier. Cleveland, like most politicians, was willing to use other people's money and acquiesce to their agenda while gaining personal financial benefits.[631]

Daniel S. Lamont, a Whitney protégé, was Cleveland's first War secretary in his second administration. Cleveland appointed attorney Hilary A. Herbert, a congressman and cofounder of Lehman Brothers, as Navy secretary. During his second administration (1888-1892), US foreign policy shifted from peaceful, nonintervention to aggressive economic and political interference and expansionism, provoked by bankers who were competing with the London bankers. They initially targeted Latin America, where they sought to subsidize new export markets, increase investment opportunities, and secure government bonds.

In 1894, British bankers economically assaulted the United States again, causing another depression and high unemployment. America's hardworking independent farmers became urbanized wage slaves, especially between 1880 and 1890. Self-employed individuals began working for big corporations, in manufacturing and industry. The

---

[631] Ferdinand Lundberg, America's 60 Families, The Citadel Press, 1937, p. 55-57

depression affected this group the most. The number of unemployed doubled to 4,712,000.[632] Rothschild's *Hazard Circular* (July 1862) referred to his European plan, wherein capital controlled labor by controlling wages.[633] People then began to look to the government, another entity outside of themselves, for problem solution.

People expected that the Cleveland administration would do something to revitalize the economy before any severe social turmoil occurred. Washington residents engaged in disorder, and people spoke of a reign of terror. Government officials canceled scheduled leaves, and the Treasury directed special military personnel to stand guard at the sub-treasuries in Chicago and New York, where there was public dissent against the economic situation. Railroad magnate James J. Hill wrote War Secretary Lamont about engaging state and federal troops to halt potential strikes. *The Bankers' magazine* took a dim view of Cleveland's use of military force to end the Pullman Strike, which set a very dangerous precedent.[634]

Things appeared to improve by the last day of January 1895, when the stock market soared upward, and the dollar gained strength in the foreign markets. Foreign business interests canceled their existing orders for gold, and laborers unloaded the $9 million in gold already aboard ships. The naïve masses failed to recognize what caused the sudden shift in their fortunes.[635] Morgan had simply exercised his influence on both sides of the Atlantic. Author Ron Chernow explains that it was Morgan's orchestrated plot to retain the gold standard. Cleveland, between his presidential terms, had worked adjacent to Morgan's bank, and they were close neighbors in a posh Princeton, New Jersey suburb.[636] Cleveland probably conspired with

[632]   Walter Lafeber, The New Empire: An Interpretation of American Expansion, 1860-1898, Cornell University Press, 1998, pp. 173-175

[633]   Charles A. Lindbergh, Banking and Currency and the Money Trust, National Capital Press, Inc., Washington, DC, 1913, p. 32

[634]   Walter Lafeber, The New Empire: An Interpretation of American Expansion, 1860-1898, Cornell University Press, 1998, pp. 173-175

[635]   Peter L. Bernstein, The Power of Gold: The History of an Obsession, Wiley, New York, 2000, pp. 274-275

[636]   Ibid. 274-275

Morgan during this economic fiasco and exercised the full limits of his military power against the workers at Pullman and elsewhere. A national monetary crisis, always devised, provides an opportunity to increase and exercise government power.

Gold outflow recommenced in early February 1895. The president's cabinet steadfastly opposed a bond issue that indebted the US government to foreign bankers. Morgan was enraged when he notified his London partners that the United States was in the midst of the great financial chaos. Morgan and Belmont, in a private railroad car, arrived in Washington, where an assistant told them the president was unavailable. Morgan said, "I have come down to see the president, and I am going to stay here until I see him." Almost immediately, Cleveland, John G. Carlisle, the Treasury Secretary, and Secretary Olney were in a meeting, during which a clerk entered and informed Carlisle that there was only $9 million in gold coin remaining in the vaults. There seemed no choice. Cleveland accepted financial indebtedness, owed indirectly, via its agents, to the Rothschilds, on behalf of the US taxpayers.[637]

Morgan's plan included selling a Treasury bond issue of about $65 million to a European Rothschild/Morgan consortium, with payment to be made in 3.5 million ounces of gold coin, about one hundred tons. About half of this gold would come from European banks with an interest rate nearly a full percentage point higher than the New York banks had previously received in Carlisle's 1894 negotiations.[638]

Presumably, the US treasury would protect the gold against withdrawal, pending completion of the contract. The Morgan-Rothschild syndicate manipulated the gold market and loaned its stash of European currencies to Americans, who owed money to Europeans, to halt the demand for the conversion of dollars into gold. Finally, the syndicate combined every banking house in New York City with European connections, making them a part of the bond issue.[639] Meanwhile, in 1894, Olney, with Cleveland's consent,

---

[637] Ibid. 274-275
[638] Ibid. 274-275
[639] Ibid. 274-275

used the navy to seize Britain's Latin America markets. It disrupted Britain's blockade and placed warships in the harbor at Rio de Janeiro to end the British-backed rebellion intent on restoring Brazil's monarchy. The United States, Britain, and Nicaragua had long battled over Nicaragua's Caribbean coast. Britain wanted to make the area a protectorate, establish a colony, and possibly construct a canal to the Pacific Ocean. However, Nicaragua had always claimed the area, and José Santos Zelaya sent forces to occupy and annex it in 1894. Britain relinquished it when the United States sent the marines and forcefully ousted the British and brought Zelaya into line in order to take over the Miskito Coast, an independent reservation and home for the Indians.

Between 1895 and 1896, the United States and Britain almost came to blows over a longtime territorial dispute between Venezuela and British Guiana. Venezuelan officials granted concessions to US businesses in the gold fields in the disputed area. Henry Cabot Lodge used his best rhetoric to pressure fellow senators, who then pressured Cleveland. Secretary Olney sent a note to the British, delivered in London on July 20, 1895, in which he bragged, "The United States is practically sovereign on this continent," which the British did not receive very well. In December, Cleveland asked Congress to consider using military force against British aggressiveness in the Caribbean, which made Lodge ecstatic. Theodore Roosevelt, then president of the Board of New York City Police Commissioners, was prepared to go to war. The United States could have held British Canada hostage, so the two countries negotiated. Britain would stay out of Latin America and would share whatever Asian resources they acquired through military force with the United States.[640]

Britain financed Japan's plundering, beginning in 1895 in Korea. Presumably, the United States, according to that agreement, was a copartner with Britain and a recipient of the pillaging. Given relatively recent Anglo American history, and the elite's resource-seizure agenda, they are still partners in their world plunder.

---

[640] Warren Zimmerman, First Great Triumph, How Five Americans Made Their Country a World Power, Farrar, Straus and Giroux, New York, 2002, pp. 153-154

Cleveland's close friend, Democrat Don M. Dickinson, gave a speech in May 1895, at the banquet of the Loyal Legion in Detroit. He said, "We need and must have open markets throughout the world to maintain and increase our prosperity."[641] In 1899, Secretary of State John Hay said, "In the field of trade and commerce we shall be the keen competitors of the richest and greatest powers, and they need no warning to be assured that in that struggle, we shall bring the sweat to their brows."[642] He had an "open-door" policy for China, which signaled US interest in the Pacific. His unabashed Anglophilia launched a lengthy alliance with Britain.

Monopolies and Trusts—the Standard Oil Trust

Author Larry Abraham wrote, "If you wish to establish national monopolies, you must control national governments; if you wish to establish international monopolies or cartels, you must control a world government."[643] The Rockefellers and their multiple industrial interests are a prime example of a monopoly trust.

In 1861, John D. Rockefeller and Henry M. Flagler set up a small oil refinery in Cleveland, and, by 1870, Standard Oil Company of Ohio had absorbed all of its rivals. Rockefeller controlled the entire oil trade of the country from his Cleveland headquarters.[644] He attempted to control the US oil and natural gas industries and crush his competitors through illegal price rebates.[645]

Oil was the fourth-largest US export by 1872 and the number one man-made export product. Within five years, Rockefeller was selling millions of gallons of oil and making millions of dollars and paying

[641] Dickinson Sounds the Note; His Warning to Watch the Attitude of Great Britain, New York Times, May 15, 1895, p. 13
[642] William Appleman Williams, The Contours of American History, World Publishing, Cleveland, Ohio, 1961, p. 346
[643] Larry Abraham, Call It Conspiracy, Double A Publications, Seattle, Washington, 1971, p. 89
[644] James Harrison Kennedy, A History Of The City Of Cleveland: Its Settlement, Rise, and Progress, 1796-1896, The Imperial Press, 1896, pp. 391-392
[645] Charles R. Morris, The tycoons, Macmillan, Henry Holt and Company, New York, 2005, pp. 83-84

huge dividends, as much as 50 percent.[646] He negotiated and obtained better freight prices and preferential treatment from the Pennsylvania, New York Central, and Erie Railroads, which agreed to give him rebates giving him incredible competitive advantages. Standard controlled a majority of the pipelines, engaged in price-cutting, and maintained a spy network to report on his competitors' operations, many of whom he bankrupted. By 1879, he would control about 90 percent of the US refining business and every important pipeline in the oil fields.[647] [648]

Independent craftsmen and laborers left the small towns and farms, and arriving immigrants soon became the part of the factory system in rapidly growing cities, living in cheaply constructed tenements. Meanwhile, the innovative industrialists and their corporations supplanted independent entrepreneurs. By the 1870s, of the 10,395 businesses in Massachusetts, only 520 (five percent) were incorporated. However, this minority possessed 96 percent of the total capital and employed 60 percent of all the labor.[649]

European buyers resented Standard's practices and terms, but Standard had a monopoly. The Germans were particularly anxious to disentangle themselves from Standard. By the late 1870s, other European countries were also seeking to break Standard's hold on them, especially when Standard raised its domestic and foreign prices for refined oil. Germans held meetings to determine how to manage the elevated prices and the devious policies, and they then began purchasing crude oil from independents who escaped Standard's

---

[646]   Stephen Pelletière, Iraq and the International Oil System: Why America Went to War in the Gulf, Praeger, Westport, Connecticut, 2001, pp. 6-7

[647]   Harry W. Laidler, Concentration of Control in American Industry, Thomas Y. Crowell, New York, 1931, pp. 15-18

[648]   Stephen Pelletière, Iraq and the International Oil System: Why America Went to War in the Gulf, Praeger, Westport, Connecticut, 2001, pp. 4-6

[649]   E. Richard Brown, Rockefeller Medicine Men, Medicine and Capitalism in America and the World, University of California Press, Berkeley, Los Angeles, 1979, pp. 16-17

competitive clutches. The Germans built refineries and processed the crude themselves, which infuriated Rockefeller.[650]

On January 2, 1882, Rockefeller created the Standard Oil trust, where trustees controlled the entire stock of fourteen companies and the majority stock of twenty-six others. Soon Ohio state officials, aware of this trust, took court action.[651] Yet the courts, controlled by complicit lawyers, failed. Rockefeller simply moved the company from Ohio to New Jersey which had lenient laws regarding corporations, thanks to numerous lawyers who served the industrial moguls and maintained close connections to state and federal governments. In New Jersey, the trust became a holding company, which functioned exactly like a trust.[652]

Standard had a capital stock of $97,500,000. The original board of directors was composed of John D. Rockefeller, Henry M. Flagler, Samuel Andrews, Stephen V. Harkness, and William Rockefeller. As early as 1884, the Board of Trade reported that the capital invested in the manufacture of oil in Cleveland was $27,395,746. There were eighty-six establishments, employing 9,869 individuals. Yearly wages totaled $4,381,572. The establishments used $34,999,101 worth of raw material. Crude oils costs totaled $16,340,581, while they paid $811,618,307 for barrels, $2,792,997 for tin cans, $906,911 for cases, and $645,412 for bungs, paint, glue, etc. The combined value of the products manufactured from crude petroleum totaled $43,705,218. Illuminating oils brought in $36,839,613. In the previous year (1883), they refined about 3,263 barrels of crude oil in Cleveland.[653]

While Ohio allowed the creation of holding companies, New Jersey allowed corporations to hold each other's stock. Standard Oil, in New

---

[650] Stephen Pelletière, Iraq and the International Oil System: Why America Went to War in the Gulf, Praeger, Westport, Connecticut, 2001, pp. 8-11

[651] Harry W. Laidler, Concentration of Control in American Industry, Thomas Y. Crowell, New York, 1931, pp. 15-18

[652] Stephen Pelletière, Iraq and the International Oil System: Why America Went to War in the Gulf, Praeger, Westport, Connecticut, 2001, pp. 8-9

[653] James Harrison Kennedy, A History Of The City Of Cleveland: Its Settlement, Rise, And Progress, 1796-1896, The Imperial Press, 1896, pp. 391-392

Jersey, could enjoy shared ownership, which perpetuated the incidence of monopolies, apparent in both industry and banking. A holding company allowed industrialists and bankers to avoid the Sherman Anti-Trust Act of July 2, 1890. With a holding company, companies bought each other's stock and camouflaged the actual ownership of many firms. Further, larger, wealthier companies maneuvered and controlled prices, upset competition, and then acquired their rival's companies.[654]

Circumstances throughout the country made riots common and the environment ripe for strikes and protests. Laborers were tired of the depressed wages and exploitation and began to organize into unions and make demands. Employers responded by using their influence with the local and federal governments, who hired thugs like the Pinkerton Agency or used federal troops. Strikes continued, from the first nationwide strike (July 14, 1877), when railroad workers struck in the middle of an economic depression, to local strikes and major disturbances, such as Haymarket Square bomb (May 4, 1886), the Homestead strike at Carnegie's Homestead steel mills (June 29, 1892), and the Pullman Strike (May 11, 1894). Farmers in the Midwest and in the South were especially hard hit, as they had to consider railroad rates to transport their produce and depend on credit lines from bigger banks located elsewhere rather than local state banks. These factors kept many farmers, especially those in the South, in continuous debt.[655]

These neophyte corporate owners were greedy for their share of the market and, in an effort to accumulate capital, decreased wages and prices to quash their competitors. Almost 16,000,000 recent immigrants, anxious for employment and a new life composed almost 15 percent of the population by 1890 and about 25 percent of the population of the more industrialized Northeastern states. Machines replaced many of the functions that skilled craftsmen

---

[654] Charles R. Geisst, Wall Street: A History from Its Beginnings to the Fall of Enron, Oxford University Press, New York, 2004, p. 127

[655] E. Richard Brown, Rockefeller Medicine Men, Medicine and Capitalism in America and the World, University of California Press, Berkeley, Los Angeles, 1979, pp. 16-17

previously employed to earn their living. Thus, many faced insecurity and unemployment. They, along with migrants, farmers, immigrants, and recently unemployed workers, soon resorted to working in the factories. By 1900, difficult times had compelled about 20 percent of the nation's women to abandon full-time household chores to work long hours in the factories, where oppressive owners paid them low wages.[656] By 1900, corporations produced three-fourths of all manufactured goods. The Civil War produced an industrial system, and the predatory men who devised the corporations were ultimately the real victors.[657]

Without the post-Civil War legislation, moguls, collaborating with lawmakers, could not have created their monopolies. The new corporations used loopholes in the law to suppress competition and regulate the refinement of natural resources, like gold, diamonds, sugar, or oil and the production, distribution, and pricing of specific products. Devised underproduction increases profits and creates shortages, a hardship for consumers, while calculated overproduction eliminates beleaguered, underfunded competitors. Ultimately, control of resources and manufactured products culminates in the unconditional management of labor and population, particularly true when the state serves the interest of a small minority. Monopolies also exist in the service industry—medical education and practice, banking, insurance, public transportation, communication, general education, and in consumer utilities—gas, water, electricity, garbage collection, and other services.

In 1897, the Standard Oil Company of New Jersey emerged as a corporation, with a capitalization of $100,000,000. To avoid competition and duplication of effort, the subsidiary companies had specific operations or market areas. It divided the United States into eleven marketing districts where each Standard company operated. In 1904, Standard controlled over 86 percent of the refined illuminating oil in the United States, which left little for the independent refineries. This large percentage produced huge profits. From 1897 to 1906, the

---

[656] Ibid
[657] Ibid. 16-17

profits were between $790,000,000 and $850,000,000.[658] Rockefeller never drilled for oil himself, but let others invest their time, effort, and money in that hazardous business. Only one in ten wells actually ever produces oil. He eliminated the potential losses experienced by others and restricted his efforts to refining, where the big profits were. Whoever controls refining and product distribution regulates the oil industry.[659]

Congressman Charles A. Lindbergh Sr. said, "We absolutely know that the trusts, as a result of the centralizing of the control of the industrial agencies and material resources, operated in connection with their juggling of credits and money, have made us dependent upon the trusts for employment. This is the industrial slavery that the capitalistic interests prefer to chattel slavery. If we were chattel slaves, they would have to care for us in sickness and old age, whereas now they are not concerned with us, except for the time during which we work for them."[660]

Trusts benefit a small select minority at the expense of the majority. Lindbergh claimed that the banks practice a type of socialism, because they have a monopoly on dollars. While they denounce socialism, they practice it. They operate their combinations for their joint advantage. Socialism allows the monopolists to control the material products "resulting from the toil of the people, the right to charge for the use of this material and to make of us industrial slaves. They are practical socialists in the interests of the few."[661]

On April 11, 1914, Henry H. Klein wrote to President Woodrow Wilson regarding Standard Oil's greedy, oppressive monopolization of business that was crushing the nation's economic life. He told Wilson that, during the last twenty-five years, Standard Oil had

---

[658]   Harry W. Laidler, Concentration of Control in American Industry, Thomas Y. Crowell, New York, 1931, pp. 15-18

[659]   Stephen Pelletière, Iraq and the International Oil System: Why America Went to War in the Gulf, Praeger, Westport, Connecticut, 2001, pp. 6-7

[660]   Charles A. Lindbergh, Banking and Currency and the Money Trust, National Capital Press, Inc., Washington DC, 1913, p. 46

[661]   Ibid. 46

distributed $800,000,000 in dividends to its stockholders, and the value of its shares had increased from $1,000,000 to $1,300,000,000. Its annual profits were $150,000,000, and only twenty people owned a majority of the stock. He said that Standard and its beneficiaries controlled the major railroads, mines, public utilities, key banks, and other financial institutions and were the leading stockholders in most of the large industrial corporations.[662]

Rockefeller had invested a significant amount of money into the public-service corporations. Without his oil, every large city in America would have been dark. Additionally, with his and his associate's investments in transportation, he could have halted transportation, essential to the vast majority of American businesses. Regarding public services, before the beginning of World War II, people in the cities paid in excess of one billion dollars a year for light, heat, and local transportation to respective corporations. Rockefeller and Standard Oil owned the largest share, or controlling interest, in those corporations. People in New York City annually paid $152,000,000 to public-service corporations, which obviously benefitted John D. Rockefeller, the largest individual shareholder.[663]

The American Medical Monopoly

For a more complete disclosure on the medical monopoly, numerous books on the subject are available including *Rockefeller Medicine Men, Medicine and Capitalism in America* by E. Richard Brown; *The Medical Mafia* by Ghislaine Lanctôt; and *Copeland's Cure: Homeopathy and the War between Conventional and Alternative* by Natalie S. Robins. I also like Dr. Peter Glidden's book, *The MD Emperor Has No Clothes*. I will give a brief history of how the industrialists created a profit-based "medical" system that has always focused on addressing patient symptoms with chemicals or surgery instead of investigating the foundational causes of disease, not only in America but in other highly-populated countries, like China.

---

[662] Henry H. Klein, Standard Oil or the People, the End of Corporate Control in America, Tribune Building, New York, 1914, pp. 11-15

[663] Ibid. 19-20

On the evening of May 7, 1847, delegates to the national medical convention approved of a resolution to establish the American Medical Association (AMA), a private organization of allopathic physicians, currently based in Chicago. As a large unified group, a white-coated trade union, it would later effectively influence advantageous legislation to eliminate non-union competition. In April 14, 1897, officials incorporated the AMA in Chicago. Dr. George H. Simmons, a reform leader, was the AMA's general manager (1899-1924) and the editor of its *Journal.*

In June 1901, John D. Rockefeller Sr. founded the Rockefeller Institute for Medical Research, similar to France's Pasteur Institute (1888) and Germany's Robert Koch Institute (1891), the first such institution in America. Simon Flexner, a former Johns Hopkins University student and brother of Abraham and Bernard, was the institute's first director (1901-1935). Bernard Flexner was a key member of the Zionist Organization of America, an advisor for the Zionist delegation to the Paris Peace Conference (1918-1919), president of the Palestine Economic Corporation and one of the founders of the Council on Foreign Relations (CFR). Simon Flexner, after studying poliomyelitis, would later direct the development of a serum treatment for meningitis. He later became a trustee of the tax-exempt Rockefeller Foundation, chartered on May 14, 1913 by New York Governor William Sulzer, who the New York Assembly voted to impeach on August 13, 1913. Louis Marshall headed Sulzer's defense team.

Rockefeller and other industrialists sought dominance over many resources including the petroleum and petrochemical industries and could envision the possibilities in a pharmaceuticals market. Therefore, in 1909, with cooperation from the AMA, the Carnegie Foundation for the Advancement of Teaching funded Abraham Flexner's investigative tour of 155 medical schools in America and Canada. He planned to evaluate the entrance requirements, the qualifications of the staff, the financial endowments, the quality and suitability of the laboratories, and the relationship between medical schools and hospitals. He concluded that medical education in America was abysmal. [664]

Flexner submitted his 364-page report, *Medical Education in the United States and Canada (Carnegie Foundation Bulletin Number Four)*, to the Carnegie Foundation, a Rockefeller collaborator, which published it in 1910. The results of his investigation resulted in a drastic reform of America's medical education for the benefit of the profit-seeking industrialists. He wrote: "It is necessary to install a doorkeeper who will, by critical scrutiny, ascertain the fitness of the applicant, a necessity suggested, in the first place, but consideration for the candidate, whose time and talents will serve him better in some other vocation, if he be unfit for this, and in the second, by consideration for a public entitled to protection from those whom the very boldness of modern medical strategy equips with instruments that, tremendously effective for good when rightly used, are all the more terrible for harm if ignorantly or incompetently employed." [665]

Flexner emphasized the need for the increasing importance of the AMA's Council on Medical Education and its inspection and ratings of medical schools. The Council, an elite group, had initially requested that the Carnegie Foundation fund an objective, unbiased view of the nation's medical schools. Nathan P. Colwell, the Council's secretary, accompanied Flexner on many of his trips. However, the Council had to maintain a fragile balance, as the AMA then only represented a very small percentage of America's physicians. Council Members, a minority within the organization, intended to achieve its established objective of educational reform through Flexner and the Carnegie Foundation. [666]

---

[664] Barbara Barzansky and Norman Gevitz (editors) Beyond Flexner: Medical Education in the Twentieth Century, Greenwood Press, New York, 1992, p. 1

[665] Medical Education in the United States and Canada, a Report to the Carnegie Foundation for the Advancement of Teaching by Abraham Flexner, with an introduction by Henry S. Pritchett, President of the Foundation, New York, Bulletin Number Four, 1910, p. 22

[666] Barbara Barzansky and Norman Gevitz (editors) Beyond Flexner: Medical Education in the Twentieth Century, Greenwood Press, New York, 1992,

Flexner determined that any instruction that failed to utilize the new progressive drugs to treat their patients amounted to quackery. Officials at the AMA informed medical schools that offered a curriculum that included studies in bioelectric Medicine, Homeopathy or Eastern Medicine that they would have to discontinue these courses or forfeit their accreditation and underwriting support. Some schools maintained their right to offer alternative classes but ultimately, the majority of the schools either closed their doors or adapted.

Because of Flexner's efforts, philanthropists were willing to grant sufficient money to create schools comparable to Johns Hopkins University, founded January 22, 1876, which was Flexner's ideal school. Hopkins had bequeathed $7 million, a fortune he obtained primarily from his investments in the Baltimore and Ohio Railroad. [667] Andrew D. White (S&B), one of the three individuals who incorporated the Russell Trust, repudiated Christianity in his *The History of the Warfare of Science with Theology in Christendom*. White finagled Daniel C. Gilman's appointment, occurring on February 22, 1876, as the first president of Johns Hopkins University, a medical school promoting surgery and drugs rather than holistic and natural methods. Drugs simply manage disease instead of helping individuals to maintain good health or regain health in a natural, safe manner without harmful side effects. The University also established one of the nation's oldest schools of nursing in 1889.

Accordingly, the members of Congress, always happy to acquiesce to the demands of deep-pocketed industrialists and the imminent establishment of their tax-exempt foundations, readily accepted Flexner's recommendations and the need for public protection. Congress decided that the AMA would function as the ever-vigilant doorkeeper and authorized it to officially approve or disapprove of any of the nation's medical schools based on its criteria. In 1906, there were 160 medical schools in America. By 1920, there were eighty-five and by 1944, there were only sixty-nine medical schools in the country.

---

pp. 13-14
[667] Ibid. 1

Abraham Flexner was a capable fund raiser, especially for medical education. In 1920, he convinced George Eastman to grant $5 million to create the University of Rochester, School of Medicine. Flexner, as a member of the General Education Board of the Rockefeller Foundation, controlled the distribution of about $50 million. He anticipated that the philanthropic grants would stimulate competition among the nation's medical schools. Naturally, when schools received foundation funds, they were obligated to support a certain scientific or progressive track even if it countered previous proven methods. Many individuals questioned Flexner's motives and those of the contributing foundations, and suggested that their philanthropy supported reform to diminish the influence, or to outright abolish opposing medical philosophies. AMA members controlled the licensing boards, and designed the examination questions to differentiate students who graduated from unscientific schools. Many of the decreased incidents of infectious diseases of the time were due to better hygiene and nutrition rather than medical intervention by those educated in the foundation-funded schools. [668]

Rockefeller, promoted as an altruistic humanitarian, launched the International Educational Board with $21 million to fund educational activities in foreign universities. In 1927, he established the China Medical Board, and built the Peking Union Medical College and then spent another $45 million in an attempt to westernize Chinese medicine by replacing inexpensive herbal remedies in favor of the American-made carcinogenic and teratogenic miracle drugs. When people discovered the drug's lethal side effects, manufacturers simply replaced the old pharmaceuticals with new, equally costly, questionable drugs. [669]

Foreign missionaries, supported by their respective governments, established hospitals and medical schools in China—England (Hong Kong), Germany (Shanghai, Tsingtao), France (Canton),

---

[668] Barbara Barzansky and Norman Gevitz (editors) Beyond Flexner: Medical Education in the Twentieth Century, Greenwood Press, New York, 1992, pp. 13-14

[669] The Truth About the Rockefeller Drug Empire: The Drug Story By Hans Ruesch, http://www.whale.to/b/ruesch.html

and Japan (Peking, Shanghai, Hankow, and Mukden) which helped the development of Western medicine in China. Additionally, the Rockefeller Foundation, in conjunction with the Chinese government, established the China Medical Board. By 1921, there were twenty-six medical schools in China, the most notable facilities being the Peking Union Medical College (Rockefeller Foundation), the Medical Department of the University of Hong Kong, the Japanese Medical School at Mukden and the Army and Naval Medical Schools at Peking and Tientsin respectively. [670]

Charles W. Eliot, President of Harvard University (1869-1909), who had lengthy experience in a specific form of educational administration, was also cognizant of the social and industrial conditions in America. The Carnegie Endowment for International Peace sent Eliot as an envoy from an allegedly peace-promoting organization on a cursory inspection, a special errand to evaluate the industrial, social, and political conditions in what it deemed as semi-civilized China where he met a considerable number of educated Chinese and Japanese. [671]

Eliot, during a two and a half month tour of China, declared that China's most urgent need, given the millions of citizens, was medical education. By 1911, in Shanghai, a few graduates of Harvard Medical School created the first western medical school in China, the Harvard Medical School of China. In 1916, the Rockefeller Foundation sent medical equipment, in conjunction with the medical establishment of the University of Nanking. In 1916, they laid the cornerstone of the Hunan—Yale Medical School. The Chinese government directed the National Medical College at Peking, the schools of military and naval medicine, and five other provincial schools. The South Manchuria Railway owned the Japanese Medical School at Mukden, under governmental control. In 1920, the Rockefeller Foundation spent $7

---

[670] Fielding Hudson Garrison, An introduction to the History of Medicine: With Medical Chronology, Suggestions for Study and Bibliographic Data, Saunders Publishing, 1921, p. 68

[671] The Means of Unifying China, Charles W. Eliot, The Journal of International Relations, Volume 3 by Clark University, Worcester, Massachusetts, The Waverly Press, 1913, pp. 237-238

million to adapt the Peking Union Medical College, a facility "destined to be the nucleus of advanced medical teaching in China." [672]

The corporate media, in conjunction with the AMA, waged a ruthless campaign of disinformation and deception while deliberately concealing successful alternative remedies, and the practitioners who helped their patients improve or regain their health. Other monopolies and regulatory organizations include the American Dental Association (ADA), the American Academy of Pediatrics (AAP) and the American Psychiatric Association (APA), the American Cancer Society (ACS), and the American Diabetes Association (ADA). There are also unelected officials staffing countless bureaucratic agencies, functioning as a formidable regulating force that impacts every American. These corporations include but are not limited to the Centers for Disease Control (CDC), the Food and Drug Administration (FDA), the National Institutes of Health (NIH), the National Cancer Institute (NCI), the Institute of Medicine (IOM) and the National Academy of Sciences (NAS). These agencies disseminate propaganda and cooperate with the corporations who hold a monopoly over America's health and the other nations that depend on technical support from the US government.

Institutionalizing Cancer for Continuous Profit

On May 17, 1884, they laid the cornerstone for the New York Cancer Hospital, founded and funded by various notables, like John J. Astor, John E. Parsons, Joseph W. Drexel, Morris K. Jessup, William Astor, Isidor Cohnfield, Abram S. Hewitt and others, with Parsons as president. They later expanded and named it the Memorial Sloan-Kettering Cancer Center (MSKCC) after Alfred P. Sloan, Jr., a long-time president, chairman, and CEO of General Motors Corporation and Charles F. Kettering, vice president and director of research for General Motors.

---

[672] Fielding Hudson Garrison, An introduction to the History of Medicine: With Medical Chronology, Suggestions for Study and Bibliographic Data, Saunders Publishing, 1921, p. 68

On April 14, 1898, Colonel Oliver H. Payne, Tobacco Trust member, with a huge endowment, founded the Cornell University Medical College. James S. Ewing, the first pathology professor at Cornell Medical, in 1899, developed it into a cancer research center. He later helped to establish the present-day Memorial Sloan-Kettering Cancer Center. In 1900, John D. Rockefeller financed the establishment of a medical laboratory on the campus of Cornell Medical which led to the further development of MSKCC as the nation's "modern American industrial research techniques to cancer research."

On January 26, 1909, the *New York Press* published the findings of an Indiana physician, Dr. W. B. Clark. His report stated, "Cancer was practically unknown until cowpox vaccination began to be introduced. I have seen 200 cases of cancer, and I never saw a case of cancer in an unvaccinated person . . . We don't usually associate vaccinations with cancer, but there are many citations in the medial literature where vaccines caused cancers."

According to *The New Times*, in April 1913, a committee of laymen decided to found an organization to fight cancer. This committee included James Speyer, son of a Jewish banker, V. Everit Macy, an industrialist, Thomas W. Lamont, a partner at J.P. Morgan, George C. Clark, a banker, Dr. Frederick L. Hoffman, a statistician for the Prudential Life Insurance Company (1894-1934), John E. Parsons, and Thomas M. Debevoise, a Rockefeller attorney. Hoffman, in the *Journal of Cancer Research*, notes that, in 1900, the cancer death rate per 100,000 was sixty-three people. [673] He was also a consulting statistician for the Biochemical Research Foundation of the Franklin Institute of Philadelphia.

During the yearly conference of the American Gynecological Society, May 6-8, 1913, members resolved to establish a national society called the American Society for the Control of Cancer. Dr. Hoffman, later a member of the Society's Executive Committee, delivered a

---

[673] The Journal of Cancer Research, Volume 6, The American Association for Cancer Research, Baltimore, Maryland, 1921, p. 251

speech entitled *The Menace of Cancer.* [674] On May 22, 1913, ten prominent physicians and five business leaders in New York City founded a national agency, the American Society for the Control of Cancer (ASCC), later renamed the American Cancer Society. George C. Clark, of Clark, Dodge & Company was its first president (1913-1919). Its objectives were to distribute information about cancer's symptoms, treatment and prevention. The Congress of American Physicians and Surgeons, the Clinical Congress of Surgeons of North America and the American Medical Association approved of the new organization.

In 1913, the Rockefeller Foundation sponsored a conference addressing the necessity of public health education in the America. A collaborative effort between public health leaders and foundation officials led to the Welch-Rose Report (1915) mandating the need for trained public health workers. They also proposed a US institute of hygiene. Yale and Columbia-educated William H. Welch (S&B) focused on scientific research while Wickliffe Rose wanted to stress the development of a public health agency. In June 1916, per the approval of the executive committee of the Rockefeller Foundation, Welch and Rockefeller founded the Johns Hopkins School of Hygiene and Public Health. The design of the institute, depicted in the Welch-Rose Report, was its alliance with a medical school and state public health services but purportedly independent of both. One objective of the institute was the training of public health officials in bacteriology, immunology, parasitology, physiology and epidemiology. By 1922, Harvard, Columbia and Yale established schools of public health patterned after the Hopkins model. The Rockefeller Foundation sponsored the formation of public health schools throughout the United States and in Brazil, Bulgaria, Canada, England, Czechoslovakia, Hungary, India, Italy, Japan, Norway, the Philippines, Poland, Rumania, Sweden, Turkey, and Yugoslavia during the 1920s and 1930s, all modeled after the Johns Hopkins School of Public Health.

---

[674] David McBride, From TB to AIDS: epidemics among urban Blacks since 1900, State University of New York Press, 1991, p. 183

In the early 1920s, the ASCC established branches in several European countries. In 1924, Dr. George A. Soper, managing director of ASCC, toured Europe to evaluate the existing cancer societies and various research and treatment facilities. After that, he wrote a report about his findings. The Executive Committee, under the direction of Dr. Howard C. Taylor, decided to convene an international cancer symposium, occurring September 20-24, 1926 at Lake Mohonk, New York. In May 1926, John D. Rockefeller Jr. gifted $100,000 to the ASCC, in addition to $10,000 to partly fund the Lake Mohonk conference. Winthrop W. Aldrich was Chairman of the Campaign Committee, part of a larger committee, directed by Thomas W. Lamont. Other committee members included Calvert Brewer, Robert S. Brewster, Dr. Nicholas Murray Butler, Dr. S. Parkes Cadman, Lewis L. Clark, Dr. Henry S. Coffin, James Speyer, Frederick Strauss, Owen D. Young and others. [675] Lamont and Aldrich announced that attendees gave a combined amount of $199,500, out of the total of $338,515, that they had hoped to raise. The donations came from Edward S. Harkness, $100,000; J.P. Morgan & Co., $50,000; Walter C. Ladd and V. Everit Macy, $11,000 each, and many others.

About 250 American and European physicians attended that international meeting held at Lake Mohonk, with the objective of arriving at a concise statement for publication. They enumerated fifteen specific issues in their statement. Dr. Wendell Phillips, AMA President said, "This meeting has done much to stabilize the knowledge that we have of cancer, and it will clarify the opinions, not only of medical men, but of the public." Dr. Welch, at the Mohonk symposium, emphasized the importance of teaching the community about cancer, and the inevitable fatality, if people did not get proper treatment. [676]

I have only listed a few of the most long-lasting declarations from Dr. Welch's statement.

---

[675] Rockefeller Aids Cancer Study Fund, The New York Times, May 3, 1926, p. 9
[676] The Canadian Medical Association Journal, the Report of Societies, pp. 1383-1384

4. Persons who have cancer must apply to competent physicians at a sufficiently early stage in the disease, in order to have a fair chance of cure. This applies to all forms of cancer. In some forms early treatment affords the only possibility of cure.

7. The public must be taught the earliest danger signals of cancer which can be recognized by persons without a special knowledge of the subject, and induced to seek competent medical attention when any of these indications are believed to be present.

8. Practitioners of medicine must keep abreast of the latest advances in the knowledge of cancer in order to diagnose as many as possible of the cases of cancer which come to them.

9. Surgeons and radiologists must make constant progress in the refined methods of technic which are necessary for the diagnosis and proper treatment not only of ordinary cases but of the more obscure and difficult ones.

10. There is much that medical men can do in the prevention of cancer, in the detection of early cases, in the referring of patients to institutions and physicians who can make the proper diagnosis and apply proper treatment, when the physicians themselves are unable to accomplish these results. The more efficient the family doctor is, the more ready he is to share responsibility with a specialist.

13. The most reliable forms of treatment, and, in fact, the only ones thus far justified by experience and observation, depend upon surgery, radium and x-rays.

14. Emphasis should be placed upon the value of the dissemination of the definite, useful and practical knowledge about cancer, and this knowledge should not be confused or hidden by what is merely theoretical and experimental. [677]

Collis P. Huntington, Leland Stanford, Mark Hopkins, and Charles Crocker built the Central Pacific Railroad. In 1902, Huntington's widow gifted $100,000 to establish the Collis P. Huntington Fund for

[677] Ibid. 1383-1384

Cancer Research at the General Memorial Hospital in New York City. She also gave $250,000 to the Harvard Medical School to construct a building in the name of her late husband. Ewing, later a co-founder of the American Association for Cancer Research in 1907, became its first director. In 1918, James Douglas, president of Phelps-Dodge Co., donated $600,000 with the stipulation that they drop the word "General" from the name of the hospital and only treat cancer patients. The hospital's focus was on radiotherapy, which Ewing pioneered. In 1937, the Rockefeller Institute permitted the construction of a new hospital on land that they owned which later evolved into the Sloan-Kettering Cancer Center. [678]

In 1921, Dr. Francis C. Wood, Director of the Institute of Cancer Research, Columbia University, participated in the National Cancer Week movement, sponsored by the ASCC, to publicize their efforts. He publically castigated people that he called "quacks," those who treated cancer with therapies other than radium and X-rays. He stated that "improperly treated cancer is always fatal." Dr. Wood said that one of the goals of the ASCC was to disseminate these "facts" and to persuade people to have frequent medical examinations after they reach the cancer age, about forty-five, and to always employ a reputable physician and to "shun quacks." [679]

In 1926, Senator Joseph E. Ransdell (1913-1931) introduced a bill to create the National Institute of Health. In May 1928, he reintroduced the bill and the Senate passed it on May 21, 1930. President Herbert Hoover signed it five days later. Several people advocated its passage, including former President Calvin Coolidge, Treasury Secretary Andrew W. Mellon, and Francis P. Garvan, President of the Chemical Foundation, established during the First World War, in order to acquire German dye patents. The Foundation was a regular contributor to Johns Hopkins University, designated for Dr. Joseph C. Bloodgood's

---

[678]   James Stuart Olson, The history of cancer: an annotated bibliography, Greenwood Press, Inc., Westport, Connecticut, 1989, p. 370

[679]   Says Quacks Kill Victims Of Cancer; Dr. Francis Carter Wood Tells of Their Methods and Why They Work Great Harm. Delay Aid Until Too Late American Society Spreading the Truth in Effort to Reduce Mortality From Dread Disease, The New York Times, October 16, 1921

work dealing with dyes and stains for diagnosis of cancer. Garvan financed *The American Journal of Cancer*, the voice of the American Society for the Control of Cancer, and the American Society of Cancer Research. In 1930, Ransdell, chairman of the Committee on Public Health and National Quarantine, authored a bill to appropriate $100,000 for cancer research. He later became the executive director of the National Institute of Health, and asked the ASCC to furnish board members to consult on cancer issues.

Five radiologists have functioned as president of the American Cancer Society (ACS), an agency that actively promotes the financial interests of Siemens, DuPont, General Electric, Eastman Kodak, and Piker, the major manufacturers of mammogram machines and films. [680] Dr. Samuel S. Epstein and Rosalie Bertell, Ph.D., of the International Physicians for Humanitarian Medicine, both emphasize that mammographies are a "significant and cumulative risk" for developing breast cancer in premenopausal women. Not only are they incredibly dangerous, but they are an avoidable cause of breast cancer. [681]

However, the very profitable mammography industry conducts research for the ACS, sits on its boards, and donates substantial funds. DuPont financially supports the ACS Breast Health Awareness Program, sponsors TV programs, advocates the ACS literature for hospitals, clinics, medical organizations, and doctors, and produces educational films, and lobbies Congress for regulation for nationwide access of mammography services. The ACS, while collecting massive contributions, maintains firm connections to the mammography industry, while ignoring safer options, including breast self-examination (BSE). [682] As long as cancer treatment remains enormously profitable, the medical industry will actively conceal numerous effective safe treatment methods, and vilify, and

---

[680] American Cancer Society (ACS), http://www.whale.to/cancer/american_cancer_society_h.html as of May 2012

[681] Mammograms and Cancer Risk, http://www.healthy-communications.com/MammogramsandCancer-Dr.Epstein,20Feb2002.htm as of May 2012

[682] American Cancer Society (ACS), http://www.whale.to/cancer/american_cancer_society_h.html as of May 2012

even prosecute those they castigate as quacks, people with proven and effective remedies for a disease that continues to kill millions a year, despite the phony but profitable war on cancer.

Managing Competition and Other Petty Annoyances

Andrew Carnegie, a Pilgrims Society member, wrote, "To leave monopolists in control would not be tolerated by the people, therefore, there must be control and that control, as far as one sees, must be in the hands of the general government." [683] Carnegie, like other industrialists, hated competition; thus he purchased local and federal politicians, who could use brute force, to help Carnegie control his competition.

Carnegie wrote, in his two-part essay, *Gospel of Wealth* (1889), "The problem of our age is the proper administration of wealth, that the ties of brotherhood may still bind together the rich and poor in harmonious relationship." In discussing the "haves" and the "have-nots," he said that the critical issue in the "progress of the race," was the accumulation of wealth. While capitalism, with the associated competition, "may be sometimes hard for the individual, it is best for the race, because it insures the survival of the fittest in every department." Presumably, society must accept, and even welcome this "great inequality of environment" and the "concentration of business, industrial and commercial, in the hands of a few." People should not regret that capitalists would "soon be in receipt of more revenues than can be judiciously expended upon themselves." [684]

In 1848, Scottish-born Carnegie, from a family of radical reformers, emigrated with his family, and settled in Allegheny, Pennsylvania. His father, William Carnegie, was a member of the Chartist Movement, a British-based group of radical socialists who demanded revolutionary

---

[683] Charles R. Geisst, Monopolies in America: Empire Builders and Their Enemies, from Jay Gould to Bill Gates, Oxford University Press, Oxford, 2000, pp. 47-48

[684] E. Richard Brown, Rockefeller Medicine Men: Medicine and Capitalism in America, University of California Press, Berkeley and Los Angeles, California, 1979, pp. 30-31

changes. [685] In February 1855, Allan Pinkerton, also from Scotland, started the National Detective Agency, which later functioned as the basis of the Union's Intelligence Service (1861-1862.) [686] Possibly, he knew Carnegie, who censored government communications during the war.

Thomas A. Scott, a superintendent at the Pennsylvania Railroad, hired Carnegie, then a telegraph messenger boy, as his assistant. When Abraham Lincoln appointed Scott as Assistant Secretary of War, Carnegie became Scott's assistant. In their official capacities, they financially profited during the war by exploiting their railroad connections. Because of accusations of price fixing, and profiteering, Congress conducted an inquiry but War Secretary Simon Cameron owned Northern Central Railroad stock. Ultimately, the government was unable to prove any misconduct, purportedly due to faulty record keeping, evidently an ongoing problem, given the vast amounts of money missing from the Pentagon, immediately before 9/11. [687]

Following the war, the iron industry shifted from individual ironmasters, with a small team of workers, and a stone furnace to a growing industry, as the railroads required more iron than the independent furnaces could produce. In the 1850s, people like Daniel J. Morrell constructed their furnaces close to the railroad tracks, and hired several ironmasters, along with their crews, the early composition of the factory. Soon, the railroads wanted huge amounts of steel, a much stronger variety of iron. William Kelly, in Johnstown, and Henry Bessemer, in England, both designed a method of converting substantial amounts of iron into steel. Both the Kelly and Bessemer Converters were large contraptions requiring more workers who were not required to know all the steps of making iron.

On a trip to England, in the spring of 1872, Carnegie visited Bessemer, the ironmaster who patented his process in 1855. He returned home,

---

[685] Ray Boston, British Chartists in America, 1839-1900, Manchester University Press, Manchester, England, 1971, pp. 43, 78, 90, 96

[686] Ibid. 26, 78, 81

[687] Peter Krass, Carnegie, Wiley, New York, 2002, p. 65

and acquired investors, William Coleman, Andrew Kloman, Henry Phipps, David McCandless, William P. Shinn, John Scott, David A. Stewart, and Thomas Carnegie to build his first steel mill, using Bessemer's process. They called their firm Carnegie, McCandless, and Company and capitalized it with $700,000. Carnegie contributed $250,000, the majority of which came from selling bonds. McCandless was highly respected locally and using his name added respectability to the project. [688] Carnegie had begun selling stocks and bonds in Europe and sold $30 million of them within five years. Right before the Panic of 1873, starting on October 4, 1873, he abruptly abandoned his career as a speculator, during which time he had associated with people like Jay Gould and George Pullman. [689]

Henry Phipps, later a Pilgrims Society member, made $75 million or more, by 1901, working with Carnegie. Phipps had been a partner, in 1861, in Bidwell & Phipps, the Pittsburgh agents for the DuPont Powder Company, which supplied explosives during the Civil War, through which he became associated with Carnegie. He later became one of the largest stockholders in the United States Steel Corporation, and a Director at the Mellon National Bank. [690] The Phipps family created the Bessemer Investment Company as a holding company for their interests. Phipps was a major owner of New England Power, International Hydroelectric, and International Paper. [691] They now call that holding company the Bessemer Trust which controls billions of dollars in investment funds. Most of their directors are Pilgrim Society members.

In 1800, Joseph Schantz (Joseph Johns), a German immigrant, founded Johnstown, the location of the Cambria Iron Company,

---

[688]   Ibid. 117

[689]   Harold C. Livesay, Andrew Carnegie and the Rise of Big Business, Addison Wesley Longman, Inc., New York, 2000, pp. 69-82

[690]   John William Leonard (editor) Who's who in finance, banking, and insurance, A Biographical Dictionary of Contemporaries, 1920-1922, Volume 2, Joseph and Sefton, New York, 1911, p. 538

[691]   Ferdinand Lundberg, The Rich and the Super-Rich, a Study in Power and Money Today, Lyle Stuart, Inc. New York, 1968, p. 199

founded in 1848, just fifty miles from Pittsburgh. [692] By 1858, Cambria was a major source of rails for the nation's growing railway system. It adopted the Bessemer process in 1869. [693] Thousands of workers, primarily from southern and eastern Europe, immigrated to Pennsylvania, to work in the steel mills and coal mines. Cambria eliminated the country's dependence on English rails and drew the most innovative leaders in the industry.

On January 1, 1873, Carnegie broke ground for the J. Edgar Thomson Steel Works, in North Braddock, Pennsylvania, eleven miles east of Pittsburgh. He wanted to "pay homage to the great man" and perhaps ingratiate himself to the Pennsylvania Railroad, of which Thomson was the president (1852-1874). In 1857, the railroad, incorporated in 1847, spent $7.5 million to purchase the entire system of state-owned transportation works, consisting of 278 miles of canals and 117 miles of railroad, along with all of the associated real estate, and rail equipment. It then dominated the state and controlled most of the traffic in the many towns along its heavily populated route.

Carnegie offered Daniel J. Morrell, Cambria's general manager, since 1855, and a partner, the job of general manager for a huge salary of $20,000. He initially accepted, but then relented and stayed with Cambria. Morrell, a member of the House of Representatives (1867-1871), was also the president of the local gas and water company (1860-1884) and president of the First National Bank of Johnstown (1863-1884). Instead, Carnegie hired William Jones, a Welshman, with a volatile temper, a war veteran, and former Cambria employee. Morrell had fired him over some serious conflicts. Jones was the steel master, behind Carnegie. [694]

Railroads heavily invested in the steel companies, and were deeply committed to the financial health of that industry, because railroads profited from hauling coal, coke, iron ore and limestone to the steel companies. Industrialists determined rail prices during their backroom negotiations. The steel mills shared the same patents and

---

[692] Peter Krass, Carnegie, Wiley, New York, 2002, pp. 115-117
[693] Ibid. 115-117
[694] Ibid. 125

organized themselves as the Bessemer Association, with divided royalties, patents and licenses. The association had the power to block the construction of new steel mills. [695]

When Thomson died in 1874, Scott, former president of the Union Pacific Railroad (1871-1872) became president of the Pennsylvania Railroad (1874-1880). In June 1875, Carnegie was disappointed to discover that his old friend, Scott, had already made freight commitments to Cambria, now his competitor. The railroad also had financial interests in Cambria and in Pennsylvania Steel, the founding members of the Bessemer Association. Not one to be outmaneuvered, Carnegie negotiated with John Garrett, the president of the Baltimore and Ohio Railroad, which was cash-strapped, a situation that Carnegie was going to exploit. [696]

The Commonwealth of Pennsylvania, between 1838 and 1853, built the South Fork Dam on Lake Conemaugh, an artificial body of water located near South Fork, Pennsylvania. The Pennsylvania Railroad now owned that dam. In 1879, Henry C. Frick, Carnegie's partner, purchased the dam from the railroad, to use as a recreational site. A small group of wealthy Pittsburgh businessmen raised the lake level, built cottages, a clubhouse, and created the South Fork Fishing and Hunting Club. The membership of the elite club was never to exceed over a hundred people and their families. The membership was $800 and people referred to the club as the "Bosses Club." [697]

It was a playground for America's wealthiest capitalists, including Benjamin Ruff, Frederick H. Sweet, Charles J. Clarke, Thomas Clark, Walter F. Fundenberg, Andrew Mellon, Howard Hartley, Henry C. Yeager, James B. White, Henry C. Frick, Edwin A. Meyers, Christopher C. Hussey, Daniel R. Euwer, Casper A. Carpenter, William T. Dunn, Philander C. Knox, James H. Reed, Walter L. McClintock, and Jesse H. Lippincott. John G. A. Leishman, of Carnegie Steel, was the US

[695] David Nasaw, Andrew Carnegie, Penguin Group, New York, 2006, pp. 169-174
[696] Ibid. 169-174
[697] David G. McCullough, The Johnstown flood, Simon and Schuster, New York, 1968, pp. 56-60

ambassador to Turkey (1899-1901) and other countries—Switzerland, Italy, and Germany. Americus V. Holmes, a member, and Frick, Mellon, Lippincott, and Knox were directors of local banks. Knox and future senator, James Hay Reed, had a successful law practice in Pittsburgh, Knox and Reed is now a huge international law firm, Reed Smith LLP.

Frick, by 1880, through his own company, employed 1,000 workers and controlled eighty percent of Pennsylvania's coal output. Carnegie and Frick merged around 1881. Knox, Carnegie's attorney, would play a prominent role in incorporating the United States Steel Corporation on February 25, 1901. Cambria, Carnegie's chief competitor, had the world's largest annual steel production in the 1880s. People regarded Cambria as one of the greatest of the earliest modern iron and steel works, and a forerunner to Bethlehem Steel Company, and United States Steel Corporation.

The South Fork Dam, about sixty-five miles east of Pittsburgh, was poorly built and maintained since 1857, and had broken open in 1862. The club emptied the reservoir, and rebuilt the dam and reservoir, all without the benefit of suitable engineers or specialists. After the flood of 1880, an engineer warned the club that the repairs were inadequate. Severe flooding would occur again in 1885, 1887, and 1888. The dam lacked a proper drainage pipe, which created predictably high unsafe levels. Despite all of the professional warnings, and long-term safety issues, the club repeatedly failed to maintain or make proper repairs, regardless of their awareness of the problems, and their adequate resources. [698]

Morrell, Cambria's general manager became a member of the South Fork Fishing and Hunting Club in order to monitor the dangerous situation at Lake Conemaugh. He continuously warned the Club's officials and insisted on inspections of the dam by his own engineers, and those from the Pennsylvania Railroad. Regrettably, club president Benjamin Franklin Ruff ignored his warnings, and rejected his offers

---

[698]   Jed Handelman Shugerman, The Floodgates of Strict Liability: Bursting Reservoirs and the Adoption of Fletcher V. Rylands in the Gilded Age, Yale Law Journal, Volume: 110, Issue: 2, 2000, p. 333

to partially pay for repairs. Morrell died on August 20, 1885, and Cyrus Elder, legal counsel for Cambria, purchased his membership.

At around 3:10 p.m. on May 31, 1889, the earthen South Fork Dam, located in the mountains above Johnstown, burst after a high snowmelt, and a torrential spring storm. It took about forty minutes for the water to drain from Lake Conemaugh and cascade down into the Little Conemaugh River. This predictable collapse released 20,000,000 tons of water from the 450-acre lake. A forty-foot wall of water rushed into the valley twenty miles downstream at 100 miles per hour. This ravaging catastrophe, due to willful neglect, totally destroyed the town, killed about 2,200 people, and wrecked 1,600 homes causing $17 million in property damages. [699]

Just before hitting the main part of Johnstown, the wall of water crashed into Cambria Iron, in the town of Woodvale, with a population of 1,100, out of which, 314 died. Boilers exploded at the Gauliter Wire Works. It was the worst flood to occur in the United States in the nineteenth century. The rushing water demolished downtown Johnstown, stretching over four miles. The water heavily damaged Cambria, but did not completely destroy the large facility. However, the firm could not return their workers to full production for two years. By that time, Carnegie had surpassed Cambria's production.

Carnegie was at the World's Fair in Paris at the time of the flood. Frick, Mellon, and other club members donated thousands of dollars but officials never charged them for their long-term negligence. [700] Frick and others organized the Pittsburgh Relief Committee to collect financial aid for the flood victims. This is a typical, distracting strategy—charity makes for good publicity and counteracts culpability while making the benefactors appear magnanimous. After every disaster, war, or famine, the elite set up charitable assistance to regulate the circumstances, redistribute resources, and control the outcome. The club members maintained silence about the club, the

[699] Ibid.
[700] Peter Krass, Carnegie, Wiley, New York, 2002, p. 267

dam, and the flood. Knox and Reed deflected all lawsuits that placed any accountability on the Club's negligent officers.

In 1892, the Carnegies and their friends, including the president of the New York Chamber of Commerce, Charles Smith, were on a month-long tour of California and Mexico, with private accommodations on the Southern Pacific, provided by his railroad friend, George Pullman. The party visited the most famous sites, dined with mining millionaires, and visited Beringer Brothers winery, where Carnegie ordered twenty-five gallons of brandy and four cases of white wine. From there, they went to northern Mexico and the Baja Peninsula. The Carnegies planned to leave for their annual trip to Scotland in April where they planned to spend the summer. [701] While in Aberdeen, Carnegie would dedicate a library and receive the *Freedom*, akin to the key to the city. Then the Carnegies planned to spend time at Sir Robert Menzies' Lodge on Loch Rannoch. [702]

Meanwhile, Frick attempted to consolidate Carnegie's rivals into one organization—Carnegie Steel Company with its base, the J. Edgar Thomson Steel Works, and Furnaces, with Charlie Schwab as general superintendent. Investors capitalized the new organization at $25 million, with Carnegie holding $13,833,333.33 or fifty-five percent with nineteen other shareholders. Frick was happy with eleven percent. The workers were not happy; they began a strike on June 30, 1892. The merger took effect July 1, 1892, the day after Carnegie's contract expired, with his Homestead laborers, represented by the Amalgamated Association of Iron and Steel Workers (AAISW). The union was more concerned about worker safety than Carnegie and Frick. Carnegie also sought to reduce wages by fifteen percent to eighteen percent, despite the fact that he had just acquired a very profitable government contract to supply some armor, probably in preparation for imminent warfare. The skilled workers were Irish, Welsh, English, and German while regular laborers were predominantly Hungarians, Italians, and Poles who were content just to have work. [703]

---

[701] Ibid. 275-276
[702] Ibid. 278-280
[703] Peter Krass, Carnegie, Wiley, New York, 2002, pp. 27-277

Carnegie drafted a rather hostile memo, quite different from his labor essay of 1886, in which he had pledged to take no man's job and professed that every man had the right to organize, apparently just not in any of his plants. Despite his humble background and his rhetoric, his employees worked long hours for low wages. He did not want the union at Homestead, and he claimed that unions were too discriminatory and that Amalgamated hindered efficiency. He sent a note to Frick, vowing his support for whatever he decided to do to halt any opposition. [704]

Frick ordered the construction of a three-mile-long fence along the Homestead perimeter, complete with portholes measuring five to six inches in diameter, just the right size for a rifle barrel. Workers strung barbed wire, allegedly electrified, across the top, and built sniper towers within the compound, completely equipped with searchlights. It had all the appearances of an intimidating military complex which some dubbed as Fort Frick. He prepared for a lengthy lockout that might turn violent. The new wage scale affected only 325 out of 3,800 men. However, Frick did not want another rampage like the previous one. Individuals alerted him that the men were going to strike and he expected violence. According to Frick, the men had no choice; they had to accept the new wage scale. [705]

Frick met with union reps and a committee of twenty-five Homestead men. The union created an Advisory Committee of forty men to oversee their battle, and appointed Hugh O'Donnell as their chairman. He had witnessed numerous unnecessary deaths in the mill, and was ready to oppose the greedy owners. [706] Tempers flared, ill feelings and arguments erupted between the skilled and unskilled workers, and the various ethnic groups. The rhetorical battle was heating up to ignite into a bloody confrontation mimicking the battle of 1889. Four thousand workers divided into three military-style divisions, with sentries posted at mill entrances, ready to dispel any strikebreakers. Frick had created an antagonistic environment and the workers followed his lead. Carnegie and Frick assumed that the

---

[704]   Ibid. 278-280
[705]   Ibid. 278-280
[706]   Ibid. 278-280

conflict would be restricted to the union men and failed to understand that, despite ethnic differences, the workers united in their feelings against these exploitative industrialists, who had already advertised for strikebreakers. [707]

Frick brought in 300 Pinkerton Agency ruffians from New York, to bully the workers and act as guards, allegedly to protect the company's property. Carnegie, who had always postured as a fair tolerant man and Frick maintained that their actions were legal. On July 4, 1892, Frick asked Sheriff William H. McCleary to intervene. Knox, their attorney approved of their actions, and the sheriff dispatched eleven deputies to post handbills throughout the town, demanding the strikers to discontinue disturbing the plant's operation. The strikers refused to relinquish the plant to nonunion workers. The Pinkertons, from eyewitness testimony, took the first shots, and then an armed battle ensued. [708]

On July 7, 1892, the strike committee alerted Governor Robert E. Pattison that things were under control. Carnegie money had installed Pattison and he was obliged to protect Carnegie interests, despite the fact that Homestead residents supported the union. On July 12, the governor sent in 6,000 state militia soldiers, who occupied the area until October 13. The Homestead Strike permanently destroyed the union in Pennsylvania. Carnegie Steel was non-union for the next forty years. By 1900, Pennsylvania steel plants were all union-free. Three Pinkerton agents and seven strikers were killed, and several other men died later from their wounds, while hundreds received injuries.

In addition to the Homestead Strike, the government later used the Pinkerton Agency, currently a subsidiary of Stockholm-based Securitas Aktiebolag, against laborers during the Pullman Strike on May 11, 1894 and against the Wild Bunch Gang in 1896. In 1894, on behalf of Wall Street, President Grover Cleveland also sent 12,000 troops to Chicago, unsolicited by the Illinois Governor, under the

---

[707] Ibid. 280-282
[708] Peter Krass, Carnegie, Wiley, New York, 2002, pp. 280-282

pretense of protecting the mails. The president sent troops to halt the Pullman Strike where workers were protesting a thirty percent wage decrease, a result of the orchestrated Panic of 1893. The federal troops killed thirteen strikers and wounded fifty-seven. [709]

People accused Carnegie of supplying inferior armor to the navy for US warships, for which officials heavily fined the company. Carnegie made every attempt to keep this information from the public. Again, Knox, the attorney, defended him. [710] With Knox's help, he avoided prosecution after the president of the Pennsylvania Railroad divulged that Carnegie had received illegal kickbacks from the railroad. [711]

In 1897, Knox began arranging the merger of the railroad, oil, coal, iron, and steel interests of Carnegie, J. Pierpont Morgan, Rockefeller, and other industrialists into US Steel, the largest conglomerate in history. This huge corporation included Consolidated Iron Mines in the Mesabi Range of Minnesota, which provided sixty percent of the country's iron ore. Rockefeller had swindled that company from the Merritt family who only received a fraction of what it was actually worth. Rockefeller kept appealing the case during which time the Merritt family simply ran out of money. [712] Frederick T. Gates, who managed Rockefeller's philanthropic decisions, reorganized Rockefeller's ownership of the Mesabi Range by buying out other stockholders who were in financial trouble. [713]

Corporations have long used brute force to impose their policies, domestically, and internationally. The Colorado National Guard initially quelled striking miners in Colorado but the state soon ran out of funds. A militia consisting mostly of Colorado Fuel & Iron

---

[709] Ferdinand Lundberg, America's 60 Families, The Citadel Press, 1937, pp. 55-57

[710] Peter Krass, Carnegie, Wiley, New York, 2002, pp. 306-308

[711] Bill Benson, The Law That Never Was, The fraud of the 16th Amendment and personal income tax, Volume II, Constitutional Research Association, 1985, pp. 122-135

[712] Ibid. 122-135

[713] Paolo Lionni, The Leipzig Connection, the Systematic Destruction of American Education, Delphian Press, 1988, p. 47

Company (CF&I) employees in National Guard uniforms, attempted to stop the strike. This precipitated the Ludlow Massacre on April 20, 1914. Uniformed employees killed at least twenty-four striking coal miners in addition to two women and eleven children in a 14-hour confrontation. The Rockefellers, who owned CF&I, the Rocky Mountain Fuel Company (RMF), and the Victor-American Fuel Company (VAF), denied all responsibility.

In late 1915, J. Leonard Replogle, of the Pennsylvania Railroad, purchased $15 million worth of Cambria stock and then immediately shifted ownership of that stock to a group of bankers, headed by Edward T. Stotesbury, of the Drexel Company, and Andrew W. Mellon and Richard B. Mellon, of the Mellon National Bank of Pittsburgh. [714]

The Banking Trust and Congress

Even before the dubious post-Civil War legislation, Congress behaved like the most furtive of all secret societies. On January 16, 1794, It passed a resolution that prohibited anyone who owned stock or held an office in a financial institution from being in Congress. However, due to heated opposition, Congress amended the resolution to allow such people to function in a legislative body allegedly designed to serve the people's interests. [715] The original Thirteenth Amendment (1810) also prohibited lawyers from functioning in Congress. The war and other circumstances prevented that amendment, though fully ratified, from taking effect.

Representative William McKinley's Tariff (1890) increased farm equipment prices, which proved detrimental to the nation's farmers. To secure passage of it, willing Republicans promised to support the Sherman Silver Act which was supposed to help the drought-poor farmers and improve the overall economy; at least that is what they claimed.

---

[714] The New York Times, November 16, 1915

[715] Charles A. Lindbergh, Banking and Currency and the Money Trust, National Capital Press, Inc., Washington DC, 1913, p. 25

On May 22, 1871, James T. Lowenstein, William Shields and O. E. Owens organized the Bank Clerks' Association of Missouri. [716] Then on May 24, 1875, Howenstein, of the Valley National Bank in St. Louis, invited bankers from around the nation to attend a meeting to establish a banker's association. In July 1875, 349 bankers from thirty-one states met in Saratoga, New York to create the American Bankers Association (ABA). On April 2, 1876, the ABA testified before Congress for the first time. The ABA, currently in the top twenty-five lobby groups, lobbies for many of America's largest financial institutions including JPMorgan Chase, Bank of America and Wells Fargo. The ABA urged students who were associated with the B'nai B'rith Hillel Foundations located on 250 colleges throughout the United States to enter banking. The ABA developed a new program about the employment practices of fifty of the nation's largest banks and provided brochures to each Hillel chapter after the American Jewish Committee's report of September 1966. [717]

The ABA sent out a *Panic Circular*, dated March 11, 1893, to all national banks. It read, "The interests of national banks require immediate financial legislation by Congress. Silver, silver certificates, and Treasury notes must be retired and national bank notes upon a gold basis made the only money . . . You will at once retire one-third of your circulation and call in one-half of your loans. Be careful to make a monetary stringency among your patrons, especially among influential businessmen. Advocate an extra session of Congress to repeal the purchasing clause of the Sherman Law and act with other banks of your city in securing a large petition to Congress for its unconditional repeal, per accompanying form. Use personal influence with your Congressman, and particularly let your wishes be known to your Senators. The future life of national banks, as fixed and safe investments, depends upon immediate action, as there is an

[716] Howard L. Conard (editor) Encyclopedia of the History of Missouri, Volume 1, The Southern History Company, New York, 1901, p. 113
[717] Press Release, May 18, 1967, The American Jewish Committee, New York, pp. 1-2, The AJC, is the pioneer human-relations agency in the United States. It protects the civil and religious rights of Jews here and abroad, and advances the cause of improved human relations for people everywhere.

increasing sentiment in favor of Government legal-tender notes and silver coinage." [718]

British investors began withdrawing their funds, transferring gold from America to England, greatly contributing to the 1893 Panic. The United States gold reserve fell below the acceptable level of $100 million as a result of revenue losses from tariff reductions and veteran's bonuses. In February 1893, investors began dumping securities and by April, gold backed only a quarter of the currency in circulation. Railroad stocks were especially susceptible. President Grover Cleveland then instructed Congress to repeal the Sherman Silver Act in an attempt to restore trust and stability in the financial sector. [719] The Philadelphia and Reading Railroad went into receivership on February 23, 1893. The Northern Pacific Railway, the Union Pacific and the Atchison, Topeka and Santa Fe Railroads failed, which affected many businesses that relied on the railroads. Predictably, the stock market plunged. Over 15,000 companies failed, unemployment skyrocketed, mines closed, grain prices fell causing an agricultural depression, and labor strikes took place.

Predictably, strikes erupted, such as the Pullman Strike of July 1894. People could not pay their mortgages. Many abandoned their homes and moved west seeking for and hoping to find a way to care for their families. Silver from newly opened mines flooded the market. Concerned people withdrew their money from banks, causing 500 bank failures. Foreign investors who would only accept gold depleted the gold reserves, affecting the value of the US dollar. As of September 1, 1894, the bankers called in outstanding loans and refused to renew loans under any circumstances. They foreclosed on mortgages and seized about two-thirds of the farms west of and thousands on the east side of the Mississippi River. Farmers suddenly became tenants on their own land despite the size or age of the mortgage.

---

[718] Charles A. Lindbergh, Banking and Currency and the Money Trust, National Capital Press, Inc., Washington DC, 1913, pp. 33-34
[719] Charles R. Geisst, Wall Street: A History from Its Beginnings to the Fall of Enron, Oxford University Press, New York, 2004, p. 110

The McKinley Tariff had established the average tariff rate for imports into the United States at the unreasonably high rate of 48.4 percent, which contributed to the 1893 Panic. Anxious investors redeemed their silver notes for gold dollars and inevitably, their actions further decreased the nation's gold reserves and led to inflation. People blamed the Panic on the Democrats and President Cleveland, a situation that gave the Republicans huge gains in the 1894 congressional elections. On July 9, 1896, at the Democratic convention, William Jennings Bryan gave a speech, referred to as the Cross of Gold Speech, in which he strongly advocated bimetallism. McKinley supporters, principally the bankers, induced a sufficient number of manufacturers and industrialists to inform their employees that if they elected Bryan, all factories and plants would subsequently close, and there would be no work. In 1896, wary citizens elected McKinley as president, and, as planned, an economic recovery soon began. The bankers supported McKinley who, in return for their operational, and financial support, now favored the gold standard. Soon, the Spanish American War would predictably further boost the economy.

Bankers handpicked Garret A. Hobart, a freemason, a New Jersey businessman, corporate lawyer, and director of numerous Morgan enterprises, including the Liberty National Bank of New York City, to be McKinley's Vice-President (1897-1899) or more accurately, his handler. When Hobart died of natural causes, that office remained vacant for a year until Theodore Roosevelt became President. [720] Despite what happened to other banks, during these calculated financial expansions and contractions, the House of Morgan always managed to come out on top. In the bank panics of 1873, 1884, 1893, and 1907, while other banks failed, Morgan's bank not only survived but prospered. [721]

International bankers had already coerced many nations to accept the gold standard. China retained the silver standard until 1935. The

---

[720] Donald G. Lett, Phoenix Rising: The Rise and Fall of the American Republic, Author House, 2008, pp. 70-71

[721] G. Edward Griffin, The Creature from Jekyll Island, a Second Look at the Federal Reserve, American Media, 2002, pp. 408-410

Coinage Act of 1873 placed the US Mint under the jurisdiction of the Treasury Department. Mints were set up in Philadelphia, San Francisco, Carson City, and Denver. The Treasury established two assay offices, one in New York and the other in Boise City, Idaho. The United States formally adopted the gold standard in 1900, in order to accommodate the bankers, who appeared to control the vast amount of the world's gold.

In 1893, Max M. Warburg and his younger brother Paul joined the family firm, M.M. Warburg and Company (founded 1798), of Hamburg. [722] In January 1907, Paul M. Warburg, now a Kuhn Loeb partner, wrote *Defects and Needs of Our Banking System*, which *The New York Times* published in the Financial Supplement. Adolph S. Ochs (Pilgrims Society) owned *The New York Times*. Warburg claimed, "Nothing short of a modern central bank will affect a final solution of the problem." An economic panic struck New York on October 14, 1907, and it subsided on November 6, 1907. On November 12, 1907, Warburg published a seven-page pamphlet, *A Plan for a Modified Central Bank*, defining methods of preventing financial panics using "a central bank with limited powers." [723] By 1914, because of the panic, 300,000 men and women would be out of work in Greater New York and about 3,000,000 would be out of work in the United States out of a total working population of twenty million. There would be more business failures because of hard times than ever before, because a few great men needed a panic to possess the wealth that belonged to others and because big business coveted the riches of other smaller businesses. The panic accomplished both objectives. [724]

Warburg claimed that a "modified" central bank would be different from the European central banks. Again, Ochs promoted Warburg's propaganda through *The New York Times Annual Financial Review.*

---

[722] The First 100 Years, M.M. Warburg, http://www.mmwarburg.com/en/bankhaus/historie/1798_1898.html as of May 2012

[723] Paul Moritz Warburg, A plan for a modified central bank, November 12, 1907

[724] Henry H. Klein, Standard Oil or the People, the End of Corporate Control in America, Tribune Building, New York, pp. 15-16

On March 21, 1911, Warburg, recognizing that he and other bankers could manipulate the nations' currency, became a citizen.

The Aldrich Plan, Corporate Currency

We have a corporate currency, a government of the corporations, by the corporations and for the corporations—a corporate republic. [725]

Ferdinand Lundberg, referring to Senator Nelson W. Aldrich wrote, "Seven Presidents served *under* Aldrich, Republican Senate whip." He had as "unsavory a record as one could conceive." *McClure's Magazine*, February 1905, exposed the Rhode Island political machine, corrupt state senators, all dominated by Aldrich and Charles R. Brayton. "Brayton, Aldrich, and Marsden J. Perry manipulated the legislature, gave themselves perpetual public-utility franchises, and passed laws worth millions to themselves. When Aldrich gave up his wholesale grocery business in 1881 to enter the Senate, he was worth $50,000; when he died, after thirty years in politics, he was worth $12,000,000." [726] He made a fortune investing in railroads, banking, sugar, mines, and rubber during King Leopold's reign of terror in the Belgian Congo, an exploitive corporate state where slave labor, mutilations and genocide were rampant. [727]

---

[725] Alfred Owen Crozier, US Money vs. Corporation Currency, Aldrich Plan, Wall Street Confessions, The Great Bank Combine, the Magnet Company, Cincinnati, Ohio, 1912, pp. 19-23

[726] America's 60 Families by Ferdinand Lundberg, The Citadel Press, 1937, p. 61

[727] Genocide Studies Program, Belgian Congo, http://www.yale.edu/gsp/colonial/belgian_congo/index.html

Aldrich was certainly not the first or last politician to exploit his government position. In 1798, John Robison revealed that opportunists wanted to influence a country's military apparatus through the establishment of academies to teach and promote warfare. [728] Military colleges and naval academies are essential to the militarizing of a country. Congress authorized the first military school, West Point on March 16, 1802, and has established others since.

On September 18, 1775, the Second Continental Congress sanctioned the Secret Committee, whose members bought arms and gunpowder, from friends or family, for which they overcharged the government, and received a kickback. During the War of 1812, the Livingstons, Elbridge Gerry, Stephen Girard, Thomas Cushing, and Benjamin Harrison, all merchants and members of the Committee, acquired huge fortunes. They kept their transactions private, and destroyed records to maintain confidentiality. Thomas Willing, the first chairman, was a business partner of Robert Morris, the so-called "Financier of the Revolution."

Eleuthère Irénée du Pont opened the first powder factory in America, and, within four years, his mills produced 600,000 pounds of high quality powder. Prominent in the philosophical movement, he had friends amongst America's most influential politicians, including Thomas Jefferson, who helped him obtain orders. Secretary of War, Henry Dearborn saw no need to order gunpowder during peacetime. The War of 1812 erupted, and du Pont sold the country all the powder that it needed. Although he sold gunpowder to foreign countries, and to the mining industry, warfare generated the most profit. Naturally, his profits soared during the brutal fratricidal Civil War. [729]

---

[728] John Robison, Proofs of a Conspiracy Against All the Religions and Governments of Europe Carried on in the Secret Meetings of Freemasons, Illuminati and Reading Societies, Kessinger Publishing, Whitefish, Montana, 2003 (originally published in 1798), p. 112

[729] Helmuth C. Engelbrecht, Ph.D. and Frank C. Hanighen, Merchants of Death, a Study of the International Armament Industry, Dodd, Mead & Co., New York, 1934, pp. 19-20, 24 This is an excellent expose of corporate welfare and warfare

The du Ponts cemented a permanent relationship with the US government. By 1896, they made smokeless powder in several colors. In 1899, the government, collaborating with du Pont, built a smokeless powder plant at Indian Head (NH). Congress then appropriated $167,000 to build a gunpowder plant in Dover (NJ). By 1907, du Pont seized control of all existing powder companies in the nation. [730] In 1916, government officials, uniting with yet another firm, awarded Bethlehem Shipbuilding, a subsidiary of the Bethlehem Steel Corporation, a generous contract for eighty-five destroyers at a cost of $134,000,000. [731]

After World War I, the du Ponts testified before a Senate committee where they claimed that their powder won the war. Their average earnings were $6 million a year (1910-1914). During the war, they averaged $58 million a year, an increase of over 950 percent. Bethlehem Steel's yearly earnings averaged $6 million (1910-1914) but increased to $49 million a year during the war. US Steel's yearly profits went from $105 million to $240 million a year during the war. Anaconda Copper's yearly earnings went from $10 million a year to $34 million a year during the war. Utah Copper's yearly profits increased from $5 million to $21 million. [732] Senators obviously recognized exactly where to invest their money for maximum profits.

Aldrich, the grandfather of David Rockefeller, chairman of the Senate Finance Committee, managed the National Monetary Commission. He and Representative Edward B. Vreeland, a banker, sponsored the Emergency Currency Act, enacted on May 30, 1908 which created the group which they co-chaired. It was composed of nine members each from the Senate and the House. At the taxpayer's expense, it investigated the banking and currency systems of England, France and Germany, industrialized countries similar to the United States. The commission published (1909-1911) a series of twenty-one reports on banking, a compilation of 9,000 pages of material, 6,500 of which

---

[730]   Ibid. 19-20, 24

[731]   Ibid. 123

[732]   Smedley D. Butler, War is a Racket, Feral House, Los Angeles, California, 1935, 2003, pp. 27-28

dealt with the three countries. [733] Germany had one of the world's key currencies. Private bankers dominated Germany with their joint-stock banks. The central bank of issue as of 1875, was the privately-owned Reich bank. However, it was under tight government control, with a very stable currency, called the Goldmark until 1914. [734]

Paul M. Warburg helped to devise the basic principles of the infamous Aldrich Plan, the genesis of the Federal Reserve System, a plan that many bankers opposed prior to its passage. In the fall of 1910, Senator Aldrich, wanting to design a Republican alternative to the banking reforms that politicians were then proposing in the Democrat-controlled Congress, allegedly met with six influential bankers at Jekyll Island, to establish the Federal Reserve System. Those bankers represented the interests of J. Pierpont Morgan, Rothschild, Rockefeller, Warburg, and Kuhn, Loeb & Company. J. Pierpont Morgan and Kuhn, Loeb organized the conference where they drafted the Federal Reserve Act. Aldrich and Warburg, Henry P. Davison, Benjamin Strong, Frank A. Vanderlip, all Pilgrims Society members, and Charles D. Norton, attended. [735] [736] The result of that meeting was the blueprint for the Federal Reserve System. Though officials ultimately offered Warburg the job as Fed chairman, he rejected their offer, and instead served as a director until 1918.

Reportedly, Warburg developed a nationwide propaganda campaign in favor of the Aldrich Plan. Academics at Princeton, Harvard, and the University of Chicago assisted in the campaign to promote the feasibility and effectiveness of a central bank. Woodrow Wilson, Princeton's former president, became a spokesman and advocate. Nationally-chartered banks were obligated to contribute to a fund to raise $5 million to pay for the campaign to convince the American

---

[733] Annals of the American Academy of Political and Social Science, Volumes 99-101 by American Academy of Political and Social Science, England, 1932, pp. 20-21

[734] Rondo E. Cameron, Valeriĭ Ivanovich Bovykin, B. V. Ananich, International banking, 1870-1914, Oxford University Press, New York, 1991, p. 91

[735] Antony C. Sutton, The Federal Reserve Conspiracy, Emissary Publications, Clackamas, Oregon, 1995, p. 75

[736] Charles Savoie, Meet the World Money Power by, December 2004, p. 51

public that the bank plan was beneficial and that Congress should pass it into law. [737]

In November 1911, the New Orleans chapter of the American Bankers Association based in Washington, DC, officially resolved to commit itself to the "banking fraternity," and to Aldrich's central bank plan. When people, through their efforts, honestly and fairly produce wealth for themselves, there is no stigma. They are due the full protection of the law in retaining that wealth. Yet, when individuals combine, and create wealth by improperly manipulating the law to their benefit, and, in the process, confiscate the results of the people's efforts, and place burdens upon them, for the benefit of a few, they neither deserve or should receive the protection of the law. [738]

On January 8, 1912, the National Monetary Commission issued its final report and made recommendations for a proposed bill, known as the Aldrich Plan. Three days later, Senator Theodore E. Burton introduced the Aldrich bill (S. 4431). In that same year, Alfred O. Crozier published a book warning the public against Wall Street and the banking trust, who were then struggling to assume the management of both parties, by offering to finance the campaigns of friendly candidates from both parties. It already had control of many individuals from both parties, who would have blocked a legitimate investigation of the money trust. It was quite willing to spend millions, in order to acquire billions in the future, as well as political control of the nation over the next century.

The people might have defeated the proposed measure in 1912, if officials had honestly presented it for open debate. Wall Street and the banks engineered it as a secret issue to prevent all discussion in Congress, and to force the bill through before the end of the session, and the presidential term beginning on March 4, 1913. According to Crozier, the people should have "publicly pledged every delegate,

---

[737] Eustace Mullins, The Secrets of the Federal Reserve, the London Connection, John McLaughlin, 1993, p. 25

[738] Alfred Owen Crozier, US Money vs. Corporation Currency, Aldrich Plan, Wall Street Confessions, The Great Bank Combine, the Magnet Company, Cincinnati, Ohio, 1912, pp. 19-23

candidate and convention." If a candidate refused to take a stand against the bank, then he should not be in the campaign; "neutrality was not an option." The issuance of the money, government money vs. corporate currency, was of concern to every individual living then, or in the future. Congress intended to grant control of the nation's money to a private corporation owned by the banks, and controlled by Wall Street. This would create an absolute monopoly over the printing and issuing of all public currency. [739]

Crozier wrote, "Remember, those who have power to make money scarce or plenty have power over the business of every man, the happiness of every home, to make or break, to confer or destroy general prosperity. It gives them a hunger-hold on every man, woman and child." [740] Congress created a corporation and implemented a criminal plan beneficial to its members. Yet, the people could have destroyed the long-lasting, dangerous, and daring scheme, which amounted to a legalized hold-up if they had known, but even then, complicity existed between the media and the Congress. If Congress passed the Aldrich Bill, it could not repeal it, because it was a contract for at least fifty years. Congress placed Americans, then totaling 94,000,000, into financial and political bondage, to the calculating, centralized, greedy incorporated money trust. Instead of the people ruling the country, the Congress-created corporation would dominate the people, their currency, and their labor. [741]

Initially, people could redeem the currency for gold. They secured the money by a reserve of "at least one-third the volume in actual gold," dispensed through the accredited banks. The Monetary Commission, an independent group of politicians, proposed the regulations, which the government did not necessarily guarantee. The Monetary Commission recommended a debt-based, paper currency, created by a corporation, issued for profit, without any legal restraints on the quantity they could print. The Aldrich Plan, which shattered and

[739] Alfred Owen Crozier, US Money vs. Corporation Currency, Aldrich Plan, Wall Street Confessions, The Great Bank Combine, the Magnet Company, Cincinnati, Ohio, 1912, p. 9
[740] Ibid, introduction
[741] Ibid. 15-18

even destroyed all party lines, made the population subservient to Congress and their collaborators, the bankers. The money issue is the "greatest political contest" that the public should address, as it touches every human being. Cozier said, "The victors will rule the republic for all future time, the vanquished being subservient." [742]

On March 12, 1912, Andrew J. Frame, president of Waukesha National Bank, gave an address, *Diagnosis of the National Monetary Commission Bill*, before the Bankers and Business Men's Club of Memphis, Tennessee. He condemned the Aldrich bill because it would destroy independent banking, and create a great banking and money monopoly. He said it was a "scheme for wild and dangerous currency and credit inflation, certain to react on the banks, and the country in the shape of frequent panics, following periods of excessive expansion, and speculation, and that the proposed remedy is worse than the claimed disease." [743]

Aldrich Plan proponents waged an aggressive war against all opposition. Warburg was behind the establishment of the National Citizens' League led by Professor Oliver Sprague, Professor of Banking and Finance at Harvard and Harvard-educated James L. Laughlin of the Economics Department of the University of Chicago, the recipient of $50 million from John D. Rockefeller. Sprague, an advisor to the Bank of England wrote *History of Crises under the National Banking System* for the National Monetary Commission. [744] He took a leave from Harvard when the president appointed him executive assistant to US Secretary of Treasury in 1933.

The law shields the wealthy, because of their power, from the consequences of their fraudulent criminal conduct. At the time of the legislation, there were 24,392 banks, which would fall into their grasp, destined to destroy popular government, accommodate

---

[742] Ibid. 13, 16-22
[743] Alfred Owen Crozier, US Money vs. Corporation Currency, Aldrich Plan, Wall Street Confessions, The Great Bank Combine, the Magnet Company, Cincinnati, Ohio, 1912, pp. 19-23
[744] John Harold Wood, A History Of Central Banking in Great Britain and the United States, Cambridge University Press, New York, 2005, p. 138

the moneychangers by establishing the gold standard, and, largely destroy silver as a medium of exchange, while instituting a paper currency. Wall Street, the big banks and Congress, precipitated a new financial and political entity on the country, an informal branch of the government that dominated the other branches. Congress forfeited their exclusive responsibility to issue, and to regulate the supply of public funds, and bank credit for fifty years to a corporation controlled by Wall Street banks. [745] However, did Congress, a cabal of lawyers, and bankers, really forfeit its duty or create a cash cow that it could milk for decades.

The Federal Reserve, the Money Trust

President William Howard Taft (1909-1913), according to a descendant, had refused to pass the Federal Reserve legislation. Yet, Taft (S&B), who had empowered the Interstate Commerce Commission, accommodated Philander C. Knox, the Secretary of State (1909-1913), who lied about the ratification of the Sixteenth Amendment. They added it to the Constitution on February 3, 1913, just before Taft left office. In addition, Taft targeted underdeveloped Latin American and Asian nations through his Dollar Diplomacy, using US military enforcement. While he implemented some profit-producing plans, he failed to accommodate those who wanted a central bank, and was soon out of a job.

In January and February 1913, a subcommittee of the House Banking and Currency, conducted hearings. Warburg, considering his experience in foreign banking, testified before the subcommittee, along with Barton Hepburn and Victor Morawetz, [746] who in 1910, wrote the article, *The Banking and Currency Problem and Its Solution,*

---

[745] Alfred Owen Crozier, US Money vs. Corporation Currency, Aldrich Plan, Wall Street Confessions, The Great Bank Combine, the Magnet Company, Cincinnati, Ohio, 1912, pp. 16-22

[746] Banking and currency reform: hearings before the subcommittee of the Committee on Banking and Currency by United States, Congress, House of Representatives, Tuesday, January 7, 1913, Statements of Barton Hepburn, Victor Morawetz and Paul M. Warburg, Government Printing Office, Washing, 1913, p. 43

Defects of the Existing System. Morawetz noted that there were more than twenty thousand independent banks and trust companies at that time. [747]

On April 7, 1913, Republican Senator Henry Cabot Lodge introduced the Aldrich Bill. On June 23, 1913, President Wilson addressed a joint session of Congress on banking and currency reform. Senator Robert L. Owen introduced S.2639 (Senate Report, Pt. 2, pp. 33-66). Representative Carter Glass, future Treasury Secretary (1918-1920) a skilled orator, introduced H.R.6454 on June 26, 1913 (House Report, pp. 111-130), the first official introduction of Wilson's Federal Reserve Act proposal. On July 2, 1913, Representative Charles A. Lindbergh Sr. introduced H.R.6578 (HR, pp. 151-155) which included a stipulation, for the period of twenty years from its organization, unless sooner dissolved by Act of Congress. [748] Congress, co-benefactors of the Federal Reserve Act, can dissolve the Fed any time, by legislation, the same way in which it created that corporation.

Representative Arsene P. Pujo, Chairman of the House Banking and Currency Committee, and also a member of the National Monetary Commission, convened an investigation to investigate the money trust, an elite group of Wall Street bankers. The Pujo Committee conducted hearings, akin to the fox investigating chicken seizures from the henhouse, between May 16, 1912 and February 26, 1913. Its comprehensive three-volume report, with hundreds of policies and regulations, satisfied the people's trust and swayed public opinion which assisted in the passage of the Federal Reserve Act and the Clayton Antitrust Act of 1914. [749]

---

[747] Proceedings of the Academy of Political Science in the City of New York, The Economic Position of Women, Volume 1 by Academy of Political Science in the City of New York, October 1910, pp. 343-344

[748] Bills introduced in the United States Senate and the House of Representatives during the Sixty-Third Congress (March 4, 1913 to March 4, 1915) relative to Rural Credits, Government Printing Office, Washington, 1915, pp. 433-437

[749] Money Trust Investigation: Investigation of Financial and Monetary Conditions in the United States Under House Resolutions Nos. 429 and 504 : 1912-1913, http://fraser.stlouisfed.org/publications/montru as of May 2012

The actions and recorded documents of Congress, leading up to the passage of the Federal Reserve Act, amounted to 300 pages of Committee Reports and 1,300 pages in the Congressional Record. Thereafter, Congress added thousands of pages. It enacted H.R.7837, for the establishment of a Federal Reserve System, introduced by Glass, chair of the House Committee on Banking and Currency, on August 29, 1913 (CR 50, p.3925). This 166-page bill went back to the House on September 9, 1913 (CR 50, p. 4633) and it passed, 287 to 85, with 5 present, 55 not voting, on September 18, 1913 (CR 50, p. 5129), the day it referred the bill to the Senate (CR 50, p. 5126). [750] [751]

From September 2 to October 27, 1913, the Senate Banking and Currency Committee, chaired by Owen, conducted hearings during which Frank A. Vanderlip gave testimony. On November 6, 1913, Vanderlip persuaded the Senate Banking Committee to adopt some of his ideas which put the Committee into a deadlock by November 20. Senator Gilbert Hitchcock, on November 22 (CR 50, p. 5962), proposed that the Senate accept the Vanderlip plan and the Senate made such amendments to H.R. 7837 on November 24, 1913 (Senate Report, Part 3, pp. 6-24) creating Owen's 131-page substitute bill. [752]

The Senate discussed the amended H.R. 7837 and passed it on December 18, 1913 with 54 yeas to 34 nays with 7 not voting (CR 51, pp. 22, 1230). The House disagreed with the Senate amendment and opted for a conference report (CR 51, p. 1464). Both legislative bodies reached an agreement, and each voted, for the passage of the 30-page H.R. 7837 in the House (435 members), on December 22, with 298 (a majority) to 60 and on December 23, in the Senate (96 members), 43 to 25 with 27 not voting. President Wilson signed H.R. 7837 on December 23, 1913 (CR 51, p. 1688). [753] Article I, section 5, paragraph

---

[750] Guide to Legislative History of the Original Federal Reserve Act, compile in the Legal Division of the Board of Governors of the Federal Reserve System, November 1963, pp. 4-6

[751] The Federal Reserve Act of 1913-A Legislative History, http://www.llsdc.org/FRA-LH/ as of May 2012

[752] The Federal Reserve Act of 1913-A Legislative History, http://www.llsdc.org/FRA-LH/ as of May 2012

[753] Ibid.

3 of the Constitution provides that one-fifth of those present (11 Senators, if no more than a quorum is present) can order the yeas and nays—also known as a roll call vote or a recorded vote.

When the House approved the measure, Congressman Lindberg said, "The money trust caused the 1907 panic and thereby forced Congress to create a National Monetary Commission." Further, he said, "the money trust would cause a money stringency in order to force the bill through Congress . . . This bill is passed by Congress as a Christmas present to The money trust" [754]

Congressman Lindbergh, according to the Congressional record of February 12, 1917 wrote articles of impeachment for members of the Federal Reserve Board, William P. G. Harding, governor; Paul M. Warburg, vice governor; Frederick Delano, Adolf C. Miller and Charles S. Hamlin. He charged them with "high crimes and misdemeanors in aiding, abetting, and conspiring with certain persons and firms hereinafter named, and with other persons, and firms, known and unknown, in a conspiracy to violate the Constitution and the laws of the United States." Probably for retribution or his continued criticism, thugs kidnapped his grandson on March 1, 1932, and then murdered him.

Lindbergh, father of the famous aviator, criticized the banking trust and wrote a book, *Why is Your Country at War*, attempting to explain the corruptness of the banking trust, and its complicity with Congress. He also referred to the *Hazard Circular*, distributed by Jay Cooke, the government's fiscal agent, at the end of the Civil War. This pamphlet had the statement, "We lay down the proposition that our national debt made permanent and rightly managed, will be a national blessing. The funded debt of the United States is the addition of three thousand millions ($3,000,000,000) to the previously realized wealth of the Nation. It is three thousand millions added to the actual available capital." [755] Alexander Hamilton also used the phrase "national blessing" when referring to the national debt.

---

[754] June Grem, The Money Manipulators, Enterprise Publications, Inc. Oak Park, Illinois, 1971, p. 43

[755] Charles A. Lindbergh, Banking and Currency and the Money Trust, National Capital Press, Inc., Washington, DC, 1913, p. 33

Several large Wall-Street-controlled newspapers vilified Lindbergh for calling attention to the banking trust. [756]

A Pilgrims Society member typically manages the New York Federal Reserve. Many bankers, industrialists, diplomats and politicians have been Pilgrims Society members—Mellon, Rockefeller, Astor, Warburg, Rothschild, Du Pont, Harriman, Vanderbilt, Duke, Reynolds, and Cullman. These are the same family names revealed in Lundberg's *America's 60 Families*. He provides credible evidence that a hierarchy of the country's sixty richest families own and control the United States, actually a corporation. These politically incestuous families cooperate with each other, belong to secret societies, and interact at various levels. The inner circle of wealth and power often delegates others to implement certain activities. [757]

Fractional reserve banking, used by the Rothschilds with great success, is dishonest and enslaving. Federal Reserve currency replaced US Treasury Department Notes. The Federal Government does not redeem them for gold, silver, or anything else. Up to 1928, currency carried this statement, "Redeemable in gold on demand at the United States Treasury, or in gold or lawful money at any Federal Reserve Bank." Prior to 1933, the government redeemed them for gold. Before 1964, people could redeem some notes for silver. From 1934 to 1971, only foreign note holders could redeem them for gold at a fixed rate. Now, all assets held in collateral, by the Federal Reserve, including Social Security number holders and their assets, back Federal Reserve Notes. [758] The Federal Reserve's assets as of November 14, 2007, per their reports, totaled $925,309,000,000. [759]

Twenty years after they created the Federal Reserve in 1913, its influence on United States domestic and foreign policy became well

[756] John Remington Graham, Blood Money: the Civil War and the Federal Reserve, Pelican Publishing Company, Gretna, Louisiana, 2006, pp. 45-46
[757] Charles Savoie, Meet the World Money Power, December 2004, pp. 52-53
[758] Department of the Treasury, http://www.ustreas.gov/education/faq/currency/legal-tender.shtml as of May 2012
[759] Geraldine Perry and Ken Fousek, The Two Faces of Money, Wasteland Press, Shelbyville, Kentucky, 2007, pp. 152-155

established. In 1933 Congressman Louis T. McFadden wrote, *"Every effort has been made by the Federal Reserve Board to conceal its powers, but the truth is, the FED has usurped the government. It controls everything here (in Congress) and it controls all our foreign relations. It makes and breaks governments at will."* Since Wilson's presidency, the Federal Reserve has managed the majority of the US presidents. Alternatively, is it the other way around? Does the US corporation control the Federal Reserve in behalf of those few wealthy families who control Congress?

In 1901, the national debt was less than $1 billion. After World War I, it was $25 billion. Between the world wars, it increased to $49 billion. In 1952, in the midst of the Korean War, under U.N. command, the debt stood at $72 billion. In 1962, it was $303 billion, which increased to $383 billion by 1970, during the Vietnam War. By 1976, the end of the Vietnam War, it was $631 billion. During the 1980s, with the Cold War military buildup, the debt increased substantially. International bankers funded the weaponization of both the United States and the Soviet Union. President Dwight D. Eisenhower's Executive Order in 1953 classified all congressional records showing the massive banker-funded technological transfers beginning in 1916. [760] By 1998, the debt was over $5.5 trillion. Now, it is over $15 trillion and climbing. This does not include personal indebtedness such as credit cards, car loans or mortgages.

According to authors Geraldine Perry and Ken Fousek in *The Two Faces of Money*, the two kinds of money are debt-based, which is owed, and debt-free or owned money. The Federal Reserve, since its inception, has kept the nation burdened with a debt-based system. Debt-based money represents credit which includes usury. A legitimate monetary authority should create debt-free money that bears no interest which people spend into circulation as money of exchange. Owned money is based on one's own productivity. Debt-based money, used by central banks in over 170 countries, employs money of accounts. People have used many items as money including

---

[760] Antony C. Sutton, National Suicide, Military Aid to the Soviet Union, Arlington House, New Rochelle, New York, 1973, p. 49

livestock, grains, beads, shells, tally sticks, hemp, gold and silver, all owned by the people who used them which represented real wealth. People produced, owned, and circulated those debt-free items as a medium of trade. [761]

Currency printed by the Federal Reserve represents money owed to that entity by whoever borrows it, an individual, a bank, an institution or a government. Our money supply, the currency in circulation, is a result of Federal Reserve loans which means debt. It's a perpetual system in which there will never be enough money to pay the interest. Continuous currency printing creates additional debt and an unstable economic environment. The Federal Reserve is a banker's bank, a private cartel. It creates money by purchasing government securities with their money and burdens citizens with un-payable, accumulating interest and taxes with an exponentially increasing debt which has inherent instability based on flawed mathematical principles. [762]

Congress created the Federal Reserve, a corporation, to function as a central bank. Many people repeat Eustace Mullins' claims that foreign banks own and control the Federal Reserve Bank of New York, just one of twelve such banks. Dr. Edward Flaherty questions Mullins' evidence that foreign banks own and annually profit from the system. Flaherty claims that the Fed actually pays its profits to the government. At least, that was the way that Congress initially set it up. It organized the twelve FR Banks into separate corporations. Commercial banks operating within the bank's district purchase shares. Those shareholders select the president and six of the nine directors for their FR Bank. In 1983, Mullins claimed that Chase Manhattan Citibank, Morgan Guaranty Trust, Chemical Bank, Bankers Trust Company, Manufacturers Hanover Trust, National Bank of North America, and the Bank of New York owned sixty-three percent of the stock of the New York Fed's stock. He wrote that the Rothschild banking dynasty and approximately a dozen

[761] Geraldine Perry and Ken Fousek, The Two Faces of Money, Wasteland Press, Shelbyville, Kentucky, 2007, pp. 152-155
[762] Ibid. 152-155

other European banks owned those banks holding that stock. [763] [764] According to a House of Representatives 1976 report, six banks, Chase, National City, Guaranty Trust, J. P. Morgan, Hanover, and Manufacturers Trust purchased controlling stock in the Federal Reserve Bank in New York in 1914. [765]

Mullins claimed that the financial power of England, centered with the House of Rothschild controlled the most powerful men in the United States with the implications that, since 1910, England, and more specifically, the Rothschilds ruled America. [766] He further claimed that when Congress passed the FR Act, "the Constitution ceased to be the governing covenant of the American people, and our liberties were handed over to a small group of international bankers." [767] That document ceased to exist decades before when Congress began functioning in their own behalf instead of serving the citizen's needs. If the Rothschilds and their ilk currently maintain a large measure of financial influence in the United States, we need to remember that they could not function without the assent of Congress.

Mullins stated that the FR Bulletin contained the names of the New York Fed stockholders although, according to Flaherty, neither it, nor any other Fed periodical, ever published such information. The Securities and Exchange Commission (SEC), established in June 6, 1934, does not require the publication of a list of key shareholders in a non-publicly traded corporation. One may scrutinize the legalities of acquiring such stock to determine ownership. The FR Act required national and state banks to buy shares in their regional FR Bank in order to join the System. The eight nationally-chartered banks that Mullins named were within the New York Federal district, and,

[763] Who owns and controls the Federal Reserve by Dr. Edward Flaherty, http://www.usagold.com/federalreserve.html as of May 2012
[764] Eustace Mullins, The Secrets of the Federal Reserve, the London Connection, John McLaughlin, 1993, pp. 172-174
[765] Federal Reserve Directors: A Study of Corporate and Banking Influence, Staff Report, Committee on Banking, Currency and Housing, House of Representatives, 94th Congress, 2nd Session, August 1976
[766] Eustace Mullins, The Secrets of the Federal Reserve, the London Connection, John McLaughlin, 1993, pp. 46-47
[767] Ibid. 28

as such, were required to buy stock in that entity, and were, as he argued, probably the primary shareholders. [768]

Gary Kah, who claims anonymous informants, is a former Europe and Middle East trade specialist for the Indiana state government. His list of shareholders, different than Mullins' list, is the Rothschild Banks (London and Berlin), Lazard Brothers Banks (Paris), Israel Moses Seif Banks (Italy), Warburg Bank (Hamburg and Amsterdam), Lehman Brothers (New York), Kuhn, Loeb Bank (New York), Chase Manhattan, and Goldman, Sachs (New York). According to Kah, foreign owners did not purchase major interests in US banks but owned them directly despite the fact that officials never issued public stock. [769]

Title 12, US Code, Section 283, Public subscription to capital stock, states, "No individual, co-partnership, or corporation other than a member bank of its district shall be permitted to subscribe for or to hold at any time more than $25,000 par value of stock in any Federal reserve bank. Such stock shall be known as public stock and may be transferred on the books of the Federal Reserve Bank by the chairman of the board of directors of such bank." [770] According to the FR Act, officials could sell public stock only if the member banks, in 1913, failed to initially generate $4 million, which they did. Therefore, officials never sold public stock to anyone, including foreigners, but rather to banks that belonged to the FR System. [771] However, given the passage of time and congressional corruptness, what has changed since 1913?

Mullins claimed that the New York banks owned the largest percentage of stock in the New York Fed and could select the president and board of directors, giving them managerial control of the Fed's actions.

---

[768] Dr. Edward Flaherty, Who owns and controls the Federal Reserve, http://www.usagold.com/federalreserve.html as of May 2012

[769] Ibid

[770] US Law, http://law.justia.com/codes/us/2010/title12/chapter3/subchaptervi/section283/

[771] Dr. Edward Flaherty, Who owns and controls the Federal Reserve, http://www.usagold.com/federalreserve.html as of May 2012

However, official policy restricts each commercial bank to only one vote despite the number of shares it holds, as opposed to other corporations in which the biggest shareholder dominates. It is highly unlikely that any small group of member banks would spend the necessary billions of dollars to exercise control over the votes of at least half of over 1,000 member banks that make up the New York FR district. [772]

While it is easier to attribute the nation's apparent economic woes to ominous, untouchable foreign bankers, the fact is that Congress has control. Mullins and Kah claimed that foreign interests, by controlling the New York Fed, rule the FR System, and therefore manage the United States economy. Yet, the president-appointed seven-member Board of Governors and the Federal Open Market Committee (FOMC) control the System, not the New York Fed, which has only one vote out of twelve. The Senate approves the president's selection of the Board which then determines interest rates, commercial bank loans, the obligatory reserve ratio, and the issuance of new currency each year (12 USCA 248). The FOMC, composed of the Board, the New York Fed president, and four presidents from other Fed Banks, regulates the amount of government bonds that the Fed Banks may trade. The FR Bank must maintain its reserve ratio and cannot issue additional currency, or buy government bonds unless the Board or the FOMC approves. The Board and the FOMC determines United States economic policies, and not international bankers, or the Federal Advisory Council, a Board-appointed non-voting group that consults quarterly with the Board about economic conditions. Mullins attributes extraordinary power to this Council, which directly contradicts his claim that European bankers control the New York Fed, and the nation's economy. [773]

The FR System, a corporation, is incredibly successful, and accrues huge profits. According to an agreement between the Board and the Treasury, since 1947, the Fed pays the majority of those profits to the

---

[772] Dr. Edward Flaherty, Who owns and controls the Federal Reserve, http://www.usagold.com/federalreserve.html as of May 2012

[773] Ibid

US Treasury. It dispenses the remainder, less than one percent, to its stockholders as dividends.

Every issue of FR paper is a lien upon the products of labor. The federal government is responsible for the unequal distribution of wealth. Warfare is one of the biggest expenditures, currently exceeded by bureaucratic agencies. The elite view these as more important than the reasonable needs of society. The parasitic elite, who produce nothing but live off the efforts of others, use bureaucrats and brute force to control the masses. The question one should always ask is Cui bono—"To whose benefit?" or literally "as a benefit to whom?"

SECTION 5

LOCALIZED WARFARE AND ASSET EXPLOITATION

High on Drug Profits

Author Edwin C. Knuth wrote, "China, Russia, the United States and Germany are in order the most populous *independent* nations in the world, and therefore represent the most dynamic and most dangerous competition of the British Empire. All of them have been the victims of recurrent British repression." [774]

Jews settled in China as early as the seventh or eighth century AD and there were isolated communities beginning in the Tang and Song Dynasties up to the Qing Dynasty. By the ninth century, Jewish merchants traveled to China via the Silk Road through Central Asia and India. The Kaifeng Jews, who may have traveled from Persia, during the Song Dynasty (960-1127), later became indistinguishable from the Chinese population. They had synagogues in Kaifeng by 1126 and as late as 1421. [775] Many Jewish communities in China left evidence of their existence in Kaifeng, Hangzhou, Ningbo, Yangzhou, and Ningxia.

The British Empire profitably engaged in piracy, slavery and drug trafficking under various companies. British individuals, doing business as the British East India Company, just one of several early corporations, targeted China's riches in the eighteenth century. It exercised monopoly powers over territories, considered critical to Britain's interests. [776] In 1715, it implemented a mass-scale, long-

---

[774] Edwin C. Knuth, The Empire of the City, the Secret History of British Financial Power by Edwin C. Knuth, The Book Tree, San Diego, California, Originally published 1944, Wisconsin, p. 14

[775] Jonathan Goldstein (editor) The Jews of China, Volume 1, M. E. Sharpe, Armonk, New York, 1999, pp. 6-7

[776] David C. Korten, When Corporations Rule the World, Kumarian Press, 1995, p. 55

term monopoly drug addiction project in China through their newly established office in Canton. Company policies included a reign of terror, political control and all-encompassing exploitation privileges supported by the Crown who received a percentage of the highly addictive opium profits.

The British East India Company initially used silver to pay for Chinese tea, Britain's favorite hot drink of which they consumed huge amounts. However, in the 1820s, the Chinese decided they would only accept gold, which jeopardized the British treasury. Certain Chinese were willing to trade opium for tea. Before 1830, Baghdad's prominent Jewish family traded opium. In 1832, the government forced them to leave and they settled in Bombay, India, on the trade route to the interior of India and the Far East gateway. They then obtained exclusive rights from Britain to market opium in Shanghai and Hong Kong, from which the queen received a healthy share of the profits.

David Sassoon (1792-1864), an Orthodox Jew, was the son of Saleh Sassoon, a wealthy businessman, and chief treasurer (court Jew) to the pashas. David Sassoon corresponded in Judaea—Arabic script, and closed his offices on Saturday and Sunday, the official day of rest. The poorer Jews in Baghdad, Aleppo and Damascus discovered that Sassoon might provide employment in Bombay. He arranged food, housing, and medical care for his employees as well as a school for their children where they learned enough to hold jobs plus the tenets of their faith. The Sassoons also established cemeteries and synagogues. [777]

On January 1, 1824, envisioning trade opportunities, Samuel Russell established Russell and Company, with a fleet of clipper ships. He acquired opium in Turkey, then sold it in the expanding China market, and then purchased Chinese silk, porcelain and tea. On June 28, 1832, at Yale University, William H. Russell, Samuel's first cousin, co-founded the Order of Skull and Bones (S&B) with Alphonso

---

[777] Jonathan Goldstein (editor), The Jews of China, Volume 1, M. E. Sharpe, Armonk, New York, 1999, pp. 142-143

Taft, the father of William Howard Taft who later became the US president and then the Chief Justice of the US Supreme Court. In 1856, they incorporated the Order as The Russell Trust Association with Daniel C. Gilman as treasurer and Russell as president. Many member families acquired their fortunes through drug trafficking— Coffin, Sloane, Taft, Bundy, Payne, Whitney and others. The Barings Bank financed the British-based Peninsular and Oriental Steamship Company which carried opium to China. The Barings and Lehman Brothers invested in the clipper trade, from the time of the American Revolution through the Civil War, trading cotton and slaves.[778]

From 1791 to 1894, the number of licensed opium dens in Shanghai increased dramatically while opium imports into the United States were also on the rise. However, Chinese leaders adamantly opposed the growing addiction. The Emperor's attempts to halt drug trafficking led to the First Opium War (1839-1842), between Britain and Ireland and the Qing Dynasty, ending with the Treaty of Nanking, on August 29, 1842, which the Chinese referred to as one of the unequal treaties. [779] Former Prime Minister, Lord Palmerston, Henry J. Temple (1835-1841) wrote Captain Charles Elliot that the treaty was insufficient. He wrote, "After all, our naval power is so strong that we can tell the Emperor what we mean to hold rather than what he would cede." He told Elliot to demand "admission of opium into China as an article of lawful commerce." He also demanded the increase of the indemnity payments and British access to several additional Chinese ports. [780]

The Chinese, per the treaty, were compelled to open five ports to foreign trade—Canton, Amoy, Foochow, Ningbo and Shanghai. Additionally, the British received Hong Kong Island as a Crown Colony, to provide traders with a harbor and a place to unload their

---

[778] China and the Opium Wars, http://www.meta-religion.com/Secret_societies/ Groups/Order_of_Skull/part_5.htm as of May 2012

[779] Treaty of Nanking, 1842, Ratifications exchanged at Hong Kong, June 26, 1843 between Great Britain and China, http://www.international.ucla.edu/ eas/documents/nanjing.htm as of May 2012

[780] Konstandinos Kalimtgis, David Goldman, and Jeffrey Steinberg, Dope, Inc., Britain's Opium War Against the US, Ben Franklin Booksellers, 1986, pp. 15-16

merchandise. The British forced the Chinese to pay the British government $6,000,000 for the opium that officials had confiscated in 1839, $3,000,000 to pay the British merchants for debts owed by merchants residing in Canton, and, another $12,000,000 in war reparations, payable in silver, in installments over three years. If they failed to pay in a timely manner, British bankers charged an annual interest rate of five percent on the unpaid balance.

That war opened new commercial opportunities to Baghdadi trader Elias D. Sassoon (1820-1880) who immediately set sail from Bombay to Canton. He succeeded in China because of his father, David Sassoon and his company, which had begun shipping opium to Canton by 1834. They established a vast network that covered a large portion of Asia. David Sassoon's eight sons helped expand Jewish networks in Southeast and East Asia. By the early 1870s, they had facilities in the treaty ports of Shanghai and Hong Kong and in the Japanese cities of Nagasaki, Yokohama and Kobe. [781]

In the nineteenth and early twentieth centuries, leading Baghdadi families, such as the Sassoons, Eliases, Kadoories, Abrahams, Hardoons, Ezras, Solomons, and Gubbays, arrived to pursue commercial interests, especially in Hong Kong, Shanghai, the International Settlement, and in Harbin, where a branch of the Trans-Siberian Railway exists. When Western commercial interests opened China after the First Opium War, Jews, under British protection, again settled in China. Many of these Jewish settlers came from India or the Ottoman Empire, because of British colonialism in those areas. They constituted the most active and largest group of opium dealers in China. [782]

---

[781] Chiara Betta, Diaspora Entrepreneurial Networks, Four Centuries of History, edited by Ina Baghdiantz McCabe, Gelina Harlaftis and Ioanna Pepelasis Minoglou, Chapter 12, The Trade Diaspora of Baghdadi Jews: From India to China's Treaty Ports, 1842-1937, Berg Publishers, Oxford, England, 2005, pp. 270-271

[782] Jonathan Goldstein (editor) The Jews of China, Volume 1, M. E. Sharpe, Armonk, New York, 1999, pp. 142-143

The Chinese monopolized the world's tea production until the British smuggled plants out of China in the 1850s. Growing and selling their own tea helped them to recoup some of their dwindling gold reserves. They also demanded that the Chinese use silver to purchase their opium. From 1829 to 1840, $7 million silver dollars entered China, while $56 million silver dollars left, due to the expanding opium trade. [783] On July 1, 1832, William Jardine and James Matheson founded Jardine, Matheson & Company in Canton. It was the first unchartered private company to import tea into England, but they made more profit from their opium trade. In 1844, they opened a branch office in Shanghai. Opium remained their major product until 1870, when they diversified into shipping, warehousing, mining, textiles, and railroads.

Warren Delano II, the grandfather of Franklin D. Roosevelt, collaborated with Russell and Company in Canton, which delivered Sassoon's opium to China, and returned with tea. The British owned their own poppy fields in India, while their American competitors had to purchase their opium in Turkey, which decreased their profits. American traders wanted a bigger share of China's opium business, and greater concessions in that market, but it would require the US government's intervention, due to Britain's established monopoly and her treaties with China.

In order for the opium traders to get government support, they had to have willing sympathetic officials, open to receiving drug profits, as in the case of Britain's queen. Therefore, they financed and supported the campaigns of men who would replace uncooperative officials. Supplanting public figures is a very private matter. In order to ascend in certain secret societies, one also has to participate in the killing of the king, as a rite of passage. [784] John S. Dye in his 1964 book, *The Adder's Den,* claimed that agents poisoned President William H. Harrison (1773-1841), a hardy, rugged former farmer, and soldier, who

---

[783] Konstandinos Kalimtgis, David Goldman, Jeffrey Steinberg, Dope, Inc., Britain's Opium War Against the US, Ben Franklin Booksellers, 1986, p. 14

[784] New Orleans Mardi Gras Mystick Krewe of Comus Secrets Revealed by Mini L. Eustis given to her by her father, Samuel Todd Churchill on his deathbed, http://www.mardigrassecrets.com/index.html as of May 2012

enjoyed good health. Yet, two hours in the rain allegedly led to his unexpected death, after only thirty-one days in office. Vice President John Tyler, a freemason, then moved into the White House, the first to attain that office through succession. After Tyler assumed office, he appointed Caleb Cushing, a freemason, as secretary of state. The Senate rejected the appointment. Therefore, Tyler appointed him as commissioner to China (1843-1844.) [785] Cushing was one of Russell's partners, and he was possibly a member of Skull and Bones, also known as the Brotherhood of Death.

American merchants, competing with the British in China, pressured President Tyler to negotiate a more detailed treaty, allowing land acquisition and other privileges that even the British had not demanded. Tyler sent Cushing to China. In February 1844, his ship arrived in Canton with its guns blazing, just to intimidate the Chinese. He negotiated the Treaty of Wàngxià, signed on July 3, 1844 in the Kun Iam Temple. This treaty, the first between China and the United States, established five treaty ports for Chinese-Western trade, Guangzhou, Xiamen, Fuzhou, Ningbo, and Shanghai. It also permitted, for the first time, land ownership by foreigners, and foreign trading operations in China. [786]

Britain's Second Opium War (1856-1860), fought on behalf of the greedy opium traders, legalized Sassoon's opium trade into China's interior. Lord Palmerston, Britain's Prime Minister (1855-1858) instigated this war. On October 18, 1860, in their siege on Peking, Commander Lord Elgin, James Bruce, ordered his troops and the accompanying French forces to destroy the summer palace and the sacred temples and shrines, an indication of their contempt for the Chinese. [787] The resulting Treaty of Tientsin, signed on October 25, 1860, allowed for the further expansion of the opium trade to over £20 million, just in 1864 alone. Within 20 years, the opium exports

[785] Steven Sora, The Secret Societies of America's Elite, From the Knights Templar to Skull and Bones, Destiny Books, 2003, pp. 149-150
[786] Ibid. 149-150
[787] The Jewish Opium Trade and Britain, The Truth at Last: Hong Kong's opium dens, October 1, 2007, http://inpursuitofhappiness.wordpress.com/2007/10/01/the-sassoon-opium-wars/ as of May 2012

from India, mostly to China, increased from 58,681 chests in 1860, to 105,508 chests in 1880. [788] Delano was in China during both wars.

The treaty opened eleven more Chinese ports to foreign trade and permitted foreign legations in the Chinese capital of Beijing (Peking, then a closed city). The treaties allowed foreign vessels, including warships, to travel freely on the Yangtze River. Foreigners could, according to the treaties, travel into the interior of China for pleasure, trade or Christian missionary activities. They also legalized opium importation. These regulations, all designed to benefit foreigners, exempted foreigners from local and national taxes.

After Britain's First Opium War, the Soong family, agents for the multinational Sassoons, was the real power behind the Chinese Emperor. By 1890, about ten percent of the Chinese population smoked opium. [789] Ironically, in 1874, given the number of bluebloods in the business, members of the Yale School of Divinity called attention to China's pervasive decadence because of their opium addiction. [790] Later, the Chinese communists would limit China's progression and continue to harvest profit-producing dope to become, at one time, the world's largest opium producer. [791]

The Sassoons preferred to run their financial interests from their luxurious English estates in order to socialize with royalty and other elites like Arthur J. Balfour, H. G. Wells, and Winston Churchill. [792] In addition to the massive drug profits, and to exploit India's cheap labor force, Albert Sassoon established huge textile mills in Bombay.

---

[788] Konstandinos Kalimtgis, David Goldman, Jeffrey Steinberg, Dope, Inc., Britain's Opium War Against the US, Ben Franklin Booksellers, 1986, Chapter 1, Britain's First Opium Wars

[789] Tales of Old Shanghai, http://www.talesofoldchina.com/shanghai/business/t-opium.htm as of May 2012

[790] The Yale Divinity School, Lecture By Prof. Seelye—Missions—Condition of Pagan World—Fail, The New York Times, December 12, 1874

[791] Skull & Bones—The Bush's China Connection, From an article in the New Federalist, January 26, 1990, http://www.illuminati-news.com/S&B-China.htm as of May 2012

[792] Edwin C. Knuth, The Empire of "The City": The Secret History of British Financial Power, CPA Books, 1995, p. 75

This early-day outsourcing of labor destabilized the Lancashire mills and devastated Britain's working class who depended on those mills. In 1872, despite this economic assault against the commoners, Queen Victoria knighted Albert. [793] In 1887, Edward A. Sassoon, Albert's son, would marry Aline Caroline de Rothschild of the French banking family, granddaughter of Jacob Mayer Rothschild.

Jews were predominate in opium trafficking. In April 1884, out of 3,763 containers of opium headed for China, Jewish traders owned 2,918 chests. David Sassoon owned 1,040 while Calcutta merchants owned a total of 1,878. The Calcutta Jews owned and controlled such a significant amount of opium, that they could depress the market by avoiding the auctions where the government sold the raw product. When the price dropped, they purchased greater amounts. [794]

Sassoon's firm, although general merchants began acting as a banker, and acquired property, further adding to its overall prosperity. Jacob Sassoon, the son of Elias, established new mills to increase his interests in the cotton industry in Bombay, while other branches of the family immigrated to, and settled in London. Jacob recruited workers from Baghdad, promising the usual benefits and housing. He soon had fifteen thousand employees in his mills and was the largest single employer of factory labor in the vicinity. For his service in building India, and extending his commercial influence beyond India into other parts of the empire, the British government knighted Jacob Sassoon in 1909. By 1900, the two Sassoon mills represented the biggest conglomeration in India. Because of an imposing excise tax, other mill owners in Bombay had to close their businesses, but the Sassoons survived. [795]

---

[793] The Jewish Opium Trade and Britain, The Truth at Last: Hong Kong's opium dens, http://inpursuitofhappiness.wordpress.com/2007/10/01/the-sassoon-opium-wars/ as of May 2012

[794] Jonathan Goldstein (editor), The Jews of China, Volume 1, M. E. Sharpe, Armonk, New York, 1999, pp. 144-145

[795] Ibid. 144-145

Iranian Oil Exploitation, a Precursor to Further Warfare

Between 1850 and 1880, numerous individuals from rival companies in France, Belgium, Britain, Russia, and America competed for the opportunity to construct and finance railways and other projects in Persia. However, these various attempts were never productive. Persia had lost territory to Russia in the early nineteenth century so Nasser al-Din Shah Qajar, the King of Persia (1848-1896) compensated for this territorial loss by seizing Herāt, Afghanistan (1856). Britain regarded the move as a threat to British India and declared war on Iran, forcing the return of Herāt as well as Iranian recognition of the kingdom of Afghanistan.

In 1872, Shah Qajar granted a concession to Baron Julius de Reuter (born Israel B. Josephat), a British citizen, for the control of all Persian roads, telegraphs, mills, factories, extraction of resources, and other public properties. In exchange de Reuter would pay the king a specific sum over a five-year period and de Reuter would receive sixty percent of the net profits for twenty years. The public immediately protested this outrageous concession. The Russian government also opposed the agreement. Because of immense pressure, the Shah rescinded, despite his deteriorating financial condition. He was the first Persian monarch to visit Europe (1873, 1878) and was impressed with Britain's technology. In 1873, Queen Victoria made him a Knight of the Order of the Garter, the first Persian monarch to receive it. During his visit, he met with several Jewish leaders, including Sir Moses Montefiore. The Shah, possibly thinking of the financial benefits, suggested that the Jews buy land and establish a state for the Jewish people.

Others had interests in what we now refer to as the Middle East. Ferdinand de Lesseps, a French developer, initially obtained a construction concession (1854 and 1856) from Sa'id Pasha, the Khedive (viceroy) of Egypt and Sudan (1854-1863). The Frenchman visualized a canal, the Suez Canal, as a passage to ships of all nations. Later, people referred to it as the Highway to India, opening in 1869, joining the Mediterranean and Red Seas. Ismail Pasha, the Khedive of Egypt and Sudan (1863-1879), modernized Egypt through industrial investments, infrastructure projects, and expansion of the nation's borders into Africa. However, his modernization efforts came with a huge burden of debt that he could not pay. Benjamin Disraeli, Britain's first Jewish Prime Minister, borrowed £4,080,000 from his friend, Nathan M. Rothschild and bought 176,000 shares in the Suez Canal Company on November 25, 1875. The British government then assumed managerial control on December 8, 1875 through the Administrative Council of the General Company of the Suez Maritime Canal. [796]

However, Egypt was part of the Ottoman Empire, governed by the Sublime Porte, the central government in Constantinople. In 1863, the Porte initially consented to the concession for the Sweet Water Canal but in a diplomatic note objected to the use of the enforced labor that de Lesseps intended to use to build the canal. The Porte wanted to terminate the concession because it would have been cruel and injurious to the Egyptian workmen. The Porte was also concerned about its rights. Additionally, the concession awarded a large strip of land as well as the Port of Suez to the French which might prove extremely disadvantageous to the Ottoman Empire in the future. The Firman of 1879, did not change the 1863 document. Consequently, the Khedive was under the jurisdiction of the Porte and it never authorized him to sell the Suez Canal, despite Egypt's deplorable economic situation. [797] Moreover, the Firman prevented the Khedive of Egypt, an autonomous province, from contracting loans without the Sultan's approval and from retaining an army greater than 18,000 in peacetime. Further, the Khedive could not enter into a treaty with any foreign power except for minor commercial considerations. [798]

According to Muslim dogma, governments should never borrow money, to construct public projects such as the Suez Canal, from

[796] Vladimir Borisovich Lutsky, Modern History of the Arab Countries, 1969, Chapter XV, The Financial Enslavement Of Egypt Foreign Loans
[797] The Parliamentary Debates, (Authorized edition), Great Britain. Volume 282, August 9, 1883, pp. 2145-2146
[798] David Musa Pidcock, Satanic Voices, Ancient and Modern, a Surfeit of Blasphemy Including the Rushdie Report from Edifice Complex to Occult Theocracy, Mustaqim, Islamic Art and Literature, Milton Keynes, England, 1992, pp. 47-53

foreigners, presumably even those living within their boundaries. A successful government should always create its own debt-free, interest-free, domestic currency, in order to accumulate assets instead of burdensome liabilities. Author David Pidcock states that these debts, payable to a foreign power, function like a built-in time bomb which that power could activate when it needed an excuse to assault and occupy a country. [799]

Abdülhamid II, the Ottoman Sultan, outraged over foreign bankers, and corrupt officials, ousted Ismail Pasha in 1879, and Tewfik Pasha succeeded him, followed by anarchy and a military mutiny. In September 1879, Robert Gascoyne-Cecil, Lord Salisbury, the Secretary of State for Foreign Affairs, along with the French ambassador in London, decided that Britain and France would not tolerate any political influence in Egypt by what they viewed as a competing power. Both countries would take military action, to the extent necessary, to prevent such a situation. [800] Friedrich Engels viewed the British occupation of Egypt, actually under Turkish jurisdiction, as in the pursuit of human interests. [801] The British military intervened on 1882, to protect its financial interests, the Suez Canal, and to quell nationalist rioting, which resulted in the Battle of Tel el-Kebir, on September 13, 1882. Occupation authorities reinstated Tewfik Pasha twelve days later.

Winston Churchill's father, Lord Randolph Churchill, was intimate friends with Nathan M. Rothschild, the great-grandson of Mayer A. Rothschild, and head of the London branch of the family bank after his father's death in 1879. As a boy, Churchill had befriended the Rothschilds, especially his schoolmate Nathan or Natty, as they called him. Nathan paid for Randolph's trip to South Africa, to evaluate the natural resources in the area, and then lent him £65,000 to invest in

---

[799]   Ibid. 47-53

[800]   The Life of William Ewart Gladstone by John Morley, Volume 3, (1890-1898), George N. Morang & Company, Limited, Toronto, 1903, pp. 73-74

[801]   Neville J. Mandel, The Arabs and Zionism before World War I, University of California Press, Berkeley and Los Angeles, California, 1976, pp. 9-11

the mining syndicates. Randolph died before he repaid the loan. [802] Rothschild also funded Cecil Rhodes, and the creation of the British South Africa Company (1889), patterned after the British East India Company, and the De Beers diamond conglomerate. He administered Rhodes's estate after his death (1902) and helped establish the Rhodes scholarship program at Oxford University.

Randolph Churchill was a staunch supporter of Jewish causes, especially the issues that were important to his close associates, and friends. In 1881, as a member of parliament (1874-1895), he persuaded the government to investigate the reports of pogroms against the Jews in Russia. On January 11 and 13, 1882, *The Times,* now owned by a subsidiary of Rupert Murdoch's Newscorp, attracted worldwide attention to the pogroms, and prominent London citizens held a meeting on February 1, 1882, to institute fund-raising, an endeavor that ultimately amounted to over £108,000, confirming the idea that persecution might be quite profitable. In 1883, Churchill favored the political emancipation for all of the Jews living in Britain. In 1882, after Britain sent a military force to Egypt, Churchill was annoyed at Prime Minister William E. Gladstone, when he sent a member of the gentile Baring Bank to examine Egypt's financial records, instead of a Rothschild, whose money had enabled the British to attain their financial interest in the canal. [803]

In December 1886, Fabius Boital, a French engineer, obtained a concession from the Shah, to construct a small Decauville railway from Tehran southwards to Ray, a stretch of about six miles. Additionally, Boital would construct a series of tramways in Tehran. Perhaps, because of cash flow issues, Boital sold these concessions to a Belgian company, founded in Brussels on May 17, 1887. Its president was Édouard Otlet, a Belgian international executive, with substantial experience in building railroads in Europe and America.

---

[802] Michael Makovsky, Churchill's Promised Land, Zionism and Statecraft, A New Republic Book, Yale University Press, New Haven, Connecticut, 2007, pp. 43-44

[803] Michael Makovsky, Churchill's Promised Land, Zionism and Statecraft, A New Republic Book, Yale University Press, New Haven, Connecticut, 2007, pp. 43-44

On March 20, 1890, the Shah met Major George F. Talbot, who convinced him to sign a contract granting a monopoly over the production, sale, and export of tobacco, for the next fifty years. For his part, the Shah would receive an annual sum of £15,000, a quarter of the yearly net profits, and a five percent dividend on the capital. In September 1890, the Russian government protested because it violated freedom of trade in the area, as stipulated by the Treaty of Turkmanchai, of February 21, 1828, between Persia and Russia. In February 1891, Talbot visited Persia to institute the Tobacco Régie. The Shah revealed his agreement, which brought the people's immediate disapproval. In December 1891, the Grand Ayatollah Mirza Hassan Shirazi issued a fatwa against farming, trading, and consuming tobacco, which ignited a boycott, and forced the government to abandon the agreement. This demonstration was Persia's initial defense against colonialism.

After miners discovered gold in Australia, the country's population increased from 430,000 to 1.7 million within three years. [804] William K. D'Arcy's family had immigrated to Australia in 1866. He ultimately became a lawyer, and, with other individuals, created the Mount Morgan Gold Mining Company, with him as the director and largest shareholder. In 1889, he returned to London with his wife and a huge fortune, acquired by exploiting Australia's gold resources and naïve miners. He thought that oil might even be more profitable and heard that Persia was full of the black gold. [805] However, he would have to work with an obliging Persian leader. On May 1, 1896, Mirza Reza Kermani assassinated Nasser al-Din Shah Qajar. In the late 1890s, Mozaffar ad-Din Shah Qajar, the new Persian King (1896-1907), and son of the former monarch, hired D'Arcy to help modernize and develop Persia's railways. [806] Like his father, the Shah visited Europe. His chancellor encouraged him to borrow money from Nicholas II of Russia to pay for his excessive traveling expenses. Because of his

---

804 The White Star Line: Beginning Years, http://www.titanic-whitestarships. com/History_WSL.htm as of May 2012

805 Stephen Kinzer, All the Shah's Men: An American Coup and the Roots of Middle East Terror, Wiley, Hoboken, New Jersey, 2003, pp. 47-49

806 William Engdahl, A Century of War, Anglo-American Oil Politics and the New World Order, Pluto Press, Ann Arbor, Michigan, 2004, pp. 21-22

extravagant personal lifestyle, he felt compelled to sign numerous concessions to foreign interests, similar to his father.

In 1900, William K. D'Arcy agreed to finance an exploratory expedition in Persia for oil and minerals, headed by Wolff, Kitabgi and Cotte, who sent George B. Reynolds and a drilling team. D'Arcy, after offering some moderate assistance, exploited his good relationship with the new Shah and managed to acquire an oil concession for a meager £20,000. He also promised to pay the Shah a sixteen percent royalty from the sale of all future discoveries. [807] In May 1901, the Shah of Persia (Iran) sold the exclusive rights to exploit, develop, export, and sell natural gas and petroleum for a period of sixty years to D'Arcy, now a London-based financier. [808] The concession covered a 480,000 square mile area but stipulated that D'Arcy would enjoy the oil rights of the whole country, with the exception of the five provinces in Northern Iran. This concession subjected the Iranian government to the will of the British until the late twentieth century, because the British relied upon the country's vast oil reserves, and therefore interfered with Iranian politics.

In 1903, D'Arcy created a company and spent more than £500,000 for expenses. In 1904, D'Arcy, because of financial necessity, had to acquire additional financial support, and negotiated with the Burmah Oil Company, which agreed to give at least £100,000 in exchange for a sizeable amount of the stock. They drilled in southern Persia until 1907, then moved to Masjed-Soleyman, and an adjacent area where they drilled from January to March 1908. By April, with no success, D'Arcy was discouraged and nearly bankrupt. However, on May 26, 1908, they struck oil and soon created a company. In April 1909, D'Arcy became the director of the newly founded Anglo-Persian Oil Company (APOC) which would later become British Petroleum (BP). By 1911, APOC constructed a pipeline from the source to a refinery at Abadan, a city in the Khuzestan province in southwestern Iran. In 1912, D'Arcy would become board chairman, although he

---

[807] William Engdahl, A Century of War, Anglo-American Oil Politics and the New World Order, Pluto Press, Ann Arbor, Michigan, 2004, pp. 21-22

[808] Stephen Kinzer, All the Shah's Men: An American Coup and the Roots of Middle East Terror, Wiley, Hoboken, New Jersey, 2003, p. 33

was now just a shareholder, because of his influence in acquiring the concession, and for attracting the financial investments of the Burmah Oil Company, and the British Admiralty.

By 1905, British financiers had realized that petroleum was more efficient and less labor-intensive than coal, which made it strategically and financially important. Britain imported oil from Standard Oil, of Mexico, a country dominated by the US oil firm, or from Russia. Energy-poor Britain was actually behind technologically, agriculturally and industrially. British strength was in naval power, and they kept ships in the gulf to deter other countries from the resources of India, a country they had exploited for generations. [809]

In 1912, the Royal Commission charged with investigating British oil supplies, agreed with Winston Churchill who said, "We must become the owners or at any rate the controllers at the source of at least a proportion of the oil which we require." In 1912, a British, Dutch and German group created the Turkish Petroleum Company, which obtained a concession to prospect for oil in the Baghdad and Mosul Wilayet. [810]

The Committee of Imperial Defence planned for a war against Germany to begin in 1914. Individuals installed Churchill into a managerial position in the Admiralty in order to prepare for that war. [811] In 1913, Churchill, as First Lord of the Admiralty, anticipating not just a local European war, but instead a world war, recognized the necessity of oil-powered ships to win that war. Thus, on June 17, 1914, he urged the government to spend £2 million, financed in part by N.M. Rothschild, to purchase fifty-one percent of the Anglo-Persian Oil Company, founded in 1908, after an oil discovery in Masjed-Soleyman, Iran, a transaction that gave Britain the major interest in the oil company.

---

[809] William Engdahl, A Century of War, Anglo-American Oil Politics and the New World Order, Pluto Press, Ann Arbor, Michigan, 2004, pp. 21-22

[810] Peter Sluglett, Britain in Iraq: 1914-1932, Ithaca Press, London, 1976, pp. 103-116

[811] Francis Neilson, The Makers of War, C. C. Nelson Publishing Company, Appleton, Wisconsin, 1950, p. 21

On May 23, 1914, the London *Petroleum Review* published a map of Mesopotamia (Iraq) showing all of the oilfields that would conceivably fall into the hands of certain British citizens, if they triumphed in what would be a very bloody battle. [812] Mesopotamia is where the Germans had recently contracted to build the railroad between Berlin and Baghdad, a situation that provoked the British into devising a war. The Germans were also interested in cotton, oil, farming, and trade with the locals, not just a railroad. [813] In August 1914, Britain was bankrupt when it declared war against Germany. The British and other participants in the war had secret agreements, numerous credits, and systematic schemes to redistribute the vast raw materials and the "physical wealth of the entire world after the war, especially areas believed to hold significant petroleum reserves in the Ottoman Empire." [814]

British and Rothschild foreign policy were uniquely compatible. Britain's interests became inseparable from the Anglo-Persian Oil Company, the only oil producing enterprise in the Middle East until 1927. In the first few years, Britain, through Anglo-Persian extracted millions of barrels of oil, while treating thousands of indigenous workers like slaves. Britain established a system of filling stations in the UK and retailed Iranian oil to several European countries and in Australia. [815] Britain, experts at imperialistic exploitation, all but drained the life's blood out of that desert land. People know the company by various names: Anglo-Iranian, British Petroleum, or just BP, which ultimately merged with Standard Oil.

On September 17, 1928, Henry Deterding of Shell Oil, John Cadman, of Britain's Anglo-Persian Oil Company and Walter Teagle, president of the Standard Oil Company formalized the Achnacarry Agreement.

---

[812] William Engdahl, A Century of War, Anglo-American Oil Politics and the New World Order, Pluto Press, Ann Arbor, Michigan, 2004, pp. 40-41

[813] W. O. Henderson, German Economic Penetration in the Middle East, 1870-1914, The Economic History Review, Vol. 18, No. 1/2 (1948), pp. 54

[814] William Engdahl, A Century of War, Anglo-American Oil Politics and the New World Order, Pluto Press, Ann Arbor, Michigan, 2004, pp. 42-45

[815] Stephen Kinzer, All the Shah's Men: An American Coup and the Roots of Middle East Terror, Wiley, Hoboken, New Jersey 2003, pp. 47-49

It was a secret pact that established the Seven Sisters oil cartel wherein Britain and France agreed to let the United States share in the oil resources in the Middle East, which they parceled out to the three countries. By 1932, Esso (Standard of New Jersey), Mobil (Standard of New York), Gulf Oil, Texaco, Standard of California (Chevron), Royal Dutch Shell and Anglo-Persian Oil Co. (British Petroleum) had become part of the Achnacarry cartel, which set world oil prices. That pact is apparently still in effect. [816] This oil cartel is part of the global banking and financial interests of the Rockefellers, the Morgans, the Warburgs, the Rothschilds, and others.

Standard's Procedures

China, Russia, America and Germany were independent, intellectually resourceful and therefore, represented "dangerous competition" to the banker-dominated British Empire. Consequently, the British, puppets working in behalf of the international bankers, collaborating with or exploiting other nations, have methodically terrorized each target country using numerous methodologies. [817] The British included the following cycle of repression just against China:

War:	British Allies:	British Target:
First Opium War, 1839-42	France	Qing Dynasty
Second Opium War, 1856-60	France	Qing Dynasty
Revolution, 1857-58	France	Chinese Nationalists
Storming of Peking, 1860	France	Qing Dynasty
Revolution, 1860-65	France	Chinese Nationalists
Sino-Japanese War, 1894-95	Japan	Qing Dynasty
Boxer Rebellion, 1899-1901,	8-Nation Alliance,	Qing Dynasty
Revolution, 1911	France, Japan	Chinese Nationalists

---

[816] William Engdahl, A Century of War, Anglo-American Oil Politics and the New World Order, Pluto Press, Ann Arbor, Michigan, 2004, pp. 74-75

[817] E. C. Knuth, The Empire of the City, the Secret History of British Financial Power, The Book Tree, San Diego, California, Originally published 1944 by E. C. Knuth, Wisconsin, p. 14

Revolution, 1916-27,	France, Japan	Gen. Chiang Kai-Shek
	Spain, Holland	
Manchurian Conquest, 1931	Japan	Gen. Chiang Kai-Shek [818]

Standard Oil began exporting kerosene to Asia and Europe, where people used it for illumination. By 1884, nearly a quarter of Standard's oil exports encompassed the kerosene exports to the Far East. Standard's shipping and contractual policies were consistent in order to maintain domestic and foreign prices. Standard always financed its operations from within, and always used local agents, who easily worked with local buyers. In France, they used the Cartel Dix. Heinrich Riedemann led the Deutsche-Amerikanische Petroleum Gesellschaft (DAPG), later a central factor in Standard's dealings with Germany. Standard created the Anglo-American Oil Co., Ltd., their enterprise in Britain. [819]

Several factors contributed to Chinese discontent and the development and expansion of the Boxer movement, called the "Righteous Fists of Harmony" or the "Society of Righteous and Harmonious Fists" (Boxers in English). Chinese opposition, by the Boxers, initially began in 1869 when they first used the slogan "Support the Qing, destroy the foreign." These important factors were: 1) a drought and subsequent flooding in Shandong province (1897-1898) forced farmers to flee to cities to seek food; 2) an increasing number of Christian missionaries, both Protestant and Catholic; 3) the exemption of missionaries from numerous laws; 4) the French Minister, in 1899, aided the missionaries to obtain special status enabling them to ignore local officials; 5) Since 1840, foreign powers had been fragmenting sovereignty; 6) foreign powers had forced China to import opium, causing widespread addiction; 7) foreign powers appeared to be incrementally colonizing China; 8) foreigners claimed the right to promote Christianity; 9) foreigners imposed unequal treaties whereby their companies were immune from Chinese law; and 10) foreign powers seized land and demanded extraterritorial rights for their citizens living in China. This caused resentment and angry reactions

---

[818] Ibid. 14
[819] Stephen Pelletière, Iraq and the International Oil System: Why America Went to War in the Gulf by, Praeger, Westport, Connecticut, 2001, pp. 8-11

among the Chinese. One official stated it very succinctly, "Take away your missionaries and your opium and you will be welcome."

France, Japan, Russia, and Germany each had spheres of influence and it appeared, at least to the Chinese, that these countries might actually dismember and rule their country. By 1900, the Qing Dynasty, that ruled China for over 200 years, was faltering and powerful foreigners, with unfamiliar religions, were assaulting the culture and attempting to replace it with materialism. By January 1900, the Empress Dowager Cixi, of the Manchu Yehenara clan, the powerful ruler of the Qing Dynasty (1861-1908) and her supporters came to the defense of the Boxers and their expanding movement. She refused to adopt the Western style of government, although she did approve of, and supported, technological advancement, and the modernization of China's armies, which undoubtedly benefitted the same bankers and armament manufacturers who were militarizing Japan.

The Chinese were completely dependent on foreign petroleum, as they had not yet developed their own resources. By 1900, Standard Oil already had a network of local Chinese merchants, who understood the culture, and had existing business connections, thus avoiding the stigma of a foreign company. Well-compensated merchants built a complex distribution system of transport and storage facilities throughout China, of which Standard maintained indirect ownership. Local agents promoted Standard's petroleum products, especially kerosene for lamps and stoves. Standard's Asian assets totaled at least $18 million, mostly in China. With 400 million Chinese consumers, limited competition, and no taxes or tariffs, according to the stipulations of the unequal treaties, their profits rapidly soared. [820]

American Minister Edwin H. Conger cabled Washington, referring to the Chinese, "The whole country is swarming with hungry, discontented, hopeless idlers." On May 30, 1900, British Minister Claude M. MacDonald and other foreign diplomats requested

---

[820] David A. Wilson, Principles and Profits: Standard Oil Responds to Chinese Nationalism, 1925-1927, The Pacific Historical Review, Vol. 46, No. 4 (Nov., 1977), pp. 625-647

military aid to defend the foreign legations. The Chinese government unwillingly agreed. The following day, over 400 soldiers, part of the Eight-Nation Alliance, disembarked from warships, coincidentally already in the area. The 400 soldiers then traveled from Tianjin to Peking by train. Upon arrival, they established defensive boundaries around their respective missions. The alliance included Austria-Hungary, France, Germany, Italy, Japan, Russia, Britain and the United States. Given the size of their combined military forces of fifty-four warships, 4,971 US Marines and 49,255 soldiers, its intentions were obvious. These foreign forces intervened in China to forcibly suppress the pro-national, anti-foreign Boxers and halt their angry siege of the diplomatic legations in Peking.

On June 5, 1900, the Boxers cut the railroad line from Tianjin and isolated Peking. On June 13, Chinese soldiers murdered a Japanese diplomat. On the same day, under the direction of the German Minister, Clemens von Ketteler, German soldiers captured and executed a Boxer, apparently just a boy. In retaliation, thousands of Boxers broke through the walled city of Peking, and burned many Christian churches. US Marines halted a Boxer attack on the Methodist Mission, where many British missionaries had taken refuge. Soldiers at the British Embassy and German Legations killed several Boxers, which disaffected Peking's Chinese population. The Muslim Kansu braves, many Boxers and other Chinese residents killed Chinese Christians, seeing them as agents for foreigners, as a reprisal for the long-term, foreign assaults on the Chinese.

Ultimately, the US government sent 100,000 troops to protect foreign business owners during the Boxer Rebellion. By August 14, 1900, US troops, along with the other forces, crushed the short-lived rebellion against foreign exploitation.

In 1907, Standard Oil had one major competitor for China's business—the Asiatic Petroleum Company, a British-based subsidiary of the Royal Dutch Shell-Rothschild cartel. The two companies enjoyed 85 percent of the kerosene trade within China for a total of about $94 million. They attempted to equally divide the Far East market, but competition remained fierce. The oil companies designed treaties that protected them, with little thought about their Asian consumers. [821] They relied on military enforcement from their respective governments, as needed to maintain their advantageous status. Thirteen percent of the kerosene market was in Kwantung Province, a relatively small area of China, adjacent the South China Sea, whose capital is Guangzhou, known historically as Canton. This location enabled foreign merchants to develop commerce early, which resulted in extensive trade with the outside world through Guangzhou, the site of the earlier Opium Wars. It was a hotbed of anti-imperialist activity, and the major port of exit for laborers enticed to travel elsewhere to find work.

According to *The New York Times*, March 29, 1913, Standard Oil offered the Chinese government, based in Peking, a loan of $35 million in gold in exchange for the exclusive rights to all oil exploitation in China. [822] The government wisely rejected that offer as it would repay the loan, calculating the interest, many times over which might conceivably have forced them to relinquish a major portion of their vast oil resources. However, according to *The New York Times*, February 23, 1914, the government arranged for Standard Oil to help them develop the oil fields of the Shen-Si and Chi-Li provinces for a period of sixty years in exchange for that large loan.

In addition to Standard Oil's interests in China, Philander C. Knox, Secretary of State (1909-1913), using the same "Dollar Diplomacy" as he had in Central and South America, tried to coerce the Chinese to negotiate with the Harriman railroad, financed by Kuhn & Loeb, Morgan, the First National Bank and the Rockefeller-controlled National City Bank, instead of working with the British, French and the Germans as they had been doing. Edward Harriman, who used his influence with the US government, intended to establish a

---

[821] David A. Wilson, Principles and Profits: Standard Oil Responds to Chinese Nationalism, 1925-1927, The Pacific Historical Review, Vol. 46, No. 4 (Nov., 1977), pp. 625-647

[822] Standard Oil Chinese Loan, London Times Hears It Offers $35,000,000 for Concessions by Marconi Transatlantic Wireless Telegraph to The New York Times. March 29, 1913, p. 7

monopolistic, worldwide transportation system with steamship and railroad lines. [823]

The Chinese, with an upsurge of nationalism and anti-foreignism, some of the causes of the Boxer Rebellion, demanded revisions of the treaty system. The big powers considered the requests at the Washington Conference (November 1921-February 1922), and decided to allow China to gradually "regain control over the customs and to permit the interim collection of a 2.5 percent tax on imports and exports." Some of the signatories did not ratify the Washington Treaty so it was invalid. [824] [825] President Harding signed it on June 9, 1923. Officials had not invited Russia to this conclave. By 1921, the United States had assumed Britain's position as the world's super power. The conference leaders, to satisfy Standard's demands, adopted inequitable procedures, very similar to those they had used a couple of years earlier against Germany, which people referred to as the "Versailles-Washington" system of international relations. [826] The United States, while sounding agreeable and obliging, with its complicit corporate partners, quashes many countries that have attempted to develop a nationalistic self-government.

In May of 1923, the Canton government regained control of the local Salt Inspectorate from the foreigners who were using the revenues from the Maritime Customs and the Salt Inspectorate to pay off the principle and interest on the foreign debts of the Peking government.

---

[823] Who Was Philander Knox? Is It Credible That He Would Commit Fraud?, http://www.givemeliberty.org/features/taxes/philanderknox.htm as of May 2012

[824] David A. Wilson, Principles and Profits: Standard Oil Responds to Chinese Nationalism, 1925-1927, The Pacific Historical Review, Vol. 46, No. 4 (Nov., 1977), pp. 625-647

[825] Conference on the Limitation of Armament, Washington, November 12, 1921-February 6, 1922, Papers Relating to the Foreign Relations of the United States: 1922, Vol. 1, pp. 247-266

[826] The USA in the Making of the USSR: The Washington Conference, 1921-22 and 'Uninvited Russia' by Paul Dukes, The USA in the Making of the USSR shows the importance of the 'Russian question' at the Washington Conference and throws light on the emergence of the 'Versailles-Washington' system of international relations.

Any surplus funds went to the Peking warlord administration. In 1924, the Kwangtung provincial government, controlled by the Nationalist Party, collected only $8 million, compared to $21 million collected by the provincial government in 1921.

Sun Yat-sen's death, on March 12, 1925, created a crisis for the Nationalist Party, and the Canton government, whose officials decided to levy a kerosene tax to raise some much-needed money in order to gain control. [827] On March 24, 1925, they notified oil dealers in the Kwangtung Province of this kerosene tax, imposed by the Canton government, scheduled to take effect on April 1, 1925. They would levy a stamp tax of twenty cents on every five-gallon tin of kerosene. Foreign governments, and the businessmen they collaborated with, refused to allow the local governments to tax their products, because officials had not ratified the treaties during the Washington Conference. The US Minister in Peking, Jacob G. Schurman (1921-1925), fronting for the American elite, requested that the Peking government "issue strict instructions to the Canton authorities to cease at once their plans for this tax." [828]

The oil companies could either stop marketing their oil in the region, or replace the Chinese Nationalist Party with a warlord government. An embargo, supported by their respective diplomats, would act as an ominous warning to the Nationalists or warlords who might decide to levy such taxes in other regions of China. American and British oil company executives opted for military enforcement. The British considered the seizure of the Canton arsenal, or the Chinese section of the Kowloon-Canton Railway. Standard Oil's vice president Howard E. Cole and attorney, Roland S. Morris, urged the State Department's Frank P. Lockhart to initiate military force to prevent the company's loss of $800,000 a year in Canton alone. Despite these machinations, there were some Americans who strongly supported

---

[827] David A. Wilson, Principles and Profits: Standard Oil Responds to Chinese Nationalism, 1925-1927, The Pacific Historical Review, Vol. 46, No. 4 (Nov., 1977), pp. 625-647

[828] Ibid.

China's nationalistic aspirations and encouraged the Secretary of State to stop meddling in China's affairs. [829]

The US government did not immediately respond to the dictates of Standard Oil officials, so they, along with the owners of Asiatic Oil continued their embargo. Consequently, the Chinese began purchasing their oil from the Russians as the treaty adopted by the Washington oligarchs did not apply to them. On May 13, 1925, a sudden unexplained fire destroyed half of all the cases of Russian gasoline in the Canton harbor, an economic catastrophe. [830] Standard Oil has a history of using terrorism against their competitor's properties and products. In the United States, John D. Rockefeller had managed to monopolize the industry by means of bribery, coercion, dynamite explosions, and sabotage to crush or control any and all local oil refining competitors, all within a year. Certainly, the company had no qualms about using terrorism in China, when other options proved unavailable.

On May 30, 1925, British-led police in the Shanghai International Settlement slaughtered Chinese demonstrators, which led to nationalist outrage. Two weeks later, on June 13, the Chinese Nationalist Party army, with assistance from workers and peasants, defeated the Cantonese-based warlords and their armies, allowing the Nationalists to control the Canton government, which meant that they could levy taxes and diminish foreign influence and privileges. In another incident, exploited workers rebelled in Hong Kong, a center of anti-foreign outrage. About 80,000 workers left Hong Kong bound for Canton where a worker's Strike Committee provided work, housing and food. British and French troops killed fifty Chinese demonstrators in Canton on June 23, 1925. [831]

Chiang Kai-shek had organized an anti-British boycott and had threatened to rid China of all foreign imperialists. Civil war broke out between the Nationalist armies of the south and the northern warlords led by Chang Tso-lin. The Fourth US Marine Brigade set sail for

---

[829] Ibid.
[830] Ibid. 625-647
[831] Ibid. 625-647

Shanghai in February 1927 to protect any US citizens and business properties in Shanghai's International Settlement. They arrived on March 16, 1927. [832] On March 25, Brigadier General Smedley D. Butler arrived with the Third Marine Brigade, including his aide, Arthur J. Burks (the author's grandfather). They disembarked at the Standard Oil dock in the Whangpoo River, opposite Shanghai, and set up tents in Standard Oil's compound. Their mission was unclear. Butler, to keep the Marines from being involved with the fighting between the two Chinese factions, attempted to maintain cordial relations with the people. His genuine respect and kindness toward them won their appreciation and respect. He did not want another Haiti-style intervention that would put him into the position of defending United States business interests against the native rebels and he did not want to risk a single Marine's life for Standard Oil.

On December 24, 1927, the Standard Oil plant, on the outskirts of Tientsin, caught fire during a battle between rival Chinese forces. There was sufficient fuel, oil, and gasoline, to entirely destroy the city of Tientsin. It took four days and about 2,000 Marines to contain the fire, for which the citizens were grateful. A Standard Oil official, during the blaze, vowed to donate $20,000 toward a recreation hall for the Marines once they brought the fire under control. Standard Oil lost $1 million and the company thanked Butler and his men for saving it $4 million. Its promised $20,000 never materialized. [833]

Butler, author of *War is a Racket* (1935), resented the use of the US military to protect big business profits overseas. The presence of the marines in China had nothing whatsoever to do with the government's professed concern about the safety of Americans living in China. It was to defend Standard Oil property and their profits. Vietnam War critic, David M. Shoup, future Marine Corps Commandant, reached the same conclusion—the government had endangered the lives of those marines to protect Standard Oil. [834]

---

[832] Wars and Battles History of the US Marine Corps Chronology-Part 1, 1775-1939,

[833] Jules Archer, The Plot to Seize the White House, Hawthorne Books, Inc., New York 1973, p. 100

[834] Ibid. 100-101

Butler and his marines undertook a project to rebuild the Peking/ Tientsin Bridge, which a flood had destroyed. A rebuilt bridge would allow the villagers to get their produce to market. The Chinese citizenry honored Butler as a public benefactor, and awarded him an Umbrella of Ten Thousand Blessings at a special celebration. Chiang Kai-Shek became President of China on October 10, 1928, and political conditions greatly improved. A civil war no longer threatened business interests in Tientsin, and officials withdrew the Third Brigade from China in January of 1929. [835] [836] Butler publicly criticized the treatment that veterans, shattered heroes, received, and the "indifference of big business toward the men in uniform, who had so often been called upon to spill blood for corporate profits." [837] Butler died unexpectedly on June 21, 1940 at the Naval Hospital in Philadelphia. Popular military leaders who criticize the use of the military to protect corporate profits often die unexpectedly, particularly when they are receiving care in government facilities.

African Resources and the Boer Wars

The French controlled Bavarian Republic (Netherlands) owned the Cape Colony. During the Napoleonic Wars, Napoleon dispatched ships to reinforce the Cape garrison. In July 1805, the British, not wanting the sea route around the Cape to fall into French hands, sent a fleet to forestall the French and seize the colony as the sea route was essential to British dominance. The Battle of Blaauwberg, January 8-18 1806, took place near Cape Town. Though it was a minor military engagement, it established British rule in South Africa.

In 1867, individuals found the first diamonds in the vicinity of the Orange River in South Africa. In 1868, Moshesh, a refugee of the Zulu Wars, wanted British protection from the Boers and the Zulus. He allowed Britain to annex Basutoland, located in the Drakensberg Mountains, an area surrounding the Orange Free State and Natal.

---

[835] Scuttlebutt, Volume 12, Issue 4, 2002, http://www.gensdbutlerdet.org/ scuttlebutt/04_02_scuttlebutt.pdf as of May 2012
[836] General Smedley Darlington Butler, Letters of a Leatherneck 1898-1931 edited by Anne Cipriano Venzon, 1992, p. 291
[837] Ibid. 82

The Boers, the Dutch and Afrikaans, word for farmer, were the descendants of the Dutch-speaking settlers of the eastern Cape frontier. In September 1870, individuals found diamonds on the farms of Dutoitspan and Bulfontein. [838] In July 1871, merchants founded a diamond mine at Kimberley, a city in South Africa. [839] People found diamonds along the banks of the Vaal River. By October 1871, Britain annexed the Vaal/Harts region. [840] In 1880, the British attempted to annex the Transvaal which led to the First Boer War, December 16, 1880 to March 23, 1881.

Vickers and Maxim tested their weaponry in South Africa as they sold their weapons to both the Boer farmers and the British who illegally annexed and invaded the Transvaal in the First Boer War but Paul Kruger's forces defeated them at Battle of Majuba Hill on February 27, 1881. It led to the signing of a peace treaty, on August 3, 1881, and later the Pretoria Convention, between the British and the newly created South African Republic, ending the First Boer War.

In the 1880s, Germany, Britain and the Boers disagreed on the disposition of Bechuanaland, located north of the Orange River. Bechuanaland, with little economic value, was on the crossroads, Missionaries Road, to territory farther north. On March 18, 1884, Basutoland became a British Crown colony and Britain assigned Marshal James Clarke as the Resident Commissioner. Germany annexed Damaraland and Namaqualand in 1884.

German and British diplomats quarreled as Germany encouraged Boer intransigence and independence, as recognized in the London Convention, an Anglo-Boer treaty signed on February 27, 1884, in the aftermath of the war. Germany also upset Rhodes's attempts to purchase Delagoa Bay from Portugal. [841] In March 1886, an

[838] Basil Williams, Cecil Rhodes, Henry Holt & Company, New York, 1921, p. 16
[839] Robert Vicat Turrell, Capital and Labour on the Kimberley Diamond Fields, 1871-1890, Cambridge University Press, New York, 1987, pp. 1, 3-4,
[840] John Holland Rose and Henry Dodwell, The Cambridge History of the British Empire, Volume 4, Cambridge University Press, London and New York, 1959, p. 39
[841] Ibid. 495

Australian gold miner, George Harrison, discovered part of the main gold-bearing reef near Ferreira's Camp, a small mining village that soon evolved into Johannesburg, which within ten years was larger than Cape Town.

Because of the Witwatersrand gold discovery in 1886, Leander S. Jameson and his Rhodesian and Bechuanaland policemen perpetrated a raid on Paul Kruger's Transvaal Republic. The failed Jameson Raid (December 29, 1895-January 2, 1896) was a buildup to the outbreak of the Second Boer War in 1899. The Boers deeply resented the increasing number of foreigners (Uitlanders) in the Witwatersrand. The enlarged population led to heavy taxes, and, since many of the miners were foreigners, the Boer government denied them voting privileges. In response, the foreigners and the British mine owners began to agitate for the overthrow of the Boer government.

Jameson, later the Prime Minister of the Cape Colony, hoped to trigger an uprising by the British expatriate workers, known as the Johannesburg conspirators. Given the vast resources, in 1899, the British would target the Transvaal and the Orange Free State, leading to the Second Boer War. This event was a foreshadowing of the Second Boer War, and the Second Matabele War, or Matabeleland Rebellion, March 1896-October 1897. The Matabele people revolted against the British South Africa Company's authority. Jameson, the Administrator General for Matabeleland, had dispatched most of his troops and arms to assault the Transvaal Republic, leaving the country almost defenseless. The British sent troops to suppress the dissidents, which caused the deaths of many settlers.

Cecil Rhodes and Alfred Beit organized and managed the De Beers Mining Corporation and the diamond business. Rhodes and Beit played a part in provoking the war (1899-1902). The indigenous population militantly opposed British control. Germany also sought influence in the area. The Boers held two positions in Bechuanaland while Britain attempted to expand its control of the region, despite the 1884 Anglo-Boer treaty. The Transvaal relinquished its claim in Bechuanaland and withdrew. Rhodes persuaded British officials to provide protection to native chiefs against Germany, in addition to impeding the Boers' attempts to acquire a republic in Zululand that would give them access to the sea. In 1886, prospectors discovered gold on the Witwatersrand which increased Rhodes' economic and imperialistic aspirations. He obtained additional powers for his London-chartered South Africa Company, expecting that they would compel acquiescence from the Transvaal. In July 1890, Rhodes assumed the position of Prime Minister of the Cape Colony. Using his company, he added a large portion of Rhodesia to Britain's Empire and envisioned a Cape to Cairo railroad. [842]

In 1891, Cecil Rhodes wanted to purchase a large tract of land from Portugal, including a railway from Delagoa Bay to the Transvaal border. President Kruger wanted to connect this railway to his own at Pretoria, as it would connect to a shorter railway at Cape Town or Port Elizabeth for the Johannesburg traffic. However, Rhodes wanted to buy the whole province of Lourenço Marques from Portugal, including all of the railways. Portugal was tempted as its finances were in a pitiable condition. His plans failed but he still wanted Delagoa Bay. [843]

President Kruger rejected Rhodes' proposal that Transvaal join a customs union with other South African states. Rhodes then fomented Uitlander dissatisfaction in Johannesburg. In June 1895, Britain annexed Tongoland, obstructing Transvaal's potential direct access to the sea. However, the July launching of the Delagoa Bay Railroad would provide Johannesburg with a British-free route via Portuguese territory. Kruger tried to block goods from the Cape to encourage people to use the new railway, but ultimately relented to British intimidation. On November 11, 1895, London officials, urged by Rhodes, added British Bechuanaland to the Cape Colony and gave him jurisdiction over a piece of land adjacent to the western border of the South African Republic, purportedly for a railroad. [844]

---

[842] Fred R. Van Hartesveldt, The Boer War: Historiography and Annotated Bibliography, Greenwood Press, Westport, Connecticut, 2000, p. 3

[843] Basil Williams, Cecil Rhodes, Henry Holt & Company, New York, 1921, p. 198

[844] Fred R. Van Hartesveldt, The Boer War: Historiography and Annotated Bibliography, Greenwood Press, Westport, Connecticut, 2000, p. 3

Winston Churchill and Cecil Rhodes, intimate friends, shared the same Anglo-American beliefs of returning the United States to British rule. On June 2, 1899, Churchill and Rhodes had breakfast at London's Burlington Hotel and planned South Africa's war. [845] Also in 1899, Churchill, referring to the Muslims, wrote, "How dreadful are the curses which Mohammedanism lays on its votaries! Besides the fanatical frenzy, which is as dangerous in a man as hydrophobia in a dog, there is this fearful fatalistic apathy." Further he wrote, "No stronger retrograde force exists in the world . . . Mohammedanism is a militant and proselytizing faith." [846]

The Second Boer War (October 11, 1899-May 31, 1902) occurred because the bankers and industrialists, backed by an imperialistic government, lusted for the massive South African gold and diamond resources. The British government sent 400,000 propagandized soldiers who waged war against about 30,000 armed farmers, who defending their farmlands, resisted the military onslaught. Lord Alfred Milner, per Rothschild's instructions, in opposition to the wishes of the British population, arranged the Boer Wars. Kruger, the State President of the South African Republic (Transvaal), advocated the use of guerrilla warfare, which the residents used to defy the invaders in the Second Boer War. To avoid these kinds of difficulties in the future, the bankers formulated a system of managed conflict for their next warfare efforts.

When the Boers attempted to expel the British, Lord Herbert H. Kitchener used the scorched earth policy in the Second Boer War and destroyed farms and homes to prevent rebels from obtaining food and supplies, which left women and children without homes, crops, and livestock. The British then erected camps for displaced persons until the war ended. Overcrowding, insufficient food and supplies caused the death of 27,927 Boers, 26,251 of whom were women and children.

---

[845] Pat Riott, The Greatest Story Never Told, Winston Churchill and the Crash of 1929, Nanoman Press, Oak Brook, Illinois, 1994, pp. 3, 57, 72-73

[846] Winston Churchill, The River War: An Historical Account of the Reconquest of the Soudan, Volume 2, Longmans, Green & Co., London, 1899, pp. 248-250

Three factors prompted British aggression in Africa. They were, 1) Britain wanted to control the trade routes to India around the Cape; 2) the 1867-1868 discoveries of diamonds in the Kimberley area on the common borders of the South African Republic which the British called the Transvaal and a major gold find first in the Orange Free State and the Cape Colony, and, in 1886 in the Transvaal and; 3) competition with other European powers that were viewing colonial expansion into Africa. Those other countries included Portugal which controlled what is now Angola and Mozambique. Germany had influence in what is now Namibia while Belgium controlled what is now the Democratic Republic of the Congo and France had interests in what is now West and Equatorial Africa, and Madagascar.

Dam Hoover

Herbert Hoover, a graduate of Stanford University (1895) failing to secure a technical job in the gold mining town of Nevada City, worked ten-hour days as a laborer. He then obtained a clerk's position with Louis Janin, in San Francisco, above the Anglo-California Bank, where he worked for two years. [847] Janin, the author of *Leading Mining Claims of the Whitewood Mining District, in the Black Hills,* (1878), [848] was an advisor to the Anglo-California Bank, established in 1873, by Philip N. Lilienthal. [849] Mortimer Fleishhacker, the bank's president, later became the president of the Great Western Power Company.

---

[847] Will Irwin, Herbert Hoover—A Reminiscent Biography, United Feature Syndicate, Inc., New York, 1928, pp. 68-70

[848] Transactions of the American Institute of Mining Engineers, Volume 49 by the American Institute of Mining, Metallurgical, and Petroleum Engineers, American Institute of Mining, New York, 1915, p. 831

[849] Martin A. Meyer, Ph.D., Western Jewry An Account of the Achievements of the Jews and Judaism in California Including Eulogies and Biographies, Emanu-El, San Francisco, 1916, pp. 123-124

Janin was part of a group of mining engineers and metallurgists who, in the late nineteenth century, directed the development of the mineral resources of the Pacific slope. [850] On March 27, 1897, with his recommendation, Hoover left for England to work as a consultant for Bewick, Moreing & Company. [851]

In 1892, miners discovered gold in Coolgardie in Western Australia (British colony). Charles A. Moreing immediately sent Hoover to Australia. He arrived at Coolgardie in June 1897, a torrid, waterless desert, 450 miles from the coast. He made "junior partner" at Bewick Moreing by November 1897 [852] due to Bewick's death. [853] On March 17, 1898, Hoover, professing to be a mining expert unscrupulously depreciated and then claim-jumped the Sons of Gwalia gold mine in Leonora, a proven but under-funded mine. He then managed this mine while Moreing over-hyped it in the trade media and in the market. The firm made $2 million and seized complete control of the mine that ultimately produced nearly five million ounces of gold and operated until 1963. Hoover, through the seizure of thirty-two mines, created a monopoly for his company in West Australia. It later controlled over fifty percent of the country's gold mining by the summer of 1904. [854]

In June 1898, Moreing had visited the Kaiping coalmines, about ninety miles from Tientsin, China, which had a 60-mile seaport. The Chinese Engineering and Mining Company (CEMC) controlled the Kaiping coal resources, and had built a 14-mile canal and a 50-mile railway. Chang Yen-Mao, with counsel from influential Gustav Detring, a Customs Commissioner from Germany, directed CEMC. The Chinese were constructing a harbor in the ice-free port of Ching-

[850] Transactions of the American Institute of Mining Engineers, Volume 49 by the American Institute of Mining, Metallurgical, and Petroleum Engineers, American Institute of Mining, New York, 1915, p. 831

[851] John Hamill, The Strange Career of Mr. Hoover Under Two Flags, William Faro, Inc., New York, 1931, pp. 26-27

[852] Anne Beiser Allen and Jon L. Wakelyn, An Independent Woman: The Life of Lou Henry Hoover, Greenwood Press, Westport, Connecticut, 2000, p. 20

[853] John Hamill, The Strange Career of Mr. Hoover Under Two Flags, William Faro, Inc., New York, 1931, pp. 39-41

[854] Ibid. 45-47

Wan-Tao, to provide an outlet to the open sea for its coal; it was open to all nations. [855] [856] Detring was the diplomatic consultant to Li Hongzhang, the minister of Peiyang, and though he was German, he was president of the British Concession, located on the west bank of Hai He River.

Moreing, while visiting Detring, offered a fifty percent foreign investment in the Kaiping mines, while retaining Chang Yen-Mao. Moreing then contrived a high-paying job at CEMC for Hoover, the purported expert, in exchange for a million dollars of Ching Wan-Tao bonds. [857] On February 10, 1899, before heading for China, he married Iowa native, Lou Henry, a banker's daughter, and a Stanford graduate. They arrived in Shanghai on March 8, 1899, where they stayed at the Astor Hotel for four days, and then left for Tientsin, where he assumed the job of chief engineer. [858]

The Boxer Rebellion (November 2, 1899-September 7, 1901) was a nationalist movement against the domination of "foreign devils," and their resource swindling. By May 1, 1900, Hoover, because of the local chaos, halted his expeditions into the interior, despite the discovery of anthracite deposits. China had more anthracite fields than the rest of the combined world. Hoover and his wife stayed in Tientsin during the upheavals, allegedly to protect their Chinese staff. [859] Several countries, including the United States and Britain had lengthy business interests in China, including opium trading. Ostensibly, the US government, to protect Americans living in China,

[855] Ibid. 53-55
[856] Wang Yuru, Capital Formation and Operating Profits of the Kailuan Mining Administration (1903-1937), Cambridge University Press, Modern Asian Studies, Vol. 28, No. 1 (Feb., 1994), pp. 99-128
[857] John Hamill, The Strange Career of Mr. Hoover Under Two Flags, William Faro, Inc., New York, 1931, p. 55
[858] Anne Beiser Allen and Jon L. Wakelyn, An Independent Woman: The Life of Lou Henry Hoover, Greenwood Press, Westport, Connecticut, 2000, pp. 21-23
[859] Diana Preston, The Boxer Rebellion: The Dramatic Story of China's War on Foreigners That Shook the World in the Summer of 1900, Walker, New York, 2000, pp. 47-48

sent Marines to Peking on November 4, 1898. On May 31, 1900, Capt. John T. Myers arrived in Peking with two marine detachments. [860]

The US military, along with seven other nations, invaded China when nationalist leaders opposed foreign exploitation of the nation's resources. Fifty-four warships and almost 50,000 men, a combination of the military forces of several nations arrived in China whose leaders importuned US leaders for some semblance of self-government. [861]

As hostilities increased, Hoover, in talking to Chang, falsely claimed that the Russians would try to take the Kaiping mines. He persuaded him to put them under British protection. Detring agreed but Chang was uncertain, for he was partially responsible to the Empress, who detested the foreign devils. Hoover convinced Detring to give Moreing a Deed of Trust for the property. Moreing would then form an English company. However, recent Mining Regulations had stipulated that China maintain control. Hoover sent for J. B. Eames, an English lawyer, then in Tientsin, to draw up the deed. [862] He had Eames devise the deed, which he would register in China, in Hoover's name. Detring initially opposed this, but then opted to trust him, because he worked for CEMC. They drew up the Deed of Trust on July 30, 1900, conveying it to Hoover, his heirs and assignees. [863]

The new British company, per the agreement, was obliged to provide a deposit of £100,000, as working capital, to the Chartered Bank of India, Australia and China, no later than February 28, 1901. According to Hoover's estimate, just the value of the coal was about $262.5 million. Chang had no idea that Hoover now had the deed to

---

[860] The Boxer Rebellion: Coalition Expeditionary Operations in China by Major Glen G. Butler, http://www.leatherneck.com/forums/showthread.php?t=10829 as of May 2012

[861] David A. Wilson, Principles and Profits: Standard Oil Responds to Chinese Nationalism, 1925-1927, The Pacific Historical Review, Vol. 46, No. 4 (Nov., 1977), pp. 625-647

[862] Kaiping Mines: Memorandum of Agreement Between Chang Yen-Mao and Herbert Hoover, http://delong.typepad.com/sdj/2007/07/kaiping-mines-m.html as of May 2012

[863] John Hamill, The Strange Career of Mr. Hoover Under Two Flags, William Faro, Inc., New York, 1931, pp. 69-70

the company. Hoover left for Shanghai to register it with the British Consulate. He then contacted Moreing, who with his partners and associates, rejoiced until he told them that the deed was in his name, and they still had to contend with Chinese regulations. Meanwhile, the Russians sent troops to protect the mines, which led the English, who supported Hoover's unscrupulous seizure, to threaten the Russians with war. [864]

One of Moreing's associates, Edmund Davis, contacted Leopold II, the Belgian King and ruler of the Congo Free State, who had extensive financial interests, and important contacts in China. Emile Francqui, the Belgium Consul in Hankow, had been one of Leopold's toughest officers in handling the slaves in the Congo. He had previously defrauded the Americans out of their concession to the Canton-Hankow railway, and would later assist Hoover in the Belgium Relief operation. Francqui, with the help of a legal adviser to the Chinese Parliament, helped Hoover transfer the Kaiping property, while King Leopold temporarily supplied the money for Moreing's firm, which lacked the ready capital. [865]

Moreing dissolved his partnership with T. Burrell Bewick and Edward Hooper, and collaborated with Hoover and Anthony S. Rowe. Moreing made Hoover a full partner. On February 19, 1901, using legal shenanigans, Hoover obtained a directorship in the newly reorganized English Chinese Engineering and Mining Company. [866] In 1903, he had financial investments in three companies—Moreing, Chinese Engineering, and Oroya Brownhill Co., Ltd. He doubled this number of companies within a year. By 1906, he would have interests in ten companies. [867]

Hoover and his wife returned to London in September 1901. He described the Boxers as "one of those emotional movements not

[864] Ibid. 70-72
[865] Ibid. 75-77, 79-80
[866] John Hamill, The Strange Career of Mr. Hoover Under Two Flags, William Faro, Inc., New York, 1931, pp. 84-85
[867] Walter W. Liggett, The Rise of Herbert Hoover, The H. K. Fly Company Publishers, New York, 1931, pp. 366

unusual in Asia." [868] In addition to seizing the Kaiping mines for himself and his friends, he also got the ice free port and the coaling station of Ching-Wan-Tao for England, a favor that England never forgot, as shown by his influence with the British government, and his continued immunity from numerous criminal activities. [869]

Hoover, the Slave Trader

The Transvaal, in South Africa, since the Boer War, was a Crown Colony, governed by a Legislative Assembly, presided over by the governor of the Colony, Lord Alfred Milner. Ernest Williams was the manager of Hoover's South African venture, the Geduld Deep. The Transvaal Coal Mining Company had offices in London with Hoover's firm. Industrialists in the Transvaal anxiously sought cheap labor. The Kaffirs had left the mines and were earning good wages and refused to return to the mines for fifty cents a day, an amount that exceeded what the mine owners wanted to pay. Hoover suggested importing Chinese laborers, an idea that the British Colonial Secretary supported. Meanwhile, Leopold was torturing and massacring the Congolese natives who failed to supply enough coal to satisfy his greed. His officers' mutilated men, women and children, cut off sexual organs or the hands of those who did not meet the huge quotas. Francqui, the copper king of the Congo, was one of those slave drivers. [870] He sat on the board, with Hoover, of the English Chinese Engineering and Mining Company in Kaiping for ten years.

In the spring of 1904, Britain approved the importation of unskilled laborers to the Transvaal. They could not engage in any other work, could not own property, would live in isolated compounds, work ten hours a day, receive two meager meals per day, and earn twenty-five cents a day, worth about five cents in China. They could not leave the compound without a permit. If they survived for three years,

---

[868] Diana Preston, The Boxer Rebellion: The Dramatic Story of China's War on Foreigners That Shook the World in the Summer of 1900, Walker, New York, 2000, p. 24

[869] John Hamill, The Strange Career of Mr. Hoover Under Two Flags, William Faro, Inc., New York, 1931, p. 83

[870] Ibid. 155-158

their masters would ship them back to China. [871] Recruiters in Hong Kong and Tientsin, despite high unemployment, were unsuccessful in attracting laborers. Local officials viewed this scheme as slavery. In February 1903, Hoover's friends whined to him about their inabilities to find 200,000 Chinese laborers. [872]

On April 18, 1904, with help from CEMC, Hoover *sold* 200,000 poor unemployed individuals into slavery for $10 plus $25 each for transportation to South Africa. Actual transportation costs were far below the $25. When individuals naively applied, agents locked them up in a compound with an eighteen-foot wall at Ching Wan Tao. Then, they crowded them into the hold of damp hot tramp steamers, and transported them under armed guard. Hoover, always open to profit, insured each individual for $125, as he expected many of the captives to perish during the four-week trip. When the slaves arrived, the traders fingerprinted and herded them into sealed boxcars for a thirty-hour trip. Hoover was already in South Africa to see the first groups of slaves arrive at the mines in which he had a financial interest. [873]

The Chinese workers, under constant armed guards, were driven like cattle into a compound about half an acre in size, 2,000 men to each of several enclosures, surrounded by 27' by 19' feet huts in which the laborers slept on wooden shelves with one blanket, twenty to a hut. South African winters can be cold as nighttime temperatures can drop to the freezing point or lower. At the end of a 10-hour day, laborers had to climb a ladder 1,000 feet out of the damp mines. [874]

In 1906, Hoover used Chinese slaves in the Burma mines when he was Chairman of the Burma Corporation, a British-registered venture that developed an abandoned Chinese silver mine in the jungles of northern Burma. He still had financial interests in the company in October 1917. He also had another enterprise in Australia, the Zinc

---

[871] Ibid. 157-158
[872] Ibid. 158-159
[873] Ibid. 163-164
[874] Ibid. 158-159

Corporation of Australia. [875] Though he had hundreds of millions at his disposal, coolies dropped dead from long-term hunger. During this time, he wrote to a friend while he was visiting in Johannesburg on slave business about "the great science of extracting the greatest possible amount of money from some other human being." [876] The term "coolie" is derived from the Chinese "ku li" the word for bonded labor.

Hoover, a Double Dealing Scoundrel

Hoover and Edgar Rickard promoted mining stocks through a magazine they started in 1909. The London Stock Exchange soon banned Rickard for his criminal activities. Hoover's other associate, Stanley Rowe, received a ten-year prison sentence but Hoover escaped such consequences because of his political connections. [877] Hoover attracted the Rothschild's attention, and they put him to work in numerous global mining schemes and rewarded him with a directorship in the Rio Tinto Mines in Spain and Bolivia. [878] Rio Tinto, founded in 1873, is one of the world's largest mining companies, and has interests in coal, iron, copper, uranium, gold, and diamonds. It had a pre-tax profit of approximately $10.2 billion in 2006. Alfred Milner was also a Rio Tinto director. [879] England's Queen is currently one of its biggest stockholders.

Hoover was involved in numerous international stock selling schemes. Between 1908 and 1916, he sold oil, gold, copper, tin, silver, zinc, and lead stocks in Africa, Australia, Burma, California, Colombia, Cornwall, Galicia, New Zealand, Nicaragua, Peru, Siberia, Trinidad, and Mexico. He also sold worthless stock to unwary individuals in

---

[875] George H. Nash, The Life of Herbert Hoover: Master of emergencies, 1917-1918, W. W. Norton & Company, New York, 1996, pp. 433-434

[876] John Hamill, The Strange Career of Mr. Hoover Under Two Flags, New York, William Faro, Inc. 1931, p. 60

[877] Eustace Mullins, The Secrets of the Federal Reserve, the London Connection, John McLaughlin, 1993, pp. 122-123

[878] Ibid. 125

[879] Will Banyan, A Short History of The Round Table, Nexus Magazine, Volume 12, Number 1 (December 2004-January 2005)

England, Australia, France, Belgium, Germany, and the United States for millions of dollars. The majority of the companies collapsed. However, he made millions before World War I. [880]

Hoover had major investments in Russian oil wells and mines, because public officials and land-owning aristocrats were quite willing to relinquish their country's mineral wealth in return for a share in the spoils. He took an interest in Russia's oil as early as 1909, when people first drilled the Maikop wells. By 1910, he had financial interests in eleven Russian oil companies. [881] By 1912, he was associated with the famous British multi-millionaire, Leslie Urquhart. They organized three new companies to exploit timber and mineral concessions in Russia's Ural Mountains and Siberia. Urquhart negotiated with two czarist banks wherein their company, the Russo-Asiatic Corporation, would monopolize all mining operations in those two areas. Their company shares increased from $16.25 in 1913 and to $47.50 in 1914. In 1913, their corporation secured three additional concessions from the czarist regime, which included 2,500,000 acres of land, comprised of vast timberlands, waterpower, estimated gold, copper, silver, and zinc reserves of 7,262,000 tons, twelve existing mines, two copper smelters, twenty sawmills, 250 miles of railroad, blast furnaces, rolling mills, sulphuric acid plants, gold refineries, and huge coal reserves. The estimated value of these properties totaled $1,000,000,000 in 1914 dollars. [882]

By 1913, Hoover, presumably still a Rothschild minion, had large financial interests in at least sixteen major companies dealing with the natural resources of China, Burma, Russia, and other areas. By 1917, he had vast interests in the Maikop areas of Russia. [883] Fortuitously, before the 1917 Bolshevik Revolution, he had withdrawn from one of the major corporations and had sold his holdings. The

---

[880] Walter W. Liggett, The Rise of Herbert Hoover, The H. K. Fly Company Publishers, New York, 1931, p. 145

[881] Michael Sayers and Albert E. Kahn, The Great Conspiracy Against Russia, Collet's, London, 1946, pp. 111-115

[882] Ibid. 111-115

[883] Walter W. Liggett, The Rise of Herbert Hoover, The H. K. Fly Company Publishers, New York, 1931, pp. 367, 371

Soviet government confiscated his numerous concessions and mines. Hoover, at the Paris Peace Conference, criticized Bolshevism, and allegedly remained a foe of the Soviets for the rest of his life. [884]

Nevertheless, he was one of the first Americans to offer massive aid to prevent a major uprising against the faltering Bolshevik regime. On November 28, 1917, his colleague, Edward M. House cabled Wilson within days after the Bolsheviks had seized power. House told Wilson, "It is exceedingly important that such criticism be suppressed." Officials concealed the telegram for several years. [885]

An armed intervention failed in Russia because of the strong support given the Soviets by France, England and the United States. Americans were adamantly opposed to sending men, arms, food, and money to the anti-Soviet armies because the media had so thoroughly propagandized the public. People organized "Hands off Russia!" committees, and laborers and soldiers refused to fight, and support interventionist policies. Journalists, educators and businessmen protested any attack on the Soviets. On December 1, 1919, England's Chief of Staff wrote, "The difficulties of the Entente in formulating a Russian policy have, indeed, proved insurmountable, since in no Allied country has there been a sufficient weight of public opinion to justify armed intervention against the Bolsheviks on a decisive scale, with the inevitable result that military operations have lacked cohesion and purpose." [886]

Failure to intervene was due to imperialistic rivalries. The British were concerned about France's objectives in the Black Sea and Germany's aspirations in the Baltic. Americans were supposedly worrying about Japan's aims in Siberia. Any covert efforts to halt the Soviets predictably ended in disaster and created an atmosphere of hatred

---

[884] Michael Sayers and Albert E. Kahn, The Great Conspiracy Against Russia, Collet's, London, 1946, pp. 111-115
[885] Eustace Mullins, The World Order, A Study in the Hegemony of Parasitism, Ezra Pound Institute of Civilization, Staunton, Virginia, 1985, pp. 68-69
[886] Michael Sayers and Albert E. Kahn, The Great Conspiracy Against Russia, Collet's, London, 1946, pp. 111-115

and distrust in Europe. [887] Hoover, as Food Relief Administrator, initially gave aid to the White Russians, and withheld supplies from the Soviets, the Red Russians, which caused the starvation deaths of hundreds of thousands. Finally, after the fact, he, due to public pressure, sent food to the Soviets.

He raised money for food commodities, which the Soviets quickly appropriated, and which Lenin and his thugs used to manipulate the surviving starving peasants, who had previously resisted them. Hoover's unique brand of humanitarianism actually rescued the Soviet regime. The Vanderlips, Harrimans, and Rockefellers helped save the Russian economy. Frank A. Vanderlip compared Lenin to George Washington. [888]

President Warren G. Harding appointed Hoover as Secretary of Commerce (1921-1928). Hoover asked Christian A. Herter to act as his secretary. Herter was secretary at the Bilateral Relations Committee (1920-1921), as well as the secretary of the American Commission to Negotiate Peace. [889] His wife was Mary C. Pratt, the daughter of Frederic B. Pratt, head of the Pratt Institute, and the granddaughter of Standard Oil magnate Charles Pratt. Herter, later Secretary of State, attended the meeting when insiders founded the Council on Foreign Relations (CFR). Hoover, as Commerce Secretary, was responsible for the Radio Act of 1927, placing the regulation and licensing of the nation's radio stations in the hands of the federal government.

Hoover, as Commerce Secretary, exercised dictatorial supervision over the US Patent Office. He allowed his friend, Edgar Rickard, to organize the Hazeltine Corporation as a patent holding company. Hazeltine became the sole owner, with control over the production, of certain domestic and international radio tube patents. The company did not manufacture the tubes, but collected royalties on every tube sold. In 1925, it purchased eighty percent of the stock of the Latour

---

[887] Ibid. 111-115

[888] Gary Allen and Larry Abraham, None Dare Call it Conspiracy, Double A Publications, Seattle, Washington, 1971, p. 112

[889] Eustace Mullins, The World Order A Study in the Hegemony of Parasitism, Ezra Pound Institute of Civilization, Staunton, Virginia, 1985, p. 223

Corporation, formed to exploit the inventions of Professor Bruno Latour, a radio expert. By 1926, they had dozens of US patents, and made millions in royalties. [890]

Hoover used Rickard's New York office as his personal address when he began campaigning for the presidency, as he had not resided in the United States since 1895. [891] J. Schröder financed his campaign. Hoover became the US President on March 4, 1929. On March 28, Henry L. Stimson, his Secretary of State initiated efforts to assist Rockefeller's Standard Oil of California (SOCAL) to obtain oil rights in Bahrain from the Gulf Oil Company. By 1935, SOCAL had sixteen operating oil wells in Bahrain. [892] When the government built the largest public construction operation ever devised to that time, Hoover Dam, Hoover, as president, assured the selection of the California-based Bechtel Company as the head construction company. [893]

Samuel P. Bush, director of Cleveland's Federal Reserve Bank, was a close adviser to President Hoover. [894] He, for certain projects, surrounded himself with Rhodes Scholars and was a member of the infamous Bohemian Grove, to which every Republican President since Hoover has belonged. [895] He called it the "greatest men's party on Earth." [896] Some people portray him as a humanitarian who merely mismanaged the destabilizing effects of the 1929 stock market crash which forced the middle class into soup lines and onto the relief rolls. He took great pains to manage the public's perceptions about

---

[890] Walter W. Liggett, The Rise of Herbert Hoover, The H. K. Fly Company Publishers, New York, 1931, pp. 379-381

[891] Eustace Mullins, The World Order A Study in the Hegemony of Parasitism, Ezra Pound Institute of Civilization, Staunton, Virginia, 1985, p. 224

[892] Miller Center of Public Affairs, University of Virginia, Key Events in the Presidency of Herbert Hoover, http://www.millercenter.virginia.edu/academic/americanpresident/keyevents/hoover as of May 2012

[893] Eustace Mullins, The World Order A Study in the Hegemony of Parasitism, Ezra Pound Institute of Civilization, Staunton, Virginia, 1985, p. 224

[894] Jennifer Harper, Follow the Money! Bush Fortune Soaked in Blood, Washington Times, January 21, 2001

[895] Bohemian Grove, http://www.nndb.com/org/114/000052955

[896] The Modern History Project, http://www.modernhistoryproject.org/mhp/ArticleDisplay.php?Article=FinalWarn09-1 as of May 2012

him, especially after his criminal activities in China. He used what he called the noble experiment of prohibition, as an unprecedented opportunity for organized crime to amass money and power. One may compare the prohibition on alcohol to the war on drugs—both encouraged crime while confiscating public funds and generating huge profits for criminals, in and out of the government.

Japan, the Banker's Mercenary in Asia

Third parties frequently benefit from the conflict between two other parties, a situation that is applicable to people as well as nations. It works like this—conflict erupts in which two factions fight each other instead of recognizing the real troublemakers behind the scene. The obscure instigators support both factions and seek economic and political influence while initiating dissension. The strongest apparatus for generating discord is the international secret societies, like freemasonry, which functions in every nation. [897] Its machinations interlink capital, politics, economy and even religion. This is the elementary level in which the elites create nations, instigate wars, and install leaders, who if they do not function as required, they eliminate them, by assassination, by exposure of private indiscretions or crimes, followed by public humiliation, resignation or prosecution, and incarceration. [898]

On November 7, 1849, August Belmont, a key Rothschild asset, operating in America, married Caroline Slidell Perry, the daughter of Commodore Matthew Perry, a freemason. Another Rothschild agent, Aaron H. Palmer, also worked for the US government as a consultant. According to Palmer's plan, Perry, in an early example of gunboat diplomacy, left New York in the spring of 1853 bound for Japan. He arrived there on July 8, 1853, to present an official letter from President Millard Fillmore. Secretary of State Edward Everett, former

---

[897] Jan Van Helsing, Secret Societies And Their Power In The 20th Century, A Guide Through the Entanglements of Lodges with High Finance and Politics, Urs Thoenen, Zurich, 1995, pp. 5-6
[898] Ibid. 8

Harvard president, drafted the letter. [899] Perry's flotilla, evidently with other, more devious intentions, consisted of two warships and two steam-powered side-wheelers. The Navy Department was certain that Perry's ships were superior and more intimidating than anything that the Japanese possessed. [900]

Perry was prepared to use military force if the Japanese rejected the provisions in President Fillmore's letter. Perry gave the Japanese sufficient time to grasp the letter's contents. On March 31, 1854, on his next trip to Japan, Perry signed the Convention of Kanagawa which opened the Japanese ports of Shimoda and Hakodate to American trade, part of the objectives of the initial mission. This opened the country to Jewish traders and merchants who flocked to Japan. [901] The treaty ended Japan's 200-year policy of seclusion. Perry departed, mistakenly believing he had made an agreement with imperial representatives. Instead, he had negotiated with the Shogun, the de facto ruler of Japan during the Edo period (1603-1868) when the shoguns of the Tokugawa family ruled the country. [902]

The Meiji Emperor, whose personal name was Mutsuhito, Hirohito's grandfather, ruled during what people know as the Meiji period (1867-1912), also called the *Enlightened Rule*. During the early Meiji period, the military began to exert a strong influence on Japanese society. Internal revolts like the Saga and Satsuma Rebellions, and numerous peasant uprisings, gave rise to Japan's militarization. Japan, as part of its militarization development, acquired ships from England and France, often through Jewish brokers, many of which the Japanese ordered in 1868, with loans from the international Jewish bankers. Japan's leadership, in the military, politics or business, was composed of ex-samurai or their descendants. The Meiji government soon began

[899] Edward S. Mihalkanin (editor), Secretaries of State from John Jay to Colin Powell, Greenwood Press, Westport, Connecticut, 2004, pp. 188-190
[900] Robert Smith Thompson, Empires on the Pacific: World War II and the Struggle for the Mastery of Asia, Basic Books, New York, 2001, p. 23
[901] Jennifer Golub, Japanese Attitudes Toward Jews, The Pacific Rim Institute of the American Jewish Committee, p. 1
[902] Jennifer Golub, Japanese Attitudes Toward Jews, The Pacific Rim Institute of the American Jewish Committee, p. 1

to feel threatened by western imperialism. To counter this, they devised the Fukoku Kyohei policy (enrich the country, strengthen the military), in order to strengthen its economic and industrial foundations, and defend Japan against outside powers. This policy entailed long-range policies to transform Japanese society in an effort to catch up with the West.

Major Jakob Meckel claimed that the German military model was superior to the French system, and attributed it to Prussia's victory in the Franco-Prussian War (July 19, 1870-May 10, 1871). Members of the Army Staff College and the Japanese General Staff requested help from Prussia in transforming their system. Prussian Chief of Staff Helmuth von Moltke sent Meckel to Japan, where he worked closely with future Prime Ministers General Katsura Tarō and General Yamagata Aritomo. He introduced Clausewitz's military theories, the Prussian concept of war games, and made numerous recommendations. Thereafter, Japan reorganized the command structure of the army, and strengthened their transportation infrastructure.

In 1873, Japan's newly-appointed War Minister, Yamagata Aritomo introduced universal military conscription. Then in 1882, with the Imperial Rescript proclamation, the Japanese military indoctrinated thousands of men from various backgrounds with military-patriotic values in conjunction with the idea of absolute loyalty to the Emperor. The Prussian example, of transforming itself from an agricultural state to a leading modern industrial and military power, influenced Yamagata who also favored military expansion abroad, and an authoritarian government at home. However, this imperialistic expansion was/is incredibly costly.

With the emergence of political parties in the late Meiji period, there arose several secret and semi-secret patriotic societies, such as the Genyōsha (1881) and Kokuryukai (1901). Along with the political activities, paramilitary activities and military intelligence supported imperialism as an answer to Japan's domestic concerns. The development of a strong military, coupled with an aggressive foreign policy is expensive, money that was only available through the international bankers. However, with these new policies, Japan might win the respect of western nations and a revision of the unequal treaties.

Meanwhile, in Korea, Empress Myeongseong (1851-1895), also known as Queen Min, was the first official wife of King Gojong, the twenty-sixth king of the Joseon Dynasty, and the first emperor of the Korean Empire. In 1873, Queen Min overthrew the dictatorship of Heungseon Daewongun (1863-1873), but retained his closed door policy to European powers. France and the United States had already attempted, unsuccessfully, to establish commerce during the previous decade. Following that overthrow, despite Queen Min's stated policies; many new progressive officials supported the idea of commerce with foreign countries. During that period of Korea's political instability, Japan, with pressure and loans from the international bankers, initiated a plan to exert influence on that vulnerable country. On July 25, 1871, the Imperial Japanese Navy received the Un'yō, a small warship, built in Scotland. In May 1875, Japan dispatched Inoue Yoshika, in command the Un'yō to survey coastal waters without obtaining Korean permission. On September 20, 1875, the ship reached Ganghwa Island, the site of fierce confrontations between Koreans and foreigners in the previous decade.

In 1871, the United States sent a military naval force to Korea, part of an American diplomatic delegation, to try to establish trade and political relations. On June 1, 1871, seeing the intimidating US warships, a Korean shore battery fired on the ships. The US admiral commanding the expedition failed to receive an official apology from the Koreans for what he called an "unwarranted" assault. Therefore, on June 10, 1871, in retaliation, he sent about 650 Americans to shore where they immediately captured three forts, killing approximately 350 Koreans in the process, referred to as Shinmiyangyo. Only three Americans died due to their superior weaponry. Afterwards, Korean officials understandably refused to negotiate with the United States until May 22, 1882, in Incheon. Because of these prior confrontations, the Koreans would inevitably shoot at all approaching foreign ships. Perhaps to provoke an incident, Commander Inoue launched a small boat, allegedly in search of drinkable water. Predictably, the Koreans opened fire on the warship and the Japanese, with their superior firepower, responded. Then the Japanese attacked another Korean port before returning home.

Japan, using gunboat diplomacy, compelled Korean officials to sign a trade treaty that opened three Korean ports—Busan, Incheon and Wuson—which ended Korea's status as a tributary state of China's Qing dynasty (1644-1912). This would allow Japan to seize and later annex Korea without military intervention from China. Koreans, hoping to import some defense technologies to avoid future invasions, signed the Japan-Korea Treaty of Amity, also known as the Treaty of Ganghwa. Kuroda Kiyotaka, Governor of Hokkaidō, and Shin Heon, the General-Minister of the Joseon Dynasty concluded the negotiations on February 26, 1876. The treaty awarded Japan some of the same privileges in Korea that Westerners acquired, using the same tactics, from Japan, including extraterritoriality. The Japanese learned their gunboat diplomacy from Commodore Matthew Perry.

During the Meiji era, Western influences transformed Japan from a feudal society into a capitalist economy. Japanese students studied abroad to attain tactical skills, practical expertise, and an understanding of various cultures unavailable in Japan. Prussian advisors instructed Meiji army leaders, modeled after the Prussian style, whose doctrines, methods and organization were meticulously evaluated and implemented. In 1885, General Meckel reorganized the Imperial Japanese Army's command structure into divisions and regiments. He instructed them on logistics, transportation, and the establishment of artillery and engineering regiments. He taught at Japan's Army Staff College (1885-1888) and worked directly with future Prime Ministers, General Katsura and General Yamagata. A more aggressive, financially-backed Japan, once an isolationist country, soon emerged as a strong world power.

Japan restructured its Imperial Navy after the British model, the world's leading naval power. Japanese officials sent eager naval students to Britain to observe the Royal Navy and master its techniques. They were very adept students, and quickly acquired seamanship skills. Japan lacked the financial resources to build a large fleet, so the international bankers funded their purchases of warships and torpedoes from British and French shipyards. The French constructed the basic components and the Japanese assembled ships and weaponry in their own country. By the 1890s, the Japanese were prepared, trained and well equipped. By 1894, the Imperial Japanese Army had a force of 120,000 men while the number of their steamships increased from twenty-six in 1873 to 1,514 by 1913. Railroad track, in that same period, increased from eighteen miles to 7,100 miles. All they needed to execute their new skills and power was the right provocation. China's young men, severely weakened by opium use, and Britain's two opium wars, proved to be an appealing target, and China had abundant public and private plunder.

Meanwhile, the Korean peasants were disillusioned with the rule of the traditional upper yangban classes. During the nineteenth century, drought and floods devastated the rice fields and farms and created great famines. The government failed to suppress the budding revolts which led to major military conflicts. Despite this, the rulers increased taxes on farm crops, and exploited the destitute farmers to perform unpaid labor, which caused violent anti-government and anti-landlord uprisings, in 1812 and 1862, both against the local nobility, wealthy landlords, and corruption within the central government. The rebels adopted the term Donghak from a Korean religion that emphasized "the equality of all human beings," a mixture of Korean Confucianism, Buddhism, Songyo, and humanism.

The impoverished farmers killed local corrupt government officials and destroyed government buildings before troops brutally butchered and crushed them. To appease them, officials revised the land, military, and grain lending systems. Progressive revolutionaries organized peasant guerrillas into small groups that embraced nationalism and social reform and the movement spread throughout Korea. In 1892, the small groups united into the Donghak Peasant Army, who armed themselves, raided government offices, and killed rich landlords, traders, and foreigners. They seized their victims' properties and redistributed them. In December 1892, the peasants protested the abuses of local officials and petitioned King Gojong for help. The king, who they were loyal to, failed to respond.

Large numbers of farmers, like the Peasant Guerrilla Army, rose up against the landlords and the ruling elite and demanded land redistribution, tax reduction, democracy, and human rights. Many farmers had to sell their ancestral homesteads to rich landowners at bargain prices because of high taxes. Meanwhile, landlords sold the rice to the Japanese, and sent their children to Japan to study. Consequently, the peasants were intensely anti-Japanese.

Progressive-minded scholars and nationalists joined the movement. On January 11, 1894, the rebels led by Jeon Bong-jun, defeated the government forces. The Battle of Gobu continued until March 13, and was the catalyst for the First Sino-Japanese War, essentially a battle for the control of Korea. The revolution ended when government troops killed and captured peasant guerrillas, burned villages, and confiscated the peasants' properties in Gobu.

Toward the end of the Joseon Dynasty of Korea (1392-1897), other reformists and activists, such as Kim Ok-gyun, who opposed the Treaty of Ganghwa, created the Dongnipdang, or Independence Party. The objective of the reform movement was to develop Korea in government, technology, and military, by using Japanese resources, to enable Korea, in time, to withstand Japan's increasing imperialism. It also sought to engage in more open policies with the West. Hong Jong-u, possibly a freemason, who lived in Paris since 1886, returned to Asia in 1893, intending to assassinate Kim Ok-gyun and Park Yeong-hyo, two reform-minded Koreans. On March 28, 1894, in Shanghai, Hong Jong-u assassinated Kim Ok-gyun, and then others, employing false flag tactics, accused Yuan Shikai's agents of the crime. Yuan Shikai was a Chinese general, politician, and later the Emperor of China (1915-1916). Officials shipped Kim Ok-gyun's mutilated body back to Korea aboard a Chinese warship, a warning to other revolutionaries.

As news of the government's tyranny at Gobu spread, the peasant army, with increased support, re-grouped and began a new rebellion. The revived peasant army defeated numerous government garrisons, and was soon near Seoul. They wanted institutional land reform, social reform, removal of corrupt officials, and the expulsion of foreign influence from Korea, especially the Christian missionaries. They also resented the Japanese imports, which affected their ability to produce reasonably priced commodities. The peasants were attempting to 1) halt illegal extortions (taxes); 2) calling for an investigation into the crimes of corrupt officials; 3) punishment of the guilty; 4) the punishment of men of wealth who owe their fortunes to the government's extortionate practices; 5) have officials burn all documents pertaining to slaves. [903]

The anxious Korean Emperor asked the Chinese government to send troops to help suppress the Donghak Rebellion. General Yuan Shikai went to Korea with 2,800 troops after notifying the Japanese in accordance with the Convention of Tientsin. Though the Chinese government had notified the Japanese of its intentions, the Japanese, waiting for the right provocation, claimed that Chinese aid was in violation of the Treaty of Ganghwa. The Koreans reluctantly signed the unequal treaty which allowed Japan to send diplomatic emissaries to Hanseong, and open trading posts. After the Chinese sent troops, the Japanese responded by sending an expeditionary force of 8,000 troops. On June 8, 1894, Japanese thugs seized Emperor Gojong and occupied the Royal Palace, replacing the existing government with a pro-Japanese faction. Japanese troops forcibly expelled the Chinese troops and called for additional troops to subdue the remainder of the country. China rejected the legitimacy of the new Korean government, setting the proverbial platform for conflict in Asia, just as the bankers had conceived. A second uprising erupted in the Korean countryside against a new pro-Japanese government in Seoul. In late June 1894, pro-Japanese forces decided to wipe out the peasant army.

On October 16, 1894, the peasant army prepared for a final battle in Gongju. However, Japanese and the pro-Japanese government troops were waiting for them. The Donghak Peasant Army lost the Battle of Ugeumchi because the Japanese had modern weapons while the peasants had only bows and arrows, spears, swords, and some flintlock muskets. On October 22, 1894, a vicious battle began that

---

[903] The Tonghak (Donghak) Rebellion, 1894, http://koreanhistory.info/Tonghak. htm as of May 2012

lasted until November 10, 1894 when the well-entrenched Japanese beat the poorly-armed peasants who suffered heavy losses.

The control over Korea triggered the First Sino-Japanese War (August 1, 1894-April 17, 1895) between China and Japan. The Warburgs, with established bank branches in Japan, loaned money to partly fund the war. Third parties, the bankers, benefit from the bloody conflict and resulting carnage between two nations and to maximize their profits, why not have another war between two other countries. Now that the Japanese were militarily prepared, they could squander their lives in a war with China. The First Sino-Japanese War shifted the region's dominance from China to Japan. In addition, it ultimately destroyed the Qing Dynasty, which led to the 1911 revolution. The war ended with the Treaty of Shimonoseki, which stipulated that China cede Formosa to Japan and recognize Korea's independence, a move toward its later annexation by Japan. [904]

During the early morning hours of October 8, 1895, Japanese assassins entered the Geoncheong Palace and the private quarters of Korea's Queen Min. The assassins were from the terrorist organization, the Black Ocean Society, Gen'yōsha, a paramilitary group founded by former Samurai. Miura Gorō, Japan's Minister to Korea, and a member of the Yamagata clique, ordered the assassination. Many Black Ocean members, much like CIA agents, posed as business agents or ran small businesses within a network of Japanese companies in Korea, including Mitsui, the oldest zaibatsu. Queen Min preferred an alliance with Russia, to block Japanese political and commercial influence in Korea. The secret society sent agents to permanently silence all of her objections. They stabbed, slashed and then tossed the kerosene-soaked, screaming queen into a blazing fire in the palace garden. [905] Heungseon Daewongun, Min's father-in-law, on the other hand, was amenable to Japan's commercial development in Korea. The predictable turmoil provided Japan with the justification for military

---

[904] Lyon Sharman, Sun Yat-Sen His Life and Its Meaning: A Critical Biography, Stanford University Press, Stanford, California, 1968, p. 39

[905] Sterling and Peggy Seagrave, Gold Warriors, America's Secret Recovery of Yamashita's Gold, Verso Publishing, 2003, Prologue, pp., 14-15

occupation by the Kempeitai that arrested thousands of dissenting Koreans, now regarded as insurgents.

The rebellion failed, but the government's Gabo Reform addressed many of the grievances of the peasants. On October 13, 1897, as a result of the First Sino-Japanese War, officials proclaimed the Korean Empire. Foreign influence would still be a major aspect, with Japan and Russia later competing over exclusive rights in Korea.

In 1895, when Japan defeated China in the First Sino-Japanese War, Calvin S. Brice, a former senator and railway lawyer created the American China Development Company. Its shareholders included railroad mogul Edward H. Harriman, Jacob H. Schiff of Kuhn, Loeb and Company, James A. Stillman of the Rockefeller-controlled National City Bank, Levi Morton, the former US Vice President, the Carnegie Steel Corporation, and railroad expert, Charles Coster, a J. P. Morgan associate. Secretary of State Richard Olney pressured China to give the consortium two concessions, one to the Peking-Hankow Railway, and the other for the construction of a potential railway across Manchuria. However, China already granted Russia a concession to build a Manchurian railway, and had granted the Peking-Hankow concession to a Belgian syndicate. The consortium officials were determined. [906]

Following China's defeat, the nation sought to develop economic reforms in order to build a defense, something the country did not previously need. Opportunistic bankers and concession hunters from other countries offered such tempting arrangements that Chinese officials found hard to resist. China had to acquire foreign capital to finance railway construction. However, Chinese leaders also recognized that their foreign creditors would threaten their empire's dominion. The Americans claimed no political accommodations in return for their monetary advances. The United States had valuable experience in the railway field, given their transcontinental lines. Charles H. Denby, the US Minister in Peking promoted United

---

[906] Michael H. Hunt, The Making of a Special Relationship: The United States and China to 1914, Columbia University Press, New York, 1983, pp. 150-151

States involvement and simply awaited the decisions of the Chinese leadership. [907]

Secretary of State Richard Olney immediately elevated the foreign diplomatic position to the title of Embassy, to equalize America with other nations, such as Britain. Until then, the United States only used Legations, inferior to embassies, for their diplomatic relations. Ambassador Denby, a former Union officer, attorney, and expansionist, told Chinese officials that railways "strengthen and unify the government, bring frontiers near, make invasion impossible, connect distant cities, pacify remote districts, educate and elevate the people, and become sources of fabulous wealth." China could have all of these benefits "without efforts of her own" or without fear of foreign political obstacles if she just would entrust her railway development to experienced US engineers and capitalists. [908]

Secretary Olney, in discussions with British officials, agreed to join forces to besiege Asia. They manipulated Japan into providing the military manpower to attack Russia within the next decade. Then Britain and the United States would divide the spoils—one of which was an open door to the lucrative Asian resources. Britain agreed to forfeit their Latin American interests and share the Asian resources. To move forward with further imperialist expansion, Britain and America formalized their alliance in 1897, the year of the first official Zionist conference. [909]

In April 1898, Chinese officials offered the American China Development Company the southern extension of the Peking-Hankow line running down to Canton. The Americans would set up the £4 million loan, purchase the equipment, construct, and operate the line for the term of the loan, fifty years. The company had an option to construct subsidiary lines, and operate coalmines on adjacent land. This deal gave the Americans a solid economic standing

---

[907] William R. Braisted, The United States and the American China Development Company, The Far Eastern Quarterly, Vol. 11, No. 2, February 1952, p. 147

[908] Ibid. 147

[909] E. C. Knuth, The Empire of the City, the Secret History of British Financial Power, The Book Tree, San Diego, California, 1944, p. 11

in a potentially strategic and productive central southern interior area. [910]

On February 12, 1902, shortly after Theodore Roosevelt became president (1901-1909), the Japanese announced that Hayashi Tadasu, the Japanese minister in London, and Henry Petty-Fitzmaurice, representing Britain, signed the Anglo-Japanese Treaty on January 30, 1902. They had been considering this alliance, recognizing Japan's special interest in Korea, renewable in 1905 and 1911, since 1895, when Britain opted not to join France, Germany and Russia in opposition to the Japanese occupation of China's Liaotung peninsula. This alliance meant that Britain would side with Japan if any nation joined with Russia against Japan.

As part of the Anglo-Japanese agreement, 300 British-trained Japanese bankers set up the Japanese banking system, a structure that then began creating devastating hardships requiring loans from the international banking cartel. Britain, challenged with heavy war debt, to America's J. P. Morgan, would terminate the 1902 alliance, in December 1921. J. P. Morgan and other banks, flush with war profits after the First World War, focused on investment opportunities in Japan. [911]

President Roosevelt would honor the unique relationship that Britain and America had in which they would share the benefits from the countries whose doors they opened. Citizens still recognized the Constitution, and understood that the United States could not sign a similar treaty with Japan, as the Senate would never approve of it. On April 23, 1903, John Hay, the Secretary of State wrote to Roosevelt, "We could never get the treaty through the Senate the object of which was to check Russian aggression." A few days later, Hay reminded Roosevelt that citizens were unaware of the government's interests in Asia. Hay said, "I am sure you will think it out of the question

---

[910] Michael H. Hunt, The Making of a Special Relationship: The United States and China to 1914, Columbia University Press, New York, 1983, pp. 150-151

[911] Sterling and Peggy Seagrave, The Yamoto Dynasty, the Secret History of Japan's Imperial Family, Broadway Books, New York, 1999, pp. 101-102

that we should adopt any scheme of concerted action with England and Japan which would seem hostile to Russia. Public opinion in this country would not support such a course, not do I think it would be to our permanent advantage." [912]

Roosevelt believed that millions of Asians would benefit through a Japanese conquest. The Japanese accepted the Anglo-American Open Door policy, even though Britain and the United States exploited Japan because of their strategic location, which functioned as an Open Door to China, while Japan expanded their power and influence into Korea. The whole objective was cooperative opposition to Russia. [913] Roosevelt anxiously awaited Japan's invasion, and even bragged that he "would not hesitate to give Japan something more than moral support against Russia." Despite his bravado, he recognized that Congress would probably not authorize him to use military force in North Asia. Because of Hay's deteriorating health and advanced age, Roosevelt essentially functioned as his own Secretary of State in addition to having excessive influence in the War Department. [914]

During a cruise to Asia, in company with President Roosevelt, War Secretary William Howard Taft met for confidential meetings in Tokyo with Japanese Prime Minister Katsura Tarō from July 27-29, 1905. They discussed three items during the meeting. They were, 1) Katsura wanted the support of the United States and Britain for Japan's foreign policy; 2) Concerning the Philippines, Taft indicated that it would be best to have a strong nation like the United States govern the Philippines; and 3) Katsura maintained that the Japanese colonization of Korea was vital as he claimed that Korea caused the recent Russo-Japanese War. Katsura claimed that Korea, unsupervised, would imprudently enter into agreements and treaties with other countries. Therefore, with Japan directing Korea's affairs, it would not create circumstances that forced Japan to fight a foreign war. Taft agreed that the creation of a Japanese protectorate over Korea would stabilize East Asia. Taft said that President Roosevelt,

[912] James Bradley, The Imperial Cruise, a secret History of Empire and War, Little, Brown and company, New York, 2009, pp. 209-210
[913] Ibid. 209
[914] Ibid. 211-212

who would never win Senate approval for such a constitutionally illegal treaty, would accept Taft's decisions on these matters.

This dastardly agreement sealed Korea's fate—forty-five years under Japanese subjugation and sanctioned Japan's plundering of Asia. Britain and the financiers readily approved, as they funded Japan's vicious warfare. [915] The Taft-Katsura Agreement or Memorandum, dated July 29, 1905, consisted of documents, carrying the weight of an international treaty, regarding a meeting between Secretary of War Taft and Prime Minister of Japan Katsura Taro. People did not discover the papers until 1924. Establishment historians, regardless of the historical events that corroborate such an agreement, claim that the official records fail to show that the two people involved made any such agreement.

They renewed the alliance after the Russo-Japanese War, an agreement that lasted from February 8, 1904 to September 5, 1905, and, in 1911, after Japan annexed Korea. As directed, Japan adopted the gold standard. Taft returned to San Francisco on September 27, 1905, aboard the *Korea*. *I*ronically, the ship was named for the country that he had just relinquished to Japan. [916] Taft, upon his arrival told reporters, "American tax dollars are hard at work to make Manila Harbor as convenient as any in the Orient." The newsmen did not ask why the Chinese developed commercial relations with every country except America. The Chinese, while Roosevelt's party was in China during their Asian cruise, negatively depicted his daughter, and Chinese officials refused to dine with Taft who assured the reporters that America would deal justly with China. Taft and Roosevelt gifted Korea to Japan while turning Japanese opinion against America. [917]

Japan claimed Korea as a protectorate, formalized by the Eulsa Treaty of November 17, 1905. Japan annexed Korea on August 22, 1910 through the Japan-Korea Annexation Treaty, effective August 29,

---

[915]   The 1905 Secret Taft-Katsura Agreement: America's Betrayal Of Korea, http://dokdo-research.com/temp25.html as of May 2012

[916]   James Bradley, The Imperial Cruise, a secret History of Empire and War, Little, Brown and company, New York, 2009, p. 320

[917]   Ibid. 322

1910. In Korea, they remember this day as the day of national shame. The majority of the propagandized Japanese citizens believed that Japan was in Korea to help. Japanese officials recalled Miura Gorō, the man who had ordered Queen Min's gruesome assassination. A military court tried him and summarily acquitted him for lack of evidence. He soon accepted a plush job in the emperor's Privy Council. After the United States had assaulted Korea in 1871, the two countries signed a friendship agreement on May 22, 1882. America's 1905 agreement with Japan violated that 1882 agreement with Korea. [918]

Japan would be "the Crown's policeman in Asia," to do the dirty work—the killing and the dying. The alliance included high-interest loans from Rothschild-controlled British banks to finance Japan's armament purchases and ships from British firms. Britain then demanded that Russia abandon the Kwantung Peninsula, territory leased from China six years before. Russia had already spent $300 million on improvements. [919]

Dividing the Spoils, Japan's War against Czarist Russia

President Theodore Roosevelt (1901-1909), intimately connected to J.P. Morgan and Company, manipulated Japan into attacking Russia.

Sir Ernest Cassel, by absorbing the Maxim-Nordenfelt Company, created Vickers-Maxim. Cassel, a phenomenally wealthy German-born Jew, interested in South-American finance, reorganized Uruguay's finances, lent money to Mexico, acquired the Royal Swedish railway and built the Central London railway. He loaned money to the Chinese after the war with Japan. He was the personal banker to Edward VII (1901-1910) whose advisory staff included

---

[918] Report of Rear Admiral John Rodgers Detailing the Events Leading Up to the US Assault on the Korean Forts; http://www.shinmiyangyo.org/ as of May 2012, See also The 1871 US-Korea Conflict: Cause and Effects by Thomas Duvernay

[919] Des Griffin, Descent into Slavery, Emissary Publications, Clackamas, Oregon, 2001, pp. 190-199

various members of the Sassoon family and Leopold and Alfred de Rothschild, who was a violent Russophobe. Cassel was a close friend of Winston Churchill and his father, Randolph, who was an intimate friend of Nathaniel Rothschild. [920] Cassel made a vast fortune in Siberian gold mines, steel concerns, and railway companies. [921]

Since the Boer Wars, the bankers focused on other countries, like Japan, receptive to heavy weaponization, a windfall to these bankers of death and their cronies, the merchants of death. Peace conferences always follow warfare, and prudent disarmament, attended by bankers and their politicians. Governments then dispose of their costly weapons, often to armament resellers, like Francis Bannerman & Sons, and then governments replace those weapons with newer, more deadly, more expensive weapons, all of which the bankers finance. [922]

Bannerman also supplied the Japanese in the Russo-Japanese War. He said, "We personally submitted samples to the Japanese War Department in Tokyo of 10,000 McClellan army saddles, 100,000 army rifles, 100,000 knapsacks, 100,000 haversacks, 100,000 sets of equipment, 150,000 gun slings, 20,000,000 cartridges, together with a shipload of assorted military goods." [923]

On February 6, 1904, Japan suspended all contact with Russia. Roosevelt, though he sided with Japan, pretended to maintain neutrality, but would apply the Roosevelt Corollary to Korea. He wrote that impotent nations were appropriate prey for civilized nations. A naïve official in Seoul told a reporter, "We have the promise of America.

---

[920] Martin Gilbert, Churchill's London: Spinning Top of Memories of Ungrand Places and Moments in Time, An address to The International Churchill Society, London, England, 17 September 1985, http://www.winstonchurchill. org/i4a/pages/index.cfm?pageid=376 as of May 2012

[921] Ernest Cassel, http://www.economy-point.org/e/ernest-cassel.html as of May 2012

[922] Helmuth C. Engelbrecht, Ph.D. and Frank C. Hanighen, Merchants of Death, a Study of the International Armament Industry, Dodd, Mead & Co., New York, 1934, pp. 88-89

[923] Ibid. 64

She will be our friend whatever happens." [924] On February 8, 1904, without a declaration of war, Japan attacked Russian ships at Port Arthur and Incheon. The surprised Russians accused the Japanese of violating international law while Jews in America were quite pleased. After Japan's assault, Roosevelt quickly warned Germany and France against assisting Russia, "I should promptly side with Japan and proceed to whatever length was necessary on her behalf." [925]

On February 10, 1904, Japan officially declared war on czarist Russia, referred to as the Russo-Japanese War, lasting a little more than a year and a half. Jacob H. Schiff of Kuhn, Loeb and Company, with $196 million, financed Japan's invasion of Russia while the European Rothschilds financed Russia. Unfortunately, and probably purposefully, Russia failed to receive timely armament deliveries, which greatly affected their defense capabilities. Russia's objectives, in 1895, were an ice-free Pacific port and the acquisition of just enough leased territory in Manchuria for the continuation of her transcontinental railway. [926] Warfare decimated her economy, preparatory to the Marxist revolution in 1905. [927]

Baron Kaneko Kentarō, who roomed with Komura Jutarō at Harvard, made various contacts in America before returning to Japan, where he taught at Tokyo Imperial University. [928] He had studied the constitutions of various western nations in order to create a similar document for Japan. In 1884, he was working at the Office for the Investigation of Institutions. In 1899, Harvard awarded him an honorary doctorate for his work on the Meiji Constitution. In 1900, he became the Minister of Justice, under the fourth Itō Hirobumi administration. In the spring of 1904, during the war, Itō Hirobumi,

[924] James Bradley, The Imperial Cruise, a secret History of Empire and War, Little, Brown and company, New York, 2009, p. 213
[925] Ibid. 216
[926] Archibald R. Colquhoun, China in Transformation, Harper & Brothers, New York, 1912, p. 147
[927] The House of Rothschild, Paris Conference, October 11, 1863, The New York Times
[928] James Bradley, The Imperial Cruise, a secret History of Empire and War, Little, Brown and company, New York, 2009, p. 219

who supported the First Sino-Japanese War (1894-1895), requested that Kaneko return to the United States as a special envoy to solicit diplomatic support to end the war. He met with President Roosevelt, another Harvard graduate, to request his assistance in mediating a beneficial peace treaty.

On April 2, 1904, Justice Oliver Wendell Holmes held a dinner party for his former protégé, Kaneko Kentarō. At George Washington University, Kaneko lectured on the similarities in the United States and Japanese constitutions, a speech that *Century Magazine* published. He also spoke to the Wall Street barons at the University Club in Manhattan, and at a dinner at the home of Oscar S. Straus. [929]

The war, which would last until September 5, 1905, though relatively short, resulted in—Japanese, 47,387 dead; 173,425 wounded; 27,192 deaths from disease. Russia: 31,458 dead; 146,032 wounded; 12,128 deaths from disease. The Chinese suffered 20,000 non-combatant, civilian deaths. Other sources give alternative death figures. *The New York Times*, dated July 26, 1905, reported that on the previous day, the Japanese spokesman Aino Sato said, "Both countries are in favor of a termination of the war for the sake of humanity and the general prosperity. It is natural that they should be. The war has already cost 570,000 men, of whom 370,000 were Russians. On the side of peace is your president. This will carry great weight." Sato reported the Japanese cost of the war at $700 million or about $1million per day and said that Japan wanted "an indemnity to cover all losses, including loss of warships, loss of lives and the tremendous cash outlay." [930]

Further Sato remarked about the "disturbed political conditions in Russia." He said, "Our terms have been forwarded by the Emperor with the counsel of his Ministers. I do not know what they are." Further, he said, "In Japan we have a strong feeling of gratitude toward the American people, who have done so much for us. England is our ally, but we regard the United States as an ally without a treaty.

---

[929] Ibid. 219
[930] Baron Komura Here to Ask Big Indemnity, Spokesman says Japan Wants all Losses Made Good, The New York Times, July 26, 1905

There is no chance of any difficulty arising between your country and ours." When someone asked, "What about the Philippines" Sato responded, "We would not take them as a gift." [931] Oscar S. Straus, a friend and later Roosevelt's Secretary of Commerce and Labor, wrote to the president that he hoped Japan would be victorious. Roosevelt wrote his son, "I was thoroughly well pleased with the Japanese victory, for Japan is playing our game." [932]

According to the Taft-Katsura Agreement, July 29, 1905, Japan would relinquish economic control of the resource-rich Hawaiian and the Philippine Islands to US dominance while Japan targeted adjacent Asiatic countries and colonized Korea. That agreement, without Congressional sanction, divvied up countries and manipulated unsuspecting people. [933] Japan fared well in the Treaty of Portsmouth because of that agreement, signed at the conclusion of the meetings between Taft and Prime Minister Katsura Tarō in Tokyo where the United States sold out Korea.

On September 5, 1905, officials of the victorious and the vanquished parties met at the Portsmouth Naval Base in Portsmouth, New Hampshire. Roosevelt, advised by attendee, Jacob H. Schiff, the major financier of Japan's warfare, mediated the post war peace agreement, ending the Russo-Japanese War. Count Sergei Witte, a freemason, [934] was the architect of the October Manifesto, [935] of October 17, 1905, in response to the Russian Revolution of 1905. Witte, a decisive policy-maker, the First Prime Minister of Imperial Russia, represented his nation. Adolf Krause, of B'nai B'rith, told Witte, who was married to a Jewess, Matilda Lisanevich, during the peace negotiations in the summer that the Jews in Russia would revolt

---

[931]   Ibid

[932]   James Bradley, The Imperial Cruise, a secret History of Empire and War, Little, Brown and company, New York, 2009, pp. 214-215

[933]   The 1905 Secret Taft-Katsura Agreement: America's Betrayal Of Korea, http://www.geocities.com/mlovmo/temp25.html as of May 2012

[934]   Jüri Lina, Under the Sign of the Scorpion: The Rise and Fall of the Soviet Empire, Referent Publishing, Stockholm, Sweden, 2002, pp. 141-142

[935]   Manifesto of October 17, 1905, http://www.dur.ac.uk/a.k.harrington/octmanif. html as of May 2012

again if the Russian government failed to appropriately accommodate them. [936]

Russia relinquished the Manchurian railway concession and all of their Manchurian investments. Japan received Manchuria, a huge base from which to attack mainland China. Roosevelt allowed Japan to maintain dominance in Korea and Manchuria with the understanding that Japan would safeguard US economic interests in the area. Ironically, in 1906, officials awarded Roosevelt, a legendary war hawk, the Nobel Peace Prize for his negotiation efforts.

Japan, represented by Kogoro Takahira, Minister to the United States, and Japan's chief negotiator Baron Komura Jutarō, Minister for Foreign Affairs, gained control of all Russian business interests in Manchuria, which financially destabilized thousands of Russian residents, who the Japanese soldiers and their crime partners soon victimized. The Portsmouth Treaty allocated the commercial port of Dalian and the naval base at Port Arthur to Japan. Mitsui Group, a Japanese conglomerate (zaibatsu) and Black Dragon, a paramilitary, right-wing group, collaborated with Japan's fiscally independent Kwantung Army, to seize the Chinese concessions that Mitsui had previously analyzed and found financially attractive. The army traded weapons for concessions with Chang Tso-lin, and then Manchuria's most powerful warlord, which accounted for the army officer's increasing wealth. [937]

The zaibatsu consisted of large family-controlled monopolies managed by a holding company. They included a banking subsidiary to accommodate their financial needs, and numerous industrial companies focused on specific markets. Mitsubishi, Mitsui, Sumitomo and Yasuda are the most influential and largest zaibatsu groups. Japanese innovators created the Mitsui and Sumitomo during the Edo period (1603-1868), rule by the shoguns of the Tokugawa family. The Mitsubishi and Yasuda zaibatsu came into existence following

[936] Jüri Lina, Under the Sign of the Scorpion: The Rise and Fall of the Soviet Empire, Referent Publishing, Stockholm, Sweden, 2002, pp. 141-142
[937] Sterling and Peggy Seagrave, Gold Warriors, America's Secret Recovery of Yamashita's Gold, Verso Publishing, 2003, pp. 25-28

the Meiji Restoration (May 3, 1868). The government relied on the
financial powers and expertise of the zaibatsu for tax collection,
military procurement, and foreign trade.

Japan's acquisition included the South Manchurian branch of the
China Far East Railway, which became the South Manchurian
Railway (Mantetsu), spoils that Edward H. Harriman wanted to
purchase. Half of the railroad went to Emperor Hirohito, the largest
private shareholder, followed by the Mitsui Bank, Japan's first private
bank, established on July 1, 1876, during the Meiji period, and the
Mitsubishi industrial and banking conglomerates. Mitsui heavily
invested in weapons and profited from Japan's aggression, disguised
as a patriotic effort, reportedly to help whatever country it waged
war against. [938]

Some Japanese citizens believed that Roosevelt had forced them into
a peaceful settlement without enacting a war indemnity from Russia,
and held mass meetings where they demanded a rejection of the treaty.
Crowds destroyed the newspaper offices whose editors defended
the treaty. Rioting in Tokyo resulted in more than 1,000 casualties
and many arrests. [939] Disturbances there began in September 1905,
following the signing of the Treaty of Portsmouth. Black Dragon
thugs staged riots, burned churches, and engaged in other destructive
activities to intimidate the government, who was already considering
selling part of the South Manchurian Railway to Harriman, who
reportedly witnessed, with amusement, the riots in the company of
Baron Matsui. [940]

South Manchurian Railway (Mantetsu) employees, while adroitly
managing the economy, according to company policies, built a
massive intelligence network, and began documenting resources for
future confiscation. Manchuria had abundant natural resources such

---

[938] Ibid. 23-31
[939] Paul Hibbert Clyde, A History of the Modern and Contemporary Far East:
A Survey of Western Contacts with Eastern Asia during the Nineteenth and
Twentieth Centuries, Prentice-Hall, New York, 1937, pp. 413-415.
[940] Sterling and Peggy Seagrave, Gold Warriors, America's Secret Recovery of
Yamashita's Gold, Verso Publishing, 2003, pp. 23-31

as forests, land, and mineral deposits. It was also home to many poor farmers who grew sorghum, and other hardy crops. Tairiku Ronin, Japanese thugs, turned South Manchuria into a poppy-producing paradise to supply thousands of Japanese-established opium dens throughout China, to demoralize, and diminish potential opposition, to the impending seizure of that country. [941]

Harriman, intent on owning a worldwide railroad and steamship service, sought control of the Trans-Siberian system, then owned by Russia, and the Chinese Eastern, and the South Manchurian Railway, then under Japanese ownership, as a result of the Portsmouth Treaty. On October 12, 1905, Prime Minister Katsura Tarō agreed to Harriman's plan, and wrote up a sales contract for the transfer of the line from Port Arthur to Changchun. According to this arrangement, a syndicate composed of the Japanese government, and Harriman would have equal ownership, and share in the practical operation of the railroad. Upon discovery of this plan, the Japanese public, still enraged over the Portsmouth Treaty, condemned its government. [942] Baron Komura Jutarō returned to Tokyo on October 16, 1905, entering Tokyo under heavy guard. The government ratified the Portsmouth Treaty despite its unpopularity. [943]

The Root-Takahira Agreement, signed on November 30, 1908, with Secretary of State Elihu Root (Pilgrims Society), was evidence of the official recognition of Japan's territorial status. It affirmed the open door policy to China, clarification of the free trade and commercial investments, Japan's acknowledgment of the United States annexation of Hawaii, the control of the Philippines, and the US recognition of Japan's status in northeast China. This agreement sanctioned Japan's annexation of Korea and its dominance over southern Manchuria. In addition, Japan would limit immigration to California. This treaty

---

[941] Sterling and Peggy Seagrave, Gold Warriors, America's Secret Recovery of Yamashita's Gold, Verso Publishing, 2003, pp. 25-28

[942] Paul Hibbert Clyde, A History of the Modern and Contemporary Far East: A Survey of Western Contacts with Eastern Asia during the Nineteenth and Twentieth Centuries, Prentice-Hall, New York, 1937, pp. 413-415.

[943] Ibid. 413-415

established political, economic, and territorial boundaries between Japan and the United States. [944]

Baron Komura acknowledged that the Japanese public would not accept the railroad plan, and claimed that Japan could not conclude the agreement because China had not yet consented to the legal transfer of the line to Japan. He also reminded the cabinet that the railroad was the only tangible asset that Japan had acquired in the war. It would be unwise to relinquish fifty percent of it to US investors. The government concurred and notified Harriman that it was voiding the arrangement. [945] Despite Jacob H. Schiff's influence, and the new Secretary of State Philander C. Knox's diplomacy, Japan rejected Harriman's offer. People knew Knox for his Dollar Diplomacy, and loan brokering in Nicaragua, Honduras and Cuba for the bankers, and for lying about the ratification of the Sixteenth Amendment. His clients included Carnegie, Vanderbilt, J.P. Morgan, Rockefeller and Harriman. [946]

United States and British investors intended to exploit Manchuria. Hoping to displace the Japanese, Chinese officials encouraged foreign investment, which violated the Peking Treaty (November 17, 1905), in which the Chinese agreed not to construct a competitive line in the same vicinity as the South Manchurian Railway. On October 2, 1909, the provincial authorities of Manchuria agreed to the construction of the Chinchow-Aigun Railway, financed by US investors, like Harriman, but built by the British firm of Pauling and Company, which had previously secured the contract for the Hsinmintun-Fakumen Railway. Britain and the United States would control the railway company. However, the Chinchow-Aigun line would cut directly across the Japanese and Russian areas, which the Japanese viewed as a threat to their South Manchurian Railway profits. [947] Knox planned to internationalize all existing and future

---

[944] Ibid. 425

[945] Ibid. 413-415

[946] Naomi Wiener Cohen, Jacob H. Schiff: A Study in American Jewish Leadership, Brandeis 1999, pp. 32-35

[947] Paul Hibbert Clyde, A History of the Modern and Contemporary Far East: A Survey of Western Contacts with Eastern Asia during the Nineteenth and

Manchurian railways. That would guarantee an open door policy to China and access to all of the country's resources. [948]

On November 6, 1909, Knox wrote to his counterpart, Sir Edward Grey of the Milner Group, confirming the United States and British alliance for the Chinchow-Aigun Railway. Grey responded with his approval on November 25. Talks had already convened for a large loan to China so Grey wanted a postponement. Knox sent identical notes to Tokyo, Peking, Paris, Berlin, and St. Petersburg on December 14. Knox failed to alert Japan and Russia about the special alliance that Britain and the United States had developed regarding China's railroads. Premier Katsura, using the Portsmouth Treaty, objected to US plans. [949]

On January 21, 1910, Foreign Minister Komura formally objected to Knox's proposals. Japan's involvement in the 1905 treaty caused negative public sentiment and had required heavy sacrifices in blood and wealth. Former President Roosevelt wrote to President Taft about Knox's proposal. He wrote, "if the Japanese choose to follow a course of conduct to which we are averse, we cannot stop it unless we are prepared to go to war, and a successful war about Manchuria would require a fleet as good as that of England plus an army as good as that of Germany." [950]

Twentieth Centuries, Prentice-Hall, New York, 1937, pp. 423-426

[948] Seiji Hishida, Japan among the Great Powers: A Survey of Her International Relations, Longmans, Green, New York, 1940, pp. 185, 189

[949] Ibid. 189-191

[950] Ibid. 189-191

SECTION 6

PREPARING FOR REVOLUTION, WORLD WAR ONE

Germany, Historical Perspectives

Officials of the Congress of Vienna (1815) created the German Confederation, which was an alliance of German-speaking countries in Central Europe, in order to coordinate their economies, and function as a safeguard against the powerful states of Austria and Prussia, the two dominant member states. International bankers living in Britain encouraged this alliance as a way of providing peace and stability, and to prevent Russia or France from making hostile moves. Continuous rivalry and the failure of the several member states to compromise would contribute to the 1848 revolution, an early attempt to establish a unified Germany, among other things. However, French officials had other plans.

In the July 1830 Revolution, the liberals ousted Charles X (1824-1830) and replaced him with the Citizen King Louis Philippe (1830-1848), who was initially friendly to Masonic principles. Paris lawyer, André Marie Jean Jacques Dupin, a member of the Supreme Council of France, was his principle advisor. However, the Citizen King's increasing political unsuitability provoked the revolution of February 1848, which freemasons directed. After Louis Philippe abdicated, on March 6, 1848, and fled to England, of the eleven individuals composing the provisional government, nine were freemasons, [951] with Jacques-Charles DuPont de l'Eure as Chairman and Adolphe I. Crémieux, as Minister of Justice, the individual who compelled the Orleans family to leave France. Crémieux also abolished the death penalty for political offenses, and made the office of judge permanent. Especially from 1848 forward, freemasonry largely

---

[951] John Daniel, Two Faces of Freemasonry, a Picture Book Supplement to Volume One, Third Edition of Scarlet and the Beast, a History of the War between English and French Freemasonry, Day Publishing, Longview Texas, 2007, pp. 114-115

influenced political and cultural policies in France, [952] the country that Dr. Heinrich Pudor referred to as the "Scourge of Europe" since the freemasonic Revolution of 1789. [953]

After the 1848 revolution, Crémieux announced, "Citizens and brothers of the Grand Orient, the Provisional Government accepts with pleasure your useful and complete adhesion. The Republic exists in freemasonry. If the Republic does as the freemasons have done, it will become the glowing pledge of union with all men, in all parts of the globe, and on all sides of our triangle." [954] The freemasons installed one of their own, Louis—Napoleon Bonaparte, through a coup d'état on December 2, 1851. He ascended the throne as Napoleon III on December 2, 1852.

Napoleon III's lodge policies aroused adamant antagonism when he attempted to install as a Grand Master, Marshall Magnan, a person without any experience as a freemason. Crémieux, the Grand Commander of the Supreme Council and founder of the exclusively Jewish organization, the Alliance Israélite Universelle, thereafter became a dangerous enemy. The Franco-Prussian War (July 19, 1870-May 10, 1871) began France's long-term anti-German policies. [955] Crémieux belonged to the French Masonic Lodge, Alsace Lorraine, reportedly the lodge from which someone stole the Protocols of the Learned Elders of Zion, a document that some scholars say was written in 1901-1902, after the formal development of the Zionist movement. Additionally, as a thirty-third degree ruling freemason,

---

[952] Dieter Schwarz, Freemasonry, Ideology, Organization and Policy, Central Publishing House of the NSDAP, Berlin, 1944, pp. 24-25

[953] Fred Scherbaum and Veronica Clark (translators), Warwolves of the Iron Cross, the Hyenas of High Finance, the International Relationships of French and American High Finance, Vera Icona Publishers, 2011, pp. 52-53

[954] John Daniel, Two Faces of Freemasonry, a Picture Book Supplement to Volume One, Third Edition of Scarlet and the Beast, a History of the War between English and French Freemasonry, Day Publishing, Longview Texas, 2007, pp. 114-115

[955] Dieter Schwarz, Freemasonry, Ideology, Organization and Policy, Central Publishing House of the NSDAP, Berlin, 1944, pp. 24-25

he was on the Supreme Council of the Ancient and Primitive Rite of Mizraim freemasonry in Paris. [956]

Satisfied people do not rise up against their governments, demanding change. Others, notably certain internationalist Jews, supported and participated in the revolutions of 1789 and 1848, reinforced by many writers and recently-positioned radical politicians who were attempting to reshape national governments. The Jews were the most vociferous in the press, but not because they demanded religious freedoms or the cessation of religious prejudice. In 1848, they did not advocate for equality but for extra special "material advantages for its members." [957]

Up until 1848, the Jews living in Germany had, for whatever reason, perhaps to infiltrate the culture, adopted democratic convictions and thereafter many supported "National Liberalism," and joined the ruling Conservative ruling parties. Then they monopolized the literary field and at least seventy-five percent of the popular press where they pursued their own interests while working to disintegrate the Germanic state. They patterned their journalistic objectives to serve their own commercial interests, shaped public opinion, critiqued the theater and art, and wrote about politics and religion. After emancipation, the Jews further exploited the press and reduced journalism to gossip and scandal and instituted unionism. Although they made fun of their own idiosyncrasies, they viewed such conduct from the German population as a malicious demonstration of religious hatred. [958]

Germans outwardly resigned "in favor of Judaism" after 1848 when they allowed Jewish mediation to rule every aspect of their lives

---

[956] John Daniel, Two Faces of Freemasonry, a Picture Book Supplement to Volume One, Third Edition of Scarlet and the Beast, a History of the War between English and French Freemasonry, Day Publishing, Longview Texas, 2007, p. 113

[957] Wilhelm Marr, The Victory of Judaism over Germanism, Viewed from a Nonreligious Point of View, Rudolph Costenoble, Bern, Switzerland, 1879, pp. 16-17

[958]

wherein Jewry collected a commission. According to writer, Wilhelm Marr, Jewry staged a war against the Germans, beginning in 1848, over a thirty-year period, with their revolutionary activities, not only in Germany, but in other European countries. [959] After 1848, a culture struggle began in which many Germans felt ostracized, as they could not criticize "anything Jewish." Marr maintained that the Germans did not oppose foreign rule sufficiently, nor the Judaic struggle to obtain world domination. The Jewish-owned press prohibited the Germans from addressing the obvious "culture struggle." Editors printed political-cultural analyses and suppressed publications about Christianity while ignoring the anomalies of Jewish statutes and rituals, like the brutalities of kosher slaughtering, which would have generated accusations of "hatred" against the Germans. According to Marr, it was "quite a different matter" if Jews criticized Germany's religious practices. The cartelized press, even in letters to the editor, excluded the German citizen's right to free expression. [960]

In 1848, Jewish banker and freemason, Ludwig Bamberger, educated at Gießen, Heidelberg, and Göttingen, edited the *Mainzer Zeitung* and was one of the leaders in the republican party which participated in the revolution in Germany. He fled to Paris to escape execution and gained banking expertise while working for the bank of Bischoffheim & Goldschmidt. Germany's general amnesty enabled him to return in 1866. He joined the National Liberal Party and people elected him as a member of the Reichstag where he advocated free trade, the Reichsbank, promoted a gold currency, and opposed bimetallism. On January 22, 1870, along with private banker Adelbert Delbruck, he founded Deutsche Bank in Berlin, specializing in foreign trade, and also founded the Group for the Promotion of Free Trade. By 1878, he would oppose Bismarck's policies of protectionism and state socialism.

The Jewish dailies in the German-speaking lands supported Jewish industrial interests and securities speculation. Meanwhile, England allied with Judaism. The Slavs dismissed the Germans and viewed

---

[959] Ibid. 19-21
[960] Ibid. 19-21

them as the Jewish newspaper depicted them. The German spirit had become a stranger in the press where the majority of journalists were Jewish. Since 1866, because of Bismarck's policies, and because he typically acquiesced to their demands, most Jews held him in high esteem. [961]

The Franco-Prussian War was a military conflict between the French Empire and the Kingdom of Prussia. The North German Confederation assisted Prussia, along with the South German states of Baden, Württemberg, and Bavaria. The victorious Prussians brought about the final unification of Germany even before the war's end and the downfall of Napoleon III. The unification of the German states occurred on January 18, 1871, when the princes of the various German states proclaimed Wilhelm I as the German Emperor when they gathered at the Versailles Palace's Hall of Mirrors in France.

Following the unification, Wilhelm of Prussia became Emperor Wilhelm of the German Empire, consisting of Prussia, Bavaria, Wurttemberg, and Saxony, each sovereign, with its own army, flag, and titles of nobility. Regional states had their own parliaments, a Prime Minister and a cabinet. [962] There were twenty-seven constituent territories, ruled by royal families. The Kingdom of Prussia was the most populous and had the most territory. The Empire's rivals, Imperial Russia was to the east, France to the west, and her ally, Austria-Hungary was in the south. From 1850 forward, German industry accelerated, because of its coal, iron, (later steel), chemicals and railways. The German Empire had the world's most powerful army, and its navy became second to Britain in less than a decade.

From 1870 onward, because Germany opposed French freemasonry, France implemented revenge and encirclement policies against Germany, as determined by liberal and democratic politicians with

---

[961] Wilhelm Marr, The Victory of Judaism over Germanism, Viewed from a Nonreligious Point of View, Rudolph Costenoble, Bern, Switzerland, 1879, pp. 22-23
[962] Leon Degrelle, How Hitler Consolidated Power in Germany and Launched A Social Revolution, The First Years of the Third Reich, The Journal of Historical Review, volume 12, no. 3, pp. 299-370

freemasonry connections. Leon Gambetta, a freemason and the head of the Republican Party, laid the foundation for the French Triple Alliance policy wherein the French would accept any ally in their efforts against Germany, including Russia. Edward VII, the head of English freemasonry as Prince of Wales, welcomed these Masonic associations. These international alliances overwhelmed Wilhelm II. The Jewish and Masonic-controlled world press initiated a hateful anti-German campaign incredibly similar to the propaganda campaign they waged against National Socialist Germany. [963]

The press exaggerated and exploited any errors the German Empire made and created propagandistic slogans and spoke of its alleged barbaric militarism as a threat to democracy, as it would before and during World War I. The press originated the myth of blind Prussian obedience, a danger to civilization, as compared to the professed ideals of Masonic individualism. Meanwhile, German lodges maintained their philosophy regarding the brotherhood of Folks and Races. Early on, due to the logistics and composition of the German Empire, there existed the Jewish Question, what to do about their powerful influence. Following the war, Masonic politicians discussed world peace and international unity at several congresses, an early attempt by internationalists to establish world governance. The same Masonic politicians who were expounding world peace hypocritically sought Germany's complete destruction. Even German freemasons, especially the Jewish Masons and the smaller lodges, abandoned their national loyalties and obligations in favor of the liberal democratic Masonic Internationale. [964]

While diplomats made concessions during the Congress of Berlin, following the Russo-Turkish War (April 24, 1877-March 3, 1878), internal warfare was brewing in Germany where the victor was a minority of the population but they controlled a majority of the communications apparatus. Frequently when one country conquers another nation, the conquerors either assimilate, thus losing their ethnic identity, or the victor exterminates the indigenous population,

---

[963] Dieter Schwarz, Freemasonry, Ideology, Organization and Policy, Central Publishing House of the NSDAP, Berlin, 1944, pp. 30-31
[964] Ibid. 30-31

and then assumes control over the government, and that nation's resources. [965]

In 1879, author Wilhelm Marr repeatedly referred to Jewish "foreign rule" in Germany because, every year, Jews traditionally say, "Next year in Jerusalem" which seems to affirm their foreign character and loyalties elsewhere although they, unassimilated aliens by choice, had lived in Germany for several generations. Marr maintained that while the above statements are often the case, Jewish assimilation had not occurred. Rather, he claims that Judaism had absorbed Germanism. He further stated that the Jews relocated, via their deportation, from Spain and Portugal into the Slavic countries, and then they emigrated from the Slavic countries via Holland into Germany. During their sojourn in the Slavic countries, Marr asserts, they socially undermined the Slavic culture, a society unprepared for foreign influence. The German-speaking states, following warfare and unification, were also vulnerable due to a lack of national identity. Consequently, while there were already Jews in Germany, incoming Jews found the newly unified country, wherein it was easier to extend their web of influence. [966]

The Germans, mostly an agricultural people, resented "the Semitic craftiness and its practical business sense" and reacted accordingly as this foreign opportunistic tribe, who viewed all Gentiles as unclean, exploited the basic German character. While this provoked the common folk, the nobility borrowed hefty amounts of money, relying on the people to pay it back via taxation. The Jews have always been "highly gifted," particularly in trade and finance, and they began to dominate in the retail and wholesale trades beginning in the middle ages. They could easily outmaneuver "the hard working common folk." [967] Other ethnic groups, like Slavs, immigrated to Germany and blended in with the native population. Yet the Jews remained separate, but still attempted to diminish their image to conceal their influence. In 1879, according to Marr, "Without a stroke of the sword,

---

[965] Wilhelm Marr, The Victory of Judaism over Germanism, Viewed from a Nonreligious Point of View, Rudolph Costenoble, Bern, Switzerland, 1879, p. 1

[966] Ibid. 11-12

[967] Ibid. 11-12

peacefully, in spite of political persecution over centuries, Judaism is today the political-social dictator in Germany." [968]

Marr maintains that diplomats coerced Rumania to "officially open floodgates to the corrosive influence of Semitism." Yet, they did not dare make the same demands of Russia. That would come later. In Germany, the Jews, represented by a handful of Jewish bankers, controlled many of the raw materials. [969] In 1879, Marr said, following the Russo-Turkish War, "Among all the European states only Russia is left to still resist the frank foreign invasion. As current events and circumstances indicate, the final surrender of Russia is only a question of time. In this multifaceted, huge state Jewry will find the cardinal point which it needs, to completely unhinge the Western world . . . and plunge Russia into a revolution like the world might never have seen before . . . Are we not witnessing today that under the gentle and humane Czar Alexander, who has abolished serfdom, it is nihilism which flourishes?" [970]

Marr said, "The future and life belongs to Judaism, Germany is of the past and will die. This is the meaning of the historical-cultural development of our German people. There is no way to fight this iron law of world order. From the very beginning it was not a religious war, it was a battle for survival against the foreign rule of Judaism, of whose character we only now have become clearly aware. In addition, we lack allies which might assist us in the peaceful and deliberate emancipation of Germanism." [971]

Further, Marr wrote, "In our parliaments, where the topic of usury is paraded about as of burning importance, one can as usual, only hear, twaddle. The dogma of 'individual freedom,' which really stands for the impertinence and gall of the most unbridled avarice, has become such a basic tenet of society, that our valiant representatives, what

---

[968] Wilhelm Marr, The Victory of Judaism over Germanism, Viewed from a Nonreligious Point of View, Rudolph Costenoble, Bern, Switzerland, 1879, pp. 17-18
[969] Ibid. 22-23
[970] Ibid. 25-27
[971] Ibid. 25-27

a despicable picture they offer . . . One might also have to curb the unbridled manipulations of big industry and of big capital and this is the reason why the question of usury remains without practical response and does not advance beyond theoretical resolutions. The doctrinarism of our Judaized society is an aid in getting around the cliff of usury. The impoverished members of every layer of our society remain victims of usury and of its corrupted German helpers, who with the help of Jews would love to make 20-30 percent per month from the hardship and misery of the poor! The cancer of usury spreads ever farther in society." [972]

The Germans had inadvertently voted for foreign rule when they voted for the Jews, made them legislators and judges and allowed them to dominate the nation's finances. The Germans relinquished the press to the Jews who transformed journalism from serious news to frivolity and decreased standards of morality. [973]

On May 23, 1863, Ferdinand Lassalle founded the General German Workers' Association. In 1869, August Bebel and Wilhelm Liebknecht founded the Social Democratic Workers' Party. In 1875, the two parties merged as the Socialist Workers' Party of Germany. On October 19, 1878, Otto von Bismarck enacted the Anti-Socialist Laws, outlawing the party due to its anti-monarchy attitudes. In 1880, Karl Kautsky, a Czech-German Jew, joined a group of Marxists in Zurich, financially supported by Karl Höchberg. Kautsky began smuggling materials into the Empire. Eduard Bernstein, Höchberg's secretary, influenced his decision to become a Marxist. Kautsky founded the monthly *Die Neue Zeit* (*The New Times*) through which he disseminated Marxism (1883-1917).

By 1890, authorities allowed the existence of the Social Democratic Party of Germany (SPD), the nation's most prominent political party with Bebel as the co-chairman (1892-1913). In 1891, Bernstein, Bebel, and Kautsky co-authored the Erfurt Program of the SPD. Kautsky

---

[972] Ibid. 29-30
[973] Ibid. 29-30

became influential, along with Bebel, in devising a Marxist theory of imperialism after Engels' death in 1895.

On October 9, 1895, in Breslau, in southwestern Poland, the Socialists held a Congress during which Dr. Wilhelm Ellenbogen, the Austrian Delegate, campaigned for Socialism. Clara Zetkin, a member of the Marxist faction of the SPD, had a lifelong friendship with Lenin, She edited the *Stuttgart Gleichheit*. She gave a speech on the emancipation of women at the Congress. [974]

Bebel authored *Woman and Socialism* in which he said, "The Socialist Party is the only one that has made the full equality of women, their liberation from every form of dependence and oppression, an integral part of its program; not for reasons of propaganda, but from necessity. For there can be no liberation of mankind, without social independence and equality of the sexes." [975] He characterized revolution as "the great crashing mess." The working masses were not interested in revolting but preferred to whine about their lot in life. Socialists, in principle, are typically all internationalists, not recognizing borders. [976]

Even though the German government was Protestant, it recognized the Vatican's significance as the basis for European society. By 1905, Russia, Germany, and the Holy See, all strongly opposed to freemasonry, enjoyed friendly relations and could have presented a formidable influence against any anti-monarchical and anti-Christian movements in Europe. [977] The Vatican, with a good relationship with Poland, could have rendered substantial help to Russia, especially since the Pope had given an Encyclical to the Polish Bishops, which

---

[974] Socialist Meeting at Brelau, The New York Times, October 10, 1895,

[975] August Bebel, Women and Socialism, Socialist Literature Company, New York, 1910, Introduction

[976] Guido Giacomo Preparata, Conjuring Hitler, How Britain and America Made the Third Reich, Pluto Press, London, England and Ann Arbor, Michigan, 2005, pp. 44-45

[977] Lucien Wolf, Notes On The Diplomatic History Of The Jewish Question, With Texts Of Protocols, Treaty Stipulations And Other Public Acts And Official Documents, Jewish Historical Society of England, Mocatta Library and Museum, London, 1919, pp. 59-60

Russians believed would provoke Polish authorities to suspend the Jewish freemasonry network, and its Paris-based organization, the Alliance Israélite Universelle. In French freemasonry, advancement to the eighteenth degree automatically enrolled the recipient in the Alliance. Of the nine members of the Supreme Council in that particular jurisdiction of freemasonry, five had to be Jews. [978]

Russian Count, Vladimir Lamsdorf knew that the Russian government was naïve and uninformed about freemasonry. The Vatican was fully cognizant of its inherent dangers and devious activities. [979] Provocateurs use tactics to alter and ultimately extinguish established governments in order to create a Sanhedrin-style world government. According to Lamsdorf, given the terrible consequences, government officials had an obligation to challenge international Jewry to save Russia. Jewry, upheld by money, unarguably would next undermine the German Empire because Judaism and Christianity have a centuries-old tradition of irreconcilable hostility. [980]

European countries, with their alliances, created a balance of power that seemed to benefit Britain. In the process, it divided Europe into two hostile camps when these countries should have united to combat Anarchism. The alliances included the secretive Franco-Russian Alliance Military Convention of August 18, 1892,[981] the Triple Entente of August 31, 1907 between Britain, France and Russia and the Triple Alliance of May 20, 1882 between Germany, Austria-Hungary and Italy[982] and the Entente Cordiale of April 8, 1904 between England and France. [983]

---

[978] Ibid. 59-60

[979] Ibid. 61-62

[980] Ibid. 59-60

[981] The Franco-Russian Alliance Military Convention—August 18, 1892, http://www.yale.edu/lawweb/avalon/frrumil.htm as of May 2012

[982] First Treaty of Alliance between Austria-Hungary, Germany, and Italy, Vienna, May 20, 1882, http://users.dickinson.edu/~rhyne/232/Six/Triple_Alliance_1882.html as of May 2012

[983] The Entente Cordiale Between The United Kingdom and France, http://wwi.lib.byu.edu/index.php/The_Entente_Cordiale_Between_The_United_Kingdom_and_France, as of May 2012

Germany had an alliance with Austria-Hungary and Italy but not with Russia. Germany, the next Marxist target, was sympathetic to what was happening in Russia. According to Count Lamsdorf, many German officials, and others, with great apprehension, recognized the hostile power of the movement toward Russia and in the Provinces of Prussian Poland. [984]

In May 1905, the Congress of the German Social-Democratic Workers' Party held a meeting in Jena, in central Germany. There and in other meetings, they passed resolutions that enabled them to accomplish, in Germany, what they were currently achieving in Russia with their anti-monarchical war through strikes and riots. This would ultimately result in chaos and a political seizure. They intended to use these tactics, and the promise of gender equality, everywhere. [985]

Lamsdorf, in a document called *The Proposed Anti-Semitic Triple Alliance*, wrote that they did not bother to conceal their aims. By January 1906, they planned to initiate an assault against Germany, to achieve success on May 1, 1906. They began their assault in Prussia and in Saxony using the motto "Universal Suffrage." [986]

Berlin to Baghdad, the Railway Concession

Wilhelm von Pressel expertly supervised railway construction in Switzerland, the Balkans and elsewhere and had an international reputation. The Ottoman Public Debt Administration (OPDA) contacted him, and he soon became one of Abdülhamid's technical advisors. In 1872, the Ottoman government had hired him to formulate plans for railways in Turkey, because of his experience during the construction of the trans-Balkan lines of the Oriental Railways Company. He understood Turkey's railway problems, and

---

[984] Lucien Wolf, Notes On The Diplomatic History Of The Jewish Question, With Texts Of Protocols, Treaty Stipulations And Other Public Acts And Official Documents, Jewish Historical Society of England, Mocatta Library and Museum, London, 1919, pp. 61-62

[985] Ibid. 1919, 61-62

[986] Socialist Meeting at Brelau, The New York Times, October 10, 1895,

the cultural and commercial importance of developing transportation in the area. [987]

During the Commercial Revolution, from the late fifteenth through the eighteenth century, the world's cultural and educational center shifted from the Mediterranean to Western Europe. Sea routes and maritime trade replaced the caravan trails. A modern transportation system might help restore a measure of the prosperity the area lost during that era. Railroad development could economically enhance Mesopotamia (Iraq) which would result in political and cultural stability. With modern transportation, the Sultan's Government could suppress the rebellions of the independent turbulent tribesmen of Kurdistan, Mesopotamia, and Arabia. [988]

While most of Europe languished in the dark ages, as early as the ninth century, educators in Spain, and the cultural centers of the Middle East, were teaching physics, algebra, medicine, surgery, anesthesiology, pharmacology, geography, philosophy, and literature to a highly literate population. Their cities had huge, well-stocked libraries, grade schools, high schools, and universities. Anyone, of any ethnicity, brown, black or white, could attend. Christopher Columbus, because of his attendance at one of Spain's schools, knew that the world was round. [989]

Abdülhamid and von Pressel envisioned a trunk line from the existing Anatolia railways, along with the new Syrian railways that would link Constantinople with Smyrna, Aleppo, Damascus, Beirut, Mosul, and Baghdad. In 1886 and in 1888, the Ottomans queried the British lessees of the Haidar Pasha-Ismid Railway, to see if they would build the extension. The Sultan offered to pay a subsidy to guarantee sufficient returns on their investment, but the British showed no interest. Sir Vincent Caillard, the OPDA Chairman, was

---

[987] Edward Mead Earle, Turkey, the Great Powers, and the Bagdad Railway: A Study in Imperialism, Macmillan, New York, 1924, pp. 18-19

[988] Ibid. 18-19

[989] Dr. Kasem Khaleel, The Arabian Connection, a Conspiracy Against Humanity, Institute of Scientific Wisdom, Lincolnshire, Illinois, 2000, pp. 149-164

also unsuccessful in his attempts to organize an Anglo-American syndicate for the construction of the railway. [990]

Beginning in the summer of 1888, Turkey had direct railway transportation to the rest of Europe from Constantinople and Salonica. The Oriental Railways began operations, running from the Austrian border across the Balkan Peninsula through Belgrade, Nish, Sofia, and Adrianople, to Constantinople. The railway connections to Austria-Hungary, and other European countries suddenly put the Ottoman capital in communication with Vienna, Paris, Berlin, and London. In 1888, French and British financiers owned all railways in Asia Minor. The oldest railway, owned by the English, was the SmyrnaAidin line, which opened in Anatolia in 1866. British investors also owned the Mersina-Adana Railway in Cilicia, and leased the Haidar Pasha-Ismid Railway. French investors controlled the Smyrna-Cassaba Railway. In autumn 1888, after others turned down the investment opportunities, Germans developed a financial interest in Asiatic Turkish railways. [991]

Dr. George von Siemens, a founder and Managing Director of the Deutsche Bank, with others, formed a German consortium, the Anatolian Railway Company, to assume control of the railway running from Haidar Pasha to Ismid, and to build an extension from Ismid to Angora. On October 6, 1888, the Ottoman government awarded the group a concession for that extension. The government intended to ultimately extend that railway to Baghdad. The Anatolian Railway Company elected financier Sir Vincent Caillard, Chairman of the OPDA, to their board hoping that he might attract other British investors. The group incorporated in Zurich, and with the aid of Swiss bankers, secured additional funding of eighty million francs, one fourth of which English bankers underwrote. German engineers began the construction of the Anatolian Railway. It began operations by January 1893. [992] They planned to make Serbia the last northern link.

---

[990] Edward Mead Earle, Turkey, the Great Powers, and the Bagdad Railway: A Study in Imperialism, Macmillan, New York, 1924, pp. 30-31
[991] Ibid. 29-30
[992] Ibid. 30-32

Before 1887, German companies had no financial interests in Turkey's railways. Yet, within five years, the Deutsche Bank and its partners financially controlled Turkey's railways from the Austro-Hungarian border to Constantinople. They had built a line from the Asiatic shore of the Straits to Angora and were developing numerous other railway projects. Now, the inaccessible parts of Asia Minor were within reach. Turkey was an important area of German economic interest. The Ottoman government, the resident population, and the German investors benefitted from these enterprises. They envisioned a whole network of German-controlled railways running from Berlin to Baghdad and from Hamburg to the Persian Gulf. [993]

In December 1899, the Ottoman government awarded the Baghdad concession to German financiers. Certain British elites were gratified that the Germans were in the Middle East and not Russia. Joseph Chamberlain and Cecil Rhodes were even willing to collaborate with them in their economic projects. The British government preferred working with Germans instead of Frenchmen. However, conditions changed in the early years of the twentieth century and British financiers were no longer interested in any Anglo-German agreements, especially after the Ottomans finalized the Baghdad concession with the Germans in 1903, which included the mineral rights on both sides of the Baghdad railway line. [994]

According to a correspondent for *The Standard*, in Constantinople, the German Anatolian Railway Company offered to purchase the Smyrna-Aidin Railway Company from its London shareholders, a proposal that disturbed the investors. Such a sale might impact British trade monopolies in the area. However, according to the original agreement, the railroad reverted "unconditionally" to Turkey. It was now time for the London shareholders to relinquish their control of the Smyrna-Aidin Railway for which the government would pay £4 million, money it did not possess. The Germans controlling the Anatolian Railway supported Turkish interests in conjunction with their own investments, unlike the British who seemed totally profit-

---

[993] Ibid. 33-34
[994] Ibid. 178-179

driven. Further, British shareholders wanted to prevent the trade in Asia Minor from falling into German hands. [995]

The bankers and freemasons who controlled the British government wanted to avoid any kind of positive, cooperative, economic alliance between Germany, France, Turkey, Russia, Japan, and China. The construction of a railroad system, linking east and west, would make such a liaison possible and eliminate Britain's lengthy domination of the seas. The Baghdad concession would link Berlin to Baghdad, the intellectual center of the Arab world and allow Germany to bypass the ongoing British naval blockades and gain direct access to oil. [996] The railway would bypass the Suez Canal, managed by the British and French. Germany was progressing, and clearly threatened Britain's global hegemony.

Stephen Kinzer wrote, "Internal combustion engines would soon revolutionize every aspect of human life, and control over the oil needed to fuel them would henceforth be the key to world power. Individuals had discovered and utilized oil around the Caspian Sea, in the Dutch East Indies, and in the United States, but neither Britain nor any of its colonies produced or showed any promise of producing it. If the British could not find oil somewhere, they would no longer be able to rule the waves or much of anything else." [997]

British bankers resented Germany's extraordinary emergence as a world power represented by her commercial interests in the Middle East. It interfered with British domination of the area and its plans for Africa. Another interloper was Portugal, especially in Africa. On January 11, 1890, the British presented an ultimatum to Portugal's King Carlos, claiming a breach against the Treaty of Windsor (1386), a rejection of Portugal's territorial claims in Africa that conflicted with British aspirations to construct a Cape to Cairo Railway. King

[995] Railway times, Volume 75, January to June 1899, London, book now housed at Stanford University, p. 466
[996] William Engdahl, A Century of War, Anglo-American Oil Politics and the New World Order, Pluto Press, Ann Arbor, Michigan,2004, pp. 16-27
[997] Stephen Kinzer, All the Shah's Men: An American Coup and the Roots of Middle East Terror, Wiley, Hoboken, New Jersey, 2003. pp. 47-49

Carlos acquiesced to their demands, and relinquished the claim to a large area of land. On August 20, 1890, Portugal and Britain signed the Treaty of London, which angered Portuguese citizens and gave the ideological Jacobins justification to criticize the monarchy. Portugal declared bankruptcy twice, on June 14, 1892, and on May 10, 1902, which created further domestic and industrial disturbances.

Portugal's Jacobins, the Republican Party, had connections to the Carbonária, a Masonic organization that wanted regime change. On January 28, 1908, authorities would imprison several rebels for their participation in the Municipal Library Elevator Coup. They were members of the same group that attempted a coup d'état. On February 1, 1908, Alfredo Costa and Manuel Buiça assassinated Carlos and one of his sons. The queen escaped injury. The police and bodyguards shot and killed the two assassins. Several days later, officials proclaimed Prince Manuel the King of Portugal. He would be the last king of that nation.

On February 12, 1911, Leon Furnémont, of the Grand Orient Lodge of Belgium, said, "Do you recall the deep feeling of pride which we all felt at the brief announcement of the Portuguese revolution?" The freemasons, with the murder of the king, destroyed the monarchy and proclaimed a republic. Furnémont indicated that local freemasons understood that it was "the marvelous organization of our Portuguese brothers, their ceaseless zeal, and their uninterrupted work." Dr. Manuel B. Grainha wrote that the "outstanding men during the religious, political, and literary upheavals of Portugal during the last two centuries belonged to freemasonry." He said freemasons led the revolution of October 5, 1910. In Spain, Russia, Turkey, Germany, Holland, England, America, and elsewhere, freemasons and those associated with the Alliance Israélite Universelle worked to overthrow all governments and abolish religion. [998]

Meanwhile, Germany's naval intentions challenged Britain's control of the oceans. Germans also disapproved of England's egregious

---

[998] Vicomte Léon De Poncins, Freemasonry and Judaism, Secret Powers Behind Revolution, A & B Publishers Group, Brooklyn, New York, pp. 60-61

policies toward the Boers in South Africa. After the Boer War (1899-1902), Britain intended to annex two very resource-rich African Free States, Orange Free State and the Transvaal. Germans viewed the British Empire as a menace. The German consortium, because of these moral concerns, did not want to accept British investments in the Baghdad Railway project. Yet, on April 7, 1903, Prime Minister Arthur J. Balfour informed the House of Commons about the Baghdad project, and suggested that British financiers might invest in it. Heated discussion over such an alliance erupted as many viewed the German enterprise as unwanted competition. Whoever controlled the railways controlled the area's political and economic future. Mesopotamia was far too important now that oil had become an economic factor. The consensus was that the Germans had to understand that Britain was there first. [999]

The German concession for the Baghdad Railway, in addition to the Anatolian line from Konya to Adana, Mosul, Baghdad, and Bursa, wanted to extend a branch to a port on the Persian Gulf. The Turkish government transferred its concession to the Anatolian Railway to the Baghdad Railway Company, located in Constantinople. They opened the first section of 125 miles between Konya and Ereğli in October 1904. They extended the Smyrna-Aidin railway seventy-five miles. They connected with the Beirut-Damascus line in the railway from Rayak to Homs, Hama, and Aleppo. The Turkish government bought back the concession for the Haifa Railway, which extended to Daraa (Syria) and joined the Mecca Railway. They opened the Damascus-Mecca Railway in February, 1907, which extended to Al Akhbar (Lebanon) and northwards. They also provided electric tramways in and about Smyrna." [1000] Thus we see why Britain greatly resented Germany.

[999] Edward Mead Earle, Turkey, the Great Powers, and the Bagdad Railway: A Study in Imperialism, Macmillan, New York, 1924, pp. 179-181

[1000] J. Scott Keltie, The Statesman's Year-book, Statistical and Historical Annual of the States of the World for the Year 1908, edited, Macmillan and Co., Limited, London, 1908, pp. 1576

German Ingenuity, a Threat to British Hegemony

In comparison to other European countries, Germany has more natural resources, including lignite, anthracite, timber, peat, iron ore, and currently, hydroelectric power. However, Germany has very few natural gas or petroleum deposits and must import large amounts of them. Germany has two forms of coal, lignite and anthracite. Lignite, or brown coal, related to peat, has a higher moisture content. Germany is the number one worldwide producer of lignite in addition to supplying anthracite, which has the highest heating capacity of any coal. Germany presently ranks ninth in the production of this type of coal. Besides coal, Germany has an abundance of iron, nickel and copper, along with barite, cadmium, selenium, feldspar, bentonite, peat, and salt.

Historically, Germany played an important part in the development of wood frame construction and woodworking expertise. With all of its forests, Germany helped develop techniques used in modern forestry. Today, Germany, with a third of its land covered with forests, has the largest standing forest in Europe. Germans developed the necessary technological skills in order to manufacture numerous hard, and soft wood products.

In the beginning of the eighteenth century, people began to synthesize organic dyes. In 1704, Heinrich Diesbach produced Berlin or Prussian blue, and in 1740, Karl Barth produced the semi-synthetic dye powder blue. The introduction of the two sulfo acid groups created an insoluble indigo water-soluble, which proved much easier to use. [1001] In the 1760s, Germany made advances in technical education by establishing a commercial college at Hamburg, and mining colleges in Freiberg (Saxony) and Clausthal (Harz). On November 21, 1765, Prince Franz Xavier of Saxony agreed to establish a Mining Academy, the Bergakademie Freiberg, the world's oldest specialist school for mining and metallurgy. [1002]

[1001] Jaime Wisniak, Dyes From Antiquity to Synthesis, Indian Journal of History of Science, 39.1, 2004, pp. 75-100
[1002] Technische Universität Bergakademie Freiberg—Modernity rooted in Tradition, http://www.geophysik.tu-freiberg.de/3dem4/venue/the_university.

In the second half of the eighteenth century, in Germany, population shifts from rural areas to urban areas occurred. Prussia's population increased from 2,380,000 to 5,750,000, during the same time that Berlin's population increased from 29,000 to 141,000. Rural peasants and about 13,000 foreign craftsmen relocated to the industrial regions. Between 1740 and 1783, people founded some 200 villages in Silesia, the center of the linen industry which spurred the growth of Germany's textile and metal industries. This population growth and the expansion of industry made it necessary to efficiently increase agriculture production, to feed the population, and to provide raw materials such as wool, flax, hemp, hides timber, the madder plant, and other items. Farmers in some areas reclaimed land and introduced new crops like clover, beet, hops, and tobacco. Meanwhile less-productive peasants in areas such as Eifel and the Senne had poorer farming standards. Overall, the farmers were able to produce sufficient food for a growing population, and enough raw materials for industry. [1003]

England advanced its textile industry with new inventions such as the mule and Edmund Cartwright's power loom (1785) and people used Abraham Darby's earlier invention of the coke blast furnace to construct cast iron for the world's first iron bridge in 1779. In the 1740s, Benjamin Huntsman, whose family had moved from Germany to Epworth, Lincolnshire, invented the Huntsman process for making cast-steel or crucible steel, replaced by the patented Bessemer process, first announced on August 24, 1856. It was the first inexpensive process for the mass-production of steel derived from molten pig iron. In Germany, Georg Winterschmidt developed the water pressure engine that could drain a whole mining district near Zellerfeld. [1004]

---

htm as of May 2012

[1003] William Otto Henderson, The Rise of German Industrial Power, 1834-1914, University of California Press, Berkeley and Los Angeles, California, 1975, pp. 23-24

[1004] Ursula Klein, Materials and Expertise in Early Modern Europe: Between Market and Laboratory, Emma C. Spary, University of Chicago Press, Chicago, 2010, p. 95

The industrial age in the primarily agrarian Germany began with the establishment of the customs union on January 1, 1834, and the opening of the Nürnberg-Fürth railway on December 7, 1835. Three-quarters of the population lived in villages and small towns. Independent artisans manufactured textiles and metal products. By 1900, before World War I, only America surpassed Germany's production of iron and steel. The removal of tariffs and the construction of railroads fueled the development of industry. [1005]

In 1865, Friedrich Engelhorn founded Badische Anilin & Soda-Fabrik (BASF) as a joint-stock company, which later developed vital petrochemical products. BASF became a mainstay of the German economy. [1006] BASF poured all of its profits and efforts into expansion and research, kept dividends low, and avoided dependence upon banks. In 1876, BASF had 1,140 employees, which grew to 6,360 by 1900. By then BASF was the world's leading manufacturer of artificial dyes. BASF created the first telephone connection to Bavaria in 1882, and was Germany's first electrical customer. By 1913, BASF was the world's largest chemical company and produced twenty-four percent of the world's coal-tar dyes. [1007]

The international bankers in London and New York recognized that control of petroleum was essential. After Britain's Rothschild-orchestrated depression of 1873, which coincided with the US stock market crash of September 18, 1873, a growing divergence existed between the efficient German Reich, an emerging industrial European economy, and the British Empire's depressed economy. [1008] By 1885, a German engineer, Gottlieb Daimler (1834-1900), used petroleum for a road vehicle that he had developed. Karl Benz, along with

[1005] William Otto Henderson, The Rise of German Industrial Power, 1834-1914, University of California Press, Berkeley and Los Angeles, California, 1975, pp. 23-24
[1006] Werner Abelshauser, Wolfgang von Hippel, Jeffrey Allan Johnson and Raymond G. Stokes, German Industry and Global Enterprise BASF: The History of a Company, Cambridge University Press, Cambridge, 2004, pp. 16-17
[1007] Ibid. 75
[1008] William Engdahl, A Century of War, Anglo-American Oil Politics and the New World Order, Pluto Press, Ann Arbor, Michigan, 2004, pp. 11-18

Daimler, invented the modern gasoline engine. The German ports of Hamburg and Bremen-Bremerhaven were two of the most highly efficient facilities in Europe.

Kaiser Wilhelm admired Albert Ballin, a Jew born in Hamburg, who, as the owner of an emigration agency, was the richest man in Germany. In 1901, he financed the construction of Emigration Halls, a reception and departure center, on the Hamburg island of Veddel, to assist the thousands of Europeans who arrived at the Port of Hamburg each week to immigrate to North America, on ships owned by the Warburg-financed Hamburg Amerika Line (HAPAG, Hamburg-Amerikanische Packetfahrt Actien-Gesellschafta). In 1899, Ballin became the Director of HAPAG, established in 1847, to accommodate German immigration to America. He and the Kaiser agreed that Germany should be constructing their own ships instead of depending on English shipyards, materials, and engineers. [1009] M. M. Warburg and Company financed this new ship construction industry.

Individual entrepreneurs, encouraged by state intervention, contributed to Germany's industrial expansion. Industrialists like Werner Siemens, Emil Moritz Rathenau, father of Walther Rathenau, August Thyssen, Emil Kirdorf, Wilhelm Cuno, Bernhard Dernburg, Carl Fürstenberg, and Ballin built great commercial and financial empires. Rathenau founded the Allgemeine Elektrizitäts-Gesellschaft (AEG), an electrical-engineering company. Meanwhile, the Federal States controlled the majority of the railways and inland waterways, in addition to the extensive forests. In 1906, Prussia supervised thirty-nine nationalized mines, twelve ironworks, five saltworks, and three stone quarries. Numerous states operated banks, breweries, amber works, tobacco factories, porcelain workshops, and medicinal baths. [1010]

[1009] Daniel Grossman, Public Symbols and Private Enterprise, Transatlantic Ocean Liners, 1897-1914, http://www.ocean-liner.com/nationalism/german-ocean-liners as of May 2012

[1010] William Otto Henderson, The Rise of German Industrial Power, 1834-1914, University of California Press, Berkeley and Los Angeles, California, 1975, pp. 173-174

Between 1873 and 1914, according to author William O. Henderson, Germany was "the leading industrial state on the Continent and challenged Britain's supremacy in the markets of the world." Henderson cited the book, *Made in Germany* (1890) by F. E. Williams, claiming that many people in Britain were becoming alarmed over what they viewed as "Germany's invasion of Britain's traditional overseas markets." During that period, Germany's national income rose from 15,195 million marks to 49,501 million marks, and her foreign investments increased to over 30,000 million marks. Her per capita income grew by 21.6 percent in each decade, compared to Britain with a 12.5 percent increase. The undistributed income of Germany's joint-stock companies increased from seventy-nine million marks in 1879 to 712 million marks by 1912. German production for the export of manufactured products increased from thirteen percent in 1870 to sixteen percent in 1900. Meanwhile, Britain's production decreased from thirty-two percent to eighteen percent. [1011]

As early as 1897, Britain wanted to neutralize and eventually eliminate Germany's power and therefore formulated a pervasive operation to encircle the Eurasian land mass and prevent a formidable alliance between Germany and Russia, both Christian nations, which would jeopardize Britain's imperialistic status. [1012]

Francis Neilson, a former member of the British Parliament, in his book *The Makers of War*, explains that Arthur J. Balfour, then a Member of Parliament for the City of London, and Henry White, then the US Ambassador to France, met in London. White's daughter, Muriel, who married a German count in 1909, often functioned as her father's hostess. Possibly, her father asked her to eavesdrop and she recorded the following conversation, which transpired in June 1907:

[1011] Ibid. 173-174

[1012] Guido Giacomo Preparata, Conjuring Hitler, How Britain and America Made the Third Reich, Pluto Press, London, England and Ann Arbor, Michigan, 2005, pp. xvii—xix

Balfour: "We are probably fools not to find a reason for declaring war on Germany before she builds too many ships and takes away our trade."

White: "You are a very high-minded man in private life. How can you possibly contemplate anything so politically immoral as provoking a war against a harmless nation which has as good a right to a navy as you have? If you wish to compete with German trade, work harder."

Balfour: "That would mean lowering our standard of living. Perhaps, it would be simpler for us to have a war."

White: "I am shocked that you of all men should enunciate such principles."

Balfour: "Is it a question of right or wrong? Maybe it is just a question of keeping our supremacy."

White later met with the Secretary of State, Elihu Root, and reported the details of his conversation with Balfour. [1013]

In 1910, with South Africa subdued, Lord Alfred Milner and his Round Table cohorts now focused on initiating an imminent war against Germany using the same vile tactics as they had in Africa. Philip Kerr (Lord Lothian) directed the recruitment of new members to the group. Sir Francis S. Oliver, Sir Alfred E. Zimmern, Sir Reginald Coupland, Simon J. Fraser (Lord Lovat), and William Waldorf Astor (1st Viscount Astor) responded favorably to the invitation. Meanwhile Lionel G. Curtis, Milner's secretary and others organized Round Table groups in the key British dependencies and special allies. [1014]

Germany, with hard work and technology, skillfully utilized her natural resources, such as coal in the Ruhr, iron-ore in Lorraine, and potassium salts in Stassfurt and Wittelsheim. By 1913, Germany excelled Britain as a manufacturer of pig iron and steel, in addition to challenging Britain in the production of coal and lignite. Germany successfully began exporting large amounts of

---

[1013] Francis Neilson, The Makers of War, C. C. Nelson Publishing Company, Appleton, Wisconsin, 1950, p. 19

[1014] Carroll Quigley, Tragedy And Hope, A History of the World in our Time, The Macmillan Company, New York, 1966, p. 144

woolen cloth and semi-manufactured woolens. German scientists made significant discoveries and contributions in the chemical, electrical and shipbuilding industries. In 1913, Germany supplied about nine-tenths of the world's synthetic dyes and exported more electrical appliances than any other country. Germany, from meager beginnings, expanded its shipbuilding industry, its mercantile marine and its navy. Numerous German inventions, such as the electric dynamo, aniline dyes, and petrol and diesel engines, energized the country's industrialization. [1015]

While the shipping facilities, harbors and natural waterways, were inadequate in comparison to other industrialized countries, Germany's greatest asset in terms of natural resources was "an industrious, healthy and intelligent population." In this regard, Germany had significant advantages over some of her neighboring countries with the exception of France, along with smaller nations like Belgium. [1016] German Emperor, Wilhelm I had unified Germany with the birth of the German Empire on January 18, 1871, with a proclamation, the period known as the Second Reich (1871-1918). By 1914, it was Europe's most powerful industrial nation. That industrialization, especially in scientific and engineering technology, and the resulting petrochemical industry, made Germany a powerful competitor to Britain, which targeted Germany for destruction. British bankers, adept at involving countries in war, manipulated France, Russia and ultimately the United States to wage war against Germany.

Marxism, Terrorism and Assassinations

Aleksandr I. Herzen (1812-1870), a freemason, heir to his father's vast fortune, provided the ideological dogma that the Narodniks, Socialist-Revolutionaries, Trudoviks, and even the agrarian American Populist Party later adopted. He said, "It is possible to lead a whole generation

[1015] William Otto Henderson, The Rise of German Industrial Power, 1834-1914, University of California Press, Berkeley and Los Angeles, California, 1975, pp. 173-174
[1016] Thorstein Veblen, Imperial Germany and the Industrial Revolution, The Macmillan Company, London, England, 1915, pp. 174-175

astray, blind it, blunt it, and guide it toward the wrong goals . . . ." [1017] Because he immigrated to France in 1847, the Russian government froze his assets. However, his family had ties to Baron James Mayer de Rothschild who interceded in his behalf and negotiated a release of Herzen's assets.

The Rothschilds, along with their salaried agents, conducted preferential business with numerous banks. By the end of the 1840s, they associated with banks in Baltimore, New York, Amsterdam, Berlin, Cologne, Constantinople, Florence, Hamburg, Milan, Odessa, Rome, and Trieste. The owners of the German banks, Warburg and Bleichröder, were, by 1848, part of a vast network. The Rothschilds valued the services of smaller banks and the influence and trust those banks had developed in their respective communities. [1018] By 1850, despite Russia's gold mines in the Urals and Altai, and "inexhaustible treasures" in the Petropavlovsk vaults, even the czar had no immediate money and had to extract silver reserves from the vaults to cover the paper issue. He also offered government bonds on the Paris Bourse (exchange). He then approached the City of London for a loan of 30 million silver rubles to cover expenses associated with the revolutions of 1848-1849. [1019]

Karl Marx, with a Doctorate in Philosophy (1841), was obscene and vulgar in his correspondence with Frederick Engels, [1020] and could not secure a teaching job because of his revolutionary activities. Marx, though a Jew, regularly voiced his hatred of them, especially Jewish capitalists. [1021] He wrote *On the Jewish Question* (1843), *A World without Jews* (1844) and *Das Kapital* (1867). He derived many of his

---

[1017] Jüri Lina, Architects of Deception, Referent Publishing, Stockholm, Sweden, 2004, pp. 338-339

[1018] Niall Ferguson, The House of Rothschild, Money's Prophets: 1798-1848, Penguin Books, New York, 1999, pp. 284-285

[1019] Karl Marx and Frederick Engels in Neue Rheinische Zeitung Politische-Ökonomische Revue No. 2, the Collected Works of Karl Marx and Frederick Engels: Volume 10, January-February 1850, http://www.marxists.org/archive/marx/works/1850/01/31.htm as of May 2012

[1020] Richard Wurmbrand, Marx & Satan, Living Sacrifice Book Company, Bartlesville, Oklahoma, 1986, p. 35

[1021] Ibid. 42

ideas from Adam Weishaupt, François-Noël Babeuf, Louis Blanc, Étienne Cabet, Robert Owen, William Ogilvie, Thomas Hodgkin, John Gray, Robert Thompson, William Carpenter, and Clinton Roosevelt. [1022] Roosevelt, of the New York banking family, wrote *The Science of Government Founded on Natural Law.*

Marx's tenets appealed to the Khazar Jews who readily accepted his ideals of state control and equality as most of them were accustomed to authoritarian rabbinic rule, having lived under the Babylonian Judaic Pharisaic Talmud, consisting of at least 5,894 pages. Because of their unique lifestyle, self-imposed exclusivity, and predatory monetary practices, people had ostracized them for centuries. Marx, descended from rabbinical families on his paternal and maternal sides, understood the unique character and atmosphere of living under Talmud tenets. [1023] The multi-volume Talmud includes over 12,000 regulatory restraints so people did not object to or question further rigorous regimentation.

Because of the revolutions (1848-1849), Russia, by necessity, became involved in European politics to avoid losing its influence in Constantinople. In early 1850, Marx and Engels predicted a Russo-Turkish War. They stated that "the war against Turkey will necessarily be a European war." This, they said would allow Russia "a firm foot in Germany," to complete the counter-revolution and help the Prussians to capture Neuchâtel, in northern Switzerland, then march to the "center of the revolution, Paris." Neuchâtel claimed independence from Prussia in 1848, and was a refuge for German revolutionaries after their defeat of May and June 1849. [1024]

[1022] Terry Melanson, Perfectibilists, the 18th Century Bavarian Order of the Illuminati, Trine Day, Walterville, Oregon, 2009, p. 147

[1023] John Beaty, The Iron Curtain Over America, Chestnut Mountain Book, Barboursville, Virginia, 1968, p. 26

[1024] Karl Marx and Frederick Engels in Neue Rheinische Zeitung Politische-Ökonomische Revue No. 2, the Collected Works of Karl Marx and Frederick Engels: Volume 10, January-February 1850, http://www.marxists.org/archive/marx/works/1850/01/31.htm as of May 2012

From France, Herzen, an associate of Vissarion Belinsky and the Russian anarchist, Mikhail Bakunin, the founder of collectivist anarchism, traveled to Italy where he stayed from December 1847 to April 1848, until he heard about the sweeping revolutions. Herzen immediately left for Paris, and then traveled to Switzerland. He championed the revolts and was disillusioned when they failed. In August 1852, he relocated to the safe political haven of London where he resided for about twelve years, promoting socialism, and where Karl Marx befriended him. [1025] In London, Herzen and Bakunin worked on the journal *Kolokol* (*The Bell*). Herzen would greatly influence the political environment that ultimately led to the emancipation of the serfs in Russia in 1861.

In June 1853, Henry J. Temple, known as Lord Palmerston, the Earl of Shaftesbury, and Lord John Russell, gathered George Sanders, a former Bank of England employee, and now the American Consul in Liverpool, along with August Belmont, the Ambassador to Holland, James Buchanan, a freemason and future US president (1857-1861), and Senator Pierre Soule for a series of meetings in London. There, they met with Giuseppe Mazzini, a freemason and the organizer of Young Italy, Giuseppe Garibaldi, a freemason, and Felice Orsini, leader of the Carbonária. Others joined them, including Arnold Ruge of Young Germany, Herzen, of Young Russia, and Lajos Kossuth, a freemason, [1026] of Young Hungary. Reportedly, during that meeting, they organized the international assassination bureau of the Scottish Rite Order of Zion. [1027]

On February 21, 1854, George Sanders, while not a member, but enthusiastic about their revolutions played host to freemasons, Mazzini, Garibaldi, Kossuth, Ruge, co-editor with Marx of a revolutionary magazine for Young Germany, Orsini, a contract

[1025] Terry Melanson, Perfectibilists, the 18th Century Bavarian Order of the Illuminati, Trine Day, Walterville, Oregon, 2009, p. 147
[1026] Vicomte Léon De Poncins, Freemasonry and Judaism, Secret Powers Behind Revolution, A & B Publishers Group, Brooklyn, New York, pp. 64-65
[1027] Paul Goldstein, B'nai B'rith, British Weapon Against America, http://www.campaigner-unbound.0catch.com/bnai_brith_british_weapon_against_america.htm as of May 2012

terrorist and assassin for Mazzini, and Herzen who had initiated Bakunin, a freemason, into Mazzini's Young Russia, and Buchanan, President Pierce's Ambassador to England. [1028]

Czar Alexander II (1818-1881) ascended the throne in 1855 during the midst of the Crimean War (1853-1856), a conflict over the Holy Land, between Russia, and an alliance of Britain, France, the Ottoman Empire, and Sardinia. On March 28, 1854, France and Britain declared war on Russia, the Jew's longtime enemy, as France demanded recognition as the sovereign authority in the Holy Land. Russia had been the protector of the Orthodox Christians in the Ottoman Empire and had assisted Austria-Hungarian efforts in suppressing the 1848 revolutions. Benjamin Disraeli blamed Prime Minister George Hamilton-Gordon (1852-1855) and Lord Stratford Canning, the British Ambassador to the Ottomans (1841-1858) for the conflict. The French and the British, unlike the Austrian and Prussian officials, refused to negotiate, making war inevitable. The Crimean War saw the first tactical use of railways, the electric telegraph and modern military tactics. [1029] The czar ended the conflict via the Treaty of Paris on March 30, 1856.

Russia relinquished control of the left bank of the mouth of the Danube River, including part of Bessarabia. Russia also had to abandon their protection of Christians in the Ottoman Empire to accommodate France. The Turkish sultan promised to improve the status of the Christians in his empire. The Crimean War, along with the revolutions of 1848, would be a factor in the emancipation of the Russian serfs. The czar witnessed Russia's military defeat by Britain and France's free troops. [1030]

[1028] John Daniel, Two Faces of Freemasonry, a Picture Book Supplement to Volume One, Third Edition of Scarlet and the Beast, a History of the War between English and French Freemasonry, Day Publishing, Longview Texas, 2007, p. 301

[1029] David Moon, The Abolition of Serfdom in Russia, 1762-1907, Pearson Education, Harlow, England, 2001, pp. 49-55

[1030] Ibid. 49-55

On January 14, 1858, as Napoleon III and the Empress were on their way to the theatre, Felice Orsini and others tossed three bombs at the imperial carriage. The couple was unhurt, but the assault killed eight people and wounded 142 others. Authorities discovered that individuals in Britain had constructed the bombs which led to anti-British sentiment for a brief time. Officials captured and tried Orsini and then sent him to the guillotine on March 13, 1858. One of his accomplices met the same fate while they sentenced two others to hard labor for life. Carlo di Rudio (later changed to Charles DeRudio) escaped from Devil's Island, and ultimately immigrated to America where he later became an officer in the Seventh Cavalry, and participated in the Battle of the Little Big Horn in 1876.

Czar Alexander II attempted to appease the Jewish minority who were willing and anxious to hold Russian citizenship, even though they were ethnic and cultural separatists. The czar approved of many new liberties for them and the serfs. On March 3, 1861, he issued the Edict of Emancipation abolishing serfdom throughout Russia, one of his most notable acts, increasing Russia's esteem throughout the world. People referred to him as "the Czar Liberator." However, the majority of the land was still in the possession of the nobles and the massive proletariat population still possessed no property. [1031]

The czar, to win the Jewish minority, offered them citizenship and other liberties. However, his policies contributed to Christian Russia's ultimate collapse. He removed many regulations and allowed Jews unrestricted travel and to attend any school they wished. He failed to anticipate the consequences, as this allowed them, still a "state within a state," to develop influential anti-government power. Through the use of terror, specifically assassinations, they advanced their goals. The czar attempted to halt their antagonism through additional concessions but it was unsuccessful and it soon cost him his life. [1032]

[1031] Charles Downer Hazen, Modern European history, Henry Holt & Company, New York, 1917, pp. 561-562
[1032] John Beaty, The Iron Curtain Over America, Chestnut Mountain Book, Barboursville, Virginia, 1968, pp. 24-25

Theoretically, everyone was free. The peasants, now wage slaves were still miserable, and they were no different from the peasants of Prussia and Austria, where the government had also granted liberation. The government established schools, and, together with media officials, reduced the incidence of censorship, but failed to totally eliminate it. Certain interests enthusiastically encouraged a process of Russification and the adoption of nationalism or statism, the aggrandizement of the state over individual desires and needs. [1033]

After emancipation, many serfs adopted narodnism, a political force whose advocates accused the government of imposing wage slavery on them. The Narodniks opposed the bourgeoisie, those who then controlled capital, and who replaced the landowners. The Narodniks, though resentful of the previous land ownership system, contested the displacement of the peasants from the traditional communes. The Narodniks concentrated on the mounting divergence between the peasantry and the prosperous farmers. The Marxist groups promised to destroy the monarchy, the wealthy, and then redistribute their wealth among the poor.

In 1863, Nikolai A. Ishutin, a utopian socialist, propagandist and advocate of terrorist tactics, organized a revolutionary society, known as the Ishutin Society. Dmitry Karakozov, a member, attempted to assassinate Alexander II on April 4, 1866, in St. Petersburg. On April 8, 1866, the authorities arrested Ishutin following that incident. The Supreme Criminal Court sentenced him to death by hanging, but instead, the court, right before the hanging was to take place, incarcerated him for the remainder of his life. He died in the Kara Katorga prison in 1879.

The Narodniks acknowledged that they could not achieve revolutionary changes on their own but would need extraordinary leaders. There were other Narodniks who demanded an immediate revolution without considering philosophical and political discussions with

---

[1033] Charles Downer Hazen, Modern European history, Henry Holt & Company, New York, 1917, p. 564

political leaders. In the spring of 1874, the Narodnik intelligentsia left the cities to try to persuade the peasants in the villages to revolt, but the peasants initially refused to support the Narodniks who were from the middle and upper middle classes, and who could not relate to the peasants. The Narodniks revised their tactics, learned about the peasant culture, and in 1877, initiated a revolution, assisted by thousands of peasants.

Professor Georg Wilhelm Friedrich Hegel (1770-1831), a freemason, promoted the philosophy that ultimate peace comes only through conflict. Rhetorical conflict and physical warfare (or pogroms) are theoretically essential for ultimate peace achieved through globalization. Author David Icke, simplifies the process with the term—Problem, Reaction, Solution (P-R-S). He explains, 1) Provocateurs create a problem and shift the blame elsewhere. 2) They use the media to present a false version of the problem. 3) They maneuver the public by creating fear and outrage. 4) The public demands a solution. 5) Those who "engineered the problem" offer a solution that they wanted all along. This successful tactic motivates people to accept and even plead for changes they would have rejected prior to the problem. [1034]

The government suppressed the revolt and imposed additional regulations, which led to the formation of the first organized revolutionary party, the Narodnaya Volya, or the People's Will. The party used secret society-directed terrorism to exert pressure on the government for change and improvement and to demonstrate the czar's vulnerability. Despite the fact that many peasants participated in the revolution, many still idolized the czar and regarded him as a benefactor. The party leadership hoped to engender a revolutionary spirit within the people and then determine those who were willing and able to fight.

Alexander Soloviev attempted to kill Czar Alexander II on April 14, 1879. He fired at him five times, but missed and authorities soon

---

[1034] David Icke, The David Icke Guide to the Global Conspiracy (and how to end it), David Icke Books Ltd., Isle of Wight, 2007, pp. 210-211

captured and executed him. On November 19, 1879, Leo Hartmann, Grigory Goldenberg, Sophia Perovskaya, all Narodnaya Volya members arranged an explosion on the railroad line but they missed the czar's train. They may have used dynamite, invented by Alfred Noble, patented in 1867. In another attempt, on February 17, 1880, when the explosive detonated, it killed Ignacy Hryniewiecki, one of the Polish terrorists. Three people admitted to making the explosives— Alexander Mikhailov and Andrei Zhelyabov, both on the Executive Committee of the Narodnaya Volya and Nikolai Kibalchich. [1035] [1036] Hartman escaped to France where he celebrated with French revolutionaries and avoided extradition, but later authorities expelled him. [1037] On November 18, 1890, Stanislaus Padlewsky, a Nihilist, murdered General Michael de Seliverstoff, the former St. Petersburg police chief, in Paris. Padlewsky, in a story in *The New York Times*, on January 30, 1892, claimed that Hartman ultimately found refuge in America among other Nihilists.

Alexander II, with numerous reforms, improved conditions but in 1880, key Jewish leaders, Samuel Poliakov, Horace Gintsburg and Nikolai Bakst petitioned him to allow them to start a fund for the Jews in the Pale of Settlement to provide education and occupational training to help people become self-sufficient. He granted permission and Poliakov, Gintsburg, Abram Zak, Leon Rosenthal, and Meer Fridland sent out an appeal for funds. The Russian authorities created the Society for Trades and Agricultural Labor among the Jews in Russia, now known today as ORT, exclusively for Jews.

Educated, liberal Jews became an influential political and social force. They viewed Marxism, using persuasive propaganda, mixed with violence, as a way of altering or eliminating established institutions, and the existing culture, and replacing it with a new society, based

[1035] Ernest Alfred Vizetelly, The Anarchists, Their Faith And Their Record, John Lane, London and New York, 1911, pp. 66-67
[1036] Israel Smith Clare, The World's History Illuminated: Containing A Record Of The Human, Volume 8, Western Newspaper Syndicate, St. Louis, 1897, p. 3136
[1037] Ernest Alfred Vizetelly, The Anarchists: Their Faith and Their Record, John Lane, London and New York, 1911, pp. 69-70

on Marxist principles. Jews joined with revolutionary non-Jewish radicals, the professed intelligentsia, and practiced terrorism and assassination as they believed that progress was only possible by purging certain officials. Alexander II attempted to immobilize the terrorist's hostility by permitting even greater concessions. However, on the day that he proposed his latest resolution, March 13, 1881, after four earlier attempts, the terrorists, the very people he was trying to help, murdered him. [1038]

The Narodnaya Volya assassination of Alexander II horrified the peasantry. The government hung many of the Narodnaya Volya leaders, most of whom were Jews, which left the group without strong effective leaders. Later, other groups, the Socialist-Revolutionaries, the Popular Socialists, and the Trudoviks embraced the same philosophies and used the same terrorist tactics. These revolutionary groups laid the foundation for the revolutions of 1905 and 1917.

The government brought the other assassins to court, where they found them guilty. In April 1881, the government hung Nikolai Rysakov, a Russian, and Sophia Perovskaya, a Russian woman. The other Russian woman, Gesya M. Gelfman, escaped hanging because she was pregnant. She died of peritonitis within six months after giving birth. Nikolai A. Sablin, another revolutionary and Gelfman's common law husband shot himself to avoid arrest. In June 1881, Bavarian-born Marxist, Johann Most, expressed his approval of the czar's assassination in the Communist-Anarchist, *Die Freiheit* (*Liberty*) in London. Shortly afterward, he immigrated to the United States. [1039] [1040]

The people justifiably blamed the revolutionary Jews for the assassination. Czar Alexander III, the czar's son, replaced him on

---

[1038] Charles Downer Hazen, Modern European history, Henry Holt & Company, New York, 1917, pp. 565-567

[1039] Ernest Alfred Vizetelly, The Anarchists, Their Faith And Their Record, John Lane, London and New York, 1911, pp. 66-67

[1040] Israel Smith Clare, The World's History Illuminated: Containing A Record Of The Human, Volume 8, Western Newspaper Syndicate, St. Louis, 1897, p. 3136

March 13, 1881, and would be in power until his death on November 1, 1894. Within a month, pogroms in the Ukraine, in response to the terrorism, destroyed thousands of Jewish homes and injured hundreds of people in approximately 166 towns as latent anti-Semitism erupted. Nationwide pogroms would begin in earnest in Russia around 1890. Alexander III accused Jewish provocateurs of starting the riots in which non-revolutionary Jews were victims. Resentful Cossacks slaughtered thousands of men, women and children. Pogroms occurred simultaneously in Poland, Romania, and Bulgaria, seemingly in a well-organized fashion.

The government and the emancipated serfs viewed the pogroms as a protest against Jewish economic exploitation. Ilya G. Orshanski, a jurist and author, part of the Petersburg Jewish elite, as not all Jews lived in the Pale, evaluated and wrote about the Jewish question. Gintsburg, one of the ORT founders, chairman of the Jewish Congress, actively participated in discussions, and designed petitions regarding the issue. Orshanski's judicial perceptions helped formulate the reaction to the pogroms of the Jewish elites in St. Petersburg. Gintsburg and others supported his opinion, as Benjamin Nathans states, "official discrimination against Jews was the root cause of popular violence against them." When the czar severed his relationship with Gintsburg and other representatives of Jewry, Gintsburg concentrated on using Jewish lawyers and the reformed Russian judiciary as the basis of his new approach of exploiting state institutions to challenge the state. [1041]

Because of the pogroms, Nicolai Ignatyev, the Minister of Internal Affairs, in a Problem, Reaction, Solution (P-R-S) response, proposed regulations for the Jews. Alexander III approved and enacted the May laws on May 15, 1882:

1) Authorities forbid Jews to create new settlements outside of towns and boroughs, except in the case of existing Jewish agricultural colonies.

[1041] Benjamin Nathans, Beyond the pale: the Jewish encounter with late imperial Russia, University of California Press, Berkeley, 2004, pp. 321-324

2) People could not issue mortgages and other deeds to Jews, or register Jews as lessees of real property situated outside of their towns and boroughs; or issue powers of attorney to Jews to manage and dispose of such real property.

3) Jews could not transact business on Sundays and on the principal Christian holy days, the existing regulations concerning the closing of places of business belonging to Christians on such days to apply to Jews also.

4) The measures laid down in 1, 2, and 3 shall apply only to the governments within the Pale of Jewish Settlement. [1042]

Regarding the May Laws and other legislation, Aleksandr Solzhenitsyn claims that the government's objective was social stability, and not religious persecution or anti-Semitism. For instance, the edict forbidding rural settlement applied only to new Jewish settlers, while exempting many villages. Ignatyev stated, "The inhabitants of the countryside may know the government is protecting them from the Jews." Also, the "governmental power is unable to defend (the Jews) against pogroms which might occur in scattered villages." According to Solzhenitsyn, the government enacted the May Laws to protect the Jews, rather than oppress them. [1043] These temporary precautions, which actually lasted for thirty years, caused considerable resentment among them.

Members of the Narodnaya Volya attempted to kill Alexander III. On May 5, 1887, the state executed Vladimir Lenin's older brother, Aleksandr Ulyanov, because he had participated in that attempt. Perhaps Vladimir Lenin, born Vladimir Ilyich Ulyanov, felt an obligation to retaliate against the Romanovs, especially Nicholas II, the grandson of Alexander II, if only for the sake of his brother. Lenin, while attending the University of Kazan, adopted Marxism. [1044]

[1042] Elliot Rosenberg, But Were They Good For The Jews?: Over 150 Historical Figures Viewed from a Jewish Perspective, Citadel Press, New York, 2000, p. 182

[1043] Ibid. 184

[1044] A. Ralph Epperson, The Unseen Hand, Publius Press, Tucson, Arizona, 1985, p. 101

Grand Duke Sergei Alexandrovich, son of Czar Alexander II, the Liberator, was very influential during the reigns of his brother Alexander III and his nephew Nicholas II. As the Governor General of Moscow (1891-1905), the revolutionaries targeted him for his policies. He shared his brother's belief in a strong, nationalist government. When he became governor, he initiated the expulsion of Moscow's 20,000 Jews which started four weeks before his arrival. Ivan Durnovo, the Minister of the Interior published an Imperial ukase. The city's Jewish population learned of the expulsion decree on March 29, 1891, the first day of Passover.

In 1893, Emanuel Levin, former secretary to the Gintsburgs, after using the judicial approach to point out discriminatory legislation directed against the Jews, retired. He had published some of the initial examples of the Russian laws. However, he lacked practical experience in the Courts. Genrikh B. Sliozberg, a secularized Jewish intellectual, a young lawyer, and a graduate of St. Petersburg University, succeeded him and was quite capable in interceding for the Jews. [1045] Sliozberg, a common Jewish surname in Russia, Ukraine and Belarus, whose family lived in the Pale, decided to study in St. Petersburg in the 1880s. He said, "How attractive the capital seemed to me—the center of the country's intellectual life where, so I thought, one could meet writers, where life was in full swing, and enlightenment poured forth in broad streams, drawing all to culture and progress." [1046]

Because of expulsion orders, in 1886, in Kiev, and in 1891, in Moscow, a huge number of Jews, possessing a globalist strategy, immigrated to other European countries and to America. It was not the first time that governments had deported Jews because of their activities. Emigration accelerated even more under Nicholas II. However, many Jews opted to stay in Russia despite the persecution, hoping that it would dissipate. In 1913, Russia's Jewish population would total

---

[1045] Benjamin Nathans, Beyond the pale: the Jewish encounter with late imperial Russia, University of California Press, Berkeley, 2004, pp. 324-325

[1046] Ezra Mendelsohn, People of the City: Jews and the Urban Challenge edited, Oxford University Press, New York, 1999, p. 108

6,946,000. [1047] Over 2,000,000 Jews left Russia between 1880 and 1920. The majority of them immigrated to the United States.

By 1905, Russia suffered a great loss in the Russo-Japanese War, causing increased revolutionary turmoil and discontent which Alexandrovich, Moscow's Governor General believed he had to stifle to maintain order. Because of the riots, Nicholas II felt compelled to make concessions but Alexandrovich opposed the czar's conciliatory policies. Thus, after thirteen years in his position, he resigned on January 1, 1905, but continued to function as the Commander of the Moscow military district. Alexandrovich and his family moved to the safety of the Nicholas Palace because of numerous threats and domestic disturbances. They rarely left their home. Yet, on the afternoon of February 17, 1905, Alexandrovich, with only his coachman, went to the Governor General's mansion to finish closing his office there. Someone alerted the waiting terrorist of the carriage's imminent arrival. As the Grand Duke passed through the gate to the Kremlin, Ivan Kalyayev threw a nitroglycerin bomb into Alexandrovich's lap which detonated, ripping and tearing his body into pieces.

His wife, the Grand Duchess, Elizabeth Feodorovna, hurried to the location, gave instructions, and, probably in a state of shock, assisted in gathering the bloody remains, parts scattered here, and there, of her husband's body which they placed on a stretcher. She retired from public life, and later, during Russia's Civil War, soldiers brutally murdered her and her maid.

1905 Revolution, Funded by International Bankers

By 1860, the Jews had the Alliance Israélite Universelle, headquartered in Paris, with massive monetary means, a huge membership, and various Masonic lodges which represented an organization that promoted equality and universal suffrage. The Alliance directed its efforts toward anti-Christian and anti-monarchist activities using socialism, an easy tool for the "ignorant masses." Russia, a land of

---

[1047] John Beaty, The Iron Curtain Over America, Chestnut Mountain Book, Barboursville, Virginia, 1968, p. 25

laborers, Orthodoxy and monarchism proved to be an obstacle. In order to impose Marxism, rebels had to debilitate the existing government, which they would do, using Japan as a mercenary. The State Duma temporarily removed the existing obstacles to the triumph of Jewry in Russia yet hostility erupted right after the October Manifesto, which presumably alleviated those concerns. The Jews subsequently engaged in terrorism against the state. Angry Russians then assaulted innocent Jews in numerous pogroms in retaliation. [1048]

Because of the Alliance Israélite Universelle, well-organized Jews in every country acted in concert as one determined body. They had efficient intelligent leaders, weapons and sufficient financing all promoting a revolution. Time and experience reveals the international character of the movement. If one evaluates the revolutionary spirit in France (1789), numerous countries in Europe (1848), America (1861), Russia (1905, 1917), and the Ottoman Empire (1908) and again in Germany (1921) it becomes apparent that a common source exists that uses similar tactics. They use strikes, military force, assassination, media control, education, and they seize or infiltrate the government. Afterwards, they control credit, currency, production, and distribution. They create civil or class warfare, debase the culture, degrade ethical standards, and promote the patriotic participation in foreign warfare to morally, and financially desecrate a country. [1049]

In 1864, explorer George Kennan (1845-1924), employed by the Russian-American Telegraph, surveyed a route for a possible overland telegraph line starting in San Francisco under the Bering Sea and across Siberia to Moscow. He spent two years on the Kamchatka Peninsula, in the Russian Far East, and then returned to Ohio and began lecturing and writing about his travels.

For years, John D. Rockefeller (1839-1937) and Standard Oil aggressively competed with the Royal Dutch Company for the

---

[1048] Lucien Wolf, Notes On The Diplomatic History Of The Jewish Question, With Texts Of Protocols, Treaty Stipulations And Other Public Acts And Official Documents, Jewish Historical Society of England, Mocatta Library and Museum, London, 1919, pp. 58-59

[1049] Ibid. 59-60

worldwide oil reserves and markets, particularly those under the control the British, especially in Saudi Arabia. The British Crown, the Dutch Crown and the Isaacs, Samuels, Rothschilds and the Sassoons controlled Royal Dutch. The czar gave Royal Dutch an exclusive oil concession in the Baku oilfields making those fields inaccessible to Rockefeller. There were three ways that he could gain access 1) support the destruction of Russia through revolution; 2) create a division between the czar and Royal Dutch; 3) and the least feasible, destroy the British to acquire access to Arabia and the Middle East. [1050]

In May 1885, Rockefeller sent Kennan back to Russia, including Siberia, where he joined with many of the revolutionaries who had remained in Russia following the 1880s pogroms. He encouraged their rebellion against the czar, who he had earlier supported. He returned to the United States in August 1886 and spent the next twenty years promoting a revolution in Russia, primarily through lectures. He spoke before a million or more people during the 1890s. He joined the Society of American Friends of Russian Freedom (SAFRF), a group of British and American politicians, public figures and reformers, founded in April 1890. Its members included Thomas W. Higginson, Julia W. Howe, Mark Twain, John Greenleaf Whittier and James R. Lowell. Kennan helped found *Free Russia*, the SAFRF journal opposing czarist Russia. Officials in Russia banned him from returning to Russia in 1891 after he wrote *Siberia and the Exile System*, an exposé of the prison system. George F. Kennan (1904-2005), the diplomat and historian, and a cousin to his namesake, the explorer, wrote a two-volume report to justify intervention following the Soviet Revolution, *The Decision to Intervene: Soviet-American Relations 1917-1920.*

[1050] Dr. Emanuel M. Josephson, Roosevelt's Communist Manifesto, incorporating a reprint of The Science of Government Founded on Natural Law (Clinton Roosevelt), originally published by Chedney Press, New York, 1955, pp. 34-37 While Josephson, a Jew, is right in some of his facts, his conclusions are extremely biased as he shifts culpability away from the real culprits and gives far too much credit to Rockefeller.

London's wealthy Anglo-Jewish community voiced its concerns over the reported pogroms and organized a protest meeting where Samuel Montagu, an Orthodox Jew, whose daughter Lily founded Liberal Judaism and Nathaniel M. Rothschild spoke and advocated political intervention. By 1891, Baron Maurice de Hirsch, part of Britain's Jewish elite founded the Jewish Colonization Association (JCA). Influential Anglo-Jews used it as a vehicle to demand improvements in the living conditions of the Jews in the Pale of Settlement. It also provided assistance for immigrants. Rothschild, involved in the JCA, facilitated contributions through N M Rothschild & Sons through their foreign branches located in Russia.

Lev D. Bronstein, born October 26, 1879 in Yanovka (now Ukraine), to a rich farmer, was a revolutionary student in Odessa. He helped re-establish the South Russia Workers Union in 1897, which had disbanded in 1881. Several hundred workers, including Russians, Poles, Jews, and Ukrainians comprised the original group. The group demanded extensive economic changes, collective ownership of land and factories, shorter working hours, and it used terrorism to achieve its aims, including sabotage, and the murder of factory managers and owners. [1051]

On October 7, 1897, in Vilna, individuals founded the General Jewish Labour Bund, a secular party, to exclusively represent the Jewish working class. About 315,000 Jews were illegally living outside the Pale, mostly in St. Petersburg and Moscow. In 1897, revolutionaries founded the Bolshevik Party in Russia, which then included Lithuania, Latvia, Belarus, Ukraine and most of what is now Poland. Jews participated in revolutionary activities on a huge scale in those areas. At the same time, American and British officials agreed to share intelligence, weaponry and military spoils. The establishment of Cecil Rhodes' Pilgrims Society cemented the alliance to purportedly facilitate "the extension of British rule throughout the world." In 1897, with the imminent Spanish American War, the Second Boer War and the Russo-Japanese War, a military power trust consisting of Vickers,

---

[1051] Encyclopedia of Ukraine, volume 4, 1993

DuPont, Nobel, Koln, Kottweiler and others, began preparing for a major world war.

In 1898, Bronstein helped found the Russian Social Democratic Labour Party (RSDLP) in Minsk, which had its First Congress, March 13-March 15, 1898, to oppose the Narodniks. It later split into the Bolshevik and Menshevik factions. In January 1898, authorities arrested him and incarcerated him in Odessa, [1052] where, over the next two years, he initiated his investigation of freemasonry. He read articles about it in the prison library in back issues of *Orthodox Review* and compiled over a 1,000 pages of notes. Alexander Parvus (born Israel L. Gelfand) later recruited him to the Illuminati. Jüri Lina says that he found Bolshevism appealing because of his exploration of freemasonry. [1053]

Through Parvus' mentoring, Bronstein concluded that freemasons intend to eliminate nations and their cultures in order to institute a world government. Apparently, elevation to the thirty-third Degree indicates acceptance of this goal. Freemasonry necessitates revolution. Bronstein, through Parvus, understood that Jews would dominate the world's population through multiculturalism and the eradication of national borders. They had to create a Jewish-ruled international republic because no other group was capable of controlling the masses. [1054] In 1902, Bronstein escaped to London where he met Vladimir Lenin (born Vladimir I. Ulyanov); Bronstein changed his name to Leon

[1052] Trotsky on Freemasonry, Grand Lodge of British Columbia and Yukon, http://freemasonry.bcy.ca/public_perceptions/trotsky.html as of May 2012

[1053] Jüri Lina, Under the Sign of the Scorpion The Rise and Fall of the Soviet Empire, Referent Publishing, Stockholm, Sweden, 2002, p. 136

[1054] Ibid. 135-136

Trotsky. [1055] In July 1898, Lenin married Nadeshda Krupskaya, a Marxist revolutionary.

Parvus, then living in a Munich suburb, provided the money for the 1905 coup attempt and made Lenin the editor of the Russian Social-Democrats' newspaper *Iskra* in 1901, in addition to allowing him to live in his flat. Parvus organized a printing office in Leipzig and ascertained that the newspaper reached Russia. [1056] Trotsky and Lenin collaborated on *Iskra*. Lenin led the Bolsheviks at the Second Congress of the RSDLP, July 30-August 23, 1903, while Trotsky acted as one of the Menshevik leaders. [1057] This congress finalized the formation of the Marxist party in Russia, first proclaimed at the First Congress of the RSDLP.

Russia annexed Batumi in accordance with the Treaty of San Stefano with the Ottoman Empire. [1058] In exchange, per a secret Anglo-Ottoman Cyprus Convention, the British occupied Cyprus. The Russians occupied Batumi beginning on August 28, 1878, and declared the town a free port until 1886. In 1883, they began the construction of the Batumi-Tiflis-Baku railway which they completed in 1900, along with the Baku-Batumi pipe-line. Batumi, 439 miles from Baku, soon became the chief Russian oil port on the Black Sea, and it population rapidly expanded from 8,671 in 1882, to 16,000 by 1902, when 1,000 men worked in Rothschild's Caspian and Black Sea oil refinery. On June 1, 1903, officials placed the region of Batumi under the General Government of Georgia's direct control.

In 1902, Joseph Stalin (born Ioseb Besarionis dze Jughashvili), began working at Rothschild's refinery in Batumi. The next day, someone, probably Stalin or his cohorts, deliberately set Rothschild's refinery

---

[1055] Trotsky on Freemasonry, Grand Lodge of British Columbia and Yukon, http://freemasonry.bcy.ca/public_perceptions/trotsky.html as of May 2012

[1056] Jüri Lina, Under the Sign of the Scorpion: The Rise and Fall of the Soviet Empire, Referent Publishing, Stockholm, Sweden, 2002, p. 182

[1057] Trotsky on Freemasonry, Grand Lodge of British Columbia and Yukon, http://freemasonry.bcy.ca/public_perceptions/trotsky.html as of May 2012

[1058] Treaty of San Stefano, http://pages.uoregon.edu/kimball/1878mr17.SanStef.trt.htm as of May 2012

ablaze. Stalin organized and engaged in creating strikes, mayhem, espionage, banditry, extortion, agitation, and murder in Batumi where he ordered the first killings of those he considered traitors. [1059] During the revolution, the Rothschilds had their termites, possibly Stalin, in Russia who destroyed and sabotaged the oil wells and refineries, even their own. Economic disaster and joblessness followed industrial sabotage.

At the Communist Party's Brussels-London conference (1902-1903), Lenin endorsed the more violent Marxist program, and won the group's support by a vote of twenty-five to twenty-three. [1060] More pogroms erupted beginning in 1903 through 1906. Jews, a distinct cultural minority, readily endorsed the three aims of International Communism, 1) seizing power in Russia, 2) Political Zionism and, 3) sustained migration to the United States, while retaining their nationalistic separatism.

Lenin and Trotsky disagreed on one very important policy; Lenin supported violent revolution, adapted for expediency, to alter society while Trotsky and his followers favored a non-violent approach. The Trotskyites evolved into what Americans currently refer to as neo-conservatives. Lenin retained the leadership after the demise of the less violent faction in 1903. The communist Jews, along with other Russian revolutionaries, were such a force that success was sure but timing and funding was everything. [1061]

Marxists exploit religion and labor through unions. In 1903, Father Georgiy A. Gapon, an Orthodox priest, organized the Assembly of Russian Factory and Mill Workers of St. Petersburg, which the Department of the Police and the St. Petersburg Okhrana supported, as they believed it was the way to control it. Gapon intended, through the Assembly, to defend workers' rights and increase their moral and religious status. His organization, composed exclusively of members of the Russian Orthodox community, had twelve branches

---

[1059] Simon Sebag Montefiore, Young Stalin, Random House, New York, 2007, p. 62

[1060] John Beaty, The Iron Curtain Over America, Chestnut Mountain Book, Barboursville, Virginia, 1968, p. 26

[1061] Ibid. 26-27

and 8,000 members. His friend, Pinhas Rutenberg, an associate of Alexander Parvus, and a freemason[1062] and a member of the Socialist-Revolutionary Party, was a workshop manager at the Putilov plant, the center of the Assembly of Russian Factory and Plant Workers.

Rutenberg, an engineer, businessman, Marxist and a Zionist leader, participated in the two revolutions, in 1905 and 1917. During World War I, he helped found the Jewish Legion of the American Jewish Congress. Later, in the British Mandate of Palestine, he obtained an exclusive concession for the production and distribution of electric power and founded the Palestine Electric Company, currently the Israel Electric Corporation. He would also participate in the formation of Haganah, a nucleus of the future Israel Defense Forces, and would serve as a President of the Jewish National Council.

Liberals formed the Union of Zemstvo Constitutionalists (1903) and the Union of Liberation (1904) both of which called for a constitutional monarchy. Socialists formed the Socialist-Revolutionary Party and the Marxist Russian Social Democratic Labour Party. In late 1904, liberals began demanding political reforms and a constitution. On December 13, 1904, the Moscow City Duma created a national legislature for popular representation, freedom of the press, and religious freedom. On December 25, 1904, the czar promised insurance for industrial workers, the emancipation of Inorodtsy (aliens), and cessation of censorship. Poles, Finns and other nationalists sought autonomy and resisted Russification. They wanted to use their own national languages and advance their culture. Increasing ethnic confrontation in the Caucasus led to the Armenian-Tatar massacres, damaging the cities and the Baku oilfields.

Gapon, an obedient police instrument, began, by the end of 1904, to cooperate with radicals, and champion the czar's abolition. On December 29, 1904, a foreman fired four at the Putilov plant, St. Petersburg's largest industrial plant, which produced military supplies during the Russo-Japanese War. Workers organized a strike,

---

[1062] Jüri Lina, Under the Sign of the Scorpion: The Rise and Fall of the Soviet Empire, Referent Publishing, Stockholm, Sweden, 2002, pp. 139-140

beginning on January 3, with more than 12,000 workers. Sympathetic workers in other city plants organized strikes so there were over 80,000 striking workers. On January 2, 1905, Russia relinquished Port Arthur, while the Japanese critically hurt the Russian Baltic Fleet at Tsushima. On January 7-8, the strike became a general one and according to the incomplete data of the factory inspectorate, it affected about 456 companies with 113,000 workers (150,000 by some sources). It paralyzed the city's industrial and commercial life. By January 8, 1905, the city was without electricity and the newspapers had stopped publishing. The authorities closed all public areas. This well-timed strike impacted Russia's ability to fight the Japanese, a war that Japan initiated without a declaration of war on behalf of the international banking cartel.

On Bloody Sunday, January 22, 1905, in St. Petersburg, during the depression that was sweeping Russia, more than 300,000 unarmed, striking workers and their families, organized and led by Father Gapon, along with Rutenberg, marched to the Winter Palace. They intended to present a petition to Czar Nicholas II demanding an end to the war, and the introduction of universal suffrage. The workers were peaceful, singing religious and patriotic songs and proceeded without the police interfering in their march. According to official documents, Parvus and Rutenberg positioned some Jewish terrorists in the trees in Aleksandrovsk Park and ordered them to shoot at the guards. [1063] The Imperial Guard then fired warning shots, in self-defense, and then opened fire on the crowd. Rutenberg took Gapon out of harm's way. Reports state that about ninety-six people died while 333 others were injured. Another report claims that the guards killed or wounded 1,000 while the frightened crowd trampled others. Although the czar was not present, people blamed

[1063] Jüri Lina, Under the Sign of the Scorpion: The Rise and Fall of the Soviet Empire, Referent Publishing, Stockholm, Sweden, 2002, pp. 139-140

him for the massacre. The people generally supported him but this massacre had serious consequences. Czar Nicholas II described the day as "painful and sad." [1064] He awarded a subsidy to the families of those who the guards had shot. However, the revolutionaries claimed that "thousands of people lost their lives." [1065]

Polish Marxists called for a general strike. By the end of January 1905, more than 400,000 workers in Russian Poland were on strike. Half of European Russia's industrial workers went on strike. They called for strikes in Finland and the Baltic coast. In Riga, police killed eighty protesters on January 26, 1905, and in Warsaw, police shot over 100 strikers. In March, authorities closed all higher academic institutions for the rest of the year. Then radical students joined the workers.

After Trotsky heard about Bloody Sunday, he returned to Russia, and, in December, the people elected him as the President of the St Petersburg Soviet. Immediately, the Russian people resented his autocratic rule. Authorities arrested, tried him and sent him to Siberia in 1907. Reportedly, the protesters were unarmed, but others claim that some of them had guns and took the first shots at the Imperial Troops. They then retaliated. This incident provoked the first Russian Revolution of 1905. Gapon and Rutenberg fled to Europe where prominent Russian emigrants Georgy Plekhanov, Vladimir Lenin, Peter Kropotkin, and French socialist leaders Jean Jaurès and Georges Clemenceau welcomed them.

In the spring of 1905, the British Fabian Society, a group founded on January 4, 1884, to incrementally introduce socialism into society, met in London, with the Bolsheviks, and arranged additional loans for them so they could proceed with their nefarious plans. Many notable people were Fabians, as well as freemasons, including George Bernard Shaw and Sidney Webb (pro-Soviet historian), two of the four founders of the London School of Economics (1895).

[1064] Peter Kurth, Tsar: the Lost World of Nicholas and Alexandra, Back Bay Books, New York City, 1998, p. 81

[1065] Jüri Lina, Under the Sign of the Scorpion: The Rise and Fall of the Soviet Empire, Referent Publishing, Stockholm, Sweden, 2002, pp. 139-140

Rothschild, Julius Wernher, a governor of the De Beers Diamond Mines, and Ernest Cassel financed the London School. In September 1902, Beatrice and Sidney Webb had formed the Coefficients, which included Herbert George "H. G." Wells, key ideologist, Leopold M. Amery, Richard B. Haldane, Robert Cecil, Edward Grey, Bertrand Russell, Alfred J. Balfour and Alfred Milner, most of whom were freemasons. [1066]

In 1929, Wells, a spokesman for the international conspiracy, wrote the pamphlet, *The Open Conspiracy: Blueprints for a World Revolution,* in which he defined the Masonic objectives, 1) Control of the world's natural resources; 2) reduction of world population through warfare; 3) the destruction of sovereign nations; and 4) imposition of a world dictatorship through the instrumentality of a superior race. Wells maintained that the elite, through control of information, would manipulate people who would willingly, incrementally accept the New World Order, gradually, one precept at a time. The conspiracy operates as a sinister system, existing as a nation within a nation, working to eradicate each nation in order to institute world government. [1067]

The Fabian philosophy spread to other countries—America, India, Australia, Canada, New Zealand, Spain, Denmark, and Germany. Dean Acheson clerked for Justice Louis D. Brandeis (1919-1921), having been recommended by one of his Harvard professors, Felix Frankfurter. By 1933, Acheson was a Fabian and the Undersecretary of the US Treasury. He advocated US recognition of the Soviet Union. [1068] Joseph Fels, a Fabian and an American-based soap manufacturer, loaned the Bolsheviks a huge amount of money. He also financed the Jewish Territorialist Organization, founded in 1903, by author, activist and freemason, Israel Zangwill and Jewish journalist, Lucien Wolfe. Fels funded it from 1906 to 1912, when he died. Fabians helped finance the Bolsheviks while Jacob H. Schiff financed the Russo-Japanese War, Japan's assault against Russia.

[1066] Jüri Lina, Architects of Deception, Referent Publishing, Stockholm, Sweden, 2004, pp. 336-337
[1067] Ibid. 340-341
[1068] Ibid. 336-337

On February 5, 1905, Czar Nicholas II had agreed to the formation of a State Duma. During the Battle of Mukden (February 20-March 10, 1905) the Japanese Army defeated Russia which lost almost 80,000 men. In June and July 1905, peasants seized land and tools. Railway workers called a strike on October 21, 1905, that evolved into a general strike in Saint Petersburg and Moscow. Trotsky set up the Saint Petersburg Soviet of Workers' Deputies, a Menshevik group that organized a strike in more than 200 factories. By October 26, 1905, over two million workers were on strike and they had deactivated rail travel throughout Russia. The strikes provided chaotic pressure from below. Accordingly, people refused to pay taxes and they withdrew their money from the banks. Sergei Witte and Alexis Obolenskii devised the *October Manifesto of 1905*, a response to the revolution, which they presented to the czar on October 14. It granted basic rights, the development of political parties, universal suffrage, and the continuation of the Duma. The czar, after resisting for three days, ultimately signed it on October 17, 1905, to circumvent another massacre. He lacked the military force to stop further rebellion. The workers in St. Petersburg and in other areas ended their strikes.

The revolutionaries initially ignored the majority of the Russians who then, because of the Jew's actions against the government, waged warfare against the Jews in the form of pogroms, killing as many as 3,000 Jews. Count Vladimir Lamsdorf confirmed the connection between the revolutionaries and foreign Jewish organizations through items that appeared in the press. Arms dealers in Europe transferred goods through England. In June 1905, in England, the Anglo-Jewish Committee began collecting money for the Russian Jews at the same time that Rothschild and his group collected money in France, England, and Germany to aid the pogrom victims in Russia. Jewish bankers in America collected funds for the victims and "for the arming of the Jewish youths." [1069]

[1069] Lucien Wolf, Notes On The Diplomatic History Of The Jewish Question, With Texts Of Protocols, Treaty Stipulations And Other Public Acts And Official Documents, Jewish Historical Society of England, Mocatta Library and Museum, London, 1919, pp. 57-58

The *October Manifesto* and imminent elections did not satisfy the revolutionaries who criticized the elections and demanded an armed uprising. In November 2005, in Sebastopol, retired naval Lieutenant Commander Pyotr Schmidt directed a mutinous uprising against the government. As many as 2,000 sailors died during the restoration of order. He said that he was a weapon of the Jews. [1070] Between December 5 and 7, the government sent in military forces when Russian workers organized a general strike. On December 18, after military troops had killed about a thousand people and destroyed portions of the city, they surrendered. By April 1906, the authorities had executed over 14,000, and imprisoned 75,000 people. That same month, the government, with the Fundamental Laws, established the parameters of this reformed political structure. The czar, still the absolute leader, maintained control of the executive, foreign policy, church, and the armed forces.

The Bolshevik revolution, January 22, 1905-July 16, 1907, failed miserably despite the financial and ideological support of the bankers and the Fabians. Thereafter, authorities sent Stalin to Siberia, Lenin fled to Switzerland; Trotsky lived in exile in London, Vienna, Zurich, Paris, and then he ultimately went to New York. He maintained connections to B'nai B'rith, a Masonic order that assisted the revolutionaries. Jacob H. Schiff, of Kuhn, Loeb, managed the communications between B'nai B'rith and the Jewish revolutionaries in Russia. [1071]

Simon Wolf, the Washington DC representative for the B'nai B'rith during the Civil War, worked with President Theodore Roosevelt to organize Jewish-American backing for the collapse of Russia. In his autobiography, Wolf revealed that he visited with Roosevelt at his estate, Sagamore Hills. They devised an international operation to accuse the czarist regime of anti-Semitism. Roosevelt regularly communicated with Count Sergei Witte, Russia's First Prime Minister, November 6, 1905-May 5, 1906. Witte presided over

---

[1070] Jüri Lina, Under the Sign of the Scorpion: The Rise and Fall of the Soviet Empire, Referent Publishing, Stockholm, Sweden, 2002, pp. 141-142

[1071] Jüri Lina, Under the Sign of the Scorpion: The Rise and Fall of the Soviet Empire, Referent Publishing, Stockholm, Sweden, 2002, pp. 135-136

extensive industrialization within Russia while serving under Czar Nicholas. According to their plan, Wolf accused the Russian regime of defaulting on its pledge to curtail the anti-Jewish pogroms. The B'nai B'rith then managed several American Jewish organizations that sent guns to the insurrectionists. [1072]

Before the end of 1905, Rutenberg and Gapon returned to Russia. A few months later, in a rented cottage outside of St. Petersburg, Gapon disclosed his police contacts to Rutenberg and attempted to recruit him as a double agent for the workers' cause. Three party members were listening from an adjacent room. Rutenberg summoned them into the room, and then he left the cottage. His comrades hung Gapon.

Count Lamsdorf, a Russian diplomat of German descent, was the Foreign Minister of the Russian Empire, during the critical time of the Russo-Japanese War and the revolution. On January 3, 1906, he produced a document called *The Proposed Anti-Semitic Triple Alliance* which detailed the activities of the anarchists in 1905, especially beginning in October following a number of strikes culminating in an armed revolt in Moscow and other cities. He asserts that the revolutionary movement, although there were serious internal issues, had an international character, supported largely from abroad, by Jewish capitalist circles that fund revolutionary movements. [1073]

Lamsdorf claims that the rebels, hostile to the government, acquired a huge quantity of arms from abroad and considerable financial support to use in organizing various kinds of strikes. This support did not originate from governments but from foreign organizations. Further, an alien racial nature characterizes the revolutionary movement. Jews are the most active in such endeavors, and are more likely to use aggression and revolution, either as individuals, or as leaders, or

---

[1072] Executive Intelligence Review (editors), The Ugly Truth About the ADL, Washington DC, 1992, pp. 26-28

[1073] Lucien Wolf, Notes On The Diplomatic History Of The Jewish Question, With Texts Of Protocols, Treaty Stipulations And Other Public Acts And Official Documents, Jewish Historical Society of England, Mocatta Library and Museum, London, 1919, pp. 57-58

they create organizations, such as the Jewish Bund, for revolutionary activities. [1074]

Lamsdorf maintained that, not only was the revolutionary movement financed from abroad but certain people also supervised it from abroad. The strikes erupted in October 1905, at the same time that the Russian government was attempting to secure a large foreign loan without having to deal with the Rothschilds. Additionally, panic surfaced among the holders of Russian securities when they tried to sell those securities. The Jewish bankers speculated openly in the Paris market on the fall of Russian securities. The hostility against the government heated up immediately after it proffered the *October Manifesto*. [1075]

Lamsdorf was certain of the connection between the Russian revolution and the foreign Jewish organizations. Many of the Jews attending the Russian universities accepted the dogma of Ferdinand Lassalle, a member of the Communist League, and Karl Marx. The revolutionary movement was completely under Jewish control, a fact not published in Russian newspapers. However, members of the Jewish Workingmen's Union in Amsterdam and Jewish groups in other countries understood that they controlled the movement in Russia. Essentially, international Jewry supports revolution in all countries. [1076]

Czar Nicholas II agreed to a State Duma and the first constitution, or Fundamental Laws, enacted on April 23, 1906. Lenin and his cronies, though they now sat in the Duma, were more of a criminal cult than a party. Trotsky, Lenin, Stalin, Zinoviev, Kamenev, Molotov and Kirov were all assumed names. Joseph Stalin, a terrorist gangster, kept the party in funds. Vyacheslav M. Molotov was born Vyacheslav M. Skryabin. Lev B. Kamenev was born Lev B. Rozenfeld, Sergei M. Kirov was born Sergei M. Kostrikov and Grigory Zinoviev was born Yevsei-Gershon Aronovich Radomyslsky.

[1074] Ibid. pp. 57-58
[1075] Ibid. 57-58
[1076] Ibid. 58-59

The czar dissolved the Duma in July 1906, as it was nothing but a podium for agitators. By June 1907, the revolution was over and the autocracy returned. Thereafter, the government hung over a thousand people. Between 1904 and 1907, there was a dramatic increase in political terrorism with revolutionary groups committing frequent assassinations and robberies. Between 1906 and 1909, those terrorists killed 7,293 people while wounding 8,061.

In 1907, Stalin was again working as a laborer in the Rothschild's refineries in Batumi. He settled his first wife, Ekaterina "Kato" Svanidze, who he had married in 1906, into an apartment close to Baku on the Bailov Peninsula. He edited two newspapers, *Bakinsky Proletary* and *Gudok;* he dominated the party and used his terrorist intimidation to raise money for the cause. [1077] Baku was a melting pot of "pitiful poverty" and "incredible wealth." [1078] The Rothschilds and local oil officials gave money to the Bolsheviks. David Landau, their managing director, contributed to them on a regular basis. While he directed the party in Baku, Stalin probably met Landau. Dr. Felix Somary, a Rothschild kinsman, banker and executive, went to Baku to settle a worker's strike which ended as soon as he paid off Stalin. [1079]

Rockefeller targeted Russia's oil but Robert and Alfred Nobel, Alphonse Rothschild, Czar Nicholas and Prime Minister Sergei Witte, who oversaw Russia's industrialization, were not about to allow Rockefeller to monopolize Russia's oil resources. The Bolsheviks, unsuccessful the first time, would, with sufficient financing, succeed the next time. Lenin and Trotsky met with US industrialists between 1907 and 1910. Rockefeller, Andrew Mellon, Andrew Carnegie and J. Pierpont Morgan founded the American International Corporation and capitalized it with $50 million for Russia's Bolshevik revolution and the ultimate destruction of the czar's family.

[1077] Simon Sebag Montefiore, Young Stalin, Random House, New York, 2007, pp. xxxii, 178
[1078] Ibid. 188
[1079] Ibid. 189

Rockefeller, whose banker was Schiff, promoted revolution to further his business interests. Ideology is insignificant. Per congressional testimony, Rockefeller helped finance the 1905 revolution. State Department records, later destroyed, show that US bankers helped finance the Bolsheviks, including Max Breitung, Benjamin Guggenheim, Kuhn, Loeb and Company whose directors were Schiff, Felix M. Warburg, Otto H. Kahn, Mortimer Schiff and Jerome J. Hanauer. Other contributors include the Lazard Brothers of Paris, the Westphalian-Rhineland Syndicate, and Speyer Brothers of London and others. [1080] Warburg was a grandson of Moses M. Warburg, one of the founders of the M. M. Warburg bank (1798).

The ruling class, concurrently, in different locations, use both Capitalism and Bolshevism as governing structures. In reality, the two do not diametrically oppose each other but are two alternative, ambitious methods of achieving world domination, by subtle, deceptive infiltration, or through violent revolutions, followed by the obliteration of the legitimate governments of one sovereign country after another. The theoretical conflict between them is a misleading, terrible deception, creating enmity among peoples who would otherwise share common aspirations. Capitalism is not the solution for Bolshevism, which is, in reality, a violent, impatient extension of Capitalism. [1081]

Woodrow Wilson, a Zionist Puppet

Woodrow Wilson was the son of one of the founders of the Southern Presbyterian Church. Sigmund Freud and William C. Bullitt, an interesting coupling, in their book, *Thomas Woodrow Wilson, a Psychological Study*, claim that Wilson was a "laughed at mama's boy," a sensitive "bundle of nerves." [1082] Bullitt (CFR), a Yale graduate, attended the Paris Peace Conference with Wilson where

---

[1080] Louis Marschalko, The World Conquerors, the Real War Criminals, Joseph Sueli Publications, London, 1958, pp. 51-52

[1081] Ibid. 51-52

[1082] Sigmund Freud and William C. Bullitt, Thomas Woodrow Wilson, twenty-eighth President of the United States: A Psychological Study, Houghton Mifflin, New York, 1967, pp. 10-12

he advocated official recognition for the Bolsheviks. Wilson, while attending Princeton, edited the *Daily Princetonian,* and he was a speaker for the American Whig Society, founded in 1769 by James Madison, William Paterson, and Aaron Burr. After graduation from Princeton (1879), he attended law school at the University of Virginia, and then attended Johns Hopkins University for graduate work in political science and history. He wrote his doctoral dissertation on *Congressional Government.* [1083]

Fabian Socialist, James Ramsay MacDonald, [1084] later England's Prime Minister (1924, 1929-1935), visited the United States as early as 1897 with his new wife, Margaret Gladstone, a feminist, social reformer, and daughter of John H. Gladstone. Her substantial inheritance enabled them to enjoy extensive travel. MacDonald felt that the US Constitution was obsolete and needed replacing. Wilson, in his first book, *Congressional Government: a Study in American Politics* (1901), also criticized what he called outdated principles. He promoted a centralized government with increased control over the citizen's lives. MacDonald, Wilson and British-educated Edward M. House (Huis), Wilson's controller shared similar views.

Wilson's classmate at Princeton was Cleveland H. Dodge, whose father, William E. Dodge, Jr., a wealthy industrialist, helped organize the YMCA in America. Cleveland H. Dodge succeeded his father as its national president. Dodge became a director at National City Bank, and a trustee of Princeton. He flattered Wilson by telling him that many Wall Street bankers viewed him as good presidential material. [1085] In 1890, to enhance his credibility for the potentiality of high public office, Dodge and his mother donated heavily to

---

[1083] Princeton University, The Presidents of Princeton University, Woodrow Wilson, http://www.princeton.edu/pr/facts/presidents/18.htm as of May 2012

[1084] Terry Melanson, Perfectibilists, the 18th Century Bavarian Order of the Illuminati, Trine Day, Walterville, Oregon, 2009, p. 103

[1085] Antony C. Sutton, The Federal Reserve Conspiracy, Emissary Publications, Oregon, 1995, pp. 82-83

Princeton,[1086] apparently with the understanding that Wilson would secure a professorship there. Thereafter, Dodge and the other trustees selected Wilson as president of Princeton, a very coveted position. [1087] Wilson, after his selection, invited J. Pierpont Morgan, George W. Harvey, Walter H. Page, Grover Cleveland, Cyrus H. McCormick Jr., Thomas B. Reed, Speaker of the House, Samuel Clemens and others to his celebratory luncheon, on October 25, 1902. [1088] [1089] Dodge and Moses T. Pyne, a Princeton trustee and the director of four banks subsidized Wilson with $5,000 a year during his tenure at Princeton.

George B. M. Harvey, a Morgan-Ryan henchman, owned *The North American Review* (1899-1926) and used it as a platform to promote Wall Street's views. He owed his position to Thomas F. Payne and William C. Whitney. In the 1880s, he had worked for them as managing editor of *The New York World* during Cleveland's second presidential campaign. Harvey then became the advertising manager and publicity agent for the Whitney-Ryan Metropolitan Street Railway, pushing bogus securities to the unsuspecting public. The appreciative Whitney cabal awarded his efforts and made him an insider in their stock-market pools. Harvey persuaded newspapers to publish positive material about investing in the market. After more than a decade of promoting the stock market, he attracted the attention of J. P. Morgan and Company. [1090]

In 1887, Harvey went to work for *The Newark Journal,* operated by James Smith Jr. In 1888, he returned to *The World* as editor and aide-de-camp to the New Jersey governor. In 1890, officials appointed him as State Commissioner of Banking and Insurance, making him

[1086] Princeton University, Department of Geosciences, 1900-1930, http://www.princeton.edu/geosciences/about/history/1900-1950/ as of May 2012
[1087] Eustace Mullins, The Secrets of the Federal Reserve, the London Connection, John McLaughlin, 1993, p. 204
[1088] Ferdinand Lundberg, America's 60 Families, The Citadel Press, New York, 1940, pp. 115-118
[1089] Donald Hoffmann, Mark Twain in Paradise: his Voyages to Bermuda, University of Missouri Press, Columbia, Missouri, 2006, p. 96
[1090] Ferdinand Lundberg, America's 60 Families, The Citadel Press, New York, 1940, pp. 115-118

very useful to Whitney and Ryan who intended to seize control of the Jersey Traction (streetcar) Company, along with the electric and gas companies, attractive businesses with long-term appeal. In 1892, Harvey introduced Smith to Whitney, the power behind Cleveland's Administration. Whitney, flush with cash, coerced the New Jersey Legislature to send Smith to the US Senate, where he functioned as a Whitney-Ryan agent until 1899. [1091]

In 1901, Harvey purchased and edited *Harper's Weekly* (1901-1913). *Harpers* then published Wilson's *History of the American People* (1901). Harvey expertly marketed Wilson to his Wall Street cronies who soon invited him to join them for lunch at Delmonico's Restaurant in Manhattan. Thomas F. Payne, William M. Laffan, Dr. John A. Wyeth, and Francis L. Stetson hosted the event. During lunch, Senator Elihu Root (1909-1915) stopped by to examine the potential candidate. [1092] Laffan, a close friend of Marxist Charles A. Dana, co-owned *The New York Sun,* and shared Dana's views. [1093] When Laffan died in 1909, J. Pierpont Morgan, honored him by giving $100,000 to Yale to establish a literature professorship, announced in *The New York Times* on January 3, 1910. [1094]

Wilson publicly endorsed Morgan following the banker-orchestrated crash of 1907. He said, "All this trouble could be averted if we appointed a committee of six or seven public-spirited men like J. P. Morgan to handle the affairs of our country." [1095] Politically, Harvey supported Wilson while Rockefeller supplied the money. Cleveland H. Dodge, J. Ogden Armour, James A. Stillman, George F. Baker, Jacob H. Schiff, Bernard Baruch, Henry Morgenthau, Sr., and Adolph S. Ochs, publisher of *The New York Times* also supported Wilson.

[1091]   Ibid. 115-118

[1092]   Ibid. 115-118

[1093]   Frank Michael O'Brien, The story of the Sun: New York, 1833-1918, George H. Doran Co., New York, 1918, p. 427

[1094]   J. P. Morgan Gives $100,000 To Yale To Establish a Professorship in Assyriology in Memory of William M. Laffan., The New York Times, January 14, 1910, p. 9

[1095]   H. S. Kenan, The Federal Reserve Bank, The Noontide Press, Costa Mesa, California, 1970, p. 105

[1096] Harvey endorsed him for the Democratic presidential nomination for 1908 but the Party would select William Jennings Bryan as its candidate. Harvey predicted that the citizens would elect Wilson as Governor of New Jersey in 1910 and President in 1912. [1097]

In January 1908, according to his doctor, Wilson needed a vacation to relieve the daily stress of his position. His wife, Ellen Axson Wilson, stayed behind to care for a sick daughter. Wilson arrived in Bermuda on January 20. Mary Peck (born Mary Allen), from Pittsfield, Massachusetts, a vivacious, trim, sophisticated, musically talented, unhappily married 45-year-old woman, rented one of Bermuda's historic houses every year. [1098] Wilson, usually an idealistic, reticent preacher's son, saw her as often as possible. She stayed at a house across the harbor from the Hamilton Hotel where he was staying. She knew many people who regularly visited the island, including Samuel Clemens who was there, accompanied by his secretary, Isabel Lyon. [1099]

Peck found Wilson rather "stilted and puritanical" but enjoyed his "continuing adoration." Lyon described Peck as "a bewitching woman, and a snare for men folk." Lyon's friend, Miss Wallace, noticing no husband present, said of Peck, "There was a little restless look of unfulfilment about her eyes and mouth that gave grounds for romantic speculation." [1100] Peck, as opposed to Wilson's wife, shared

---

[1096] Dr. W. Cleon Skousen, The Urgent Need for a Comprehensive Monetary Reform, 1982, The Freemen Institute

[1097] Ferdinand Lundberg, America's 60 Families, The Citadel Press, New York, 1940, pp. 115-118

[1098] Betty Boyd Caroli, First ladies, Oxford University Press, New York, 1987, p. 430; Another source, The Woodrow Wilson I Knew, The True Story of the Mysterious Mrs. Peck's Long Friendship with the War President, for Years the Target of Innuendoes and Malicious Gossip, as Written by Herself to Silence the Whispering of Tongues by Mary Allen Hulbert, December 20, 1924, gives the year 1907, She also says the Justice Department confiscated the letters. http://www.libertymagazine.com/presidential_hulbert.htm as of May 2012

[1099] Donald Hoffmann, Mark Twain in Paradise: his Voyages to Bermuda, University of Missouri Press, Columbia, Missouri, 2006, pp. 95-96, 107

[1100] Ibid. 95-96, 107

his political enthusiasm and aspirations. By February, he referred to her as "My precious one, my beloved Mary." [1101] After his trip, Wilson regularly wrote to her. In December 1911, she would file for divorce from wealthy industrialist, Thomas D. Peck and resume her former name, Hulbert. [1102]

After years of financially manipulating campaigns and elections in Texas, Edward M. House decided to exercise his skills nationally. In 1910, to prepare for World War I, he began "to look about for a proper candidate for the Democratic nomination for President." Concurrently, Budapest-born Rabbi Stephen S. Wise, a former Republican, and the chief Zionist organizer in America, announced to a New Jersey audience, "On Tuesday Mr. Woodrow Wilson will be elected governor of your State; he will not complete his term of office as governor; in November 1912 he will be elected President of the United States; he will be inaugurated for the second time as president." He had it on good authority from House, neither of whom had met Wilson, but others had studied his philosophies and his private life and were satisfied that he was their man. [1103]

Morgan cronies had encouraged Wilson to enter politics. George W. Harvey's former boss at *The Newark Journal*, former Senator James Smith Jr. (1893-1899) was now New Jersey's Democratic leader, and got Wilson's name on the ballot for governor in the Trenton Democratic State convention in October 1910. With the financial support of Rockefeller, Schiff, Baruch, and others, he won the governorship of New Jersey. Dodge donated $75,000 to Smith for getting him nominated. [1104]

[1101] Kenneth S. Lynn, The Hidden Agony of Woodrow Wilson, The Wilson Quarterly, Volume: 28, Issue: 1, Publication Date: Winter 2004, p. 59+

[1102] Wife Sues Thomas D. Peck.; Charges Woolen Manufacturer with Desertion, and Asks Alimony, The New York Times, December 9, 1911, p. 1

[1103] Douglas Reed, The Controversy of Zion, Dolphin Press, Durban, South Africa, 1978, pp. 166-167

[1104] Ferdinand Lundberg, America's 60 Families, The Citadel Press, New York, 1940, pp. 115-118

In the spring of 1912, Wilson spent the weekend at Beechwood, Frank A. Vanderlip's estate in Scarborough, on the Hudson River, along with William Rockefeller and others. Vanderlip and Rockefeller, in Wilson's presence, elaborated on the role of American capital in the world. Cyrus H. McCormick Jr., another former Princeton classmate, was then president of McCormick Harvesting Machine Company. He donated $12,500 to Wilson's campaign through Dodge. Wilson returned it, a ploy to convince people that big corporations could not influence him. [1105]

With encouragement from the bankers, Wilson ran for president in 1912. President William Howard Taft, though popular and usually acquiescent to the banker's plans, opposed the Aldrich Plan. They were anxious to maneuver him out of the White House. Harvey continued to extol Wilson's virtues during his gubernatorial term. People knew that Harvey was a Morgan agent so Wilson asked him to limit his editorial praises as it might jeopardize his presidential chances. Therefore, Harvey acted disenchanted with Wilson, and even supported the opposition at the 1912 Convention while Wilson pretended to oppose the bankers. [1106]

To split the Republican vote, the bankers persuaded Theodore Roosevelt to run on his new Bull Moose Party, in order to put Wilson, a Democrat, into the White House. Newspaper publisher Frank A. Munsey and George W. Perkins funded Roosevelt and Taft. Perkins was the vice-president of New York Life Insurance Company and the Morgan partner who negotiated the creation of International Harvester, International Mercantile Marine Company, the Northern Securities Company and the restructuring of Carnegie's steel operation. He sat on the board of Carnegie's company. Paul M. Warburg, a Republican, contributed substantial funds to Wilson's campaign while his brother contributed to Taft's campaign. [1107]

[1105] McCormick Money Returned, Harvester Head Withdrew contribution for Wilson's Nomination, The New York Times, October 26, 1912, p. 4
[1106] Ferdinand Lundberg, America's 60 Families, The Citadel Press, New York, 1940, pp. 115-118
[1107] Pat Riott, The Greatest Story Never Told, Winston Churchill and the Crash of 1929, Nanoman Press, Oak Brook, Illinois, 1994, pp. 21-22

The third party candidate assured Wilson's triumph in the Electoral College. He took 41.8 percent of the popular vote and won 435 electoral votes from forty states. Wilson, exhibiting a characteristic psychopathic grandiose sense of self-worth, told his campaign manager, ". . . God ordained that I should be the next president of the United States." [1108] Two-thirds of his financial support came from only seven people—all affiliated with Wall Street. Dodge, McCormick, Morgenthau, Abram I. Elkus, Frederick C. Penfield, William F. McCombs, and Charles R. Crane promoted him as a "man of peace." Like most politicians, he concealed his affiliation with the banking cabal. [1109] He would appoint both Morgenthau and Elkus as Ambassadors to the Ottoman Empire, recently targeted by the Young Turks (cryptic Jews).

Colonel House, never legitimately employed, used his inheritance to influence Texas politics. He helped elect five governors (1893-1911). In 1911 he supported Wilson for president and maneuvered the very decisive Texas delegation which ensured Wilson's nomination. [1110] House's long-term scheme all but guaranteed the presidential victories (1912, 1916), as well as the election of Franklin D. Roosevelt (1932, 1936, 1940, and 1944) and Harry S. Truman (1948). The colonel's electoral plans included the exploitation of the political ideas of others. He implemented a brilliant strategy whereby the Democrats gained the loyalties of the new foreign-born immigrants by appealing to their unique racial feelings and their challenges in becoming part of the societal makeup of their respective communities while still remaining culturally distinct. Garnering voter loyalty was not mere happenstance but rather a very detailed plan where he targeted foreigners for specific propaganda according to their circumstances. [1111]

[1108] Sigmund Freud and William C. Bullitt, Thomas Woodrow Wilson, twenty-eighth President of the United States: A Psychological Study, Houghton Mifflin, New York, 1967, p. 148

[1109] Pat Riott, The Greatest Story Never Told, Winston Churchill and the Crash of 1929, Nanoman Press, Oak Brook, Illinois, 1994, pp. 82-83

[1110] Eustace Mullins, The Secrets of the Federal Reserve, the London Connection, John McLaughlin, 1993, pp. 44-45

[1111] Douglas Reed, The Controversy of Zion, Dolphin Press, Durban, South Africa, 1978, pp. 167-168

Most of the Jews in America were from Germany and were adamantly opposed to Zionism. However, by 1910, one million out of less than 15,000,000 worldwide, [1112] new Zionist Jews had arrived from Russia. They soon became an important group of voters. Rabbi Wise remarked, after the election, "We received warm and heartening help from Colonel House; close friend of the president . . . House not only made our cause the object of his very special concern but served as liaison officer between the Wilson administration and the Zionist movement." [1113]

During a thirty-day period, House wrote a novel in New Haven, the site of Yale University. [1114] The novel, from which Wilson developed his program, [1115] *Philip Dru: Administrator*, a title that might refer to the Protocols of the Elders of Zion, which state, "The Administrators whom we shall choose . . ." His book, published anonymously (1912), elaborated on plans for America's overthrow by establishing "socialism as dreamed by Karl Marx." House wrote, ". . . (It) cannot be entirely brought about by a comprehensive system of state ownership and by the leveling of wealth . . . (but not) without a spiritual leavening." [1116] [1117] He quoted Giuseppe Mazzini, "No war of classes, no hostility to existing wealth, no wanton or unjust violation of the rights of property, but a constant disposition to ameliorate the condition of the classes least favored by fortune." He dedicated his book "to the unhappy many who have lived and died lacking

---

[1112] Sigmund Freud and William C. Bullitt, Thomas Woodrow Wilson, twenty-eighth President of the United States: A Psychological Study, Houghton Mifflin, New York, 1967, p. 154

[1113] Douglas Reed, The Controversy of Zion, Dolphin Press, Durban, South Africa, 1978, pp. 166-167

[1114] Antony C. Sutton, America's Secret Establishment, An Introduction to the Order of Skull & Bones, Trine Day, Walterville, Oregon, 2002, p. 96

[1115] Sigmund Freud and William C. Bullitt, Thomas Woodrow Wilson, twenty-eighth President of the United States: A Psychological Study, Houghton Mifflin, New York, 1967, p. 152

[1116] Edward Mandell House, Philip Dru: Administrator, A Story of Tomorrow, 1920-1935, B. W. Huebsch, New York, 1912, p. 22

[1117] Douglas Reed, The Controversy of Zion, Dolphin Press, Durban, South Africa, 1978, pp. 167-168

opportunity, because, in the starting, the world-wide social structure was wrongly begun." [1118]

In 1831-1832, Mazzini, a Marxist, organized Young Italy, a Masonic organization of males, ages sixteen to twenty. Giuseppe Garibaldi joined the group and then proceeded to become a thirty-third degree freemason; people later referred to him as Italy's "liberator." To finance their revolutionary activities, like the Bolsheviks, they robbed banks, performed high-level assassinations, kidnappings for ransom, and they demanded "protection money" from numerous businessmen to prevent the thugs from burning or bombing their buildings. They called themselves "Mazzini's Association for Insurrection and Assassination later shortened to MAFIA, perhaps the first Political Action Group. Organized crime and politics have long been associated in nearly every country. [1119]

In August 1912, during the presidential campaign, Louis D. Brandeis and Wilson first met for a private three-hour conference in New Jersey to discuss economic issues. Afterwards, Brandeis supported Wilson and urged his friends to do likewise and Wilson began using Brandeis' term "regulated competition." The bankers installed House as Wilson's mentor when he entered the White House on March 4, 1913. The Schiffs, Warburgs, Kahns, Rockefellers and Morgans had complete confidence in House's abilities to properly manage Wilson. While the bankers sought the passage of the Federal Reserve Act, they pretended to oppose it to keep the public from suspecting that they were actually behind it. [1120]

In addition to House, others greatly influenced Wilson-Brandeis, Felix Frankfurter, Walter Lippmann, Bernard Baruch, Sydney Hillman,

[1118] Edward Mandell House, Philip Dru: Administrator, A Story of Tomorrow, 1920-1935, B. W. Huebsch, New York, 1912, title page
[1119] John Daniel, Two Faces of Freemasonry, Day Publishing, Longview, Texas, 2007, p. 296
[1120] W. Cleon Skousen, The Naked Capitalist, Buccaneer Books, Cutchogue, New York, 1970, pp. 20-21

and Florence Kelley. [1121] Allegedly, Brandeis was instrumental in developing the Federal Reserve Act and he decisively argued to break the deadlock on the issue. He convinced the Wilson administration to devise proposals for further legislation that would allow the Justice Department the authority to enforce antitrust laws. He helped create the Federal Trade Commission and was Wilson's Key economic adviser (1912-1916).

Two days after Wilson took office, William G. McAdoo (Pilgrims Society), a lawyer and businessman became Treasury Secretary. J. Pierpont Morgan and his associates previously befriended and helped McAdoo resolve his difficult financial problem, for which he was very grateful. [1122] Thereafter, they appointed him as the President of the Hudson and Manhattan Railroad Company, now known as the Port Authority Trans-Hudson. The bankers introduced him to Wilson in 1910 and McAdoo later worked on his campaign. McAdoo married Wilson's daughter, Eleanor R. Wilson at the White House on May 7, 1914. He was the first chairman of the Federal Reserve Board and was part of the Morgan cabal for the rest of his financial and political career.

Cleveland H. Dodge, President of the Winchester Arms Company and Remington Arms Company, was Wilson's key supporter. On February 12, 1914, during the Mexican Revolution (1910-1920) wherein 2.1 million people died, Wilson lifted the embargo on arms shipments to enable Dodge to ship a million dollars' worth of munitions to Venustiano Carranza, the opposition leader. Kuhn, Loeb bankers, owner of the Mexican National Railways System, were disgruntled with President José Huerta's policies so they eliminated him using dissident internal forces and the US military. [1123] By 1901, about twenty-seven percent of the land in Mexico belonged to Americans while Americans held forty-five percent of all industrial investments.

[1121] Eustace Mullins, The Secrets of the Federal Reserve, the London Connection, John McLaughlin, 1993, p. 174

[1122] Charles Savoie, Pilgrims, Silver Investor, May 2005, www.silver-investor. com/charlessavoie/cs_may05_pilgrims.htm as of May 2012

[1123] Eustace Mullins, The Secrets of the Federal Reserve, the London Connection, John McLaughlin, 1993, pp. 169-170

Therefore, both Taft and Wilson intervened in Mexico's affairs in behalf of the corporations that put them in office.

Samuel Untermeyer, a prominent New York City lawyer, member of the Tammany Society, and later the president of Keren HaYesod, donated generously to Wilson's campaign. He approached President Wilson with an interesting collection of letters that Bernard Baruch had purchased for $65,000. [1124] Wilson's friend, Mary Hulbert, retained Untermeyer to initiate a breach of promise action against Wilson. Her son, a bank employee, desperately needed $40,000 to avoid arrest. She would be willing to drop her suit for $40,000. Apparently, the $65,000 she received for the letters was insufficient. Perhaps this shakedown was part of an operation, beginning with the meeting in Bermuda. Untermeyer would pay the bribe if Wilson appointed Brandeis to the Supreme Court when the next vacancy occurred. [1125] This occurred on June 1, 1916. A *New York Times* article dated December 8, 1922, reported that Untermeyer had financial investments in the Mosul oil fields in Palestine. [1126]

Congress passed the Federal Reserve Act on December 23, 1913. On July 28, 1914, after assassins killed Franz Ferdinand and his wife in Sarajevo, the warmongers, now that the United States had a central bank with money to loan, began the Great War. On that same day, *The Wall Street Journal* reported the exportation of $14,750,000 in gold, mainly to London. It was a new record for "a single day's consignment." Three other ships left at about the same time carrying $25,450,000 in gold, the German ship *Kronprinzessin Cecilie* going to Bremen, the *Carmania* heading for Liverpool, and the steamship *La Savoie* headed for Le Havre. [1127]

[1124] Pat Riott, The Greatest Story Never Told, Winston Churchill and the Crash of 1929, Nanoman Press, Oak Brook, Illinois, 1994, p. 20
[1125] How Does Samuel Untermeyer Fit Into The Scheme? http://www.historicist.com/untermeyer/wilson.htm as on May 2012
[1126] Push Mosul Oil Claims, Ex-British Officers Say They are Representing Americans, The New York Times, December 8, 1922
[1127] William L. Silber, When Washington Shut Down Wall Street: The Great Financial Crisis of 1914 and the Origins of America's Monetary Supremacy, Princeton University Press, 2007, pp. 26-29

The Austrian Ultimatum of July 23, 1914, to Serbia triggered this huge exportation, of gold in less than a week. Guaranty Trust Company sent $10 million; National City Bank sent $6.5 million; Lazard Frères sent $2.5 million; and Goldman Sachs sent $1.75. [1128] Skull and Bones members headed Guaranty Trust Company almost entirely. This same firm financially supported the Bolsheviks. [1129] The total sum exported out of New York, July 23, 1914 to July 29, 1914, was $27,850,000 (*Wall Street Journal*, July 29, 1914). The Treasury regularly provided monthly data on all gold exports and imports in its yearly reports. They show that from the beginning of 1900 to the end of 1913, the United States exported an average of $5,338,784 in gold each month, with a standard deviation of $6,556,493.

The United States, a debtor nation, now with a central bank and a system of national loans, ultimately gave the Allies $25 billion dollars. Actually, one cannot call it a loan, as they never repaid it. However, the New York bankers collected interest on it which was the whole point. Despite the fact that almost half of all US citizens were of German descent, because of official propaganda targeting Germany, US citizens would soon begin fighting Germans. [1130]

On Friday, July 31, 1914, many European investors placed at least $100 million American securities into the market. The *Wall Street Journal* reported that brokers had huge volumes of buy orders and there were bargain hunters wanting to buy at low prices. People feared a market crash. J. Pierpont Morgan Jr. called McAdoo that morning at 9:30 and convened a meeting of Wall Street bankers to discuss the overnight developments. The New York Stock Exchange Governing Board voted to close at 9:45, that morning. Secretary McAdoo approved the closing of the Stock Exchange for four months. This allowed the Federal Reserve System to entrench itself. McAdoo

---

[1128] Ibid. 26-29

[1129] Webster G. Tarpley & Anton Chaitkin, George Bush: The Unauthorized Biography, Executive Intelligence Review, 1991, p. 97

[1130] Eustace Mullins, The Secrets of the Federal Reserve, the London Connection, John McLaughlin, 1993, pp. 143-144, 147

rescued the bankers in New York City in 1914 which established the precedent for future bailouts. [1131]

McAdoo pushed Wilson's nominees, Paul M. Warburg and Frederick Delano, through the Senate Banking Committee. He accommodated the desires of Benjamin Strong and Warburg, an expert on central banking. Strong was the Governor of the New York Reserve Bank. [1132] In October 1915, J. P. Morgan issued a $500 million bond for Britain and France. This joint Anglo-French loan was very suitable for the US population in denominations of $100, $500, and $1,000 and put the United States into the position of an international moneylender, mostly to foreign countries. Between January 1, 1915 and April 5, 1917, New York bankers issued $2.6 billion. The United States also joined Britain in accepting gold as the standard. [1133]

Wilson's worldviews included four main components, 1) the League of Nations as a global forum for the settlement of territorial disputes through arbitration, along with the power of enforcement; 2) free global trade, as later elucidated in his Fourteen Points, "equality of trade" and "removal . . . of all economic barriers." Wilson, a friend to big corporations wanted an absence of war, and market expansion for US industries through a binding global treaty; 3) a regional integration of both political and economic levels, as noted in his "Pan-American Pact" proposal of 1914-15, a welding of North and South America together as a union. Both House and Wilson viewed the Pan-American Pact as a model for the political organization of Europe; 4) the US should assume global leadership to enforce peace and justice throughout the world. [1134]

There was not a hint of any of these concepts in Wilson's campaign rhetoric. Like other politicians, he had promised to oppose imperialism

---

[1131] William L. Silber, When Washington Shut Down Wall Street: The Great Financial Crisis of 1914 and the Origins of America's Monetary Supremacy, Princeton University Press, 2007, p. 124
[1132] Ibid. 139
[1133] Ibid. 158
[1134] Will Banyan, Rockefeller Internationalism, Part 1, Nexus Magazine Volume 10-Number 3, (April-May 2003)

and warfare. His indiscretions, useful knowledge for blackmail, his complicity in the establishment of the Federal Reserve, and his disdain for the Constitution, and the fact that the bankers, through Edward M. House, managed his perceptions, led to the bloodshed of World War I. The public elected him through the machinations of Roosevelt's third party charade and through the maneuverings of the international bankers.

Assassination in Sarajevo

Wars—organized mass slaughter—require meticulous political planning, which often includes contrived emotionally charged incidents, like an assassination, or an enemy attack blamed on another country, which we know as a false flag operation. Corrupt politicians use such incidents to gain popular acceptance from a propagandized population. The deaths of two people, and other politically provoked powder keg issues, helped to ignite a war that caused massive unemployment, poverty, pandemic diseases, a decline in agriculture leading to famine, currency devaluation, the emergence of new countries, the disintegration of governments, disruption of communications, and the deaths and serious injuries of millions.

Mihailo Obrenović, the Prince of Serbia (1860-1868), supported the concept of a Balkan federation against the Ottoman Empire. On June 10 1868, assassins, probably the Karađorđevićs shot and killed him. Milan Obrenović succeeded him as the Prince of Serbia. In 1876, Obrenović declared war on Turkey and unified with Bosnia. The delegates of the Congress of Berlin, with the Treaty of Berlin, formally recognized Serbia's independence but prohibited it from uniting with Bosnia and Raška and placed them under Austro-Hungarian occupation. In June 1881, Obrenović signed a secret agreement with Austria-Hungary, vowing that Serbia would not act against the interests of Austria-Hungary in Bosnia and Herzegovina, and would not make political agreements with other countries. In 1882, Serbia became a kingdom, Obrenović declared himself king. Meanwhile bankers in London and Paris were worried that, with the Ottoman Empire's diminishing power, Russia would expand to the south. By 1878, Britain and France had already targeted Egypt and Palestine for colonization.

In the 1880s and 1890s, Germany and Austria-Hungary allied with Russia, Serbia, and Italy. By the early 1900s, Russia and Serbia had issues as the Young Turks had enacted reforms that would weaken Austrian positions in Bosnia and Herzegovina. On October 6, 1908, Austria-Hungary annexed Bosnia and Herzegovina, which Serbia and Russia opposed. German support for Austria-Hungary, and financial aid to Constantinople from Vienna convinced Russia, Serbia, and the Ottoman Empire to consent to the annexation, and resolve the crisis in Bosnia by amending the Treaty of Berlin of April 1809. After the Bosnian Crisis, Vienna's pro-war party viewed a war with Serbia as unavoidable and pushed for a preventative war. [1135]

Colonel Edward M. House allegedly had a working copy of the Protocols of the Learned Elders of Zion in his personal papers. House, representing President Woodrow Wilson, arrived in Europe in January 1914, where he remained until the end of July. In mid-June, he had what he considered a very pleasant visit with Kaiser Wilhelm II, in Potsdam, the residence of the Prussian kings until 1918. Based on claims from certain entities in Europe, he believed that the German leader threatened Europe's peace, but he soon discovered that the Kaiser had no intentions of starting a war. In fact, he was the only European politician who was open to mediation. Leaders in Paris and London did not want to discuss peace but were primed to go to war. [1136]

By June 1914, according to Dr. Harry Elmer Barnes, Germany and England had settled their differences regarding Mesopotamia, and the Baghdad Railroad. The two countries were getting along better than they had in the previous eighteen years. This Anglo-German alliance would likely prevent Britain from joining France and Russia,

---

[1135] Gábor Ágoston and Bruce Alan Masters, Encyclopedia of the Ottoman Empire, InfoBase Publishing, New York, 2009, pp. 64-65

[1136] Leon Degrelle, Hitler: Born at Versailles, Volume 1, of the Hitler Century, Institute for Historical Review, Torrance, California, 1992, pp. 219-221

if they decided to go to war. Germany and England had no reason to fight each other. [1137]

Wilhelm did everything he could to prevent war and for his efforts, the victors ultimately made him the scapegoat, and accused him of the crimes that they had committed. Winston Churchill, always looking for a battle, waited for the right justification, even if he had to maneuver the circumstances. He did not wait long as the conspirators had a plan, followed by huge reparations—the Treaty of Versailles and the sequel, a second world revolution. Upon receiving orders from Paris telling him to be ready for a full-scale war, the future French Marshal, Hubert Lyautey, said, "They are completely insane; a war between Europeans is a civil war. It is the most colossal folly the civilized world has ever committed!" [1138]

Franz Ferdinand was the oldest son of Archduke Karl Ludwig of Austria, the younger brother of Maximilian and Franz Joseph. Italian anarchist Luigi Lucheni assassinated Franz Joseph's wife, Empress Elizabeth, on September 10, 1898, in Geneva. Numerous people viewed the prospect of Franz Ferdinand ascending to the throne as very grave, especially those in the upper circles of government. If he came to power, he planned to drastically revise the constitution of the whole Hapsburg Empire by creating a "United States of Austria," and federalizing the government. He believed in giving autonomy to ethnic groups within the Empire and advocated listening to their grievances, particularly the Czechs in Bohemia and the Slavic peoples in Croatia and Bosnia. [1139]

[1137] Dr. Harry Elmer Barnes, Who started World War One?, The Barnes Review, Washington, DC, 2009, p. 7
[1138] Leon Degrelle, Hitler: Born at Versailles, Volume 1, of the Hitler Century, Institute for Historical Review, Torrance, California, 1992, pp. 98-99
[1139] Frederic Morton, Thunder at Twilight: Vienna 1913/1914, Da Capo Press, Cambridge, Massachusetts, 2001, pp. 181-183

If he controlled the Hapsburg Empire, he would remove the Hungarian Prime Minister Kálmán Tisza (1875-1890), who was married to a Jewess, Ilona Degenfeld-Schomburg, and who, through his decisions, accommodated the Jews. Franz Ferdinand would alter the election laws that allowed Tisza, part of the landed gentry, and his base to maintain power. The masses attributed the national misery to his policies which triggered widespread anti-Semitism. [1140] Franz would allow equal rights and permit agricultural workers, the non-property owners to vote. This would allow the 3,000,000 Croats within the Hungarian borders to have a voice against their oppressors. Officials did not invite Croat delegates to the Austro-Hungarian compromise of March 30, 1867, which reestablished the sovereignty of the Kingdom of Hungary and separated it from the Austrian Empire. [1141] After 1867, Tisza formed a coalition of the nobility, business interests, and small landowners into the new Liberal Party. István Tisza, Kálmán's son was Prime Minister of the Kingdom of Hungary (1903-1905).

Emperor Franz Josef's son, Rudolf, committed suicide with his lover Marie Vetsera on January 30, 1889, which made Franz Ferdinand the heir to the throne. In 1895, in Prague, Ferdinand met the former Countess Sophie Chotek from an old Czech family. Her family failed to meet the eligibility standards for marrying into one of the reigning European families. Despite this, and amid family pressure, they married on July 1, 1900. Emperor Franz Joseph reluctantly agreed to the marriage but compelled his nephew to renounce all possibilities to the Hapsburg throne, for himself, his wife, and their future children.

Archduke Ferdinand, while reserving the right of succession to the throne, despite his marriage, systematically increased Austria's power, while eliminating German influence. State officials within the German districts gradually promoted the integration of languages. The Czechs, traditionally hostile to the Germans, viewed Vienna as "their" biggest city. Because of the Archduke's marriage, the royal

---

[1140] Raphael Patai, The Jews of Hungary: History, Culture, Psychology, Wayne State University Press, Detroit, Michigan, 1996, p. 356

[1141] Frederic Morton, Thunder at Twilight: Vienna 1913/1914, Da Capo Press, Cambridge, Massachusetts, 2001, pp. 181-183

family favored the Czech language. Evidently, the Archduke was determined to institute a Catholic Slav State in Central Europe to function as a fortification against Orthodox Russia. During other times in Habsburg history, officials exploited religion to attain political objectives, a disastrous policy to German interests. Ultimately, this proved a detriment to the House of Habsburg, which lost the throne, and to the Catholic Church, which lost the state. The monarchy's mingling of religion and politics, to quench Germanism, instead, ignited the Pan-German Movement in Austria. [1142]

In 1912, leading freemasons met in Switzerland, a neutral country where people devise international schemes. They purportedly decided to assassinate Ferdinand in order to initiate worldwide warfare. On September 15, 1912, the *Revue Internationale des Sociétés Secretes,* a Catholic anti-Masonic, anti-Jewish publication edited by Ernest Jouin, in discussing Ferdinand, a prominent Swiss freemason stated, "The Archduke is a remarkable man. It is a pity that he is condemned. He will die on the steps of the throne." [1143]

Archduke Ferdinand and his wife, Duchess Sophie, arrived in Sarajevo on June 28, 1914 to observe military maneuvers in his official capacity as commander-in-chief of the Austro-Hungarian army. The couple's car, part of a four-car procession, was traveling on the quay alongside the Miljach River toward town hall, their first destination. Hardly had they begun, when a terrorist threw a bomb at the archduke. It bounced off the back of the car and exploded under the vehicle behind them, injuring two officers. The alarmed couple continued traveling to the town hall. Upon their arrival, the archduke indignantly reprimanded the mayor. Then the motorcade left to visit the hospital where one of the wounded officers was receiving medical attention.

The mayor then joined the procession sitting in the lead car. The driver turned on the wrong street and the driver of the archduke's car followed him. General Oskar Potiorek, the military governor of

---

[1142] Adolf Hitler, Mein Kampf, Hurst and Blackett Ltd., New York, 1939, p. 83

[1143] William Guy Carr, Pawns in the Game, Noontide Press, Newport Beach, California, 1978, pp. 87-88

Bosnia, corrected the driver who backed up to return to the correct route. When the driver stopped, Gavrilo Princip, a 19-year-old Serbian, took careful aim, and fired two shots into the open car, a Gräf and Stift luxury automobile. One bullet hit Ferdinand in the neck, while the other bullet struck Sophie in the stomach. She immediately collapsed against her husband, he whispered, "Sophie, live for our children." They both died within a few moments on June 28, 1914. [1144] Their children were Princess Sophie von Hohenberg (1901), Maximilian, Duke of Hohenberg (1902), and Prince Ernst von Hohenberg (1904).

Allegedly, the assassination was retaliation for the annexation of Bosnia and Herzegovina in 1908, which the Serbs had already claimed. Sarajevo, the capital of the Austro-Hungarian province of Bosnia and Herzegovina, was a quiet Balkan town in Bosnia, previously the seat of a province of the Ottoman Empire. There were mosques rising above the meandering streets of the marketplace. The Austro-Hungarian Empire had administered the area since 1878.

Nedjelko Čabrinović, a freemason, and Trifko Grabež, militants associated with the Pan Serbian Black Hand threw the initial bomb that failed to explode under the vehicle transporting the royal couple. [1145] The notes taken during the military trial of the assassins seem to corroborate freemasonry involvement. On October 12, 1914, Čabrinović, of the Narodna Odbrana, part of the Young Bosnia faction, admitted that freemasons, Major Vojislav Tankosić and Milan Ciganović, had influenced his decision to participate. He said that freemasonry tenets permitted people to kill. He said, "Ciganović told me that the freemasons had condemned the Archduke Franz Ferdinand to death more than a year before." [1146]

[1144] Leon Degrelle, Hitler: Born at Versailles, Volume 1, of the Hitler Century, Institute for Historical Review, Torrance, California, 1992, pp. 3-6

[1145] R. J. W. Evans and Hartmut Pogge Von Strandman, The Coming of the First World War, Clarendon Press, Oxford, 1990, pp. 19-25, 28, 32, 40-41

[1146] William Guy Carr, Pawns in the Game, Noontide Press, Newport Beach, California, 1978, pp. 87-88

Chief of Serbian Military Intelligence, Dragutin Dimitrijević Apis, from Belgrade, directed Princip and the other assassins, all members of the Black Hand Society, [1147] and all of whom, were under twenty. [1148] This terrorist brotherhood, created by army officers, used a skull and bones insignia and had a constitution. [1149] Dimitrijević, a leader of the Black Hand, had sent the three men to kill the Archduke and his wife, furnishing the culprits with a revolver, two bombs and sufficient cyanide to commit suicide afterwards, to prevent them from revealing the identity of the organizers. All three men suffered from terminal tuberculosis.

On July 5, 1914, Wilhelm II received a letter from Emperor Franz Josef explaining Austria's objections against Serbia, the southern Slavic state. Franz Josef feared that Serbia's actions would destroy the Austrian-Hungarian Empire, which might also affect the German Empire. Franz Josef, through his letter to a man he had a friendly relationship with, was assessing Wilhelm's attitude about the murders. According to Dr. Harry Elmer Barnes, their "dynastic fortunes" were also "closely linked." The Kaiser quickly met with his advisors and wrote back on the same day, "Austria may judge what is to be done to clear up her relation to Serbia; whatever Austria's decision may turn out to be, Austria can with certainty upon it that Germany will stand behind her as an ally and a friend." Kaiser Wilhelm thought it inconceivable that the assassination would lead to a European war. He thought that the czar was unprepared for a war, and would not oppose "the proper punishment of Serbia." He also believed that England would remain neutral. [1150]

[1147] R. J. W. Evans and Hartmut Pogge Von Strandman, The Coming of the First World War, Clarendon Press, Oxford, 1990, pp. 19-25, 28, 32, 40-41

[1148] Guido Giacomo Preparata, Conjuring Hitler, How Britain and America Made the Third Reich, Pluto Press, London, England and Ann Arbor, Michigan, 2005, pp. 20-22

[1149] The Constitution of the Ujedinjenje ili Smrt—Unification or Death, http://wwi.lib.byu.edu/index.php/Constitution_of_the_Black_Hand as of May 2012

[1150] Dr. Harry Elmer Barnes, Who started World War One?, The Barnes Review, Washington, DC, 2009, pp. 9-10

On July 9, 1914, Colonel House wrote a "brush-off" letter to the Kaiser. His last sentence read, "I left Germany happy at the thought that Your Majesty would use its high influence in favor of peace." Wilson, in a letter was "elated" by House's success with the Kaiser in Germany. On July 31, 1914, House wrote to Wilson, before returning home. He said, "If my project could have been advanced further Germany could have exerted pressure on Austria and the cause of peace might have been safe." Had they followed his proposals, they could have negotiated before the murders in Sarajevo. The Kaiser, in his post-war exile said, "House's visit in Berlin during the spring of 1914 almost prevented the war." [1151]

German and Austria-Hungarian citizens viewed the assassination as a local police matter that they could settle peacefully, without diplomatic clashes. However, the politicians had other ideas. They made unreasonable demands, flung accusations, and told incendiary lies. Serbian politicians failed to meet the demands, known as the July Ultimatum, so Austria-Hungarian politicians declared war on Serbia on July 28, 1914, on the grounds that it had a role in the assassinations. Russia declared war on Germany on July 29, 1914. Max M. Warburg, Albert Ballin, Arthur Zimmermann, and Chancellor Theobald von Bethmann-Hollweg advised Kaiser Wilhelm to support Austria-Hungary by declaring war on Russia, which he did on August 1, 1914. Britain entered the war on August 4, 1914 theoretically to protect Belgian neutrality. Austria-Hungarian politicians declared war against Russia on August 6, 1914. Citizens never declare war; they just fight and die in them!

Henry Kissinger said, "Military men are just dumb, stupid animals to be used as pawns for foreign policy." [1152] Trotsky, who held similar views, said, "An army cannot be built without reprisals. Masses of men cannot be led to death unless the army-command has the death penalty in its arsenal. So long as those malicious tailless apes that are

---

[1151] Leon Degrelle, Hitler: Born at Versailles, Volume 1, of the Hitler Century, Institute for Historical Review, Torrance, California, 1992, pp. 221-222

[1152] Monika Jensen-Stevenson and William Stevenson quoted Henry Kissinger in Kiss the Boys Goodbye: How the United States Betrayed Its Own POW's in Vietnam, Plume Publishing, New York, 1999

so proud of their technical achievements—the animals that we call men—will build armies and wage wars, the command will always be obliged to place the soldiers between the possible death in the front and the inevitable one in the rear." [1153] Trotsky placed troops in the rear, behind his front-line troops, to shoot deserters and stop the front line from retreating.

By the fall of 1914, US business interests recognized that they could gain windfall profits from the European war. [1154] President Wilson said the United States would "remain neutral in fact as well as in name." [1155] However, now that the United States had the Federal Reserve, he loaned $500 million to the Triple Entente in October 1914. US bankers eventually loaned the Triple Entente $2.3 billion. Loans originating in the United States to the Triple Alliance totaled $27 million. On April 15, 1915, Sir Gilbert Parker, a Member of Parliament, addressed the Pilgrims Society of London. He confidently assured them that the United States would enter the war on Britain's side. [1156]

Colonel House, for eight years, was the power behind Wilson and was the key figure between 1914 and 1918. In the *Intimate Papers of Colonel House*, he wrote, "There were few citizens of the United States who could claim any knowledge of European affairs of state or who had any interests in them." House would deliver two million young men and billions of dollars to the Allies. Wilson was indifferent to and had absolutely no experience or interest in European problems. [1157] The Allies lusted for war and refused to negotiate, despite the deaths it would cause. House, whose loyalties were always with those who controlled Britain, knew exactly who had started the war. On

---

[1153] Leon Trotsky, My Life: The Rise and Fall of a Dictator, Thornton Butterworth Limited, London, 1930, p. 351

[1154] Leon Degrelle, Hitler: Born at Versailles, Volume 1, of the Hitler Century, Institute for Historical Review, Torrance, California, 1992, pp. 222-223

[1155] Woodrow Wilson, Message to Congress, 63rd Cong., 2d Session., Senate Doc. No. 566 (Washington, 1914), pp. 3-4

[1156] Charles Savoie, Meet the World Money Power, December 2004, pp. 47-48

[1157] Leon Degrelle, Hitler: Born at Versailles, Volume 1, of the Hitler Century, Institute for Historical Review, Torrance, California, 1992, p. 217

April 15, 1915, he wrote, "I never commit myself. But here I can say what I think; I do not believe the Kaiser wanted the war." [1158]

The so-called "Great War" was the first global war. Although it began in Europe, it quickly spread throughout the world. The hostilities ensnared several countries within a month while others joined during the next four years. Honduras declared war against Germany on July 19, 1918 and Romania entered the war, for the second time, on November 10, 1918.

The Lusitania Incident, Live Bait

The British, with naval superiority since 1815, felt threatened by German competition and their growing influence in the North Atlantic, through the efforts of the German lines, Hamburg-Amerika and Norddeutscher Lloyd. Samuel Cunard had founded the Cunard Line in 1840, as a British and North American mail packet line. In 1903, Prime Minister Arthur J. Balfour (1902-1905) authorized a twenty-year loan at 2.5 percent interest for £2.6 million to Cunard Line chairperson, James Burns, Lord Inverclyde, to construct the *Lusitania* and *Mauretania*, which would be the largest and fastest liners afloat. Upon completion of the ships, the government subsidized Cunard with £150,000 to keep both ships in a "state of war readiness." In August 1914, they retained the *Lusitania*, due to its size and heavy fuel consumption, as a merchant vessel. [1159]

In 1902, the J. Pierpont Morgan-owned conglomerate, the International Mercantile Marine Company, had absorbed the White Star Line, Cunard's British rival. He purchased many of White Star's rival companies to control freight prices. In 1926, He would fortuitously sell the line, just before the stock market crash for a very handsome profit. Although he owned the line since 1902, the government mandated that all British marine properties maintain British registration. While Morgan owned the line, as a financial investment, the British government retained management of all vessels in the event of a war.

[1158] Ibid. 222-223

[1159] The Lusitania Timeline, http://web.rmslusitania.info:81/pages/timeline.html as of May 2012

The US Government had no privileges except those conceded by Britain through friendship. [1160]

The White Star Line began construction on the *Titanic* on March 31, 1909. Nearly three years later, the *Titanic* sank on her maiden voyage across the Atlantic on April 15, 1912. Officials attributed the high death toll to a belated emergency response and insufficient lifeboats, a huge factor in the survival rate. Over 1,500 people perished, including Benjamin Guggenheim, Isador Straus and John J. Astor. An American and British Commissioner's Inquiry concluded, "The loss of the said ship was due to collision with an iceberg, brought about by the excessive speed at which the ship was being navigated." A much greater proportion of third class passengers were lost than of first and second-class passengers. [1161]

Winston Churchill, First Lord of the British Admiralty (1911-1915), wrote to the President of the Board of Trade, saying it's "most important to attract neutral shipping to our shores, in the hopes especially of embroiling the United States with Germany." Churchill had been President of the Board of Trade (1908-1910) and certainly had influence and connections. He asked Commander Joseph Kenworthy, of Naval Intelligence, to prepare a report on the possible "political results of an ocean liner being sunk with American passengers on board." Later, Kenworthy, in his book *Freedom of the Seas* (1927), wrote, "The *Lusitania* was deliberately sent at considerably reduced speed into an area where a U-boat was known to be waiting and with her escorts withdrawn." British officials knew that there were U-boats in that shipping lane and deliberately withdrew the destroyer escorts. Additionally, a U-boat had recently sunk two ships, the *Candidate* and the *Centurion*, in the same path in which the *Lusitania* was traveling. [1162]

[1160] White Star, Time Magazine, Business: White Star, December 6, 1926
[1161] Titanic Inquiry Project, British Wreck Commissioner's Inquiry Report on the Loss of the Titanic, http://www.titanicinquiry.org/BOTInq/BOTReport/BOTRep01.php as of May 2012
[1162] Richard Sanders, The American Use of War Pretext Incidents (1848-1989), http://www.mindfully.org/Reform/2002/How-To-Start-A-WarMay02.htm as of May 2012

Several months before the ill-fated voyage, Churchill described the *Lusitania* as "live bait." In his World War I memoirs, *The World Crisis*, he wrote, "There are many kinds of maneuvers in war, some only of which take place on the battlefield . . . There are maneuvers in time, in diplomacy; in psychology; all of which are removed from the battlefield . . . The maneuver which brings an ally into the field is as serviceable as that which wins a great battle." [1163]

Initially, the Germans attempted to honor international law regarding the destruction of merchant vessels but it was not very effective because Britain controlled the high seas. Britain blockaded Europe in order to starve the Germans. British officials instructed the officers on merchant ships to assault German submarines whenever possible. It was difficult to discern the difference between British ships and neutral ships. The British designated the North Sea, essential to German imports, as a war zone in the winter of 1915. The United States and other neutral countries did not protest their actions. Britain detained, searched and confiscated the non-contraband cargoes of all neutral countries. They made certain that Germany did not receive foodstuffs. Yet, international law dictates that belligerent governments allow the passage of all food destined for civilian populations. [1164]

The British blockade violated international law in addition to laws of human decency. The Germans were bound to retaliate. On February 4, 1915, Germany declared the waters around Britain and Ireland a war zone and issued a warning that they would sink all enemy ships in that area after February 18, 1915. Britain responded by declaring its goal of starving 120,000,000 Germans and Austrians. [1165]

Britain's *Lusitania*, then the world's largest and fastest passenger ship deceptively flew the US flag. In February 1915, the British

---

[1163] Winston Churchill, The World Crisis, 1911-1918, Martin Gilbert, free Press, Simon and Schuster, New York, 1931, pp. 293-294

[1164] "Sinking Justified, Says Dr. Dernburg; Lusitania a "War Vessel," Known to be Carrying Contraband, Hence Search Was Not Necessary," The New York Times, May 9, 1915

[1165] The New York Times Current History, Volume 2, April 1915 to September 1915, New York Times Company, 1915, pp. 426-429

Admiralty, under Churchill's direction, ordered British merchant ships, like the *Lusitania*, to ram German submarines on sight. The British government borrowed the *Lusitania,* equipped it with bases for mounting guns and reclassified it as an auxiliary cruiser. [1166] Germany knew of Churchill's orders by February 15, 1915. On April 22, Germany, through its US Embassy warned Americans not to travel on British ships in the war zone. On that same day, they also submitted a notice to *The New York Times.* [1167] It read, "Travelers intending to embark on the Atlantic voyage are reminded that a state of war exists between Germany and her allies and Great Britain and her allies; that the zone of war includes the waters adjacent to the British Isles; that, in accordance with formal notice given by the Imperial German Government, vessels flying the flag of Great Britain, or of any of her allies, are liable to destruction in those waters and that travelers sailing in the war zone on ships of Great Britain or her allies do so at their own risk." [1168]

The newspaper published the warning on the day the *Lusitania* was to depart from New York, May 1, 1915. [1169] On that day, there was a two and a half hour delay due to the suspicious transfer of passengers from the *Cameronia* to the *Lusitania.* [1170] A number of prominent passengers received anonymous warnings against traveling on the *Lusitania.* [1171] Alfred G. Vanderbilt (S&B) received a telegram the morning of the sailing, which said, "The *Lusitania* is doomed. Do

[1166] Carroll Quigley, Tragedy and Hope, a History of the world in Our Time, The Macmillan Company, New York, 1966, pp. 250-251
[1167] Winston S. Churchill, 1874-1965: A Comprehensive Historiography and Annotated Bibliography by Eugene L. Rasor, Greenwood Press, Westport, Connecticut, 2000, pp. 74-75
[1168] The New York Times Current History, Volume 2, April 1915 to September 1915, New York Times Company, 1915, p. 413
[1169] German Embassy Issues Warning; Advertises Notice of Danger to Travelers in the War Zone, Building Up A Defense? Suggestion That Notice May Be Cited Against Possible Claims for Damages—Cunard Agent Says Travel Is Safe. New York Times, May 1, 1915
[1170] S. S. Cameronia, The Ship and List of Transfers, http://web.rmslusitania. info:81/pages/cameronia.html as of May 2012
[1171] The Lusitania Timeline, http://web.rmslusitania.info:81/pages/timeline.html as of May 2012

not sail on her." The telegram was signed Morte (death). [1172] He disregarded the warning; no one ever recovered his body following the disaster. His sister, Gertrude Vanderbilt, who had married into the wealthy Whitney family, flew into a rage when she learned that Cleveland H. Dodge had packed the civilian ship with ammunition. She blamed him for her brother's death. This incident ultimately pitted the fortunes of the Vanderbilts and the Whitneys against the Dodges and the Rockefellers.

The night of May 7, 1915, the 32,000-ton *Lusitania*, allegedly because of fog, was not operating at full speed but rather at a substantially reduced speed. In addition, the ship did not execute the usual defensive zigzag course to evade German submarines known to be in the area. Later, during the liability hearings, Cunard's lawyers fought to conceal the ship's slow speed while it traveled through dangerous waters. Two of the surviving passengers, Belle Naish and Maude Thompson witnessed the military vessel accompanying the *Lusitania* inexplicably increase its speed and quickly withdraw. Evidently, British officials ordered the withdrawal of the military escort as the ship approached England.

The *Lusitania*, now an easy target, was traveling directly into the gun sights of a German submarine. They converged at about 2 PM, about eleven miles off of Ireland's coast, near Kinsale. Captain Walther Schwieger, the U-20 commander, after observing the *Lusitania* for an hour, released one torpedo. There was an immediate, unexpected second explosion on the *Lusitania*. [1173] The powerful ship surprisingly sank in just eighteen minutes, which contributed to a great loss of life. There were 1,198 passengers, including 128 Americans. German submarines had torpedoed ships much smaller. Some never sank while others sank only after several hours. Overnight, any sympathy that Americans had for Germany was lost. It works every time—kill some Americans and the government will declare war!

[1172] Mr. Alfred Gwynne Vanderbilt, Saloon Class Passenger, http://web. rmslusitania.info:81/pages/saloon_class/vanderbilt_ag.html as of May 2012

[1173] The Sinking of the Lusitania, 1915, http://www.eyewitnesstohistory.com/ lusitania.htm as of May 2012

In addition to the passengers, reportedly, there were six million rounds of US ammunition bound for Britain. This was in addition to the massive amounts of ammunition that Remington Arms produced for the Allied powers. They manufactured the M1916 Berthier rifles for France, the Pattern 1914 Enfield rifles for Britain, and Model 1891 Mosin-Nagant rifles for Imperial Russia. The ship was carrying armaments from the factories under the jurisdiction of Dodge, president of Winchester Arms Company, and Remington Arms Company, one of Wilson's chief financial supporters. As the war intensified, profit and production for Remington dramatically increased. Cunard admitted to carrying 4,200 cases of ammunition but no one ever told the public, either before or after the incident. [1174] The DuPont family also had a controlling financial interest in the Remington Arms Company. [1175]

Dodge of Kuhn Loeb, who controlled National City Bank of New York, profited immensely from his ammunition factories. Like other politicians and bankers, he exploited the tragedy and chaired the Survivors of Victims of the Lusitania Fund, whose humanitarian efforts with its accompanying propaganda, predictably aroused anger toward Germany. Dodge was the heir to one of the nation's leading copper mining operations. Its products were in great demand for making armaments. He was infamous for using thugs against strikers in his plants. [1176]

The *Lusitania*, according to an underwater exploration fifty years later, carried a hull full of ammunition. The arms dealers and the British sacrificed almost 1,200 lives to hide their contraband. The Germans were well aware of this, and were within their international rights to attack an arms-carrying enemy vessel. The British, not the Germans, were responsible for the passenger deaths on the *Lusitania*,

---

[1174] Eugene L. Rasor, Winston S. Churchill, 1874-1965: A Comprehensive Historiography and Annotated Bibliography, Greenwood Press, Westport, Connecticut, 2000, pp. 74-75
[1175] Smedley D. Butler, War is a Racket, Feral House, Los Angeles, California, 2003, pg. 16
[1176] Eustace Mullins, The Secrets of the Federal Reserve, the London Connection, John McLaughlin, 1993, p. 170

as they disguised a warship as an ocean liner. They used a neutral flag to cover their arms trafficking. [1177] Gregg Bemis, who financed the salvaging operation, told the British press, "Now that we've found it, the British can't deny that there was ammunition aboard." He said that there was literally tons and tons of ammunition, all marked as food commodities. He said, "That's what sank the ship . . . those four million rounds of .303s . . ." [1178]

Dr. Quincy Wright, in *A Study of War*, defined how peace-loving countries maintain peace. Britain, from 1800 to 1941, participated in thirty-four wars; France fought in twenty-nine wars and Germany (Prussia) fought in ten wars. [1179] Yet, people have always deceptively characterized the Germans as the aggressors. Germany had a more peaceful, less aggressive history, and had participated in "less than one quarter of the wars" in which Britain had engaged. Britain now targeted Germany for the gravest ethnic cleansing in history. The English press, through militant propaganda, soon transformed them into murderous villains. Warmongers within two governments were impatient to entrench America into a costly, deadly foreign war. [1180] The United States resisted war, even after the *Lusitania* incident. [1181]

To provoke outrage, the *Times of London* declared that "four-fifths" of the passengers were US citizens instead of the actual proportion. The British produced and circulated a medal that German officials purportedly created to award the crew of the U-boat crew for their actions. A French newspaper published a photo, taken much earlier, under totally different circumstances, of German crowds rejoicing, purportedly over the news of the sunken *Lusitania*. Americans

---

[1177] Leon Degrelle, Hitler: Born at Versailles, Volume 1, of the Hitler Century, Institute for Historical Review, Torrance, California, 1992, pp. 232-233

[1178] History You May Have Missed, New Info on HMS Lusitania, The Barnes Review, March/April 2009, p. 32

[1179] Francis Neilson, The Makers of War, C. C. Nelson Publishing Company, Appleton, Wisconsin, 1950, p. 28

[1180] Hysteria Part 1, Before They Sprouted Horns and Fangs, http://www.exulanten.com/hysforward.html as of May 2012

[1181] Carroll Quigley, Tragedy & Hope, A History of the World in Our Time, G. S. G. & Associates, Incorporated, San Pedro, California,1975, pp. 250-51

vehemently objected to Germany's submarine warfare, while ignoring Germany's justifiable opposition to the illegal, inhumane British blockade. [1182] The German ambassador met with President Wilson on June 2, 1915, and diplomatically resolved the problem. On June 10, 1915, William Jennings Bryan, the Secretary of State resigned. He adamantly believed that Americans, by law, should not travel on the ships of belligerent nations, especially when they had several other options. [1183]

Colonel House and British Foreign Minister Sir Edward Grey exchanged information, using a secret code, and bypassed government channels, with their letters and cables. On July 8, 1915, House wrote, "The nation continues to show itself clearly opposed to war and I seriously doubt that Congress would support the president if he decides otherwise." In another message, he explained America's situation to Grey, "It goes without saying that I will not let the Germans know we are in agreement with the Allies, but I will attempt on the contrary to convince them that they (the Allies) will reject our proposals. This could influence them in accepting them. If they did not, their refusal would be enough to justify our intervention." Wilson told Brand Whitlock, the US Ambassador to Belgium that he sided with the Allies. However, he had to keep his feelings to himself until after the next year's elections. He said, "I have no right to force the American people to participate in a war they do not understand." [1184]

The Board of Trade Official Commission convened on June 15, 1915, and presented their report, dated July 17, 1915. The commission concluded, after studying the circumstances of the disaster, that the loss of the ship, as well as the great loss of lives was due to damage caused by torpedoes fired by a German submarine. Further, "In the opinion of the Court the act was done not merely with the intention of sinking the ship, but also with the intention of destroying the lives of the people on board." The number of passengers on board

---

[1182] Ibid. 251

[1183] John Cornelius, The Hidden History of the Balfour Declaration, Washington Report on Middle East Affairs, November 2005, pages 44-50

[1184] Leon Degrelle, Hitler: Born at Versailles, Volume 1, of the Hitler Century, Institute for Historical Review, Torrance, California, 1992, pp. 236-237

was 1,257, consisting of 290 saloons, 600 second-cabin, and 367 third-cabin passengers. Of these, 944 were British and Canadian, 159 were Americans, and the remainder consisted of seventeen other nationalities. British and Canadian losses were 584, United States losses were 124, and other losses were 77. Total deaths were 785, with 472 survivors." [1185]

Colonel House wrote to the US Ambassador to London, Walter H. Page, "We will be at war with Germany within a month." Page (Pilgrims Society) responded on July 21, 1915, "It is strange to say but I only see one solution to the present situation: a new outrage like the *Lusitania* sinking that would force us into war." [1186]

On August 4, 1915, about 90 percent of the US public was against participating in the European War. House again wrote to Page, describing "his sadness" that so many US citizens were opposed to going to war. [1187] A large percentage of those citizens had German ancestors. People were neutral until the media launched a barrage of anti-German atrocity stories depicting the worst human brutality imaginable. The US government published highly emotional propaganda pamphlets to evoke public anger against Germany. The war did not affect American citizens and Germany was not a threat so why should the US government spend vast amounts of money and send its youth off to fight and die in a foreign country.

On August 26, 1915, Colonel House warned Americans, "German agents will no doubt try to blow up hydroelectric plants, gas and electricity stations, subways and bridges in cities like New York. He urged Wilson to exploit the *Lusitania* sinking to the degree that "the rupture with Germany" would become "inevitable and the

---

[1185] Formal Investigation into the circumstances attending the foundering on the 7th of May, 1915, of the British Steamship "Lusitania," of Liverpool, after being torpedoed off the Old Head of Kinsale, Ireland. Presented to both Houses of Parliament by Command of His Majesty, http://www.titanicinquiry. org/Lusitania/Report/Rep01.php as of May 2012

[1186] Leon Degrelle, Hitler: Born at Versailles, Volume 1, of the Hitler Century, Institute for Historical Review, Torrance, California, 1992, pp. 232-233

[1187] Ibid. 236-237

United States would be forced to enter the war on the side of the Allies." [1188]

Judge Julius M. Mayer, a Zionist, of the District Court of New York, wrote an official decision claiming that a German submarine torpedoed and sunk the *Lusitania*. He said a "common enemy of mankind," assaulted an unarmed merchant vessel with 1,959 souls, "which had no explosives aboard." Further, the judge stated that the Cunard Line was not liable. [1189] President Wilson, who promised to keep us out of war, did not ask for a declaration of war against Germany after this incident. The isolationists, who always viewed Germans as friends, resisted a war against them. Others demanded war. By November 1915, Congress strongly opposed the war and the more isolationist areas of the country were against the "growing spirit of militarism." [1190]

On January 11, 1916, House cabled Wilson, "England should be grateful for all acts of terrorism committed by Germany because each person—man woman or child—killed on land or sea, is dying for England." House's prediction about entering the war in a month had not yet occurred. [1191]

House felt that the United States was "the only nation on earth" to get the Allies "out of trouble." Germans received him very well when he returned to Paris on February 3, 1916. However, the Germans were losing their patience over the withdrawal of their submarines from combat, due to pressure from the United States. This cut their remaining supply lines, and the continued British blockade deprived German citizens of food. Millions were hungry, and many died

---

[1188] Ibid. 237

[1189] Finds Lusitania The Victim Of An Act Of Piracy; US Court Declares Germany Alone Responsible for Lives and Property Lost, Cunard Line Is Absolved, The New York Times, August 26, 1918, p. 1

[1190] John Whiteclay Chambers, The Eagle and the Dove: the American Peace Movement and United States Foreign Policy 1900-1922, Syracuse University Press, New York, 1991, pp. 69-70

[1191] Leon Degrelle, Hitler: Born at Versailles, Volume 1, of the Hitler Century, Institute for Historical Review, Torrance, California, 1992, pp. 232-233

of starvation. This was despite Herbert Hoover's Belgian Relief operation. House wrote, "I find it fair war for the Entente to try to starve the Germans and reduce them to sue for peace." On February 14, 1916, House had dinner with Grey, Balfour, David Lloyd George and Herbert H. Asquith. He told them, "The Germans are at peak efficiency and they can strike a decisive blow, break through the lines and occupy Calais or Paris. If they do, it is possible that the war will end." Lloyd George was unconcerned and retained his opinion that the war "could go on indefinitely." His policy during the Battle of Verdun demonstrated his indifference, as 650,000 men died to gain territory the size of a football field, only to lose it again. [1192]

In February 1916, German officials apologized to the Americans for the loss of life resulting from the *Lusitania* incident. The Gore-McLemore Resolution, of February 17, 1916, made it illegal for Americans to travel on armed belligerent ships. However, Wilson publicly denounced it and aggressively lobbied to get Congress to defeat it. He wrote to Senator William J. Stone, Chairman of the Senate Foreign Relations Committee, dated February 24, 1916, which the media published. [1193]

The *Sussex*, a French steamer, provided passenger service between Dover and Calais. During a crossing in March 1916, officers on a German U-boat mistook the ship for a minelayer and torpedoed it. Rescuers towed *The Sussex* into the French port of Boulogne. Fifty people died in the incident but none were US citizens. However, the incident injured several Americans. President Wilson addressed both houses of Congress and notified the German government with an ultimatum. German officials responded on May 4, 1916, with what people called the *Sussex Pledge* in which they assured Wilson that they would search all merchant ships and make provisions for passenger ships and crews.

[1192] Ibid. 241-242

[1193] John Whiteclay Chambers, The Eagle and the Dove: the American Peace Movement and United States Foreign Policy 1900-1922, Syracuse University Press, New York, 1991, pp. 68-69

The Germans did not want a war with the United States. They were fighting the Russians in the east; they were in Serbia, in Romania, in Italy, on the Dardanelles and in Asia Minor as well as on the French front. In March 1916, they sank eight allied vessels, all with Americans aboard, but none died, due to Germany's extraordinary precautions. On April 14, 1916, Germany's US Ambassador wrote, "My dear Colonel House: My government is ready to conduct submarine warfare with all due respect to the rights of neutrals. It is standing by the assurances already provided to your government and it had given such precise instructions to its submarine commanders that within the bounds of human foresight errors can no longer be committed. If, contrary to our intentions, some do occur our government is committed to correct them by all the means in its power." [1194]

On June 1, 1916, Zionist Louis D. Brandeis became a Supreme Court Judge. Representative Julius Kahn sponsored the National Defense Act of June 3, 1916, increasing the size of the army from 108,000 to 175,000 while expanding the National Guard to 450,000. In August 1916, Congress authorized a huge buildup of the navy to make it the largest and best in the world. [1195] In 1919, Kahn would be very critical of Wilson's endorsement of Israel and Zionism. He said, "One of the great dangers of Zionism is that the non-Jew will begin to look upon the American Jew as having a lurking desire to return to the so-called Jewish homeland." [1196]

Germany, whose citizens were suffering from famine, no longer restrained their submarines. They demanded that Britain halt their blockade. Over 100,000 Berlin workers went on strike, which shut down strategic industry. Over 33 percent of German deputies were Socialists and against the war—they had two choices, either famine or revolution which presented a terrible dilemma. Secretary of State,

---

[1194] Leon Degrelle, Hitler: Born at Versailles, Volume 1, of the Hitler Century, Institute for Historical Review, Torrance, California, 1992, pp. 241-242

[1195] John Whiteclay Chambers, The Eagle and the Dove: the American Peace Movement and United States Foreign Policy 1900-1922, Syracuse University Press, New York, 1991, p. 70

[1196] Kahn Opposes Zionism, Californian Regrets That President Has Indorsed It, Special to The New York Times, February 6, 1919, p. 24

Robert Lansing, said on December 21, 1916, "We are on the eve of war." [1197]

On January 22, 1917, Wilson addressed the Senate and said, "We must reach a peace without victory. Peace must be based on the right of each nation to decide its own destiny without the intervention of a more powerful external enemy." While his speech reflected public opinion, British officials were unhappy. Sir William Wiseman, Balfour's agent, told House, "By insisting too much on peace among the Allies, you (the Americans) are doing great harm to the cause of democracy." On January 30, 1917, House urged Wilson, "If I were you I would be cautious enough to hasten the state of readiness of the navy and the army." On January 30, 1917, the German Ambassador announced that Germany was going to break the British blockade despite US reaction. [1198]

On January 16, 1917, the British had claimed that they had intercepted a German message to Washington's German Ambassador who then sent it to Mexico's German Ambassador, known as the Zimmermann Telegram, which was allegedly proposing an alliance with Mexico with a promise to help Mexico recover land that they had earlier ceded to the United States in the Treaty of Guadalupe-Hidalgo. Someone leaked the contents of the telegram to US newspapers, and they subsequently published the information on March 1. President Wilson asked Congress for a declaration of war on April 2, 1917; Congress complied on April 6. He deceptively told Congress that Americans had died when the *Sussex* sank, when, in fact, people had towed it into a French port. [1199]

Edward Rothschild and his associates made more than $100 billion dollars during World War I. [1200] It brought death to between sixteen

---

[1197] Leon Degrelle, Hitler: Born at Versailles, Volume 1, of the Hitler Century, Institute for Historical Review, Torrance, California, 1992, pp. 255-259

[1198] Ibid. 255-259

[1199] Francis Neilson, The Makers of War, Flanders Hall Publishers, New Orleans, Louisiana, 1950, pp. 149-150

[1200] General Cherep-Spiridovich, The Secret World Government or "The Hidden Hand," The Anti-Bolshevist Publishing Association, New York, 1926, p. 2

and twenty million people, mostly civilians, including a half million in Britain. However, the war planners had met their objective—they cut Germany off from Russian, and Middle-Eastern oil. Rockefeller provided the oil necessary to win the war. Following the war, France and Britain carved up the Middle East, as per their agreement prior to the war. Britain received a protectorate over Palestine and Iraq. [1201]

Yehuda Bauer said, "World War I was evidence of the massive brutalization of the twentieth century; it was a major new departure in the history of mankind. For the first time in history, there had never been such a mass killing of such proportion taken place between civilized societies. The killing, mutilation and gas poisoning of millions of soldiers on both sides had broken taboos and decisively blunted moral sensitivities." [1202]

Churchill, a thirty-third degree freemason, purportedly viewed World War 1 as an ideological struggle between the Christian civilization and scientific barbarism. He intended to obliterate Germany's militant aggressiveness, which he characterized as Prussian Militarism, by imposing social changes within Germany. He maintained this opinion throughout both world wars and blamed Germany even though Britain had adopted what he considered Prussian-style strategies. [1203]

[1201] Alan B. Jones, How The World Really Works, ABJ Press, Paradise, California, 1997 pp. 6-7

[1202] Eric Markusen and David Kopf, The Holocaust and Strategic Bombing: Genocide and Total War in the Twentieth Century, Westview Press, Boulder, Colorado, 1995, p. 30

[1203] Tuvia Ben-Moshe, Churchill, Strategy and History, Lynne Rienner, Boulder, Colorado, 1992, pp. 71-72

SECTION 7

THE REVOLUTION, WORLD WAR ONE

Media and Wartime Propaganda, Fomenting Hatred

The House of Rothschild purchased the London-based Reuters International News Agency in the late 1800s, in time to propagandize the masses for World War I. They also owned the controlling interest of Havas of France, and Wolff in Germany. [1204] Propaganda includes deliberate distortions, exaggerations or outright fabrications in order to manipulate our emotions and/or prejudices or intentionally mislead the uninformed. Among other types of propaganda, there is political, economic, literary, drama and entertainment, all perpetuated during peaceful times but especially disseminated during wartime against a purported enemy. [1205]

Édouard Quartier-la-Tente, a former Protestant preacher, was the State Councilor of Neuchâtel (1898-1922), in Switzerland, and the Grand Master of the Grand Lodge Alpina Swiss. When war erupted, he condemned the disloyalty of German freemasons. He helped found the Masonic World Business Office and participated in disseminating the atrocity stories against the German Army. [1206]

Even before Germany declared war, the hate-mongers began targeting the German people. They dehumanized them by portraying them as a "tribe of cannibals." Charles Maurras, a French politician, denounced "the innate savagery of the instincts of flesh and blood" of the Germans. Henri Bergson, the prominent philosopher, proclaimed "the brutality and cynicism of Germany, a regression to the savage

---

[1204] Eustace Mullins, The Secrets of the Federal Reserve, the London Connection, John McLaughlin, 1993, pp. 107-108

[1205] Larry Tye, The Father of Spin, Edward L. Bernays and the Birth of Public Relations, Henry Hold & Co., New York, 1998, p. 7

[1206] Dieter Schwarz, Freemasonry, Ideology, Organization and Policy, Central Publishing House of the NSDAP, Berlin, 1944, pp. 32-33

state." Georges Clemenceau, a French diplomat, wrote, "I wish to believe that civilization will carry the day against savagery, and that is sufficient for me to rule out the German from a life of common dignity." [1207]

Georges Clemenceau, in describing the Germans, implied that they were a bunch of drunkards who worshipped in the beer-gardens, including the men, women, and children. He said they were "just a conglomeration of buffoons, gluttons, and drunkards capable only of the eternal violence of fundamentally savage tribes for purposes of depredation by every means of barbarism." When the war began, officials characterized the Germans as heinous and cruel to convince their armies that they were fighting against extreme evil. Those officials spread their hatred abroad, to win support and arouse the wrath of the world. [1208]

The Allied media accused the German soldiers of slaughtering citizens as they marched through Belgium on their way to France in August 1914. Many villagers fired at them and the soldiers retaliated in kind and often burned down the homes of the Belgian aggressors. They reacted no differently than the British, the French, or the Americans in the same situation. Sometimes the villagers used sniper fire, provoking bloody reprisals. To conceal Belgian culpability, the media denied civilian participation while claiming the unmitigated massacre of innocents. [1209]

Baron Oscar von der Lancken, the German Political Minister in Brussels, consulted the official reports of the soldiers who the Belgian civilians had wounded. He thoroughly investigated the hospital records wherein every man wounded in Belgium received medical care in August 1914. They revealed that buckshot or shotgun pellets, not bullets or shrapnel injured hundreds of soldiers. The Hague Convention explicitly allows only recognizable soldiers, not civilians, to bear arms and engage in combat. The civilian use of a weapon

---

[1207] Leon Degrelle, Hitler: Born at Versailles, Volume 1, of the Hitler Century, Institute for Historical Review, Torrance, California, 1992, pp. 133-141
[1208] Ibid. 133-141
[1209] Ibid. 133-141

was and is justification for execution. The international conventions do not allow unauthorized combatants such as civil guards or town militias. On August 4, 1914, authorities warned the Belgians not to organize such groups. Those who refused to comply created a newspaper, *Le Franc-Tireur* (*The Sniper*). [1210]

The same situation occurred in World War II, when citizens in Belgium, Holland, and France killed German soldiers. They were members of the civilian "resistance." Often, in such circumstances, the perpetrators, outside of international law, retreat as soon as they have attacked, and the enemy soldiers retaliate against ordinary citizens. In Belgium in 1914, the citizens and the media fabricated stories to create hatred against the Germans. The French even accused the Germans of cutting down their apple orchards. Such a campaign would take an enormous effort. Following the armistice, the Allies confiscated foodstuffs, cattle, and milk in Germany, where people were already starving, due to the British blockade during the entire four-year war. [1211]

Minus sentiment, passion and bias, in the most ordinary circumstances, human testimony is frequently very unreliable. Fervent patriotism, questionable but favorable notoriety, and personal statements, no matter how emotional, are often not credible. Yet, agents repeatedly disseminate atrocity stories through flyers, letters, pamphlets, and fiery speeches. Prominent people, typically non-judgmental and silent about the transgressions of their worst enemies, quickly became vociferous over the purported evidence and do not hesitate to lead a hateful campaign against an entire nation over the professed evidence, based largely on hearsay. [1212]

The Times published "Marching Songs" to escalate the outrage of the populace. The stanza of one song had the following lines,

---

[1210] Leon Degrelle, Hitler: Born at Versailles, Volume 1, of the Hitler Century, Institute for Historical Review, Torrance, California, 1992, pp. 133-141

[1211] Ibid. 133-141

[1212] Arthur Ponsonby, Falsehood in War-Time, Containing an Assortment of Lies Circulated Throughout the Nations During the Great War, E. P. Dutton & Company, New York, 1928, pp. 128-129

He shot the wives and children,
The wives and little children;
He shot the wives and children,
And laughed to see them die. [1213]

Reportedly, thirty to thirty-five German soldiers forcefully entered David Tordens' home in Sempst, Belgium. They bound Tordens, then five or six of them gang raped his thirteen-year old daughter in his presence, and then slaughtered her with their bayonets. They then bayoneted his nine-year-old boy, and murdered his wife. Some Belgian soldiers arrived just in the nick of time and saved his life. German soldiers reportedly ravished every young female in Sempst. [1214]

Paul van Boeckpourt, the commune's secretary and Peter van Asbroeck, the mayor and his son Louis, testified on April 4, 1915, at Sempst, that no one by the name of David Tordens, or his family ever lived there. They also testified, under oath, that during the war, German soldiers had not killed any woman or child under the age of fourteen in Sempst. Given their position in the commune, they would certainly have been aware of such events. [1215]

War itself is an atrocity, with numerous individual acts of cruelty and barbaric violence. Exaggeration and blatant deceptions are a component of propaganda. Agents widely distributed tales of German brutality, to furnish sufficient evidence of the horrendous cruelty of their army, in order to foment outrage against them. James Bryce, a former US Ambassador and Member of Parliament, chaired a commission created to collect witness affidavits regarding atrocities, ostensibly conclusive proof. He used these to shape opinions. Gullible Americans accepted the heart-rending stories in those affidavits. [1216] On May 12, 1915, he issued his official *Report of the Committee*

[1213] Ibid. 128-129
[1214] Ibid. 128-129
[1215] Arthur Ponsonby, Falsehood in War-Time, Containing an Assortment of Lies Circulated Throughout the Nations During the Great War, E. P. Dutton & Company, New York, 1928, pp. 128-129
[1216] Ibid. 128-129

on Alleged German Outrages. Prime Minister Herbert H. Asquith commissioned it, suspiciously early in the war, but the purpose, to outrage American sensibilities, worked quite effectively. [1217]

Emile Vandervelde, a Belgian diplomat, based on hearsay, claimed that Germans cut off the hands of thousands of Belgian children. Allied propagandists continued the enormous slander to poison the minds of entire populations. Establishment historians, among the Allies, repeated the dreadful tale for several decades, as if Vandervelde had conducted a scientific examination. Yet, no one ever found a single Belgian child, or other nationality, without hands. In 1915, shops in Italy sold statues of a little "Belgian girl with her hands cut off, holding out her bloody arms to Mary, the Holy Virgin, begging her to make them grow again." [1218]

Italian freemasons, working with their French "brothers," engaged in vehement anti-German propaganda in the Italian press before and after the war began, admittedly to provoke Italy's entry into the war on the Allied side. They proudly admitted their contribution in getting their country into World War I. [1219]

In the spring of 1915, Vandervelde, head of Belgian's socialist party and the president of the Second International, visited Benito Mussolini, on behalf of the Allies, to persuade Italy to fight on their side. Mussolini admitted that his story about the children convinced him to commit his country to battle. Yet, there must have been other motives as Mussolini doubted the story and asked him if he had actually seen any of these pitiful children, or if he knew of any reliable man who had seen any of these children. He soon recanted his story. In the occupied areas, individuals observed that the Germans were generally kind and courteous to children. Despite the lack of

---

[1217] Primary Documents—Bryce Report into German Atrocities in Belgium, May 12, 1915, http://www.firstworldwar.com/source/brycereport.htm as of May 2012

[1218] Leon Degrelle, Hitler: Born at Versailles, Volume 1, of the Hitler Century, Institute for Historical Review, Torrance, California, 1992, pp. 133-141

[1219] Dieter Schwarz, Freemasonry, Ideology, Organization and Policy, Central Publishing House of the NSDAP, Berlin, 1944, p. 32

physical evidence, the sinister story, traveled throughout the world and contributed to America's entry into the war. Following Germany's defeat, the allies could not find even one mutilated child who had experienced maiming by the Germans. [1220]

Britain did not have an official propaganda program at the beginning of the war, as it was theoretically antithetical to British values. In 1917, they established the Department of Information and on February 10, 1918, they created the Ministry of Information, headed by William M. Aitken. By the war's end, Britain had a highly developed propaganda apparatus, superior to any of their opponents. Their press played an integral role in the diffusion of misinformation before, during and after the war. Reuters was a key component of Britain's media operations, especially in the overseas distribution of propaganda masquerading as news. [1221] H. G. Wells, a key spokesman of internationalism, intended to demoralize society by destroying the concept of God. An intelligence agent, he insisted that the elite should kill "the less worthy." During the war, he directed the propaganda operation of the British intelligence service and advised the British on the creation of military equipment in both world wars. [1222]

Newton D. Baker, Jr., Cleveland's former mayor, was Secretary of War (1916-1921) under President Woodrow Wilson. On June 9, 1916, evidently anticipating the United States entry into the war, Baker instituted the military draft and created the Bureau of Information headed by Major Douglas MacArthur. This agency was the only source from which the press could obtain any war-related news. On August 11, 1916, Baker sent the draft of a law sanctioning extensive censorship to Edwin Y. Webb, chairman of the House Judiciary Committee. Before the Declaration of war on April 2, 1917, Congress

[1220] Leon Degrelle, Hitler: Born at Versailles, Volume 1, of the Hitler Century, Institute for Historical Review, Torrance, California, 1992, pp. 133-141

[1221] Peter Putnis and Kerry McCallum, The Role of Reuters in the Distribution of Propaganda News in Australia During World War I, a Paper presented to the Australian Media Traditions Conference November 24-25, 2005 Canberra, University of Canberra

[1222] Jüri Lina, Architects of Deception, Referent Publishing, Stockholm, Sweden, 2004, pp. 338-339

initiated censorship policies, to ensure intelligence security, and the War Department manipulated the media, throughout the war. [1223]

On April 13, 1917, Wilson, the so-called peace candidate, as directed by Colonel House, created the Committee on Public Information (CPI) to acquire support for the war. He appointed publisher George Creel as its director. He had a staff of persuasive wordsmiths, journalists, writers, intellectuals and advertisers, who later admitted they were quite willing to lie, use emotional appeal and enemy demonization to generate hate and fear to elicit support for the government's war. [1224] They used popular phrases like, "Bleeding Belgium," "The Criminal Kaiser," and the always-useful slogan, "Make the World Safe for Democracy." They filled propaganda posters and CPI pamphlets with fictitious atrocity stories, which proved useful in recruiting troops. [1225] Howard Lasswell said, "If at first they do not enrage, use an atrocity. It has been employed with unvarying success in every conflict known to man . . . Unlike the pacifist, who argues that all wars are brutal, the atrocity story implies that war is only brutal when practiced by the enemy." [1226]

The CPI staff distributed 6,000 "news releases," emotionally charged propaganda, disguised as "news." It was so successful that the majority of citizens responded with inordinately self-righteous nationalistic enthusiasm, the kind of nationalism that avoids self-evaluation while glaring at government-targeted "evil-doers." [1227]

Austrian-born Edward Bernays, master manipulator, headed the CPI's Export Section and co-headed the Latin American Section of the Foreign Press Bureau. Bernays, a close friend of H. G. Wells and

---

[1223] James R. Mock, Censorship, 1917, Princeton University Press, Publication, New Jersey, 1941, p. 42

[1224] Wartime Propaganda, World War I, "The War To End All Wars, http://www.100megspop3.com/bark/Propaganda.html as of May 2012

[1225] Ibid

[1226] War Propaganda: World War I, Demons, atrocities, and lies, http://www.propagandacritic.com/articles/ww1.demons.html as of May 2012

[1227] Shawn J. Parry-Giles, The Rhetorical Presidency, Propaganda, and the Cold War, 1945-1955, Praeger Series in Presidential Studies, 2002, Introduction

Sigmund Freud's nephew, employed his uncle's views on behavior to manage people in the marketplace. Freud, a member of B'nai B'rith, when working on his psychoanalysis theory (1880-1890), used cocaine daily and freely gave it to his friends. [1228] Bernays, the "Father of Public Relations," contacted Ford, International Harvester and other US firms in order to distribute pro-war literature to foreign contacts. He concocted atrocity stories in Germany to engender dissent and affect morale. He organized rallies and printed propaganda in other languages for insertion into export journals. His tenacious persuasion skills changed America's views toward a very unpopular war. [1229]

Bernays said, "If we understand the mechanisms and motives of the group mind, it is now possible to control and regiment the masses according to our will without their knowing it . . . . Those who manipulate this unseen mechanism of society constitute an invisible government, which is the true ruling power of our country . . . . It is they who pull the wires which control the public mind." [1230] He apparently agreed with Benjamin Disraeli's *Coningsby* because he wrote, "We are governed, our minds are molded, our tastes formed, our ideas suggested, largely by men we have never heard of. This is a logical result of the way in which our democratic society is organized." [1231] To give the right spin on the war, a CPI press team, including Bernays, attended the Paris Peace Conference. In 1920, Creel wrote *How We Advertised America,* in which he described how "he and his committee used the principles of advertising to convince Americans to go to war with Germany." [1232]

[1228] Jüri Lina, Architects of Deception, Reverent Publishers, Stockholm, Sweden, 2004, pp. 22-23

[1229] Larry Tye, The Father of Spin, Edward L. Bernays and the Birth of Public Relations, pp. 15-20

[1230] Larry Tye, The Father of Spin: Edward L. Bernays & The Birth of PR, PR Watch, Second Quarter 1999, Volume 6, No. 2

[1231] Edward Bernays, Propaganda, Ig Publishing, Brooklyn, New York, 1928, p. 37

[1232] Anthony Pratkanis and Elliot Aronson, Age of Propaganda, the Everyday Use and Abuse of Persuasion, University of California, Henry Holt and Co., New York, 1992, pp. 9-10

Hollywood director, Rupert Julian, associated with Universal Studios, founded in 1912 by Carl Laemmle, made a propaganda film *The Kaiser, the Beast of Berlin,* which proved to be extremely popular. Other hate pieces from Hollywood include *To Hell with the Kaiser,* directed by George Irving, and *Wolves of Kultur,* directed by Joseph A. Golden, both produced in early 1918. One propagandist of the time typified the average German in Hollywood movies as "the hideous Hun," a sadistic rapist of pre-teen girls. Hollywood portrayed the Germans in the same way that atheist Ilya Ehrenburg, the Soviet Minister of Propaganda, would in the next war when he told the Russian soldiers, "The Germans are not human beings."

We usually assign a later date to formalized mind management. However, from John Robison's 1798 exposé, certain people determined, early on, to shape general perceptions through deceptive propaganda. Someone had given Robison a copy of the Illuminati conspiracy defining its so-called beneficial dictatorial objectives. [1233] In 1922, Walter Lippmann, an ardent disciple of H. G. Wells, [1234] argued that the "so-called omni competent citizen making rational, objective judgments based simply on facts is a myth . . . A democratic polity demands definers, people who give shape to our feelings and impressions, people who give meanings for our facts." [1235]

Obviously, there were occasional Germans who committed unnecessary acts of violence. Just as the French, the Belgians, the British, and the Americans engaged in war crimes. Actually, the Allies committed more war crimes, and on a greater scale than the defeated Germans. However, the victors write the history, seize the glory, medals, and they collect the pensions. They attribute the most

---

[1233] Myron C. Fagan, The Illuminati and The Council on Foreign Relations One-World-Government Conspiracy and the Protocols of the Learned Elders of Zion, p. 12, http://jahtruth.net/illumin.htm#Protocols%20Proof as of May 2012

[1234] Dr. John Coleman, Conspirator's Hierarchy, the Committee of 300, World in Review, Carson City, Nevada, 1991, p. 166

[1235] Stig Förster and Jorg Nagler (editors), On the Road to Total War: The American Civil War and the German Wars of Unification, 1861-1871, German Historical Institute 1997, Cambridge University Press, New York, 2002, pp. 357-359

horrendous acts to the defeated nations. Decades after World War I, the Allies repeat the accusations of mutilation of children, civilian massacres, and the apple orchard destruction. These acts pale in comparison to the later terrorist bombings of Hamburg, Dresden, and dozens of other German cities, in addition to Tokyo, and the atomic bombings of Hiroshima and Nagasaki after Japan offered to surrender. [1236]

The Allies' propaganda was so flagrant as to be wholly unbelievable under normal conditions but in wartime, even reasonable men accepted the falsehoods. Millions of naïve individuals fell for the deceptions and felt utter contempt and outrage. Children heard their parents discussing "the terrible Germans" which influenced them. It seemed that everyone believed that Germany was responsible for World War I, which made it easier to believe that they caused World War II. The media characterized the real warmongers as peace-loving heroes merely responding to the aggressive, savage Germans. The deceptive propaganda was so pervasive that naïve people simply accepted it. Because of popular perceptions, people thought Germans were totally evil and capable of any despicable act. History books in most nations repeat the atrocity stories. During and after World War II, people readily accepted lies because of the foundation cemented in the Great War. People, conditioned by false history, expected them to behave like murdering brutes. [1237]

Belgian Relief, a Platform for War, Profits and Position

In early 1914, Mansfield Smith-Cumming, the director of the Secret Intelligence Service (MI6), created in 1909, as a joint initiative of the Admiralty and the War Office, sent Sir William Wiseman, a future partner (1929-1960) of Kuhn, Loeb & Company to America to establish a branch. He enjoyed any-time access to Edward M. House, Wilson's handler, and to President Wilson himself. House and Wiseman correlated British and US intelligence operations before

---

[1236] Leon Degrelle, Hitler: Born at Versailles, Volume 1, of the Hitler Century, Institute for Historical Review, Torrance, California, 1992, pp. 133-141
[1237] Ibid. 133-141

and during the war. [1238] Max Warburg, Paul's brother, directed the German espionage system. Jacob H. Schiff's two brothers financed the war efforts in Germany. The bankers wanted to delay warfare until their agents could create America's central bank, the Federal Reserve, in order to guarantee a permanent, healthy fiscal return for financing continuous warfare thereafter.

Armies need food as much, or maybe even more, than they need ammunition. Germany had a bumper grain crop in 1914, but the nation had 67,000,000 people to feed which necessitated the importation of at least one-fifth of all of their food during normal times, requiring access to available ports. England, using one of its usual population-starving strategies, blockaded all of those ports. British warmongers anticipated that Germany would go through neutral Belgium to attack France. On August 3-4, 1914, German troops did just that. British oligarchs, like David Lloyd George, expressed pious indignation. German soldiers lived off the land while they occupied Belgium. They rationed Belgian citizens and shipped the nation's produce to Germany. [1239] Belgium was a rich agricultural country that produced far more than her citizens consumed.

On August 28, 1914, the Commission for Relief in Belgium (CRB), a private unincorporated, organization that was unaccountable to anyone, created the Brussels Relief Committee. Emile Francqui, the commission chairman, was the director of the Société Générale de Belgique, a private banking firm. On September 1, 1914, Francqui met with Brand Whitlock, US Minister, and Marquis de Villalobar, the Minister from Spain, the to seek their support. Francqui sent Millard K. Shaler, an American engineer residing in Brussels, to London as a representative of the Comité Central. He arrived in London on September 26, 1914. Shaler described the functions of the Comité Central to Edgar Rickard, who introduced Shaler to Herbert Hoover, just back from the Congo. Hoover, Rickard, John B.

[1238] Roger Z. George and Robert D. Kline, Intelligence and the National Security Strategist: Enduring Issues and Challenges, Rowman & Littlefield, Lanham, Maryland, 2006, p. 432
[1239] John Hamill, The Strange Career of Mr. Hoover Under Two Flags, William Faro, Inc., New York, 1931, pp. 309-310

White, Clarence Graff, Colonel Millard Hunsiker, and others were then directing the American Relief Committee in London, with the support of US Ambassador Walter H. Page. [1240]

Francqui arranged for the Belgium government to advance him $500,000 from the British Relief Fund, then under its direction. British officials gave him another $500,000 and the Belgium banks in London gave him $600,000 for Shaler to buy food in London. Shaler purchased food but still needed permission from the Foreign Office to bypass England's blockade. [1241]

On October 1, 1914, Hugh Gibson, the Secretary of the American Legation in Brussels, arrived in London and joined Shaler in convincing the British to allow food exportation. The US Ambassador in London would ship the supplies to the US Minister in Brussels. On that day, Page and Hoover drafted a memo to the State Department, requesting the protection of the supplies as the British required it before issuing an export permit. Additionally, Hoover asked that those working for refugee relief in America direct their efforts to Belgian relief. On October 12, they formed an American Committee to facilitate that relief work. The very next day, Hoover, using the press, appealed to Americans. He asked Minister Whitlock to reinforce his appeal by speaking with President Wilson. [1242]

Francqui presided over the National Relief and Food Committee, and held total executive control. The British government agreed to export foods, but required a letter, dated October 16, 1914, from General Rüdiger von der Goltz, head of the German infantry in France, insuring that the Germans would not *requisition* food brought

---

[1240] George I. Gay, Public Relations of the Commission for Relief in Belgium Documents, Commission for Relief in Belgium with the collaboration of H. H. Fisher, Stanford University, Stanford University Press, California, 1929,

[1241] John Bach McMaster, The United States in the World War, D. Appleton, New York, 1918, pp. 44-45

[1242] George I. Gay, Public Relations of the Commission for Relief in Belgium Documents, Commission for Relief in Belgium with the collaboration of H. H. Fisher, Stanford University, Stanford University Press, California, 1929, http://net.lib.byu.edu/estu/wwi/comment/CRB/CRB1-TC.htm as of May 2012

into Belgium. They also agreed to work with Francqui's bank to prevent financial losses, as Francqui, seeking profit, did not want any losses. On October 17, 1914, Hugh Gibson and Francqui, with the required authorization, left for London accompanied by Baron Léon Lambert, a Rothschild relative by marriage, who headed their Belgian operations. With obvious Rothschild influence, Prime Minister Herbert H. Asquith quickly granted permission for the humanitarian venture. [1243]

On October 22, 1914, they formally organized, according to Hoover's guidelines, and under American leadership, the Comité Central which followed the recommendations of the Commission for Relief in Belgium. Francqui and Lambert returned to Brussels in early November and created the Comité National de Secours et d'Alimentation with the necessary organizational changes and responsibilities. [1244]

Herbert Hoover, one of the Rothschild's longtime agents, was the Director of the Belgian Relief Committee (BRC). The only Belgians he knew were those he had associated with during his slave trading ventures in the Belgian Congo. [1245] He had resided in Britain for at least thirteen years, and he knew Walter H. Page. On October 31, 1914, Hoover sent an appeal to the United States from King Albert of Belgium asking for aid for the BRC. He soon received donations of food and other essentials, the majority of which the BRC sent to Germany, via the Rothschild rail lines. [1246] Soon, Senator Elihu Root became the honorary president of the Committee of Mercy, with August Belmont Jr., as Treasurer. Jacob H. Schiff was the Chairman

[1243] John Hamill, The Strange Career of Mr. Hoover Under Two Flags, William Faro, Inc., New York, 1931, pp. 310-311
[1244] George I. Gay, Public Relations of the Commission for Relief in Belgium Documents, Commission for Relief in Belgium with the collaboration of H. H. Fisher, Stanford University, Stanford University Press, California, 1929, http://net.lib.byu.edu/estu/wwi/comment/CRB/CRB1-TC.htm As of May 2012
[1245] John Hamill, The Strange Career of Mr. Hoover Under Two Flags, William Faro, Inc., New York, 1931, pp. 307-309
[1246] Eustace Mullins, The Secrets of the Federal Reserve, the London Connection, John McLaughlin, 1993, pp. 122-123

of the New York branch of the Red Cross. Both groups worked with
the BRC. [1247]

The BRC sent food from England to Belgium where they offered to
sell it but the Belgians had sufficient food. The German occupiers
purchased it, and per their agreement, they paid Francqui top price for
it. On February 22, 1915, Sir Edward Grey, Britain's Foreign Minister,
notified Hoover that Britain reneged on its offer to participate with
the BRC, in as much as the British discovered that the Germans
received some of that food. Hoover responded with a press release on
February 24, 1915, referring to the destitute in Belgium, the "wards
of the world. In as much as the BRC had failed to sustain government
help, only charity, said Hoover, would assuage their abject misery.
It was a blatant lie, as Belgium had reserved $5,000,000 a month
for relief for its citizens. By October 1915, the government would
increase the amount to $7,500,000. [1248]

By March 1915, Germany, short of money, energy, and food, attempted
to declare peace. However, absent Germany's participation, Britain's
ambition to control oil, and exercise power in the Middle East
following a certain victory at the war's end would not materialize.
Britain had to crush Germany, so that Germany's ally, the Ottoman
Empire would fall. Politicians planned to bring America into the war
to subtly transfer its gold to Europe. Paul Warburg, Vice Governor
of the Federal Reserve, rescued Germany monetarily, with credit
arranged through his brother, Max Warburg, director of M. M.
Warburg and Company. To resolve Germany's food problem and
continue the war, they would resort to greater assistance from the
banker-financed a front group, the profit-producing Belgium Relief
Commission (BRC). [1249]

[1247] Duchess Will Tell Needs of England; Former Consuelo Vanderbilt to Act for
the Committee of Mercy in Britain. Red Cross Fund $180,645 Jacob H. Schiff
Acknowledges Gifts of $1,770 Received Yesterday—Belgian Fund $79,034,
The New York Times, October 1, 1914, p. 6
[1248] John Hamill, The Strange Career of Mr. Hoover Under Two Flags, William
Faro, Inc., New York, 1931, pp. 325-326, 341
[1249] Ibid. 309-310

The German newspaper, *Nordeutsche Allgemeine Zeitung*, of March 4, 1915, reported the quantities of food arriving from Belgium, and applauded the German authority's efforts there for solving the food shortages through their relationship with the United States. Further, the newspaper reported, "The German government was therefore glad to help in obtaining provisions from neutral countries of the needy inhabitants in order to save German home supplies, and insure its own troops against going short." [1250] *Schmollers Yearbook for Legislation*, for 1916, reported the amounts of food shipped to Germany, just during the first four months of the war—963,600,000 pounds of meat, 1,445,400,000 pounds each of potatoes and bread, 400,000 tons of flour, and 121,000,000 pounds of butter, and other fats, and 1,000,000 tons of other provisions. Hoover's BRC shipped about 600,000 tons of US grain into Belgium, sustaining the German occupiers, and keeping them fighting. [1251]

A few months into the war, German officials offered to transport all English doctors and nurses who wanted to leave Belgium, back to England. Edith L. Cavell, the matron of the nursing school L'École Belge d'Infirmières Diplômées in Brussels remained in Belgium. On April 15, 1915, having missed the attention of the censor, London's *Nursing Mirror* published Cavell's article, criticizing the BRC's scheme. The Germans did not view her as a threat and simply ignored her. However, Ambassador Page and British Intelligence demanded that the Germans arrest her as a spy. [1252] On August 5, 1915, they arrested her [1253] and her assistant, who they later released. They incarcerated Cavell at St. Giles. [1254]

[1250] Ibid. 307-308
[1251] Ibid. 329-330
[1252] Ibid. 330-331
[1253] Francis Whiting Halsey, The Literary Digest History of the World War: Compiled from Original and Contemporary Sources American, British, French, German, and Others, Volume: 10, Funk & Wagnalls Company, New York, 1920, pp. 433-434
[1254] Gerald Herman, The Pivotal Conflict: A Comprehensive Chronology of the First World War, 1914-1919, Greenwood Press, New York, 1992, p. 155

Sir William Wiseman, a British Intelligence agent in New York since 1914, was the liaison between President Woodrow Wilson and the British government. The British agency demanded that the Germans execute Cavell in order to silence her. Accordingly, they falsely accused her of assisting approximately 200 Allied prisoners to escape to Holland and Britain from the hospital where she worked, usually punishable by three months' imprisonment. [1255]

Brand Whitlock and Hugh Gibson, were supposed to help British subjects who had difficulties, like Cavell. Whitlock made a few inquiries and the authorities informed him of her trial date, but he made no effort to intervene. [1256] Francqui's National Relief Committee offered to handle her defense. Francqui's committee appointed numerous lawyers who, for various reasons, failed to qualify as defense attorneys or lacked the authorization to plead a case before a German military tribunal. Finally, Sadi Kirschen took the case. Officials scheduled the trial and arranged interviews between Kirschen and Cavell, but he neglected to appear for the interviews and on the day of the trial, he was relaxing in the country. [1257] Despite international opposition and appeals from Baron Oscar von der Lancken, a firing squad executed Cavell on October 15, 1915. [1258]

While Germany had economically and militarily prepared for war, its military leaders apparently underestimated its length, and miscalculated the quantity of materials essential to fight a modern war. After Britain entered the war, Dr. Walther Rathenau, a top official in the Raw Materials Department of the War Ministry, in conjunction with the German War Office, revised their calculations

---

[1255] Eustace Mullins, The Secrets of the Federal Reserve, the London Connection, John McLaughlin, 1993, pp. 127-128

[1256] John Hamill, The Strange Career of Mr. Hoover Under Two Flags, William Faro, Inc., New York, 1931, pp. 331-332

[1257] Ibid. 332-333

[1258] Francis Whiting Halsey, The Literary Digest History of the World War: Compiled from Original and Contemporary Sources American, British, French, German, and Others, Volume: 10, Funk & Wagnalls Company, New York, 1920, pp. 433-434

for a longer war. Yet, as early as mid-1915, they experienced a munitions shortage. [1259]

Germany, the most industrialized country in Europe, depended on imported raw materials. The nation's prosperity emanated from the diligence and technical ability of its people, who utilized the imported raw materials to manufacture products. They relied on the importation of industrial raw materials and semi-manufactured items and imported fabrics, cotton, wool, silk, flax, hemp and jute. By the fall of 1915, due to war shortages, Germans were wearing clothing constructed from paper-woven fabrics and used clothing. They were able, through these alternatives, to clothe the army. Germany also suffered a shortage of leather, furs, and rubber, despite the claims that they had discovered artificial rubber. They lacked shoe and boot leather, an absolute necessity for the army, especially when fighting in the Flanders mud. Ultimately, the German War Office requisitioned church bells and other articles, public or domestic, to melt down for military use. [1260]

In December, 1915, Dr. Rathenau, stated, "On the fourth of August of last year, when England declared war, a terrible and unprecedented thing happened—*our country became a besieged fortress.*" Germany was isolated. On August 8, 1914, he had met with Colonel Heinrich Scheuch, the head of the War Department and explained to him that Germany, with limited materials, could only sustain a war for a few months. He asked him what measures they had taken *"to avert the danger of the throttling of Germany."* The Chief of the General Staff, Erich von Falkenhayn sent Rathenau a telegram inviting him to meet the next morning, during which they organized a department to procure sufficient raw materials. With this organization, Germany acquired the necessary supplies to execute the war, "at the expense of the civilian population," until December 1915. [1261]

[1259] Alfred Eckhard Zimmern, The Economic Weapon in the War Against Germany, Allen & Unwin Ltd., London, 1918, pp. 8-9
[1260] Alfred Eckhard Zimmern, The Economic Weapon in the War Against Germany, Allen & Unwin Ltd., London, 1918, pp. 9-11
[1261] Ibid. 3-7

During the war, Rathenau structured Germany's economic system in such a way as to make it feasible for Germany to continue fighting, despite declining resources. He based it on scarcity for the population in preference of supplies devoted to warfare. [1262] On December 25, 1913, Rathenau, referring to potential central African colonies, had said, "The opportunity for great German acquisitions has been missed. Woe to us that we took nothing and received nothing." [1263] He apparently had some imperialistic proclivities.

Regarding the BRC, Lewis L. Strauss of Kuhn, Loeb, Hoover's assistant managed the operation. Strauss was married to Alice Hanauer, daughter of Kuhn Loeb partner, Jerome J. Hanauer. Wiseman worked closely with Edward M. House who vowed to get the United States into the war ten months before the country reelected Wilson. The president had promised to keep America out of the war, yet he sanctioned our entry into the foreign war on March 9, 1916, while he was still campaigning. [1264]

On December 12, 1916, German officials approached US officials to see if President Wilson would persuade the Allies to meet together. Edward M. House ruled out the possibility of peace negotiations. [1265] On December 18, 1916, US Ambassador to Britain Walter H. Page relayed a peace offer from Germany, and the other Central Powers, to British officials. On January 9, 1917, Prime Minister David Lloyd George repudiated the offering and declared that

[1262] Carroll Quigley, Tragedy And Hope, A History of the World in our Time, The Macmillan Company, New York, 1966, pp. 61, 233

[1263] Fritz Fischer, World Power or Decline: The Controversy over Germany's Aims in the First World War, translated by Lancelot L. Farrar, Robert and Rita Kimber, W. W. Norton, New York, 1974, pp. 13-16

[1264] Eustace Mullins, The Secrets of the Federal Reserve, the London Connection, John McLaughlin, 1993, pp. 153-154

[1265] Leon Degrelle, Hitler: Born at Versailles, Volume 1, of the Hitler Century, Institute for Historical Review, Torrance, California, 1992, pp. 255-259

Britain would fight to the victory, which possibly prompted the Germans to re-initiate submarine warfare. Given Britain's collapsing financial situation, the United States should have remained neutral. America's promised entry into the war would allow Britain to avoid financial disaster and continue the war. [1266]

Winston Churchill had ignored every effort to avoid a war and refused to consider negotiating a quick end once it started. He obstinately opposed all of Germany's attempts to end the war. In 1916, David Lloyd George considered negotiations, but Churchill erupted in anger when he heard about Lloyd George's intentions. He argued, "Not to win decisively is to have all this misery over again after an uneasy truce and to fight it over again, probably under less favorable circumstances and, perhaps, alone." However, Germany wanted to compromise, especially after America had entered the conflict. Russia withdrew at the end of 1917. [1267]

Hoover, continuing the profitable food fraud, appealed to the governments of Britain and France for relief for Belgium, which actually needed no relief. It was, like now, a major shift of taxpayer funds, to well-connected scam artists. Britain granted £500,000 per month and France pledged 12,500,000 francs each month. French institutions also promised 25,000,000 francs per month, for the relief of the inhabitants in German-occupied Northern France. On June 1, 1917, the United States took responsibility for the contributions for the Belgian and Northern France relief efforts. The BRC received £89,500,000 from Britain and $66,000,000 from the French, for Belgium and $108,000,000 for use in the occupied territory. Private organizations and individuals in England donated $16,000,000 in cash and clothing. US citizens donated $11,500,000 while donations from the rest of the world totaled $3,000,000. On June 1, 1917, the United States loaned $75,000,000, payable in six monthly installments

---

[1266] John Cornelius, The Hidden History of the Balfour Declaration, Washington Report on Middle East Affairs, November 2005, pages 44-50
[1267] Tuvia Ben-Moshe, Churchill, Strategy and History, Lynne Rienner, Boulder, Colorado, 1992, pp. 71-72

of $12,500,000, of which $7,500,000 was to go to Belgium, and $5,000,000 to France. [1268]

Hoover and Francqui, both Rothschild front men, designed the BRC as a profitable commercial endeavor to enrich themselves. This sham kept the war going for two additional years, which enriched the banks that funded the war. By then, America had entered the war. [1269] This was very significant in that the United States had abandoned any semblance of isolationism and came to Britain's rescue. Britain, now economically drained, passed the warfare baton to the United States, the banker's new global enforcer for confiscating and controlling the world's resources.

Justice Louis D. Brandeis, a friend of Paul M. Warburg, Colonel House, Lord Arthur J. Balfour, Louis Marshall, and Baron Edmond de Rothschild, lauded praise on Hoover. In early February 1917, Brandeis had arranged for Senator William G. McAdoo, Wilson's son-in-law, to help to secure Hoover's appointment as US Food Administrator. [1270] After America entered the war, Wilson issued Executive Order 2679-A, on August 10, 1917, to create the US Food Administration, operational in each state, actually part of the elaborate government expansion. Hoover became the agency's administrator, the food dictator. [1271]

Meanwhile in Germany, Dr. Heinrich Pudor, of Leipzig, an economist, inventoried the supplies of iron ore, copper, wolfram, and nickel in the Raw Materials Department. He wrote an article, in the July-August, 1917 issue of *Weltwirtschaft,* a publication of the German Association for Promoting Foreign Trade. He wrote, "We must face

---

[1268] John Bach McMaster, The United States in the World War, D. Appleton, New York, 1918, p. 50

[1269] John Hamill, The Strange Career of Mr. Hoover Under Two Flags, William Faro, Inc., New York, 1931, pp. 314-315

[1270] Eustace Mullins, The World Order A Study in the Hegemony of Parasitism, Ezra Pound Institute of Civilization, Staunton, Virginia, 1985, p. 222

[1271] The National Archives, Teaching With Documents: Sow the Seeds of Victory! Posters from the Food Administration During World War I, http://www. archives.gov/education/lessons/sow-seeds/ as of May 2012

the fact that our apprehensions about (the) shortage of raw material are well founded, both as regards our manufactures and our military requirements. We must realize that we are now living not only on the remains of our stocks of raw material, but even in large part on shoddy or resurrected materials ; neither of these sources of supply can last forever, and both will be practically exhausted at the end of the war." Essentially, at war's end, Germany's cupboard would be bare. Her military authorities were eager for peace. [1272]

Although Germany conquered Belgium, Poland, Serbia, Lithuania, Courland and Friuli, the Allies held a stronger economic weapon, as they controlled cotton, wool, jute, leather, copper, and food. German diplomats recognized that the Allies, including the United States, with their control of the sea and a ready supply of goods, maintained economic leverage. The Allie's powerful economic weapon ultimately made them victorious. During war and peace, those who control the resources and the finances, control everything else, including who wins and who loses, deciding factors in every war before any soldier fires the first shot. [1273]

On November 13, 1918, Hoover asked President Wilson to appoint his associate, Edgar Rickard, to function in his place while Hoover was in Europe, for the beginning of the Paris Peace Conference. [1274] Per the president's Executive Order, officials divided the US Food Administration into four factions—the Sugar Equalization Board, Belgian Relief, the US Grain Corporation, and the US Shipping Board. On December 16, 1918, Wilson directed the State Department to the US Food Administration's Grain Corp. $5 million from his fund for National Security and Defense. [1275] Hoover insisted on directing the agency without oversight. He had Lewis L. Strauss, and two assistants, Prentiss N. Gray, and Julius H. Barnes, President of the Grain Corporation (1917-1918). Gray had collaborated with Hoover

---

[1272] Alfred Eckhard Zimmern, The Economic Weapon in the War Against Germany, Allen & Unwin Ltd., London, 1918, pp. 3-7

[1273] Ibid. 20

[1274] Eustace Mullins, The World Order A Study in the Hegemony of Parasitism, Ezra Pound Institute of Civilization, Staunton, Virginia, 1985, p. 221

[1275] Ibid. 221-222

in the BRC swindle, which he adopted as a food relief model. [1276]
Gray would become the president of J. Henry Schröder Banking in
New York in 1923. Sullivan and Cromwell, where the Dulles brothers
worked, represented Schröder. Barnes also had a post-war position
with the bank. They both amassed huge fortunes, principally in grain
and sugar. [1277]

Hoover told Americans to, "Go back to simple food, simple clothes,
simple pleasures. Pray hard, work hard, sleep hard and play hard. Do
it all courageously and cheerfully." The Lever Act, enacted August
10, 1917, authorized him to regulate the distribution, export, import,
purchase, and storage of food. He called for patriotism and self-
sacrifice. He set wheat prices, bought and distributed wheat, and
supervised the federal corporations, and national trade associations.
The Council of Defense exhorted all homeowners to sign pledge
cards to verify their efforts to conserve food. [1278] Personal sacrifice
psychologically binds people to the cause they are making the
sacrifices for; in this case the government and its war.

The Belgian National Committee reported that as of December 31,
1918, the BRC had spent $260 million. During a 1921 audit, there
was a $182 million discrepancy between the amount collected and
the amount expended. Francqui revised the figure. In December 1918,
after the war, he submitted expenditures of $40 million. On January
13, 1932, *The New York Times* revealed the extensive attacks made
against Hoover in the Belgian media; it accused him of being part
of the BRC scheme to make huge wartime profits. [1279] Barnes, Gray,
and Hoover invested "their" funds in numerous US corporations.
Gray had connections to the Prudential Investors, and International

[1276] The National Archives, Teaching With Documents: Sow the Seeds of Victory!
Posters from the Food Administration During World War I, http://www.
archives.gov/education/lessons/sow-seeds/ as of May 2012

[1277] Eustace Mullins, The Secrets of the Federal Reserve, the London Connection,
John McLaughlin, 1993, pp. 128-129

[1278] The National Archives, Teaching With Documents: Sow the Seeds of Victory!
Posters from the Food Administration During World War I, http://www.
archives.gov/education/lessons/sow-seeds/ as of May 2012

[1279] Eustace Mullins, The World Order A Study in the Hegemony of Parasitism,
Ezra Pound Institute of Civilization, Staunton, Virginia, 1985, p. 221

Holdings and Investment Corporation, two companies that Francqui's Société Générale de Belgique controlled. [1280]

Hoover suggested that the United States offer $100 million in aid to post-war Europe. On January 21, 1919, *The New York Times* reported that some Senators were critical of his scheme to dump surplus foodstuffs in Europe. They speculated about his US citizenship and asked whether he had even registered or voted in an election. He had never paid taxes or taken an oath of office. He was so annoyed over the criticism that he threatened to resign from his political position. [1281]

In April 1919, Gray organized the P. N. Gray Company. Mr. M. E. Bunge, head of Belgium's largest grain firm, and Carolus Falk, a former Bunge manager joined his firm. Alexander Hempbill, board Chairman of the Guarantee Trust Company, also allied with Gray. After he started his company, the Guarantee Trust Company, he created a syndicate with National City Bank, the National Bank of Commerce, and J. Pierpont Morgan. It gave the Belgium government a credit of $50,000,000, perhaps an attempt to silence its criticism of Hoover. Gray contracted with Belgium officials to purchase post-war supplies, which he shipped to them via the US Shipping Board, for bargain basement prices. [1282]

Hoover probably invested several million dollars in international banking concerns, which had major holdings in public utility stocks in the United States and abroad. [1283] In December 7, 1919, he and Barnes purchased the *Washington Herald,* later acquired by the Patterson-McCormick family. Eugene I. Meyer, Bernard Baruch's partner, then purchased the newspaper. Barnes bought the Penobscot Paper Company for $750,000 in 1919. [1284]

[1280] Ibid. 222-223

[1281] Ibid. 222

[1282] Walter W. Liggett, The Rise of Herbert Hoover, The H. K. Fly Company Publishers, New York, 1931, pp. 379-381

[1283] Ibid. 379-381

[1284] Eustace Mullins, The World Order A Study in the Hegemony of Parasitism, Ezra Pound Institute of Civilization, Staunton, Virginia, 1985, pp. 224-225

Some researchers maintain that freemasons instigated World War I, causing millions of deaths, while 20,000,000 soldiers received serious wounds and 3,000,000 were permanently disabled. In addition to the deaths, disease, and disabilities, the war cost $100 million a day. The freemasons, along with the profit seekers, Hoover and others, sold food to Germany, just to prolong the war, at a time when Germany attempted to halt the war due to its inability to feed the nation. [1285]

Ethnic Dissension and Polarization

Establishment historians elaborate on the massacres of Bulgarians, Armenians, and Greeks but typically ignore the massacres, and forced exile of Muslims. Western writers disregard the history, the misery, and the pain of the Balkan, Caucasian, and Anatolian Muslim populations. [1286]

During the nineteenth century, the Bulgarians revolted against the Ottoman government, and by the time of the Russo-Turkish War, April 24, 1877-March 3, 1878, they, with Russia's help, gained their freedom. Before the war, those revolutionaries began slaughtering Bulgarian Muslims. On May 2, 1876, while the Ottoman military was busily engaged in putting down an uprising in Bosnia, they exploited the opportunity to wage a revolution in several towns in central Bulgaria, never anticipating the possibility of Turkish retaliations afterwards. For the ethnic Bulgarians, it was always essentially genocide against the Muslims. [1287]

The minority Ottoman Armenians, most of them Christians, lived in the Six Provinces, called Ottoman Armenia, composed of seventeen percent Armenian and seventy-eight percent Muslim. Russia intended to seize that northern area, after their success during the Russo-

[1285] Jüri Lina, Architects of Deception, Referent Publishing, Stockholm, Sweden, 2004, pp. 341-342
[1286] Justin McCarthy, Death and Exile: The Ethnic Cleansing of Ottoman Muslims, 1821-1922, Darwin Press, Princeton, New Jersey, 1995, p. 2
[1287] Ibid. 59-60

Turkish War. [1288] The war ended with the signing of the Treaty of San Stefano, a document that Russian officials viewed as a rough draft. However, that treaty served as a warning to the Ottomans that the Western powers were concerned about the conditions of the Armenians, the beginning of the politicized *Armenian Question*, which evolved around the issue of whether they would become an independent nation. [1289] An independent Armenian state inevitably meant the deportation of the Muslims. [1290]

After England accepted Bismarck's invitation to the Congress of Berlin, June 13-July 13, 1878, Russia followed suit. Rather than face a possible Anglo-Austrian coalition, the czar acquiesced to British concessions and consented to discuss the Treaty of San Stefano, and renounced a partition between the Serbian states, and agreed to allow the congress to determine the question of Montenegrin access to the sea. The delegates, representing the European powers, Turkey, and all of the Balkan countries, ratified the Treaty of Berlin, and eliminated eighteen of the twenty-nine articles in the Treaty of San Stefano. The World Powers also delivered a fatal blow to the growing pan-Slavism movement, a trend that worried officials in Berlin and Vienna, who were concerned that the Slavic nationalities would rebel against the Habsburgs. Even before the conference, officials resolved the most critical issues. Russia yielded to the demands of Austria, and Britain, who disagreed with the original stipulations of the Treaty of San Stefano. [1291] [1292]

[1288] Dr. Justin McCarthy, Armenian Rebels—Effects & Consequences, a transcription of a speech given at the Turkish Grand National Assembly, March 24, 2005, http://www.tallarmeniantale.com/mccarthy-armenian-rebels.htm as of May 2012

[1289] Gábor Ágoston and Bruce Alan Masters, Encyclopedia of the Ottoman Empire, InfoBase Publishing, New York, 2009, pp. 52-53

[1290] Dr. Justin McCarthy, Armenian Rebels—Effects & Consequences, a transcription of a speech given at the Turkish Grand National Assembly, March 24, 2005, http://www.tallarmeniantale.com/mccarthy-armenian-rebels.htm as of May 2012

[1291] David MacKenzie, The Serbs and Russian Pan-Slavism, 1875-1878, Cornell University Press, Ithaca, New York, 1967, pp. 299-300

[1292] Gábor Ágoston and Bruce Alan Masters, Encyclopedia of the Ottoman Empire, InfoBase Publishing, New York, 2009, p. 29

Abdülhamid had, for a long time, regarded the Armenians as a threat, not the wealthy ones in Constantinople or Smyrna, but the peasant populations in the six provinces, who the Empire had reduced to poverty. In the late 1880s, the British foreign office sent Arminius Vámbéry (born Hermann Bamberger), a Hungarian Jew, to Turkey to discuss the Armenian question with the Sultan. He then reported the details of those conversations back to British officials. They found commonality in their hatred of Russia. Vámbéry began submitting reports about the Armenian's situation beginning in 1889. On October 22, 1889, he reported that when he raised the Armenian question, the Sultan blamed his pashas for the Armenian agitation, yet he failed to replace them. Abdülhamid told him, "Tell your English fiends, and particularly Lord Salisbury, for whom I have a great consideration, that I am ready to cure the evils in Armenia, but I will sooner allow to severe (sic) this head from my body than to permit the formation of a separate Armenia." [1293]

Vámbéry, who hated Russia, saw Armenian independence as an expansion of Russia, and that is how he presented it in his reports to the British, and their best interests. He presented Abdülhamid as a tyrant with regards to the Armenians, and the Russian danger, who still needed Britain's assistance. Since the Sasun incident, officials in Constantinople were understandably uneasy. Abdülhamid, according to a document of December 25, 1894, directed his subordinates to carry out actions against the Armenians. Adam Block, Chief Dragoman at the British embassy, in a confidential report, said that "The sultan has from the first known that a massacre of some kind took place in consequence of his orders, and hence his aversion to any inquiry." According to Block, Abdülhamid believed that widespread sedition existed among his Armenian subjects. [1294]

Armenian terrorists participated in political assassinations of dozens of Ottoman and Russian officials between 1860 and the beginning of World War I. They also occupied and threatened to blow up public buildings if the authorities failed to meet their demands. Armenian

---

[1293] Christopher J. Walker, Armenia, the Survival of a Nation, Routledge, London, 1980, pp. 145-146
[1294] Ibid. 145-148

terrorists, in August 1896, seized control of the Ottoman Bank in Beyoglu, Istanbul, took hostages, and made demands. Between 1904 and 1906, just in one area of the Ottoman Empire, Armenian terrorists assassinated 105 people, of whom 56 were Armenian informers. They killed 32 Russian and Turkish officials, and officers, and others for various reasons, political or otherwise. They assassinated two Armenian victims for every one non-Armenian. Terrorists frequently, even today, destroy their own people for intimidation purposes— to intimidate the majority of peaceful Armenians to remain silent regarding the activities of the terrorists. [1295]

Propagandists colored the Armenians as a persecuted minority attempting to exist. They always described them as poor, innocent, and martyred, yet they prospered in the Ottoman society because they controlled a large part of the economy. Lawless bands did victimize people, mostly the Kurds in Eastern Anatolia, and other areas where government officials had little control. The British and French, envisioning the resources of the economically prostate Ottoman Empire saw an opportunity to castigate the Turks and their purported Christian prejudices. Armenians, outsiders in the empire, participated in the cultural and economic assault. [1296]

Prior to the European politicization of the Armenian question, there were four distinct groups of Armenians—1) the rich Armenians in Constantinople or Smyrna who rarely interacted with their fellow nationals in Turkish Armenia. Then there were 2) the traders and artisans in the interior towns, 3) then the villagers and finally 4) the independent mountaineers who the Ottoman Empire and its tax-collectors largely ignored. They were the residents of Zeitun, Cilicia, and the inhabitants of about forty other Armenian villages. In Sasun,

---

[1295] Professor Heath W. Lowry, Nineteenth and Twentieth Century Armenian Terrorism: 'Threads of Continuity,' International terrorism and the drug connection: Armenian terrorism, its supporters, the narcotic connection, the distortion of history by Ankara University, The Press, Information and Public Relations Office, Ankara University, 1984, pp. 71-83, http://www.tallarmeniantale.com/lowry-threads-continuity.htm as of May 2012

[1296] The Black Hand of the Armenians, http://www.tallarmeniantale.com/black-hand.htm as of May 2012

the mountaineers paid tribute to local Kurdish beys (lords). By 1854, the Armenian minority in Turkish Armenia, probably numbering about 2,400,000, had intermingled with Kurds and Turks who outnumbered them. In 1882, the Armenian patriarchate of Constantinople said the total Armenian population in the empire was 2,660,000, of whom 1,630,000 lived in the provinces of Turkish Armenia. In 1912, he put the population of the empire at 2,100,000, the decrease due to massacre and the relocation of the Armenians to Russian Armenia. During most of the nineteenth century, the Armenians made up about one-third of the total population of Turkish Armenia, and were the largest minority in the area. [1297]

In the nineteenth and early twentieth centuries, while many Turks and Muslims were suffering at the hands of the Serbs, Russians, Bulgarians, and Greeks, Ottoman laws guaranteed equal rights to Jews and Christians who became very influential in numerous official positions. They had greater autonomy and freedom than the Muslims because Europeans demanded exclusivity for Christians. Following hundreds of years of peace, the Armenians, despite their abundant advantages, rebelled against the Ottoman Empire following the invasion of the Russians into the Caucasian Muslim lands during the Russo-Turkish War. [1298]

During that war, many Armenians favored the Russians and even functioned as spies and military forces for the Russians. They even had a base in Russia, where they could transfer men and guns into the Ottoman Empire. In 1828, the Russians had seized the Erivan Province, expelled the Turks, and repopulated the area, tax-free, to the friendlier Armenians. They expelled the Turks because they would have naturally opposed their conquerors. [1299] The Muslim deportees, from 1828, to the beginning of World War I, amounted to 300,000 Crimean Tatars, 1.2 million Circassians and Abkhazians, 40,000 Laz, and 70,000 Turks. At that time, there was an amicable closeness

---

[1297] Christopher J. Walker, Armenia, the Survival of a Nation, Routledge, London, 1980, pp. 94-97
[1298] Justin McCarthy, Death and Exile: The Ethnic Cleansing of Ottoman Muslims, 1821-1922, Darwin Press, Princeton, New Jersey, 1995, pp. 109-110
[1299] Ibid. 16-18

of Jews and Muslims in Ottoman Europe. [1300] When the Russians invaded Anatolia in 1877-78, many Armenians again sided with their invaders and became the intimidating and persecuting force in the Russian-occupied territories. The 1878 peace treaty relinquished a large portion of Northeastern Anatolia back to the Ottomans, causing many of the Armenians who had assisted the Russians to flee, fearing that the Turks would justifiably retaliate.

Armenians received free land, acquired prosperity, and protection because of the Russian invasions while the Muslims recognized that if the Russians invaded and triumphed again, they would lose their lands and their lives. They also knew that the Armenians would favor the Russians, as they had before. The Armenian rebels also exploited, threatened, and punished the common people. They compelled peasant farmers to become unwilling soldiers and forced them to purchase smuggled over-priced weapons from Russia. The rebels forced the young women, and girls in the villages, to submit to their demands, and murdered people who incurred their displeasure. The callous and uncaring rebels retaliated against resistant villagers by destroying property or farm animals. They attacked Kurdish villages and subjugated the poorest of their own people, while recognizing that the Kurdish tribes would retaliate against innocent Armenian villagers. Absent the influence of external Marxist forces, Armenians in Anatolia could have dwelled in relative harmony with the Turks and Kurds. The Dashnaks, the Armenian rebels, caused the unrest. The desperate Ottoman Government, feeling it had no options, was fully aware of the problem's foreign origin, but failed to oppose the rebels for a variety of reasons. A foreign country financially supported the rebels and helped to organize a rebellion that would allow the minority radicals to create a political environment wherein they would exclude the majority population from rule. [1301]

[1300] Ibid. 87-88

[1301] Dr. Justin McCarthy, Armenian Rebels—Effects & Consequences, a transcription of a speech given at the Turkish Grand National Assembly, March 24, 2005, http://www.tallarmeniantale.com/mccarthy-armenian-rebels.htm as of May 2012

Kurdish tribes had previously assaulted the Armenians living in southeastern Anatolia, along with other Kurds and Turks, and, as a result of their experience, the Armenians did not trust the Ottoman government, and abhorred the tribal Muslims. [1302] Around 1890, the Armenians hoping that Russia might rule them, began asking for the implementation of the protections promised them at the Congress of Berlin, especially in as much as they were now paying taxes. In 1891, Abdülhamid, fearful of Armenian nationalism, authorized the recruitment of an armed Kurdish militia, the Hamidiye, which aligned itself with Kurds. Then, they settled Muslim refugees, angered at their former Christian neighbors, into the eastern provinces, close to the minority Christians, creating a potentially volatile environment. [1303]

The Armenians viewed this militia suspiciously, not as a peace-keeping unit, and assumed that the government was against them. The Armenian radicals, at war with the State, had already murdered police chiefs and other officials. The Russian radicals, in the 1890s, began smuggling arms and dynamite across the borders. The debt-ridden Ottomans were poorly equipped for such armed infiltration, as they were still attempting to recuperate financially from the war with Russia. Predatory European bankers had stripped them of the essential resources to supply police and military units to counter anyone, including the Armenian rebels. [1304]

In 1893, hostilities erupted in Anatolia with skirmishes between armed Armenians and Muslims. Rumors abounded among the Muslims that the Armenians were going to rebel, causing the Kurdish militia to attack, kill, and plunder them. The Armenians retaliated by withholding their taxes, payable to the Kurds and the empire. The local governor, with Abdülhamid's approval, declared that the

---

[1302] Justin McCarthy, Death and Exile: The Ethnic Cleansing of Ottoman Muslims, 1821-1922, Darwin Press, Princeton, New Jersey, 1995, pp. 116-117

[1303] Gábor Ágoston and Bruce Alan Masters, Encyclopedia of the Ottoman Empire, InfoBase Publishing, New York, 2009, pp. 52-53

[1304] Dr. Justin McCarthy, Armenian Rebels—Effects & Consequences, a transcription of a speech given at the Turkish Grand National Assembly, March 24, 2005, http://www.tallarmeniantale.com/mccarthy-armenian-rebels.htm as of May 2012

Armenians were in a state of rebellion and authorized the Hamidiye to attack, resulting in a series of massacres (1894-1896), over which the Ottoman officials had little control, until Western authorities pressured them to use the Ottoman army to intervene. Tensions between the Kurds and the Armenians remained tense, although they had co-existed peacefully for many decades. [1305]

The Ottoman Empire's existence was at stake. The Europeans had already seized control in Serbia, Bosnia, Romania, Greece, and Bulgaria, and had almost apportioned the Empire in 1878. The Europeans feared that Russia would become too powerful. Top Armenian revolutionaries hoped that the Ottomans would retaliate against minor Armenian rebels so that European newspapers could accuse the Ottoman government of political discrimination against innocent people. The Muslims reacted to Armenian lawlessness by opportunistically killing them. Predictably, the European newspapers reported the murders, but remained silent about the slaughter of Muslims. Given this media influence, European citizens petitioned Britain and France to cooperate with Russian, to dismember the Ottoman Empire. Therefore, the Ottomans tried to conceal the pervasive criminality of these foreign rebels and curbed its punishment of them. If they had governed appropriately, foreign military forces would have destroyed their state. [1306] They were damned, no matter how they governed.

Because of the Treaty of May 10, 1830, and up until World War I, America claimed the right to send missionaries to the Ottoman Empire. Ottoman officials suspected them of circulating anti-Ottoman propaganda among the Ottoman Christians, which intensified during the nineteenth century. The Protestant Congregationalist and Presbyterian churches, through their American Board of Commissioners for Foreign Missions, sponsored most of the

---

[1305] Gábor Ágoston and Bruce Alan Masters, Encyclopedia of the Ottoman Empire, InfoBase Publishing, New York, 2009, pp. 52-53

[1306] Dr. Justin McCarthy, Armenian Rebels—Effects & Consequences, a transcription of a speech given at the Turkish Grand National Assembly, March 24, 2005, http://www.tallarmeniantale.com/mccarthy-armenian-rebels.htm as of May 2012

missionaries. That agency had missions in İzmir, Constantinople, Trabzon, Erzurum, Sivas, Diyarbakır, Adana, Gaziantep, Maras, Urfa and Van. By 1914, it had sponsored 151 missionaries, 1,204 Ottoman Christians, operated 137 churches, 8 colleges, 9 hospitals, 46 secondary schools and 369 elementary schools with an enrollment of 25,199 mostly Christian, and some Muslim students. [1307]

The organization's purpose was to promote American-style progress, economic development, and Christianity in the Ottoman Empire. Merchants joined the educators and missionaries to perpetuate US economic interests, such as the exportation of products Americans wanted, while securing a foreign source for natural materials. By 1914, the United States imported over $20 million from Turkey, while selling about $3 million to Turkey. Americans were mainly interested in oil and tobacco. Some American-based tobacco firms invested millions of dollars and owned warehouses in Constantinople and İzmir. Standard Oil sold oil to Turkey, while seeking oil drilling concessions there. US investors, like Admiral Colby Chester and his sons targeted mineral resources, and began negotiations, unsuccessfully, in 1909, for the right to build a railroad from Aleppo to Iskenderun, to exploit resources in eastern Anatolia. Following the war, under different circumstances, Admiral Chester, with the State Department's help, successfully negotiated a new project which included oil exploration. [1308] Warfare opens all kinds of economic opportunities.

Before World War I, the Turks and the Armenians had inhabited the same area for 800 years and the Armenians residing in Anatolia had been Ottoman subjects for almost 400 years without significant problems until outside interference created dissension and polarization. This ultimately led to the destruction of the empire, causing great suffering for the Turks and other Muslims. The Armenians, earlier proselyted by American missionaries, compared to others, advanced economically and educationally while living under Ottoman rule. This

---

[1307] John M. Vander Lippe, The Other Treaty of Lausanne: the American Public and Official Debate on Turkish-American Relations, The Turkish Yearbook, Volume 23, 1993, pp. 31-38

[1308] Ibid. 31-38

was due to the European merchants who chose Christian Armenians to function as their agents, while European consuls interceded in their behalf. [1309]

According to British sources, as early as 1913, in anticipation of a war, certain Armenian groups, meeting with the Russian authorities in Tiflis, organized their rebellious endeavors against the Ottomans. They had already abandoned whatever loyalties they may have had, and demonstrated their ready acceptance of a potential Russian occupation of the Armenian Vilayets. Dashnak leaders acknowledged their alliance to Russia, and, in 1910, distributed pamphlets throughout Eastern Anatolia with instructions on how villages should organize into regional commands in order to engage in guerilla warfare against adjacent Muslim villages. According to Ottoman intelligence, while the Dashnaks asserted their loyalty to the Ottoman State, they were instructing armed Armenian soldiers to desert to the Russians, if the Russians declared war. Russia distributed arms to the Armenians in the Caucasus and Iran as early as September 1914. [1310]

Russia had taken the fortress of Kars from the Turks during the Russo-Turkish War and the Ottomans wanted to recover their territories in the Armenian Highland, Artvin, Ardahan, Kars, and the port of Batum. During the Battle of Sarıkamış December 22, 1914 to January 17, 1915, then in Russian Armenia, the Turks lost 75,000 troops out of a total of 95,000. Instead of fighting for their country, the Armenians sided with the Russians. When war erupted, the Ottoman Army mobilized but Armenians from certain villages refused their conscription obligations or the call to enlist. Instead, more than 50,000 of them traveled east and joined the Russian military. Had the Armenians fought for their resident country, Russia might not have defeated Turkey at Sarıkamış. [1311]

[1309] Justin McCarthy, Death and Exile: The Ethnic Cleansing of Ottoman Muslims, 1821-1922, Darwin Press, Princeton, New Jersey, 1995, pp. 109-110

[1310] Dr. Justin McCarthy, Armenian Rebels—Effects & Consequences, a transcription of a speech given at the Turkish Grand National Assembly, March 24, 2005, http://www.tallarmeniantale.com/mccarthy-armenian-rebels.htm as of May 2012

[1311] Ibid

Tens of thousands of Armenians fled to the Greek islands, Egypt, or Cyprus to avoid military service in the Ottoman Empire. Those young Armenian men who did participate in the war fought on the side of the empire's enemies, instead of protecting their homeland. The Armenians who remained in Turkey functioned as the biggest threat to the Ottomans and their efforts to defend their state and the lives of the Muslims of Eastern Anatolia. [1312]

Armenian deserters formed groups to attack state officials and Muslims traveling on the roads. By December, they began burning Muslim villages, and slaughtering their inhabitants. Then, the Armenians attacked a military unit and killed 400 Ottoman soldiers. In February 1915, in another attack, 1,000 Armenians cut telegraph lines to the front and attacked supply convoys to the troops. On April 20, well-armed, uniformed Armenians seized the city of Van, drove Ottoman forces into the citadel, and torched much of the city. On May 17, the Ottomans evacuated the citadel while soldiers and civilians attempted to escape the city in boats on Lake Van, half of whom the Armenians killed. The fighting between the Muslims and the Armenians was vicious, and thousands perished. The Armenians fled to Russia when the Ottomans recaptured the area. Those who fled often starved or died from disease because when the Russians seized the Van and Bitlis Provinces, they prohibited the Armenians from returning because they wanted the land for themselves. The Armenians, who remained, especially in Erzurum Province, slaughtered the Muslims residing there, toward the end of the war. [1313]

The Ottoman Armenians rebelled in the areas that the Russians wanted, and exactly in the path of the Russian advance from the North including in Sivas Province and in Sebinkarahisar, an area where the Muslims outnumbered the Armenians by ten to one. The men, with their supplies, passed through this area along one particular road, making it easy for the Armenians to ambush the Ottoman supply route. They rebelled at the exact place that the British intended to invade, to cut the rail links southward, places that an experienced military

---

[1312] Ibid
[1313] Ibid

planner would have chosen to most effectively impair the Ottoman war effort. Due to these rebellions, the Ottomans withdrew their much needed troops from the Russian front, to fight the Armenian rebels. Had the Ottomans not been compelled to take these measures, the war in the east might have ended differently. [1314]

The Revolutionary Young Turks

In 1862, Giuseppe Mazzini, a proponent of Italian unification and a member of the Carbonari, sent agents to Russia to instigate chaos to create problems for the czar. Shortly thereafter, with the assistance of Young Poland, he organized a Young Ottoman movement in Paris. By 1876, after his death, these rebels emerged in Constantinople, a community that received the wealthy Maranos and Jewish exiles of Spain, Italy, and Portugal. [1315] The rebels paid off the British, initiated free trade, and brought in some Anglo-French bankers. Although another power toppled them, the movement emerged under the Young Turks, an alliance that would destroy the Ottoman Empire within seven years after it formally seized power. [1316]

In 1865, the Ottoman government granted the Jews of Constantinople the Constitution of the Jewish Nation. A İ akam Bashi (Chief Rabbi) governed the Jews of Constantinople, along with two assemblies, the Civic Communal Council, and the Spiritual Council, both elected for three years by an assembly of notables. [1317] In that same year, influenced by the Jacobean philosophy of the French Revolution, dissidents formed the Young Ottomans, a secret organization that

---

[1314] Dr. Justin McCarthy, Armenian Rebels—Effects & Consequences, a transcription of a speech given at the Turkish Grand National Assembly, March 24, 2005, http://www.tallarmeniantale.com/mccarthy-armenian-rebels.htm as of May 2012

[1315] Constantinople, The Jewish Encyclopedia, http://www.jewishencyclopedia.com/articles/4623-constantinople as of May 2012

[1316] Joseph Brewda, Palmerston launches Young Turks to permanently control Middle East, Schiller Institute/ICLC Conference, The Palmerston Zoo, Presidents Day, February 1994, http://www.schillerinstitute.org/conf-iclc/1990s/conf_feb_1994_brewda.html#brewda as of May 2012

[1317] Constantinople, The Jewish Encyclopedia, http://www.jewishencyclopedia.com/articles/4623-constantinople As of May 2012

began abroad. They backed a constitutional regime that opposed Abdülhamid II. Following that brief First Constitutional Era, from November 23, 1876-February 13, 1878, people referred to them as the Young Turks. [1318] The government banned the group's activities in 1867, yet it evolved into a strong force and developed some of the concepts associated with the First Constitutional Era, which ended when the sultan suspended the parliament, a month before the Russo-Turkish War. [1319]

In the summer of 1886, Avetis Nazarbekian's radical articles appeared in the journal *Armenia*, published in Marseille by Mekertitch Portugalian, a former teacher who inspired his students to found the first Armenian revolutionary party in Van in 1885. He left for France and established the Armenian Patriotic Union. [1320] Nazarbekian, a student at the St. Petersburg and Paris (Sorbonne) Universities, financed by his wealthy uncle, was engaged to Mariam Vardanian (Maro). As a student in St. Petersburg, she had joined a secret revolutionary band, and, due to her activities, fled to Paris where they met, and where she also met Lenin. During that summer of 1886, they went to Geneva. By summer's end, they, with four dissident Russian Armenian students, Gevorg Gharadjian, Christopher Ohanian, Ruben Khan-Azat, and Gabriel Kafian, decided to form a revolutionary organization headquartered in Geneva. Nazarbekian wrote a pamphlet, *Armenian Eating Chameleon*, which the group published and distributed. [1321] He also translated some of the works of Karl Marx, Friedrich Engels and Georgi Plekhanov.

Meanwhile, Portugalian's former students created the Armenakan Party, a small local group. The Geneva group intended to devise

---

[1318] Gábor Ágoston and Bruce Alan Masters, Encyclopedia of the Ottoman Empire, InfoBase Publishing, New York, 2009, pp. 605-606

[1319] Ibid. 52-53

[1320] Şerif Mardin, Religion and Social Change in Modern Turkey: the Case of Bediüzzaman Said Nursi, State University of New York Press, Albany, 1989, pp. 62-63

[1321] Louise Nalbandian, The Armenian Revolutionary Movement—The Development of Armenian Political Parties through the Nineteenth Century, University of California Press, Berkeley, Los Angeles, London, 1963, pp. 104-107

a powerful revolutionary party in Turkish Armenia, the Hunchak Party, with foreign branches. It acquired the funds to publish its own journal and circulars for mail distribution to potential Armenian revolutionaries and drafted a program for the first socialist party in Turkey and Persia. It promoted an ideological, humanitarian, socialistic society, a new order, absent inequalities, and where a small privileged minority did not exploit and oppress the impoverished majority. A revolution, according to them, was necessary in order to destroy the current system. The party advocated violent revolution in Turkish Armenia, and the destruction of the existing system as the way of obtaining its objectives. [1322]

Initially, the party, created in August 1887, wanted the political and national independence of Turkish Armenia. They felt that the Ottoman government, the aristocracy, and the parasitical capitalists exploited the acquiescent, silent masses by high taxes, land seizure, and the confiscation of the fruits of one's labor. Further, the people could not selectively worship. In order to save the enslaved Armenians, it wanted to shift the population to socialism with the promise of a popular Legislative Assembly, free elections, universal suffrage, and representatives from all classes of society, freedom of the press, of speech, of conscience, of public assembly, of organizations, universal military service, and a culture wherein people could feel secure in their homes. Additionally, the party would establish a progressive income tax and universal compulsory education. The party intended to implement propaganda, agitation, and terror to achieve its goals. [1323]

The Hunchak Party would use terror and the pretenses of protection in order to manipulate the people to trust its program. It would terrorize the Ottoman government to discredit it in the eyes of the masses to bring about its collapse. The Hunchaks wanted to destroy certain Armenian and Turkish politicians, and all spies, and informers. The party created a special group dedicated to executing its terrorist deeds. They would begin by gaining the support of the peasants and

---

[1322] Ibid. 108-112
[1323] Ibid. 108-112

workers, divided into two revolutionary factions. They planned to create guerrilla bands to fight during the projected revolution, best instituted at a time when Turkey was involved in a war. [1324]

The Hunchaks intended to gain the sympathy of non-Armenians and other minorities, like the Assyrians and Kurds, who might later assist in the revolution. They were not concerned about the Turks. The great powers politicized the conditions of the Armenians, the majority of who lived under Ottomans, and mandated reform in Article 61 of the Treaty of Berlin. The Hunchaks, seeking to impose a worldwide socialistic system, concluded that all dissident groups should first champion the independence of Turkish Armenia, as opposed to their own self-serving interests. It projected that, after the collapse of the bankrupt Ottoman regime, the European Powers would partition it for themselves. With solidarity, they might avoid having Turkish Armenia exchange one oppressive master for another. [1325]

The Hunchakian Revolutionary Party, part of the Second International, formalized in 1890, was both socialistic and nationalistic, and advocated the Marxian class struggle and sought the victory of the subjugated classes via revolution. Its economic program was pure Marxist. It adopted the same centralized administration as the Russian Narodnaya Volya (People's Will), as well as the use of propaganda, agitation, terror and the future use of guerrilla bands. Because the founders were either born or studied in Russia, the activities of the Narodnik also influenced them. The intellectually-gifted Mariam Vardanian (Maro), who devised the organizational structure, participated with the Jewish revolutionaries in St. Petersburg. [1326]

[1324] Ibid. 108-112
[1325] Louise Nalbandian, The Armenian Revolutionary Movement—The Development of Armenian Political Parties through the Nineteenth Century, University of California Press, Berkeley, Los Angeles, London, 1963, pp. 108-112
[1326] Louise Nalbandian, The Armenian Revolutionary Movement—The Development of Armenian Political Parties through the Nineteenth Century, University of California Press, Berkeley, Los Angeles, London, 1963, pp. 112-116

The Young Turks operated in Europe and British-ruled Egypt during Abdülhamid's reign and founded numerous political parties, committees, and leagues, in order to overthrow his regime and change it first to a constitutional monarchy, in order to later alter the entire political power structure. In 1889, the Young Turks established the Royal Medical Academy in Constantinople, called the Ottoman Union Committee. Mehmed Talaat (known as Talaat Bey) helped found a Masonic lodge, that he later called the Committee of Union and Progress (CUP). He was a friend of Ziya Gökalp, a freemason, and a well-known newspaper columnist, political figure, and a primary ideologue of the CUP. [1327]

In 1890, in Tiflis, Russia, Christapor Mikaelian, Stepan Zorian, and Simon Zavarian created the Armenian Revolutionary Federation (ARF), known as the Dashnaks, which gained significant strength and generated sympathy among Russian Armenians and the Russian government. With the advent of European nationalism, the Ottoman Armenians, backed by the two political groups, demanded equal rights, an end to discrimination, and their own autonomous state. [1328] Both groups, according to their manifestos, called for terrorist activities, including the assassination of Ottoman officials and Armenians who opposed them. Though Marxist, they used nationalism to accomplish their objectives. [1329]

On Sunday, July 15, 1890, the Hunchaks organized the Demonstration of Kum Kapu to call attention to the government's mistreatment of the Armenians. The Hunchaks compelled the unwilling Patriarch Khoren Ashegian to participate in their protests against Abdülhamid. Turkish forces blocked the demonstration and a riot erupted during which the soldiers killed a number of people and wounded many

---

[1327] Mason olsalardı ülke bu hale gelmezdi, http://www.milliyet.com.tr/2001/05/16/yazar/yilmaz.html as of May 2012

[1328] Gábor Ágoston and Bruce Alan Masters, Encyclopedia of the Ottoman Empire, InfoBase Publishing, New York, 2009, pp. 52-53

[1329] Dr. Justin McCarthy, Armenian Rebels—Effects & Consequences, a transcription of a speech given at the Turkish Grand National Assembly, March 24, 2005, http://www.tallarmeniantale.com/mccarthy-armenian-rebels.htm as of May 2012

others. The authorities incarcerated many activists. The demonstration and the Armenian question captured the attention of the European powers. Turkey's internal problems made the empire and its resources vulnerable to the tentacles of Russia and England, which sought control of Crete. Russia wanted to annex Turkish Armenia, which the Hunchaks adamantly opposed as they wanted an independent Armenia. [1330]

In early 1894, the Hunchak leader Murat (Hambardsum Poyadjian) encouraged the Armenians to refuse to pay taxes which the government viewed as rebellion and deployed troops. Murat and his Armenians resisted the Turkish forces for over a month but the much better prepared Turks overwhelmed and captured Murat and many of his men. This latest violence provoked Britain, France, and Russia. These nations convened a Commission of Inquiry which concluded that the Armenians were guilty of sheltering Murat and his band and resisted the government troops. It also decided that the Turkish authorities overreacted while the Hunchaks felt that the Sassun Rebellion was a victory. The European Powers recognized the party's revolutionary activities and issued a memo to Abdülhamid admonishing reforms in the Armenian provinces. The Sultan refused. In August 1894, after other demonstrations, the authorities arrested and hung some revolutionaries and prominent Armenians. [1331]

The European powers, England, France, and Russia, supported by Germany, Austria, and Italy, demanded that Abdülhamid implement the Armenian Reform Program of May 11, 1895. The sultan never effectively implemented the reforms but reportedly responded with the massacres (1894-1895) which almost destroyed the terrorist Hunchakian Party. The Hunchaks arranged the Demonstration of Bab Ali in Constantinople on September 18-30. [1332] On October 12, the Hunchaks rebelled again. The sultan was supposed to sign the

---

[1330] Louise Nalbandian, The Armenian Revolutionary Movement—The Development of Armenian Political Parties through the Nineteenth Century, University of California Press, Berkeley, Los Angeles, London, 1963, pp. 116-120

[1331] Ibid. 120-124

[1332] Ibid. 120-124

Armenian Reform Program on October 17, assenting to the prescribed program. Turkish troops retaliated and a four-month battle ensued in several villages that ended on February 1, 1896, after European intervention, with the sultan accepting the peace terms offered by six European consuls. In 1896, the terrorists ended much of their activities as they erroneously believed that they had met the goal of attracting intervention in support of an independent Armenia.[1333]

European politicians and bankers used the media to influence public opinion to oppose the Turks who they had targeted for destruction. Europeans demanded that Ottoman officials tolerate this poor minority population, despite their actions. They even arranged for the release of the armed Dashnaks who seized the Ottoman Bank in Constantinople on August 26, 1896, using pistols, grenades, dynamite and hand-held bombs. They killed ten people and held hostages for fourteen hours. European leaders demanded amnesty and pardons, even for those who would later attempt to kill Abdülhamid on July 21, 1905. The terrorists, during that assassination attempt, killed twenty-six, and wounded fifty-eight people with their bomb. The Russian consuls prohibited the Ottoman courts from trying Dashnaks because they were Russian subjects. One of them even functioned as their weapons instructor. [1334]

Emanuel Karasu (Emanuel Qrasow), a lawyer and a Sephardic Jew, was a key member of the Young Turks in the 1890s, in Salonica, where he later became the president of the Macedonian Risorta Masonic lodge, and where he sought the support of several Jewish organizations. He launched the development of freemasonry in the Ottoman Empire. freemasons in Salonica sympathized with the Young Turks, including Mehmed Talaat. Karasu joined the Ottoman Freedom Society, later a part of the CUP.

[1333] Ibid. 126-130

[1334] Dr. Justin McCarthy, Armenian Rebels—Effects & Consequences, a transcription of a speech given at the Turkish Grand National Assembly, March 24, 2005, http://www.tallarmeniantale.com/mccarthy-armenian-rebels.htm as of May 2012

One of those Jewish organizations was the Alliance Israélite Universelle which had eleven schools in Constantinople, with at least 3,000 students. About 1,000 children studied the Talmud in special private schools, of which there were thirty. In 1898, Abraham Danon founded a Jewish seminary. Many Jews attended state schools to study medicine, law, pharmacy, fine arts, and agriculture. The Alliance, though they instructed young Jews in many practical skills, preferred to place people into influential positions such as secretaries or accountants in European companies, including public service firms. [1335]

In 1900, the Grand Orient assumed control of the Young Turk Party, composed almost entirely of Jews, Greeks, and Armenians. It was only then, that the party began to be a considerable force. Most freemasons in Constantinople associated themselves with the CUP and the Young Turk movement, following the pattern of continental freemasonry. The Young Turkey movement in Paris was more benign than that in Salonica. The population in Salonica, 140,000, was composed of about 80,000 Spanish Jews, and 20,000 Crypto-Jews, who professed Islamism. Many of the Spanish Jews affiliated with Italian Masonic Lodges, associated with the Scottish rite. Both the Young Turks and the Italian freemasons used the motto Liberté, Equalité and Fraternité. After the revolution in July 1908, the CUP established headquarters in Constantinople. Its principle members were Jewish freemasons. Jews from other countries enthusiastically supported the events occurring in Turkey. It was obvious to many that the movement was a Jewish Revolution rather than a Turkish one. [1336]

Karasu and others, Aref Hikmat, Aram Afandi (Armenian), and As'ad Tobatani, would later inform Abdülhamid of his overthrow in April 1911. Aref Hikmat read the Fatwa and Aram Afandi said, "The nation has removed you from your office." Abdülhamid responded, "The nation has removed me from my office, that is okay . . . but why

---

[1335] Constantinople, The Jewish Encyclopedia, http://www.jewishencyclopedia. com/articles/4623-constantinople as of May 2012

[1336] Vicomte Léon De Poncins, Freemasonry and Judaism, Secret Powers Behind Revolution, A & B Publishers Group, Brooklyn, New York, pp. 66-67

did you bring the Jew to the Quarters of the Khilafa?" pointing at Qrasow. Apparently, because the sultan refused to sell Palestine to the Jews, they were going to have the last word by removing him from office. Following his removal, many writers attacked his character, called him a tyrant, and accused him of numerous disreputable, immoral activities. [1337]

While some important Armenian groups moderately assisted the Hunchaks in their activities, they rejected many principles, and withdrew all backing. This did not alter their intentions to launch a revolution in Turkish Armenia, starting in Constantinople, where they moved their headquarters. They recruited 700 well-educated, influential members in the capital and disseminated agents from Geneva to various towns and villages in Turkey to consolidate the Armenians. Before long, the Hunchaks attracted hundreds of young Armenians in Turkey, Russia, Persia, Europe, and the United States. The party published the *Communist Manifesto* and other Marxist works in the Armenian language. [1338]

The successful rebellious Dashnaks, led by Russians, shaped the Armenians of Anatolia into a military force, people who initially had no desire to rebel but rather preferred peace. The rebels, in an attempt to unite the Armenians against the government, used terrorism to destroy church and community leaders, people who opposed the Dashnaks. They killed Armenian clergymen, loyal Ottoman subjects, then ended religious education and imposed a system with "teachers" who promoted revolution. They extorted money from the merchant class who typically favored the government. From 1902 to 1904, the Dashnak Party, active throughout the Empire, officially sanctioned assassination and extortion to fund their activities, similar to the

---

[1337] Khondakar Golam Mowla, The Judgment Against Imperialism, Fascism and Racism Against Caliphate and Islam, Volume 2, Author House, Bloomington, Indiana, 2008, pp. 332-333

[1338] Louise Nalbandian, The Armenian Revolutionary Movement—The Development of Armenian Political Parties through the Nineteenth Century, University of California Press, Berkeley, Los Angeles, London, 1963, pp. 116-120

Bolsheviks. Merchants then paid their taxes to the rebels. They would pay the government if they furnished protection from the rebels. [1339]

In 1905-1906, the ARF participated in armed activities and massacres which some claim that the Russian government incited to reinforce its authority, part of a larger anti-Armenian policy. In February 1905, violence broke out in Baku. The ARF blamed the Russians for the massacres. On May 11, 1905, rebels assassinated Russian governor general, Prince Giorgi Nakashidze, a supporter of the policies of Prince Grigori Golitsyn, the General Governor of the Caucasus. The Armenians, who relied on the ARF for protection, considered Golitsyn the main instigator of hate. Russia's General Governor of Caucasus, (1905-1915), Illarion I. Vorontsov-Dashkov, blamed the ARF for the massacres. The ARF argued that it organized the defense of the Armenian population against Muslim attacks. Its terrorist activities, supposedly necessary to implement political goals, served as a catalyst to consolidate the Muslim community of the Caucasus.

In 1905, Dr. Bahaeddin Şakir, a founding member, led the CUP. Some members advocated gradual reform while others promoted revolution. In 1906, Şakir changed the organization into a political association and allied with the Young Turks, a group that affiliated with secret societies, like Italy's Carbonari. They opposed traditional government and wanted to reshape the intellectual, political and cultural life of the area. In September 1907, the CUP merged with the Ottoman Freedom Society, established by Mehmed Talaat, along with army officers and bureaucrats in Salonica in 1906. The Young Turks expanded and infiltrated the elite Ottoman officer corps. [1340] Talaat exerted significant control within the CUP, especially during the dissolution of the Ottoman Empire (1908-1922).

[1339] Dr. Justin McCarthy, Armenian Rebels—Effects & Consequences, a transcription of a speech given at the Turkish Grand National Assembly, March 24, 2005, http://www.tallarmeniantale.com/mccarthy-armenian-rebels.htm as of May 2012
[1340] Gábor Ágoston and Bruce Alan Masters, Encyclopedia of the Ottoman Empire, InfoBase Publishing, New York, 2009, pp. 8, 605-606

In 1907, in the Ottoman Empire, Mehmed Talaat was the Grand Master of the Scottish Rite Masons, in which numerous Young Turk leaders were high officials. Adolphe Isaac Crémieux, head of the B'nai B'rith in France, helped found the Scottish Rite in Turkey. He had formerly headed Mazzini's Young France, and helped to install Napoleon III on the throne. [1341] The Young Turks were typically part of a progressive university clique, similar to Leo Strauss' disciples at the University of Chicago. Most of them were Jewish scientists, influential state officials, journalists, doctors, administrators, and political activists.

Mustafa Kemal, born in Salonica, a freemason, a supporter of the Young Turk movement, would later be the first President of Turkey (1923-1938). He was a Spanish Jew by ancestry, an Islamic Marrano, and an orthodox Moslem by birth. [1342] According to Encyclopedia Judaica, he was of Dönme origin, an assertion that many Salonica Jews made. On June 20, 1907, he became a Senior Captain, and on October 13, 1907, they assigned him to the headquarters of the Third Army in Manastır. He joined the CUP, although, later, he opposed some of its policies. On June 22, 1908, he became the Inspector of the Ottoman Railways in Eastern Rumaila, and, in July 1908, he participated in the Young Turk Revolution which seized power from Sultan Abdülhamid.

The Armenian revolutionaries began rebelling as early as 1908 when their Committee in Tiflis informed them that, if war erupted, they should unite with Russia against Turkey. In the City of Van, the Ottomans uncovered a cache of Dashnak weapons, with 2,000 guns, a significant amount of ammunition, and 5,000 bombs to support an imminent revolt. Even without Russia, they had the capacity to

[1341] Joseph Brewda, Palmerston launches Young Turks to permanently control Middle East, Schiller Institute/ICLC Conference, The Palmerston Zoo, Presidents Day, February 1994, http://www.schillerinstitute.org/conf-iclc/1990s/conf_feb_1994_brewda.html#brewda as of May 2012

[1342] The Literary Digest, United States, October 14, 1922, p. 50

assemble roughly 3,500 fully-armed sharpshooters at the border to target the Turks, and obstruct their communication connections. [1343]

The Young Turks launched a publication, *The Acacia*, in October 1908, in Salonica, from which, they directed the entire movement. Salonica was the most Jewish town in Europe where the Jews numbered 70,000 out of a population of 100,000. There were several Masonic lodges, under the shelter of European diplomacy, in Salonica, where the revolutionaries made plans for their future activities. The sultan had no defenses against the united power of the freemasons. On May 1, 1909, a very significant date, individuals representing forty-five Turkish lodges convened in Constantinople and created the Grand Orient Ottoman. They nominated Mahmoud Orphi Pasha as the Grand Master. Thereafter, members founded a Supreme Council of the Ancient and Accepted Scottish Rites. [1344]

Ismail Enver, a military officer, also helped organize the Young Turk Revolution, the beginning of the Second Constitutional Era and the ultimate dissolution of the Ottoman Empire. He was a leader of the CUP that would control the Ottoman Empire during the First World War, the conspiratorial nucleus of the Young Turk movement. The revolution began in the Balkan provinces, and quickly spread throughout the empire resulting in the restoration of the 1876 constitution and a new parliament, on July 3, 1908, consisting of 142 Turks, 60 Arabs, 25 Albanians, 23 Greeks, 12 Armenians, 5 Jews, 4 Bulgarians, 3 Serbs and 1 Vlach. At least sixty deputies supported the CUP, the force behind the revolution. The CUP, or Young Turks, gained dominance over the others and became the biggest party, despite the fact they only had 60 of the 275 seats.

[1343] Dr. Justin McCarthy, Armenian Rebels—Effects & Consequences, a transcription of a speech given at the Turkish Grand National Assembly, March 24, 2005, http://www.tallarmeniantale.com/mccarthy-armenian-rebels.htm as of May 2012

[1344] David Musa Pidcock, Satanic Voices, Ancient and Modern, a Surfeit of Blasphemy Including the Rushdie Report from Edifice Complex to Occult Theocracy, Mustaqim, Islamic Art and Literature, Milton Keynes, England, 1992, pp. 47-53

Vladimir Jabotinsky, a Russian Zionist fluent in several languages including Hebrew, became an editor for *The Young Turk*, one of several newspapers that the group owned. He went to Constantinople after the Young Turk coup, specifically to edit the paper, which the Russian Zionist federation funded, and the B'nai B'rith managed. He ultimately created the Irgun, a terrorist organization. [1345] He visited Palestine and considered moving his family there in 1908-09, but soon returned to Turkey. [1346] The Second Constitutional Era began after Abdülhamid restored the monarchy after the Young Turk Revolution. Thereafter, through a series of elections, the CUP dominated politics and Prince Sabahaddin led the second largest party, the Liberal Union, a coalition. There were three significant events, 1) the Young Turk Revolution, mid-April to July 24, 1908, 2) the Counter-coup (1909), led by Dervish Vahdeti, and 3) the Counter Revolution, April 13, 1909.

After nine months of parliamentary government, dissidents staged a Countercoup, and then in Constantinople, reactionaries rebelled against the restoration of the constitutional monarchy brought about by the Young Turks in 1908. Sections of the army mutinied in Constantinople and the Chamber of Deputies convened in a secret session to unanimously vote to depose Abdülhamid, on April 27, 1909, exile him to Salonica, and replace him with his younger brother, Mehmed V Reşad. The CUP, now very influential, claimed that the sultan had organized the countercoup and accused him of corrupting the troops in order to restore the old regime, yet they lacked any evidence of their allegations. Using ambiguities in the constitution,

---

[1345] Joseph Brewda, Palmerston launches Young Turks to permanently control Middle East, Schiller Institute/ICLC Conference, The Palmerston Zoo, Presidents Day, February 1994, http://www.schillerinstitute.org/conf-iclc/1990s/conf_feb_1994_brewda.html#brewda as of May 2012

[1346] Lenni Brenner, The Iron Wall, Zionist Revisionism from Jabotinsky to Shamir, AAARGH Publisher, 1984, p. 29

they removed him from the throne, and consolidated the parliament's powers. The CUP soon initiated anti-minority movements which would culminate in the Balkan wars (October 8, 1912-July 18, 1913) in southeastern Europe.

In 1905-1906, Alexander Parvus, who supported the Soviet revolutions, had relocated to Constantinople, to become the economics editor of a Young Turk newspaper, *The Turkish Homeland*. He became business partners with Emanuel Karasu, who supplied foodstuffs and arms to the Turkish army during the Balkan wars, during which they made a fortune. The socialists reportedly lost respect for Parvus after he became a millionaire. He would later return to Europe, where he arranged for the secret train that returned Lenin to Russia in 1917. [1347]

Parvus functioned as the financial and political advisor for the Young Turks. In 1912, he became the editor of *Turk Yurdu*, the group's daily newspaper. He collaborated with Ismail Enver, Mehmed Talaat, the CUP Secretary General, Ahmed Djemal, and Djavid Bey, a Dönme. In 1909, Bey became Minister of Finance in the cabinet of Grand Vizier Tevfik Pasha. Enver, Talaat, and Bey would organize the Armenian Massacres in 1915. In addition to his business with Karasu, Parvus was a partner of the Krupp concern, of Vickers Limited, and, of the arms dealer, and financier, Basil Zaharoff, (born Zacharie B. Zacharias), possibly "the offspring of an obscure Anatolian Jew." Zaharoff became a French citizen in 1913, worked for the Vickers munitions firm (1897-1927), and was a Knight of the British Empire. People thought that Parvus, also a war profiteer, was a British intelligence asset. [1348]

Since the new constitution banned all secret societies, the CUP modified its rules, and ceased to be a secret association, seen as

---

[1347] Joseph Brewda, Palmerston launches Young Turks to permanently control Middle East, Schiller Institute/ICLC Conference, The Palmerston Zoo, Presidents Day, February 1994, http://www.schillerinstitute.org/conf-iclc/1990s/conf_feb_1994_brewda.html#brewda as of May 2012

[1348] Guiles Davenport, Zaharoff, High Priest of War, Lothrop, Lee and Shepard Company, Boston, 1934, pp. 4, 12-16

evidence of its confidence in the parliament, the foundation of imminent financial and administrative changes. Authorities closed the lodges in 1911, but the freemasons soon revitalized them, including two lodges in Salonica, and others in Macedonia and other areas that had connections to the Grand Orient of Italy and France. [1349] Soon, there arose tensions and clashes between Zionist colonists and Palestinian farmers near Nazareth. A Palestinian deputy residing in Jaffa broached the Zionist issue for the first time in the new Ottoman parliament. The CUP presented numerous new initiatives to modernize the Ottoman Empire, by the imposition of a strong central government, and the elimination of all foreign influence.

The CUP began secularizing the legal system, and subsidizing women's education, while altering the foundation of state-supported primary schools. They also wanted to modernize the communications and transportation networks. Germany already had an interest in the Anatolian Railway, but the Ottoman Empire had defaulted in some of its loans held by some international bankers.

When the Young Turks gained control, the multi-ethnic Ottoman Empire was composed of Syria, Iraq, Jordan, Palestine, the Arabian Peninsula, a large part of the Balkans, half of Greece, Bulgaria, Serbia, and all of Albania. Most of the population was Turkish, along with sizeable numbers of Arabs, Armenians, Greeks, Kurds, and Slavs. The Zionist, Arminius Vámbéry, a double agent between Turkey and Britain, mentored the Young Turks. Vámbéry befriended and counseled Abdülhamid, and soon promoted pan-Turkism, a nation for all the Turkish populations of Asia, including some people who lived in Russia, certain to create a conflict with that nation. The Young Turks also supported a pan-Islamic state, and policies designed to create a confrontation with Russia. Meanwhile, the British supported Arab nationalism, led by Lawrence of Arabia, and an Armenian nation created from parts of Turkey, Iran, and Russia, even if the Kurds opposed population relocation schemes.

[1349] David Musa Pidcock, Satanic Voices, Ancient and Modern, a Surfeit of Blasphemy Including the Rushdie, Report from Edifice Complex to Occult Theocracy, Mustaqim, Islamic Art and Literature, Milton Keynes, England, 1992, pp. 47-53

The CUP leaders, Ahmed Djemal and Ismail Enver organized the coup d'état. On January 23, 1913, during the Balkan war, Enver and his accomplices interrupted the cabinet as it was in session. Yakup Cemil, an Ottoman army officer, shot Hussein Nazim Pasha, Chief of Staff of the Army, during the First Balkan War. He altered the military doctrine that Colmar Freiherr von der Goltz had created. In the event of war with the Balkan states, der Goltz wanted the Ottoman forces to remain on the defensive in both the western and eastern fronts. Nazim Pasha abandoned that more realistic approach and developed an offensive plan which had grave consequences for the Ottoman Empire.

The Young Turks forced Mehmed Kamil Pasha to resign and Mahmud Şevket Pasha replaced him as Grand Vizier (like a Prime Minister) to Mehmed V Reşad (January 23-June 15, 1913), when someone assassinated him. He previously worked with der Goltz Pasha, had been to Germany, and had brought military aviation to the empire in 1911, as well as the first car to the capital. Said Halim Pasha succeeded him (1913-1917). On January 23, Mehmed Talaat became the Minister of Interior Affairs, now Talaat Pasha, until February 4, 1917 when he became the Grand Vizier. Pasha is a term meaning Lord.

The new Young Turk government focused on minority issues, like those pertaining to the Armenians. Armenian politicians had always supported the CUP, and, expected that, when it organized Parliament, they would have some influence. However, the tensions that arose during the Balkan Wars, in south-eastern Europe, changed what was a multi-ethnic and multi-religious Ottoman Empire, into a Muslim-oriented society. These wars enabled Bulgaria, Greece, Serbia, Montenegro, and the nations of the Balkan League, to achieve independence from the Ottoman Empire. The CUP's majority in parliament now became a disadvantage to the minorities as they soon became outcasts. Instead of having the anticipated adequate representation, democracy placed them in the minority.

In 1913, politicians in Constantinople concentrated on resolving the demands of Arab and Armenian reformist groups. By then, most of the Christian population had already relocated out of the empire following the Balkan Wars, when the new politicians redefined policies, and placed greater emphasis on Islam. This is interesting given that the imperialistic external forces that were driving policy were predominantly Christian countries. The CUP employed populist politics, and propagated Islamic propaganda, in order to increase their legitimacy with the majority of the population. The CUP clubs, challenging traditional forces, emerged throughout the Empire. By 1914, Mehmed Talaat, the Interior Minister, Ismail Enver, the Minister of War, and Ahmed Djemal, the Minister of the Navy controlled all government power. People referred to Talaat, Enver and Djemal as the Three Pashas. Parvus, freemasonry, and Marxist policies guided them in their control of the Ottoman government, until October 1918, when they all fled.

Enver Leads Turkey into the War

Following the Young Turk Revolution, the relationship between Germany and the Ottoman Empire became uncertain. Previously, Kaiser Wilhelm and Abdülhamid had a good relationship and the sultan approved of the railway concessions and armament contracts. The Young Turks held the sultan responsible for the empire's problems and they, the empire's new rulers, mistrusted Germany because of the Austrian annexation of Bosnia and Herzegovina. The counterrevolution, and a new sultan using affable diplomacy, managed to gain German support for Ottoman interests in the Balkans. In 1909, Ottoman officials invited Colmar von der Goltz to the capital to serve as an army inspector and to reform the Ottoman military. [1350]

Ismail Enver Pasha, like others in the military and the bureaucracy, was pro-German. Enver and a faction within the CUP devised a secret alliance between the Ottoman Empire and Germany, the Ottoman-German Alliance, on August 2, 1914, which caused the Empire to enter World War I, as an ally of the Central Powers. When Bulgaria collapsed and Germany capitulated, the isolated

---

[1350] Gábor Ágoston and Bruce Alan Masters, Encyclopedia of the Ottoman Empire, InfoBase Publishing, New York, 2009, pp. 230-231

Ottomans were at the mercy of the British and the French. Germany and the Ottomans already had a relationship due to the railway concession which strengthened the Ottoman Empire's connection to industrialized Europe, and facilitated Germany's easier access to its African colonies.

When hostilities broke out between the Austro-Hungarian Empire and Serbia, Admiral Wilhelm Souchon, to avoid conflict, took his two ships to the western Mediterranean. In the event of war, his squadron was to intercept the French who were transporting colonial troops from Algeria to France. On July 30, 1914, Winston Churchill directed the Malta-based British Mediterranean Fleet, eleven cruisers and fourteen destroyers, commanded by Admiral Sir Archibald B. Milne, to safeguard the French transports, because of a pre-war agreement, and contain the German cruisers. If necessary, Churchill authorized Milne to engage the Germans but Churchill had to cancel his authorization, as the British Cabinet had not yet declared war against Germany.

The British Admiral, Sir Ernest Troubridge, and four British cruisers were to prevent Admiral Souchon from entering the Adriatic and joining the Austro-Hungarian fleet. Admiral Souchon positioned his ships off the coast of Africa, ready to engage if necessary. On August 3, Germany declared war on France, and troops predictably headed for France through Belgium, the only logical route. On August 4, 1914, Admiral Alfred von Tirpitz reported to Souchon that Germany had allied with the CUP. On August 4, Admiral Souchon bombarded the French-Algerian ports of Bone and Philippeville. Later that day, England declared war on Germany, following an unsatisfactory reply to Britain's ultimatum regarding Belgium's neutrality. Souchon eluded the British, and on August 10, 1914, the two cruisers arrived at the Dardanelles and from there, he proceeded to Constantinople, as instructed. Troubridge, with a superior force, could have prevented his escape. Troubridge's actions were indirectly instrumental in Turkey's entrance into the war on the side of the Central Powers. Fawcet Wray, his Flag Captain, persuaded him to allow the German ships safe passage.

Upon arrival in Constantinople, as directed, Admiral Souchon officially transferred his ships to the Ottoman navy and the CUP appointed him as the Commander-in-Chief of the Ottoman navy, where he functioned until September 1917. When war erupted, Churchill requisitioned, without compensation, two nearly completed Turkish battleships, in British shipyards and then commissioned them into the Royal Navy. On August 15, 1914, Turkey cancelled its maritime agreement with Britain. The Royal Navy left by September 15. With German assistance, Turkey fortified the Dardanelles and the Bosporus and on September 27, officials closed the Straits to all international shipping.

German officials expected Admiral Souchon and Otto Liman von Saunders, the son of a Jewish nobleman, and Baron von der Goltz, also in Turkey, to consider German national interests while serving with the Ottoman Empire. However, Souchon had to report directly to Turkish Minister of Marine, Djemal. The Young Turks, especially Enver, distrusted Saunders who appeared to put German interests first. Enver authorized a military offensive in the Black Sea. On October 29, 1914, he instructed Souchon to attack the Russian ports of Odessa, Sevastopol, and Theodosia, which initiated a war with the Entente Powers. Russia declared war on the Ottoman Empire on November 2, 1914, and Britain and France declared war on November 5. The majority of the Turkish cabinet members opposed entering the war. Souchon, dissatisfied with his role, consistently requested submarine support to challenge Russian dominance of the Black Sea. He returned to Germany in September 1917, where officials appointed him head of the Fourth Battleship Squadron with the High Seas Fleet. As Governor of the Kiel naval base, he witnessed, with despair, the mutiny of the German navy bent on revolution. [1351]

Enver directed all military-age men to report to the army recruiting offices, which were unable to accommodate the huge number of men who wanted to enlist. Because so many young men left the fields, it ruined the harvest for the year. However, within six months, the

---

[1351] Who's Who—Wilhelm Souchon, http://www.firstworldwar.com/bio/souchon. htm as of May 2012

Ottoman Empire had an army of 800,000 men, who were fighting on a four-front war.

Enver depended heavily on the support of the Germans during the next four years. German generals and military advisers, Otto Liman von Sanders, Erich von Falkenhayn, Colmar von der Goltz, and Friedrich von Kressenstein provided military expertise while the Germans also furnished military supplies, soldiers, and fuel. Enver expected a military victory but the Russians countered with incredible strength during an assault against them in the Caucasus, where Enver hoped to encircle them and recover lost territory ceded to Russia after the Russo-Turkish War. Meanwhile, at home, living conditions deteriorated, and people became disheartened and discouraged. The government of the CUP overspent for the war and inflation was rampant.

Sykes-Picot Agreement

Bankers in Britain and France benefited through extending their financial influence into Turkish territory. They devised massive projects such as railroads, and the Suez Canal, which kept the Arab countries deeply in debt, allowing Britain and France to usurp authority over the Middle East. By 1900, Britain ruled Egypt, the Sudan, and parts of the Persian Gulf. France controlled Lebanon and Syria, where there was a significant Christian minority. The bankers behind the British government divided Iran between the British and Russians. The dismemberment of the Ottoman territories (from Turkey to the Arabian Peninsula), was the top priority of the imperialist powers. [1352]

In 1900, Theodor Herzl began negotiating with Abdülhamid, the sultan of the Ottoman Empire, for either a charter or an outright purchase of land in Palestine for the Zionists. The sultan rejected Herzl's request. Dr. Chaim Weizmann later headed the Zionist Movement. At the beginning of World War I, Edmond Rothschild

---

[1352] Behind the War on Iraq: Research Unit for Political Economy, Monthly Review. Volume: 55. Issue: 1. May 2003, p. 20

told Weizmann that the coming war would spread to the Middle East, where things of great significance to political Zionism would occur. [1353] Apparently, if the Zionists could not obtain a charter or buy land in Palestine, they would simply go to war and seize it.

Politicians, provoked by influential Jews in England and America, used World War I as a political catalyst to gain Palestine as a Jewish homeland. Author Hasia R. Diner wrote, "The Jews of Palestine, regardless of whether they were yeshiva students in Jerusalem, halutzim (pioneers) in the Jordan River valley, or dwellers in the new Jewish cities of Tel Aviv and Haifa, like the Jews of central and eastern Europe, stood trapped among the great powers fighting for control of land, waterways, and resources of the crucial region. The direct clash between the British forces and those of the Ottoman Empire under whom the Jews of Palestine lived often put them in harm's way." [1354]

In the event of a World War I victory, per the Constantinople Agreement, of March 18, 1915, France and Britain officially promised the port city of Constantinople and the Dardanelles (occupied by the Ottoman Empire) to Russia, as supported in documents between Russia, France, and Britain. The other Allies, for their warfare efforts, would receive compensation elsewhere in Turkey, and Britain would maintain the neutral zone in oil-rich Persia. Later, when the Bolsheviks seized Russia, they relinquished the booty promised in the treaty. During the Peace Conference, Balfour described the Treaty of London, signed on April 26, 1915, as "unmatched in the annals of friendly international negotiations." Italy, for joining the Allies, received territory in the Austrian Empire, the finest port in Albania, territorial extensions in Africa, the Dodecanese Islands, and territory in Turkey. Italy also insisted on a share of the German reimbursement, and a £50 million loan from Britain. In the Agreement of St.-Jean-de-Mauriennean, on April 26, 1917, the Allies promised Italy, represented by Sidney C. Sonnino, a Jew, an even larger area

---

[1353] Douglas Reed, Far And Wide, former foreign correspondent for the London Times, 1951, p. 285

[1354] Hasia R. Diner, The Jews of the United States, 1654 to 2000, University of California Press, Berkeley, California, 2004, pp. 182-183

in Anatolia and Smyrna. [1355] They never executed the agreement but rescinded it because of the Bolshevik Revolution, financially and logistically supported by United States and British bankers. Lenin later discovered a copy of the agreement, the actual justification for the war, among Russia's state papers and made it public.

When the Italians attempted to take the said land in Smyrna, Greece sent a military expedition, on May 15, 1919, to thwart them. These actions generated the Turkish Nationalist movement, which later quashed the Christian powers. In the absence of these damnable secret treaties, the current crisis in the Middle East would be non-existent. In March 1916, Russia and France signed the Sazanof-Paleologue Treaty, giving the land located between Persia and the Black Sea, to Russia, and giving France territory in Turkey, including Syria. Then France and Britain negotiated the Sykes-Picot Agreement a couple of months later, which gave Syria to France, all the way to the port of Acre. Britain received Haifa and Lower Mesopotamia. [1356]

By 1912, Mark Sykes, a Second Boer War veteran, and an honorary attaché to the British Embassy in Constantinople, was a Member of Parliament. He advocated the British Conservative's policy of supporting the Ottoman Empire as a safeguard against Russian development and expansion into the Mediterranean area. Britain worried that Russia had plans for India, its longtime colony. British fleets controlled the oceans, and feared that a strong Russian fleet would impede its trade routes to India. British diplomats, Henry J. Temple

[1355] Turkey-World Center of News Interest, Originally printed in Editor & Publisher, V.55, No. 27, 2nd Section, December 2, 1922, http://www.codoh. com/incon/inconkcintro.html as of May 2012

[1356] Turkey-World Center of News Interest, Originally printed in Editor & Publisher, V.55, No. 27, 2nd Section, December 2, 1922, http://www.codoh. com/incon/inconkcintro.html as of May 2012

(Lord Palmerston), Benjamin Disraeli, and Robert Gascoyne-Cecil (Lord Salisbury) embraced that mentality. The Liberal Party leader, William E. Gladstone, along with David Lloyd George, criticized the Ottoman government, its misgovernment, and its alleged recurrent slaughter of minorities, especially Christians.

Given that Britain was engaged in war with Turkey, Sykes and Lord Herbert H. Kitchener saw fit to alter British policies, and develop new alliances. Many British leaders favored the Arabs over the Turks when considering the postwar settlements, because of the location of those states along the coast, adjacent to the sea route to India and in the Persian Gulf. Other diplomats wanted to retain their relationship to Turkey to avert any Russian influence in Constantinople, and in the Straits.

Additionally, France wanted to acquire lands in the Middle East, particularly in Syria, which had a Christian minority. Italy wanted possession of the Aegean Islands to protect Christian minorities in Asia Minor. Russia wanted control of the Straits leading from the Black Sea to the Aegean to protect the Christians of Turkish Armenia and the Black Sea coast. Greece wanted to claim the historic Byzantine territories of Asia, Minor and Thrace, which conflicted with the claims of Russia, Italy, and Turkey. British Prime Minister David Lloyd George (1916-1922) preferred to ally with Greece. There were also the Zionists who wanted to establish a Jewish homeland in Palestine.

Mark Sykes had the position of negotiating an agreement with Britain's most important ally, France, a country that was carrying a disparate responsibility in the war efforts against Germany. In July 1915, Sykes and François Georges-Picot worked on the secret agreement, which people later referred to as the Sykes-Picot Agreement, officially signed on May 16, 1916. Sykes was sympathetic toward the Armenians, Arabs, Turks, and Jews. As an officer, Sykes worked at the War Office as a protégé of Lord Herbert H. Kitchener, the Secretary of State for War. After negotiating the agreement, the British promised Sherif Hussein bin Ali that they would support Arab independence as a single unified state if the Arabs would join the

British, under Lieutenant Colonel Thomas E. Lawrence (Lawrence of Arabia), against the Ottoman Empire, Germany's ally. Sir Arthur H. McMahon, the British High Commissioner in Egypt (1915-1917) and a British administrator to India, clarified this promise in a letter dated October 24, 1915 to India, to the Sherif, who thought that the promise included Palestine. [1357]

Sherif was the sultan's regent in Mecca. Sherif's objective was the establishment of a single, independent, unified Arab state, stretching from Aleppo (Syria) to Aden (Yemen), including Palestine. Based on this understanding, the Arabs supplied the British with thousands of men, considered invaluable military assistance, during which their opponents slaughtered 100,000 of them. [1358] The Sykes-Picot Agreement deceptively internationalized the bulk of Palestine, and divided the land into protectorates, vehicles for resource exploitation by the victors. British politicians predictably reneged on every single promise. [1359]

Sir Mark Sykes, a budding Zionist and co-author of the agreement, was good friends with Dr. Chaim Weizmann, the head Zionist. The Sykes-Picot Agreement conformed to the Rothschild agenda. Britain intended to seize control of all of the undeveloped oil-rich Arabian Gulf after the war. [1360] Ultimately, Britain gained Jordan, southern Iraq, part of Haifa and direct access to the Mediterranean Sea. France gained control of Syria, Lebanon, southeastern Turkey, northern Iraq and Mosul. Russia was supposed to get Constantinople, the Turkish Straits and the Armenian vilayets, the unique subdivisions within the Ottoman Empire. Leaders initially designated Palestine as an area for

---

[1357] Avi Shlaim, The Balfour Declaration And its Consequences, http://users. ox.ac.uk/~ssfc0005/The Balfour Declaration and its consequences.html as of May 2012

[1358] The Great Arab Revolt, http://www.kinghussein.gov.jo/his_arabrevolt.html as of May 2012

[1359] Behind the War on Iraq: Research Unit for Political Economy, Monthly Review, Volume 55, Issue: 1, May 2003, p. 20

[1360] William Engdahl, A Century of War, Anglo-American Oil Politics and the New World Order, Pluto Press, Ann Arbor, Michigan, 2004, pp. 40-42

international administration after discussion with Russia and others, including the Sherif.

On November 7, 1918, even after the exposure of the double dealing-duplicity of inducing Sherif's men to fight against the Ottoman Empire, France and Britain (both bankrupt), issued statements claiming that they were fighting for the freedom of those who the Turks had allegedly oppressed for such a long time.

The predetermined divisions closely correspond to the current Middle East borders. Those partitions created the countries of Syria and Lebanon, designated as French protectorates, a status they held until 1946 for Syria, and 1943, for Lebanon, when they finally gained their freedom. Britain predictably betrayed Sherif Hussein bin Ali, and allotted him control only over Iraq, along with Trans-Jordan, and Kuwait, which were effectively British entities. The British ultimately handed Palestine over to the Zionists in 1948. [1361]

Britain's Middle East Objectives

British Prime Minister, Herbert H. Asquith and Herbert H. Kitchener, the War Minister, were not interested in fracturing Europe in order to help British bankers develop commercial interests or political influence in the Middle East. Lord Alfred Milner, an Anglophile, had alternative plans. On November 22, 1915, his Round Table placed a notice in the *Manchester Guardian,* which intimated, "The whole future of the British Empire as a Sea Empire" hinged on taking control of Palestine, a buffer state and peopling it with "an intensely patriotic race." They also claimed that Palestine was the missing link that would complete the boundaries of the empire, from the Atlantic to the Pacific. [1362] The war's major function was the destruction of the Ottoman Empire, to free Palestine in order to create the state of Israel. The dismemberment of that empire would include genocide and ethnic cleansing.

[1361] David Livingston, Terrorism And The Illuminati, A Three Thousand Year History, BookSurge LLC, Charleston, South Carolina, 2007, p. 180

[1362] William B. Ziff, The Rape of Palestine, Longmans, Green and Company, New York, Toronto, 1938, pp. 54-55

The Milner faction had to manipulate the United States into fighting against Germany. Given the growing influence of America's Jewish population, chances of dragging them into the war were good. Asquith and Kitchener opposed that plan. On June 6, 1916, Kitchener died on his way to Russia when his ship went down, apparently due to an explosion. Reginald B. Brett, who orchestrated many lethal reforms during World War I, as a member of the monarch's Privy Council, helped replace Asquith with a more willing pawn. Brett, a founding member of the Pilgrims Society, was close to the Rothschilds [1363] and a leading member of the Rhodes-Milner group. [1364] On December 7, 1916, David Lloyd George became Britain's Prime Minister. Before long, the Round Table had positioned several of their most effective members into government posts. Milner became the chief strategist of the War Cabinet. Soon British troops left for the Middle East to fight the Turks.

Prime Minister Lloyd George's astute legal skills immeasurably enhanced his career in behalf of the World Zionist Organization. Sir Philip Sassoon, whose mother was a Rothschild, was his secretary. [1365] Winston Churchill and Arthur J. Balfour, of Milner's Round Table, were also elevated in power. Lord Rothschild, James de Rothschild, the son of Edmund de Rothschild of Paris, former owner of the Rothschild colonies in Palestine, and Sir Mark Sykes attended the first official meeting of the Political Committee, where they discussed the future mandates of Palestine, Armenia, Mesopotamia, and Arabia. [1366]

The Grand Chessboard, a major globalist blueprint by the audacious globalist, Zbigniew Brzezinski, describes the United States Geostrategic Imperatives in the Middle East. One key premise of the

---

[1363] Charles Savoie, Meet the World Money Power, December 2004, pp. 13-14, http://freedom4um.com/cgi-bin/readart.cgi?ArtNum=20574 as of May 2012

[1364] Carroll Quigley, Tragedy And Hope, A History of the World in our Time, The Macmillan Company, New York, 1966, p. 144

[1365] Arnold Leese, Gentile Folly: the Rothschilds, Reception, February 17, 1937, p. 55

[1366] David Livingston, Terrorism And The Illuminati, A Three Thousand Year History, BookSurge LLC, Charleston, South Carolina, 2007, pp. 178-179

book is the control of the world's resources. Naval strategist, Alfred Thayer Mahan, long ago proposed that whoever secured Egypt would obtain all the coasts, and the islands in the Indian Ocean. Egypt, he felt, held the key to the East. [1367] Total control of all resources includes the protection and control of oil pipelines, and transportation routes such as the Suez Canal. This apparently necessitates a permanent US military presence, with dozens of bases, since the US military is currently the banker's global enforcers. Immediately after World War I, and every major conflict since, the elites shuffle territory and people, which generates turmoil, often requiring military control and occupation.

While thousands of ordinary French and German soldiers were slaughtering each other in Europe, British politicians, ostensibly concerned about the Suez Canal's security, removed 1,400,000 British soldiers. and scarce war materials to the Mediterranean and the Persian Gulf. The French were irate over this maneuver. They had already lost almost 1,500,000 soldiers while another 2,600,000 were severely injured. About a million British troops remained in the Middle East until *after* the end of hostilities, even in the French area, protecting petroleum resources. France's leader, Georges Clemenceau, agreed to the Prime Minister's request to allow the British to have complete control of the Mosul Wilayet (Iraq), and Palestine, from Dan to Beersheba. France would control Greater Syria and receive half of the Mosul oil, along with the guarantee of British post-war support if Germany ever challenged France regarding the Rhine area. [1368]

By the last quarter of 1916, the allies depended wholly on American supplies, and Federal Reserve financing. By 1917, Britain was bankrupt, and ready to relinquish her imperialistic role to the United States, to transfer the wealth from America, as warfare requires huge amounts of cash and credit. They consummated the power transfer with the clear understanding that British officials would retain the exclusive right to command the current struggle. The United States

---

[1367] A. T. Mahan, The Influence of Sea Power upon History, 1660-1783, Little, Brown, Boston, 1918, p. 142

[1368] William Engdahl, A Century of War, Anglo-American Oil Politics and the New World Order, Pluto Press, Ann Arbor, Michigan, 2004, pp. 35-45

would commit troops to prevent Britain from losing the war. Britain had a superior navy, and America was not yet ready to assume naval power. Britain owed money to the Federal Reserve, and had to win to pay the war debts, and keep the banks from losing the money they had loaned.

Colonel Edward M. House had managed Woodrow Wilson's political campaign, including his deceptive promise to keep the United States out of the war. However, he opted to comply with his handlers, which included appointing Louis D. Brandeis, a leading Zionist, to the Supreme Court. Warfare necessitated the removal of Zionist headquarters from Berlin to New York. Then, Wilson, House, J. Pierpont Morgan, Churchill, and others collaborated to provoke Germany into sinking the *Lusitania*, a passenger ship. Wilson, the *man of peace*, largely relying on Brandeis' opinions and encouragement, addressed Congress on April 2, 1917, where he poignantly pleaded for a declaration of war against Germany, which it granted on April 6, 1917. Brandeis was Felix Frankfurter's uncle. Later, Frankfurter dominated the Supreme Court.

Wilson told Congress, "The world must be safe for democracy." The United States entered the war when Britain was close to defeat. The real reasons included the division of the oil-rich Ottoman Empire, and the seizure of Palestine for the creation of Israel, a prospective military presence in the oil-rich gulf. [1369] J. Pierpont Morgan was the US financial agent for all the Allied countries. He also funded France's participation in the war. [1370] Britain owed millions to US banks and businesses who sold war-related components, some shipped on the fated *Lusitania*. Aiding Britain, our debtor nation, protected the banker's loans and business profits. [1371] US citizens died for the bankers and the businessmen.

[1369] David Livingston, Terrorism And The Illuminati, A Three Thousand Year History, BookSurge LLC, Charleston, South Carolina, 2007, pp. 178-179

[1370] 1914-1915, US Policy on Loans to the Belligerents, http://wwi.lib.byu.edu/index.php/US_Policy_on_War_Loans_to_Belligerents as of May 2012

[1371] Carroll Quigley, Tragedy & Hope, A History of the World in Our Time, G. S. G. & Associates, Incorporated, San Pedro, California,1975, p. 250

On June 15, 1917, Congress passed the Espionage Act, the twentieth century version of the 1798 Sedition Law. Congress devised it to squelch internal dissent, rather than protect the United States from any external threats. The current version of this domestic suppression vehicle is the National Defense Authorization Act (NDAA) that Obama signed into law on December 31, 2011. Allegedly, the 1917 act was to punish those who interfered with foreign relations, neutrality, or foreign commerce, and to punish espionage. In fact, it was to suppress war opposition, which Wilson considered to be treasonous behavior. [1372] Officials arrested and incarcerated Eugene Debs, head of the Socialist Party, for "speaking and writing against war." Oddly, the Socialist Party, under Debs, promoted many ideologies that average Americans embraced. The party declined in popularity, prestige, and principles when Norman Thomas took over the leadership.

Vladimir Lenin, Russia's Bolshevik leader, announced an armistice, and sent Trotsky to Brest-Litovsk in November 1917, to negotiate a peace deal with Germany and Austria. They were unable to reach an agreement after nine weeks. As a result, on March 3, 1918, German troops moved toward Petrograd to encourage Russia to accept the terms of the Central Power's (Germany, Austria-Hungary, Bulgaria, and the Ottoman Empire) Brest-Litovsk Treaty. [1373]

Because of the Brest-Litovsk Treaty, the Allies could not impose the Treaty of Versailles upon the new Bolshevik government in Russia, a great benefit. The Bolsheviks now controlled a huge quantity of untapped oil, which would not fall under the control of Standard Oil, British Petroleum, or Royal Dutch Shell, the world's first oil cartel. The Bolsheviks relinquished most of their oil rights in Iran, and forgave all Iranian indebtedness owed to czarist Russia. With Russia out of the way in Iran, Britain and their Anglo-Persian Oil Company seized control of oil exploration and development. Britain extracted

[1372] Clyde E. Willis, Student's Guide to Landmark Congressional Laws on the First Amendment, Greenwood Press, Westport, Connecticut, 2002, p. 12
[1373] Russia and the First World War, http://www.spartacus.schoolnet.co.uk/RUSfww.htm as of May 2012

massive amounts of Iranian oil. Churchill called it "a prize from fairyland beyond our wildest dreams." [1374]

Millions of Americans participated in the war including Smedley D. Butler, who went to France as commander of the Thirteenth Marines. They arrived at Brest on September 24, 1918, and were under the jurisdiction of the US Army. [1375] Butler's marines relocated after two weeks, and his superiors promoted him to Brigadier General on October 7, 1918,[1376] and given charge, by A.E.F. Commander General John J. Pershing, of the army debarkation camp at Pontanezen, France, a filthy, 1700-acre pestilence-infested mud flat, where 75,000 US soldiers were crammed together trying to share inadequate sanitation facilities.

At least 16,000 of those soldiers suffered from influenza. An average of twenty-five soldiers died each day from that, and other diseases. In usual Butler fashion, he turned the camp into a model of efficiency. His treatment of the troops was admirable—he gave them double rations of food, an adequate number of blankets, and provided them with a dry sleeping area. He cared more about the men than the regulations he broke to make them comfortable. He always favored his men, the powerless against the brass. [1377]

Toward the end of the war, technicians had gathered up all of the vaccines on the lab shelves and vaccinated every single US soldier, the first time in history that a government had mandated compulsory inoculations in the military. This poisonous medical assault, the Schick diphtheria vaccine, outlawed years before in Austria, due to the deaths of several children, killed more US soldiers than the war.

[1374] Stephen Kinzer, All the Shah's Men: An American Coup and the Roots of Middle East Terror, Publisher: Wiley. Hoboken, NJ. 2003, p. 39
[1375] David T. Zabecki, Paths to Glory: Medal of Honor Recipients Smedley Butler and Dan Daly, http://www.historynet.com/magazines/military_history/12833262.html?page=1&c=y as of May 2012
[1376] Who's Who in Marine Corps History, http://www.tecom.usmc.mil/HD/Whos_Who/Butler_SD.htm as of May 2012
[1377] Jules Archer, The Plot to Seize the White House, Hawthorne Books, Inc., New York 1973, pp. 77-80

The Austrian government banned the use of Béla Schick's vaccine and banished him from the country. [1378] By 1923, Schick, a Hungarian Jew, directed the Pediatric Department at Mount Sinai Hospital, New York. In 1936, he became a professor at Columbia University. He headed the Pediatric Department of Beth-El Hospital, Brooklyn (1950-1962). Doctors still use the Schick test, invented in 1910-1911, to determine whether a person is susceptible to diphtheria. Later, Gerta Ries (Wiener) created a sculpture as a tribute to Schick, for the Jewish-American Hall of Fame.

Despite recruiting propaganda, the military were and are now underpaid, used as medical guinea pigs, exposed to death, disease, toxic depleted uranium, and, often abandoned as POWs or MIAs. When discharged, the government typically leaves the men and women to battle war's inevitable emotional trauma without assistance.

Butler, disturbed by what he witnessed, wrote, "The wounded and maimed pass through Pontanezen, some with their nervous systems irreparably shattered . . . Gradually it began to dawn on me, to wonder what on earth these American boys are doing getting wounded, and killed, and buried in France." He began to doubt "the ethics of his chosen calling." [1379]

Alexander Parvus and his German Accomplices

Alexander Parvus, who wanted to establish revolutionary fifth columns among the allies, befriended Baron Hans von Wangenheim, Germany's Ambassador in Constantinople. Parvus presented a proposal to Germany via Wangenheim. He suggested that Germany finance Russia's destabilization through a general strike during its war with Russia and its allies. On January 9, 1915, Wangenheim sent a telegram to Arthur Zimmermann, the Under State Secretary to the State Secretary. The ambassador told him that Parvus, who wanted to meet with them, was one of the main leaders of the last Russian

---

[1378] Dr. Eleanor Elben McBean, Vaccination Condemned by all Competent Doctors, Book One, Better Life Research, Los Angeles, California, 1981, pp. 41, 45

[1379] Ibid. 77-80

Revolution, an exile from Russia, and that officials had, on several occasions, expelled him from Germany. Now, Parvus was active as a writer, "concerning himself chiefly with questions of Turkish economics." He was assisting a Dr. Zimmer in his support of the Union for the Liberation of Ukraine, formally founded in Lemberg (Lviv) by socialists on August 4, 1914. [1380]

Arthur Zimmermann responded to the telegram on January 10, 1915, asking that officials keep Parvus' visit a secret. By January 13, they arranged to have Kurt Riezler, a Permanent Assistant in the Foreign Ministry, meet with Parvus when he arrived. In September 1917, Riezler went to the Legation in Stockholm as a Counselor to direct the newly-formed Russian consul there. In April 1918, officials would recall Riezler to Berlin, and in the same month he left to work with Count Wilhelm von Mirbach, the Minister in Moscow. [1381] After the war, Riezler avidly supported the Weimar Republic (1918-1933), and joined the Social Democratic Party (SPD). He regularly contributed to the newspaper *Die Deutsche Nation,* and helped develop the Weimar Constitution. He was Chief of Cabinet (1919-1920) to President Friedrich Ebert, and played a big part in quashing the Kapp Putsch.

Von Wangenheim sent Parvus to Berlin where he arrived on March 6, 1915. He met with certain officials and proposed a twenty-page strategy describing the implementation of massive political strikes in Russia. Parvus advised the division of Russia by supporting the

---

[1380] Hakan Kirimli, The Activities of the Union for the Liberation of Ukraine in the Ottoman Empire during the First World War, Middle Eastern Studies, Volume 34, No. 4, Turkey before and after Atatürk: Internal and External Affairs, October 1998, pp. 177-200

[1381] Z. A. B. Zeman (editor), Germany and the Revolution in Russia 1915-1918, Documents from the Archives of the German Foreign Ministry," Oxford University Press, Oxford, England, 1958, pp. 1-2

Bolshevik faction of the Social Democratic Labor Party, by urging ethnic exclusivity in various Russian regions, and by championing writers who criticized the czar during the war. Considering his experience in 1905, he imagined that class division in Russia, following a devastating war defeat, would be the most effective method of instituting a socialist revolution.

Alexander Parvus, after influencing and contributing to the fomenting of the Bolshevik Revolution of 1917 in Russia, would become an adviser to the Weimar Republic in postwar Germany. He joined the German Social Democratic Party, and he developed close relationships with Karl Kautsky, Clara Zetkin, Rosa Luxemburg, and Karl Radek. Parvus quickly became one of the best theoreticians of the party. Others regarded him, and Luxembourg, as hotheads. In the 1890s, and early 1900s, he participated in the politics surrounding German and Russian Marxism. He also wrote extensively on imperialism, agrarian matters, and capitalism. [1382] The German Foreign Ministry, controlled by Lenin assets, transferred the first five million marks to the Bolsheviks for revolutionary propaganda on June 7, 1915, via Aleksander Keskula, the Estonian agent who began his association with the Germans on September 12, 1914. He initially met Lenin on October 6, 1914. [1383]

Dr. Johannes Lepsius arrived in Constantinople in late July to visit Ismail Enver. Henry Morgenthau Sr., the US Ambassador to the Ottoman Empire (1913-1916), in his memoirs, and elsewhere, criticized Wangenheim and painted him as a villain. [1384] He claimed that Kaiser

---

[1382] M Asim Karaömerlioglu, Helphand-Parvus and his Impact on Turkish Intellectual Life, Middle Eastern Studies Publication, Vol.40, No.6, November 2004, pp. 145-165

[1383] Jüri Lina, Under the Sign of the Scorpion: The Rise and Fall of the Soviet Empire, Referent Publishing, Stockholm, Sweden, 2002, pp. 183-186

[1384] Christopher J. Walker, Armenia, the Survival of a Nation, Routledge, London, 1980, pp. 231-235

Wilhelm, who he claimed sought "world domination," personally chose Wangenheim to try to subjugate Turkey, and transform its army, and its territory into "instruments of Germany." He wrote, "Wangenheim worshipped the Prussian military system." He claimed that Germany's "ambitions had transformed the world into a place of horror," and "Wangenheim's every act and every word typified this new and dreadful portent among the nations." He claimed that Wangenheim "divided mankind into two classes, the governing and the governed" and believed that "Germany was inevitably destined to rule the world." [1385]

Morgenthau claimed, "For twenty years the German Government had been cultivating the Turkish Empire. All this time the Kaiser had been preparing for a world war and in this war it was destined that Turkey should play an almost decisive part." [1386] He said of Wangenheim, "Like the government which he served so loyally, he was fundamentally ruthless, shameless, and cruel . . . with the realism and logic that are so characteristically German, (he) would brush aside all feelings of humanity and decency that might interfere with success." [1387] He claimed that Wangenheim, by the spring of 1914, controlled Talaat and Enver, who represented the CUP, and "dominated the Turkish Empire." [1388]

On August 14, 1915, German Minister in Copenhagen Ulrich Graf von Brockdorff-Rantzau addressed a letter to the German vice-state secretary, trying to convince him and other officials to financially support the Bolsheviks. The letter summarized a conversation between Brockdorff-Rantzau and Alexander Parvus wherein the ambassador advocated using Parvus to destabilize Russia. [1389]

[1385] Henry Morgenthau, Ambassador Morgenthau's Story, Doubleday, Page & Co., New York, 1918, pp. 5-6

[1386] Ibid. 5-6

[1387] Ibid. 7-8

[1388] Ibid. 14-15

[1389] Jüri Lina, Under the Sign of the Scorpion: The Rise and Fall of the Soviet Empire, Referent Publishing, Stockholm, Sweden, 2002, pp. 183-186

A State Department document, dated February 15, 1916, discusses the czar's overthrow and mentions Max Breitung and Isaac Seligman, both freemasons, as participating in that event. Max Warburg, a Zionist, a banker and a freemason, helped fund the communist propaganda in Russia. Warburg, one of the most powerful men in Germany, and other wealthy Jews supported Communism. Parvus planned for the Bolshevik seizure in 1916, and made certain that Lenin had sufficient money, as much as six million dollars in gold. Karl Kautsky, a German Jew, said that "the Jews in Russia had only one true friend—the revolutionary movement." They comprised about thirty to fifty percent of the party. [1390]

The American International Corporation, headed by J. Pierpont Morgan Jr. also assisted the revolutionaries. Jacob H. and Mortimer Schiff, Felix Warburg, Otto H. Kahn, Max Warburg, Jerome J. Hanauer, Alfred Milner and the Guggenheim family also financed the Bolsheviks. Most of these people were Jews and freemasons. Max Warburg established a Russian publishing house, along with German industrialist, Hugo Stinnes, who, on August 12, 1916, agreed to contribute two million rubles for the financing of that publishing house. [1391]

In April 1917, the German General Staff, and the German Supreme Command, unknown to the Kaiser, facilitated and financed Lenin and his revolutionaries on their train journey from Switzerland through Germany and Sweden, to Petrograd, Russia, with money funneled from Parvus through Jakub Fürstenberg (Yakov Ganetsky), both Jews. There, they would meet Leon Trotsky to complete the revolution, to destroy the Russian Army, and to eliminate it from World War I. Chancellor Bethmann-Hollweg, who, in 1917, lost the Reichstag's support, directed State Secretary Arthur Zimmermann to approve of the passage of the Bolsheviks. He allegedly never anticipated that they would later oppose Germany and Europe. He facilitated the

---

[1390] Ibid. 184-185

[1391] Jüri Lina, Under the Sign of the Scorpion: The Rise and Fall of the Soviet Empire, Referent Publishing, Stockholm, Sweden, 2002, pp. 183-186

diplomatic details with Fürstenberg, the German minister in Bern, and Brockdorff-Rantzau in Copenhagen. [1392]

Bethmann-Hollweg and Zimmermann, in Berlin, communicated with Brockdorff-Rantzau, a thirty-third degree freemason, [1393] a Parvus associate, then residing in Copenhagen. Lenin's direct link was Fürstenberg. Lenin was not a German agent, despite the help that Chancellor Bethmann-Hollweg awarded him, because his objectives were then compatible with certain people in the Foreign Ministry. Additionally, each entity had alternative motives—Germany sought access to postwar markets in Russia, and Lenin sought to establish a Marxist dictatorship. [1394] Lenin and Parvus, who worked with German intelligence, privately collaborated but carefully avoided meeting in public.

On April 16, 1917, Lenin, his wife Nadeshda Krupskaya, Grigory Zinoviev, Grigori Sokolnikov, and Karl Radek left Bern for Stockholm. When the train arrived at the Russian border, authorities denied entrance to Fritz Platten, a Swiss socialist, and Karl Radek, but allowed everyone else admittance. Several months later, the authorities allowed almost 200 Mensheviks into the country. Trotsky had been a Menshevik, but adopted Bolshevism in 1917, perhaps because of the German funds. [1395]

German intelligence established Parvus' financial network via offshore operations in Copenhagen, to shift money to Russia between front organizations. The majority of the transactions were genuine, yet still helped to conceal Bolshevik funds. Scandinavian fiscal and customs offices were overburdened, and inadequate for the booming black market during the war. There is no conclusive evidence showing that the Germans supplied the money for this financial network.

[1392] Antony C. Sutton, Wall Street and the Bolshevik Revolution, Buccaneer Books, Cutchogue, New York, 1993, pp. 27-29

[1393] Jüri Lina, Under the Sign of the Scorpion: The Rise and Fall of the Soviet Empire, Referent Publishing, Stockholm, Sweden, 2002, p. 183

[1394] Antony C. Sutton, Wall Street and the Bolshevik Revolution, Buccaneer Books, Cutchogue, New York, 1993, pp. 27-29

[1395] Ibid. 27-29

Historians recently examined the records from Alexander Kerensky's Government and found them to be inconclusive or utter forgeries.

On October 27, 1917, Edgar Sisson, a former *Chicago Tribune* reporter, former managing editor of *Collier's Weekly* and past editor of *Cosmopolitan,* left the United States to become the Petrograd-based representative of the government's propaganda apparatus, the Committee on Public Information (CPI) or the Creel Committee, and a special envoy of President Woodrow Wilson. In early 1918, after the Bolsheviks had seized power, he acquired a set of 68 Russian-language documents. These papers appeared to provide evidence of a German-Bolshevik conspiracy during World War I, claiming that Trotsky, Lenin, and other Bolshevik leaders were agents of the German government. Sisson recruited Russians to disseminate US propaganda in Germany, in addition to distributing a million Russian-language prints of President Wilson's war message to the US Congress.

On December 3, 1917, Richard von Kühlmann, Minister of Foreign Affairs, said, "It was not until the Bolsheviks had received from us a steady flow of funds through various channels and under varying labels that they were in a position to be able to build up their main organ Pravda, to conduct energetic propaganda and appreciably to extend the originally narrow base of their party." [1396] The Kaiser's Zionist adviser Walter Rathenau (1867-1922), a rich industrialist, also suggested that Germany should finance the Bolsheviks. [1397]

Sisson returned to the United States in May, to head the CPI's Foreign Section. On May 9, 1918, President Wilson had Sisson's report on the Russian documents, which the CPI released to the media on September 15. The press dutifully and unquestioning reported that the German General Staff had hired Lenin and Trotsky. On September 21, 1918, *The New York Evening Post* questioned the validity of the Sisson Documents, and claimed that Santeri Nuorteva, member of

[1396] Antony C. Sutton, Wall Street and the Bolshevik Revolution, Buccaneer Books, Cutchogue, New York, 1993, pp. 27-29
[1397] Jüri Lina, Under the Sign of the Scorpion: The Rise and Fall of the Soviet Empire, Referent Publishing, Stockholm, Sweden, 2002, p. 183

the Finnish Socialist Federation, and a former Soviet propagandist, actually wrote them. *The New York Times*, certainly a biased opinion-making newspaper, reported that the Sisson Documents, in possession of the CPI, verified that Lenin and Trotsky, heads of the Bolshevist government, were German agents. Further, that the German Great General Staff arranged for the German Imperial Bank, and other financial institutions, to fund the revolution. Moreover, German agents Lenin and Trotsky betrayed the Russian people by signing the Treaty of Brest-Litovsk.

Germany allegedly selected a commander to defend Petrograd against the German Army, and provided German officers to advise the Bolshevik government, command its armies, spy on the embassies of Russia, and to direct Bolshevik foreign and domestic policy. *The New York Times* claimed that the Bolshevik government was in fact German, representing the best interests of Germany. The CPI published a pamphlet, based on the Sisson Documents, *The German-Bolshevik Conspiracy*, of which it distributed 137,000 copies. John F. Jameson, a gatekeeper historian, associated with the Carnegie Institution, and the American Historical Association, founded by Andrew D. White (S&B), and Professor Samuel N. Harper, validated the authenticity of most of the documents. [1398] Not surprisingly, after World War II, the Allies discovered documents in the German Foreign Office that purportedly confirmed that Imperial Germany had financed the Bolsheviks.

In 1956, George F. Kennan examined and scientifically evaluated the Sisson Documents, and categorically stated that they were forgeries. He wrote a very persuasive technical article but, by then, the public paid very little attention to a decades-old controversy. Some academics appreciated his scholarship but, for the most part, the entertainment and news media, the schools, and typical government officials raised on propaganda pabulum, continue to compare every totalitarian institution, or government, to Nazism or Communism, as if each shared the same characteristics, but with different names.

[1398] Christopher Lasch, The New Radicalism in America 1889-1963: The Intellectual As a Social Type, Norton & Company, New York, 1965, pp. 178-179

The Armenian Genocide, Relocation and Extermination

The Jews took power during their Young Turk Revolution, a movement entirely overshadowed by the Chinese Revolution (1911), and the Russian Revolutions (1905, 1917). Young Turk leaders then organized and executed the Armenian Genocide wherein between 600,000 and 1,500,000 perished.

The United States sends ambassadors to foreign countries to intimidate, cajole, or threaten local leaders to serve the corporate, cultural, and political interests of politically-connected entities. Since 1831, the United States has sent ambassadors to Turkey, including Lew Wallace (1881-1885), the author of *Ben-Hur: A Tale of the Christ* (1880). President Grover Cleveland appointed Oscar S. Straus, a B'nai B'rith member, as Ambassador (1887-1889), followed by Solomon Hirsch (1889-1892). Straus represented certain interests so well that three succeeding presidents appointed him to Turkey (1898-1899, and 1909-1910). Henry Morgenthau Sr., a member of both the Pilgrims Society, and B'nai B'rith, was a Harlem real estate mogul and a leader in New York City's Reform Jewish community. His money helped to install Woodrow Wilson into the White House, and the new president asked him to accept the ambassadorship to Turkey.[1399] Though lacking experience, Morgenthau reluctantly accepted the position (1913-1916), with the encouragement of his good friend, Rabbi Stephen S. Wise, a founder, and leading member of the Zionist Organization of America, founded in 1897, to do everything necessary to secure a Jewish homeland in Palestine. Wilson appointed Abram I. Elkus (1916-1917), a key member of the American Jewish Congress.

Not only do the United States and other industrialized countries send ambassadors, they also send intelligence agents, such as the CIA, to engage in terrorist activities. In March 1915, Eitan Belkind, Aharon and Sarah Aharonson, his sister, and Avshalam Feinberg founded Nili, a Jewish espionage network that provided information to the allied forces during World War I. Sir Mark Sykes assisted

---

[1399] Kerry M. Olitzky and Ronald H. Isaacs, A Glossary of Jewish Life, Jason Aronson Inc., New Jersey, 1991, p. 155

them during the organization's assault against the Ottoman Empire in Palestine. Belkind infiltrated the Ottoman army, and became an officer assigned to the headquarters of Ahmed Djemal, Minister of the Navy. Belkind, the British agent, relates that, in early 1915, a few Circassian soldiers ordered some Armenians to gather sufficient thorns and thistles to create a tall pyramid. Thereafter, the soldiers tied almost 5,000 Armenians together around the pyramid and then torched it. He fled in order to escape the tortuous screams but returned two days later to find the charred bodies. Belkind was a cousin to the Chief Rabbi of Turkey, Chaim Nahum, who "rejected any involvement or contact" in the Armenian issue. [1400] [1401]

Belkind also wrote, "On Friday in late March 1915, about 10,000 Jewish were exiled from Israel. They were taken to Jaffa and forced to board ships belonging to neutral states such as Italy, USA, etc. The deportation was carried out with great cruelty. The deportees left all their property behind, women and children were hurled into the ships. It was a tragic and oppressing sight. Feinberg, a witness to the deportations, went to Jerusalem to the Anti-Locust Department, and urged Aharonson to start an uprising; because the Jewish settlements were on the brink of annihilation. Avshalom insisted that, in his opinion, that it had been the Germans that advised Turkey to deport the Jews." [1402]

On April 24, 1915, Mehmed Talaat Pasha, a freemason, while posing as an orthodox Moslem, was actually descended from a Spanish-Jewish family. He had collaborated with the Young Turks, also Jews. He ordered the closure of all Armenian political organizations within the Ottoman Empire, and the arrest of all Armenians associated with those organizations. He justified his actions by acknowledging that foreign influences were controlling those organizations and provoking disturbances in collaboration with Russian forces. On the night of April 24/25, 1915, Young Turk authorities arrested between 235

[1400] Yair Auron, The Banality of Indifference: Zionism & the Armenian Genocide, Transaction Publishers, New Brunswick, New Jersey, 2000, pp. 181-183

[1401] That's How It Was, Narrated by Eitan Belkind, member of the NILI, Published by the Ministry of Defense of Israel, 1979, pp. 77-78, 115-116, 118-120, 124, 127

[1402] Ibid. 77-78, 115-116, 118-120, 124, 127

and 270 Armenian leaders in Constantinople, including politicians, clergymen, physicians, authors, journalists, lawyers, and teachers. Several weeks earlier, the government allegedly organized the mass killings of Armenian civilians in the Van vilayet.

On May 27, 1915, Talaat Pasha, CUP Minister of the Interior issued the Tehcir Law or Temporary Law of Deportation authorizing the government to deport anyone that it "sensed" was a threat to national security. The order covered the period from June 1, 1915 to February 8, 1916. It legalized the mass deportation of Armenians from the empire's eastern provinces to Syria. Many historians maintain that Ismail Enver Pasha should share equal responsibility for the "extermination" of the Armenians. Reportedly, Ismail Enver Pasha told Ambassador Morgenthau, "I have accomplished more toward solving the Armenian problem in three months than Abdülhamid accomplished in thirty years!"

Ismail Enver Pasha, because the Armenians were plotting against the government, introduced repressive measures against them, and implemented the deportation of about 2,000,000 Armenians, which culminated in a massacre. Ethnic Turks and Kurds attacked their villages and murdered vulnerable refugees. Many Armenians relocated in Iran, now the residence of about 100,000 of them. [1403] Armenian nationalists claim that the government did not deport them because of their rebellion, and, as proof, point to the date of the deportation law, about the same time that the Armenians seized the City of Van. They further claim that the Ottomans intended to deport them long before they published their intentions. However, the authorities considered the deportation shortly before May 1915. [1404]

[1403] Anahit Khosroeva, Assyrian Massacres in Ottoman Turkey and Adjacent Turkish Territories, from the book Assyrian Massacres in Ottoman Turkey and Adjacent Territories, http://www.aina.org/articles/amitaatt.htm as of May 2012

[1404] Dr. Justin McCarthy, Armenian Rebels—Effects & Consequences, a transcription of a speech given at the Turkish Grand National Assembly, March 24, 2005, http://www.tallarmeniantale.com/mccarthy-armenian-rebels.htm as of May 2012

The German Ambassador to the Ottoman Empire, Baron Hans von Wangenheim stated that a systematic genocide of the Armenians would have obstructed the war effort. It would have withdrawn troops and military supplies, needed by the Central powers, and weakened the army. He did not want to insult the Young Turk rulers and their efforts to win the war. On May 31, 1915, he notified officials in Berlin to block Armenian espionage and their extensive risings. İsmail Enver Pasha intended to close many Armenian schools, suppress their correspondence and newspapers as well as relocate uninvolved Armenian families to Mesopotamia. He requested that Germany not interfere. Governments hostile to Germany, would exploit anything that Turkish officials did. He said that he thought that Germany should try to modify its methods, but not hinder the Turkish government on its principles. [1405]

On June 17, 1915, Wangenheim changed his opinions. He wrote, "It is obvious that the banishment of the Armenians is not due solely to military considerations." Talaat Bey (born Mehmed Talaat), the minister of the interior, told Dr. Johannes Mordtmann of the embassy that "the Porte intended to make use of the world war to deal thoroughly with its internal enemies, the Christians in Turkey, and that it meant not to be disturbed in this by diplomatic intervention from abroad." Wangenheim arranged for Dr. Johannes Lepsius to visit the Porte. On July 1, Count Johann von Pallavicini, Ambassador at the Sublime Porte, told Talaat that the deportations "seemed hardly justified." On July 4, Wangenheim sent a memo to the grand vizier telling him that Germany would not hide the consequences "created by these harsh measures and mass deportations, which include guilty and innocent without distinction, especially when they accompany these measures by acts of violence, such as massacres and pillages." [1406]

On Saturday, June 26, 1915, authorities posted the deportation proclamation pertaining to all Armenians. Women and children wept. Some of these people were wealthy and accustomed to luxury and ease. There were clergymen, bankers, merchants, lawyers, mechanics,

---

[1405] Christopher J. Walker, Armenia, the Survival of a Nation, Routledge, London, 1980, pp. 231-235
[1406] Ibid. 231-235

tailors, and men from every occupation. [1407] Young Turk officials subjected the Armenian Christians, as part of the deportation, to forced marches, massacres, starvation and rape.

Wangenheim said that it was imperative that the provincial authorities take measures to protect the life and property of evacuated Armenians, during their deportation and in their new location. He reminded the Turkish authorities that their activities could damage German interests, and asked that the deportees be given a grace period before they were actually deported. The Turkish government rejected the Austrian or German appeals. On July 12, 1915, Wangenheim again wrote to Talaat Pasha demanding that he take measures against Reshid Bey, who was organizing large-scale massacres. Talaat later told Aubrey Herbert of the British Parliament that he opposed the attempted extermination of the Armenians. Yet, he claims that when he protested the policy, others overruled his objections. Wangenheim also wrote to Chancellor Bethmann-Hollweg telling him that diplomatic pressure failed to influence the government and therefore, "Turkey must accept full responsibility for her actions." Wangenheim soon left for Berlin and his successor, Paul Wolff Metternich, reiterated Germany's opposition to the Ottoman's treatment of the Armenians. [1408] In August 1916, Young Turk leaders, İsmail Enver Pasha and Mehmed Talaat Pasha, demanded Metternich's recall citing his stance on the Armenian Question.

The Young Turk government allegedly did not provide the deportees with shelter, food, water or supplies during the march. The Turkish guards accompanying them reportedly robbed, raped, and killed many of them and allowed bystanders to participate. On August 18, 1915, *The New York Times*, published by Adolph S. Ochs, reported, "The refugees will have to traverse on foot a distance, requiring marches of from one to two months . . . the roads and the Euphrates are strewn with corpses of exiles, and those who survive are doomed to certain death. It is a plan to exterminate the whole Armenian people." The

---

[1407] Samuel Sidney McClure, Obstacles to Peace, Houghton Mifflin Company, Boston and New York, 1917, pp. 400-402

[1408] Christopher J. Walker, Armenia, the Survival of a Nation, Routledge, London, 1980, pp. 231-235

Times reported, "Hundreds of women and young girls . . . have been pillaged, defiled and destroyed. At the beginning of this month all the inhabitants of Karahissar were pitilessly massacred, with the exception of a few children." [1409]

Bahaeddin Şakir said, "We are in war, there is no threat of intervention by Europe and the Great Powers, and the world press either will not be able to voice a protest. Even if we do not succeed, the problem will become an accomplished fact, the voices will calm down, and no one will dare to express a protest. We should make use of this exceptional situation as much as possible. This kind of opportunity is not always available . . ." [1410] Talaat Pasha told Johannes Mordtmann, "Turkey is intent on taking advantage of the war in order to thoroughly liquidate its internal foes, the indigenous Christians, without being thereby disturbed by foreign intervention." [1411]

Samuel S. McClure wrote, "The shortest method for disposing of the women and children concentrated in the various camps was to burn them. Fire was set to large wooden sheds in Alidjan, Megrakon, Khaskegh, and other Armenian villages, and these absolutely helpless women and children were roasted to death . . . And the executioners, who seem to have been unmoved by this unparalleled savagery, grasped infants by one leg and hurled them into the fire . . . the stench of the burning human flesh permeated the air for many days after." In the Baibourt area, "The worst and most unimaginable horrors were reserved for us at the banks of the Euphrates and in the Erzindjan plain. The mutilated bodies of women, girls, and little children made everybody shudder." [1412]

[1409] Armenians are Sent to Perish in Desert; Turks Accused of Plan to Exterminate Whole Population People of Karahissar Massacred, Special Cable to The New York Times, August 18, 1915, p. 5
[1410] Anahit Khosroeva, Assyrian Massacres in Ottoman Turkey and Adjacent Turkish Territories, from the book Assyrian Massacres in Ottoman Turkey and Adjacent Territories, http://www.aina.org/articles/amitaatt.htm
[1411] Ibid
[1412] Samuel Sidney McClure, Obstacles to Peace, Houghton Mifflin Company, Boston and New York, 1917, pp. 400-402

The Young Turks also allegedly used cattle cars to transport the Armenians, at least 20,000 by August 1, 1915. Peter Balakian, an author on *The New York Times Best Seller's List*, relates that there was a twenty-five mile stretch between Urfa and Arab Pournar, where "the beaten paths are lined with corpses of the victims." [1413]

After deportation, the government could legally confiscate the abandoned properties, livestock, and land and assets, as sanctioned by the new Temporary Law of Expropriation and Confiscation, enacted on September 13, 1915. [1414] On September 29, 1915, Jesse B. Jackson, American Consul in Aleppo, sent Morgenthau many charts and tables enumerating the railway deportations by city, town, and Armenian religious sect . . . giving the numbers of children and adults." Jackson wrote, "The deportation of Armenians from their homes by the Turkish government has continued with a persistence and perfection of plan." [1415]

According to Balakian's book, government officials put Virginia Meghrouni, a thirteen year old, and her mother onto an eastern-bound, windowless, stuffy cattle car to Ras ul-Ain with a group of people suffering with dysentery which made the air foul with the smell of excrement. When the car arrived at Ras ul-Ain the guards shoved the occupants out of the cattle car into the desert, calling them "infidel dogs" and telling them "You're on your way to slaughter valley." Virginia and her mother were surprised to find "miles of large black tents in which thousands of people were dead or barely breathing." When they looked into one of the tents, they found people languishing, waiting for death, stretched out, on the bare earth, while flies, insects and birds of prey feasted on nearby corpses. [1416] Other Armenian deportees attempted to stay alive, sheltered in grass huts [1417]

[1413] Peter Balakian, The Burning Tigris: The Armenian Genocide and America's Response, Harper Collins, New York, 2003, pp. 256-257

[1414] Ibid. 186-188

[1415] Ibid. 256-257

[1416] Ibid. 256-257

[1417] Yair Auron, The Banality of Indifference: Zionism & the Armenian Genocide, Transaction Publishers, New Brunswick, New Jersey, 2000, pp. 181-183

According to Jackson, officials were evacuating every "Christian" in the Turkish Empire. Almost all of the Armenians, Catholics, Caldeans and Protestants, from the provinces of "Van, Erzaerum, Bitlis, Diarbekir, Mamouret ul-Aziz, Angora and Sivas . . . have already been practically exterminated." The death toll was reportedly already over 500,000 by August 15, 1915. The survival rate of the forced marches was about fifteen percent; about one million Armenians were missing. [1418] Military personnel who refused to kill defenseless Armenians were relieved of duty and court-martialed or murdered. [1419]

On October 6, 1915, Lord James Bryce, former Member of Parliament, a former Ambassador to the United States (1907-1913), a friend of President Woodrow Wilson, and a popular figure in America, told Parliament about the premeditated murder of "around 800,000" Armenians. He said that officials in Constantinople ordered the massacres, which carried a penalty for non-compliance. Aneurin Williams, of the British Parliament, presented a similar account on November 16. Denys Cochin, a French writer, wrote about the massacres. He was the Minister of State (1915-1916) under Aristide Briand, a leader of the French Socialist Party. Cochin was then under-secretary for foreign policy matters responsible for dealing with the blockade of Germany. Other writers disseminated Cochin's material. One such individual wrote, "Germany's ally was committing the vilest atrocities," and compared the fate of the Armenians to that of the Belgians. [1420]

Senate Concurrent Resolution of February 9, 1916, resolved that the US President designate a day on which US citizens give an expression

---

[1418] Peter Balakian, The Burning Tigris: The Armenian Genocide and America's Response, Harper Collins, New York, 2003, pp. 256-257

[1419] Jeremy Hugh Baron FRCP FRCS, Genocidal Doctors, Journal of the Royal Society of Medicine, Volume 92, November 1999, p. 590

[1420] Christopher J. Walker, Armenia, the Survival of a Nation, Routledge, London, 1980, pp. 231-235

to their sympathy by contributing funds for the relief of the Armenians who were enduring starvation, disease, and untold suffering. [1421]

When Dr. Johannes Lepsius returned to Germany after a trip to Constantinople, he campaigned to get fifty pastors to petition Germany's foreign ministry to attempt to alter Turkey's policy. They also questioned why Germany would ally itself with a government that had such policies. Bethmann-Hollweg responded that he would direct his ambassadors in the capital to further appeal to the government. This intervention hardly absolved Bethmann-Hollweg from what his ally was doing to its Armenian population. The German Foreign Ministry allowed Dr. Lepsius full access to their archives following the war. As a result he wrote *Germany and Armenia 1914-1918: Collection of Diplomatic documents*. J. Ellis Barker, author of several books, concluded, from reading Lepsius' book, that Germany participated in the genocide. Ulrich Trumpener, author of *Germany and the Armenian Persecutions, 1914-1918*, resolved that Germany was uninvolved and instead attempted to halt it. [1422]

Other German ambassadors to the Turkish capital, despite their efforts, also encountered the same inflexibility, and inaction regarding the Armenian question. Both Enver Pasha and Khalil Pasha refused to discuss the issue. Talaat agreed that innocent people had suffered, but that did not change the policies, although he promised to alleviate their plight. Talaat furiously responded in December, that their policies regarding the Armenians were issues of the internal administration, and not a diplomatic matter, and that military necessities, and a legitimate self-defense against subversion dictated these measures. Therefore, the government rejected Germany's recommendations. The German foreign ministry did not respond to Talaat's memorandum. [1423]

[1421] Affirmation Of The United States Record On The Armenian Genocide Resolution, House of Representatives, to accompany H. Res. 596, October 4, 2000, http://thomas.loc.gov/cgi-bin/cpquery/T?&report=hr933&dbname=106& as of May 2012

[1422] Christopher J. Walker, Armenia, the Survival of a Nation, Routledge, London, 1980, pp. 231-235

[1423] Ibid. 231-235

Ambassador Morgenthau gave a speech at the Wise Center Forum in Cincinnati on May 21, 1916, regarding the sale of Palestine, after the war. As ambassador, he said he broached the subject of the Armenians with Turkish officials who were very receptive, even eager. He said, "Turkish officials will do anything if they have no fear of punishment or censure. The Turks gladly would have made a bargain with me that they would protect the Jews and do what they desired with the Christians." He went on to say, "It is utterly impossible to place several millions of people in Palestine. There would be grave danger from the Arabs. It is a good idea to have a model colony here. If Jews continue there as at present, at the end of the war there will be no friction. I believe the Zionists will not provoke the Government. Turkey needs the Jews. They have lost the Armenians and must fill the gap." [1424]

Chaim Nahum, Chief Rabbi of Turkey (1909-1920), associated with the Young Turks, especially Talaat Pasha, who was a good friend. He was Morgenthau's political counterpart, in as much as Turkey considered sending him to the United States as an ambassador, which concerned some British officials, who feared that World Jewry would ally with the Central Powers. The Jews were such a strong influence, and held enough power to bring United States into the war on the side of Germany, and the Turkish Empire. To counter that possibility, on May 24, 1916, *The London Times* reported that the English Zionist Federation planned to commemorate June 4, 1916, as "Declaration Day." It read, "We earnestly desire the establishment of a publicly-recognized, legally-secure Home for the Jewish People in Palestine, as officially formulated by the First Zionist Congress in 1897."

The government ended the deportations by early 1916, though survivors still experienced violent outbreaks against them. Germany decreased its protests. The German Ambassador continued his reports of the internal workings of the Turkish government to Berlin. On June 30, 1916, he described how the CUP was directing the affairs

---

[1424] Found Turks Eager To Sell Palestine; Mr. Morgenthau, in Speech, Discloses Fact That They Discussed the Matter. Even Got Down To Figures Ministers Argued Whether the Holy Land Should Be an International State or a Republic, The New York Times, May 22, 1916, p. 2

of the country, and implementing its philosophical preferences in every aspect of society, while enriching itself by the annihilation of the Armenians. [1425]

While Morgenthau was US Ambassador, though he claimed otherwise, he remained relatively silent during what people refer to as the systematic Armenian Genocide. In June 1917, he and Felix Frankfurter, representing the War Department, traveled to Turkey on a secret mission to convince its leaders to abandon the Central Powers. After the war, Morgenthau attended the Paris Peace Conference as an advisor regarding Eastern Europe and the Middle East issues.

Perhaps Morgenthau's statements in Cincinnati were an attempt to push the British to accept the Zionist goals. They were going to take Palestine, no matter who won the war, Britain or Germany. However, the Zionists played both sides of the war to guarantee their own objectives, despite the costs to anyone else. On November 12, 1917, *The New York Times* reported that the Germans recognized that Morgenthau, Walter Rothschild, Frankfurter and President Wilson had conspired to get the United States to enter the war in exchange for the Balfour Declaration. [1426]

In August 1919, Woodrow Wilson sent General James Harbord on a fact-finding mission to the Middle East to investigate the feasibility of the Balfour Declaration, in support of a Jewish state. On April 13, 1920, Harbord, later RCA president (1922-1930), and Board Chairman (to 1947), reported to the Senate on the mutilation, violation, torture, and death, that occurred in a hundred Armenian valleys. He referred to it as "this most colossal crime of all the ages." [1427]

[1425] Christopher J. Walker, Armenia, the Survival of a Nation, Routledge, London, 1980, pp. 231-235

[1426] Christopher Jon Bjerknes, Jewish Genocide of Armenian Christians, 2007, p. 188

[1427] AffirmationOfTheUnitedStatesRecordOnTheArmenianGenocideResolution, House of Representatives, to accompany H. Res. 596, October 4, 2000, http://thomas.loc.gov/cgi-bin/cpquery/T?&report=hr933&dbname=106& as of May 2012

In 1919, Morgenthau wrote an incredibly anti-Muslim book detailing the genocidal horrors of the Armenian genocide, actually carried out by the Dönmes, which, at the time, the United States and Britain apparently ignored. He described Sheik-ul-Islam's alleged appeal for a total *Jihad* or *Holy War* against all infidels. The Sheik's proclamation purportedly summoned the complete Muslim world to arise and annihilate their Christian oppressors, except for the Germans and Austrians. [1428] Interestingly, certain parties, attempting to ignite hatred, republished his book in 2003, perhaps to provoke US sensibilities against the Muslims.

Morgenthau explained how the Turkish government instigated the massacre, and reiterated how officials "enthusiastically approved this treatment of the detested race." They had "even delved into the records of the Spanish Inquisition and other historic institutions of torture and adopted all the suggestions found there." He claimed that the atrocities "were merely the preparatory steps in the destruction of the race." The Turks preferred to use death through deportation instead of wholesale slaughter by announcing their intentions "of gathering the two million or more Armenians living in the several sections of the empire and transporting them to this desolate and inhospitable region," to the desert of what is now Syria. They understood that "the great majority would never reach their destination and that those who did would either die of thirst and starvation." He wrote, "When the Turkish authorities gave the orders for these deportations, they were merely giving the death warrant to a whole race; they understood this well." [1429]

About the atrocities, he wrote, "they were the product of religious fanaticism and most of the men and women who instigated them sincerely believed that they were devoutly serving their Maker. Undoubtedly, religious fanaticism was an impelling motive with the Turkish and Kurdish rabble who slew Armenians as a service to Allah, but the men who really conceived the crime had no such motive. Practically all of them were atheists, with no more respect

---

[1428] Henry Morgenthau, Ambassador Morgenthau's Story, Doubleday, Page & Co., New York, 1918, p. 112
[1429] Ibid. 211-212

for Mohammedanism than for Christianity, and with them the one motive was cold-blooded, calculating state policy." [1430]

President Wilson encouraged Congress to create the Near East Relief, which contributed $116,000,000 (1915-1930) to aid the Armenian survivors, including 132,000 orphans who became America's foster children. Senate Resolution 359, dated May 11, 1920, stated "the testimony adduced at the hearings conducted by the sub-committee of the Senate Committee on Foreign Relations have clearly established the truth of the reported massacres and other atrocities from which the Armenian people have suffered." [1431]

Barbara W. Tuchman, a Radcliff graduate, wrote the best-selling book, *The Guns of August*, covering the prelude to and the first month of World War I for which she received the credibility-building Pulitzer Prize in 1963. She won another Pulitzer for *Stilwell and the American Experience in China* in 1972. Tuchman was the daughter of banker, Maurice Wertheim, a first cousin of New York district attorney Robert M. Morgenthau, a niece of Henry Morgenthau, Jr. and the granddaughter of Ambassador Morgenthau. Her daughter is Jessica Tuchman Mathews, the president of the Carnegie Endowment for International Peace.

Tuchman was a research assistant at the Institute of Pacific Relations in New York and Tokyo (1934-1935) then became a journalist before turning her attention to writing books on "official" history. Tuchman was the editorial assistant for *The Nation* and an American correspondent for the Office of War Information (1944-1945). She was a trustee of Radcliffe College, a lecturer at Harvard University and the US Naval War College, all logical activities for a court historian.

[1430] Ibid. 263
[1431] AffirmationOfTheUnitedStatesRecordOnTheArmenianGenocideResolution, House of Representatives, to accompany H. Res. 596, October 4, 2000, http://thomas.loc.gov/cgi-bin/cpquery/T?&report=hr933&dbname=106& as of May 2012

The New Republic of Turkey

Mustafa Kemal, a freemason, the commander of the Nineteenth Turkish Division, actually contributed to Turkey's World War I defeat. Establishment historians have exaggerated his "heroic" actions during the Gallipoli Campaign (April 25, 1915 and January 9, 1916), what the Allies considered a major failure. The losses were similar, the Ottoman Empire and her allies suffered a sixty percent casualty rate of 251,000 while the Allies had a fifty-nine percent casualty rate of 220,000. Kemal planned the Turkish Army's retreat across the Middle East to Aleppo, where the British bombarded them. Following that defeat, the Allies supported a Greek invasion to generate Muslim support for Kemal. After he secured his position, the Allies withdrew their cooperation from Greece. Purportedly, Kemal deliberately positioned his men to ensure that the enemies killed a large number of them.

On October 30, 1918, the Ottoman Empire and the Allies signed the Armistice of Mudros, ending hostilities in the Middle Eastern theater at the end of World War I. The Allies claimed territory even before signing the Armistice. French troops entered Constantinople on November 12, 1918 and the British arrived in the city on November 13, 1918. Early in December 1918, the Allies created a military administration. The Allies occupied Constantinople and Smyrna, November 13, 1918-September 23, 1923. Sir Somerset A. Gough-Calthorpe was the High Commissioner and military adviser in the city. He quickly arrested between 160 and 200 Turkish officials associated with the military or government of Tevfik Pasha and sent thirty of them to Malta.

The military occupation encouraged the establishment of the Turkish national movement and the Turkish War of Independence, May 19, 1919-October 11, 1922. Many members of the Ottoman Parliament escaped the Allied round-up and joined with other resisters. On

January 28, 1920, Nationalist Turkey signed the National Pact which stipulated the withdrawal of British. The document functioned as a declaration of independence. It included the integrity of all territories inhabited by "an Ottoman Islamic majority," the protection of Constantinople, recognition of minority rights in exchange for reciprocal rights for Muslim minorities in other countries; and the recognition of the country's independence and sovereignty. On February 17, 1920, the Ottoman Parliament adopted a resolution declaring support for the Nationalist Movement led by Kemal. In March 1920, rebels declared the formation of a Turkish nation with a Parliament in Ankara, the Grand National Assembly (GNA), founded on April 23, 1920, under Mustafa Kemal's leadership.

The Armistice of Mudros did not authorize the government's dismantlement or the banishment of the Ottoman Sultan. The new Turkish government signed the Treaty of Sèvres, August 10, 1920, drafted by the London Conference, finalized the San Remo conference, and was the Mandate for Palestine. The British originally conceived of this declaration for Palestine on November 2, 1917. The other Allied Powers adopted plan for the establishment of a national Jewish home in Palestine.

France, Britain, and Italy also signed the Tripartite Agreement on August 10, 1920, which defined Britain's oil and commercial interests, including the former German ventures in the Ottoman Empire. Negotiations for these properties began at the Paris Peace Conference, continued at the Conference of London, February 12-24, 1920, and ended at the San Remo conference, with the San Remo Resolution on April 24, 1920. However, France, Italy, and Britain began envisioning their acquired booty in the Ottoman Empire by 1915. The three countries could not make a final determination until the conclusion of the Turkish national movement. During the Turkish War of Independence, the Turks voided the Treaty of Sèvres, the peace treaty between the Ottoman Empire and Allies at the war's end. The Turks also fought in the Greco-Turkish War (1919-1922), in the Turkish-Armenian War, September 24-December 2, 1920, and in the Franco-Turkish War, May 1920-October 1921. During those wars, perhaps as many as 1,000,000 people died.

By September 18, 1922, the Turks, duped by the Dönmes (crypto Jews), into believing they were fighting for their best interests, expelled the occupying forces, and established the new Turkish state with representative democracy.

On August 6, 1923, Joseph Grew, America's negotiator at the Lausanne Conference, and Mustafa İsmet İnönü, the Foreign Minister of the new nationalist government of Ankara, signed the Treaty of Amity, and Commerce in Lausanne, Switzerland, home of the second branch of the International Masonic Association. They designed the treaty to institute political and business relations between the United States and the new Turkish Government. The United States entry into the war voided any previous agreements with the Ottoman Empire. The treaty sanctioned the US government's recognition of the new independent Turkish state. [1432]

The Treaty of Lausanne, July 24, 1923, fostered international recognition of the Republic of Turkey, the successor of the Ottoman Empire. Officials proclaimed the republic on October 29, 1923, with the new capital in Ankara. On November 1, the new parliament, under the influence of the Dönmes pretending to be Muslims, without violence, officially abolished the Sultanate and terminated 623 years of Ottoman rule. On March 3, 1924, it dissolved the Caliphate and exiled the sultan and his family. Kemal, who deceived the Muslims into thinking he supported the sultan, became the first President, and soon introduced numerous radical reforms in order to create a new modern, secular republic, including the founding of state banks. On June 21, 1934, the Turkish Parliament, with the Surname Law, would confer the surname Atatürk (Father of the Turks) upon Mustafa Kemal.

France promised that Cilicia would become an Armenian state. Kemal annexed a large portion of the Province of Aleppo and Cilicia to Turkey in his War of Independence, supported by the Arabs and the Kurds against the French. He supplied weapons to, and, coordinated

---

[1432] John M. Vander Lippe, The Other Treaty of Lausanne: the American Public and Official Debate on Turkish-American Relations, The Turkish Yearbook, Volume 23, 1993, pp. 31-38

his activities with Ibrahim Hananu, who had collaborated with the Young Turks. However, the Treaty of Lausanne had disastrous consequences because most of the Province of Aleppo became part of Turkey except for Aleppo and Alexandretta. This isolated Aleppo from the Anatolian cities, from which it obtained many essentials. The Sykes-Picot also partitioned Aleppo from most of Mesopotamia, a huge economic disadvantage for Aleppo. In 1939, Turkey annexed Alexandretta which deprived Aleppo from access to its main port of Iskenderun, isolating it within Syria.

The Treaty of Lausanne settled the Anatolian and East Thracian, parts of the partitioning of the Ottoman Empire, and voided the Treaty of Sèvres, previously signed by the Constantinople-based Ottoman government. Via the Treaty of Lausanne, the British swapped prisoners with Kemal's new Turkish government. Because an International Tribunal was relatively non-existent, those responsible for the Armenian Genocide were free to travel wherever they wished.

Documents in the British Embassy in Constantinople, and published accounts in a Masonic periodical, claim that between 70,000 and 80,000 occult Masonic Jews and 20,000 crypto-Jews brought down the entire city of Constantinople almost without firing a single shot. [1433]

The Military Tribunals, the Terrible Turks

The *Christian Science Monitor* and other US media reported on Turkey's brutal atrocities against the Armenians, which ignited massive pro-Armenian sentiments, the very purpose of claims. This predictable response engendered Armenian confidence in an

---

[1433] David Musa Pidcock, Satanic Voices, Ancient and Modern, a Surfeit of Blasphemy Including the Rushdie Report from Edifice Complex to Occult Theocracy, Mustaqim, Islamic Art and Literature, Milton Keynes, England, 1992, pp. 47-53

Armenian-American alliance, which discouraged them from seeking a connection with their neighbors. [1434]

Imaginative Americans viewed the Ottoman Empire and Islam as exotic and mysterious, a perception that businessmen, diplomats, and marketing campaigns reinforced. Because of popular literature, many people perceived the East as overflowing with filth, disease, and totally inferior in every way compared to the superior West, a rationalization for intervention and expansionism. Greek and Armenian immigrants to America supported the ideas of the barbaric, fanatical "Terrible Turk" and the alleged slaughter of Christians. These tales characterized the entire Muslim population as enemies of Christianity. Some people argued that the Young Turk's reforms would transform the Empire into a stable progressive nation conducive to open trade and American interests. [1435]

At the beginning of World War I, when the CUP was in power, reports revealed the circumstances of the Siege of Van, on May 24, 1915, perpetrated by an insurgency against the government's attempts to massacre Armenian citizens. Apparently, the CUP created the Special Organization to destroy the Armenians. The Triple Entente issued this warning, "In view of these new crimes of Turkey against humanity and civilization, the Allied Governments announce publicly to the Sublime Porte that they will hold personally responsible for these crimes all members of the Ottoman Government, as well as those of their agents who are implicated in such massacres." [1436]

[1434] Christopher J. Walker, Armenia, the Survival of a Nation, Routledge, London, 1980, pp. 231-235

[1435] John M. Vander Lippe, The Other Treaty of Lausanne: the American Public and Official Debate on Turkish-American Relations, The Turkish Yearbook, Volume 23, 1993, pp. 31-38

[1436] Affirmation of the United States Record on the Armenian Genocide Resolution, 106th Congress Report, House Of Representatives, October 4, 2000, http://thomas.loc.gov/cgi-bin/cpquery/T?&report=hr933&dbname=106& as of May 2012, One should never assume that the congressional record, the government's version of any event, is an accurate account but rather it is the official justification for political policies, partitioning a country, meting out reparations and resource seizures. This is a must read document created several decades after the event.

The British government published the official James Bryce and Arnold J. Toynbee Blue Book, (1916), commercially published as *The Treatment of Armenians in the Ottoman Empire*. Toynbee later admitted that Britain published it as war propaganda to discredit Germany's chief ally. [1437] Bryce, a former Member of Parliament, published the *Report of the Committee on Alleged German Outrages* a year earlier, also British propaganda. [1438]

On May 30, 1918, Hovhannes Kachaznuni and Alexander Khatisyan, Russian Armenians, members of the Armenian Revolutionary Federation (ARF), who led the Armenian National Council, in Tiflis, declared the Democratic Republic of Armenia's independence with Yerevan, the largest city of Armenia, as the capital.

As part of the Armistice of Mudros, the Ottomans surrendered their garrisons outside Anatolia, and granted the Allies occupational rights to the forts, as well as the control of the Straits of the Dardanelles and the Bosporus, The Allies could also occupy any other area "in case of disorder" in the Ottoman territory. Officials demobilized the Ottoman army, and the Allies took control of all ports, railways, and other strategic points. In the Caucasus, the Ottomans had to retreat to within the pre-war borders between the Ottoman and the Russian Empires. Per the Armistice, the Allies convened the Turkish Courts-Martial of 1919-20, to try the CUP leadership and other selected former officials on charges of subversion of the constitution, wartime profiteering, and the massacres of Armenians and Greeks.

Aram Andonian, an Armenian military censor in 1914, allegedly transcribed from Turkish, *The Memoirs of Naim Bey: Turkish Official Documents Relating to the Deportation and the Massacres of Armenians*, published in London, in English, by Hodder & Stoughton in 1920, with an introduction by Herbert J. Gladstone, the youngest son of Prime Minister William E. Gladstone. After the war, Andonian

---

[1437] Christopher J. Walker, Armenia, the Survival of a Nation, Routledge, London, 1980, pp. 379-389

[1438] Primary Documents—Bryce Report into German Atrocities in Belgium, May 12, 1915, http://www.firstworldwar.com/source/brycereport.htm as of May 2012

gathered the testimonies of many deportation survivors. He claims that an official, Naim Bey, part of the deportations committee in Aleppo, gave him his personal papers, containing official documents, telegrams, during his term of office, which Andonian translated into Armenian. These various items provided the most damning evidence of a deliberate system of genocide. The documents revealed that Talaat Pasha had ordered the extermination of the Armenians. One telegram, dated September 16, 1915, indicts the CUP and its "decision" to destroy them. [1439]

On July 26, 1937, Walter Rössler, the German consul in Aleppo, sent a letter in which he referred to Aram Andonian. He said, "I believe that the author is not capable of being objective; he is carried away by his passion." Andonian admitted that his book was not a historical one, but rather "aiming at propaganda." He attributed whatever "errors" in the book were due to publication characteristics. He further disclosed, "I would also like to point out that the Armenian Bureau in London, and the National Armenian Delegation in Paris, behaved somewhat cavalierly with my manuscript, for the needs of the cause they were defending."

There are numerous sources pertaining to the Armenian/Christian Genocide, and the subsequent trials. Dr. Guenter Lewy, a Jew born in Germany, in his *The Armenian Massacres in Ottoman Turkey: A Disputed Genocide* (2005), questioned the validity of the genocide, and the criminal charges. He referred to the evidence as dubious, often based on eyewitness testimony. He condemned the judicial procedures, and the lack of due process. He was critical of the deportee's testimonies, and especially negated the idea that CUP officials had engaged in a premeditated Armenian extermination. Andonian's published work, which cited questionable documents, supplied much of this evidence.

Dr. Lewy mentioned that, despite the citizen's disdain for the government, the Turkish people still expressed antagonistic feelings

---

[1439] Guenter Lewy, Revisiting the Armenian Genocide, Middle East Quarterly, Fall 2005, Volume XII, Number 4, pp. 3-12

about the tribunals for CUP officials. On April 4, 1919, Lewis Heck, the US high commissioner in Constantinople, was in charge of American affairs. He said, "It is popularly believed that many of (the trials) are made from motives of personal vengeance or at the instigation of the Entente authorities, especially the British." The Turks especially opposed the trials after the Greek army occupied Smyrna on May 15, 1919. [1440]

Dr. Lewy reminds us that the Allied authorities convened the Turkish Courts-Martial in Constantinople for the trial and prosecution of the key perpetrators of the Armenian Genocide. Several hundred thousand Armenian Christians died during their deportation, when the government forced them from their homes in Anatolia. Thousands died of starvation and disease, while individuals murdered many others. The Allies wanted military tribunals to exact reparations and retributions for the Armenian massacres. The first trial had begun on February 5, 1919, when they charged three Turkish officials with the mass murder and plunder of the deportees. The main trial began in Constantinople on April 28, 1919. [1441]

Dr. Lewy said that on May 6, 1919, a defense lawyer defied the court's frequent mention of the indictment as if it was a proven fact. Yet, it made no difference because, during the trial, due process for the defendants was non-existent. Officials authenticated "official documents" before they introduced them as evidence. [1442] This lack of original source documentation set a precedent for the questionable evidence presented during the Nuremberg trials, less than three decades later, but with more dire penalties, and long-lasting economic, and social consequences.

Dr. Lewy concludes that the big question is whether the Ottoman government engaged in the premeditated extermination of the Armenians. Dr. Lewy said that people base this idea on three issues, 1) the policies of the Turkish military courts of 1919-20,

---

[1440] Guenter Lewy, Revisiting the Armenian Genocide, Middle East Quarterly, Fall 2005, Volume XII, Number 4, pp. 3-12

[1441] Ibid. 3-12

[1442] Ibid. 3-12

which convicted Young Turk officials, 2) the role of the "Special Organization" as perpetrators of the murders, and, 3) the Memoirs of Naim Bey, containing the alleged telegrams of Interior Minister Talaat Pasha, with orders for the Armenian destruction. According to Professor Guenter Lewy, when people carefully examine the sources, they discover "a shaky foundation from which to claim, let alone conclude, that the deaths of Armenians were premeditated." [1443]

Dr. Lewy said that Mustafa Kemal had emboldened a nationalist movement that ultimately helped depose the sultan. Abdülhamid's followers accused him of acquiescing to the Allies. They claimed that the Allies devised the trials in an attempt to prove criminality, part of a devious plan to discredit, and then partition, the empire. On August 11, 1920, Kemal's regime, in Ankara, demanded that the Allies discontinue all court-martial proceedings. The last Ottoman cabinet member resigned on October 17, 1920, the day the Allies ended the trials. [1444]

Dr. Lewy wrote of the many Turkish authors who have discredited the military tribunals as tools of Allied retribution. He points out that even Somerset A. Gough-Calthorpe remarked that they were a farce. Commissioner John de Robeck, of the British Royal Navy, regarded the tribunal and its findings as a failure. The British government chose not to use any of the evidence from the Turkish Courts-Martial for any potential trials of purported Ottoman war criminals in Malta. In some of the trials, people referred to the Special Organization, created between 1903 and 1907, by Ismail Enver Pasha. They claim that he placed Süleyman Askeri Bey in charge of the agency on November 17, 1913. Vahakn N. Dadrian, without proof, assumed that the CUP used it to exterminate the Armenians. Yet, it was a Special Forces outfit, composed of about 30,000 men used for special military operations in the Caucasus, Egypt, and Mesopotamia. [1445]

Dadrian, currently the director of Genocide Research at Zoryan Institute, author of five books on the Armenian Genocide, is purportedly

---

[1443] Ibid. 3-12
[1444] Ibid. 3-12
[1445] Ibid. 3-12

the leading scholar on the Armenian Question. Interestingly, he is the author of *German Responsibility in the Armenian Genocide: A Review of the Historical Evidence of German Complicity.* Dr. Lewy reminds us that Dadrian relates how General Vehib Pasha, commander of the Turkish Third Army, personally viewed Bahaeddin Şakir, a leading CUP official, as a rather bloodthirsty "butcher," as if a personal evaluation is credible evidence of behavior that, otherwise, no one has proven. Yet, Dr. Lewy states, someone used a portion of that deposition, almost Tabloid-type material, in an indictment but as Professor Lewy states, "an indictment is not proof of guilt." [1446]

Dadrian claimed that "mostly secret reports of German and Austrian diplomats" validated the documents. The statements of German and Austrian diplomats and representatives of the Turkish state support the book's claims. Whether there were factual errors or forgeries in the book, other sources verify the policies. The court-martial proceedings that tried Young Turk leaders for their conduct of the war, and the extermination policy supported the book's claims. While the documents are significant, he says there were other sources that substantiate the genocide. [1447]

Guenter Lewy, in 1938, was a fifteen-year old German Jew, who began to encourage his family to leave Germany. After Kristallnacht, November 9-10, 1938, they immigrated to Palestine. During World War II, Lewy joined a Jewish Brigade fighting against Germany. In 1964, he wrote *The Catholic Church and Nazi Germany,* a controversial anti-Catholic book published the year after Rolf Hochhuth's play *The Deputy, a Christian Tragedy.* Hochhuth's play, praised by Deborah E. Lipstadt, indicted the Vatican for failing to save the Jews from the Holocaust. Lewy cites the "long tradition" of the Church's "moderate anti-Semitism" as the reason it did not "view the plight of the Jews with a real sense of urgency and moral outrage." He said it is a "conclusion difficult to avoid." [1448]

[1446] Ibid. 3-12

[1447] Ervin Staub, The Roots of Evil: the Origins of Genocide and other Group Violence, Cambridge University Press, New York, 1989, pp. 183-184

[1448] Margherita Marchione, Pope Pius XII: Architect for Peace, Paulist Press, Mahwah, New Jersey, 2000, pp. 16-17 this book actually gives credibility to

The Vatican has responded to the allegations with a series of documents refuting the Vatican's perceived collaboration in the Holocaust. One priest said that Lewy founded his conclusions "not on the record but on a subjective conviction." [1449] Is Lewy asking legitimate questions based on real objectivity or is he attempting to minimize the crimes of the CUP officials, his co-religionists? While he argues that there was insufficient evidence regarding the Young Turks and the Armenians, he does not apply that same critical standard to Germany and its purported treatment of the Jews, also based on limited eyewitness testimony, hearsay, questionable, faulty, contrived documentation and total lack of judicial equity.

Some people argue that authorities would never have put the Ottoman leaders on trial following World War I if they had not been responsible for genocide. Yet, the British had jurisdiction over Constantinople and over local government lackeys when these trials took place. Local politicians would do whatever it took to satisfy the British who, unlike the locals, admitted that they could find no indication of any systematic genocide. Further, according to Dr. Justin McCarthy, they did not allow the defendants to select their own defense lawyers. [1450] One must remember that death and destruction are a part of every war—Muslims, Christians, Turks, Kurds, and others died by the thousands in the Ottoman Empire during the war.

The Ottomans gladly relinquished CUP members to the courts of justice to gain more lenient treatment at the Paris Peace Conference. The occupational forces scrutinized the trial proceedings, which abandoned due process, individual legal rights, and where defenders and lawyers feared for their lives, while the Ottoman penal code did

---

the holocaust which numerous scholars, with verifiable scientific evidence, have proven did not take place nor was there an official Nazi program designed to exterminate the Jews despite popular belief. Just try to question its validity in a country in which the Jews have dominant control of the government, the judicial system and the media. Truth should not fear investigation.

[1449] Ibid. 17-17

[1450] Dr. Justin McCarthy, Armenian Rebels—Effects & Consequences, a transcription of a speech given at the Turkish Grand National Assembly, March 24, 2005, http://www.tallarmeniantale.com/mccarthy-armenian-rebels.htm as of May 2012

not allow the opportunity for cross-examination. Many people have questioned the validity of the evidence and the eyewitness accounts particularly in the absence of defendant rights. Witnesses submitted much of their evidence during the preparatory phase of the trial without the defendant being present.

No one verified the evidence as the witnesses presented it. Experts have since testified that some of the evidence, such as letters and military orders, were, in fact, forgeries. In other cases, the judges accepted hearsay, as direct evidence without ever validating the alleged direct source. During the trials, the court did not allow lawyers to cross-examine the witnesses, and the court presented some materials as "anonymous court material," in other words, a witness who has sworn to tell the truth did not present the material. The British either dismissed, or exonerated members of the ARF, supposedly the perpetrators of the deliberate genocide, individual the Ottoman military tribunal prosecuted.

The Armenian Revolutionary Federation (ARF) staged its Ninth General Conference in October 1919, where delegates discussed the issue of retribution against the authorities responsible for the Armenian Genocide. Despite the objections of many of the Russian Armenian delegates, they decided to seek justice using force. Shahan Natalie, working with Grigor Merjanov, created a black list of about 200 individuals they deemed responsible for organizing the genocide.

Politicians fabricated a history relating to the Armenian Question that many have accepted. The British Propaganda Office, to support the false history, created credible-looking documents, while others placed articles in the Dashnak newspaper, which some people who fail to look at authentic records might find credible. Typically, people believe the first accounts of a particular event, even if scholars discover and reveal solid scientific data that counters those first oft-repeated reports. Establishment historians continue to reproduce the falsehoods as confirmation that the Ottoman Empire engaged in genocide against the Armenians. [1451]

Mustafa Kemal falsified population and other statistics while Talaat Pasha transmitted deceptive telegrams. Talaat created fraudulent reports in a Blue Book, and in court records. Neither of them divulged how many Turks the Armenians killed. For over a century, the Armenian Nationalists planned to create their own state in Eastern Anatolia, and the Southern Caucasus, despite the wishes of the local residents. According to their plan, Turkish officials would report that an Armenian Genocide had occurred for which they apologized, and would have to pay reparations. Because of this genocide, Turkish officials would have to create an Armenian state with specific borders in an area populated by twice as many Turkish citizens as the total number of Armenians in the world. [1452]

Court officials dismissed most of the convictions and relocated the more serious cases to the International Courts-Martial in Malta. The trials were Turkish because of their selective, politicized prosecution of former Ottoman officials. The trials functioned to replace the CUP with the Liberal Union Party. In the second stage of the international trials, the Allies relocated Ottoman politicians, generals, and intellectuals from Constantinople jails to the British colony of Malta. These Malta exiles, remained incarcerated for three years, during which time, the Allies searched the archives in Constantinople, London, Paris, and Washington to find proof of their guilt. The Allies used the trials to devise the principle claims in the Treaty of Sèvres, the document used for the partitioning of the Ottoman Empire.

The ARF or the Dashnaks created Operation Nemesis (1920-1922), an agency to stalk and assassinate previous members of the Young Turk Government who were behind the Armenian Genocide. On June

---

[1451] Dr. Justin McCarthy, Armenian Rebels—Effects & Consequences, a transcription of a speech given at the Turkish Grand National Assembly, March 24, 2005, http://www.tallarmeniantale.com/mccarthy-armenian-rebels.htm as of May 2012

[1452] Ibid

19, 1920, Aram Yerganian killed Fatali Khan Khoyski. On March 15, 1921, Soghomon Tehlirian killed Talaat Pasha. On July 18, 1921, Misak Torlakian killed Bihbud Khan Jivanshir. On December 5, 1921, Arshavir Shirakian killed Said Halim Pasha. On April 17, 1922, Aram Yerganian killed Bahaeddin Şakir. On April 17, 1922, Arshavir Shirakian killed Jemal Azmi. On July 21, 1922, Stepan Dzaghigian killed Djemal Pasha. On August 4, 1922, Yakov Melkumov, an Armenian member of the Red Army, killed Ismail Enver Pasha.

Officials acquitted Soghomon Tehlirian of the murder of Talaat Pasha and to the day he died, Armenians regarded him as an "Armenian National Hero." [1453] Dr. Bahaeddin Şakir led the Special Organization (East) and the killer units which massacred the Armenians in Baku, between September 15-17, 1918. Judges sentenced top Ittihad leaders and government officials, in absentia, to death in 1919 and 1920. Fifteen Turks received death sentences for their genocidal massacres but officials executed only three of the fifteen. Dr. Riza Nur, part of the Turkish delegation at the Lausanne Conference, July 24, 1923, denied the Armenian genocide. The Allies accepted this denial, despite Lloyd George's critical berating. [1454]

In 1984, Yves Ternon convened a Permanent Peoples' Tribunal and insists that experts authenticated the telegrams. However, they were lost when they sent them back to Andonian in London. That is akin to the negligent student saying that "the dog ate my homework."

In 1986, Şinasi Orel published his book, *The Talaat Pasha "telegrams:" Historical fact or Armenian fiction?* Orel pointed out that the signature of Mustafa Abdülhalik Bey, the Aleppo governor, did not match existing examples of his signature. Whoever drafted

---

[1453] Professor Heath W. Lowry, Nineteenth and Twentieth Century Armenian Terrorism: 'Threads of Continuity,' International terrorism and the drug connection: Armenian terrorism, its supporters, the narcotic connection, the distortion of history by Ankara University, The Press, Information and Public Relations Office, Ankara University, 1984, pp. 71-83, http://www.tallarmeniantale.com/lowry-threads-continuity.htm as of May 2012

[1454] Jeremy Hugh Baron FRCP FRCS, Genocidal doctors, Journal of the Royal Society of Medicine, Volume 92, November 1999, p. 590

these documents demonstrated an obvious ignorance of the variations between the Ottoman and European calendar. Forgers produced the majority of the documents on plain paper, rather than the official paper that the Ottoman government used during World War I. Additionally, Andonian's document numbers do not correspond, and are inconsistent with the numbers that officials used on cyphered telegrams between Aleppo and Constantinople.

Additionally, Orel could find no mention of the name of Naim Bey in any official records. Further the grammar and language idiosyncrasies were those that only a non-Turkish writer would make. Orel implies that Andonian created a fictitious person, or he was a very low-level bureaucrat in which case he would not have had custody or access to such important records. Based on the other documents that Orel produced, there is no evidence that the Ottoman government intended to implement a mass genocide against the Armenians. Other researchers, such as Erik-Jan Zürcher agree with Orel regarding the person of Naim Bey. However, Zürcher argues that there were other corroborating documents that suggest that certain key CUP members executed the premeditated killing of thousands of Armenians. Professor Paul Dumont, of Strasbourg University and director of French Institute of Anatolian Studies (1999-2003), questions the authenticity of the Andonian documents. Michael M. Gunter calls the documents "notorious forgeries." Bernard Lewis, in referring to the Talaat Pasha telegrams, says they are "historical fabrications." Others, Andrew Mango, Jeremy Salt, Norman Stone and Giles Veinstein, consider the spurious documents as forgeries and fakes.

In 1986, Armenian sociologist Vahakn N. Dadrian, Niall Ferguson, and Richard Albrecht argue that the court did not find any discrepancies in the authenticity of the telegrams in 1921. However, no one introduced the thirty-one telegrams as evidence. The British claimed to have intercepted several telegrams which incriminated Talaat and other Turkish officials. Guenter Lewy claims that Turkish historians and many western students have discredited the thirty-one telegrams contained in the Naim-Andonian volume as "crude forgeries." Some of those telegrams ordered the killing of all Armenians. [1455]

Michael M. Gunter wrote, "The manifest inconsistencies in the Naim-Andonian documents indicate that they are likely forgeries. Indeed, in all fairness to the Armenian position in the hoary controversy over whether the Ottomans intended to commit genocide against them, one would think that the Armenians and their supporters could come up with a better smoking pistol." [1456]

In 1997, Christopher J. Walker maintained that one must critically question the data unless someone produces the original documents or creditable papers with similar information. Guenter Lewy notes that Andonian's demonization of Talaat Pasha is a drastic change from how many Armenians viewed him prior to 1915. Lewy, justifiably skeptical over the legitimacy of the Andonian documents concludes that the unearthing and publication of pertinent Ottoman documents would resolve the issue but, in fact, may never occur. He praises Orel's painstaking analysis and subsequent work. Lewy regards those who promote Andonian's claims lack scholastic credibility. Meanwhile others, like David B. MacDonald, regard Lewy in the same way that some people view Holocaust deniers.

Confronting Denial

By the late 1970s, Turkey failed to acknowledge, or discuss the Armenian Genocide, while others deny the extent of the event, as well as the number of victims. Turkish officials state that the Armenians had been in a state of revolt and possibly received what they deserved. Others have ignored the policies of the government at the time, and the reports from neutral ambassadors and relief-workers that describe the Armenian's plight and the authority's attitude.

[1455] Guenter Lewy, Revisiting the Armenian Genocide, Middle East Quarterly, Fall 2005, pp. 3-12

[1456] Michael M. Gunter, A Reply to Judith Tucker's Excerpt of Vahakn Dadrian's Article, International Journal of Middle Eastern Studies, Volume 40, Issue 4, 2008, p. 728

Generations later, Armenians living in America and elsewhere, who readily accepted the idea of a policy of deliberate genocide, wanted some kind of response from the Turkish government. [1457]

Other minority groups successfully used terrorism to bring attention to their grievances, so Armenians decided to use those same tactics to force the world to remember the Armenian genocide. Moreover, they wanted to suppress what they considered denial about a deliberate policy, as many people assumed that the Armenian deaths in 1915 were war-related. Between 1974 and 1983, two Armenian terrorist groups assassinated about forty-five Turkish diplomats and state personnel worldwide. [1458] Reportedly, they resorted to violence because everyone had ignored their peaceful overtures. Generally, the Armenians did not begin to organize a narrative of the genocide until the 1980s. Historians did not investigate the archives in order to write an account of why it transpired, what occurred, who dictated it, and who carried it out. Certain Armenians want the world to know what occurred and are using outrage and violence to extract justice. [1459]

Kevork Donabedian, the editor of the *Armenian Weekly*, an American-based newspaper, as reported in the *Christian Scientist Monitor* on November 18, 1980, said, "As an Armenian, I never condone terrorism, but there must be a reason behind this. Maybe the terrorism will work. It worked for the Jews. They have Israel." [1460] President Ronald Reagan, on April 22, 1981, stated that the Armenian Genocide and the lessons of the holocaust must never be forgotten." The US Holocaust Memorial Council, an independent Federal agency, unanimously resolved on April 30, 1981, that the tax-payer-funded United States

[1457] Christopher J. Walker, Armenia, the Survival of a Nation, Routledge, London, 1980, pp. 379-389
[1458] Ibid. 379-389
[1459] Ibid. 379-389
[1460] Professor Heath W. Lowry, Nineteenth and Twentieth Century Armenian Terrorism: 'Threads of Continuity,' International terrorism and the drug connection: Armenian terrorism, its supporters, the narcotic connection, the distortion of history by Ankara University, The Press, Information and Public Relations Office, Ankara University, 1984, pp. 71-83, http://www.tallarmeniantale.com/lowry-threads-continuity.htm as of May 2012

Holocaust Memorial Museum would include the Armenian Genocide in the Museum. [1461]

On August 29, 1985, in Geneva, the United Nations Sub-Commission on the Prevention of Discrimination and the Protection of Minorities accepted Benjamin Whitaker's report on genocide wherein he stated that at least one million, and possibly over half the Armenian population, perished during a death march. Fourteen nations, including Britain, France and the United States, favored the resolution which did not substantiate genocide against the Armenians but that "the sub-commission would accept the report for future reference" even though, as one member stated, the massacre was not "adequately documented" but relied on biased eyewitness accounts to draw conclusions regarding the official policies. [1462]

In 1985, the U.N. Commission on Human Rights adopted a report entitled *Study of the Question of the Prevention and Punishment of the Crime of Genocide*, which stated "the Nazi aberration has unfortunately not been the only case of genocide in the twentieth century. Another example qualified—the Ottoman massacre of Armenians in 1915-1916. This report claimed that the Ottomans killed at least one million and possibly more than half of the Armenian population during a death march according to independent authorities and eyewitnesses as corroborated by the United States in addition to records in the German and British archives and by contemporary diplomats in Turkey, including those of its ally Germany." [1463]

On June 18, 1987, in Strasbourg, the European Parliament voted to recognize the Armenian Genocide. It concluded, without

---

[1461] AffirmationOfTheUnitedStatesRecordOnTheArmenianGenocideResolution, House of Representatives, to accompany H. Res. 596, October 4, 2000, http://thomas.loc.gov/cgi-bin/cpquery/T?&report=hr933&dbname=106& as of May 2012

[1462] Christopher J. Walker, Armenia, the Survival of a Nation, Routledge, London, 1980, pp. 379-389

[1463] AffirmationOfTheUnitedStatesRecordOnTheArmenianGenocideResolution, House of Representatives, to accompany H. Res. 596, October 4, 2000, http://thomas.loc.gov/cgi-bin/cpquery/T?&report=hr933&dbname=106& as of May 2012

acknowledging the circumstances in Turkey at the time that the Turkish government, by failing to admit to the genocide, was depriving the Armenians "of the right to their own history." The resolution stated that the events in 1915-1917 constituted genocide according to the US's adoption of Raphael Lemkin, a Polish-born Jewish lawyer's definition of the crime of genocide on December 9, 1948. The Parliament stated that it could not hold the Turkish Republic responsible for those past events. The resolution only wanted an acknowledgement of the genocide, along with other stipulations such as the provisions of the 1923 Treaty of Lausanne regarding minorities. If Turkey failed to oblige, the European Community would not admit the country. [1464]

In 1987, coinciding with the European Parliament's actions, the US House of Representatives passed a resolution declaring April 24, as a day of remembrance for genocide victims. In other words, the US Congress officially recognized the Armenian Genocide. Alex Manoogian, an Armenian millionaire wrote that ten US presidents confirmed these truths and records in the US State Department, including eyewitness accounts, documented the event. [1465]

Turkish officials reported that the CUP was in power then and it created the Special Organization to destroy the Armenians. The Turks claim that many Armenians were in a state of revolt in 1915, in Anatolia, and that those in Van provoked the Ottoman government's anti-Armenian policies. Others point out that many Muslims died as well as Armenians in the world war. The British government published the official James Bryce and Arnold J. Toynbee Blue Book, (1916) and later commercially published it as *The Treatment of Armenians in the Ottoman Empire*, which functioned as the key evidence of the Ottoman's ethnic slaughter. Toynbee later admitted that the government published it as part of its war propaganda, designed to discredit Germany's chief ally. Naturally, officials in Washington accepted it. [1466] Interestingly, Bryce, a former Member of Parliament,

[1464] Christopher J. Walker, Armenia, the Survival of a Nation, Routledge, London, 1980, pp. 379-389
[1465] Ibid. 379-389
[1466] Ibid. 379-389

published the *Report of the Committee on Alleged German Outrages* a year earlier as part of the British propaganda operation. [1467]

In 1988, President George H. W. Bush, regarding the Armenian Genocide, stated "we must consciously and conscientiously recognize the genocides of the past." Further, he said, "the United States must acknowledge the attempted genocide of the Armenian people in the last years of the Ottoman Empire, based on the testimony of survivors, scholars, and indeed our own representatives at the time, if we are to insure that such horrors are not repeated." [1468]

Hundreds of thousands of Turkish soldiers died of hunger, cold, and war-related diseases as a result of the absence of clean facilities and hygiene, a common occurrence during any war. A million Muslims died during a typhus epidemic. Turkish officials offered to open their state archives in January 1989. However, they suppressed the records between 1894 and 1923, those most pertinent to the Armenians. Even so, the most important records are not those within their archives, but those in the archives of the CUP, the party in power in the Ottoman Empire during the Armenian Genocide. [1469]

On August 13, 1992, President Bill Clinton stated "the Genocide of 1915, years of communist dictatorship, and the devastating earthquake of 1988 have caused great suffering in Armenia during this century." In 1982, the US State Department stated that the facts regarding the Armenian Genocide were ambiguous. In 1993, the US Court of Appeals for the District of Columbia retracted the "assertion on ambiguity" as it contradicted the US record about the Armenian Genocide. Stuart Eizenstat, then Under Secretary of

---

[1467] Primary Documents—Bryce Report into German Atrocities in Belgium, May 12, 1915, http://www.firstworldwar.com/source/brycereport.htm as of May 2012

[1468] AffirmationOfTheUnitedStatesRecordOnTheArmenianGenocideResolution, House of Representatives, to accompany H. Res. 596, October 4, 2000, http://thomas.loc.gov/cgi-bin/cpquery/T?&report=hr933&dbname=106& as of May 2012

[1469] Christopher J. Walker, Armenia, the Survival of a Nation, Routledge, London, 1980, pp. 379-389

State for Economic, Business, and Agricultural Affairs in a letter of April 9, 1999 pledged that the administration would raise the issue of the recovery of Armenian assets from the genocide period held by the Imperial Ottoman Bank with the Republic of Turkey. [1470] Eizenstat was the Head of US delegation on the Holocaust Era Assets Conference.

On September 27, 2000, Representative George P. Radanovich and David E. Bonior, of the Committee on International Relations, presented House Resolution 596 to address "the result of a purposeful campaign of genocide against the Armenian nation." [1471] Benjamin A. Gilman chaired the Committee on International Relations. He had close ties to the ultra-Orthodox Jewish community, supported gays in the military [1472] and despite being Jewish, was a huge congressional supporter of the Church of Scientology from which he received huge contributions.

The House of Representatives concluded that the Ottoman Empire conceived and carried out the Armenian Genocide (1915-1923), through the deportation of nearly 2,000,000 Armenians, killing 1,500,000 men, women, and children. They expelled another 500,000 survivors from their homes, and eliminated a 2,500-year Armenian presence in their historic homeland. On May 24, 1915, England, France, and Russia, had issued a joint statement charging, for the first time, a government of committing crimes against humanity. [1473] The US National Archives and Record Administration has records of the event, under Record Group 59, of the Department of State, which the public may access. Henry Morgenthau, US Ambassador to the

---

[1470] AffirmationOfTheUnitedStatesRecordOnTheArmenianGenocideResolution, House of Representatives, to accompany H. Res. 596, October 4, 2000, http://thomas.loc.gov/cgi-bin/cpquery/T?&report=hr933&dbname=106& as of May 2012

[1471] Ibid

[1472] Kurt F. Stone, The Jews of Capitol Hill: A Compendium of Jewish Congressional Members, Scarecrow Press, Maryland, 2001, pp. 280-281

[1473] AffirmationOfTheUnitedStatesRecordOnTheArmenianGenocideResolution, House of Representatives, to accompany H. Res. 596, October 4, 2000, http://thomas.loc.gov/cgi-bin/cpquery/T?&report=hr933&dbname=106& as of May 2012

Ottoman Empire described the race extermination policy to the State Department. His son later developed the infamous Morgenthau Plan for Germany. [1474]

Making Money the Old Fashioned Way, War Profiteering

Evidently, the financial cost of World War I amounted to almost $38 billion for Germany alone; Britain spent $35 billion, France $24 billion, Russia $22 billion, USA $22 billion and Austria-Hungary $20 billion. In total, the war cost the Allies around $125 billion and it cost the Central Powers about $60 billion.

On November 23, 1913, John D. Rockefeller, Andrew Mellon, Andrew Carnegie, and J. Pierpont Morgan, Frank A. Vanderlip and other bankers, financiers, and industrialists created the American International Corporation (AIC), capitalized with $50 million specifically to assist the Bolsheviks in their revolution. AIC moved to the forty-story Equitable Building, located at 120 Broadway, New York City, owned by Silverstein Properties since 1981. AIC's objectives were to develop and promote US foreign trade. AIC soon acquired interests in the Panic Mail Steamship Company, the International Mercantile Marine Company, United Fruit Company, and the New York Shipbuilding Company. It owned all of the stock in the Allied Machinery Company of America, invested in other companies and had controlling interest in many others. [1475]

AIC created, controlled, owned, or purchased the following companies to fulfill their objectives, Allied Machinery Company of America; American International Shipbuilding Corporation; [1476] American International Steel Corporation; American Balsa Company; Allied Construction Machinery Corporation; Allied Sugar Machinery Corporation; American International Terminals Company;

[1474] Ibid (no page numbers)

[1475] Financial News Association, Manual of Statistics, Stock Exchange Handbook, New York, 1917, p. 369

[1476] The Saga of Hog Island,1917-1921: The Story of the First Great War Boondoggle by James J. Martin, http://tmh.floonet.net/articles/hogisle.shtml as of May 2012

Carter Macey & Company; F. W. Horne & Company; The China Corporation; The Latin American Corporation; Ulen Contracting Company; Grace Russian Company; Holbrook, Cabot & Rollins Corporation; International Merchant Marine; International Products Company; New York Shipbuilding Corporation [1477]; Pacific Mail Steamship Company; Rosin & Turpentine Export Company; Siems Carry Railroad and Canal Company; United Fruit Company; United States Rubber Company; United States Industrial Alcohol Company; Jones Laughlin Steel Corporation; Midvale Steel Corporation; G. Amsinck & Company; Symington Forge Corporation; Remington Arms; and the Robert Dollar Company. [1478] [1479]

Individuals associated with the Federal Reserve and Wall Street assumed control of AIC, all attempting to profit from imminent war. These included—Stone & Webster (railroad builders), the Rockefeller family, and those who made up the AIC board. Charles A. Stone was the president of AIC. Its Board of Directors was composed of James J. Hill, Theodore Vail, P.A. Rockefeller, Edwin F. Webster, Otto H. Kahn, Ambrose Monell, James A. Stillman, Beekman Winthrop, Henry S. Pritchett, Robert S. Lovett, Joseph P. Grace, Cyrus H. McCormick, Charles H. Sabin, W.E. Corey, J. Ogden Armour, and Charles A. Coffin, Chairman of the Board of Directors of the General Electric Company. [1480] Coffin succeeded Judge Robert S. Lovett as the head of the Committee on Cooperation appointed by the Red Cross to negotiate with independent war relief organizations. [1481]

Frank A. Vanderlip was the chairman of AIC while Charles A. Stone was President with the following Vice-Presidents George J. Baldwin, Philip W. Henry, Robert F. Herrick, Frederick Holbrook,

[1477] A Place Called Yorkship—History of New York Ship, http://yorkship.home.comcast.net/~yorkship/NYSB_history.htm as of May 2012

[1478] Business & Finance: Anniversary, March 19, 1928, Time Magazine, http://www.time.com/time/magazine/article/0,9171,786781,00.html as of May 2012

[1479] Revenue for A.I.C. in 1919, $8,153,112, New York Times, March 23, 1920

[1480] Frank A. Vanderlip and Boyden Sparkes, From Farm Boy to Financier, D. Appleton-Century Co., Incorporated, 1935, pp. 267-271

[1481] Brings Honor to C. A. Coffin, M. Godart Confers Rank of Officer of Legion of Honor, The New York Times, May 14, 1918, p. 13

William S. Kies, and Willard Straight. The Secretary and Treasurer was Richard P. Tinsley, Ames Higgins was the Assistant Secretary, and the Assistant Treasurer was P. Mayes. The AIC Directors, all powerful bankers, politicians or industrialists, included J. Ogden Armour, Charles A. Coffin, Pierre S. DuPont, Joseph P. Grace, Otto H. Kahn, Robert S. Lovett, Henry S. Pritchett, Percy A. Rockefeller (S&B), James A. Stillman, among others. [1482] Robert A. Lovett (S&B), son of Robert S. Lovett, was Defense Secretary (1951-1953). George H. Walker was a founder and Director of AIC until 1952.

By 1915, AIC was doing business in Australia, Argentina, Uruguay, Paraguay, Colombia, Brazil, Chile, China, Japan, India, Ceylon, Italy, Switzerland, France, Spain, Cuba, Mexico, and other Central American countries. By 1917, AIC's foreign investments totaled over $27 million and it had agents in London, Paris, Buenos Aires, Peking, and Petrograd, Russia. AIC's United Fruit Company played a role in various Central American Marxist revolutions in the 1920s. [1483] By November 1917, AIC owned Amsinck and Company, also located at 120 Broadway. [1484] Amsinck funded German wartime espionage in the United States and supported the Bolshevik Revolution. [1485]

Churchill's US counterpart, Navy Secretary Franklin D. Roosevelt claimed that US industry had been preparing for war for about a year. The Army and Navy Departments started purchasing supplies by early 1916. [1486] In 1916, AIC purchased New York Shipbuilding, a navy contractor that, by 1918, owned the world's biggest shipyard. The National City Bank, a year later, reorganized Remington Arms and installed Samuel F. Pryor who presided over the company as

---

[1482] Manual of Statistics, Stock Exchange Hand-book by Financial News Association, New York, 1917, p. 369

[1483] Antony C. Sutton, Wall Street and the Bolshevik Revolution, Buccaneer Books, Cutchogue, New York, 1993, p. 108

[1484] Buys Out Control Of G. Amsinck & Co.; American International Corporation Takes Over Firm Mentioned in Bolo Pacha Case, The New York Times, October 27, 1917, p. 18

[1485] Frank A. Vanderlip and Boyden Sparkes, From Farm Boy to Financier, D. Appleton-Century Co., Incorporated, 1935, pp. 267-271

[1486] Eustace Mullins, The Secrets of the Federal Reserve, the London Connection, John McLaughlin, 1993, pp. 146-147

general manager and then president. Remington produced sixty-nine percent of all American-produced rifles used by US troops fighting in World War I. The firm also manufactured over fifty percent of all the small-arms ammunition for the United States and her Allies. [1487]

President Woodrow Wilson placed the nation's monetary system into the hands of the international bankers through the Federal Reserve System. When the United States entered into World War I against Germany, on April 6, 1917, Wilson relinquished further economic control of the government to three of his financial backers, all Jews, Eugene I. Meyer, Paul Warburg, and Bernard Baruch. Meyer was Baruch's partner in the Alaska Juneau Gold Mining Company. [1488]

In 1890, Bernard Baruch had worked on Wall Street for A.A. Housman & Co. In 1896, he merged the six top US tobacco companies into the Consolidated Tobacco Company, which forced James Duke and the American Tobacco Trust into another trust. He delivered the copper industry to the Guggenheim family, and collaborated with Edward H. Harriman, Jacob H. Schiff's agent in managing America's railway system for the Rothschild family. Baruch and Harriman seized control of the New York City transit system. Baruch Brothers of New York changed their name to Hentz Brothers in 1917 when Bernard became Chairman of the US War Industries Board, established on July 28, 1917. [1489] Baruch wrote, ". . . in the view of many, I became a virtual dictator." [1490]

On August 31, 1917, the Emergency Fleet Corporation awarded contracts to AIC, the Submarine Boat Corporation, and the Merchants Shipbuilding Company. W. Averell Harriman Company owned Merchants Shipbuilding, located at Chester. AIC would conduct its shipbuilding operations at Hog Island, a 1,000-acre piece of

---

[1487] Kevin Phillips, American Dynasty, Aristocracy, Fortune, and the Politics of Deceit in the House of Bush, Penguin Books, 2004, p. 179

[1488] Eustace Mullins, The Secrets of the Federal Reserve, the London Connection, John McLaughlin, 1993, pp. 161-162

[1489] Ibid. 157-158

[1490] Bernard M. Baruch, Baruch, the Public Years, My Own Story, Holt, Rinehart and Winston of Canada, Limited, 1960, p. 53

land along the Delaware River between Philadelphia and Chester, Pennsylvania. The firm would build at least 200 ships. Submarine Boat would operate out of Port Newark, New Jersey. [1491] Matthew C. Brush, a thirty-second degree freemason and a Knight Templar became chairman of AIC in 1918. He worked for Franklin MacVeagh & Company in Chicago. MacVeagh attended Yale and belonged to the Order (S&B). Members of the Order directed Guaranty Trust and Brown Brothers. Active members of Skull and Bones, the Brotherhood of Death, established both the W. A. Harriman Company and Guaranty Trust. [1492]

President Charles A. Stone, according to a report in *The New York Times*, foresaw great opportunity in world trade. According to the newspaper report, "The balance sheet of the company for December 31, 1919 shows current assets of $48,396,145 and current liabilities of $25,249,553 making a working capital of $23,146,592, an increase from $6,052,550 in the preceding year. Inventories of merchandise total $15,049,126 compared with $7,474,400 in the preceding year and securities advanced to $30,815,836 from $27,847,508. [1493]

Stone believed that the war, once the European economies "convalescence" by means of "balanced budgets and sound currency policies" would provide great opportunities for American capital. Additionally, the war enriched the South American nations "materially" and has given them a wide and "profitable market for their natural resources." Regarding war, Stone stated, "All this spells opportunity for the United States which, among the great nations in the world, possesses not merely enormous natural resources but also, under normal conditions, a large available capital." Stone, reviewing the work of the corporation at Hog Island Maryland, said they had

[1491] James J. Martin, The Saga of Hog Island,1917-1921: The Story of the First Great War Boondoggle, http://tmh.floonet.net/articles/hogisle.shtml as of May 2012
[1492] Antony Sutton, America's Secret Establishment: An Introduction to the Order of Skull & Bones, Trine Day, Walterville, Oregon, 2002, pp. 136-137
[1493] Revenue for A.I.C. in 1919, $8,153,112, The New York Times, March 23, 1920

launched sixty-six ships during 1919, all delivered to the Emergency Fleet Corporation. [1494]

On February 8, 1918, some senators convened a committee to hear the views of Treasury Secretary William G. McAdoo regarding Senate bill No. 3714, providing for the establishment of a War Finance Corporation. Other attendees who favored the bill's passage were banker, William Proctor Gould Harding, Chairman of the Federal Reserve (1916-1922) and Paul M. Warburg, Vice Governor Federal Reserve Board. [1495] Warburg relinquished his $500,000 a year job at Kuhn, Loeb to accept the paltry $12,000 a year job as governor of the Federal Reserve. [1496] On March 7, 1918, the Senate passed the bill, which authorized the extension of $4 billion in credit to firms and corporations engaged in war-related industries. [1497] Eugene I. Meyer directed the War Finance Corporation. The President would later propose his name as the Governor of the Federal Reserve Board. [1498] Congress created the US Government agency on April 5, 1918 in order to give financial support to industries deemed essential for World War I, and to the banks that financed them. It functioned in that capacity, between the wars, until Congress abolished it on July 1, 1939.

Meyer, head of the War Finance Corporation, administered the loans that financed the war. Presumably, he worked with banks with which he already had a personal connection. His father had been a partner at Lazard Frères, headquartered in Paris and Lazard Brothers of London.

[1494] Ibid

[1495] Establishment of a War Finance Corporation: Hearings before the Committee by United States Congress, Senate Committee on Finance, February 8, 1918, Washington, DC, Government Printing Office, pp. 3-4

[1496] Gary Allen with Larry Abraham, None Dare Call it Conspiracy, Double A Publications, Seattle, Washington, 1971, p. 58

[1497] War Finance Bill Passed By Senate; Corporation Measure Modified in Many Respects Before Being Adopted, 74 to 3. Change Aimed At Warburg Power to Name Capital Issues Committee Is Shifted in Order to Bar New York Banker, Special to The New York Times, March 8, 1918, p. 1

[1498] Eustace Mullins, The Secrets of the Federal Reserve, the London Connection, John McLaughlin, 1993, pp. 161-162

[1499] Lazard Frères, sharing the same goals as the Rothschilds, was an expert in international gold movements and managed the fortunes of many political families. [1500] The *New York Times*, August 10, 1918, reported that Warburg, the first Federal Reserve vice Governor (1913-1918), authored the plan for the War Finance Corporation. [1501]

That agency executed financial transactions with the Treasury prior to June 20, 1920, which included purchases and sales, facilitated by Meyer, the Managing Director with the Assistant Treasury Secretary. The records indicate that the government paid over $1,894 billion for bonds through the War Finance Corporation. They did not sell these bonds at the market price. Meyer, during the investigations, stated that he and Jerome J. Hanauer, Assistant Treasury Secretary and Kuhn, Loeb Co. partner agreed to the arbitrary price, set by Hanauer. Meyer, through the War Finance Corporation, sold approximately $70 million worth of bonds to the government and purchased about $10 million in bonds in his official capacity. He paid select brokers a commission on each transaction. Ernst and Ernst certified public accountants hired by the War Finance Corporation, audited and altered the agency's books. After June 1921, the officials at the War Finance Corporation destroyed about $10 billion worth of securities. [1502]

Regarding his personal interests, Baruch admitted, "I carried through the war three major investments, Alaska Juneau Gold Mining Company, Texas Gulf Sulphur, and Atolia Mining Company (tungsten)." On February 21, 1921, Representative Mason told the House of Representatives that Baruch made over $50 million just in copper during the war. Baruch, as chairman of the War Industries Board, directed the affairs of all US factories. He chose Clarence Dillon, a Wall Street lawyer as his assistant. [1503] William P. G. Harding, Chairman of the Federal Reserve, was the Managing Director of the War Finance Corporation under Meyer. George R. James, member of

---

[1499] Ibid. 130

[1500] Ibid. 165-166

[1501] Ibid. 150

[1502] Eustace Mullins, The Secrets of the Federal Reserve, the London Connection, John McLaughlin, 1993, pp. 161-162, 169

[1503] Ibid. 150

the Federal Reserve Board (1923-1924) had been Chief of the Cotton Section of the War Industries Board. [1504]

There were at least two Congressional investigations, in 1925 and 1930-The Select Committee to Investigate the Destruction of Government Bonds. On March 2, 1925, it was reported, "Duplicate bonds amounting to 2,314 pairs and duplicate coupons amounting to 4,698 pairs ranging in denominations from $50 to $10,000 had been redeemed to July 1, 1924. Some of these duplications have resulted from error and some from fraud." This chicanery enabled Meyer to purchase control of Allied Chemical and Dye Corporation and *The Washington Post*. The duplication of bonds, "one for the government, one for me" in denominations as high as $10,000 each, amounted to a fortune. [1505] Meyer's daughter Katharine Graham later became publisher of the *Washington Post*. President Herbert Hoover appointed Meyer as Chairman of the Federal Reserve (1930-1933). [1506] In 1920 Meyer and William H. Nichols, owner of General Chemical, merged five smaller chemical companies to create the Allied Chemical and Dye Corporation later known as the Allied Chemical Corp. After World War II, President Harry S. Truman, a freemason, appointed Meyer as the first head of the World Bank in June 1946. [1507]

On September 13, 1937, in a congressional investigation, Baruch testified before Congress and admitted that all wars are economic in nature, despite the political or religious reasons repeatedly used to justify war. He made $750,000 in just one day during World War I when he headed the purchasing agency for the Allies. In that capacity, he spent $10 billion per year and was the primary member of the Munitions Price-Fixing Committee, and as such, he determined how much money the US government spent and the companies from which they would purchase. President Wilson also gave him a letter authorizing him to seize any US industry or plant. During Congress'

[1504] Ibid. 161-162, 169
[1505] Ibid. 161-162
[1506] Ibid. 130
[1507] Ibid. 165-166

investigation, officials asked him about the specific skills that qualified him for the job. He responded that he was a speculator. [1508]

Samuel P. Bush, of Columbus, Ohio, father of Prescott, was the chief of the Facilities Division on the War Industries Board. This division was in charge with developing facilities outside of the congested northeastern part of the United States. The government had overloaded the private railroad industry, located primarily in the northeast. The Government Railroad Administration decided the problem was unsolvable. Treasury Secretary McAdoo urged President Wilson to relieve the railways from the burdensome government contracts. Wilson gave the problem to the War Industries Board, which had already begun to work on the issue of diverting a portion of the government's demand to other parts of the country. [1509]

Samuel P. Bush was president of Buckeye Steel Castings (1908-1927), a railroad equipment-manufacturing firm that had supplied the Morgans, Harrimans, and Rockefellers and the railroads they controlled. Frank Rockefeller, brother of John D. and William, was Buckeye's former president. Bush, who helped co-found Columbus Academy, a private prep school, made certain that his own children had superior educations at private schools. He was a director of the Pennsylvania Railroad's Ohio subsidiaries, of the Hocking Valley Railway, the Norfolk & Western Railway, and the Huntington National Bank. He was also a director of the Federal Reserve Bank of Cleveland.

Bush was associated with the US Chamber of Commerce and was the first president of the National Association of Manufacturers, a lobbying group founded in Cincinnati, Ohio in 1895. He worked with Baruch on the War Industries Board where he was the national chief of the Ordnance, Small Arms, and Ammunition Section. He negotiated with the nation's munitions companies, including

[1508] Eustace Mullins, The Secrets of the Federal Reserve, the London Connection, John McLaughlin, 1993, pp. 156-158

[1509] Grosvenor B. Clarkson, Industrial America in the World War: The Strategy behind the Line, 1917-1918, Houghton Mifflin, Boston, Massachusetts, 1923, pp. 198-199

Remington Arms, in securing weaponry. The War Industries Board directed the militarization of the country's civilian industry. The National Archives destroyed most of the War Industries Board records relating to his activities. [1510]

After the war, Remington Arms executives sought other major markets and looked to Germany for business. In 1919, National City Bank helped establish W. Averell Harriman and Company, with George H. Walker, as president, because of his many European contacts. Harriman, Walker, and National City had business dealings with Germany in the 1920s. Percy A. Rockefeller of National City Bank helped to reorganize Remington Arms, and afterwards became one of its directors. He also joined Harriman and Company as a director. [1511]

Other War Industries Board officials included Clarence Dillon, Robert Brookings, Judge Robert S. Lovett, and their friend George H. Walker. Bush knew top executives at Du Pont, Remington, Winchester and Colt Arms. Between the wars, he was an advisor to President Herbert Hoover. Unlike the Spanish American War, World War I brought together the nation's industrial, military and business components. These connections grew even stronger with the next war and helped to further militarize America. [1512]

It was AIC then; now it is Carlyle and other such groups. On May 16, 2008, Booz, Allen & Hamilton, a privately held corporation owned by about 300 senior executives announced the sale of the majority of its US government business division to the Carlyle Group (established 1987), a multibillion dollar private equity firm for $2.54 billion. [1513] Carlyle Group invested in the Bin Laden family's extensive construction projects in Saudi Arabia and other areas in the Middle

---

[1510] Kevin Phillips, American Dynasty, Aristocracy, Fortune, and the Politics of Deceit in the House of Bush, Penguin Books, 2004, pp. 182-183
[1511] Ibid. 182-183
[1512] Ibid. 182-183
[1513] Booz Allen To Separate US Government and Global Commercial Business, http://www.boozallen.com/news/39856120 as of May 2012

East. [1514] In September 2007, the Mubadala Development Company, a sovereign wealth fund of the Abu Dhabi government specializing in acquisitions, paid 1.35 billion for a 7.5 percent ownership stake in Carlyle. [1515] The politically connected, bi-partisan, buyout firm, Carlyle Group, is stacked with war profiteers, numerous former politicians, and has massive assets. [1516] [1517]

George H. W. Bush, a profiteer like his progenitor, joined Carlyle in 1993, and was the Senior Advisor to their Asia Advisory Board (April 1998-October 2003). He reluctantly resigned, under pressure due to the company's massive Iraqi war profits. He retained his Carlyle stock, and gave speeches in Carlyle's behalf, for a $500,000 fee. Carlyle is notorious for buying defense companies and "doubling or tripling their value" due to abundant, frequently no-bid, defense contracts. In 2002, Carlyle got at least $677 million in government contracts, and by Bush's 2003 Iraqi invasion, Carlyle contracts were worth $2.1 billion, netting sizeable profits for the investors—friends and family. [1518]

Notable people associated with Carlyle include James Baker III, former US Secretary of State under George H. W. Bush. Baker was also a staff member under George W. Bush. Others associated with Carlyle include Frank C. Carlucci, Deputy Director of the CIA under Carter; Richard Darman, former Director of the US Office of Management and Budget under George H. W. Bush; Randal K. Quarles, former Under Secretary of the US Treasury under George

---

[1514] Corporate Crime Reporter, Interview With Dan Briody, Author Of The Iron Triangle: Inside The Secret World Of The Carlyle Group, (Wiley, 2003), http://www.corporatecrimereporter.com/briodyinterview.html as of May 2012

[1515] Andrew Ross Sorkin, Carlyle to Sell Stake to a Mideast Government, The New York Times, September 21, 2007

[1516] The Carlyle Group, Aerospace & Defense, http://www.carlyle.com/Industry/Aerospace%20&%20Defense/item8359.html as of May 2012

[1517] The Carlyle Group, http://www.carlyle.com/Company/item1677.html as of May 2012

[1518] Congress Must Cut Off Bush Family War Profits by Evelyn Pringle, Global Research, April 10, 2007, http://globalresearch.ca/index.php?context=va&aid=5337 as of May 2012

W. Bush; Allan Gotlieb, Canadian ambassador to the United States; William Kennard, Chairman of the Federal Communications Commission (FCC) under Clinton; Arthur Levitt, Chairman of the Securities and Exchange Commission (SEC) under Clinton; Mack McLarty, White House Chief of Staff under Clinton, President of Kissinger McLarty Associates and many others.

After 9/11, no-bid contracts and privatization, accelerated. The war on terror, the creation of numerous new agencies and bureaucracies was never about freedom or security. All of it, the programs, and the Iraq reconstruction are all a colossal assault on the federal budget, facilitated by the politically connected, selectively efficient contractors who collect up-front then frequently, sub-contract projects to unskilled workers who often never complete the work.

The Bankers of World War I

The City of London, the financial core within London, financed America's trade before World War I, which made the United States a debtor nation, a country that had invested fewer resources in other countries than they had invested in America. With the advent of World War I, and the creation of the Federal Reserve, the bankers transformed the United States into a net creditor nation of $3.7 billion. American banks established foreign branches and made foreign loans. Europe shifted their investments from the United States while the US government and banks extended loans to the Allies, France and Britain. With the war, J. P. Morgan, National City Bank and others exploited the new federal legislation to enlarge their foreign operations. [1519]

Cordell Hull, House of Representatives (1907-1921; 1923-1931), who authored the federal income tax laws of 1913 and 1916, remarked in his memoirs, that the enactment of the income tax law and the Federal Reserve System had to be rushed through, "just in the nick of time," to meet the economic demands of the war. Further, administrators

---

[1519] David Reynolds, From World War to Cold War, Oxford University Press, 2006, pp. 294-295

had to train bank staffs to meet the demand of their services. The drafters of the Federal Reserve Act decided that Federal Reserve Banks would function as fiscal agents of the government. [1520]

When war broke out in Europe in 1914, the United States was a debtor nation, with outstanding debts of about $3.5 billion dollars. The United States was inexperienced in raising large amounts of capital for lending abroad. Beginning in July 1913, a steady exportation of gold concerned US bankers, some of which had fallen below their required gold reserves. This was serious because drafts, payable in gold, were due on railway and industrial securities sold abroad starting on July 31, 1914. The bankers and the US Treasury created a gold fund of $100 million to protect the country's foreign credit. The warring nations were purchasing huge amounts of American products, which normalized the inequitable exchange rate. Then gold started flowing into the United States. [1521]

In 1915, President Woodrow Wilson informed the banks, "The government sees no objection in opening banking credits to all belligerents." While that might have sounded neutral, the international bankers made 95 percent of their loans to the Allies and only 5 percent to Germany. Professor Pierre Renouvin admitted, "American economic and financial relations were almost exclusively tied to Great Britain and France. How could such a situation not have political consequences? The neutrality of the United States is no longer impartial." Colonel Edward M. House said, "We will act not only to save civilization but also for our own benefit." [1522]

In September 1915, New York bankers loaned England and France a combined amount of $500 million, payable on April 15, 1917. Then, between September 1, 1915 and April 17, 1917, they loaned England and France over $1,650 billion dollars. The net balance of

---

[1520] Eustace Mullins, The Secrets of the Federal Reserve, the London Connection, John McLaughlin, 1993, pp. 146-147

[1521] Liberty Loan Publicity Campaigns, http://www.1911encyclopedia.org/ Liberty_Loan_Publicity_Campaigns as of May 2012

[1522] Leon Degrelle, Hitler: Born at Versailles, Volume 1, of the Hitler Century, Institute for Historical Review, Torrance, California, 1992, pp. 231-232

gold imports into the United States in that same period was $1,075 billion. Our entry into the war required funding the US military, either through taxation or the sale of a series of four "liberty" bonds, a voluntary contribution which functioned as a loan to the government. The Treasury Secretary, William G. McAdoo, a former New York lawyer, the first Chairman of the Federal Reserve Board, issued Liberty Loan bonds. They had varying maturation dates, some as long as thirty years. [1523]

German loans generated within the United States included $400,000, from Kuhn, Loeb & Company in September 1914, backed by the collateral of twenty-five million marks deposited with Max M. Warburg, Kuhn, Loeb's German affiliate. Chase National Bank, part of the Morgan group, loaned Germany $3 million. Mechanics and Metals National Bank loaned $1 million dollars. These loans funded Germany's espionage activities in Mexico and the United States Felix A. Sommerfeld, a German agent, had an account with the Guaranty Trust Company, which made direct payments to Western Cartridge Co. of Alton, Illinois, for ammunition used in Mexico by Pancho Villa's bandits. [1524]

The Central Liberty Loan, within each of the twelve Federal Reserve Districts Committees, aggressively marketed the bonds to the American public. Benjamin Strong, head of J.P Morgan's Bankers Trust Company and governor of the Second Reserve Bank (1914-1928) headed the Committee in his district, assisted by J. P. Morgan, Jacob H. Schiff, and Frank A. Vanderlip and others. Trusted men directed the bond sales in each Federal Reserve District. The nation-wide National Woman's Liberty Loan Committee enrolled about 800,000 women. [1525]

[1523] Liberty Loan Publicity Campaigns, http://www.1911encyclopedia.org/ Liberty_Loan_Publicity_Campaigns as of May 2012

[1524] Antony C. Sutton, Wall Street and the Bolshevik Revolution, Buccaneer Books, Cutchogue, New York, 1993, pp. 48-49

[1525] Liberty Loan Publicity Campaigns, http://www.1911encyclopedia.org/ Liberty_Loan_Publicity_Campaigns as of May 2012

People competed against each other and got on the patriotic bandwagon to support the war by selling and buying bonds. Loyalty typically follows one's money. Every man, woman and child was encouraged to do their part for the war effort. There were bands, parades, processions, and airplanes dropping leaflets. They used every imaginable selling device, including the use of endorsements from movie stars, Douglas Fairbanks and Mary Pickford, with phrases like "Your money must win the war." They filled newspapers and magazines with full-page ads to "Buy a Bond." It was the cultural slogan of the day, in every public place—restaurants, theaters, clubs and schools. Purchasing a bond was not about earning the promised interest but about "helping" the country in its patriotic fight for freedom. Purchasers without available funds could borrow money—"Borrow, buy and save." One could even buy bonds on the installment plan using coupon books. After the Armistice, prices for all commodities increased and merchants required more cash to increase their inventories. People redeemed their bonds below par. [1526]

Treasury Secretary William G. McAdoo placed his Assistant Treasury Secretary Jerome J. Hanauer in charge of the Liberty Loans. The two Treasury Under-secretaries were S. Parker Gilbert and Roscoe C. Leffingwell from the law firm of Cravath and Henderson, lawyers for Kuhn Loeb Co. They both later obtained partnerships in J.P. Morgan Co. [1527] Liberty Loans were a government scheme for the US taxpayers to assist Europe in paying its debts to the House of Morgan. [1528]

On October 1, 1895, Paul Warburg had married Nina Loeb, the daughter of Solomon Loeb of Kuhn, Loeb and Company, an international banking firm. Felix M. Warburg, a senior partner at Kuhn, Loeb, married Frieda Schiff, the daughter of Jacob H. Schiff, also of Kuhn, Loeb. The Schiffs and the Rothschilds were neighbors in Frankfurt. Schiff used Rothschild money to secure a partnership

---

[1526] Ibid

[1527] Eustace Mullins, The Secrets of the Federal Reserve, the London Connection, John McLaughlin, 1993, pp. 165-166

[1528] Jules Archer, The Plot to Seize the White House: The Shocking True Story of the Conspiracy, Hawthorne Books, New York, 1973, p. 224

with Kuhn, Loeb and Company. After frequent trips to the United States, Paul Warburg, along with his brother Felix, immigrated to the United States from Germany in 1902. [1529]

American citizens, in 1915 and 1916, were anti-British and pro-German. Paul Warburg, a naturalized citizen (1911), and Kuhn, Loeb Company were prominent United States fixtures. Max, Paul's brother stayed at home in Frankfurt to manage the family business, M.M. Warburg & Company, which their great-grandfather founded in 1798. Paul was a partner in the family firm in 1895. Max supervised the German Secret Service during the war. [1530] He was working in Switzerland for German Intelligence. [1531] From the proceeds of the First Liberty Loan, J. P. Morgan advanced Britain $400 million at the beginning of the war. [1532] By 1917, the Morgans and Kuhn, Loeb Company had loaned the Allies $1.5 billion in addition to financing numerous front organizations designed to embroil America into warfare. Morgan also offered to give the Allies credit. [1533]

On October 13, 1917 Woodrow Wilson gave an address, "It is manifestly imperative that there should be a complete mobilization of the banking reserves of the United States. The burden and the privilege (of the Allied loans) must be shared by every banking institution in the country. I believe that cooperation on the part of the banks is a patriotic duty at this time, and that membership in the Federal Reserve System is a distinct and significant evidence of patriotism." [1534]

[1529] Gary Allen with Larry Abraham, None Dare Call it Conspiracy, Double A Publications, Seattle, Washington, 1971, pp. 52-53

[1530] Ibid. 52-53

[1531] War Finance Bill Passed By Senate; Corporation Measure Modified in Many Respects Before Being Adopted, 74 to 3. Change Aimed At Warburg Power to Name Capital Issues Committee Is Shifted in Order to Bar New York Banker, Special to The New York Times, March 8, 1918, p. 1

[1532] Eustace Mullins, The Secrets of the Federal Reserve, the London Connection, John McLaughlin, 1993, p. 147

[1533] Ibid. 147

[1534] Ibid. 147-148

On December 12, 1918, after they signed the armistice, the US Naval Secret Service presented a report detailing Paul Warburg's questionable connections while we were at war with Germany. The report noted that he had resigned from the Federal Reserve in May 1918. [1535] In June 1918, he wrote to Wilson, "I have two brothers in Germany who are bankers. They naturally now serve their country to their utmost ability, as I serve mine." According to the *New York Times*, dated August 10, 1918, he resigned because his term expired, not because of his brother's position. He assumed Morgan's position on the Federal Advisory Council and continued to administer the Federal Reserve for the next ten years. [1536]

Paul Warburg was a Council on Foreign Relations (CFR) Director since its founding in 1921, until his death and was trustee of the Institute of Economics (1922), which merged with the Brookings Institution (1927), for which he was a trustee until his death. He promoted German-American relations and helped found the Carl Schurz Memorial Foundation in 1930. James Warburg, Paul Warburg's son, was one of Franklin D. Roosevelt's financial advisers.

Kuhn, Loeb Company was the country's biggest owner of railroad properties in the United States and Mexico and had controlling interest in *The New York Times*. [1537] They instructed President Wilson to establish the US Railroad Administration, under the jurisdiction of McAdoo, Comptroller of the Currency in order to protect their interests during the war. In 1918, the Federal Transportation Council replaced this agency. These agencies prevented railroad workers from earning suitable wages, a travesty, given the increased profits that Kuhn, Loeb was making from the US government as a result of the war. [1538]

On May 1, 1918, Sir William Wiseman sent a cable to Colonel House from London suggesting Allied assistance to help organize the Bolshevik forces. During the years 1917-1920, Lt. Col. Norman

---

[1535] Ibid. 150-151

[1536] Ibid. 178

[1537] Ibid. 154-155

[1538] Ibid. 167

Thwaites often consulted with Otto H. Kahn on political and economic issues. He also sought advice from Wiseman, the advisor on United States issues to the British delegation at the Peace Conference. He functioned in Britain in the same capacity as House did in this country. Wilson appointed House to head the American War Mission to the Inter-Allied War Conference in the summer of 1917. Gordon Auchincloss, House's son-in-law, was his assistant. Paul Cravath, a Kuhn, Loeb Co. lawyer accompanied House and Auchincloss on a European tour, guided by Wiseman. [1539] He was a protégé of Canadian Round Table founder Lord Beaverbrook, and was prominent in the Zionist movement." [1540]

Representative Charles A. Lindbergh, of the House Banking and Currency Committee, impeached five members of the Federal Reserve Board. Lindbergh said that Paul M. Warburg, of the Federal Reserve Board, the National City Bank and other banking firms conspired to enact currency legislation in the interest of big business in order to make industrial slaves of the population. However, the House did not act on the impeachment resolution. [1541]

Communism, a Banker's Perfect Political System

Leon Degrelle wrote, "Unlike conventional imperialists, who sought to grab a piece of land, communist imperialism sought to conquer the entire world. It was a basic difference that would transform the world." [1542]

Freemason Friedrich Adler, who assassinated Austrian Prime Minister Karl von Sturgkh, on October 21, 1916, maintained contact "with the masonic leader Rothschild." Austrian Viktor Adler, father of Friedrich, warned Leon Trotsky, who was then exiled in Vienna

[1539] Ibid. 171-172
[1540] US Labor Party Investigating Team, Dope Inc. Britain's Opium War Against the US, New York, 1978, p. 45
[1541] Eustace Mullins, The Secrets of the Federal Reserve, the London Connection, John McLaughlin, 1993, pp. 177-178
[1542] Leon Degrelle, Hitler: Born at Versailles, Volume 1, of the Hitler Century, Institute for Historical Review, Torrance, California, 1992, p. 298

[1543] that the authorities were going to capture him the next day, so he fled to Switzerland. Lenin stayed in Switzerland until March 1917. [1544] Ultimately, Trotsky arrived in New York City in January 1917, where he collaborated with Jacob H. Schiff, who ensconced him in an apartment and provided him with a chauffeur-driven limousine. After Trotsky had gathered a group of 300 Marxist revolutionaries from Manhattan's Lower East Side, Rockefeller allowed them to train in the Standard Oil compound in New Jersey. Then, they sailed from New York on the *S.S. Kristianiafjord*, chartered by Schiff, who also supplied Trotsky with $20 million in gold. It was a paltry sum to acquire control of Russia and her vast natural resources. Rockefeller gave Trotsky $10,000 for traveling expenses and arranged a special passport for him with President Woodrow Wilson. [1545]

Trotsky joined Vladimir Lenin, Joseph Stalin, Lazar Kaganovich, and Maxim Litvinov (Meyer H. Wallakh) for a strategy meeting in Switzerland before going to Russia. At the Congress of Vienna, officials guaranteed perpetual neutrality, to Switzerland, in the heart of Europe, due to the Rothschild's meticulous long-range planning. [1546] Industrialists, bankers, and politicians supported the Bolsheviks. On April, 2, 1917, President Wilson said ". . . Assurance has been added to our hope for the future peace of the world by the wonderful and heartening things that have been happening in the last few weeks in Russia . . . Here is a fit partner for a League of Honor." [1547]

US State Department records document that National City Bank, controlled by Stillman and Rockefeller interests, and the Guaranty Trust, controlled by Morgan interests, both provided substantial loans

[1543] Jüri Lina, Architects of Deception, Referent Publishing, Stockholm Sweden, 2004, pp. 316-317

[1544] Leon Degrelle, Hitler: Born at Versailles, Volume 1, of the Hitler Century, Institute for Historical Review, Torrance, California, 1992, p. 98

[1545] Eustace Mullins, Murder by Injection, the Story of the Medical Conspiracy Against America, the National Council for Medical Research, Staunton, Virginia, 1988, pp. 326-327

[1546] Des Griffin, Descent into Slavery, Emissary Publications, Clackamas, Oregon, 1980, pp. 64-69

[1547] Wilson's War Message to Congress, April 2, 1917, http://wwi.lib.byu.edu/index.php/Wilson's_War_Message_to_Congress as of May 2012

to belligerent Russia before America entered World War I on April 6, 1917. The State Department told the banks that the loans were contrary to international law. However, they conducted the loan negotiations through official US government communications facilities, and the State Department allowed the message transference. [1548]

On April 13, 1917, officials waylaid the ship in Halifax and they arrested Trotsky. People had warned Canadian officials that Trotsky would halt Russia's participation in the war, which would free up the German armies who would then attack Canadian troops on the Western Front. Prime Minister David Lloyd George (1916-1922) cabled them and ordered the immediate release of Trotsky. They ignored him. John D. Rockefeller then directed Canadian Minister Mackenzie King to intervene, and he maneuvered Trotsky's release. [1549]

In April 1917, after nine years, Lenin was returning to Russia to join Trotsky, the person with the connections to the bankers. Germany did not anticipate that Lenin, with perhaps 200 followers, could challenge their enemy, Russia. Lenin arrived at the Russian frontier in a sealed train from Switzerland. Trotsky arrived from the United States a while later. [1550] Kurt Riezler was the conduit for German subsidies to the Bolsheviks and negotiated with Lenin's agents, Karl Radek, and Alexander Parvus. Riezler later claimed that it was his idea to transport Lenin in the sealed train from Zurich, through Germany to Russia.

A few Germans considered supporting Stalin, as they believed they could influence him more than Lenin could. They wanted to destroy both Lenin and Stalin without destroying Russia. The Germans had two objectives, 1) get Lenin to end Russia's participation in the war, and 2) eliminate Lenin and his revolutionary goals. However,

---

[1548] Antony C. Sutton, Wall Street and the Bolshevik Revolution, Buccaneer Books, Cutchogue, New York, 1993, p. 39

[1549] Eustace Mullins, Murder by Injection, the Story of the Medical Conspiracy Against America, the National Council for Medical Research, Staunton, Virginia, 1988, pp. 326-327

[1550] Nesta H. Webster, The Surrender of an Empire, Boswell Printing and Publishing Company, Ltd., London, p. 73

Lenin was incredibly deceptive. While he played along with them, he implemented his revolution, and he intended to manipulate them and then turn against them. [1551]

To allay the fears of his colleagues, Alexander Kerensky claimed that Lenin was a German agent to discredit him. The patriots in the Duma said, "The very fact that Lenin came back via Germany will harm his prestige to such an extent that there will be nothing more to fear from him." Lenin expected such an indictment and so, before boarding the German train, he asked others to attest to his credentials. Paul Levi, a Jewish political leader, a member of the Social Democratic Party (SPD), along with Rosa Luxemburg, who kept kosher, and Karl Liebknecht verified Lenin's legitimacy as a Marxist. One person wrote, "The Russian internationalists who are now leaving for Russia to serve the revolution will be helping us by fostering uprisings among the proletarians of other countries, particularly those of Germany and Austria, against their own governments." Lenin requested the writer of that endorsement to add the reference to Germany and Austria to refute the claim that he was a German agent. [1552]

German bankers, through their agents, gave Lenin money before he boarded the train. Lenin exploited everyone for his own objectives, one of which was to destroy imperial Germany, after he had seized power in Russia. In September 1917, Schiff gave Trotsky funds through the Warburg Bank, his correspondent in Stockholm, which managed Trotsky's account. While the bankers invested in Lenin and Trotsky's revolutionary activities, they did not anticipate getting revolutions in their own countries. If certain German and Jewish bankers had not given Lenin millions of dollars, his revolution and plans for world subversion would have failed. With Lenin, it was always the ends justify the means. [1553]

Max Warburg, the head of the German Secret Service, allowed Lenin's train with $20 million in gold to cross the border on its way

[1551] Leon Degrelle, Hitler: Born at Versailles, Volume 1, of the Hitler Century, Institute for Historical Review, Torrance, California, 1992, pp. 278-279
[1552] Ibid. 280-281
[1553] Ibid. 280-281

to Russia. [1554] The bankers and industrialists did not espouse the Marxist ideology but recognized that it is the ultimate monopoly for controlling the government, the monetary system and all property. [1555] Less than ten percent of the population had imposed a dictatorship on the rest of the country. [1556] The occupants of Lenin's train, of the 165 names published, twenty-three were Russian, three were Georgian, four were Armenian, one was a German, and 128 were Jewish. [1557]

Henry P. Davison, as Chairman of the War Council of the American Red Cross, assisted the Bolsheviks by sending food. Davison, who helped found the Bankers Trust Company, was a senior partner at J.P. Morgan & Company, and participated in the meeting on Jekyll Island in 1910, where plotters devised the creation of the Federal Reserve. The contrived reason for the revolution was that starving Russian workers revolted against the oppressive czarist regime. However, the Bolsheviks manipulated the workers just as revolutionaries in France, exploited the destitute workers during the French Revolution. Prior to the Bolshevik revolt, Russia had become a producer in the world's oil market. [1558]

Thomas D. Thacher (S&B), whose brother worked for Henry L. Stimson (S&B), was a partner in the Wall Street law firm of Simpson, Thacher & Bartlett. He represented the Soviet State Bank and assisted the Soviets to circumvent the law with the government's full cooperation. People at the Equitable Trust Building, 120 Broadway, in New York City, home of numerous firms, including the American International Corporation, developed the plan to participate in the brewing revolution. Thacher's 1917 memorandum, in consultation

---

[1554] Eustace Mullins, The Secrets of the Federal Reserve, the London Connection, John McLaughlin, 1993, pp. 83, 150

[1555] Eustace Mullins, Murder by Injection, the Story of the Medical Conspiracy Against America, the National Council for Medical Research, Staunton, Virginia, 1988, pp. 326-327

[1556] Leon Degrelle, Hitler: Born at Versailles, Volume 1, of the Hitler Century, Institute for Historical Review, Torrance, California, 1992, p. 300

[1557] Nesta H. Webster, The Surrender of an Empire, Boswell Printing and Publishing Company, Ltd., London, p. 77

[1558] Gary Allen, The Rockefeller File, the Untold Story of the Most Powerful Family in America, 76 Press, Seal Beach, California, 1976, pp. 106-107

with Alfred Harmsworth, Lord Northcliffe, in London, called for assistance to the Bolsheviks. Thacher, who had visited Russia with William B. Thompson's Red Cross Mission, called for official recognition of the Soviet government. Because the Bolsheviks only controlled a small portion of the huge country, they required military and financial assistance to conquer the rest of the country. [1559]

The Thatcher Memorandum suggested the following, 1) The Allies should discourage Japanese intervention in Siberia, 2) the US government should render its full assistance to the Soviets in organizing a volunteer revolutionary army, 3) the Allied governments should give moral support to the Russians in choosing their own political systems uninfluenced by any foreign power, and, 4) until the Soviets and Germany engage in conflict, "there will be opportunity for peaceful commercial penetration by German agencies in Russia." Absent open conflict, it would be almost impossible to inhibit trade. The Soviets should impede, as far as possible, the transport of grain and raw materials to Germany from Russia. [1560]

Thacher thought that the United States should keep Japan out of Siberia, while giving assistance to the Soviets to build an army. He suggested that the Allied forces supply moral support to the Russian people in their political choices. Further, they should make every effort to maintain peace between Germany and the Soviet Union, until the inevitable conflict, in order to allow the Soviets to expand technologically and commercially. The Soviets would be unable to develop their natural resources without western assistance. The czar had rejected Rockefeller's help in developing the country's vast oil resources after Alphonse Rothschild died. President Woodrow Wilson sent US troops, under General William S. Graves to secure the Tran-Siberian Railroad for which the Soviets were grateful. [1561]

Guaranty Trust and Brown Brothers saw a profitable opportunity with the Bolshevik Revolution, for which they supplied cash, guns,

---

[1559] Antony Sutton, America's Secret Establishment: An Introduction to the Order of Skull & Bones, Trine Day, Walterville, Oregon, 2002, pp. 138-143

[1560] Ibid. 138-143

[1561] Ibid. 138-143

ammunition, and discreet political support from London, Washington, DC, and Paris, which gave minimal support. International bankers often finance both sides to incur major indebtedness. By their lending policies, the bankers decide which nation will be victorious. They loan the predetermined loser nation(s) enough money to participate but insufficient funds for a victory. Meanwhile, the banks lend the inevitable victor plenty of money with the understanding that the winner will honor the debts of the defeated countries, via the victor's seizure of the vanquished nation's natural and manufactured assets. The bankers invariably win while nations, even victorious nations, mount up unpayable debt and squander their people in warfare.

William B. Thompson sent a document to Prime Minister David Lloyd George in December 1917. He wrote, "The Russian situation is lost and Russia lies entirely open to unopposed German exploitation unless a radical reversal of policy is at once undertaken by the Allies. Because of their shortsighted diplomacy, the Allies since the Revolution have accomplished nothing beneficial, and have done considerable harm to their own interests." [1562]

Catherine Breshkovsky, the so-called Grandmother of the Russian Revolution, wrote to President Wilson, "A widespread education is necessary to make Russia an orderly democracy. We plan to bring this education to the soldier in the camp, to the workman in the factory, to the peasant in the village." Further, they could only maintain a democracy in Russian by militarily defeating and overthrowing Germany. She maintained that a free Russia could not survive if the people were untrained, unprepared and uneducated for governmental responsibilities, especially with Germany as "her next door neighbor." Thompson reiterated, "Russia would become speedily the greatest war prize the world has even known." [1563]

Thompson's agents disseminated Bolshevik literature. He wrote to Lloyd George, "After the overthrow of the last Kerensky government

---

[1562] Selected Documents from Government Files of the United States and Great Britain, http://www.reformation.org/wall-st-bolshevik-app3.html as of May 2012
[1563] Ibid

we materially aided the dissemination of the Bolshevik literature, distributing it through agents and by airplanes to the German army. If the suggestion is permissible, it might be well to consider whether it would not be desirable to have this same Bolshevik literature sent into Germany and Austria across the West and Italian fronts." Further, he wrote, "If you ask for a further programme I should say that it is impossible to give it now. I believe that intelligent and courageous work will still prevent Germany from occupying the field to itself and thus exploiting Russia at the expense of the Allies. There will be many ways in which this service can be rendered which will become obvious as the work progresses." [1564]

In March 1918, President Wilson sent a telegram addressed to the Soviet Congress which read, "Let me take the opportunity on the occasion of this Soviet gathering to express the sincere sympathy felt by the American people for the Russian People. The American people are heartily with the Russian people in its determination to be forever free of autocratic government and to be master of its own destiny." [1565] Wilson sent Elihu Root to Russia with $100 million from his Special Emergency War Fund to prop up the faltering Bolshevik regime. The evidence of Kuhn, Loeb and Company's support in the establishment of Communism is extensive. After their victory, the Bolsheviks transferred 600 million rubles in gold between the years 1918 and 1922, to Kuhn, Loeb.

American Jews such as the Warburg family funded Lenin and Trotsky. Armand Hammer, son of Russian-born Jewish immigrants, Julius and Rose (Lipshitz) Hammer, whose parents named him after the arm and hammer symbol of the Socialist Labor Party of America (SLP), was a Bolshevik agent. He later assisted in the formation of the American Communist Party, and advocated support for the Bolsheviks. In 1921, Armand Hammer went to the Soviet Union and stayed until late 1930. Jews were deeply involved in the revolution to destroy the czar and Christian Russia. Some individuals claim that British freemasons directed the B'nai B'rith in their installation

---

[1564] Ibid
[1565] Leon Degrelle, Hitler: Born at Versailles, Volume 1, of the Hitler Century, Institute for Historical Review, Torrance, California, 1992, p. 297

of the Bolsheviks to destroy the possibility of a Eurasian alliance among France, Germany, Russia, Japan, and China, which would jeopardize British economic and geopolitical objectives. Germany, in the late 1800s, won a concession to build the Baghdad to Berlin railway, which would decrease Britain's importance as the dominate power. [1566]

On November 30, 1918, Trotsky addressed the Petrograd Soviet during which he spoke of two Americans with close connections to Wall Street, probably Thompson and Raymond Robins, a mining promoter. New York Federal Reserve Bank director (1914-1919), Thompson, left Petrograd on December 4, 1918, two days after he cabled a request for $1 million to Morgan. The three key Soviet financiers were Thompson, Thomas W. Lamont, and Charles R. Crane (King Crane Commission). Without the help of J. Pierpont Morgan, and the Guaranty Trust Company, the Bolshevik Revolution would have failed as it did in 1905. [1567]

Financing any movement implies controlling that movement. The bankers initially financed the communists, but who controlled them thereafter? Wall Street kingmakers decide who gets to be the king, in the United States and elsewhere. Then they control the king. They hire, fire, and/or assassinate him. In October 1964, David Rockefeller went to the Soviet Union, ostensibly for a vacation. Within days, minor officials summoned Nikita S. Khrushchev home from a Black Sea resort. He returned home to discover that Rockefeller had fired him as of October 14, 1964. Few people have the authority to fire a dictator. [1568]

Jacques Attali, the Jewish historian, academician and freemason, author of *The Jews, the World, and the Money,* confirmed in the magazine *L'Express* that the Jews invented capitalism. The Jews

---

[1566] Executive Intelligence Review (editors), The Ugly Truth About the ADL, Washington DC, 1992, pp. 26-28

[1567] Antony C. Sutton, Wall Street and the Bolshevik Revolution, Buccaneer Books, Cutchogue, New York, 1993, pp. 8-9

[1568] Gary Allen with Larry Abraham, None Dare Call it Conspiracy, Double A Publications, Seattle, Washington, 1971, p. 121

also developed state capitalism, which is communism, two diabolical systems that have caused the death of millions. [1569] Elizabeth Dilling wrote, "Marxism, Socialism, or Communism in practice are nothing but state-capitalism and rule by a privileged minority, exercising despotic and total control over a majority having virtually no property or legal rights." [1570]

As long as currency creation, with its inherent debt structure, remains in the hands of the families that funded communism, the United States will never escape from the tyranny of the international money cabal. Experts say this about every country in which a central bank controls the currency and credit. The control of a nation's currency must be in the hands of the people who labor, not by those who seize the products of their labors. Communism, under other names, exists in every country, particularly the United States, and has been since the secretive, private Federal Reserve was established.

The Bolshevik Revolution, 1917

Dr. Ray M. Jurjevich, who called the Soviet Union the first Judaic State, wrote, "The real Judaic aim of World War I was to advance their conquest of the world. The chief weapon of that advancement was the Bolshevik Revolution." The revolution initially accomplished the destruction of the Russian Empire and ultimately the brutal deaths of millions of its people. [1571] In 1910, Vladimir Lenin and Leon Trotsky participated in the International Masonic Conference in Copenhagen, where the Socialization of Europe was part of the presentation. [1572]

[1569] Jüri Lina, Architects of Deception, Referent Publishing, Stockholm, Sweden, 2004, pp. 141-142
[1570] Elizabeth Dilling, The Jewish Religion: Its Influence Today, formerly titled The Plot Against Christianity, Noontide Press, Newport Beach, California, 1983, p. 121
[1571] Ray M. Jurjevich, Ph.D., Five Bloody Revolutions by Judeo-Bankers and their own Judeo-Masonry, Ichthys Books, Inc., Overland Park, Kansas, 2000, pp. 163-164
[1572] Jüri Lina, Under the Sign of the Scorpion: The Rise and Fall of the Soviet Empire, Referent Publishing, Stockholm, Sweden, 2002, pp. 98-99

The Bolsheviks were unsuccessful in taking over the Russian government during their 1905 revolution. However, with sufficient financing, they would eventually succeed. To acquire the needed financing, Vladimir Lenin and Leon Trotsky met with US industrialists twice, in 1907 and in 1910. The Bolsheviks wanted to establish a land base from which to wage a destructive worldwide revolution. After regrouping and gaining additional funding, they secured influential positions within the government, and by 1917, after the nation was emotionally and economically weakened by warfare, Stalin, Lenin, and Trotsky, all assumed names, prepared for another onslaught against Russia and the Romanov family, who had ruled Christian Russia for 500 years.

Robert Grimm invited thirty-eight Socialists to attend a pacifist conference in Zimmerwald, from September 5-8, 1915. Attendees came from Russia, Poland, Italy, Switzerland, Bulgaria, Romania, Germany, France, the Netherlands, and Sweden. Lenin, Trotsky, Grigory Zinoviev (Gerson Radomyslsky) and Karl Radek, infiltrated the conference to present the Zimmerwald Manifesto that Trotsky helped draft. It summoned the working people of the warring countries to wage a civil war within their respective countries to achieve power toward the implementation of a Marxist society. Over forty delegates from various countries attended the Second Zimmerwald Conference, April 24-30, 1916, in the village of Kienthal. The delegates again opposed Lenin's doctrine in favor of a more pacifist position. While Lenin failed to gain full support, this meeting increased his influence in the Zimmerwald movement.

Trotsky wrote in the Manifesto, "The war has lasted more than a year. Millions of corpses cover the battlefields. Millions of human beings have been crippled for the rest of their lives. Europe is like a gigantic human slaughterhouse . . . Proletarians of all countries, unite!" [1573] Lenin encouraged the working-class soldiers to shift the war toward the czar and his monarchy. Then, if they were victorious,

---

[1573] Bob Blaisdell, The Communist Manifesto and other revolutionary writings: Marx, Marat, Paine, Mao, Gandhi and Others, Courier Dover Publications, New York, 2003, pp. 223-227

they should wage a revolution for the oppressed masses of Europe in other countries.

From June 4, 1916, until late September, Russian General Aleksei A. Brusilov waged one of the most lethal battles in world history, a major offensive against the armies of the Central Powers, Germany and Austria-Hungary, on the Eastern Front. This forced Germany to stop its attack on Verdun, and shift its forces to the East. Brusilov's strategy overwhelmed the Austro-Hungarian Army, which suffered 750,000 casualties. That army then had to rely on the Germans. Meanwhile, Russian casualties totaled about 1.4 million, which the population viewed as a military failure. At least 58,016 Russian soldiers deserted. While the Brusilov Offensive demonstrated good leadership, and military planning, the Russian Army's effectiveness began a steep decline because of Russia's declining economic and political situation.

The Brusilov Offensive and the huge loss of life contributed to the massive demonstrations in St. Petersburg in March 1917, during which the Bolsheviks, in an initial attempt to manage the masses, mingled amongst the crowd yelling, "All power to the soviets!," until other demonstrators took up the cry. Trotsky, after the authorities detained him in London, joined Lenin as his right hand man. Both were fervent speakers who drew massive crowds. [1574] For three years, the Russians had fought with inadequate guns, and deficient ammunition. Its army, by 1917, had lost more men than Britain, France, and Italy together with 2,762,064 dead, 4,950,000 wounded and 2,500,000 missing. The army was disbanding despite Minister of War Alexander Kerensky's promises of pending peace. He toured the Eastern Front trying to convince them to keep fighting, assuring them that "victory, democracy and peace" were imminent. [1575]

Turkey's entry into World War I on October 28, 1914, on the side of the Central Powers, deprived Russia of its chief trade route through

[1574] Leon Degrelle, Hitler: Born at Versailles, Volume 1, of the Hitler Century, Institute for Historical Review, Torrance, California, 1992, p. 283

[1575] Michael Sayers and Albert E. Kahn, The Great Conspiracy Against Russia, Collet's, London, 1946, p. 11

Turkey, which prevented Russia from obtaining needed munitions for its army and sparked other economic hardships. Hungry, weary Russians blamed Czar Nicholas for the crisis and for the continued warfare that disrupted agriculture, making access to food a significant dilemma, not due entirely to the cessation of agriculture but by 1917, to the over-printing of currency to fund the war and the resulting monetary inflation that increased food costs by approximately four times what it cost in 1914.

The peasantry, who grew the grain, had higher food costs without a corresponding increase in the wholesale price, through intermediaries, of their produce. Rather than relinquishing it, the farmers hoarded their grain or simply returned to subsistence farming in an attempt to meet their own needs. Hence, food was in short supply in urban areas, in addition to increasing prices, which, like a domino effect, provoked factory workers to demand higher wages. In January and February 1916, socialist propaganda and well-placed agitators triggered pervasive strikes, creating mass unrest and mounting criticism of the government. People abandoned their patriotic war fervor, yet still objected to the people who opposed the war. The heavy losses associated with it made people, especially the workers, question their religious faith and lose confidence in the czar's ability. Irreligion and the atheistic pseudo-religion of socialism began to replace Christianity after almost three years of war with millions dead, maimed, sick, and hopeless. People regress and abandon their noble intentions and often adopt new ideas, even primitive, less humanitarian notions that they would have rejected in healthier stress-free circumstances.

The Revolution, March 8-12, 1917, as far as the Russian population was concerned, was a demonstration against the war and general dissatisfaction. On March 15, revolutionaries halted the czar's train and informed him that his reign was over. [1576] The revolution, during the military mutiny, allowed certain members of the Duma to seize control and create the Russian Provisional Government. The army

---

[1576] Nesta H. Webster, The Surrender of an Empire, Boswell Printing and Publishing Company, Ltd., London, p. 73

leadership felt powerless in suppressing the revolution. Prince Georgy L'vov initially headed the government. Soon, Kerensky, a high-ranking freemason, [1577] and a key figure in the Duma, a leader in the efforts to depose the czar and the first Minister of Justice headed the new government. The Soviets (workers' councils), led by Marxists, shared dual power with Kerensky, who maintained state power while they relied on their influence with the lower-class and the political left.

Christian Rakovsky, a longtime Trotsky cohort, Soviet Ambassador to France, and the First Chairman of the Council of People's Commissars of the Ukrainian (1919-1923), claimed that Kerensky was the banker's inside man in Russia as false opposition, and only pretended to oppose Communism, but actually would later surrender the whole country to the Bolsheviks. Rakovsky, a participant, said, communism is indebted to Kerensky, much more than to Lenin." He said that Jacob H. Schiff, who had financed Japan's warfare with Russia in 1905, along with the Warburg brothers, and Kuhn, Loeb ultimately financed Russia's collapse. [1578]

While Lenin successfully indoctrinated the Russian workers, there remained a huge population who opposed his views. In June 1917, people rebelled against the provisional government established by the March revolution. Though Lenin had not participated in the March incidents, he viewed this revolt as a potential means to power, as he viewed the crowds as ignorant and undisciplined. He decided to exploit and develop this opportunity to wage a second revolution. To cover his subsequent failure in carrying out his objectives, Trotsky wrote, "Lenin was sick and had lived in a Finnish country house since June 19. Neither on this day nor on the following days did he go to Petrograd." [1579]

[1577] Jüri Lina, Under the Sign of the Scorpion: The Rise and Fall of the Soviet Empire, Referent Publishing, Stockholm, Sweden, 2002, pp. 136-137

[1578] Dr. J. Landowsky, Red Symphony, translated by George Knupffer, Christian Book Club of America, Palmdale, California, 1968, pp. 36-37

[1579] Leon Degrelle, Hitler: Born at Versailles, Volume 1, of the Hitler Century, Institute for Historical Review, Torrance, California, 1992, pp. 285-287

On June 18, 1917, in St. Petersburg, workers and soldiers participated in a huge demonstration that affected people throughout Russia. Trotsky wrote, "The manifestation of June 18 had revealed to everybody that the government was without support." [1580] During the next few days, fierce conflicts erupted between the anarchists, communists and the anti-communists. The authorities released jail prisoners and the soldiers revolted. Frightened middle class revolutionaries finally opposed the Bolsheviks. On June 25, 1917, Lenin, at the scene and not in Finland, savagely denounced them for their rage against the Bolsheviks. While Lenin may have been in Finland, it had nothing to do with ill health. [1581]

Lenin was in Finland between June 29 and July 3, 1917, where he met with German agents, representing Max Warburg, the brother of Paul Warburg, who gave him additional funds. When Lenin returned to St. Petersburg, he directed his agents to take to the streets on July 4, 1917, a tactic he had previously prohibited. He understood that anarchy could destroy a revolution, but he now had the money to impose a dictatorship. On that day, the second revolution erupted. He addressed the crowds, standing in the pouring rain, from a balcony of the ballerina Kshesinskaya's palace, where he persuaded the masses to storm the Taurid Palace. He ordered his people to mingle with the anti-war protesters. Many Russians still believed that they had a moral obligation, to fight the enemy. In the Duma, when Trotsky, Zinoviev, and Kamenev demanded that the army give up its arms, other members called them anti-Russian Jews, who were attempting to devastate the fatherland. People accused Lenin of being a German agent. Trotsky wrote, "In the shops, in the street, everybody was talking about German money." Angry citizens ransacked Bolshevik headquarters and the office of their newspaper *Pravda* and Lenin fled. [1582]

[1580] Leon Trotsky, The History of the Russian Revolution, Volume Two: The Attempted Counter-Revolution, Chapter 24, The July Days: Preparation and Beginning, http://www.marxists.org/archive/trotsky/1930/hrr/ch24.htm as of May 2012

[1581] Leon Degrelle, Hitler: Born at Versailles, Volume 1, of the Hitler Century, Institute for Historical Review, Torrance, California, 1992, pp. 285-287

[1582] Ibid. 285-287

Kerensky, instead of terminating the floundering war, ordered what people now refer to as the Kerensky Offensive, from July 1-19, 1917, during which troops attacked the Austro-Hungarian and German forces in Galicia. The Russian advance collapsed by July 16. On July 18, the Germans and Austro-Hungarians counterattacked, and by July 23, the Russians retreated. This military catastrophe weakened the new government, and made a Bolshevik coup d'état possible. The army's morale was low and the soldiers no longer followed directions.

Within two weeks, people recognized Lenin and Trotsky, previously lauded as heroes, as the criminals they were. Now the crowds yelled, "Death to the Jews, death to the Bolsheviks." Lenin, through his miscalculations and eagerness, underestimated the citizen's reactions. Even as war-weary and demoralized as they were, they were unwilling to betray the military and the fatherland. Lenin's treacherous July revolution failed and the officials deported him and incarcerated his collaborators. The Russians, considering the least of the two evils, then readily accepted the existing partially socialist government. Officers absolved Kerensky of the Brusilov catastrophe, and appointed him as Prime Minister on July 21, 1917. As autumn approached, Lenin planned to destroy Russia and Germany. [1583]

The Grand Orient of France and Italy had established a network of Masonic lodges in St. Petersburg and other large cities, as a foundation to consolidate their power for the revolution. All of the officials in Kerensky's Provisional Government were freemasons. [1584] The government, now under Kerensky preferred to remain in the war against Germany while the Bolsheviks and socialists wanted to abandon it. Kerensky, a member of the Socialist-Revolutionary Party, and a brilliant orator, who stage-managed the operation to depose the czar, collaborated with Genrikh Sliozberg, the alleged Grand Master

[1583] Ibid. 285-287
[1584] David Musa Pidcock, Satanic Voices, Ancient and Modern, a Surfeit of Blasphemy Including the Rushdie Report from Edifice Complex to Occult Theocracy, Mustaqim, Islamic Art and Literature, Milton Keynes, England, 1992, pp. 47-53

for Russia for the B'nai B'rith. [1585] His major accomplishments, as Prime Minister, were the abolition of the death penalty, universal suffrage, and the granting of equal freedoms to women.

The Bolsheviks established and controlled militias, the Red Guards, under the Military Revolutionary Committee, later known as the Red Army. On September 14, the Directorate suspended the State Duma. On October 24, 1917, these forces began the takeover of government buildings. They captured the Winter Palace the next day. By fall 1917, despite Kerensky's energetic pro-war speeches, two million Russians deserted. On October 25, 1917, the Bolsheviks stormed the Winter Palace and arrested members of Kerensky's cabinet. He fled to France. [1586]

Thereafter, Trotsky seized control of the government and became President of the Petrograd Soviet, from October 8, to November 8, 1917. The Bolshevik Revolution, a political coup, on November 7, 1917, allowed the Bolsheviks to maximize the Russian Revolution of February 1917. Trotsky and Lenin ordered the killing of the members of the Provisional government. Lenin announced a general amnesty for the Bolshevik leaders and about 250,000 revolutionaries, who had been in exile since 1905. They had received financial support from the same American industrialists and bankers who had funded the 1905 revolution.

The Bolsheviks petitioned the masses to accept the new authority and recognize Lenin as the person who reinstated the land and peoples from the previous empire. They claimed that they facilitated this reinstatement in the name of solidarity so that the centralized uniform government could rule in Moscow. Nikolai V. Ustrialov said, "The first and most important thing is . . . the restoration of Russia as a great and united state. All else will follow." He was referring to the adjacent states that the Bolsheviks wanted incorporated into Russia, even if it required war. Surely, Russian patriots, despite ideological

[1585] Jüri Lina, Architects of Deception, Referent Publishing, Stockholm, Sweden, 2004, p. 308
[1586] Russia and the First World War, http://www.spartacus.schoolnet.co.uk/RUSfww.htm as of May 2012

differences, would "fight for the same thing, in the name of a great and united Russia." He concluded, "Their practical course is the same." The ends justify the means. [1587]

Lenin's Bolshevik party and the workers' Soviets assumed the leadership of numerous government positions. On December 19-20, 1917, he authorized the creation of The All-Russian Extraordinary Commission for Combating Counter-Revolution and Sabotage, known as Cheka, to suppress any dissent. This agency, which murdered at least 20,000,000 people, ultimately evolved into the KGB. They randomly slaughtered independent farmers, ethnic minorities, members of the bourgeoisie, senior officers, intellectuals, artists, labor movement activists, and even members of the Communist Party. The Menshevik Marxists ultimately abandoned the whole movement. The term *Bolshevik* refers to the larger majority faction. After 1918, they would call their organization the Communist Party. [1588]

On July 17, 1918, at the Ipatiev House in Yekaterinburg, Filipp I. Goloshchekin (Jew), Peter Z. Yermakov (Russian), Yakov Yurovsky (Jew), the murderer-in-chief and others murdered Czar Nicholas II and the his entire family. Some of the conspirators were Lenin's fellow train passengers. Yakov M. Sverdlov (Jew) was the Soviet's uncrowned czar. People in Yekaterinburg described Goloshchekin, a longtime close friend of Sverdlov (Yankel-Aaron Solomon), as a bloodthirsty homicidal sadist. [1589] Bolsheviks later renamed Yekaterinburg as Sverdlovsk in his honor. Sverdlov, the chairman of the All-Russian Central Executive Committee, had, the day before, ordered the execution of the czar, his wife, Alexandra, and their children Olga, Tatiana, Maria, Anastasia, and Alexei. [1590]

[1587] Roman Szporluk, Communism and Nationalism: Karl Marx Versus Friedrich List, Oxford University Press, New York, 1991, pp. 217-219

[1588] John Beaty, The Iron Curtain Over America, Chestnut Mountain Book, Barboursville, Virginia, 1968, p. 26

[1589] George Gustav Telberg, The Last Days of the Romanovs, Read Books, Vancouver, BC, 2007, pp. 228-229

[1590] William Guy Carr, Pawns in the Game, Noontide Press, Newport Beach, California, 1978, pp. 91-92

Following the revolution, Russia was the first country in the world to make anti-Semitism a crime. [1591] On July 27, 1918, Lenin outlawed all anti-Semitism, a law, if broken, might result in execution. [1592] Quite possibly the reason for this law was to officially prevent skeptical citizens from openly associating the Jews with what had befallen their nation. The brutal communists slaughtered the entire royal family and many religious and professional people. Those same people, the Jews, were the most predominant faction within the government. In the 1930s, Marietta Shaginyan, a writer, discovered that Lenin was Jewish and certain individuals instructed her not to publicize this state secret. [1593] In 1935, the court ruled anti-Semitism a penal offense. [1594]

After the revolution, a civil war erupted between the Bolsheviks and the Whites. As many as half a million former czarist officers and members of the old regime joined the Bolsheviks. They did not adopt Marxism but promoted the idea of a great and indivisible Russia. The Bolsheviks regarded the unification of adjacent provinces as an ideological triumph. However, the dedicated Marxists waged war for world conquest, not to instill their power in just one country. Therefore, national interests took a back seat to rampant militancy directed at other nations. The Bolsheviks began an aggressive state-building campaign in which they received encouragement from the extreme right. [1595]

The Bolsheviks began a two and a half year unprecedented reign of terror which was successful only because they neutralized the

---

[1591] Louis Marschalko, The World Conquerors, the Real War Criminals, Translated from the Hungarian by A. Suranyi, Joseph Sueli Publications, London, 1958, pp. 93-94

[1592] Udo Walendy, The Jews in the Soviet Union, Part 2 of Aleksandr Solzhenitsyn's 200 Years Together, a review, The Barnes Review, Volume 15, Number 5, September/October 2008, p. 16

[1593] Jüri Lina, Under the Sign of the Scorpion The Rise and Fall of the Soviet Empire, Referent Publishing, Stockholm, Sweden, 2002, pp. 95-96

[1594] John Beaty, The Iron Curtain Over America, Chestnut Mountain Book, Barboursville, Virginia, 1968, pp. 28-30

[1595] Roman Szporluk, Communism and Nationalism: Karl Marx Versus Friedrich List, Oxford University Press, New York, 1991, pp. 217-219

masses through propaganda. Trotsky was the People's Commissar for Army and Navy Affairs (1918-1925) and directed the Red Army; a deadly device of the Rothschild (Red Shield) dominated international bankers. Given the millions that the government deliberately starved or savagely slaughtered, the color red was indeed morbidly appropriate. Moreover, there was economic chaos, an inadequate amount of raw materials, loss of crops, and credit followed by the unrestrained printing of currency, which devalued the ruble. Debauching the country's currency is the typical Marxist strategy to economically destabilize a nation. [1596]

The White Russian Armies opposed the Bolshevik seizure. They viewed Jews and Bolsheviks as common enemies. The number of Jews compared to other ethnic groups represented in the early days of communist rule in Russia is as follows, according to the Soviet press, out of 556 important officials of the Bolshevik State, in 1918-1919, there were 457 Jews. Predominant in the Soviet government, Jews built a totalitarian bureaucracy complete with a government-controlled press which regularly "issued numerous and violent denunciations of anti-Semitic episodes, either violence or discriminations. [1597]

There was sufficient funding to purchase the loyalties of the leaders of Nicholas's army who were then able to defeat the Czarist White generals in Russia's Civil War (1918-1923). The outnumbered Whites had little chance of winning against the Bolsheviks who consolidated their official position and controlled most of the military resources. [1598] W. Averell Harriman (S&B) secretly financed the Bolsheviks while America, Britain, and White Russian troops allegedly opposed communism, the most efficient, yet the most merciless of all political systems.

[1596] Des Griffin, Descent Into Slavery, Emissary Publications, Clackamas, Oregon, 1980, pp. 64-73
[1597] John Beaty, The Iron Curtain Over America, Chestnut Mountain Book, Barboursville, Virginia, 1968, pp. 28-30
[1598] Geoffrey Swain, The Origins of the Russian Civil War, Longman, London, 1996, p. 2

After Russia's Civil War, Lenin was the Soviet's first chairman, and was personally responsible for the deaths of millions of Russian citizens. He appointed Felix E. Dzerzhinsky, a radical revolutionary, who in 1894 had begun a fanatical study of the words of Karl Marx. He founded the first revolutionary group in Kaunas, Lithuania, where he published an illegal Polish language newspaper. On July 17, 1897, the authorities had arrested Dzerzhinsky and kept him in solitary confinement for a year. In August 1899, he fled to Warsaw where he helped to rebuild the Social Democratic Party, and where officials arrested him in 1900. He spent several months incarcerated in the Warsaw Citadel, and then they banished him to Eastern Siberia, from where he escaped. He did not meet Lenin, Stalin, or Trotsky until the fourth Congress of the Russian Social Democratic Workers' Party in Stockholm in 1906 where he supported Lenin unconditionally. To better understand, one should read *The Uses of Terror, the Soviet Secret Police 1917-1970* by Boris Levytsky. [1599]

Dzerzhinsky created and headed the Cheka, which, beginning on September 2, 1918, perpetrated the mass murders of the Red Terror and the fratricidal Russian Civil War, complete with concentration camps, even for children. Dzerzhinsky, under Lenin and Stalin, devised the gulag system, and helped to enforce, and strengthen the Bolshevik's power. [1600] In the first years of the Soviet regime Louis Marschalko, the Hungarian writer and author of *The World Conquerors, the Real War Criminals*, claims that the communists killed the following people: 28 Bishops and Archbishops, 6,776 priests, 8,500 doctors, 6,765 teachers, 54,000 army officers, 260,000 soldiers, 150,000 police officers, 48,000 gendarmes, 355,000 intellectuals, 198,000 workers, and 915,000 peasants. According to Marschalko, these figures came from US congressional records. [1601]

[1599] Boris Levytsky, The Uses of Terror, the Soviet Secret Police 1917-1970, Coward, McCann & Geoghegan, Inc. New York, 1972, pp. 14-16 This is possibly the most authoritative and complete treatise of this subject

[1600] Alexander N. Yakovlev, A Century of Violence in Soviet Russia, Anthony Austin, Paul Hollander, Yale University Press, New Haven, Connecticut, 2002, pp. 15-16

[1601] Louis Marschalko, The World Conquerors, the Real War Criminals, Joseph Sueli Publications, London, 1958, p. 53

Specific targets included the clergy and the intelligentsia. Lenin instructed Stalin, Dzerzhinsky, and Nikolai A. Semashko to create tactics to employ against dissidents. Lenin said, "The more representatives of the reactionary clergy we manage to shoot, the better." The Bolsheviks, to replace the exterminated clergy, began to create a Red church, with Red priests, and branches throughout the country. Dzerzhinsky and Emilian Yaroslavsky, the President of the League of Militant Atheists in the Soviet Union, decided that the church was already disintegrating and that they should not try to reconstitute it, even with an alternative. "Our stake is on Communism and not on religion." The Orthodox Church also had acquired vast riches over the centuries from wealthy merchants and aristocrats. The Bolsheviks had their greedy eyes on those valuables, as well as the solid gold, associated with the sacred books. [1602] Yaroslavsky, the editor of *Pravda*, said, "The program of the Communist International also clearly states that communists fight against religion. Remember that the struggle against religion is a struggle for socialism."

Under the New Economic Policy, beginning on October 3, 1921, the Central Executive Committee established the first central State bank of the Russian Soviet Federative Socialist Republic or Gosbank, which began operations on November 16, 1921. In 1923, the government placed the Gosbank under the jurisdiction of the People's Commissariat of Finance, which allowed the bank to extend industrial and commercial loans. In November 1921, the State Bank received the exclusive right to exchange foreign currency and develop correspondent agencies abroad. It set the price of gold, silver, and foreign currency on stock exchanges, and checks and bills of exchange executed in foreign currency. The USSR adopted the gold standard, and, in 1923, began minting gold coin.

Lenin, in his *Collected Works*, wrote: "The World War (1914-1918) will see the establishment of Communism in Russia; a second world war will extend its control over Europe; and a third world war will be necessary to make it worldwide." Lenin died on January 21,

---

[1602] Alexander N. Yakovlev, A Century of Violence in Soviet Russia, Anthony Austin, Paul Hollander, Yale University Press, New Haven, Connecticut, 2002, p. 157

1924. Genrikh Yagoda, a dreaded Soviet official, directed Joseph Stalin's Secret Political Police, the NKVD (1920-1936). Leon Trotsky, with twenty-one agents, while in exile, fought against Stalin. He almost succeeded in remaking the maps of Asia and of Europe by disconnecting from the Soviet Union, and attaching to adjoining Capitalist countries, territories with a total area of 625,000 square miles. Trotsky also opposed Lenin and officials implicated him in the attempted murder of Lenin in 1919, which may have contributed to his own assassination and death on August 21, 1940 in Mexico. Yagoda, directing the official Kremlin physicians, ordered the deaths of many Bolsheviks by slow poisoning. [1603] Stalin seized complete power and was the General Secretary from April 3, 1922 until his death, probably by poisoning, on March 5, 1953.

Marxist Subversion throughout Europe

Zalka Máté (born Béla Frankl), a Hungarian revolutionary and writer, known for his extraordinary brutality, was, along with Gerö Ernö, Béla Kuhn (born Béla Kohn), and others, a member of the notorious Hungarian, Mátyás Rákosi's, brigade. [1604] In February 1918, during the Russian Civil War, Máté created an international group of Red Guards in Khabarovsk, Russia, composed of Hungarians, and was involved in the punitive operations in Siberia. His squadron participated in brutal atrocities. Following World War I, Máté remained in Russia instead of returning to Hungary.

By November 1918, every country in Europe was experiencing economic chaos, and the destabilization associated with warfare, just as the Bolshevik criminals intended. On November 24, 1918, Béla Kuhn, a former journalist, a communist politician, and a Bolshevik revolutionary founded the Communist Party of Hungary (KMP) in Budapest. There was rampant inflation, mass unemployment, housing

---

[1603] Russia: Lined With Despair, Time Magazine, Monday, March 4, 1938, http://www.time.com/time/magazine/article/0,9171,759286,00.html as of May 2012

[1604] Louis Marschalko, The World Conquerors, the Real War Criminals, Translated from the Hungarian by A. Suranyi, Joseph Sueli Publications, London, 1958, p. 59

shortages, food and energy shortages, and widespread protests, a highly suitable environment in which to establish socialism. In his early travels, including to Petrograd and Moscow, Kuhn met Vladimir Lenin, who was more to the right than Kuhn. He created an ultra-radical left-wing faction in opposition to Lenin, and the conventional Bolsheviks. Kuhn and others, such as the Italian Umberto Terracini, and the Hungarian Mátyás Rákosi (born Mátyás Rosenfeld), joined with the very ruthless Grigory Zinoviev (born Apfelbaum), the dominating force of the Political Bureau of the Central Committee, and Karl Radek (born Karol Sobelsohn) who endorsed revolutionary offensive by any means possible.

The Bolsheviks declared Bremen, Germany, as a Soviet Republic, which existed from November 1918 to February 1919. On April 6, 1919, they declared a Bavarian Soviet Republic, which lasted until May 3, 1919. They created a Red Army, and established secret police squads to commit terrorist activities against every citizen and to liberate neighboring countries. The Soviet Ukraine waged war on Romania and prepared to march west to meet Soviet Hungary. [1605]

Anarchy, hunger, and hardships made every European country vulnerable to communist infiltration as numerous governments collapsed, including the German Empire. As quickly as the Soviets had declared peace, they now declared war, and sent the Red Army to take over the governments of Estonia (November 29, 1918), Latvia (December 4), Lithuania (December 8). The revolution in Germany would begin at the end of World War I. On December 17, 1918, the Marxists published a manifesto in Riga describing the war-weary vulnerable German Empire as the main target of their immediate assault. Lenin said, "We are at the doorstep of world revolution." [1606]

Lenin and Trotsky began to construct a World Soviet Socialist Republic, their ultimate goal, by creating communist factions on

---

[1605] Viktor Suvorov (pseudonym of Vladimir Bogdanovich Rezun), The Chief Culprit, Stalin's Grand Design to Start World War II, Naval Institute Press, Annapolis, Maryland, 2008, pp. 5-6

[1606] Ibid. 3-4

each continent. They funded this from Russia's gold reserves. The communist ideology stated—the old world must be destroyed and replaced by a new one; this destruction requires gaining political control through any means possible—peaceful, violent, open or secret; the struggle for this new world must unfold on a world scale rather than a national one. Their stated philosophy is, "The interests of the World Revolution are more important than the interests of individual countries." [1607]

After World War I, Jewish-led revolutionary movements peopled by the propagandized poverty-stricken working classes swept across war-torn Europe. On March 4, 1919, at a Congress in Moscow, Lenin and Trotsky devised the Communist International, or Comintern, with the objective of creating a World Soviet Socialist Republic. [1608] According to official Hungarian documents, Bolshevism in Hungary was a Judaea-Masonic movement. On March 21, 1919, communists established the Hungarian Soviet Republic. The new government had numerous freemasons headed by Hungarian Béla Kuhn, who Vicomte Léon de Poncins wrote was the "Jewish-Masonic-Hungarian butcher of Christians, who was a criminal of the first order and who operated under the protection of his Masonic connections." The Hungarian Commissariat consisted of twenty-six, eighteen of who were Jewish freemasons, a disproportionate number given the size of the Jewish population in Hungary, 1.5 million out of 22 million. [1609]

Hungarian Prime Minister Mihály Károlyi relinquished the reins of government to the Socialist Party of Hungary, a coalition of Social Democrats and Communists. He believed he was awarding political power to the Social Democrats, but instead, he was giving it to the communists, led by Kuhn, the first communist government following the Bolshevik's Revolution in Russia. Kuhn's new Hungarian Soviet Republic promised equality and social justice. It only lasted until August 6, 1919, collapsing when Romanian forces occupied Budapest

---

[1607] Ibid. 6
[1608] Ibid. 5-6
[1609] Vicomte Léon De Poncins, Freemasonry and Judaism, Secret Powers Behind Revolution, A & B Publishers Group, Brooklyn, New York, pp. 121-124

during the Hungarian-Romanian War. Officials created the Kingdom of Hungary after the Romanian Army withdrew.

On March 24, 1919, the communist infiltrators seized control of the government buildings in Hamburg. In other industrialized cities in central Germany, they sequestered court buildings, municipal buildings, banks, and police headquarters. Their official newspaper, *Die Rote Fahme* advocated a general revolution. Despite their success and their propaganda efforts, their revolution failed to achieve their objectives. [1610] On June 20, 1919, members of the Hungarian Red Army entered Slovakia and declared the Slovak Soviet Republic. The Communist Party of Russia, with all of the confiscated gold reserves of Russia, financed the activities of the Marxist regimes in other countries. Comintern officials at the Kremlin made the decisions, and the Soviet secret police enforced them. They eliminated those who opposed the tyrannical central control. [1611]

On August 5, 1919, Trotsky issued a memo stating, "The road to Paris and London lies through the cities of Afghanistan, Punjab, and Bengal." [1612] On March 6, 1920, Lenin said, "Victory will be ensured in the not-too distant future." [1613] Lenin prepared to invade India. Trotsky thought it essential to have an Asian command center from which to conduct a revolution in India, in conjunction with, and support of local revolutionaries. While the Bolsheviks wanted to immediately initiate another world war, the Russians were engaged in a civil war (1918-1919). Because they were expending the nation's resources on fighting against dissident Russians, they were unable to initiate another world war. Moreover, Trotsky and Lenin could not send financing to the communist leaders they had installed in

---

[1610] Viktor Suvorov, The Chief Culprit, Stalin's Grand Design to Start World War II, Naval Institute Press, Annapolis, Maryland, 2008, pp. 10-11, 13

[1611] Ibid. 5-6

[1612] Ibid. 5

[1613] Joachim Hoffmann, Stalin's War of Extermination, 1941-1945, Planning, Realization and Documentation, Theses & Dissertations Press, Capshaw, Alabama, 2001, pp. 26-27

Central European countries nor could they send the Red Army to Germany. [1614]

On July 23, 1920, Lenin cabled Stalin, who was at the Polish front, "Situation in Comintern is outstanding. Zinoviev (Grigory), Bukharin (Nikolai), and I think that it would be proper to encourage a revolution in Italy. My personal opinion is that to do so, Hungary has to be sovietized, possibly along with Czechoslovakia and Rumania." Lenin told some French delegates in the Comintern congress, "Yes, the Soviet troops are in Warsaw. Soon, Germany will be ours. We will conquer Hungary again; the Balkans will rise against capitalism. Italy will tremble. Bourgeois Europe is crackling at the seams in the storm." [1615]

Hungarian, Gerö Ernö (born Ernö Singer), although Jewish, later denounced his religion and backed Stalin's persecution of Jews. An early Bolshevik, he fled from Hungary to the Soviet Union after the fall of Kuhn's government. He lived in the USSR for over twenty years and was a KGB agent who was involved in the Comintern in France. He fought in the Spanish Civil War, and became known as the Butcher of Barcelona, for his brutal war crimes. He was a Hungarian Communist Party leader in the period after World War II.

The Egyenlöség (Equality), a Hungarian newspaper for the elite, praised Trotsky as follows, "Jewish intellect and knowledge, Jewish courage and love of peace saved Russia and perhaps the whole world. Never has world historical mission of Jewry shone so brightly as in Russia. Trotsky's words prove that the Biblical and prophetic Jewish spirit of Isaiah and Micah, the great peacemakers, with that of the Talmudic Elders is inspiring the leaders of Russia today." [1616] While

---

[1614] Viktor Suvorov, The Chief Culprit, Stalin's Grand Design to Start World War II, Naval Institute Press, Annapolis, Maryland, 2008, pp. 5-6

[1615] Ibid. 8-9

[1616] Louis Marschalko, The World Conquerors, the Real War Criminals, Translated from the Hungarian by A. Suranyi, Joseph Sueli Publications, London, 1958, p. 50

the Bolshevik slaughter in Russia horrified the Christian world, others, especially in Europe, viewed it as heroic. [1617]

In 1920, hundreds of communist agitators entered a disheartened, economically ruined Germany, the perfect crisis environment to emphasize class struggle, and provoke a revolution against the status quo. In March 1920, about twelve million workers participated in a strike. On December 6, 1920, Lenin said that in order to have soviet communist world dominion or "victory of socialism all over the world," that they would have to incite the conflicts and contradictions between the capitalist states, to let them exhaust themselves fighting each other. [1618]

The red army was also on the move in 1920, marching toward Germany, through Poland, the country that separated Russia and Germany. This constituted the Polish-Soviet War (February 1919-March 1921). On March 22, 1921, the communists organized a general strike throughout the industrialized part of central Germany. In other cities in central Germany, they seized courts, municipal buildings, banks, and police headquarters. Their official newspaper, *Die Rote Fahme* advocated a general revolution. Despite their attempts, the revolution failed to achieve the communist's objectives. [1619]

On December 30, 1922, in Moscow, the Bolsheviks created the Union of Soviet Socialist Republics with the implications that there were no geographic limitations but rather worldwide with global image on its coat of arms. Their first target was Germany. They had a regular commission just to concentrate on Germany composed of the top leadership—Trotsky, Stalin, Zinoviev, Nikolai Bukharin (Moshe Pinkhus-Dolgolevsky), and Karl Radek. Stalin, who had taken over the party from Lenin, felt that it was imperative that they conceal the fact that the Bolsheviks in the USSR had instigated and dictated the

[1617] Ibid. 60
[1618] Joachim Hoffmann, Stalin's War of Extermination, 1941-1945, Planning, Realization and Documentation, Theses & Dissertations Press, Capshaw, Alabama, 2001, pp. 26-27
[1619] Viktor Suvorov, The Chief Culprit, Stalin's Grand Design to Start World War II, Naval Institute Press, Annapolis, Maryland, 2008, pp. 10-11, 13

circumstances of the revolution in Germany which they planned for November 9, 1923. [1620]

In almost every nation, the Comintern helped to establish communist parties, all dictated by policies from Moscow. For the most part, delegates from the various nations representing communist parties were trade union members, members of legislative bodies, and other government officials. communists engaged in open terrorism, and assassinations, followed by coup d'état and infiltration of existing governments. Their ideology advocates the following:

1) They must destroy the old world and build a new one in its place.
2) To do that, it is necessary to gain political power which requires using all measures, ranging from the most peaceful to the most violent, from the most open to the most secretive.
3) They must impose a new world on a world scale. "The interests of the World Revolution are more important than the interests of individual countries." [1621]

Marxist Infiltration in Germany

The Social Democratic Party of Germany (SPD), the strongest party in Germany, steadily increased in membership, from 384,327 in 1906 to 1,085,905 by 1914. In 1912, it had 110 seats in the Reichstag, the German parliament. Trade unions were also very strong. In 1892, at least 237,000 workers belonged to a union. The number grew to 2,600,000 by 1912. [1622]

When Russia declared war on Germany, needing funds for defense, Germany attempted to borrow money from Wall Street, but found that the international financial markets excluded her. However, they funded France and Britain's warfare. Germany resorted to domestic borrowing, mainly from institutions and large corporations. Thus the

---

[1620] Ibid. 10-11, 13
[1621] Ibid. 5-6
[1622] Stan Crooke, The German Revolution, November 1918, November 22, 2008, http://www.workersliberty.org/germany1918 as of May 2012

Reichstag passed a series of war credits (bonds). On August 4, 1914, Friedrich Ebert, August Bebel's successor as SPD co-chairman, and other party members, like Karl Liebknecht, supported these bonds to finance Germany in World War I, despite the party's supposed anti-war position. [1623] These bonds only covered two-thirds of the costs and carried interest, a growing expense which required further resources to pay.

In 1915, the SPD advocated German participation in World War I. The avid Marxists who dominated the SPD tried to legitimize their support of the war in the Reichstag. Heinrich Cunow, Paul Lensch, and Konrad Haenisch led this group, individuals who were close to Alexander Parvus (born Israel L. Gelfand), a wealthy Jewish freemason and revolutionary from Odessa, who had joined the SPD by 1886. Conversely, in June 1915, Marxist, Karl Kautsky appealed to his colleagues, Eduard Bernstein and Hugo Haase, asking them to oppose the pro-war leaders in the SPD. He also denounced the German's alleged annexationist aims. [1624]

In early 1915, Franz Mehring, sympathetic to the Bolsheviks, and their October Revolution, and Rosa Luxemburg, a Polish Jew, edited and published the magazine *Die Internationale*. She, Liebknecht, Clara Zetkin, and others, officially founded the anti-war Spartacus League on January 1, 1915. They quietly funded a conference in Berlin to attract a growing number of like-minded people. Meanwhile, they worked to instigate strikes. There had been none between August and December 1914. However, in 1915, about 13,000 workers participated in 140 strikes. [1625]

In 1915, Karl Artelt, a Marxist and a SPD party member, worked in the Germania shipyard in Kiel as an iron fitter. The continuous Allied blockade created a drastic reduction in the food supply in Kiel. He led a strike of his fellow workers on June 15, 1916, demanding

---

[1623] Jüri Lina, Under the Sign of the Scorpion: The Rise and Fall of the Soviet Empire, Referent Publishing, Stockholm, Sweden, 2002, pp. 100-101

[1624] Ibid. 100-101

[1625] Stan Crooke, The German Revolution, November 1918, November 22, 2008, http://www.workersliberty.org/germany1918 as of May 2012

peace and better food. On May 1, 1916 (a communist holiday), Luxemburg and Liebknecht organized an anti-war demonstration, with 10,000 workers in Berlin. In June, in Berlin, 55,000 munitions workers went on strike. Concurrently, strikes erupted in Bremen and Braunschweig. In 1916, there were 125,000 workers who participated in 240 strikes. [1626]

In January 1917, given their success instigating strikes and demonstrations, Luxemburg, Liebknecht and Haase left the SPD and founded the anti-war Independent Social Democratic Party of Germany (USPD). Kautsky, whose wife was close to Luxemburg, soon left the SPD and joined them. After the November revolution in Germany, Kautsky would become the under-secretary of State in the Foreign Office where he would attempt to find documents proving Germany's war guilt. Author Fritz Fischer purportedly *discovered* secret archival documents long after the war. He described the *September Plan* in two books, claiming that Germany had expansionary goals, its alleged goals for going to war, the claim that Kautsky had made in 1915. Initially, Matthias Erzberger, a key assistant of Chancellor Theobald von Bethmann-Hollweg, supported the war and drafted war objectives, the *September Program*, with staffer Kurt Riezler's help. They published it on September 9, 1914, a plan that top officials never implemented.

Over the winter, the food situation worsened and by March 1917, the government had to decrease bread rations. From January through April of 1917, more than 400,000 workers were involved in more strikes than had taken place in the previous year. In April 1917, decreased bread rations ignited another wave of strikes. In Berlin, over 300,000 workers refused to work, demanded peace, the release of all political prisoners, and more food. As a result of the strikes of April 1917, and January 1918, the USPD instituted the office of Revolutionary Shop Stewards whose stewards would maintain regular connections to the USPD and play a big part in the strikes. [1627] Artelt,

---

[1626] Ibid

[1627] Stan Crooke, The German Revolution, November 1918, November 22, 2008, http://www.workersliberty.org/germany1918 as of May 2012

one of those stewards, led a work strike with a combined group of 5,450 workers from the Howaldt and Germania shipyards.

By mid-1917, Matthias Erzberger, of the Centre Party, began opposing the war which, with the concurrent strikes, seriously undermined military morale. He authored the Peace Resolutions that the Reichstag adopted on July 17, 1917, seeking a negotiated peace. In October 1918, he would become Secretary of State after he helped oust Chancellor Bethmann-Hollweg.

In the summer of 1917, Max Reichpietsch and Albin Köbis of the *Friedrich der Grosse* led 4,000 sailors in a revolt. They complained about the food and other conditions, calling for the establishment of a democratic peace and the war's end. Authorities executed Reichpietsch and Köbis in Cologne on September 5, 1917, inadvertently making them Marxist heroes. On August 2, 1917, about 400 sailors from the battleship *Prinzeregent Lutipold*, anchored at Wilhelmshaven, abandoned their stations and marched into town declaring their unwillingness to continue fighting. The crews of several ships in Wilhelmshaven joined the rebellion. On August 16, 1917, the firemen of the *Westphalia* quit working while the crew of the *Nürnberg*, at sea, began an uprising. Authorities quickly responded and arrested many of the participants and sentenced them to hard labor.

The German army was slowly losing ground, not because of Allied strength but to the undermining actions of officials. General Erich Ludendorff blamed the government and certain civilians for the military surrender and the subsequent armistice, claiming they withheld support. Additionally, Vladimir Lenin's Marxist agitators had infiltrated the unions and had waged a relentless drive of subversion and sabotage. Officials arrested some of them and found incriminating documents. Jewish managers provided considerable funds to Liebknecht and Luxemburg to conduct espionage activities in order to instigate an insurrection. Over 70,010 Jews were among

Russia's communist leadership and they made certain to disseminate a majority of Jewish agents throughout Europe. [1628]

While they were negotiating for peace in Brest-Litovsk, February-March 1918, the Bolsheviks in St. Petersburg published 500,000 inflammatory copies of *Die Fackel* (*The Torch*) for distribution in German. This subversion facilitated instability while German soldiers were fighting a bloody battle in the West. [1629] The Bolsheviks may have procrastinated signing the Brest-Litovsk Treaty to allow their agents more organizational time. Liebknecht, along with Luxemburg, a dedicated Marxist, and a naturalized German citizen, influenced some of the German negotiators to agree with Trotsky. The Marxists sent agitators among the steel workers unions; they were able to organize at least 500,000 workers to go on strike. General Erich Ludendorff, exasperated with this obvious foreign subversion, persuaded the workers to return to work within a week. [1630] Despite the peace treaty, the unethical Marxists still published German-language propaganda, and set up additional groups in Germany to exploit war-related political and economic instabilities. [1631]

On September 29, 1918, the Supreme Army Command informed Kaiser Wilhelm, at the Imperial Army headquarters in Spa, Belgium, about the military situation with decreased armaments and the numerous uprisings in Berlin and other places. Ludendorff asked for an immediate cease fire and suggested that Germany accept President Wilson's peace terms, which would place the nation on an equal basis with the Allies. On that same day, the Prussian Kingdom assumed its pre-war authority, which lasted until Kaiser Wilhelm's abdication. Henry Cabot Lodge had attacked Wilson's Fourteen Points as unrealistic and too weak, maintaining that they should

[1628] Leon Degrelle, Hitler: Born at Versailles, Volume 1, of the Hitler Century, Institute for Historical Review, Torrance, California, 1992, p. 325
[1629] Viktor Suvorov, The Chief Culprit, Stalin's Grand Design to Start World War II, Naval Institute Press, Annapolis, Maryland, 2008, pp. 3-4
[1630] Leon Degrelle, Hitler: Born at Versailles, Volume 1, of the Hitler Century, Institute for Historical Review, Torrance, California, 1992, pp. 297-308
[1631] Viktor Suvorov, The Chief Culprit, Stalin's Grand Design to Start World War II, Naval Institute Press, Annapolis, Maryland, 2008, pp. 2-4

militarily and economically demolish Germany, and then burden it with severe penalties to remove all possible future threats to Europe's stability. This sounds strangely similar to the vindictive Morgenthau Plan after World War II.

The Allies had success against the other Central Powers, in Bulgaria, the first to sign an armistice, Macedonia, Italy, and the Ottoman Empire which surrendered at Mudros. On November 3, 1918, Austria-Hungary surrendered and signed a truce, all of which impacted Germany's military situation.

Apparently, naval commanders were making a last-ditch attempt against the British navy to break the blockade in the North Sea. This unsuccessful effort, along with increasing pessimism, had sparked another mutiny and sabotage at Wilhelmshaven on October 29, 1918, leading to the arrest of 300 sailors, who refused to obey orders. The chaos spread to the port city of Kiel. On November 3, about 3,000 German sailors and workers, in cooperation with local unions, seized ships and buildings under the auspices of the red communist flag. The next day, the Kiel rebels, mimicking the Soviets, created the first Workers' and Soldiers' Council in opposition to the national government.

USPD members, Artelt and Lothar Popp led a group of several thousand dissidents who met on the afternoon of November 3, 1918 with workers' representatives who used the slogan *Frieden und Brot* (peace and bread). They wanted to show that they were cognizant of the desires of the sailors and workers who demanded, not just the release of the imprisoned strikers, but the end of the war and sufficient food provisions. The group, under Artelt's direction, moved toward the military prison. Sublieutenant Steinhäuser, with orders to stop the demonstrators, ordered his men to fire warning shots and then to shoot into the crowd. They killed seven people and wounded twenty-nine others. A few demonstrators retaliated with open fire. This is reminiscent of Bloody Sunday on January 22, 1905, in St. Petersburg, except that the demonstrators and the military withdrew.

Early on November 4, 1918, sailors refused to obey directions and more demonstrations erupted. Artelt organized the first soldiers' council. Wilhelm Souchon, the governor of the navy station, negotiated the release of the imprisoned men. Soldiers attempted to seize control of public and military buildings but Souchon brought in different troops to suppress them. However, by that evening, about 4,000 rebellious sailors, soldiers and workers controlled Kiel. Shortly, Wilhelmshaven experienced the same thing. When SPD deputy, Gustav Noske arrived in Kiel that evening, the rebels enthusiastically welcomed him. He helped to restore peace.

Beginning in 1916, journalist Kurt Eisner, a Jew living in Munich, had written numerous pieces about the illegalities of the war. Authorities convicted Eisner, a member of the Independent Social Democratic Party of Germany (USPD), for treason for helping to incite a strike among munitions workers. He spent nine months in Stadelheim Prison. They released him during the General Amnesty in October 1918. Munich was a city of political unrest, exaggerated economic instability, and discouraged citizens, the perfect environment for rebellion. The German Revolution soon erupted, lasting from November 4, 1918 to August 11, 1919. [1632]

On November 7, 1918, the first anniversary of the Bolshevik Revolution, Eisner attended a peace rally in Munich. In front of approximately 60,000 people he demanded the end of the war, the institution of an eight-hour work day, and assistance for the poor and unemployed. He demanded that King Ludwig III, of the Wittelsbach monarchy in Bavaria, and Emperor Wilhelm II relinquish their positions. Eisner wanted to replace them with councils, composed of workers and soldiers. The crowd, swayed by his fervency, marched to the army barracks where they persuaded many of the soldiers to join the revolution. That evening, Ludwig went into exile. On November 8, Eisner proclaimed Bavaria a free state and he became Minister-President of Bavaria. He quickly dissociated himself from the Bolsheviks and other communists.

[1632] Alan Bullock, Hitler: A Study in Tyranny, Harper & Row, New York, 1962, p. 61 Bullock is obviously not a friendly biographer of Hitler

On November 9, 1918, Luxemburg founded the *Die Rote Fahne* (*The Red Flag*), the central organ of the Spartacist League, which would evolve into the Communist Party of Germany (KPD), during a founding congress, December 30, 1918 to January 1, 1919, part of the Comintern. The expertly-trained agents, such as Luxemburg, fomented strikes in vital industries, particularly those related to the war effort. They emboldened civil disorder with rhetoric that challenged people's faith. They promoted contempt and ridicule for political and military leaders. They used rational arguments and emotional slogans that encouraged people to question traditional moral values such as honesty, sobriety, integrity and commitment.

The Kaiser appointed Prince Maximilian of Baden as the new Imperial Chancellor who then announced the abdication of the Kaiser. On November 7, 1918, the prince formed a new government, which included Friedrich Ebert, Philipp Scheidemann, a freemason, and other top SPD members. The French lodge, Art et Travail in Paris, was a study center for Scheidemann, Lenin, Trotsky, and Béla Kuhn. [1633] Recall, that in August 1914, Ebert had led the SPD to unanimously vote for war loans to fight a necessary patriotic war. On November 9, 1918, after the German Revolution erupted, Maximilian relinquished his office to Ebert, the head of the provisional government for the next several months. Maximilian appointed Secretary of State, Matthias Erzberger to represent Germany in the negotiations in the Forest of Compiègne. Scheidemann, who had also been pro-war, proclaimed the Weimar Republic (1919-1933) to replace the imperial form of government, following the Kaiser's abdication. He did this to ostensibly counter Liebknecht's declaration of a Free Socialist Republic. German nationalists referred to Ebert, Erzberger, and Walter Rathenau as November Criminals. Many Germans blamed the civilian government who they say failed to support the army who were undefeated in the field and that Marxists sabotaged and now ruled the country.

[1633] Fred Scherbaum and Veronica Clark (translators), Warwolves of the Iron Cross, the Hyenas of High Finance, the International Relationships of French and American High Finance, Vera Icona Publishers, 2011, pp. 53-54

Britain and France were war-weary, and had not penetrated Germany's western frontier and had no will to do so. Those nations were ready to capitulate even though the United States had re-supplied them. In the east, Germany had prevailed against Russia and they had signed the Treaty of Brest-Litovsk. Germany was close to winning the war in the West, with the Spring Offensive, which began on March 21, 1918, when they advanced further into enemy territory, before fresh US troops entered the war. The German armies were in France and Belgium in November 1918, when German officials surrendered. Thereafter, the armies withdrew. One of the biggest contributing factors for the surrender was the strikes occurring in the arms industry, which left the military with an insufficient supply of armaments. Further, the West's industrialization of warfare, in addition to the blockades, initiated a radical dehumanizing war that helped to defeat Germany.

German soldiers relinquished their weapons with the understanding that the government arbitrators would devise the peace treaty according to Wilson's Fourteen Points. They felt that the politicians had pressured them into putting down their arms without a legitimate military defeat. The relative ease of a deceptive unconditional surrender strengthened the conspiratorial relationship of the three major Allies. [1634]

In addition to a military loss, the Treaty of Versailles would impose further territorial and financial losses. When the new government forced Kaiser Wilhelm to abdicate, the military, under General Paul von Hindenburg, commander-in-chief, relinquished its executive power to the temporary civilian government. Ebert, telegraphed Erzberger, a civilian, authorizing him to sign the Armistice which he did on November 11, 1918, which officially ended the war and lead to the Treaty of Versailles. Then, starting in August 1919, as Finance Minister, Erzberger encouraged the parliament to honor the ratification of the Versailles Treaty. He then began making plans toward accruing funds to start reparations payments by forcing through the

---

[1634] Tuvia Ben-Moshe, Churchill, Strategy and History, Lynne Rienner, Boulder, Colorado, 1992, p. 308

new measures of taxation. [1635] People would force Erzberger from office in March 1920, and members of the nationalistic Organization Consul murdered him on August 26, 1921, in Bad Griesbach, a spa in the Black Forest. That group also assassinated Rathenau, the Foreign Minister, from February to June 24, 1922.

When the German monarchy fell, influential Jews seized control of the Bavarian government. Hugo Haase was in charge of Foreign affairs. Otto Landsberg, a member of the Weimar National Assembly, was the German Ambassador in Belgium (1920-1923), and was deputy to the Reichstag (1924-1933). Karl Kautsky was the state under-secretary in the Foreign Office under Haase. Oskar Cohn and Joseph Herzfeld were both Haase assistants. The Finance Minister, Eugen Schiffer, was also Jewish, as was Eduard Bernstein, his assistant. Dr. Ludwig Freund, an associate of Sigmund Freud assisted the Minister of the Interior, Hugo Preuß, the main author of the Weimar constitution. [1636] Fritz M. Cohen was the government's publicity agent.

The desperate middle class Germans blamed their economic troubles on the Jews, easily identified with communism because so many of them embraced Marxism. After all, Eisner helped instigate the Bolshevik revolution in Munich. Other Jews collaborated with him— Liebknecht, Luxemburg, who the Bolsheviks had sent to Germany, and Max Lowenberg, Dr. Kurt Rosenfeld, Caspar Wollheim, Max Rothschild, Carl Arnold, Hermann Kranold, Rosenhek, Birnbaum, Reis and Kaisser. Eleven of the most active revolutionaries were freemasons who belonged to a secret lodge located in Munich at No. 51 Briennerstrasse. [1637] De Poncins wrote, "The Jewish preponderance in the German revolutions of 1918 is not less irrefutable; there as elsewhere, they are directors and strategists of the movement. The Soviet Republic of Munich was Jewish; it is sufficient to mention

---

[1635] Guido Giacomo Preparata, Conjuring Hitler, How Britain and America Made the Third Reich, Pluto Press, London, 2005, pp. 74-76

[1636] Maurice Pinay, The Plot Against the Church, St. Anthony's Press, Los Angeles, California, 1967, p. 8

[1637] Ibid. 8

some of the names of leaders: Liebknecht, Rosa Luxembourg, Kurt Eisner and many others." [1638]

Hugh R. Wilson wrote, "In these conditions anti-Semitism reared its ugly head. Millions of returning soldiers out of a job and desperately searching for one, found the stage, the press, medicine and law crowded with Jews. They saw among the few who had money to splurge, a high proportion of Jews. A number of the leaders of the Demokratische Partei, that fraction of the Reichstag most closely identified with the type of government in power, were Jews. The leaders of the Bolshevist movement in Russia, a movement desperately feared in Germany, were Jews. One could sense the spreading resentment and hatred." [1639] He further wrote, "I remember writing home at the time that if there ever came a reactionary movement, whether military or monarchist, I didn't dream of a Nazi Party, that movement would be anti-Semitic in character. It has been widely assumed that Adolf Hitler and his followers invented anti-Semitism in Germany. The facts of the case do not bear this out. When Hitler inserted an anti-Semitic plank in his platform, he doubtless was acting in accordance with his own hatred and prejudice. Nevertheless, adroit politician that he is, he was inserting a plank to catch the votes." [1640]

Luxemburg viewed the Spartacist uprising, January 5-15, 1919, in Berlin as a mistake but backed it after she discovered that Liebknecht ordered it without consulting her. The government and the Freikorps, Horse Guards Division, an important unit, under Captain Waldemar Pabst, crushed the revolt, captured Luxemburg and Liebknecht and some of their supporters. On January 15, 1919, they drowned Luxemburg in the Landwehr Canal in Berlin, thereby making them Marxist martyrs. Pabst viewed Bolshevism as a world danger.

[1638] Freemasonry and Judaism, Secret Powers Behind Revolution by Vicomte Léon De Poncins, A & B Publishers Group, Brooklyn, New York, pp. 121-124

[1639] Hugh R. Wilson, Diplomat between Wars, Longmans, Green, New York, 1941, p. 115

[1640] Ibid. 115

After his party lost the election, Kurt Eisner decided to leave office. On February 21, 1919, on his way to the Reichstag to announce his resignation, Anton Graf von Arco auf Valley, a nationalist, shot him. The assassination caused continued unrest and lawlessness in Bavaria. The news of a soviet revolution in Hungary provoked communists and anarchists to seize power. Friedrich Ebert, who headed the new Weimar Republic, violently suppressed the workers' uprisings with Gustav Noske and the assistance of General Wilhelm Groener. Ebert reluctantly allowed the formation of paramilitary Freikorps throughout Germany.

Violence was pandemic in Munich in the first six months of 1919. On March 7, 1919, Johannes Hoffmann, the leader of the SPD, unsuccessfully attempted to form a coalition government in Bavaria. Then he set up and headed a Social Democratic government, which would only last until April 6, 1919. On that day, Marxists officially proclaimed a Soviet Republic, ruled by USPD members such as Ernst Toller, from a Prussian Jewish family, Gustav Landauer, a Jewish anarchist (grandfather of the television and film director, Mike Nichols), Silvio Gesell, and Erich Mühsam, influenced by Béla Kuhn's communist régime in Hungary. Toller, who was president from April 6 to April 12, viewed the revolution as the Bavarian Revolution of Love. [1641]

On April 12, 1919, the communists seized power and Eugen Leviné, a Russian-born Jew, was the leader of the Bavarian Soviet Republic. He began imposing reforms, organizing a Red Army and confiscating money, food, and expensive apartments. They requisitioned factories and assigned workers to control them. Leviné intended to reform the education system. Lenin directed Leviné to capture and execute certain individuals, but his men refused to kill the hostages. On April 30, Russian soldiers, sent by Lenin, murdered eight men, including Prince Gustav of Thurn and Taxis, and Countess Hella von Westarp.

[1641] Alan Bullock, Hitler: A Study in Tyranny, Harper & Row, New York, 1962, p. 61 Bullock is obviously not a friendly biographer of Hitler

German soldiers returned home following their inexplicable defeat and many joined one of several paramilitary organizations that had sprung up to in an attempt to suppress the communist uprisings. Minister of Defense Gustav Noske, of the SPD, gave considerable support to these military groups. He used them to crush the German Revolution and the Marxist Spartacist League.

Leviné's communist government lasted less than a month. On May 3, 1919, a combined 39,000-member force of loyal members of the German army and the Freikorps arrived in Munich where they engaged in brutal street fighting and finally defeated the communists. During the battle, they killed over 1,000 people who supported the communist government. They arrested and summarily executed approximately 700 men and women. The court also condemned Leviné for treason. A firing squad carried out the sentence at Stadelheim Prison. Germans justifiably wanted revenge, but Hoffman's government, in a wave of suppression, shot many people. These events began a decided swing to the right in Bavarian politics. [1642]

The civil conflict resulted in the replacement of Germany's imperial government with the Weimar Republic on August 11, 1919, when they officially adopted the Weimar Constitution. Following the war and the abolition of the monarchy, Ebert was the first president of Germany (1919-1925). After he assumed office, the government, the army, and the Freikorps together battled the leftist uprisings, where they killed several leftwing politicians which culminated in the affiliation of the SPD and the Independent Social Democratic Party of Germany (USPD).

Nationalists and former military leaders criticized the unconditional peace stipulations and the Weimar politicians, socialists, communists, and Jews, who they accused of betraying Germany by withdrawing support for the military, criticizing nationalism, instigating unrest and strikes, and finally relinquishing Germany to its enemies. People refer to those responsible as the treasonous November Criminals,

---

[1642] Ibid

many of whom were now functioning in the newly formed Weimar Republic.

The newly-established government attempted to address the death and destruction and other chaotic consequences of the war, the lack of infrastructure, the loss of thousands of homes, the absence of food and the starvation afflicting the entire population. It tried to provide unemployment benefits and other assistance to the soldiers who returned home to high unemployment and very little opportunity. The SPD, now part of the struggling republic, and the new Communist Party of Germany (KPD), consisting of former SPD members, became bitter enemies.

In November 1919, the Weimar National Assembly appointed a committee to investigate the causes of the war and Germany's defeat. On November 18, 1919, Paul von Hindenburg testified and referred to an article that appeared in the *Neue Zürcher Zeitung* on December 17, 1918, which cited two other articles, wherein British General Frederick B. Maurice said the civilians betrayed the German army.

Communists entered a disheartened, economically ruined Germany, the perfect environment to emphasize class struggle and provoke a further revolution against the status quo. In March 1920, at least 12,000,000 workers initiated a general strike in Germany, a nation about to explode in revolution. The Red Army, now on the move through Poland, in the Polish-Soviet War, February 1919-March 1921, was to expedite that explosive event. The Red Army, invigorated by the emotion of patriotic songs, and energetic marches, sang this popular verse:

> We are fanning the flames of a world-wide fire,
> We will raze churches and prisons to the ground.
> For from the taiga to the British seas
> The Red Army is the strongest of all! [1643]

[1643] Viktor Suvorov, The Chief Culprit, Stalin's Grand Design to Start World War II, Naval Institute Press, Annapolis, Maryland, 2008, pp. 8-9

General Mikhail Tukhachevsky began an aggressive campaign westward with his forces toward the goal of brutalizing Europe. Later, he became the commander in chief of the Red Army (1925-1928). According to excerpts from order #1423, dated July 2, 1920, regarding the western front, it said, "Fighters of the Workers' Revolution! The fate of the World Revolution will be decided in the West. The path to the world fire lies over the dead body of White (anti-communist) Poland. We will carry happiness and peace on our bayonets to the working people of the world. To the West! To decisive battles and thundering victories." [1644]

Tukhachevsky, leading the Soviet invasion of Poland in 1920, failed to understand military strategy, and his opponents, led by Józef Piłsudski, defeated his army outside Warsaw. Tukhachevsky and Stalin blamed each other for their inability to capture Warsaw. Because of this, they had to postpone their revolution in Europe. Tukhachevsky later said, "There can be no doubt that if we had been victorious on the Vistula, the revolutionary fires would have reached the entire continent." [1645]

On March 22, 1921, there was a general strike throughout the industrialized part of central Germany. On March 24, the communists took control of the government buildings in Hamburg. In other industrialized cities in central Germany, they seized courts, municipal buildings, banks and police headquarters. Their newspaper, *Die Rote Fahme* advocated a general revolution. Despite their attempts, the revolution failed to achieve communist objectives. [1646] The Marxist revolutionaries in Germany were unsuccessful in seizing power as compared to the Bolsheviks in Russia.

In 1922, Judge Hass of the People's Court tried Felix Fechenbach, Kurt Eisner's former secretary, for publishing a secret diplomatic telegram while State Secretary (1918-1919), under Eisner. The prosecution

---

[1644] Ibid. 8-9
[1645] Robert A. Pastor and Stanley Hoffmann, A Century's Journey: How the Great Powers Shape the World, Political Science, 1999, p. 175
[1646] Viktor Suvorov, The Chief Culprit, Stalin's Grand Design to Start World War II, Naval Institute Press, Annapolis, Maryland, 2008, pp. 10-11, 13

accused him and his fellow defendants, Dr. Sigismund Gorgas (Polish citizen), and Karl Lembke, both journalists who were working for a news service that actually functioned as an espionage service. Judge Hass referred to Eisner as a "forger of political documents." In 1919, Fechenbach sold a copy of the infamous Erzberger memorandum, calling for annexation of French and Belgian territory, to some French and Swiss newspapers [1647]

On April 16, 1922, Walther Rathenau, Foreign Minister of the Weimar Republic, negotiated and signed the Treaty of Rapallo, with Georgi Chicherin, the Soviet Foreign Minister, which officials reaffirmed with the Treaty of Berlin, April 24, 1926. The Weimar Republic and Soviet Russia each renounced all territorial and financial claims against each other following the Treaty of Brest-Litovsk and World War I. This new treaty recognized the secret German-Soviet collaboration, starting in 1921, which allowed for Germany's rearmament. Hitler and his associates saw Rathenau as part of the communist conspiracy for his actions.

In 1923, Jews living in Germany acquired financial power through the receipt of funds for investment from rich friends in other countries, including the United States. There was also a huge migration of Jews from the former Austro-Hungarian Empire. Germans viewed all of the Jews coming from the East as invaders, all looking for food and shelter that were unavailable. Some Eastern European Jews participated in the rampant speculation, always a factor with an unstable currency, and a decreased supply of commodities. The Germans resented the Jews, who with their increased power, now benefited from Germany's misfortunes. This Jewish influx resurrected the earlier feelings of Germans who viewed them as trespassers who were not interested in assimilating but remained exclusively separate. [1648]

Under the Weimar Republic, the SPD introduced unemployment insurance benefits for all workers, trade union recognition, and

---

[1647] Fechenbach Trial is Called a Farce, The New York Times, November 26, 1922
[1648] John Beaty, The Iron Curtain Over America, Chestnut Mountain Book, Barboursville, Virginia, 1968, pp. 11-12

shorter work hours. They also expanded educational opportunities and established health clinics. Between 1924 and 1928, workers in the Free Trade Unions helped to decrease the disparity between unskilled and skilled workers. They also implemented educational reforms, and introduced the four-year common primary school, adult education, improvements in public health, and maternity benefits. Prussia, the SPD stronghold after the introduction of universal suffrage, gave power to police officials to issue more regulations over local populations in the Reich.

Balfour: Germany is Expendable

Decades before World War I, the Zionist movement was predisposed to be pro-German. Theodor Herzl, formerly an assimilated Jewish journalist in Vienna, was part of the German-speaking world, whose first supporters resided in Germany and Austria. There were, in Germany, approximately 600,000 Jewish citizens who were better educated, a bit more assimilated, and enjoyed superior social standing compared to Jews living in Eastern Europe. Germany was the prominent power in Europe and Jews in Germany viewed themselves as the natural leaders of Jewry. Additionally, the Jewish aristocrats in America originally came from Germany and maintained cultural loyalties to that country and when war erupted, they naturally allied with Germany. [1649]

Prior to 1914, Berlin had been the foundation of Zionist activity. The Israel Institute of Technology, located in Haifa, looked to Germany for support and protection. Arthur Zimmermann, who became Under Secretary of State in 1911 in the German Empire, was in China during the Boxer Rebellion, and as acting secretary, he participated in the deliberations in 1914, with Kaiser Wilhelm and Chancellor Theobald von Bethmann-Hollweg (1909-1917), to support Austria-Hungary after the assassination of Franz Ferdinand. Hollweg, Max Warburg, and Albert Ballin advised Wilhelm to declare war. Zimmerman, famous for the Zimmerman telegram, later helped the communists

---

[1649] Klaus Polkehn, Zionism and the Kaiser's Germany: Zionist Diplomacy with the Empire of Kaiser Wilhelm, Journal of Palestine Studies, Volume 4, no. 2, 1975, pp. 77-78

to undermine czarist Russia and appreciated his close connections to the German Zionists.

Jews living in America and Britain, including Baron Walter Rothschild, favored Germany in 1914 and 1915, even to the point that Rothschild sent the Kaiser an encouraging cable when the war broke out. At the beginning of the war, most Jews favored Germany because it had attacked Russia, their mortal enemy. They viewed Kaiser Wilhelm, who treated them with deference, as the man who might potentially deliver Palestine to them. Despite minor altercations against them in Germany, they still felt more at ease there than anywhere else in Europe. They had acquired substantial influence in finance, business, and the news media and in the universities. Their language, Yiddish, was similar to German and they were culturally comfortable. The most influential members of the Reichstag were Jews. [1650]

Dr. Chaim Weizmann understood that the British government would relinquish the organization of *the Jewish commonwealth* in Palestine to the management of the Jews, but first a powerful government must militarily conquer Palestine. Thereafter, the Zionists would require the protection of the armies of that same powerful government to protect them from the indigenous population. In 1915, Dr. Weizmann already knew what would occur in the next twenty years following the war. The British would establish a protectorate and the Jews would take over the country, as anticipated by the mandate system, the devious system legalized by the League of Nations, a body concocted by freemasons. They devised this system of governing a conquered territory with Palestine as their target. They created other mandates during the war to lend procedural legitimacy to their agenda for Palestine. The mandate remained in place just long enough for the Zionists to gather sufficient weapons to slaughter the inhabitants themselves. [1651]

[1650] Leon Degrelle, Hitler: Born at Versailles, Volume 1, of the Hitler Century, Institute for Historical Review, Torrance, California, 1992, pp. 255-259
[1651] Douglas Reed, The Controversy of Zion, Dolphin Press, Durban, South Africa, 1978, p. 186

On June 1, 1916, Louis D. Brandeis joined the US Supreme Court as an Associate Judge. By October 1916, the war-torn British were exhausted and unable to expel the German Army from France. Prime Minister Herbert H. Asquith (1908-1916), was ready to negotiate to end the war. However, the Zionists, via Weizmann and Arthur J. Balfour, offered British officials another possibility. If Britain would establish a secret alliance with the Zionists, in order to transfer Palestine to them for the establishment of a Jewish state, the Zionists would maneuver America into the European war in behalf of the Allies, which would guarantee an Allied victory, an arrangement that probably occurred in October 1916. This agreement would necessitate changes in the political and military personnel in Britain and Germany, so that specific people would be in place to facilitate the necessary circumstances. [1652] In November 1916, the American citizens reelected Woodrow Wilson who campaigned on the deceptive slogan—He kept us out of war.

In early December 1916, Prime Minister Herbert H. Asquith resigned under pressure. On December 6, 1916, King George V gathered numerous politicians, including Balfour and David Lloyd George, to a special meeting at Buckingham Palace. That night, a delegation approached Balfour to see if he would accept the office of Foreign Minister under a new Prime Minister, Lloyd George, who soon enacted a war dictatorship under the direction of a five-member War Cabinet. He named Sir Mark Sykes as Secretary of the War Cabinet. [1653]

Dr. Weizmann was certain that Lloyd George, with fundamentalist Christian parents, was even more predisposed to the Zionist ideology than Balfour. Wilson's reelection also established the appropriate political circumstances to move forward. [1654] Though it certainly existed, there is little readily available evidence proving an absolute connection between freemasonry, Zionism and the initiation of World

---

[1652] John Cornelius, The Hidden History of the Balfour Declaration, Washington Report on Middle East Affairs, November 2005, pages 44-50
[1653] Ibid. 44-50
[1654] Douglas Reed, The Controversy of Zion, Dolphin Press, Durban, South Africa, 1978, pp. 186-187

War. However, freemasons in the Entente States, as well as the neutral states, because of their affiliation, would support the Allies against Germany. [1655]

Dr. Weizmann wrote a memorandum to the British Government in which he demanded that it officially recognize *"The Jewish population of Palestine"* as *the Jewish Nation."* A committee composed of nine Zionist leaders, and Sykes, the government's representative, convened privately to draft an official document, later known as the Balfour Declaration. Balfour immediately scheduled a trip to America to promote an Anglo-American protectorate but he never spoke directly to President Wilson. [1656]

Winston Churchill initiated effective naval intelligence by 1914, along with Alfred Ewing, Henry F. Oliver, and Captain Reginald Hall. The Admiralty controlled all cable communications by 1911, and had broken the German codes. When the war began, Britain cut the German cables, which forced the Germans to use an alternative means of communication. [1657] Ewing had been in charge of the British code breaking organization since the fall of 1914. In October 1916, Captain Hall, director of naval intelligence (1914-1919), replaced Ewing as the head of the organization. Balfour found Ewing another position in academia. [1658] Captain Hall, a freemason, belonged to Studholme Lodge 1591, the lodge into which they initiated Churchill on May 24, 1901, following a long standing family tradition.

In November 1916, Gottlieb von Jagow, Germany's Foreign Minister resigned in opposition to Naval Minister Alfred von Tirpitz's lobbying for the adoption of a policy of unrestricted submarine warfare.

[1655] Dieter Schwarz, Freemasonry, Ideology, Organization and Policy, Central Publishing House of the NSDAP, Berlin, 1944, pp. 32-33
[1656] Douglas Reed, The Controversy of Zion, Dolphin Press, Durban, South Africa, 1978, pp. 186-187
[1657] Eugene L. Rasor, Winston S. Churchill, 1874-1965: A Comprehensive Historiography and Annotated Bibliography, Greenwood Press, Westport, Connecticut, 2000, pp. 143-144
[1658] John Cornelius, The Hidden History of the Balfour Declaration, Washington Report on Middle East Affairs, November 2005, pages 44-50

Tirpitz, a freemason, [1659] was responsible, with Wilhelm's approval, as encouraged by Albert Ballin, for the build-up of the navy, including its submarine fleet, beginning in 1897. Jagow advocated improved Anglo-German relations and supported Austria-Hungary's dealings with Serbia. He was skeptical of the Schlieffen Plan, and opposed Germany's invasion of neutral Belgium and thought that von Tirpitz's plan of submarine warfare would ultimately bring the United States into the war. On November 22, 1916, Arthur Zimmermann replaced von Jagow as State Secretary for Foreign Affairs.

The new Prime Minister David Lloyd George, under the strong influence of the Zionists, wanted war, not negotiations. On December 10, 1916, Lord Balfour replaced Sir Edward Grey as the British Foreign Minister. Baron Sidney C. Sonnino became the Foreign Minister in Italy. Bernard Baruch enlarged his influence within President Woodrow Wilson's Administration. Georges Mandel's real name was Jeroboam Rothschild. Though reportedly unrelated to the infamous banking family, he was prosperous and Jewish. [1660] He was Georges Clemenceau's handler, just as Edward M. House managed Woodrow Wilson. Louis-Lucien Klotz, a radical Jewish socialist, became French Minister of Finance, and was later responsible for negotiating reparations from Germany. House was elated with all of these changes. Balfour visited the United States in 1916, to establish the foundation among financial and media connections. [1661] Balfour was very impressed with the strength of the US Jewish lobby and their powerful influence in financial circles.

Financial networks were already set up as well as the media that used every propaganda slogan imaginable. Colonel House, supported by American Jews, informed the British government of President Wilson's every move. House literally controlled the United States; Wilson was just a figurehead and everyone but the public knew it. On

[1659] Alfred von Tirpitz, http://freemasonry.bcy.ca/biography/tirpitz_a/tirpitz_a.html as of May 2012
[1660] Arnold Leese, Gentile Folly: the Rothschilds, Reception, February 17, 1937, p. 55
[1661] Leon Degrelle, Hitler: Born at Versailles, Volume 1, of the Hitler Century, Institute for Historical Review, Torrance, California, 1992, pp. 255-259

December 12, 1916, German officials stated that they were anxious for peace and wished to talk with their adversaries and hoped Wilson would persuade the Allies to meet together. House ruled out the possibility of peace negotiations. [1662]

On December 18, 1916, US Ambassador to Britain, Walter H. Page, relayed a peace offer to the Allies from Germany, the Austro-Hungarian Empire, the Ottoman Empire, and Bulgaria. On January 9, 1917, Prime Minister Lloyd George quickly repudiated the offering, and declared that Britain would fight to the victory, which possibly prompted the Germans to re-initiate submarine warfare. Ambassador Page, in touch with President Wilson and Secretary of State Robert Lansing, defended British policies. This was after William Jennings Bryan's resignation, after he described Britain's collapsing financial situation, and the need for American neutrality. America's entry into the war would allow Britain to avoid financial disaster. [1663]

According to author John Cornelius, British officials in London concocted the nefarious Zimmermann telegram. Apparently, Hans Arthur von Kemnitz, of the German foreign office and probably a Zionist agent, admitted to the press after the war that he devised the alliance scheme. He provided Zimmermann with the exact information for the intended telegram, written in code 7500, and instructed Zimmermann to send it. An informant had already passed the German Code 7500 to Captain Reginald Hall and his British code breaking organization a few weeks before. [1664]

Zimmermann informed the German ambassador in Washington, Count Johann Heinrich von Bernstorff that Germany was going to engage in submarine warfare so that the ambassador could alert US officials. On January 19, 1917, Zimmermann sent a second telegram to the German Embassy in Mexico City. The British intercepted and de-coded it. The Kaiser and Chancellor Hollweg were unaware of Zimmermann's telegram, as he had acted on his own authority. Later,

---

[1662] Ibid. 255-259
[1663] John Cornelius, The Hidden History of the Balfour Declaration, Washington Report on Middle East Affairs, November 2005, pp. 44-50
[1664] Ibid. 44-50

officials called him to testify about his behavior before the Reichstag. Bernstorff advised the German government to reconsider their decision to start unrestricted submarine warfare, which it refused to do. On February 1, 1917, Bernstorff told the US government that Germany was beginning submarine warfare the next day. On February 14, 1917, the US government suspended all diplomatic relations with Germany and demanded that Bernstorff leave the country, which he did. [1665]

In early 1917, three obstacles prohibited Zionist efforts from acquiring a promise from the British government to support their objectives in Palestine—1) the 1915 agreement made with Sharif Husain of Arabia regarding an independent Arab state, including Palestine; 2) the Sykes-Picot agreement; 3) an influential faction of British Jews opposed political Zionism. However, Prime Minister Lloyd George directed Sykes to negotiate with the Zionists which resulted in the British Government issuing the Balfour Declaration. Additionally, the Jews allegedly used their substantial influence to maneuver the United States into the war. The secretive details of the Balfour-Weizmann agreement of October 1916 remain a mystery.

On February 7, 1917, Secretary Mark Sykes held a meeting with Weizmann and other Zionist leaders in London. He was probably aware of the secret meeting and the resulting British-Zionist agreement in October 1916. On February 26, 1917, London officials sent a telegram to the US State Department with the text of the Zimmermann telegram, which the State Department published on March 1, 1917. On March 15, 1917, Czar Nicholas II abdicated and officials formed a provisional government later under the leadership of Alexander Kerensky. On April 2, 1917, President Wilson addressed Congress, praised the events in Russia, and remarked, "The world needs to be made safe for democracy." He asked Congress to declare war on Germany, which it did on April 6, 1917. On that day, the German government wisely replaced Zimmermann as foreign minister.

[1665] John Cornelius, The Hidden History of the Balfour Declaration, Washington Report on Middle East Affairs, November 2005, pp. 44-50

On April 8, 1917, Dr. Weizmann wrote and requested Judge Brandeis to counsel Wilson to oppose a joint protectorate but to confirm America's support of Balfour. Brandeis, author of *The Jewish Problem* (1915), no longer directed the American Zionist movement but functioned as Wilson's advisor on all Jewish issues. Weizmann requested Brandeis to counsel Wilson to favor a British protectorate. Although Balfour did not meet with Wilson, the president talked with Rabbi Stephen S. Wise who had also informed Edward M. House of their wishes. The Zionists had already recruited House to their cause. [1666]

Balfour, Brandeis, House, and Weizmann were all dedicated to establishing a British administration in Palestine. Balfour, now the British Foreign Secretary, despite a conflict of interests, personally supported Zionism. Brandeis, also in an official position, had self-interests that countered his official obligations. Brandeis and House, on behalf of Wilson, and in accordance with Weizmann's request, issued a statement denouncing secret treaties. Americans, upon hearing their announcement, assumed that their government was transparent and trustworthy, exactly the illusion that the Zionists sought. The British and the French had to defeat Turkey and win the Arabs to their side, using the deceptive Sykes-Picot agreement, a contract that would create an independent confederation of Arab States. Unfortunately, for the Zionists, that agreement would also facilitate the establishment of an international administration for Palestine rather than an exclusive British protectorate. However, Weizmann made certain that President Wilson, despite his denunciation of secret treaties, would insist that England assume the protectorate of Palestine, which targeted the Arab inhabitants. [1667]

Soon after America entered the war, President Wilson considered ending the bloody battle by separating Turkey from the Central Powers. He sent Henry Morgenthau, Sr. and other representatives on a secret mission to Britain, France, and Switzerland, and then to Turkey. In June 1917, according to Weizmann's autobiography, Brandeis

[1666] Douglas Reed, The Controversy of Zion, Dolphin Press, Durban, South Africa, 1978, pp. 186-187
[1667] Ibid. 186-187

alerted Weizmann in London about the mission and suggested that he approach British officials to determine the nature of the mission. He convinced the British to intercept the mission, so it would never reach Switzerland or Turkey. Weizmann, who wanted the war to continue while the Ottoman Empire was still intact, feared that the Zionists would lose their chance to acquire Palestine. He met with Balfour, who sent Weizmann to Gibraltar where, on July 4, 1917, he met with the US mission, as a representative of the British government. He easily persuaded Morgenthau, an avid Zionist, to scrap the mission. Thereafter, Morgenthau went to Biarritz, in France, to speak with General John J. Pershing, a freemason, and to wait for President Wilson's instructions. [1668]

The British government sent Sir William Wiseman to Washington to advise Edward M. House about Britain's desires. He informed House, "It is impossible to negotiate with the Germans since they did not specify any conditions," the very purpose of negotiations, to define the conditions. US Ambassador Walter H. Page told British officials that President Wilson was not interested in negotiating, which was a blatant lie. Wilson had written letters to British and German officials, behind House's back saying, "The belligerents each insist on certain conditions. They are not incompatible, contrary to the fear of certain persons. An exchange of views would clear the air." This was just the circumstances that the German officials wanted, but the Allies rejected this suggestion. House was not pleased when he read Wilson's note and disassociated himself from Wilson's correspondence because "the Allies were obviously not in a mood to welcome it." [1669]

After the Bolshevik Revolution of October 1917, Russia capitulated. The Kaiser's Turkish allies probably would have delivered Palestine to the Zionists. Then, the Zionists no longer needed Germany, especially since they had an alliance with Britain. Thus, Balfour viewed Germany as expendable. The Zionists were now looking at

---

[1668] John Cornelius, The Hidden History of the Balfour Declaration, Washington Report on Middle East Affairs, November 2005, pp. 44-50

[1669] Leon Degrelle, Hitler: Born at Versailles, Volume 1, of the Hitler Century, Institute for Historical Review, Torrance, California, 1992, pp. 255-259

Britain as their total benefactor, to get Palestine as a Jewish homeland, especially after House and Balfour brought America into the war to guarantee an Allied victory. Balfour's only challenge was to sway the US Jews to support Britain and relinquish their longtime loyalties to Germany. [1670]

Altering History, the Cover-up

At least five people wrote books about the betrayal and cover-up of German Code 7500 to the British. Burton J. Hendrick wrote a three-volume composition, entitled *The Life and Letters of Walter H. Page* (1922, 1925). Ambassador Page was, since 1881, friends with Woodrow Wilson who appointed him to the position in Britain. Hendrick's third volume contained Page's correspondence with Wilson and Secretary of State Robert Lansing. Balfour presented Page with a copy of the second Zimmermann telegram, dated January 19, 1917. Two versions of the telegram, from the German originals, are public but the one that Hendrick refers to, a draft of the original telegram, is only available in his book, compiled from numerous private and public sources. [1671]

In 1936-1937, Blanche Dugdale, Lord Balfour's niece, wrote the second book, *Arthur James Balfour,* in two volumes. In Chapter ten of the second volume, Dugdale refers to the first Zimmermann telegram and insinuates that the British government received the Zimmermann telegram from an informant, not by code breaking, right after Zimmermann sent it. In 1937, William F. Friedman and Charles J. Mendelsohn wrote the third book, a US Army Signal Corps Bulletin, *The Zimmermann Telegram of January 16, 1917 and its Cryptographic Background.* The US government immediately classified the book until 1965. [1672]

In 1958, Barbara W. Tuchman, granddaughter of Henry Morgenthau Sr., published the fourth book, *The Zimmermann Telegram,* with a

---

[1670] Ibid. 255-259
[1671] John Cornelius, The Hidden History of the Balfour Declaration, Washington Report on Middle East Affairs, November 2005, pp. 44-50
[1672] Ibid. 44-50

second edition in 1966, after the declassification of Friedman and Mendelsohn's book. In 1958, she claimed that the British obtained the telegram by wireless, January 17, in code 13042, one they had previously deciphered. According to Tuchman, that explains how they were able to generate a copy of the decoded telegram. Tuchman's very detailed first chapter, unchanged in both editions, describes how the British deciphered code 13042 in the telegram of January 16, 1917. Even if she failed to read Friedman and Mendelsohn's declassified book, she must have realized that her story was incorrect. Cornelius believes that she "fabricated a false story of how the British obtained the text of the Zimmermann telegram in order to conceal the fact that they obtained it by betrayal." [1673]

David Kahn wrote a 1,000-page plus book, *The Codebreakers*, published in 1967. In chapter nine, he described how the British deciphered code 7500 but he mistakenly refers to it as 0075 (as Tuchman did), perhaps to confuse the issue. He wrote a second edition (1996) but did not amend chapter nine. He claims the British somehow broke the code. Friedman and Mendelsohn were professional cryptographers, which certainly gives credibility to their version, in addition to the government's suppression of their book for almost thirty years. Kahn also claims, "to this day no one knows why Zimmermann admitted it." In as much as Zimmermann acted on his own without the knowledge of the German government, German officials investigated the matter and called him to testify before the Reichstag where they compelled him to confess. [1674]

Cornelius suggests that, by examining the evidence, we can surmise that a Zionist agent inside the German government obtained code 7500, either by photography or photographic memory, used by Zimmermann in the telegram he sent on January 16, 1917. This is consistent with what Dugdale cited in her book whereas the other authors overlooked this probability. Rather, they present incompatible accounts of British capabilities and their possession of the text of the telegram. Interestingly, in her 1966 preface, Tuchman wrote that

---

[1673]   Ibid. 44-50
[1674]   Ibid. 44-50

Kahn would analyze the decipherment of code 7500 (or 0075 as she calls it) in his forthcoming book. Does this suggest that these two authors are collaborating on some sort of cover-up? [1675]

Groundwork for the Holocaust Hoax

Jacob H. Schiff loaned Japan $200,000,000, to fund the Russo-Japanese War in an attempt to destroy the czarist government. He refused loans to Russia and used his influence to prevent other banking houses from loaning money to Russia. In 1904, America's Jews applauded Japan's assault against Russia. [1676] Almost 650,000 Jews immigrated to America between 1904 and 1908, about seventy-five percent of them from Russia, just before, during, and following the banker-funded 1905 revolution and the rest from Romania, and other Eastern European countries. They accounted for more than nine percent of the total immigration during those years. The Jewish population would expand from 0.6 percent to approximately 3.5 percent by 1930. [1677] Jewish leaders, such as Schiff, Louis Marshall, and Isidor Straus aroused national sympathy for the Jews by elaborating on and condemning Russia's barbarity. [1678]

Felix M. Warburg noted in his book, "As soon as the World War (One) started and it was obvious that a large part of the War would be fought in the zone in which six or seven million Jews lived, particularly Poland, Russia and Galicia, many worthy people started organizations to collect funds for the sufferers in the War zones." [1679]

[1675] Ibid. 44-50

[1676] Hasia R. Diner, The Jews of the United States, 1654 to 2000, University of California Press, Berkeley, California, 2004, pp. 178-179

[1677] Avraham Barkai, Branching Out: German-Jewish Immigration to the United States, 1820-1914, Holmes & Meier, New York, 1994, p. 191

[1678] Hasia R. Diner, The Jews of the United States, 1654 to 2000, University of California Press, Berkeley, California, 2004, pp. 178-179

[1679] Felix M. Warburg, A Biographical Sketch, The American Jewish Committee, New York, 1938, p. 14 as cited in The First Holocaust, Jewish Fund Raising Campaigns with Holocaust Claims During and After World War One by Don Heddeshemimer

According to *The New York Times*, Rabbi Stephen S. Wise, included the following in an address to his co-religionists, "The day will never come when I will care less for Zion, when there will be anyone who will strive more for the glorious ideals of Zionism. Two great conventions of Jews are being held tonight. In Chicago, there is a conference of charities called together by men who minister to the wants of the poor. They have assembled to see that too much charity is not given to the unworthy. Their purpose is right. But ours is the greater charity. We have assembled not to see that the Jew does not get too much, but that every Jew shall get the right to live. There are 6,000,000 living, bleeding, suffering arguments in favor of Zionism. They come not to beg, but ask for that which is higher than all material things. They seek to have satisfied the unquenchable thirst after the ideal. They ask to become once again the messengers of right, justice, and humanity." [1680]

During World War I, wealthy Jews living in America developed a rescue plan for their disadvantaged fellow religionists living elsewhere. Schiff, Marshall, and Nathan Straus were instrumental in collecting and sending money to the Jews living in Palestine. They induced government officials to permit a messenger carrying the funds to travel aboard the *USS North Carolina*, a battleship to deliver the money. [1681]

On October 19, 1919, Nathan Straus, Isidor's brother, wrote an article for the *San Francisco Chronicle* in which he claims that 6,000,000 Jews, out of the world's 16,000,000 Jews are destitute and starving in Eastern Europe. He claimed that recent reports from American Jewish relief workers indicated that the suffering of the Jews, a third of the "entire Jewish race," was so intense that they were standing in breadlines or depending on the soup kitchens of the American Jewish Joint Distribution Committee (JDC), established in 1914, for Jewish War Sufferers. The JDC, a worldwide Jewish relief organization with headquarters in New York, is active in over 70 countries. It managed

---

[1680] There are 6,000,000 living, bleeding, suffering arguments in favor of Zionism, Rabbi Wise's Address, The New York Times, June 11, 1900, p. 7

[1681] Hasia R. Diner, The Jews of the United States, 1654 to 2000, University of California Press, Berkeley, California, 2004, pp. 182-183

Operation Solomon, Operation Moses and Operation Joshua. He further wrote that every month this past summer, workers sent 27,000 Jewish children to vacation homes to recover their strength. They sent other Jewish children from Vienna to Holland or Trieste to convalesce.

Martin H. Glynn, former governor of New York, wrote an article entitled, *The Crucifixion of Jews Must Stop*, published on October 19, 1919, in *The American Hebrew*. He said, "Six million men and women are dying from lack of the necessaries of life; eight hundred thousand children cry for bread. And this fate is upon them through no fault of their own, through no transgression of the laws of God or man; but through the awful tyranny of war and a bigoted lust for Jewish blood. In this threatened *holocaust* of human life, forgotten are the niceties of philosophical distinction, forgotten are the differences of historical interpretation; and the determination to help the helpless, to shelter the homeless, to clothe the naked and to feed the hungry becomes a religion at whose altar men of every race can worship and women of every creed can kneel." [1682]

On November 12, 1919, *The New York Times* quoted Felix M. Warburg, Chairman of the JDC, which had spent $30 million to feed Jews in Europe since 1914. About the dire situation of Jewish war sufferers, he said, "The successive blows of contending armies have all but broken the back of European Jewry, and have reduced to tragically unbelievable poverty, starvation and disease about 6,000,000 souls, or half the Jewish population of the earth. The Jewish people throughout Eastern Europe, by sheer accident of geography, have suffered more from the war than any other element of the population." [1683]

On May 31, 1920, the members of American Jewish Committee elected Nathan Straus as Chairman of the group at the end of a two-day meeting. They also elected Dr. Louis S. Rubinsohn, Colonel Harry Cutler, Judge Leon Sanders, and Rabbi Moses S. Margolies, a Zionist

[1682] Martin H. Glynn, The Crucifixion of Jews Must Stop!, The American Hebrew, October 31, 1919, p. 582, http://www.codoh.com/incon/incrucifix.html
[1683] Tells Sad Plight of Jews, Felix M. Warburg Says they were the Worst Sufferers in War, The New York Times, November 12, 1919

leader and head of all the Orthodox Rabbis in America, Gedaliah Bublick and Solomon Bloomgarten as the six Vice Chairmen of what *The New York Times* called "the most important Jewish organization in the whole world." They elected Bernard G. Richards as executive secretary. [1684]

According to *The New York Times*, June 1, 1920, the AJC, with commissioners from various parts of Europe, intended to create a Jewish World Tribunal in conjunction with similar groups in other countries. Dr. Joseph Bloch, from Vienna, declared that the Jews of the world expected Jews in America to stop the persecutions that they had experienced in the past. Evidently, convening a World Tribunal to target those guilty of persecution would effectively halt further prejudice and maltreatment. Bloch requested that an American Consul go to Lemberg to give special passport assistance to Jews who wished to immigrate to America. Rabbi Wise asked for and collected money or pledges of about $70,000 to cover expenses for the next year. [1685]

Just before that 1920 meeting concluded, Louis Lipsky, journalist and author, asked the Executive Committee to adopt a resolution asking Auckland Geddes, the British Ambassador to the United States, for the release of Vladimir Jabotinsky, the founder of the Jewish Self-Defense Organization and nineteen other members of the Jewish Legion who authorities arrested during a recent "anti-Semitic" wave in Jerusalem. The court sentenced them for organizing an armed body to defend the Jews instead of notifying the British military authorities. The AJC wanted a full pardon. [1686]

It appears that after Jabotinsky left the British Army in September 1919, he trained a group of Jews for warfare in Palestine. After the riots there, April 4-7, 1920, the Arabs demanded that the British search the homes of the Zionist leadership. They found three rifles, two pistols

---

[1684] The Jewish Congress elected Schiff, Marshall, Wise, Elkus and Mack to its Executive Committee with an aim toward convening a World Tribunal, The New York Times, June 1, 1920

[1685] Ibid.

[1686] Ibid.

and 250 rounds of ammunition in Jabotinsky's home. Authorities arrested him and others for initiating the riots. They sentenced him to a 15-year prison term for possession of weapons and blamed him and Bolshevism for the riots. The majority of the victims were from the old Yishuv, composed of Jews who had lived in Palestine from about 70 AD. They were adamantly anti-Zionist Orthodox Jews. After the AJC began making public demands, the authorities awarded him amnesty and released him from Acre prison.

Before 1900, American Jews comprised less than one percent of the total United States population. The new immigrants quickly became naturalized-citizens and indoctrinated Democrats, former victims who were now grateful to their new benefactors. They assumed the role of vital factors in the nation, which they have maintained to this day. Those new voters later helped Schiff to install compliant stooges like Senator Nelson W. Aldrich, Woodrow Wilson, and later Franklin D. Roosevelt into public office. Regarding religious groups, there were more Jews in the United States by 1930, than there were Presbyterians or Episcopalians. During World War II, Jews living in America collected about $63 million, from private sources, destined to assist the European Jews. [1687]

Allegedly, ancient prophecies require that six million Jews must vanish before the Jews can create the state of Israel. They can "return minus six million." Tom Segev, an Israeli historian, declared that the six million is an effort to convert the holocaust story into a "state religion." According to the Talmud, six million had to disappear in "burning ovens." Robert B. Goldmann writes: ". . . without the Holocaust, there would be no Jewish State." If the Jews could convince the world that six million perished, in the "burning ovens" of a holocaustic war (the Greek word holocaust means burned offerings) then it would fulfill the prophecies and they could become a "legitimate state . . ."

[1687] Jonathan D. Sarna and Jonathan Golden, The American Jewish Experience in the Twentieth Century: Anti-Semitism and Assimilation, Brandeis University, http://nationalhumanitiescenter.org/tserve/twenty/tkeyinfo/jewishexp.htm as of May 2012

Dr. Robert Brock, the publisher of *The Holocaust Dogma of Judaism: Keystone of the New World Order*, in the book's foreword argues that the taxpayer-funded Holocaust Museums in America violates the Constitution as they give preferential treatment and promote one religion above others. They also insinuate that the alleged suffering of one religious and/or ethnic group excels and is more historically significant than other groups, such as the millions of black slaves seized in Africa and brought to America by Jewish slave-trade promoters before the Civil War. [1688] Public, government-paid teachers in America teach the Holocaust, again accorded a special status by the government, as historical fact and no student dare question or dispute its history despite scientific evidence. The dogma makes all willing believers participants in Holocaustianity or Holocaustians.

The US Congress allotted land and millions of dollars of financing to the tax-exempt United States Holocaust Memorial Museum which had its grand opening on April 22, 1993 and has since welcomed almost thirty million visitors. The museum has an operating budget of almost $78.7 million, of which the government supplies $47.3 million while private donations provide $31.4 million. By 2008, the museum had about 400 employees, 125 contractors, 650 volunteers, 91 Holocaust survivors, and 175,000 members. There are branch museums in New York, Boston, Boca Raton, Chicago, Los Angeles, and Dallas.

The American Civil Liberties Union should defy all institutions preaching or promoting the Holocaust in any public place and forbid all public funds from supporting what constitutes Talmudic religious dogma. The First Amendment, as interpreted by the Supreme Court, repudiates the teaching of any religion in state institutions. [1689]

The Holocaust Dogma of Judaism: Keystone of the New World Order explains why the number of Jews "missing" when they founded the State of Israel had to be six million, a magic, symbolical figure, in order to fulfill prophecy.

[1688] Ben Weintraub, The Holocaust Dogma of Judaism: Keystone of the New World Order, Robert L. Brock, 1995
[1689] Ibid. viii

"The Holocaust Doctrine is a Jewish religious belief; therefore:

1. Public institutions may not legally teach it according to the current Supreme Court interpretation of the US Constitution.
2. The museums documenting the religious belief of the Holocaust and holding liturgies and candlelight ceremonies are in reality synagogues, temples, or places of Jewish worship and therefore cannot be erected on public property or financed by Congress no matter how subservient the Congress may be to Zionist pressure." [1690]

Jews used the symbolic number, six million, before World War Two, when they claimed that Germany gassed six million Jews. The Jewish-controlled media began popularizing the idea in the early 1960s. The symbolic figure, six-million, originated during World War I and in its aftermath. That magical number is Judaic dogma. Broadcasters reported that five or even six million European Jews were sick or dying in a holocaust from starvation, epidemics, and persecution. This generated fund raising drives by notable Jewish advocacy groups, which possibly led to the very financially lucrative Holocaust industry following World War II. People did not use the capitalized word, Holocaust, for over a decade after World War II and then began referring to it as the "greatest tragedy" the world has ever known. [1691]

[1690] Ibid. xi-xii
[1691] Don Heddesheimer, The First Holocaust, Jewish Fund Raising Campaigns with Holocaust Claims During and After World War One, Theses & Dissertations Press, Chicago, Illinois, 2003, p. 31

SECTION 8

PREPARING FOR ANOTHER REVOLUTION,

WORLD WAR TWO

Concealing the History of World War I

In 1917, President Woodrow Wilson would fall in line with the warmongers and send America's youth into the carnage of the European war. In October 1916, he said, "The singularity of the present war resides in the fact that its origin and its objectives have never been revealed. History will have to search a long time to explain this conflict." [1692]

Long before World War I, revolutionaries led an assault against the Russian Empire. The czar responded but instead of exile to Siberia, Russian authorities deported at least 5,000 revolutionaries and terrorists, many of which fled to Paris. These dissidents, who may have included people like Avetis Nazarbekian and Mariam Vardanian, had more freedom in the West to carry out their subversive revolutionary actions against Imperial Russia. In 1883, to counter this activity, the Russian Imperial Police opened an office in Paris known as the Okhranka or Agentura. Okhranka's foreign bureau was composed of agents, double agents, and agent provocateurs who gathered information on the revolutionaries. [1693]

In March 1917, after the Bolsheviks overthrew the regime, they concentrated on their enemies within the Okhranka, and organized a committee to investigate czarist officials in St. Petersburg, Moscow, Warsaw, and Paris in order to prosecute them. Basil Maklakov, the

---

[1692] Sigmund Freud and William C. Bullitt, Thomas Woodrow Wilson, twenty-eighth President of the United States: A Psychological Study, Houghton Mifflin, New York, 1967, p. 280

[1693] Ben B. Fischer, Okhranka: The Paris Operations of the Russian Imperial Police, From Paris to Palo Alto, Central Intelligence Agency, 1997

last Russian Ambassador to France, closed his Paris office and boxed up its contents and placed the Okhranka files in sixteen 500-pound packing crates. The Bolsheviks seized power from the Provisional Government in November. France repudiated Moscow's new government until 1924. In 1925, the Bolsheviks sought these vital, very revealing records. Maklakov claimed to have burnt them. Christian A. Herter, an associate of Hoover's American Relief Administration (1919-1923) had a house in Paris. Maklakov coaxed Herter to stash the records there until they could get them to America. Once in the US officials transferred them to the Hoover Institution at Stanford University. [1694]

Maklakov, justifiably fearful of retaliation from the Cheka, asked that the officials conceal the records until after his death which occurred in 1957, in Switzerland. He maintained contact with the Hoover Institution which would finally open the packing crates on October 28, 1957. A team would spend five years organizing and cataloguing a vast collection containing 206 boxes, 26 scrapbooks, 164,000 cards, and thousands of photographs, all available on 509 reels of microfilm. This collection includes files and photos of Stalin, Molotov, and Trotsky. [1695]

After the bloodletting of World War I ended, to conceal the culpability of the culprits, court historians composed a falsified official version of that horrific, but very profitable event. Andrew D. White (S&B), the founder and first president of the American Historical Association (1884-1886), Daniel C. Gilman, and Stanford president, Ray L. Wilbur urged Herbert Hoover to found the Hoover Institution and Hoover Library at Stanford University. White also helped found the Carnegie Institution of Washington and was a regent of the Smithsonian Institution.

The winners write the history according to the unspoken but understood policies of the American Historical Association. Many influential tax-exempt foundations fund that association. Court

---

[1694] Ibid.

[1695]

historians regularly overlook historical facts in favor of the official version. These official guidelines for reporting history have been in place for over a century. The Eastern Establishment governs what is acceptable—in textbooks, magazines, or any other major publications targeted for libraries. The same provisions apply to the American Economic Association, the American Chemical Society, the American Psychological Association, and other prominent institutions which successfully control and manipulate society. [1696]

In mid-1918, Hoover acquired the assistance of General John J. Pershing, the commanding general of the American Expeditionary Forces (AEF) in his food distribution organization. [1697] Beginning in 1919, Hoover, with General Pershing's help, recruited at least 1,500 trusted officers from the US Army and the Supreme Economic Council and sent them throughout Europe to gather documents, in addition to the Okhranka records mentioned above. All of these records would comprise, by 1922, the Hoover War Collection. [1698]

On February 5, 1921, *The New York Times* reported that Hoover, from Stanford University's first graduating class and one of its Trustees, presented the school with a collection of secret Bolshevik documents with descriptions of their initial organizational plans, along with records from other European countries. One agent acquired many Bolshevik records for $200. These items joined a collection of 375,000 volumes and data already deposited in the university's library. The library already had more than 6,000 volumes "of court documents covering the complete official and secret proceedings of the Kaiser's war preparations and his wartime conduct of the German Empire, every record, in fact, except those of the Grand Military Headquarters itself." When Hoover began his "relief" efforts in Europe, he recognized the value of "original documents" to future

---

[1696] Antony Sutton, America's Secret Establishment: An Introduction to the Order of Skull & Bones, Trine Day 2002, pp. 1, 27

[1697] George H. Nash, The Life of Herbert Hoover: Master of emergencies, 1917-1918, W. W. Norton and Company, New York, 1996, pp. 358-359

[1698] Ephraim Douglass Adams, The Hoover War Collection at Stanford University, California; a report and an analysis, Stanford University, 1921, Adams wrote this book in 1921 to explain the contents of the collection.

historians and had agents scouring Europe for them. They evidently knew exactly what they were seeking and had been given ample funds to purchase documents. [1699]

Over the years, the Rothschilds had compensated Hoover, one of their minions, for his service to them. They, through their minions, determined when to end the war. The Carnegie Endowment Center of National Peace, as noted in their records, sent a telegram to President Wilson, another minion, to caution him not to end the war too quickly. [1700]

The CFR formalized a historical blackout to circumvent any conscientious journalists who challenged the government's cover story, the official version, after World War II, and actually write about the realities of the war as many had done after World War I. The tax-exempt Rockefeller Foundation would later allot $139,000 for a three-volume set of the history of World War II. [1701] Harry Elmer Barnes wrote, "The readjustment of historical writing to historical facts relative to the background and causes of the First World War, what is popularly known in the historical craft as 'Revisionism' was the most important development in historiography during the decade of the 1920s." The cowardly writers who wished to remain in "the profession remained true to the mythology of the war decade." [1702]

The concealment of historical events, in addition to the printed word, also applies to other media. When broadcast radio began in November 1920, the airwave spectrum, according to official theories, was in short supply. Consequently, they licensed and regulated this public commodity. People who had a political or religious message,

---

[1699] Hoover Gives Red Data to Stanford, 375,000 Volumes of Secret War Document of Bolshevik and European Governments, The New York Times, February 5, 1921, http://spiderbites.nytimes.com/free_1921/articles_1921_02_00003.html as of May 2012

[1700] Transcript of Norman Dodd with G. Edward Griffin, 1982 available at www.realityzone.com/hiddenagenda2.html as of May 2012

[1701] René A. Wormser, Foundations: Their Power and Influence, 1958, Devin-Adair, New York, pp. 209-210

[1702] Harry Elmer Barnes, Revisionism And The Historical Blackout, http://yamaguchy.netfirms.com/vegyes_/barnes.html as of May 2012

or those with a product or service to sell, wanted airtime. By 1922, there were 576 stations licensed by the Secretary of Commerce, Herbert Hoover (1921-1928). By 1925, churches or religious groups owned sixty-three stations. [1703] The Commerce Department sponsored a series of conferences for major broadcasters. At the first meeting, a Westinghouse representative complained to Hoover that certain inferior stations, according to him, lacked substance and recommended that only preferred people be allowed to broadcast with a limit of 12-15 stations. [1704]

Hoover, as Commerce Secretary, was responsible for The Radio Act of 1927, which placed the responsibility of licensing and regulating (censoring) all the nation's radio stations in the hands of the federal government. That 1927 act established the Federal Radio Commission (FRC), which, in 1929, issued a set of guidelines. Accordingly, a station was to accommodate the "tastes, needs and desires of all substantial groups among the listening public . . . in some fair proportion, by a well-rounded program, in which entertainment, consisting of music of both classical and lighter grades, religion, education and instruction, important public events, discussions of public questions, weather, market reports, and news, and matters of interest to all members of the family." [1705]

The government insisted that regulation was essential due to a barrage of signal interference. Selectively licensing broadcasters solved the dilemma of allocating the purported limited amount of airwave frequency. Government regulations stifle the free dissemination of ideas in an open marketplace. By definition, the airwaves are public property. The government placed them under the *guardianship* of a

---

[1703] Jeffrey K. Hadden, Policing the Religious Airwaves: A Case of Market Place Regulation, http://religiousbroadcasting.lib.virginia.edu/pubs/policing.html as of May 2012

[1704] B.K. Marcus, The Spectrum Should Be Private Property: The Economics, History, and Future of Wireless Technology, http://www.mises.org/fullstory. aspx?Id=1662 as of May 2012

[1705] The Public Interest Standard In Television Broadcasting, http://www.ntia.doc. gov/pubintadvcom/novmtg/pubint.htm as of May 2012

Commission that it selected. [1706] Broadcasters began acting as public trustees and evidently people naïvely assumed that broadcasters would never violate that trust.

The Communications Act of 1934 established the Federal Communications Commission (FCC) that began operating on July 11, 1934 with seven commissioners appointed by the President and confirmed by the Senate. Officials changed this to five in 1983. [1707] The 1934 Communications Act, and later the Fairness Doctrine (1949) [1708] allowed equal time to opposing opinions.

British and American publishers and broadcasters who receive the most press coverage, airtime, and accolades consistently suppress the truth. Skeptical authors, in both countries, rarely, if ever, get a manuscript published if it is contrary to official opinions. Despite the number of schools, libraries and books, there is a huge decline in the population's knowledge and understanding. The literacy statistics in America and Britain substantiate the fact that, with the increase of technology and laborsaving gadgets, allowing more discretionary time, people are more prone to believe trendy popularized, personable talking heads sponsored by multinational media corporations than their own perceptions, derived from personal examination of authentic alternative sources.

According to the official version of any event, a political assassination, a terrorist act, an airplane crash, or any other extraordinary occurrence, it can never be the result of a premeditated conspiracy. [1709] To avoid speculative questions and popular dissent, the talking heads at the government-licensed network news shows immediately and authoritatively report, within minutes of any tragedy, that the

---

[1706] B.K. Marcus, The Spectrum Should Be Private Property: The Economics, History, and Future of Wireless Technology, http://www.mises.org/fullstory.aspx?Id=1662 as of May 2012

[1707] Communications Act of 1934, http://www.fcc.gov/Reports/1934new.pdf as of May 2012

[1708] Ibid

[1709] Antony Sutton, America's Secret Establishment: An Introduction to the Order of Skull & Bones, Trine Day 2002, pp. 1, 27

event was not the result of a conspiracy. Typically, the government sanctions an investigative commission stacked with individuals who always support the government's version of any event.

Writers, who perpetuate the government's official story, are in essence, participants in a vile conspiracy, which is by definition an agreement between persons to deceive, mislead, or defraud others. Fabricating fraudulent reasons to send individuals into wars where they kill total strangers at the government's behest, while risking their lives and emotional well-being is the epitome of deception. The government creates and maintains more conspiracies than any other entity while deceiving and plundering millions of taxpayers. The government and their media cohorts have the power to consistently control and sustain the cover story of every event and all circumstances. The rewriting of history and the dissemination of disinformation is rampant.

In 1924, Bernard Baruch reportedly financed Maxwell L. Schuster and Dick Simon to form Simon and Schuster. [1710] Following World War II, just before the huge media and Hollywood emphasis on the Holocaust, William L. Shirer, worked for Edward R. Murrow, the European manager of Columbia Broadcasting System (CBS). Shirer, a corporate journalist and a Jew, provided the news coverage, or the official version, during and immediately after the war. Similarly, Hoover, with the help of leading military leaders had subsequently collected and camouflaged the real history of World War I. Simon and Schuster published Shirer's 1,200-page tome, *The Rise and Fall of the Third Reich, a History of Nazi Germany*, the source of much of the later rhetoric regarding Hitler and Germany.

Just exactly who creates some of these false histories? One such group might be the Carnegie Endowment. According to their Annual Report of the Secretary, the Trustees at the Carnegie Endowment, on the day after the attack on Pearl Harbor, following their precedent from 1917, offered its services, equipment and personnel to the US Government. Since then, it devotes its efforts and assistance, in large

---

[1710] Pat Riott, The Greatest Story Never Told, Winston Churchill and the Crash of 1929, Nanoman Press, Oak Brook, Illinois, 1994, pp. 163-166

part, to various government agencies in dealing with international business incident to warfare and in preparing useful materials for the post-war reconstruction of peace. It also offers such services to agents of other UN-associated governments with offices located in Washington. The Endowment's Washington offices are located close to the White House and the State Department and are a busy center of information, guidance, and advice by personal visits and interviews, by telephone, and by mail. It also assisted organizations such as the Institute of Pacific Relations, the Commission to Study the Organization of Peace, the American Society of International Law, the Inter-American Bar Association and the Section of International Law of the American Bar Association. [1711]

In 1946, the Rockefeller Foundation, a huge sponsor of the CFR, functioning like a government agency, issued a report. It included the following statement, "The Committee on Studies of the Council on Foreign Relations is concerned that the debunking journalistic campaign following World War I should not be repeated and believes that the American public deserves a clear and competent statement of our basic aims and activities during the second World War." [1712]

CBS Corporation owns Showtime, formerly known as Viacom, which it reorganized on December 31, 2005 to create a mega media trust. Sumner Murray Redstone (born Sumner Murray Rothstein) owns seventy percent of its voting stock. [1713] He obtained an exclusive contract with the Smithsonian Institute, an educational and research institute. Taxpayers fund the institution with about $800 million a year. Effective January 1, 2006, the Smithsonian restricted access to its archives and its scientists to Redstone's *Showtime Network*. Prior to this exclusive contract, all filmmakers relied on the vast holdings of the archives to produce accurate historical pieces. Millions of viewers now view history according to *Showtime's* version of history.

[1711] Carnegie Endowment for International Peace, Yearbook, 1944, p. 15

[1712] René A. Wormser, Foundations: Their Power and Influence, 1958, Devin-Adair, New York, pp. 209-210

[1713] Peter Phillips, Project Censored, 2006, the Top 25 Censored Stories, Seven Stories Press, New York, 2006, pp. 257-258

[1714] *Showtime* has full access to millions of historical documents, films, photographs and thousands of hours of recordings unavailable anywhere else in the world. One has to obtain permission from *Showtime*, the Smithsonian's new collaborator, to access these resources.

The Brest-Litovsk Treaty

The British, working behind the scenes, disseminated a rumor claiming that the czarina was pro-German while accusing the czar of indecisiveness. The British claimed that Russia was attempting to make a separate peace with Germany, which in fact they would after the Bolsheviks seized power. [1715]

On April 6, 1917, Congress declared war on Germany obligating that country to fight a two-front war, which was even more formidable after America joined the battle. There was no way that Germany could possibly win. However, her defeat would end the war, the profit stream, the ongoing Marxist infiltration, and the subsequent destabilization of Europe. Vladimir Lenin, in order to prolong the war, had to somehow remove Russia from the equation. Thereafter, Germany and Austria-Hungary and its allies would exhaust themselves fighting France, Britain and the United States, the remaining allies. Meanwhile, Russia, on the sidelines, would add fuel to the fiery battle. [1716]

By 1917, provocateurs were busily engaged in Berlin where they infiltrated various organizations, including the government. [1717] On July 6, 1917, in the Reichstag, Matthias Erzberger passionately called for peace. In the fall of 1917, using seventy-five newspapers,

[1714] Jacqueline Trescott, Smithsonian Deal With Showtime Restricts Access By Filmmakers, Washington Post, Tuesday, April 4, 2006; Page C01
[1715] Leon Degrelle, Hitler: Born at Versailles, Volume 1, of the Hitler Century, Institute for Historical Review, Torrance, California, 1992, p. 271
[1716] Viktor Suvorov, The Chief Culprit, Stalin's Grand Design to Start World War II, Naval Institute Press, Annapolis, Maryland, 2008, pp. 3-4
[1717] Leon Degrelle, Hitler: Born at Versailles, Volume 1, of the Hitler Century, Institute for Historical Review, Torrance, California, 1992, pp. 196-197

the militaristic Bolsheviks began an "unprecedented campaign" for peace. On October 26, 1917, after they had seized St. Petersburg and gained control of the government, Lenin presented their first official document to the Second Congress of the Soviet, the *Decree on Peace*. The next day, he had it published in the *Izvestia*, which called for an abrupt end of Russia's war with Germany and Austria-Hungary. [1718]

After Lenin's power grab, the people, fed up with war, given the well-placed anti-war campaign, almost forced him to declare peace. Concurrently, peasants increasingly resisted the Bolsheviks and their criminal cabal. His October victory was tenuous and restricted both geographically and numerically. Alexander Kerensky, allegedly hostile to Lenin, retained a group of loyalist troops that still posed a threat. Lenin admitted, "Everything is hanging by a thread." A continued war with Germany might cost Lenin the more important revolution in Russia. On November 23, 1917, in as much as their political survival was at stake, Lenin and Trotsky decided to negotiate with Germany at Brest-Litovsk, a city in Belarus. Germany finally persuaded Lenin to negotiate. Yet, for political expediency, he procrastinated for over four months. [1719]

Countries do not willingly dismantle their armies, especially during the height of warfare where there is certain victory. Yet, Lenin and Trotsky disassembled the Russian army right when Germany's situation appeared hopeless. Germany depended on imports to feed her population; the Allies had blockaded Germany, and her allies, cutting off all sea routes. On the other hand, Russia had almost inexhaustible natural resources, in addition to having the French and British as allies in its battle against Germany. The United States entry into the war against Germany assured a victory for Germany's adversaries. Under such circumstances, Germany would most certainly surrender and implore the Russian government for peace. [1720]

[1718] Viktor Suvorov, The Chief Culprit, Stalin's Grand Design to Start World War II, Naval Institute Press, Annapolis, Maryland, 2008, pp. 2-4

[1719] Leon Degrelle, Hitler: Born at Versailles, Volume 1, of the Hitler Century, Institute for Historical Review, Torrance, California, 1992, pp. 297-308

[1720] Viktor Suvorov, The Chief Culprit, Stalin's Grand Design to Start World War II, Naval Institute Press, Annapolis, Maryland, 2008, pp. 2-3

Lenin and Trotsky, implementing the total capitulation of Russia to Germany, directed the Russian army to abandon their trenches, leaving their guns, mortars, machine guns, millions of small arms, ammunition, uniforms, and other essential war supplies and return home. Lenin and Trotsky, two internationalists devoid of national loyalties to any country, with their *Peace Decree* betrayed Russia's allies, allowed Germany to focus its attention on the western front while at the same time wreaking havoc within Germany and Austria-Hungary beginning in earnest in early 1918, through well-positioned agitators. Lenin and Trotsky then came to Germany's assistance with the Brest-Litovsk Treaty. [1721]

The Bolsheviks stalled, from December 28, 1917 to January 7, 1918. Lenin faced massive opposition at home. The propagandized working classes had elected only 175 Bolsheviks out of 717 total seats in the Constituent Assembly. On January 18, 1918, Bolsheviks placed police armed with machine guns at the Taurid Palace to displace new assembly members as they arrived. They dissolved the Assembly the next morning. A few hours later, some workers organized a march to show their support for the people they had elected. The Bolsheviks machine-gunned twenty-one of them, the consequences of opposing Lenin. The Germans recognized that less than ten percent of the population had forced a dictatorship on Russia. Trotsky wanted to use those same tactics at Brest-Litovsk but that would not achieve their goals. On January 22, 1918, Trotsky, of the central committee, proposed that the Soviets should refuse to sign a peace treaty but have both sides demobilize. [1722]

On February 9, 1918, Ukrainians declared independence and soon negotiated the German-Austrian-Ukrainian treaty and then shipped a million tons of wheat to Austria. When Trotsky heard about it, he flew into a rage. He had hoped to leverage the Germans into a treaty more beneficial to the Soviets, using food, a desperate need of Germany

---

[1721] Ibid. 2-3

[1722] Leon Degrelle, Hitler: Born at Versailles, Volume 1, of the Hitler Century, Institute for Historical Review, Torrance, California, 1992, pp. 297-308

and Austria. Germany then ordered troops to St. Petersburg, about a two-week march and they met no resistance along the way. [1723]

The Bolshevik arbitrators were Adolph A. Joffe, Lev Rozenfeld (Lev B. Kamenev) and Lev D. Bronstein (Leon Trotsky). [1724] When General Erich Ludendorff met them, he asked, "How can we negotiate with such people?" He would rather have taken his troops to St. Petersburg and Moscow and eradicated their stronghold. Yet, that would mean retaining a large German force in Russia and he could not spare the forces when he needed his greatest strength on the Western front. [1725] Richard von Kühlmann, an industrialist and Germany's Secretary of State for Foreign Affairs (1917-1918) led the German delegation and Count Ottokar Czernin represented Austria-Hungary. Erich Ludendorff wanted better territorial guarantees on the eastern border and the creation of a German protectorate in the Baltic States to halt the spread of Bolshevism. On March 3, 1918, they signed the Brest-Litovsk Treaty.

Lenin agreed to recognize the anti-communist areas that were once part of the Russian Empire, mentioned above, and Rumania (including Bessarabia), the Crimea, the Caucasus, Georgia, Armenia, Azerbaijan, the Urals, and all of Siberia. He agreed to limit his rule to Moscow and the adjacent area, in addition to the city of Leningrad. However, despite his promises, he intended to expand Communism as quickly as possible. Surrounded by anti-communist countries, if the west had really wanted to crush communism, they could have at this point. [1726]

[1723] Ibid. 297-308
[1724] Proceedings of the Brest-Litovsk Peace Conference: the peace negotiations between Russia and the Central Powers November 21, 1917-March 3, 1918, Brest-Litovsk Peace Conference, United States, Department of State, Washington, pp. 12-13
[1725] Leon Degrelle, Hitler: Born at Versailles, Volume 1, of the Hitler Century, Institute for Historical Review, Torrance, California, 1992, pp. 297-308
[1726] Sigmund Freud and William C. Bullitt, Thomas Woodrow Wilson, twenty-eighth President of the United States: A Psychological Study, Houghton Mifflin, New York, 1967, p. 253

Lenin's plans fell apart and he was about to have the anti-communist Germans too close to home. They would stop his revolution so he was ready to sign anything as long as he could retain part of Russia as a base. France, his ally, through their embassy, wanted Russia to stay in the war and even offered men and millions in gold which they accepted. However, the German Army was about 100 miles from his headquarters in St. Petersburg. Trotsky wanted to fight but finally agreed with Lenin that they should sign the treaties. Lenin viewed this as a defeat but had no choice. It was either peace with Germany or extinction. [1727]

With the treaty, Lenin betrayed his allies, members of the Triple Entente, Britain, France, Belgium, Serbia, Italy, Japan, Greece, and Romania by signing the Brest-Litovsk Treaty with the Central Powers, the German Empire, the Austro-Hungarian Empire, the Ottoman Empire, and the Kingdom of Bulgaria (the Triple Alliance). Lenin relinquished Poland, Finland, Estonia, Latvia, Lithuania, Belarus, and over half of Ukraine. The treaty put Russia at a disadvantage but he focused on initiating a world revolution even if it meant sacrificing Russia's national interests. Lenin was quick to admit that establishing Communism in Russia and other countries was foremost and that it was above all national sacrifices. [1728] They also signed the Treaty of Bucharest with Austria-Hungary on May 7, 1918. [1729]

In the treaty, the Soviets relinquished the Baltic countries, Poland, Byelorussia, Ukraine, Crimea and Tiflis to Germany, who now had access to food and other raw materials. According to author, Leon Degrelle, Germany might have won the war if the United States had not intervened. General Ludendorff, Marshal Paul von Hindenburg's

---

[1727] Leon Degrelle, Hitler: Born at Versailles, Volume 1, of the Hitler Century, Institute for Historical Review, Torrance, California, 1992, pp. 297-308

[1728] Viktor Suvorov, Icebreaker, Who Started the Second World War, Hamish Hamilton Ltd., London, England, 1990, p. 17

[1729] Viktor Suvorov, The Chief Culprit, Stalin's Grand Design to Start World War II, Naval Institute Press, Annapolis, Maryland, 2008, pp. 2-4

best general, brought back 600,000 soldiers from the Eastern front to reinforce Germany's war efforts on the Western front. [1730]

Germany immediately acquired massive amounts of food to feed its starving population. In as much as they now occupied Russian land, Germans displaced Russians. Lenin and Trotsky had not consulted anyone about the forfeiture of their land and homes. Without the industrial and agricultural regions, millions of people in the remaining territory experienced severe famine. Lenin, to prolong the war, willingly sacrificed them. [1731] The stipulations of the treaty provided food and resources to Germans while it deprived Russians who adamantly opposed communism. Moreover, in as much as Germans were taking lands and homes, the fleeing Russians would develop resentment and be anxious and willing to fight Germans in another war, already planned by the communist cabal.

The French and British had blockaded Germany and her allies, cutting off all food and weapon supplies. Russia, with the Brest-Litovsk Treaty, like manna from heaven, relinquished about 387,000 square miles, about 25 percent of Russia's cultivated land to Germany. At least fifty-six million people inhabited the area, which also contained 26 percent of the nation's railways, 73 percent of their iron and steel industry and 89 percent of their coal. On August 27, 1918, Lenin and Trotsky also agreed to pay Germany war reparations in the amount of six billion marks, without which, Germany might not have lasted until November 1918. [1732]

On November 5, 1918, because of Soviet revolutionary propaganda, Germany renounced the Treaty of Brest-Litovsk and terminated diplomatic relations with the Russian Soviet Federative Socialist Republic (RSFSR) which came to power on November 7, 1917. The Bolsheviks then voided the treaty on November 13, 1918, as reported in *Pravda* the next day. Following the armistice, the German Army

---

[1730] Leon Degrelle, Hitler: Born at Versailles, Volume 1, of the Hitler Century, Institute for Historical Review, Torrance, California, 1992, pp. 297-308

[1731] Viktor Suvorov, The Chief Culprit, Stalin's Grand Design to Start World War II, Naval Institute Press, Annapolis, Maryland, 2008, pp. 2-4

[1732] Ibid. 2-4

totally withdrew from the territories obtained through the treaty. On April 16, 1922, via the Treaty of Rapallo, the two countries, with Georgi Chicherin, Soviet Foreign Minister and Walther Rathenau of Germany agreed to invalidate all territorial and financial claims against each other. On June 29, 1926, officials reaffirmed that agreement with the Treaty of Berlin.

The Balfour Deportation Declaration

Negotiations between the British politicians and the Zionists began as early as 1903, when Arthur J. Balfour was British Prime Minister (1902-1905). The Zionists retained the London law firm of Lloyd George, Roberts and Company, as David Lloyd George, a partner at the firm, was a Member of Parliament (1890-1945), allowing them influence in the Foreign Office. Politicians and moneyed individuals frequently form symbiotic relationships.

Theodor Herzl's successor, Dr. Chaim Weizmann, a freemason, recognized that Zionism could only succeed with the support of a world power. Weizmann, born in Belarus (then part of the Russian Empire), moved to England in 1905, developed an interest in Palestine and was the professed leader of a pro-Zionist faction. He was a member of the General Zionist Council. Weizmann, Chairman of the Zionist Administrative Commission in Palestine, and a chemist, offered his services to the Ministry of Munitions when war erupted. According to Lloyd George's memoirs, the Balfour Declaration was Weizmann's reward for his expertise in producing acetone. [1733] British officials told the citizens that they supported Zionism to show gratitude to Weizmann (Israel's first president). Evidently, so the story goes, he developed a process for creating synthetic acetone, theoretically an essential factor in winning the war. [1734]

[1733] Walter Laqueur, A History of Zionism, From the French Revolution to the Establishment of the State of Israel, MJF Books, New York, 1972, p. 187

[1734] Robert John, Behind the Balfour Declaration: Britain's Great War, Pledge to Lord Rothschild, The Journal for Historical Review, Winter 1985-6, Volume 6 number 4, p. 389

As the war became imminent, numerous politicians espoused Zionism and became co-conspirators while failing to inform the public about their intentions regarding Palestine. Weizmann advocated a British-Zionist alliance in October 1914. He lobbied every influential figure in the Anglo-Jewish hierarchy of the Rothschild-dominated British government, primarily Balfour, Baron James de Rothschild, Sir Herbert Samuel, and Sir David Lloyd George. Weizmann and Samuel persuaded a majority of sympathetic British citizens to create a British protectorate. [1735]

The plot that the Jews developed in Russia, could not get support there, or in Germany, but it took root in Britain. Weizmann and Balfour met again on December 14, 1914, right after war erupted. During the first few months of the war, many British and French soldiers lost their lives and by the end of the war, 3,000,000 of the youth of France and Britain would die thinking they were overthrowing Prussian militarism, or liberating small nations, and restoring freedom and democracy. Balfour told Weizmann, regarding Zionism and Palestine, "I was thinking about that conversation of ours (in 1906) and I believe that when the guns stop firing you may get your Jerusalem." [1736] [1737]

In referring to the protectorate, Dr. Weizmann repeatedly resorted to the phrase, "the Bible is our Mandate" which of course meant the utter destruction, of the indigenous population, a fact that western politicians acknowledged, yet they continued to support the Zionists. [1738] Weizmann wanted to "make Palestine as Jewish as England is English." [1739] In 1914, the population of Palestine, according to British estimates, was 689,272 of which no more than 60,000 were Jews.

[1735] Hershel Edelheit and Abfaham J. Edelheit, History of Zionism: A Handbook and Dictionary, Westview Press, Boulder, Colorado, 2000, p. 74

[1736] Douglas Reed, The Controversy of Zion, Dolphin Press, Durban, South Africa, 1978, p. 164

[1737] John Cornelius, The Hidden History of the Balfour Declaration, Washington Report on Middle East Affairs, November 2005, pages 44-50

[1738] Douglas Reed, The Controversy of Zion, Dolphin Press, Durban, South Africa, 1978, p. 19

[1739] John Mahoney, Jane Adas and Robert Norberg (editors), Burning Issues, Understanding and Misunderstanding the Middle East: A 40-Year Chronicle, Americans for Middle East Understanding, 2007, p. 2

The Zionist goal was the entire usurpation of the land; there was, he felt, no room for both the Jews and the Arabs. They planned to deport the Arabs to adjacent countries. [1740] According to some figures from eighty-five percent to ninety-three percent of the residents of Palestine were Arabs. A very small percentage of the inhabitants were Jewish. [1741]

Dr. Weizmann told Balfour that the Jews had Jerusalem when London was still a marsh. Balfour apparently supposed, if that were the case, then the Ashkenazic Jews from Russia should have Palestine. However, many of the Jews in England attempted to dissuade Balfour from getting involved in Zionism. He told Weizmann, "It is curious, the Jews I meet are quite different." Weizmann replied, "Mr. Balfour, you meet the wrong kind of Jew." Balfour never again questioned the Russian Jews' claim to Palestine. Blanche Dugdale, Lord Balfour's niece, wrote, "The more Balfour thought about Zionism, the more his respect for it and his belief in its importance grew. His convictions took shape before the defeat of Turkey in World War I, transforming the whole future for the Zionists." [1742]

The Zionists assumed that Britain, France, Russia, Serbia, and Belgium would prevail in World War I and that they would dismantle the Ottoman Empire. In May 1917, Nahum Sokolow helped negotiate for the Balfour Declaration when he met with French officials who formally agreed to support the Zionists. They secured a promise from Britain that Palestine would be a national home for the Jews. In return, the World Zionist Organization would network and pressure Jews in Austria, Germany, France, and the United States to support the Allied war effort. America entered the war on April 6, 1917, a year before the war ended. That year, Lord Balfour, a crucially important Zionist patron and the British Foreign Minister, sent a letter, drafted by Leopold M. Amery, to Lord Rothschild, which ultimately grew into the Balfour Declaration, "the key which unlocks the doors of

---

[1740] Ibid. 18-20
[1741] William Engdahl, A Century of War, Anglo-American Oil Politics and the New World Order, Pluto Press, Ann Arbor, Michigan, 2004, pp. 35-45
[1742] Douglas Reed, The Controversy of Zion, Dolphin Press, Durban, South Africa, 1978, p. 164

Palestine." Lord Balfour wrote, "Zionism . . . is of far profounder import than the desires and prejudices of the 700,000 Arabs who now inhabit that ancient land." [1743]

Amery was the son of an English father, Charles F. Amery, and a Hungarian Jewish mother, Elizabeth J. Saphir, whose parents fled after the 1848 revolution, and eventually settled in England. Amery, who concealed his Jewish roots for decades, changed his middle name from Moritz to Maurice, and was a contemporary of Winston Churchill, and a correspondent for *The Times* during the Second Boer War (1899-1902). By 1911, Amery, a pro-Zionist, a Member of Parliament, and during World War I, an assistant secretary to the British war cabinet in Prime Minister Lloyd George's government. In 1917, he authored the final draft of the Balfour Declaration. He encouraged Vladimir Jabotinsky, a Zionist leader and founder of the Jewish Self-Defense Organization in Odessa, to create the Jewish Legion of the British Army during World War I. [1744] Amery, the Secretary of State for the Colonies would help bring down Neville Chamberlain in 1940.

On June 27, 1917, Lord Edmund Allenby, took over as commander-in-chief of the Egyptian Expeditionary Force to conquer Palestine and Syria. He decided that it was inappropriate to publish the Balfour Declaration in Palestine, as his military forces had not yet subdued the area. He reorganized his troops, won the Third Battle of Gaza, October 31 to November 7, 1917, and captured Jerusalem on December 9, 1917 where he established martial law. Although the Zionists presumptuously drafted the Balfour Declaration before the end of the war, it did not become official until the San Remo Resolution on April 24, 1920, after the British Mandate established the Civil Administration. [1745]

[1743] John Mahoney, Jane Adas and Robert Norberg (editors), Burning Issues, Understanding and Misunderstanding the Middle East: A 40-Year Chronicle, Americans for Middle East Understanding, 2007, pp. 18-20

[1744] William D. Rubenstein, The Secret of Leopold Amery, Conservative Politician, History Today, February 1, 1999

[1745] The British Mandate For Palestine, San Remo Conference, April 24, 1920, http://www.mtholyoke.edu/acad/intrel/britman.htm as of May 2012

People might be more accurate if they called the Balfour Declaration, the Lord Alfred Milner Declaration because he also helped draft the document, a fact that they concealed until July 21, 1936. Nathan M. Rothschild appointed him to chair the Round Table group to implement world government, and to promote the draft in the War Cabinet. The initial Zionist draft, of July 1917, was simple. It mandated that Britain would reconstitute Palestine as the National Home of the Jewish People. Further, Britain would use its power to reach that objective, in consultation with the Zionist Organization. [1746]

Balfour wrote the contract between Britain and World Jewry as a letter to Baron Walter Rothschild who was a key figure in England's Jewish community, and he would then transmit it to the Zionist Federation of Britain and Ireland, established in 1899, as a Zionist lobby. The document disclosed the views of the British Cabinet, as discussed in a meeting on October 31, 1917. Weizmann and Sokolow, in a statement, stated that the declaration did not meet their expectations of a national home in Palestine. Officials later integrated the Balfour Declaration into the Treaty of Sèvres, of August 10, 1920, between the Ottoman Empire and Allies at the war's end, to partition the empire. They signed that treaty a year after the Versailles Treaty, which forced Germany to relinquish their concessions and economic interests in the Ottoman Empire.

The Zionists were not satisfied with the first draft as they felt that the promises of exploration of Palestine's natural resources did not guarantee the resulting financial benefits for them. They accepted another draft, of October 4, 1917, and approved it on October 31, 1917. That draft was included in a letter that Balfour sent to Baron Walter Rothschild, President of the Zionist Federation, on November 2, 1917. [1747]

William G. A. Ormsby-Gore revealed, "The draft as originally put up by Lord Balfour was not the final draft approved by the War Cabinet. The particular draft assented to by the War Cabinet and afterwards

---

[1746] Hershel Edelheit and Abfaham J. Edelheit, History of Zionism: A Handbook and Dictionary, Westview Press, Boulder, Colorado, 2000, pp. 77-78
[1747] Ibid. 77-78

by the Allied Governments and by the United States . . . and finally embodied in the Mandate, happens to have been drafted by Lord Milner. The actual final draft had to be issued in the name of the Foreign Secretary, but the actual draftsman was Lord Milner." [1748]

On December 23, 1917, at least 15,000 American Jews gathered at Carnegie Hall to celebrate the signing of the momentous Balfour Declaration on November 2, 1917. Another 25,000 American Jews paraded down the main streets of Newark, New Jersey. Anti-Zionist Jews did not celebrate but the majority of American Jews did and they, most especially Colonel Edward M. House, had been influential in persuading President Woodrow Wilson to champion the Declaration. [1749]

In his famous speech in 1919, Balfour said, "For in Palestine we do not propose even to go through the form of consulting the wishes of the present inhabitants of the country . . . The four great powers are committed to Zionism, and Zionism, be it right or wrong, good or bad, is rooted in age-long traditions, in present needs, in future hopes, of far profounder import than the desires and prejudices of 700,000 Arabs who now inhabit that ancient land." [1750]

It was pompous, pretentious, generosity to promise a well-represented, well-connected ethnic group, land that another closely related ethnic group already inhabited, and had for decades. It was sure to cause chaos, death, and destruction that would certainly require a long-term military presence in the area. The Jews in Israel and elsewhere celebrate the anniversary of the declaration, November 2, as Balfour Day. Residents of Arab countries observe the day as a day of mourning and protest.

[1748] Carroll Quigley, The Anglo-American Establishment, Books in Focus, New York, 1981, p. 169
[1749] Hasia R. Diner, The Jews of the United States, 1654 to 2000, University of California Press, Berkeley, California, 2004, pp. 182-183
[1750] Dr. Salman Abu Sitta, Balfour's Odyssey, From Betrayal to Expulsion and Quest for Return, Near Edinburg, Balfour Birthplace, November 12-13, 2005, http://www.plands.org/speechs/003.html as of May 2012

Ultimately, in 1947, with Palestine's partition, the Arabs received 4,500 square miles (2,880,000 acres) and the Jews received roughly 5,500 square miles (3,520,000 acres). Currently, the Israeli state consists of about 8,367 square miles.

The Parliament of Man, the League of Nations

Author Gary Allen wrote, "For centuries, naive idealists have dreamed of a 'parliament of man' that would put an end to poverty, ignorance and disease. Modern one-worlders have added pollution and over-population to the list of evils World Government would cure. The allure of a world super state to such starry-eyed dreamers is obvious." [1751]

George W. Kirchwey, the Dean of the Columbia University Law School and thirteen international lawyers established the American Society of International Law at the Eleventh Lake Mohonk Conference, May 31-June 2, 1905, in Ulster County, New York. It was, like today's Bohemian Grove, the elite's gathering place. They formed a committee to create a group designed to promote peace and international arbitration. The committee included Robert Lansing, a Pilgrims Society member, and future Secretary of State (1915-1920) and James B. Scott. [1752]

Consequently, on February 6, 1910, the American Society for the Judicial Settlement of International Disputes (ASJSID) convened at Theodore Marburg's residence, where the "leading men of all countries" discussed methods to promote peace. President William Howard Taft sent a letter, saying, "There is no other single way in which the cause of peace and disarmament can be so effectively promoted as by the firm establishment of a permanent international court of justice." Secretary of State Philander C. Knox, Senator Elihu Root, and Senator Theodore E. Burton all wrote similar letters praising

---

[1751] Gary Allen, The Rockefeller File, the Untold Story of the Most Powerful Family in America, 76 Press, 1976, pp. 59-60

[1752] Frederic L. Kirgis, The American Society of International Law's First Century: 1906-2006, American Society of International Law, Martinus Nijhoff Publishers, 2006, p. 6

gradual disarmament and the need to settle "controversies between nations." The group elected Dr. James B. Scott as President, John H. Hammond as Vice President, Jacob G. Schmidlapp of Cincinnati, and Theodore Marburg as Secretary. [1753] They held their first official international conference in Washington DC from December 15-17, 1910. [1754]

Baltimore-born, William A. Marburg, a director of the National Union Bank of Maryland and his son, Theodore, a friend of Andrew Carnegie, were Pilgrims Society members. [1755] Baltimore, with a unique history, is a strategic port city and transportation center. It became the Cradle of American Zionism, and is the site of the Baltimore Zionist District. [1756] Dr. Aaron Friedenwald (past president)[1757], Dr. Cyrus Alder, and Rabbi Benjamin Szold of the Congregation Oheb Shalom founded the Baltimore chapter of the Alliance Israélite Universelle. [1758] The Seligmans established their banking houses in New York and Baltimore and financed many B'nai B'rith front groups. Judah Benjamin's family allegedly financed the Baltimore Hebrew Congregation, [1759] the first Jewish organization that the State of Maryland chartered. [1760]

[1753] To Promote Arbitration: Society for the Judicial Settlement of International Disputes Organized, The New York Times, February 7, 1910, p. 2

[1754] American Society of International Law, The American Journal of International Law, Volume 5, Baker, Voorhis & Company, New York, 1911, p. 193

[1755] Anne Pimlott Baker, The Pilgrims of Great Britain, a Centennial History, Profile Books, London, England, the copyright is held by the Pilgrims of Great Britain, 2002, p. 183

[1756] Baltimore Zionist District, http://www.bzdisrael.org/ as of May 2012

[1757] American Jewish Year Book, www.ajcarchives.org/ajc_data/files/1904_1905_5_natlorgs.pdf as of May 2012

[1758] Campaigner Special Report No. 24: The US Labor Party's Freeman Goes to Congress, Campaigner Special Report, Campaigner Publications Inc., New York, p. 7

[1759] Paul Goldstein, B'nai B'rith, British Weapon Against America, http://www.campaigner-unbound.0catch.com/bnai_brith_british_weapon_against_america.htm as of May 2012

[1760] Baltimore Hebrew Congregation, http://www.bhcong.org/index.php?submenu=history&src=gendocs&ref=History&category=Welcome as of May 2012

Brothers, William A., Charles L. and Louis H. Marburg, built the Marburg Brothers Company, which manufactured tobacco. In May 1891, they sold it to the American Tobacco Company, and William became its vice-president. He was also a director in the National Union Bank of Maryland, the Bartlett Hayward Company, the American Marine Steamship Company, president of the National Water Company of Wisconsin, and vice-president and trustee of the Johns Hopkins Hospital.

Theodore Marburg, following his father's example, was a trustee of the Johns Hopkins University (1902-1945), a facility that attracted many Pilgrims Society members. He attended Princeton, Johns Hopkins, Oxford University and the University of Heidelberg. He was the US Ambassador to Belgium (1912-1914), and a member of the American Society for International Law. While he and a host of others publicly promoted peace, they secretly favored war. He belonged to Washington's Metropolitan Club. In 1896, he wrote *The World's Money Problem*. He also authored The *Peace Movement* (1910), and *The League of Nations* (1917). He collaborated with Woodrow Wilson on the League of Nations covenant, the Pilgrims Society's initial attempt for world government. [1761]

The ASJSID held its third annual meeting (December 20-21, 1912) in Washington, DC, attended by elites from America, Canada, Mexico, England, and the Argentine Republic. Speakers presented *The International Court, a Natural Incident of the Evolution of the Modem World*; *the Supreme Court of the United States, a Prototype of a Court of Nations*; *The Line of Least Resistance in the Establishment of International Tribunals* among others. President Taft, now honorary president of Marburg's Society, said, "I am glad to come here and to give my voice in favor of the establishment of a permanent international court. I sincerely hope that the negotiations which Secretary Knox has initiated in favor of an international prize court, after the establishment of that court, will involve the

---

[1761] Anne Pimlott Baker, The Pilgrims of Great Britain, a Centennial History, Profile Books, London, England, the copyright is held by the Pilgrims of Great Britain, 2002

enlargement of that court into a general arbitral court for international matters." [1762]

Theodore Marburg, who blamed the war on "Germany's assault on the peace of Europe," [1763] later became the Vice Chairman for the Committee on Foreign Organization of the League to Enforce Peace. Dr. Felix Adler, founder of the Society for Ethical Culture, the influence behind Humanistic Judaism, said, in *The New York Times*, November 6, 1916, that after the war, only a Parliament of Nations will end warfare. The ASJSID, now known as the League for the Enforcement of Peace, promoted a Parliament of Nations. Adler quoted Wilson, who said that it was "time for the American people to take this wonderful opportunity." Adler, "as a means toward peace on earth" recommended a parliament or parliaments made of the "representation of nations . . . to take power and affairs from the exploiting groups and put it back into the hands of the people where it belongs." [1764] This is reminiscent of Tennyson's poem about the Anglo-Saxon's objectives of extending its dominion and influence— "Till the war-drum throbs no longer and the battle-flags are furl'd in the Parliament of man, the Federation of the world."

Predictably, the war makers soon ensnared most of Europe in war, due to freemason complicity amongst the lodges of the Entente States, Britain, France, and Russia who supported warfare. Even freemasons in the neutral states backed war. During World War I, freemasons in both the Allied powers and neutral States held conferences to determine the circumstances under which they should accept peace. The Grand Orient and the Grand Lodge of France held a meeting, the Masonic Congress of the Allied and Neutral Nations during June 28-

---

[1762] Theodore Marburg and James Brown Scott, Proceedings of National Conference, American Society for Judicial Settlement by American Society for Judicial Settlement of International Disputes, Williams & Wilkins Company, 1913,

[1763] Theodore Marburg Wants Allies Pledged, The New York Times, November 6, 1916

[1764] Taft As Envoy For World Peace: Theodore Marburg Would Send the Ex-President to Europe as League's Emissary, The New York Times, November 6, 1916, p. 6

30, 1917 in Paris. During this event, they developed the plan to create the League of Nations, and devised the idea of self-determination and independence for the subjugated peoples of Austria and Poland. They mandated the return of Alsace-Lorraine to France and Trieste to Italy. [1765] Author Gerard Aalders claims that Walther Rathenau and Karl Liebknecht, both freemasons, attended this conference. [1766]

That congress would send President Wilson, a member of the Order Of Odd Fellows, a Masonic organization, a telegram after he proclaimed his Fourteen Points during a session of Congress on January 8, 1918. The Congress expressed their satisfaction with the president and his ideals of international justice and democratic brotherhood, the Masonic ideal. [1767] His worldview included a global forum for the settlement of territorial disputes through arbitration, along with the power of enforcement and free global trade, as elucidated in his Fourteen Points, "equality of trade" and "removal . . . of all economic barriers." [1768]

In September 1917, five months after the United States entered the war, Colonel Edward M. House persuaded Wilson, already sold on a world federation, to create a body of experts to devise the peace terms and the League of Nations Covenant. [1769] Through the winter of 1917-1918, these discreet experts met at 155th Street and Broadway in New York City, to accumulate the information they considered essential to "make the world safe for democracy." [1770] This committee, led by Colonel House, was composed of 150 college professors, lawyers,

---

[1765] Dieter Schwarz, Freemasonry, Ideology, Organization and Policy, Central Publishing House of the NSDAP, Berlin, 1944, pp. 32-33

[1766] Gerard Aalders, Nazi Looting: the Plunder of Dutch Jewry During the Second World War, Berg Publishers, Oxford, England, 2004, p. 51

[1767] Dieter Schwarz, Freemasonry, Ideology, Organization and Policy, Central Publishing House of the NSDAP, Berlin, 1944, pp. 32-33

[1768] Will Banyan, Rockefeller Internationalism, Part 1, Nexus Magazine Volume 10-Number 3, (April-May 2003)

[1769] Edward Mandell House and Charles Seymour (editors), What Really Happened at Paris: The Story of the Peace Conference, 1918-1919, Simon Publications LLC, Safety Harbor, Florida, 1921, pp. 1-7

[1770] Continuing the Inquiry, http://www.cfr.org/about/history/cfr/inquiry.html as of May 2012

economists, and other intellectuals. He referred to this assembly as The Inquiry. Some key members of this group later functioned as the American Commission to Negotiate Peace—Frank L. Polk headed the commission, House, Clive Day (S&B), Donald P. Frary, Vance C. McCormick, Sidney E. Mezes, Charles Seymour, and William L. Westermann.

The Commission, with ties to the international banking cabal, wrote the numerous peace treaties and the charter for a world organization. Others, Bernard Baruch, Louis Marshall, Julian W. Mack, joined them. [1771] Walter Lippmann, Dr. James T. Shotwell, Eugene Delano, and Jacob H. Schiff helped organize the League of Nations. In 1905, Lippmann had established the American branch of the Fabian Society, which later became the Students for a Democratic Society.

On October 9, 1918, for greater collaboration between the scientific societies, the Masonic-based Royal Society of London sponsored an InterAllied Conference on International Scientific Organizations that hosted delegates from numerous countries. They established the International Research Council to function as a central clearinghouse for the future scientific activities of each country. [1772]

On July 8, 1919, Wilson returned to the United States with jewels and other lavish gifts worth a million dollars, a reward from the appreciative Europeans for his assurance that he would convince the United States to join the League of Nations. [1773] On July 10, he presented the treaty to the Senate for ratification during which he said, "Shall we or any other free people hesitate to accept this great

---

[1771] Edward Mandell House and Charles Seymour (editors), What Really Happened at Paris: The Story of the Peace Conference, 1918-1919, Simon Publications LLC, Safety Harbor, Florida, 1921, pp. 1-7

[1772] Ralph S. Bates, Scientific Societies in the United States, The Technology Press, Massachusetts Institute of Technology, New York, 1945, pp. 159-160

[1773] Eustace Mullins, The World Order A Study in the Hegemony of Parasitism, Ezra Pound Institute of Civilization, Staunton, Virginia, 1985, pp. 46-47

duty? Dare we reject it and break the heart of the world? [1774] [1775] The Senate procrastinated on his request so he invited some members of the Committee on Foreign Relations to the White House on August 19, 1919 to discuss it. Arthur J. Balfour visited the United States in 1917 and spoke to Wilson about the existence of secret treaties. Yet, when queried, Wilson denied knowing anything about them, particularly the secret Treaty of London, a pact between Italy and Triple Entente, signed in London on April 26, 1915 by Italy, Britain, France and Russia. [1776]

Wilson did not understand why American citizens booed him during his campaign to relinquish our sovereignty to an international body. His decisions caused death and destruction throughout Europe. The French hissed and jeered him when he was in France. Deeply depressed, he later isolated himself, even from Colonel House. From September 25, 1919 to April 13, 1920, his wife ruled the United States with Colonel Rixey Smith. Baruch continued to claim that Wilson was the greatest man he ever knew, probably because Baruch made millions during the war. [1777]

On April 28, 1919, to supervise every nation's activities, the freemasons erected the international organization, the League of Nations in Paris. Freemasons James E. Drummond of England, and Joseph L. A. Avenol, of France influenced President Wilson and Prime Minister Jan Smuts, a freemason, of South Africa (1919-1924) to consent to the organization with the claim that it would end all

---

[1774] Sigmund Freud and William C. Bullitt, Thomas Woodrow Wilson, twenty-eighth President of the United States: A Psychological Study, Houghton Mifflin, New York, 1967, pp. 281-283

[1775] Treaty of peace with Germany: Hearings before the Committee on Foreign Relations of the United States Senate, Treaty of Peace with Germany signed at Versailles on June 28, 1919, Government Printing Office, Washington, 1919, pp. 58-62

[1776] Sigmund Freud and William C. Bullitt, Thomas Woodrow Wilson, twenty-eighth President of the United States: A Psychological Study, Houghton Mifflin, New York, 1967, pp. 281-283

[1777] Eustace Mullins, The Secrets of the Federal Reserve, the London Connection, John McLaughlin, 1993, pp. 176-177

warfare. On January 10, 1920, the League of Nations charter would take effect. [1778]

The ASJSID evolved into the League of Nations and then into the United Nations. America facilitated the creation of the World Bank and the International Monetary Fund (IMF), both headquartered in Washington DC. The UN's European headquarters are located in a majestic building, divided into three parts, in Geneva. From above, it looks like a peace symbol. At one time, the International Archives of freemasonry, along with the International Masonic League and International Masonic Association all had headquarters in Geneva. They remained, from the 1920s forward, in close contact with the Council of the League of Nations. [1779]

On September 25, 1919, the US Senate declined League membership, which reportedly caused Wilson to suffer a nervous breakdown followed by a paralyzing stroke. On March 19, 1920, the Senate again declined membership. German officials especially opposed the British Round Table's plans for a world government. Lord Lionel Rothschild, a member of the Round Table, funded Cecil Rhodes and Alfred Milner, a prominent freemason leader and later chairman of the board of Rothschild's Rio Tinto Zinc mine. Milner, the Secretary for War in David Lloyd George's cabinet, was a delegate at Versailles in 1919. [1780]

In 1922, the Grand Lodge of France acknowledged that freemasons designed the League of Nations to set up the "United States of Europe." [1781] Walther Rathenau, a strong proponent of internationalism, advised Kaiser Wilhelm to create a United States of Europe or the Mitteleuropa Plan to counter potential economic threats by America against Europe. On July 29, 1914, he talked about that plan to British

---

[1778] Jüri Lina, Architects of Deception, Referent Publishing, Stockholm, Sweden, 2004, pp. 341-342

[1779] E. Cahill, Freemasonry and the Anti-Christian Movement, Kessinger Publishing, Whitefish, Montana, 2003, p. 230

[1780] Jüri Lina, Architects of Deception, Referent Publishing, Stockholm, Sweden, 2004, pp. 343-344

[1781] Ibid. 343-344

Ambassador, Sir William E. Goschen, involving a customs union, incorporating Austria, Switzerland, Italy, Belgium, the Netherlands, and perhaps even France. This plan, both anti-American and anti-Russian, initially called for the economic merger of Germany with her neighbors followed by a political union to create a German hegemony over Central Europe. [1782]

In 1909, Rathenau, who had inherited his father's managerial position at the German General Electric, along with about five dozen other directorships, acknowledged the people who rule from "behind the scenes." He said, "Three hundred men, all of whom know one another, direct the economic destiny of Europe and choose their successors from among themselves." [1783]

Concurrently, Theobald von Bethmann-Hollweg, German Chancellor (1909-1917), asked Britain to maintain neutrality if Germany and Austro-Hungary declared war on Russia and France. If they agreed, Germany would retain the existing European boundaries following the war. This pact would function as the basis of an ongoing Anglo-German neutrality agreement after the war. On August 1, 1914, the day Germany declared war on Russia, Rathenau reemphasized his plan to Bethmann-Hollweg who preferred the *September Program*, Germany's war objectives and the extravagant plans for the German annexations, drafted by his key adviser, Matthias Erzberger, and staffer Kurt Riezler, a non-Jew married to Max Liebermann's daughter. The German government never implemented either the *September Program* or the *Mitteleuropa Plan*. [1784]

German historian Fritz Fischer revealed the *September Program* after he purportedly discovered Riezler's secret documents in the archives

---

[1782] Fritz Fischer, World Power or Decline: The Controversy over Germany's Aims in the First World War, translated by Lancelot L. Farrar, Robert and Rita Kimber, W. W. Norton, New York, 1974, pp. 13-16

[1783] Carroll Quigley, Tragedy And Hope, A History of the World in our Time, The Macmillan Company, New York, 1966, pp. 61, 233

[1784] Fritz Fischer, World Power or Decline: The Controversy over Germany's Aims in the First World War, translated by Lancelot L. Farrar, Robert and Rita Kimber, W. W. Norton, New York, 1974, pp. 13-16

long after the war. Fischer described the September Plan in a couple of books and concluded that Germany had expansionary goals that served as its motives for going to war.

Rathenau, who some people considered the Bernard Baruch of Germany, and who promoted Bolshevism long before, and during World War I, said, "The towns of Germany will not stand in ruins, but will exist as semi-lifeless blocks of stone partially inhabited by a few poor wretches. The streets of certain quarters will be crowded, but all joy and brilliancy will have gone forever. Wearied figures will drag along the rotten pavement toward their slum dwellings. The country roads will be broken up, the forests cut down, and scanty crops be growing in the fields. Docks, railways and canals will have decayed and everywhere the weather-beaten buildings, the monuments of our greatness, will have become homes of sadness." [1785]

The Paris Peace Conference, the Delegate's Demands

Governments that are almost certain to be victorious during a war must justify their warfare intentions to the citizens. Governments do everything possible to subvert anti-war sentiments including formulating a sub-culture of problematic pacifists, like the anti-war drug culture of the 1960s, so that the majority of the population would predictably marginalize authentic pacifists who resist war for moral reasons. Victorious nations must prove that the conquered nation was the aggressor in order to impose a punitive, even revengeful peace on the vanquished. Raymond Poincaré, later the Prime Minister of France, said regarding reparations, "If the Germans are proved innocent, why should they want to pay war damages?" [1786]

Following World War I, numerous scholars in the triumphant countries, as well as the conquered nations, otherwise accurate and credible in many of their historical interpretations, falsely claimed that Germany bore the sole responsibility for the war. Fabre Luce,

---

[1785] Gyeorgos Ceres Hatonn, Rise of Antichrist, Volume 2, Phoenix Source Distributors, Inc., Las Vegas, Nevada, 1998, pp. 72-73

[1786] Leon Degrelle, Hitler: Born at Versailles, Volume 1, of the Hitler Century, Institute for Historical Review, Torrance, California, 1992, pp. 98-99

the French historian, apparently more honest than his colleagues, admitted, "France isolated herself in a lie." [1787]

As Edward M. House's influence over Wilson decreased, Bernard Baruch's power increased, particularly in the financial decisions he made in Paris where Baruch wanted to squeeze their Allies, France, England and Italy, to accept America's terms or lose the credits upon which they were living. [1788] Jews living in America became influential with Washington's politicians including those in the State Department. A US Jewish delegation, led by Louis Marshall, requested a clause in the peace treaty concerning the civil rights of Jews and other minorities in Poland, Czechoslovakia, Yugoslavia, Hungary, Romania, and Austria. [1789]

Delegates were gearing up for the Paris Peace Conference, January 18, 1919-January 21, 1920, with the inauguration of the League of Nations. On January 4, 1919, Dr. Chaim Weizmann arrived in Paris as part of the Zionist Delegation. Nahum Sokolow would join him. The Zionists, who after years of negotiations with Middle East officials and the capitals of Western Europe, appeared to be gaining cooperation between the Arabs and Jews of Palestine. On behalf of the Zionist Organization of America, Julian W. Mack, Stephen S. Wise, Harry Friedenwald, Jacob De Haas, Mary Fels, Louis Robison and Bernard Flexner attended. Israel Rosoff attended in behalf of the Russian Zionist Organization. [1790]

The Zionist Organization submitted their draft resolutions for consideration by the Peace Conference on February 3, 1919. Their demands, officially submitted by Lord Walter Rothschild, included:

[1787] Ibid. 98-99

[1788] Sigmund Freud and William C. Bullitt, Thomas Woodrow Wilson, twenty-eighth President of the United States: A Psychological Study, Houghton Mifflin, New York, 1967, pp. 252-253

[1789] Hasia R. Diner, The Jews of the United States, 1654 to 2000, University of California Press, Berkeley, California, 2004, pp. 178-179

[1790] Statement of the Zionist Organization regarding Palestine, Paris Peace Conference, February 3, 1919, http://www.jewishvirtuallibrary.org/jsource/History/zoparis.html as of May 2012

(1) Officials would formally recognize the Jewish people's historic title to Palestine and their right to reconstitute their National Home there.
(2) The boundaries of Palestine were to be declared as set out in the attached Schedule
(3) Officials would place the sovereign possession of Palestine in the League of Nations and entrust the Government to Britain as Mandatory of the League.
(4) The High Contracting Parties would insert other provisions relating to the application of any general conditions attached to mandates, which are suitable to the case in Palestine.
(5) The mandate shall be subject to several noted special conditions, including a provision to be inserted relating to the control of the Holy Places. [1791]

A few powerful individuals, including the Rothschilds and their allied bankers, instructed their agents on the terms they sought to impose upon Germany. One important aspect of the he Versailles Treaty was the allocation of Germany's railway rights within Palestine to the Rothschilds which would then allow them to dictate policy for Palestine because they had loaned Turkey almost £100 million. Since Turkey lost the war and its government had collapsed, they were unable to pay the debt, allowing the Rothschilds to claim Palestine with its strategic location and Christian and Islam significance. The British government, habitually subservient Rothschild puppets, maneuvered the circumstances to ultimately gain political control of Palestine. As a result, the Rothschilds began to direct the formation of the Israeli nation via their power over the British politicians. [1792]

The US Delegation, headed by Herbert Hoover, Wilson's Advisor on Relief, included Bernard Baruch and Paul Warburg, as economic advisors, Colonel House, Walter Lippmann, and brothers Allen W. and John Foster Dulles. Just before the conference, Baruch accompanied Hoover to Belgium, the location of his profitable food swindle. Hoover was in Paris for another reason—to meet with several other

---

[1791] Ibid
[1792] An Afternoon With Eustace Mullins by James Dyer, Rense.com, July 15, 2003, http://www.rense.com/general39/EUSTACE.htm as of May 2012

individuals to discuss the need for a continuing council of "private bodies" to resolve international problems. On May 30, 1919, he met with Colonel House, Whitney H. Shepardson, General Tasker H. Bliss, George L. Beer, Professor Archibald C. Coolidge and Dr. James T. Shotwell and their British counterparts Lord Robert Cecil (a Jewish family), Sir Valentine Chirol, Lionel G. Curtis, Lord Eustace Percy and Professor Harold Temperley. [1793]

Hoover and Thomas W. Lamont were among twenty-one other Americans, including twelve scholars, members of The Inquiry, from Harvard, Yale and Columbia who attended the organizational meeting, at Hotel Majestic, of the Anglo-American Royal Institute of International Affairs of London which is allegedly Illuminati-based. [1794] Charles Seymour (S&B), historian and later President of Yale University (1937-1951), was a CFR founding member. He functioned as the chief of the Austro-Hungarian Division of the American Commission to Negotiate Peace and also the United States delegate on the Romanian, Yugoslavian, and Czechoslovakian Territorial Commissions. On July 29, 1921, they incorporated the Council on Foreign Relations (CFR), a RIIA branch in New York City. The CFR initially functioned as a J. P. Morgan front in association with the American Round Table Group. [1795] The institute devises domestic and foreign policies. Scholarly members promote open borders and internationalism and curtail nationalism. J.P. Morgan, Baruch, John D. Rockefeller, Otto H. Kahn, Jacob H. Schiff and Paul Warburg provided financing for its creation. [1796]

Others in the US Peace Treaty Delegation included President Wilson, Secretary of State Robert Lansing, Joseph Tumulty, George Creel, Henry White, General Tasker H. Bliss, Frank Cobb, editor of the *New York World,* Charles R. Crane, a Chicago merchant, Norman

---

[1793] Whitney H. Shepardson, Early History of the Council on Foreign Relations, The Overbrook Press, Stamford, Connecticut, 1960, pp. 1-4

[1794] Jüri Lina, Architects of Deception, Referent Publishing, Stockholm, Sweden, 2004, pp. 338-339

[1795] Carroll Quigley, Tragedy And Hope, A History of the World in our Time, G. S. G. & Associates, Incorporated, 1975, pp. 952-954

[1796] Ibid. 1-4

H. Davis, future Assistant Secretary of State and Chairman of the American Red Cross, Colonel Boyd, military secretary to General John J. Pershing, a freemason, and Major General Clarence Edwards. J. P. Morgan lawyers, Frank L. Polk and John W. Davis, attended. Albert Strauss (Federal Reserve Board) and Thomas W. Lamont, a Morgan partner and owner of the *New York Evening Post* were also part of the US Delegation.

The Peace Conference served as a social, familial gathering. Felix Frankfurter and Justice Louis D. Brandeis met with friends in Paris, Arthur J. Balfour, Louis Marshall, and Edmond de Rothschild who hosted the most prominent delegates at his Paris mansion. Minor delegates stayed at the Hotel Crillon. Paul Warburg socialized with his brother Max, who represented Germany. Dr. Carl Melchior, also of M.M. Warburg Company, and William G. von Strauss, Franz Urbig, and Mathias Erzberger, accompanied him. [1797] Baruch, head of the Reparations Commission negotiated with Max Warburg on behalf of Germany, who accepted the reparations terms. Paul Warburg, Thomas W. Lamont, John Foster and Allen W. Dulles, of Sullivan & Cromwell, and other Wall Street bankers counseled Wilson on US diplomatic policies in conjunction with this conference. [1798]

The Allies accomplished three major objectives, all in conjunction with devising the retributive treaties that had little to do with justice but led to further destabilization. Those goals were 1) implement the League of Nations, the entity favoring global governance over nationalism, located in Geneva; 2) officially recognize the Soviet regime; 3) reconfigure European countries to maximize ethnic and political discontent, a foundation for further warfare. The Versailles Treaty terms, imposed on Germany without any negotiation, included debilitating territorial changes and excessive reparations, which created the perfect environment for an anti-Soviet regime, an

---

[1797] Eustace Mullins, The Secrets of the Federal Reserve, the London Connection, John McLaughlin, 1993, pp. 174-176

[1798] Eustace Mullins, The World Order A Study in the Hegemony of Parasitism, Ezra Pound Institute of Civilization, Staunton, Virginia, 1985, pp. 21-22

inevitable situation. The treaty formalized the circumstances that would ignite the next world war. [1799]

The Versailles Treaty, Economic Warfare against Germany

In 1918, Sir Alfred E. Zimmern, of Alfred Milner's Round Table, wrote a plan for Germany, *The Economic Weapon against Germany*, in which he said, "The Central Powers are being besieged by practically the entire world and they have no means at their disposal for bringing the siege to an end." [1800] He indicated that systematic, large-scale economic warfare was yet untried and that Germany would not anticipate its effectiveness. He and his cohorts had post-war plans, devised at the peace conference. While the physical blockade would ultimately end, they would make certain that Germany would lack access to raw materials, making industrial employment impossible. Without manufacturing, the returning soldiers would not find employment. The Allies, by confiscating and managing essential supplies, they would incapacitate Germany and make it impossible for her to recover from warfare. This would cause food shortages and famine, which would affect all of civilized Europe, if not the whole world for as long as three years. He wrote, "Who more naturally than Germany? It is not as if the boycott had to be organized. It will come about almost of itself unless special provision is made in the peace." [1801]

The Allies included Britain, France, and the United States, and also Bolivia, Guatemala, Haiti, Cuba, Ecuador, Honduras, Liberia, Nicaragua, Panama, Peru, Uruguay and many others. Regardless, the countries that benefitted from the stipulations of the Versailles

---

[1799] The Weimar Republic, D.1, The Treaty of Versailles, http://www.colby.edu/personal/r/rmscheck/GermanyD1.html as of May 2012

[1800] Alfred Eckhard Zlmmern, The Economic Weapon In The War Against Germany, Allen & Unwin Ltd., London, 1918, p. 2

[1801] Stephen A. Zarlenga, The Lost Science of Money: The Mythology of Money, The Story of Power, American Monetary Institute, Valatie, New York, 2002, pp. 577-578

Treaty were Britain and France, both of which the United States supported. [1802]

On January 8, 1918, President Woodrow Wilson delivered his Fourteen Points to Congress, authored by Walter Lippmann. They functioned as a platform for a new world order, calling for transparent democracy, unilateral disarmament, free trade and self-determination. [1803] He implied the restoration of invaded territories, no annexations, no contributions, and no punitive damages. Germany would sign the Armistice based on Wilson's ideals. On November 5, 1918, six days before the signing of the Armistice, Secretary of State Robert Lansing notified the German government that they would have to compensate the Allies for all damages, including civilian property which obviously contradicted Wilson's words. [1804]

On February 6, 1919, Germany's National Assembly had selected Friedrich Ebert as its first president during the Weimar period and soon the reparations rhetoric began. [1805] The armistice disarmed Germany and they allegedly devised the document to keep a Bolshevik onslaught at bay. However, Germany sent a few units to fend off the invaders at Frankfurt on the Oder and at Breslau. On February 16, 1919, Georges Clemenceau sent in the military and forced the German units to retreat behind a provisional line, which would later function as the border between Poland and Germany, awaiting the Allied Supreme Council's final decision. They obviously favored Warsaw. If Poland wanted to annex Silesia, all they had to do was issue a statement making the provisional border permanent. [1806]

Despite the humanitarian slogans like save the children and the massive funds that charities raised to allegedly alleviate starvation

---

[1802] Viktor Suvorov, The Chief Culprit, Stalin's Grand Design to Start World War II, Naval Institute Press, Annapolis, Maryland, 2008, p. 7
[1803] Guido Giacomo Preparata, Conjuring Hitler, How Britain and America Made the Third Reich, Pluto Press, London, 2005, p. 47
[1804] Ibid. 74-76
[1805] Ibid. 74-76
[1806] Leon Degrelle, Hitler: Born at Versailles, Volume 1, of the Hitler Century, Institute for Historical Review, Torrance, California, 1992, pp. 451-462

in Germany, the ships could not penetrate the blockade. In February 1919, George E. R. Gedye traveled to inspect the situation in Germany. He reported, "Hospital conditions were appalling. A steady average of ten percent of the patients had died during the war years from lack of fats, milk and good flour . . . We saw some terrible sights in the children's hospital, such as the 'starvation babies' with ugly swollen heads . . . Our report naturally urged the immediate opening of the frontiers for fats, milk and flour . . . but the terrible blockade was maintained as a result of French insistence." [1807]

Norman H. Davis, President Wilson's Assistant Secretary of Treasury, and later Undersecretary of State, and John Foster Dulles, a well-connected New York lawyer, part of the US team, wrote the War Guilt Clause (Kriegsschuld Klausel), article 231, created on April 7, 1919. It compelled Germany to accept the responsibility, essentially a blank check, for causing all of the loss and destruction suffered by the allies. Article 231 reads, "The Allied and Associated Governments affirm and Germany accepts the responsibility of Germany and her allies for causing all the loss and damage to which the Allied and Associated Governments and their nationals have been subjected as a consequence of the war imposed upon them by the aggression of Germany and her allies." [1808]

Germany's political and economic structure, though incredibly bruised, remained a factor despite their defeat in the war. Warfare caused by external forces had not totally destroyed those responsible for Germany's strong industrial foundation or the country's resilient internal framework. The Allies' maneuvering at Versailles initiated Britain's second onslaught against Germany with the intention of bringing about the country's total obliteration.

The Allies excluded the officials of the defeated nations of Germany and her ally, Austria-Hungary from the negotiations. Russia did not participate because it had already signed the Brest-Litovsk Treaty

---

[1807] Charles Callan Tansill, Back Door to War, the Roosevelt Foreign Policy, 1933-1941, Henry Regnery Company, Chicago, Illinois, 1952, pp. 22-23
[1808] Primary Documents: Treaty of Versailles, 28 June 1919; http://www.firstworldwar.com/source/versailles.htm as of May 2012

with Germany. The Allies arranged Germany's economic future. They apportioned German spoils as follows, 50 percent to France, 30 percent to Britain and they divided 20 percent between the smaller allies. The Allies abandoned Wilson's Fourteen Points, a deceptive decoy; it had served its misleading purpose of getting the Germans to surrender. They arrived in Paris at the end of April 1919. Prime Minister David Lloyd George read the text of the Versailles Treaty on May 7, 1919. They completed it in secret, the day before. [1809] Prime Minister Georges Clemenceau submitted the potential treaty to the German delegation, which ordered the transfer of Silesia to Poland. An unauthorized group of Polish soldiers had invaded Silesia; therefore Germany had to relinquish nearly two million ethnic Germans, and its resource-rich province to the invaders. Clemenceau legalized the invasion, barred the Germans from protecting themselves and forced them back behind the Oder River. Wilson supported his conclusions because, Winston Churchill explained, "Polish voters constituted a real factor in American politics." [1810]

According to *The New York Times*, May 14, 1919, Hugo Haase and those who controlled the Weimar government fought to gain approval of the Versailles Treaty. [1811] Although officials signed the armistice, it did not end the British blockade of Germany (August 1914-1919). For months following the war's end, unknown to American and British citizens, the British government prohibited food shipments to the starving Germans in several cities and towns until they acquiesced to the stipulations of the Versailles Treaty. According to official documents in the National Archives, 763,000 German civilians died from starvation caused by the blockade with another 150,000 deaths due to the 1918 flu pandemic. While the British and US public

---

[1809] Carroll Quigley, Tragedy And Hope, A History of the World in our Time, The Macmillan Company, New York, 1966, pp. 269-270

[1810] Leon Degrelle, Hitler: Born at Versailles, Volume 1, of the Hitler Century, Institute for Historical Review, Torrance, California, 1992, pp. 451-462

[1811] Haase Followers Fight for Treaty; German Independent Socialist Committee Makes Signing a Party Measure, Hope For Revision Later Steps Taken for Assuming Power if the Present Cabinet Fails. Maneuvering for Political Power, Haase Followers Fight For Treaty Kautsky Fears War's Renewal, Hints of Worthless Promise, The New York Times, May 14, 1919, p. 1

knew about the desperate situation, no one informed them about the atrocious policies that generated it. [1812]

German officials protested but to no avail. Georges Clemenceau and Wilson sided with the Polish officials, many of whom were closet Bolsheviks. British officials tried to reason with Wilson so he temporarily distanced himself from Clemenceau and then reverted to his position of granting the same consideration to the invaders as the victim. He said, "Since Germany and Poland both claim these people (Silesian Germans), wouldn't it be wise to let them decide for themselves?" Essentially, Poland had no claim at all but Wilson ignored such a concept, no doubt counseled to do so by Colonel Edward House. [1813] Isaiah Bowman, president of the American Geographical Society (1915-1935), also advised Wilson on the reformation of Central Europe, especially Germany in accordance to the Treaty of Versailles.

The Germans were flabbergasted. Their spokesperson, Foreign Minister Count Ulrich von Brockdorff-Rantzau, who remained seated as an insult to the others, pointed out the violations of the 'pre-armistice commitments. German officials prepared a 443-page counter proposal and the German government offered $25 billion dollars and rejected the proposed territorial changes. Philip Kerr (Lord Lothian) wrote the rejection to Germany's counter proposals. Kerr, of Milner's Kindergarten, also helped co-author the treaty. The Allies refused to budge and gave Germany an ultimatum. On June 20, 1919, Georges Clemenceau, David Lloyd George and Woodrow Wilson told the Germans that unless they signed the treaty by the evening of June 23, they would direct Ferdinand Foch, who commanded the Allied forces as of March 1918, to advance on Germany. [1814]

[1812] Fred Blahut, Hidden Historical Fact: The Allied Attempt to Starve Germany in 1919, The Barnes Review, Washington DC, April 1996, pp. 11-14
[1813] Leon Degrelle, Hitler: Born at Versailles, Volume 1, of the Hitler Century, Institute for Historical Review, Torrance, California, 1992, pp. 451-462
[1814] Sigmund Freud and William C. Bullitt, Thomas Woodrow Wilson, twenty-eighth President of the United States: A Psychological Study, Houghton Mifflin, New York, 1967, p. 276

German advisors included Max M. Warburg, Oscar Oppenheimer, and Albrecht Mendelssohn Bartholdy, a great-great-grandson of philosopher Moses Mendelssohn, and grandson of the composer Felix Mendelssohn Bartholdy. [1815] Bartholdy, of the Politics Law Consortium, was part of the German delegation to the League of Nations in Geneva, beginning in 1931. He left Germany in 1933.

Philipp Scheidemann, Germany's Chancellor (February 13-June 20, 1919), rather than sign the document resigned. After Scheidemann's resignation, President Friedrich Ebert formed a new coalition government under Chancellor Gustav Bauer, former chairman of the General Commission of Trade Unions for all of Germany (1908-1918). On June 22, the Reichstag ratified the treaty. On June 28, 1919, in the Hall of Mirrors at Versailles, exactly five years after assassins killed Franz Ferdinand, the delegates, except for the Chinese, signed the Treaty of Versailles. The Chinese refused in protest of the disposition of the prewar German concessions in Shantung.

Political leaders, banker's agents, advisors and lawyers from the victorious nations had arrived and were ensconced in luxurious Paris hotels and enjoying sumptuous meals. They were prepared to spend almost a year to resolve, negotiate, and make decisions. Meanwhile, an entire population, because of a hellish war, was starving in Central Europe. The British maintained the blockade against the Germans until July 12, 1919, eight long months after the armistice. [1816] Count von Brockdorff-Rantzau addressed the Versailles assembly. "The hundreds of thousands of noncombatants who have perished since November 11, 1918, as a result of the blockade, were killed with cold deliberation, after our enemies had been assured of their complete victory." [1817]

[1815] Louis Marschalko, The World Conquerors, the Real War Criminals, Translated from the Hungarian by A. Suranyi, Joseph Sueli Publications, London, 1958, p. 62

[1816] Charles Callan Tansill, Back Door to War, the Roosevelt Foreign Policy, 1933-1941, Henry Regnery Company, Chicago, Illinois, 1952, pp. 22-23

[1817] Fred Blahut, Hidden Historical Fact: The Allied Attempt to Starve Germany in 1919, The Barnes Review, Washington DC, April 1996, pp. 11-14

Jan Smuts, one of Milner's associates, discovered a loophole in Robert Lansing's letter regarding the damages against the civilians. Smuts skewed the issues in Britain's favor and persuaded Wilson to include a pension for the soldiers' widows and orphans in the reparations package. John Maynard Keynes, representing the British Treasury, argued that those additions violated Wilson's Fourteen Points and would increase the reparations by at least two and half times. Still, the Allies expected Germany to remit a preliminary payment by May 1921. These additions totaled almost $40 billion dollars, far beyond their capacity to pay. [1818]

The war planners, those who won the war, made financial demands in the billions of dollars. Prime Minister Lloyd George (He added his uncle's surname to become Lloyd George) suggested $120 billion; Prime Minister Georges Clemenceau wanted $220 billion. Lloyd George delegated the task of calculating the final reparation figures to a panel of experts with a target date of May 1921. [1819] To lighten the suffering of war-weary Europeans, they finally made the reparations demands—the British got the equivalent of $90 billion in addition to a portion of Germany's foreign colonies and their European industries; the French got $200 billion; the United States wanted $25 to $30 billion. However, it was also important that Germany retain sufficient capital to rebuild their economy, which would help diminish destitution throughout war-torn Europe. [1820]

Georges Clemenceau and his assistant, André Tardieu encouraged Polish officials to demand chunks of East Prussia, in addition to Danzig and the corridor. British officials wanted to put this issue to a vote, which irked the Poles and Tardieu, their advocate. The vote would be in the districts of Allenstein and Marienwerder, accompanied by a massive propaganda campaign and overt intimidation. However, the Prussians voted almost unanimously, 98.73 percent, to remain German, a figure rarely mentioned in Allied history books. Next,

---

[1818] Guido Giacomo Preparata, Conjuring Hitler, How Britain and America Made the Third Reich, Pluto Press, London, 2005, pp. 74-76

[1819] Ibid. 74-76

[1820] Christopher Simpson, The Splendid Blond Beast, Money, Law, and Genocide in the Twentieth Century, Common Courage Press, 1995, pp. 43-44

they considered the annexation of Upper Silesia, a rich and highly industrialized province. Its loss would dramatically reduce Germany's power. Greedy Polish politicians had sent in armed groups by February 1919 to grab their legally sanctioned war booty. [1821]

The Allies forced Germany to relinquish a sizeable amount of territory, including vital mineral areas and the Polish Corridor, which would isolate Prussia from the rest of the county. The Allies deprived Germany of its merchant fleet. [1822] She had to terminate all military drafts and reduce her troops to 100,000 for internal peace keeping only. She had to drastically decrease her naval fleet and disband the submarine fleet. She had to destroy all military fortifications and give up the right to have heavy artillery, tanks, submarines, and all aviation. The Allies prohibited Germany's military industry from designing or owning chemical weapons and they had to destroy their stock of poisonous biological warfare weapons. International officials would have to supervise any German arms production. [1823]

The treaties signed during the conference in Paris were 1) the Treaty of Versailles, June 28, 1919 for the disposition of the German Empire; 2) the Treaty of Saint-Germain, September 10, 1919 for the disposition of Austria; 3) the Treaty of Neuilly, November 27, 1919 for the disposition of Bulgaria; 4) the Treaty of Trianon, June 4, 1920 for the disposition of Hungary; 5) the Treaty of Sèvres, August 10, 1920, later revised by the Treaty of Lausanne, July 24, 1923 for the disposition and partition of the Ottoman Empire.

The Allies forced Hungary, a quickly developing country who supported Germany, according to the Treaty of Trianon, to relinquish over two-thirds of its territory. This shifted 3.3 million ethnic Hungarians into Romania and Czechoslovakia. The newly configured Hungary also had to pay war reparations to its neighbors. Ethnic

---

[1821] Leon Degrelle, Hitler: Born at Versailles, Volume 1, of the Hitler Century, Institute for Historical Review, Torrance, California, 1992, pp. 451-462

[1822] John Beaty, The Iron Curtain Over America, Chestnut Mountain Book, Barboursville, Virginia, 1968, pp. 10-11

[1823] Viktor Suvorov, The Chief Culprit, Stalin's Grand Design to Start World War II, Naval Institute Press, Annapolis, Maryland, 2008, p. 7

Hungarians would be living in a foreign land where local residents subjected them to discrimination and difficulty in assimilating. Hungarians and non-Hungarian historians justifiably claim that the real objective of the treaty stipulations was an attempt to dismantle a major power in Central Europe. The Ally's priority was to prevent Germany's resurgence. Therefore, they surrounded Germany's allies, Austria and Hungary, with more powerful, bigger states friendly to the Allies.

The Treaty of St. Germain amputated Austria from all of its industrial areas and natural resources, which were located in the German populated areas of Austrian Silesia and the Sudetenland. Austria was nothing but a skeleton of a state with a decreased population of just seven million. The Allies reduced the multinational Austria-Hungary into numerous pieces lacking the cohesiveness they once enjoyed. This partition spawned the state of Czechoslovakia whose population consisted of Czechs (46%), Slovaks (13%), Poles (2%), Ukrainians (3%), Hungarians (8%), and 3.5 million Germans (28%). [1824]

This unproductive dissection, administered by Archibald C. Coolidge, part of Edward M. House's Inquiry but under the auspices of the American Expert Commission, placed several thousand Germans under Czech domination, and placed German industrial areas from northern Bohemia into Saxony. The Austrians, who had no voice in the matter, contested this arbitrary fracturing. Nearly 1.5 million Germans, now considered minorities, remained in Romania, Yugoslavia, Banar, Syrmia, Czechoslovakia, Batschka, and Slovenia. The provisions of the Treaty of Trianon placed 550,000 Germans into what remained of Hungary. [1825]

Commercially, Germany lost all of her African colonies; the Allies placed them under the League of Nations' jurisdiction. France received Alsace-Lorraine and all the coal resources in the Saar district, 991.8 square miles, on the border between France and Germany, with the League of Nations administering the area. Poland got the key

---

[1824] Alfred Maurice de Zayas, A Terrible Revenge, the Ethnic Cleansing of the East European Germans, Palgrave, Macmillan, New York, 2006, pp. 20-21
[1825] Ibid. 20-21

industrialized area of Upper Silesia, most of Posen Province and West Prussia, which created what people referred to as the Polish Corridor, with access to the sea. This separated East Prussia from the rest of the country.

This would cut Prussia in half and the so-called Polish Corridor and amputate the city of Danzig from Germany. Poland would receive Upper Silesia, one of Germany's richest regions (producing 20% of its coal, 57% of its lead, and 72% of its zinc). They forced Germany to relinquish Posen, another rich German province. Yet, Danzig was almost completely German in composition. Churchill wrote, "German science and capital had created a vigorous industry in this territory. German culture, imposed by the power of an energetic empire, had left its mark everywhere." He later admitted, "The commission first proposed to place Danzig entirely under Polish sovereignty, which would subject Danzigers to Polish laws and mandatory conscription in the Polish army." For centuries, there were few Poles in Danzig. Yet they gifted Poland control of the city's customs, taxes, port facilities and the city's diplomatic representation. This required that any German Danziger traveling from the area had to get a passport or visa from the Polish embassies and consulates, a group of "hateful and arrogant alien bureaucrats." [1826]

When the Danzigers finally voted, just before the Second World War, they chose Germany by a margin of 99%. Wilson had guaranteed Poland "free and secure access to the sea," not "access to the sea," as dozens of biased historians and journalists have reported thus accrediting the creation of the corridor, a piece of land 20 to 70 miles wide, right across Germany. No one would have proposed such an incursion on France but thought nothing of imposing it on Germany. For 20 years, Germans were compelled to travel from one part of Germany to the other part locked in sealed trains where they were humiliated at the two Polish borders while entering and leaving the corridor. [1827]

[1826] Leon Degrelle, Hitler: Born at Versailles, Volume 1, of the Hitler Century, Institute for Historical Review, Torrance, California, 1992, pp. 451-462

[1827] Ibid. 451-462

The British Establishment "helped themselves to the German colonial empire, German assets and her navy." Clemenceau directed that the residents of Upper Silesia cast a vote to determine if they wanted to reunite with Germany. Thereafter, the Allies forced Germany to renounce its claims to Upper Silesia, in favor of Poland, at the new border. German officials, troops and non-residents had to leave the area. An unbiased Allied commission of four members would conduct the vote. The Allies would send troops to occupy the area. The Allies would not allow the German voters access to any campaign information. Of course, the foreign troops would predictably intimidate the voters, actions that favored Poland. However, the troops did not arrive for six months, which allowed a huge influx of armed Polish agents who terrorized the disarmed Germans. On July 10, 1919, the Polish terrorists, probably Bolsheviks, destroyed the three key bridges over the Oder River. They also patrolled the railway stations. Warsaw's politicians, with their agents, controlled the Silesian vote, given the absence of the Allied troops. [1828]

The Allies forced Germany to surrender 67,273 square kilometers, comprising one-eight of its territory, which had a population of 5,138,000 people. The Allies appropriated all merchant ships over a certain size, a quarter of the fishing fleet and a fifth of the river fleet and half of all German paints and non-military chemicals as well as their production of those items for the next five years. Over the next five years, Germany had to construct merchant ships for the allies. Further, she was to supply 140 million tons of coal to France, eighty million tons to Belgium and seventy-seven million to Italy. The allies gained the right to use all German railways, ports, waterways for a very small remuneration, all in addition to huge reparations. They designed these unrealistic and inequitable provisions, not to promote peace but to instill resentment, to set the stage for more warfare. [1829]

The Allies seized Germany's merchant navy and unethically confiscated private property from many countries throughout the

---

[1828] Ibid. 451-462
[1829] Viktor Suvorov, The Chief Culprit, Stalin's Grand Design to Start World War II, Naval Institute Press, Annapolis, Maryland, 2008, p. 7

world that belonged to German citizens. The amoral Allied powers usurped the right, by virtue of the treaty, to retain or dispose of privately held companies or other assets. This occurred without any compensation to the victims of this wholesale plunder. Furthermore, the Allies held German citizens responsible for the liabilities or indebtedness on those confiscated items. Additionally, the Allies and their lawyers stipulated that Germany could not make capital investments in other countries and had to relinquish the title of any possessions in neighboring countries. The lawyers designed the agreement to force Germany to allow the Allies full access to all of their markets without paying a tariff. Conversely, Germany had to pay an outrageously high tariff for foreign goods. [1830]

Germans, already starving, were required to surrender their remaining livestock—they had to deliver their cattle, sheep, goats, pigs and even their dairy cows to France and Belgium. They left the starving children, the most vulnerable victims in any war, without milk to drink. The confiscation of Germany's coal resources caused the deaths of German children who were not only starving but would now freeze to death without a source of heat. [1831]

The Treaty of Versailles was a deliberate "instrument of continuing aggression." Francisco Nitti, Italy's Prime Minister wrote, "It will remain forever a terrible precedent in modern history that, against all pledges, all precedents and all traditions, the representatives of Germany were never even heard, nothing was left to them but to sign a treaty at a moment when famine and exhaustion and threat of revolution made it impossible not to sign." [1832]

On October 15, 1920, Vladimir Lenin declared, "The order held by the Versailles Peace Treaty lies over a volcano, since the seventy percent of the world's people who are enslaved are anxiously awaiting

---

[1830] Fred Blahut, Hidden Historical Fact: The Allied Attempt to Starve Germany in 1919, The Barnes Review, Washington DC, April 1996, pp. 11-14

[1831] Ibid. 11-14

[1832] Stephen A. Zarlenga, The Lost Science of Money: The Mythology of Money, The Story of Power, American Monetary Institute, Valatie, New York, 2002, pp. 577-578

someone to come and start a struggle for their liberation, and to rock the foundation of their countries." [1833] He said, "The war is waged by slave traders haggling over cattle." In fact, the Allies were wrangling over the Rhineland, Tyrol, Sudetenland, Prussia, Carpathia, Dalmatia, Smyrna, Armenia, Mosul, Baghdad and Jerusalem. [1834] He surmised that the turmoil caused by the Allied remapping of the world would open the door to Communism. [1835]

German Reparations and Recovery

General Charles C. Dawes, a corrupt Illinois politician and banker, with J. P. Morgan guidance, set up the Inter-Allied Reparations Commission, and devised the Dawes Plan to collect war reparations from Germany. The commission was to submit its report on how much Germany owed by May 1, 1921. [1836] Members of the Reparations Commission included Herbert Hoover, General Tasker H. Bliss, W. S. Benson, Bernard Baruch, Henry M. Robinson, Thomas W. Lamont, Whitney H. Shepardson, Norman H. Davis, Edward M. House, Gordon Auchincloss, and Vance C. McCormick.

By January 1921, as calculated by the Inter-Allied Reparations Commission, Germany owed 269 billion gold marks, which amounted to about £23.6 billion or about $32 billion (equivalent to about $393.6 billion in today's market). The commission adopted the Young Plan in 1929 to replace the failed Dawes Plan. In the late 1920s, Wall Street bankers, with Washington's blessings, exercised their new financial powers by extending loans to restructure German finances, fund the reparations debt, and stabilize the struggling European economy. Germany had been a pillar of economic and technological strength in Europe. The war and the resulting indignations and restrictions weakened all of Europe. *Time* magazine made Owen D. Young, the

---

[1833] Viktor Suvorov, The Chief Culprit, Stalin's Grand Design to Start World War II, Naval Institute Press, Annapolis, Maryland, 2008, p. 8

[1834] Leon Degrelle, Hitler: Born at Versailles, Volume 1, of the Hitler Century, Institute for Historical Review, Torrance, California, 1992, p. 298

[1835] Ibid. 298

[1836] Marshall Dill, Germany: a Modern History, University of Michigan Press, Ann Arbor, Michigan, 1961, p. 273

president of General Electric, the Man of the Year, appearing on the cover on January 6, 1930.

The Allies, according to the Versailles Treaty, specifically the "war-guilt clause" (Article 231 of the treaty), set up a schedule of reparations for Germany covering the years, 1919-1932 which one may subdivide into six periods.

1. The preliminary payments, 1919-1921
2. The London Schedule, May 1921-September 1924
3. The Dawes Plan, September 1924-January 1930
4. The Young Plan, January 1930-June 1931
5. The Hoover Moratorium, June 193 1-July 1932
6. The Lausanne Convention, July 1932 [1837]

By May 1921, Germany was to pay 20,000 million marks. The Allies, Britain, France, America and Italy contended that German had only paid 8,000 million marks of the required preliminary payments. They threatened to occupy the Ruhr in order to enforce payment. In May, dismissing the previous threat, the Allies presented Germany with a 132,000 million marks bill. To avoid another ultimatum, Germany capitulated and gave them bonds for the new amount. The Allies forgave 82 million but required Germany to pay the other 50 million in yearly installments plus interest. [1838]

Given its economic circumstances, Germany was hard-pressed to pay reparations. The international bankers refused payment in the form of German goods and services. Therefore, Germany was unable to fulfill the reparation schedule. British bankers viewed this as evidence of Germany's inability while French bankers regarded this as Germany's unwillingness to pay. The Anglo-Americans rejected Germany's offer to pay in goods to compensate for money Germany could not pay. In 1921, Britain imposed a 26% tax on all German

---

[1837] Carroll Quigley, Tragedy And Hope, A History of the World in our Time, The Macmillan Company, New York, 1966, pp. 305-306
[1838] Ibid. 305-306

imports. They could have paid the required reparations if the bankers had agreed to accept goods and services. [1839]

On May 26, 1922, per the Allies suggestion, German officials released the Reichsbank from government regulation. The absence of regulation led to horrific hyperinflation (1922-1923). [1840] The bank maintained the excessive monetary demands by printing paper currency to meet the government expenditures. [1841] On November 22, 1922, Friedrich Ebert, via a presidential decree, appointed Wilhelm Cuno, former head of Hamburg-Amerika Line (1917-1922), as Chancellor of Germany. Cuno printed excessive amounts of money which led to heavy inflation. Germany's central bank traded this currency for foreign currency to satisfy the reparations payments. Sometimes, officials derive reparations payments from taxation or an alteration of living standards. The circumstances in Germany prevented any considerations of that type.

Bankers deceptively used this example of hyperinflation to persuade people not to trust governments to print money; rather private bankers should manage the task. [1842] The League of Nations then delegated "experts" to monitor Germany's economic recovery. These experts wanted Germany's central bank to adopt free market policies. [1843] Germany's currency predictably lost its value, causing immense suffering especially in urban and industrial areas. Berlin was especially hard hit—people were scavenging the trashcans behind the hotels looking for something to eat. A cup of coffee cost one million marks one day only to rise to a million and a half the next day. [1844]

[1839] Ibid. 306-307
[1840] Stephen A. Zarlenga, The Lost Science of Money: The Mythology of Money, The Story of Power, American Monetary Institute, Valatie, New York, 2002, p. 580
[1841] Stephen Zarlenga, Germany's 1923 Hyperinflation: A "Private" Affair, The Barnes Review, July-Aug. 1999, pp. 61-67
[1842] Stephen A. Zarlenga, The Lost Science of Money: The Mythology of Money, The Story of Power, American Monetary Institute, Valatie, New York, 2002, pp. 575-576
[1843] Ibid. 579
[1844] John Beaty, The Iron Curtain Over America, Chestnut Mountain Book, Barboursville, Virginia, 1968, pp. 11-12

On January 9, 1923, the Reparations Commission declared that Germany had defaulted on her payments. Consequently, France, Belgium, and Italy immediately occupied the Ruhr with 70,000 soldiers, supposedly to protect engineers seizing telegraph poles and timber, but really to secure "the economic edge that France and Belgium had failed to secure under the Versailles Treaty." Cuno instituted a "campaign of passive resistance among the Ruhr's inhabitants." Although the British had threatened the occupation of the Ruhr in 1921, [1845] the residents did not organize or accumulate essentials for the possibility of such an occupation.

Germany stopped all reparations payments and supported those who had gone on strike in the Ruhr. The government also printed more currency. The Ruhr, 60 miles long and 30 miles wide, had 10 percent of Germany's population and generated 80 percent of Germany's coal, iron, and steel. The occupation forces seized the Ruhr's complex railway system. Armed conflict erupted and soldiers killed at least 400 people and wounded over 2,100 people. [1846]

Because of their "passive resistance," French authorities expelled or detained 46,200 uncooperative civil servants, railroad workers, and police, along with 100,000 members of their families. The residents responded by committing acts of sabotage and "low-level acts of terrorism." The occupying forces countered these actions by taking hostages, massive fines, hostile house searches, identity examinations and executions. [1847] Walther Kadow, a communist, betrayed Albert L. Schlageter, who blew up a rail line near Düsseldorf. [1848] On May 26, 1923, after a quick trial, French authorities executed Schlageter. Rudolf Höss and Martin Bormann then assassinated Kadow for which the authorities imprisoned them.

[1845] Carroll Quigley, Tragedy And Hope, A History of the World in our Time, The Macmillan Company, New York, 1966, pp. 307-312

[1846] Ibid. 307-312

[1847] Michael Burleigh, The Third Reich: a New History, Hill and Wang, New York, 2000, pp. 54-55

[1848] Ruth Fischer and John C. Leggett, Stalin and German Communism: A Study in the Origins of the State Party, Transaction Publishers, New Jersey, 2006, pp. 259, 270-272

Karl Radek attempted to exploit the situation in the Ruhr, especially to the German communists, and claimed that the strike was part of the revolt against German capitalism. Radek and other communists, like Clara Zetkin, feared that the general destruction in Europe would cause a "regrouping of forces into a united front against Russia." He felt it was necessary to cooperate with the German nationalists to protect Soviet Russia. Zetkin and Radek feared fascism. Radek decided to make Schlageter a nationalist hero and depicted him as "a courageous soldier of the counter revolution." [1849] It is possible that the Bolsheviks were hoping for a fascist overthrow of the Weimar Republic, and then they would take over. Radek, in a speech on June 20, 1923, in Moscow, adopted the national hero and lavished praise on Schlageter. The communist press accorded wide publicity to Radek's speech, designed to "appeal to disgruntled Germans who had been flocking to Hitler's NSDAP. The communists even used some of the same phrases, like "Down with the government of national shame and betrayal of the people." Ruth Fischer, a half Jewish leftist, exhorted communists to "trample the Jewish capitalists down, hang them from the lampposts." [1850]

The German government continued, year after year, to maintain an unbalanced budget. To pay their deficit, they borrowed from the Reichsbank, which continued to cause severe inflation, ruinous to the middle class but it barely touched the wealthy living in Germany. This situation predictably encouraged middle class dissent while it benefited people who owned actual wealth in the form of property. Inflation hiked up property and land values, which allowed certain people to eliminate their debts. The German mark collapsed in value from 305 to the pound in August 1921 to 1,020 in November 1921. It dropped to 80,000 by January 1923, to 20 million by August 1923, and to 20 billion by December 1923. [1851] The hyperinflation peaked

---

[1849] Ibid. 259, 270-272

[1850] Sean McMeekin, The Red Millionaire: a Political Biography of Willi Münzenberg, Moscow's Secret Propaganda Tsar in the West, Yale University Press, New Haven, Connecticut, 2003, pp. 146-147

[1851] Carroll Quigley, Tragedy And Hope, A History of the World in our Time, The Macmillan Company, New York, 1966, pp. 306-307

during the summer of 1923. A wave of strikes began in August 1923 and Cuno and his cabinet resigned on August 12, 1923.

In 1923, the League of Nations asked Charles G. Dawes, owner of Chicago's Central Republic Bank and Trust to lead a committee to address Germany's financial condition. He, along with Austen Chamberlain, received the 1925 Nobel Peace Prize. In 1932, his bank would fail, costing the US taxpayers $90 million. [1852] In April 1924, his committee followed some of John Foster Dulles' suggestions. Dulles, a lawyer with Sullivan and Cromwell, was a member of the Reparations Commission. The Inter-Allied Reparations Committee sent Dawes and Young to Europe with Dulles as their special counsel. J. P. Morgan bank initiated the entire process with a $200 million private loan. The Dawes Plan relied on private loans, not government aid. While it was ostensibly a government program, it allowed private bankers to make a financial killing in Europe. Sullivan and Cromwell, who later represented Hamburg-Amerika Line, also handled a bond for the Krupp steel company, issued through J. & W. Seligman & Company. Dulles, knowing the State Department would not interfere with his transactions, made considerable money for himself and his firm which dominated a major portion of the private loans and investments in Germany. [1853]

The Dawes Plan called for long-term, high interest loans, and a restructuring of the Reichsbank including revenue sharing, followed up, in 1924, by loans from foreign banks, based on their confidence in Hjalmar Schacht. In December 1923, he had become the bank president after a meeting with Montagu Norman, president of the Rothschild's Bank of England. Schacht initially opposed the loans but acquiesced only if they used the money to fund production, not luxury or consumption. Between 1924 and 1929, Germany established

---

[1852] Stephen A. Zarlenga, The Lost Science of Money: The Mythology of Money, The Story of Power, American Monetary Institute, Valatie, New York, 2002, p. 589

[1853] Nancy Lisagor and Frank Lipsius, A Law Unto Itself, the Untold Story of the Law Firm Sullivan & Cromwell, 100 Years of Creating Power & Wealth, William Morrow and Company, Inc., New York, 1988, pp. 90-92

a factory system. [1854] Schacht's father, a naturalized US citizen and newspaper editor, and a friend of Horace Greeley, ultimately returned to Germany. [1855]

The foreign troops in the Ruhr forced Germany to accept the Dawes Plan for reparations; then the troops left the Ruhr. Dawes, Vice President under President Calvin Coolidge (1925-1929), directed a committee of financial experts under the jurisdiction of the international bankers, to devise the plan under which Germany owed more in 1929 than before. It artificially protected the German mark in the international market. It encouraged Germany to over borrow and spend without experiencing immediate consequences, which would have occurred with a system of accurate international exchange. Germany was unable to repay the loans. US bankers loaned money to German industrialists for their recovery. The bankers also insisted that Germans build unnecessary and nonproductive equipment. [1856]

Adolf Hitler and others were certain that Germany was rushing headlong into severe inflation because of the collaboration of the black-red coalition. [1857] Hitler opposed the Dawes Pact, a devious method for the bankers to plunder all of Germany's resources. The Young Plan, with the objective of enslaving Germany, facilitated it. Hitler, while incarcerated in 1924, attempted to have his associates oppose the Dawes Pact and the Centre Party who claimed that the foreign loans associated with the plan would increase Germany's prosperity, create jobs, raise wages and benefit agriculture. He claimed that the Dawes Pact would do nothing but increase poverty. [1858] International bankers have always worked with local complicit politicians to enslave nations with excessive, usury-heavy loans.

[1854] Stephen A. Zarlenga, The Lost Science of Money: The Mythology of Money, The Story of Power, American Monetary Institute, Valatie, New York, 2002, p. 589

[1855] Ibid. 587

[1856] Carroll Quigley, Tragedy And Hope, A History of the World in our Time, The Macmillan Company, New York, 1966, pp. 307-312

[1857] Gottfried Feder, The Programme of the N.S.D.A.P., Translated by E. T. S. Dugdale, Frz. Eher Nachf, Munich, Germany, 1932, pp. 4-5

[1858] Ibid. 6-7

When this occurs, the bankers control the national resources and soon, a once resource-rich country is a dependent third world nation, relying on other countries for manufactured goods, food, and fuel.

John Perkins, in *Confessions of an Economic Hit Man*, explains that highly paid professionals, lawyers like Dulles, cheat countries out of trillions of dollars by loaning them money through government programs but it actually goes into the "coffers of huge corporations and the pockets of a few wealthy families who control the planet's natural resources." These agents use "fraudulent financial reports, rigged elections, payoffs, extortion, sex, and murder." It is a "game as old as empire, but one that has taken on new and terrifying dimensions during this time of globalization." [1859]

Owen D. Young chaired the committee that conceived, between February and June 1929, the Young Plan that mandated German reparations over a period of fifty-nine years, until 1988. Hjalmar Schacht, Emile Francqui, John Foster Dulles, later referred to as the "most dangerous man in America" established the Bank for International Settlements (BIS), chartered on January 20, 1930. The officials who designed the Hague Treaty created it to receive German reparations payments. Germany would pay these funds to the BIS in Basel, owned by the world's central banks. It functioned as a "Central Bankers' Bank" which shifted payments among national accounts. The 1929 crash ended the Dawes Plan and created an environment for another world war. By 1931, US banks terminated their loans to Germany whose gold reserve they had greatly reduced. [1860] The BIS gradually assumed control of coordinating banking and economic policy across the world.

Germany paid their war debts but did not balance their budget or pursue a trade balance. Two things would be sure to occur with this easy money, 1) when the US bankers stopped lending, Germany would collapse and, 2) they transferred debts from account to account

[1859] John Perkins, Confessions of an Economic Hit Man, Berrett-Koehler Publishers, Inc., San Francisco, California, 2004, p. ix
[1860] Carroll Quigley, Tragedy And Hope, A History of the World in our Time, The Macmillan Company, New York, 1966, pp. 307-312

without building real solvency. Germany borrowed 18.6 billion marks while paying 10.5 billion marks in reparations (1924-1931). The international bankers were the only benefactors, with their numerous commissions and fees. In January 1930, the equally nefarious Young Plan replaced the Dawes Plan because Germany's payments under that plan did not satisfy the London Schedule. This change also voided the German foreign-exchange rate, which forced Germany to experience the results of her extravagant borrowing. In addition, France demanded payment for their war reconstruction. [1861]

On September 16, 1930, President Hoover appointed Eugene I. Meyer as the Governor of the Federal Reserve Board (1930-1933). Meyer was part of his financial policy-making triumvirate. The other two members were Treasury under Secretary Ogden L. Mills and George L. Harrison, the New York Federal Reserve Bank Governor. [1862]

In April 1931, Germany and Austria united their customs while remaining separate countries, a move opposed by the French. On May 11, 1931, Rothschild's Austrian bank, the Creditanstalt that controlled 70 percent of Austria's Industry, declared its insolvency. The Rothschilds and the Austrian government bailed out the bank. However, there was still a run on the bank. To accommodate this run, Austrian banks pulled all their funds from the German banks, which then began to fail. The German banks called for their funds in London, which began to fail. Europe's gold disappeared. On September 21, 1931, Churchill removed England from the gold standard. The Reichsbank lost a huge percentage of their gold reserve, which almost destroyed German industry. [1863]

F. William Engdahl refers to Attorney George L. Harrison (S&B, CFR) as a "Germano-phobe." As president of the Federal Reserve Bank, he worked with the Bank of England's Montagu Norman and Reichsbank President Hjalmar Schacht to collapse and bankrupt the

---

[1861] Ibid. 307-312
[1862] James L. Butkiewicz, Governor Eugene Meyer and the Great Contraction, Research in Economic History, Volume 26, 2008, p. 275
[1863] Carroll Quigley, Tragedy And Hope, A History of the World in our Time, The Macmillan Company, New York, 1966, pp. 307-312

Vienna-based Creditanstalt, a Rothschild bank. It had connections to the French bankers, which in turn led to "the flight of capital out of Germany" and the ultimate failure of the Danat-Bank of Germany, the second largest bank of Germany, chaired by Jakob Goldschmidt. [1864] That was obviously the objective; the Rothschilds ultimately benefitted.

Germany wanted the United States to relieve them of their obligatory war debts. The United States falsely claimed that if Germany could buy armaments, they could pay their war debts. Treasury Secretary Andrew Mellon, then in Europe, told Hoover that Germany would collapse without some sort of relief. Hoover would give Germany a one-year moratorium but they would have to renounce their customs union with Austria, stop building a second battleship, and restrict their military organization.

On July 7, 1931, German citizens tried to pull their funds from the Reichsbank. German industry and the four largest banks suffered losses. By November 1931, the European Powers, except France, were willing to end reparations via the Lausanne Conference of June 1932. Germany was then responsible to pay three billion marks. The US Congress refused to cut the debt so the Germans never ratified the Lausanne agreement so the Young Plan was still legally in force. [1865]

However, in 1933, Hitler renounced all reparations. The Germans had already paid about 10.5 billion marks under the Dawes Plan (1924-1931). Before 1924, they had paid 56,577 billion marks. The Allies claimed that Germany had only paid 10,426 billion. In truth, Germany probably paid, before 1924, about 40 billion marks. [1866] Though reparation ended in 1933, the Allies reinstated them after World War II.

[1864] William Engdahl, A Century of War, Anglo-American Oil Politics and the New World Order, Pluto Press, Ann Arbor, Michigan, 2004, pp. 92-93
[1865] Carroll Quigley, Tragedy And Hope, A History of the World in our Time, The Macmillan Company, New York, 1966, pp. 307-312
[1866] Ibid. 307-312

Zionism and the American War Congress

In addition to Britain, France and Italy, other countries, including Serbia, supported a Zionist homeland. Italy's Ambassador to Britain worked in London with Nahum Sokolow, the representative of the Zionist International Political Committee. Jacobus Kann, President of the Dutch Zionist Federation persuaded officials in Holland to support the British. In Greece, the Zionists worked for the support of the Minister for Foreign Affairs. Officials in Siam supported the Zionists, as announced by Elly S. Kadoorie, one of the leading bankers of China and President of the Shanghai Zionist Association China. Officials in Japan, through their Ambassador to Britain, announced that they would support the establishment of a Jewish Homeland in Palestine. [1867]

Decades before in China, David Sassoon and Sons hired Baghdad-born Elly S. Kadoorie (1867-1944) who arrived in Shanghai via Bombay in 1880. He left the Sassoon firm to begin his own business, E.S. Kadoorie and Company, doing business in Hong Kong and Shanghai, amassing a vast fortune in merchant banking, real estate, hotels, utilities, and rubber. His brother Sir Ellis Kadoorie (1865-1922) of Hong Kong, was the director of the Hong Kong Hotel Company, and established several nondenominational schools in Hong Kong, Guangzhou, and Shanghai to teach Chinese students English so they could work in foreign companies in Asia. Elly and Ellis Kadoorie both contributed to Jewish and non-Jewish institutions, including hospitals all over the world. [1868]

In 1897, after the first World Zionist Congress in Basel, the Jews of Shanghai holding British citizenship, numbering several hundred people, mostly from Baghdad, supported Britain's views on Zionism and the Zionist movement. Elly S. Kadoorie generously supported

---

[1867] Reuben Fink (compiler), The American War Congress and Zionism, Statements by Members of the American War Congress on the Jewish National Movement, Zionist Organization of America, New York, February 1919, pp. 7-8

[1868] Jonathan Goldstein (editor), The Jews of China, Volume: 1, M. E. Sharpe, Armonk, New York, 1999, pp. 149, 177-178

the movement. Nissim E. Benjamin Ezra, from India, launched the Shanghai Zionist Association (SZA) in 1903, one of the three earliest Zionist organizations in Asia; the others were in Iraq and Turkey. [1869] The Kadoories were dedicated Zionists by the early twentieth century. Officials in Hong Kong appointed several Jews to government positions such as Sir Matthew Nathan, governor of Hong Kong (1904-1907). One may discover distinctly Jewish names on the list of *Past Masters of an English Masonic Lodge* in Hong Kong. [1870]

Paul S. Reinsch, the US ambassador to China (1913-1919), failed to immediately arbitrate between the Zionists and China's government. Judge Charles S. Lobingier, of the US District Court in China, was a high ranking freemason who initiated several Chinese men into the craft. [1871] He was the Preceptor, an expert in the ritual of the order, who also initiated many individuals into freemasonry in the Philippines, [1872] where he served as a judge for ten years before Wilson appointed him to China in 1914. [1873] Lobingier wrote *The Supreme Council, 33° Mother Council of the World Ancient and Accepted Scottish Rite of Freemasonry Southern Jurisdiction*. Lobingier, with his many connections, suggested that someone in one of the American Zionist organizations approach the State Department to facilitate the presentation of the letter from the Shanghai Zionist Association to the Chinese foreign minister asking for support for a Jewish homeland in Palestine. Reinsch then met with Chen Lu, China's deputy minister of foreign affairs. [1874]

[1869] Ibid. 251-252

[1870] Ibid. 149, 177-178

[1871] Bro. Charles S. Lobingier, Shanghai, China, http://masonic.wikidot.com/builder-1915-vol-1-no-12-december#toc27 as of May 2012

[1872] Albert G. Mackey, Encyclopedia of Freemasonry, Part 2, Kessinger Publishing, Whitefish, Montana, 2003, p. 772

[1873] Sustains Shanghai Judge, President Warren G. Harding, a freemason, dismisses charges filed against Lobingier, The New York Times, June 24, 1922, ; The Times: http://query.nytimes.com/gst/abstract.html?res=F10F13 FC3B5D14738DDDAD0A94DE405B828EF1D3 as of May 2012

[1874] Jonathan Goldstein (editor), The Jews of China, Volume: 1, M. E. Sharpe, Armonk, New York, 1999, pp. 255-256

On June 11, 1918, the Zionist Organization of America (ZOA), founded in 1897, to support the Jewish National Home in Palestine, sent a letter to each member of what they described as the "War-Congress" in order to assess their individual attitudes about the Zionist movement. They included a copy of the letter from British officials to Arthur J. Balfour, the Secretary of State for Foreign Affairs. It stated that French (February 11, 1918), and Italian officials (February 23, 1918), had both formally endorsed the British Declaration. This campaign, with endorsements from other countries, is a form of Sigmund Freud's crowd behavior theory. People who act as a group, like Congress or a jury, tend to blend their behavior to reach a consensus as opposed to most independent thinkers who base their conclusions on objectivity, moral principles and pertinent data. In herd mentality, each person's enthusiasm increases based on the group's subtle energy and the leadership's persuasiveness. The letters to members of Congress, undoubtedly discussed with others by leading congressional figures, requested five things.

1. Do you approve the official Declaration of England, France and Italy on the Zionist question?
2. Would you please let us have your reasons for favoring the Declaration? (If you do not favor it, please give us your reasons.)
3. Do you favor action by the United States Government in line with the British Declaration, now or within the near future?
4. Do you favor the adoption of an appropriate resolution by Congress in favor of the establishment in Palestine of a Jewish National Centre?
5. What are your views in general with regard to the effort of the Jewish people to establish a national home in Palestine? [1875]

The US government had not yet declared their position on a Jewish homeland in Palestine. A few months after the ZOA had sent its letters to Congress, President Woodrow Wilson wrote to Rabbi Stephen S.

[1875] Reuben Fink (compiler), The American War Congress and Zionism, Statements by Members of the American War Congress on the Jewish National Movement, Zionist Organization of America, New York, February 1919, pp. 4-5

Wise, Chairman of the Provisional Executive Committee for General Zionist Affairs, New York, on August 31, 1918:

"My Dear Rabbi Wise,

I have watched with deep and sincere interest the reconstructive work which the Weizmann Commission has done in Palestine at the instance of the British Government, and I welcome an opportunity to express the satisfaction I have felt in the progress of the Zionist movement in the United States and in the Allied countries since the declaration by Mr. Balfour on behalf of the British Government, of Great Britain's approval of the establishment in Palestine of a national home for the Jewish people, and his promise that the British Government would use its best endeavors to facilitate the achievement of that object, with the understanding that nothing would be done to prejudice the civil and religious rights of non-Jewish people in Palestine or the rights and political status enjoyed by Jews in other countries. I think that all Americans will be deeply moved by the report that even in this time of stress the Weizmann Commission has been able to lay the foundation of the Hebrew University at Jerusalem, with the promise that that bears of spiritual rebirth." [1876]

Regarding the letters that the ZOA sent to Congress, sixty-one senators favorably responded while 239 representatives favorably responded for a total of 300 members of Congress who supported a Zionist state in Palestine. Similarly, nearly 300 members of Congress signed a similar declaration in March 2010, addressed to Secretary of State Hillary Clinton, reaffirming their commitment to "the unbreakable bond" that exists between the United States and the Israeli State. [1877] The United States Senate and House of Representatives, for almost a century, have promoted, represented, and acted in behalf of the best interests, financially and politically, of an ethnic/religious/cultural

---

[1876] Ibid. 7-8

[1877] Nearly 300 Congress members declare commitment to 'unbreakable' US-Israel bond, Letter to Clinton underscores Biden remarks that there is 'no space' when it comes to Israel's security by Natasha Mozgovaya, http://www.haaretz.com/news/nearly-300-congress-members-declare-commitment-to-unbreakable-u-s-israel-bond-1.266652 as of May 2012

minority, comprising about two percent of the population, a group whose loyalties are to a country in another part of the world.

The King and Crane Commission

On July 4, 1918, President Woodrow Wilson provided the following direction regarding the dismantlement of the Ottoman Empire and Jewish immigration. "The settlement of every question, whether of territory, of sovereignty, of economic arrangement, or of political relationship upon the basis of the free acceptance of that settlement by the people immediately concerned and not upon the basis of the material interest or advantage of any other nation or people which may desire a different settlement for the sake of its own exterior influence or mastery." Further he said, "To subject a people so minded to unlimited Jewish immigration, and to steady financial and social pressure to surrender the land, would be a gross violation of the principle just quoted, and of the people's rights, though it kept within the forms of law" [1878]

The US government initially proposed a commission to determine if the region was capable or ready for self-government and to decide which of the victorious nations the local residents would accept as mandatory powers. France and Britain had already made plans for the area so they opted out of an investigatory commission. The United States solitarily sponsored the commission with the questionable assistance of the British army (for protection) and its translators. The commission concluded that the locals preferred independence but would accept America as a colonial power rather than the British or French.

On October 30, 1918, the Ottoman Empire and the Allies signed the Armistice of Mudros, ending hostilities in the Middle Eastern theater at the end of World War I. The Allies prolonged the war, destroyed the area's peace, allowed and promoted the relocation of unwelcome people. In February 1919, a month after the Peace Conference, the

---

[1878] Henry C. King and Charles R. Crane, 1919: The King-Crane Commission Report by, August 28, 1919, http://www.atour.com/government/un/20040205g. html as of May 2012

British and French signed a treaty which targeted Constantinople, and Mosul and its oil. [1879]

After World War I, the victors executed numerous secret treaties, where they divvied up existing countries, and combined peoples into unsustainable nations. In September 1919, Wilson appointed Dr. Henry C. King, the president of Oberlin College and Charles R. Crane, a Chicago executive and a former secretary of the original Committee on Armenian Atrocities, to head the American Section of the Peace Conference Inter-Allied Commission on Mandates, of which Colonel House was a member. King and Crane, after considerable travel, discussion with the local residents and evaluation of the cultural conditions drafted the comprehensive King-Crane Report. Afterwards, the government suppressed it as it emphatically condemned the idea that the Jews should have a homeland in Palestine. Zionists later succeeded in discrediting King and Crane as Nazi sympathizers. [1880]

Before they left on their official investigation, pro-Zionists attempted to persuade the members of the commission in their favor. King, Crane, and the commission spent forty-two days interviewing cultural, religious and political leaders in Syria, Lebanon, Palestine, Mesopotamia (Iraq) and Asia Minor. They gathered opinions and attitudes regarding territorial limits, independence, form of government, choice of mandate and Zionism. The Muslim population in Syria supported an American mandate, if their country needed help, but rejected the idea of a British mandate. Regarding Zionism, Syrian leaders adamantly opposed the partitioning of Palestine from the remainder of Syria. These leaders recognized that the Zionists intended to dispossess the indigenous population, and create a Jewish state in the future. [1881]

[1879] Turkey-World Center of News Interest, Originally printed in Editor & Publisher, V.55, No. 27, 2nd Section, December 2, 1922, http://www.codoh.com/incon/inconkcintro.html as of May 2012

[1880] Untold Story of the King-Crane Commission by Tammy Obeidallah, http://www.palestinechronicle.com/view_article_details.php?id=15355 as of May 2012

[1881] Ibid

Based on what King and Crane heard and observed, they wrote, "No British officer, consulted by the Commissioners, believed that the Zionist Program could be carried out except by force of arms. The officers generally thought that a force of not less than 50,000 soldiers would be required even to initiate the program . . . Decisions requiring armies to carry out, are sometimes necessary. But they are surely not gratuitously to be taken in the interest of a serious injustice." With regard to the holy places in Palestine, they said, "The places which are most sacred to Christians—those having to do with Jesus—and which are also sacred to Moslems, are not only not sacred to Jews, but abhorrent to them." They really thought it inappropriate to place these sites in the hands of a "Jewish authority." [1882]

In order to understand the ethnic distribution in the three Ottoman Empire districts under consideration, the Commission compiled the estimated population numbers in those districts as follows: Muslims-2,365 000; Christians-587,560; Druses-280,000; Jews-110,000; and others-45,000 totaling 3,387,560 altogether. The Commission devised petitions so that the residents could convey their wishes regarding the Zionist Program. There were eleven petitions, all from Jewish delegations, favoring the Zionist Program comprising a Jewish State and increased immigration. Eight petitions expressed approval of a partial Zionist Program with a few colonies in Palestine. Another 1,350 petitions opposed it. In percentages, those residents favoring a complete Zionist Program were 0.59 percent, those residents favoring a modified Zionist Program 0.4 percent and those residents who opposed the Zionist Program 72.3 percent. The Muslims and the Christians living in Palestine accounted for 85.3 percent of those who protested the Zionist Program. [1883]

The opposition wrote, "We oppose the pretentions of the Zionists to create a Jewish commonwealth in the southern part of Syria, known as Palestine, and oppose Zionist migration to any part of our country; for we do not acknowledge their title, but consider them a grave peril

---

[1882] Henry C. King and Charles R. Crane, 1919: The King-Crane Commission Report, August 28, 1919, http://www.atour.com/government/un/20040205g. html as of May 2012

[1883] Ibid.

to our people from the national, economical, and political points of view. Our Jewish compatriots shall enjoy our common rights and assume the common responsibilities. On the other hand, the practical obstacles to the unity of Syria are: The apparent unwillingness of either the British or the French to withdraw from Syria-the British from Palestine, or the French from Beirut and the Lebanon; the intense opposition of the Arabs and the Christians to the Zionist Program." [1884]

The King/Crane Commission were initially predisposed in favor of the Zionist Program for Palestine, including unlimited Jewish immigration and the ultimate formalization of a Jewish State. However, after it began gathering the facts, they recognized the adamant opposition and recommended serious modification. The Syrians had accepted the Ally's lofty principles. The Zionist Commission had supplied the Commission with an abundance of literature advocating its program. King and Crane acknowledged that Arthur J. Balfour and others approved of and even encouraged the Zionists. However, the Balfour Declaration calls for "the establishment in Palestine of a national home for the Jewish people." The program, given the non-Jewish communities in Palestine, "must be greatly modified." [1885]

The Commission report stated, "A national home for the Jewish people" is not equivalent to making Palestine into a Jewish State. The erection of such a Jewish State would create the "gravest trespass upon the civil and religious rights of existing non-Jewish communities in Palestine." During their interaction with Jewish representatives, commission members perceived that the Zionists anticipated the "complete dispossession of the present non-Jewish inhabitants of Palestine, by various forms of purchase." The people in Palestine were not the only inhabitants who opposed the Zionist Program. People throughout Syria expressed disapproval, as shown in the petitions previously mentioned. The General Syrian Congress, in the seventh, eighth and tenth resolutions of their formal statement, was against the Zionist Program. [1886]

[1884] Ibid
[1885] Ibid
[1886] Ibid

According to the Commissioners, the Peace Conference participants apparently ignored the intense anti-Zionist feelings in Palestine and Syria. They consulted some British officers who expressed their expert opinions that the Zionists could not accomplish their program without military force. The officers thought it would take at least 50,000 soldiers to instigate the program. Evidently, the Zionist Program, given it would require force, did not consider the injustice of it or the feelings of the non-Jewish populations. The Zionist representatives claimed that they had a "right" to Palestine based on an occupation of 2,000 years ago. The Commissioners could hardly take such a claim seriously. [1887]

Further, the Commissioners considered that if Palestine were to become an exclusive Jewish state, the Jews would have jurisdiction over the Holy Land, a significant place for Jews, Christians, and Muslims. Millions of Christians and Muslims might question whether the Jews would be appropriate guardians of the Holy Land. For Christians, the most sacred places in Palestine are associated with Jesus. These places are also important to Muslims. According to the Talmud, Jews find Jesus and his mother abominable. Therefore, Muslims and Christians would tend to feel dissatisfied having these special places under Jewish custody rather than in the custody of the people who value them most. The anti-Zionist feelings in Palestine, the Holy Land, and Syria increase this uneasiness. [1888]

King and Crane, based on interviews, concluded that while the Middle East was not ready for self-government, a colonial power would not meet the needs of the people either. King suggested that the trustworthy Americans occupy the region until the people could prove their self-sufficiency and independence. The British Foreign Office wanted either the United States or Britain to administer the proposed Palestine mandate rather than France or Italy. However, David Lloyd George and Georges Clemenceau drafted the provisions of the San Remo conference and the Treaty of Sèvres to partition the Ottoman Empire. Lloyd George, friendly toward France, agreed that

---

[1887] Ibid
[1888] Ibid

France would receive Syria and Britain would control Mesopotamia (Iraq and Palestine), an arrangement in conflict with the conclusions of the commission and the residents of the area.

Because of all of these considerations, the Commissioners were duty-bound to recommend a "greatly reduced Zionist Program" to the Peace Conference. Even if they accepted numerous moderations of their original objectives, they should implement it gradually. Further, the Commissioners felt that governments should limit Jewish immigration. They vetoed the Zionist Program, as it would not serve the best interests of the long-time residents of the area and would only create great animosity leading to death and destruction. [1889] The Muslims and Christians sought "self-determination." The unwanted intervention of the British and French, supported by the United States, demonstrated that these super powers apparently did not think these peoples were fit to rule themselves. The participants of the Peace Conference censored the findings of the King/Crane Commission.

The government released the King/Crane Commission Report to the public in 1922, after the Senate and House had already passed a joint resolution in favor of the establishment of a National Homeland for the Jews in Palestine. This may have resulted from the letter that the Zionist Organization of America sent to members of Congress in June 1918. The American public later learned that an Arab majority had requested an American mandate with a democratically elected constituent assembly. The actions covertly taken by Britain and the United States divided many citizens who disagreed with their government's actions in this matter.

The British Mandate for Palestine was composed of a commission for the administration of Palestine. The Council of the League of Nations confirmed the draft of the document on July 24, 1922 and became effective on September 26, 1923. The architects of the document based its principles on Article 22 of the draft Covenant of the League of Nations and on the resolutions of the San Remo Resolution of

---

[1889] Ibid

April 25, 1920, adopted by the key Allies following the First World War. The mandate legalized British rule in the Southern part of the Ottoman Empire (1923-1948). On September 16, 1922, under the League of Nations' jurisdiction, Britain apportioned the territory into two administrative sections comprised of Palestine, under absolute British rule, and Transjordan, under the rule of the Hashemite family from present-day Saudi Arabia.

Opposition to Jewish Settlement

On May 19, 1896, Theodor Herzl, recognizing the influence of the Catholic Church in the Middle East, met with Cardinal Antonio Agliardi in Vienna, shortly after the publication of his book *The Jewish State*. On January 22, 1904, Herzl met with Secretary of State Cardinal Rafael Merry del Val. On January 25, Herzl met with Pope Pius X who said, "We cannot prevent the Jews from going to Jerusalem but we could never sanction it. The Jews have not recognized our Lord; therefore we cannot recognize the Jewish people. If you come to Palestine and settle your people there, we will have churches and priests ready to baptize all of you." [1890]

The Vatican knew about the Sykes-Picot Agreement. For centuries, France had protected Catholic power in the Ottoman Empire. On April 11, 1917, Monsignor Eugenio Pacelli and the new Pope, Benedict XV, in talking with Sir Mark Sykes implied that the Vatican would not be adverse to Zionist settlement in Palestine. Therefore, on April 29, 1917, after talking with Sykes, Nahum Sokolow met with Pacelli and on May 1, with Secretary of State Cardinal Pietro Gasparri. On May 4, 1917, he met with the Pope. Pacelli insisted on viewing the geographical boundaries to ascertain if they were acceptable. Gasparri wanted a "reserved zone" for the church, in the cities of Jerusalem, Bethlehem, Nazareth, Tiberius, and Jericho. The Pope wanted protection of the holy places and would not accept any agreement that excluded the holy places. He also preferred to negotiate with British officials rather than with the Zionists. [1891]

[1890] The Vatican and Zionism, http://www.jewishvirtuallibrary.org/jsource/judaica/ejud_0002_0020_0_20338.html As of May 2012

[1891] Ibid

On May 20, 1917, based on Sokolow's assumptions from talking with Catholic officials, Dr. Weizmann announced at the Zionist conference in London that the Pope and other representatives supported the establishment of a Jewish National Home in Palestine. However, the Pope understood that officials were going to internationalize Palestine and that the Zionists would inhabit areas outside of Palestine. Cardinal Gasparri absolutely opposed the Jewish State in Palestine. On December 18, 1917, he said, "The transformation of Palestine into a Jewish state would not only endanger the Holy Places and injure the feelings of all Christians; it would also be very harmful for the country itself." On December 28, the Pope expressed his concern that relinquishing Palestine to the Jews would be "to the detriment of the Christian interests." [1892]

The Holy See did not participate in the Peace Conference because of the secret Treaty of London, in which Britain had offered Italy large sections of territory in the Adriatic Sea region, but Article 15 excluded the Vatican from involvement in any future "peace negotiations or negotiations for the settlement of questions raised by the present war." [1893] In March 10, 1919, the Pope told some of his advisors, "it would be a terrible grief for us and for all Christians if infidels (in Palestine) were placed in a privileged and prominent position; much more if those most holy sanctuaries of the Christian religion were given into the charge of non-Christians." Gasparri told a Belgian representative, "The danger that we most fear is the establishment of a Jewish state in Palestine. We would have found nothing wrong in Jews entering that country, and setting up agricultural colonies. But that they be given the rule over the Holy Places is intolerable for Christians." [1894]

Catholic officials reiterated to British authorities that the Holy See absolutely opposed Zionism as it would infuriate so many Christians. On May 1, 1921, Arabs attacked Jewish communists who were celebrating in Jaffa, in what people call the Jaffa riots (May 1-7)

[1892] Ibid
[1893] John A.S Grenville, The Major International Treaties, 1914-1945, a History and Guide with Texts, Routledge 1987, pp. 24-27
[1894] The Vatican and Zionism, http://www.jewishvirtuallibrary.org/jsource/judaica/ejud_0002_0020_0_20338.html As of May 2012

which spread elsewhere. The Jewish communists distributed Arabic and Yiddish fliers calling for the toppling of British rule and the creation of a "Soviet Palestine." The Ahdut HaAvoda socialist group organized, with official authorization, another large May Day parade in Tel Aviv. David Ben-Gurion originally led this group, a main predecessor of the current Israeli Labor Party.

The violence led to the deaths of about 100 people, half of whom were Arabs while other rioters injured 200. British forces accounted for most of the Arab casualties. Apparently, the Zionists brought Bolsheviks into Palestine to create chaos. A local newspaper suggested that revolutionaries had coordinated the Bolshevik Revolution with the Zionist movement.

High Commissioner Herbert Samuel, an avid Zionist, who, in 1915, submitted a memorandum suggesting that Palestine become a home for the Jewish people, declared a state of emergency. He imposed media censorship, and called for British reinforcements from Egypt. General Edmund Allenby deployed two destroyers to Jaffa, and one to Haifa. Samuel, who the Arabs deeply resented, attempted to placate their representative, Musa Kazim al-Husseini, former mayor of Jerusalem, and the leader of the Palestinian national movement (1922-1934). The British had removed al-Husseini from office because he had been involved in a riot in Nebi Musa (April 4-7, 1920). He insisted on a suspension of Jewish immigration. Samuel agreed and prohibited the landing of boats carrying 300 Jews, which he forced to return to Istanbul. [1895]

Authorities in some villages fined some of the riot participants and tried others. They convicted three Jews, including a policeman of murdering Arabs. This verdict created an international outcry and the Supreme Court ultimately acquitted them on the grounds that they acted in self-defense. The Jewish community, because of the riots and the trials, quickly lost confidence in the British and their ability to settle them in Palestine without incident. The area was under

---

[1895] Tom Segey and Haim Watzman, One Palestine, Complete: Jews and Arabs Under the British Mandate, Metropolitan Books, New York, 1999, pp. 173-190

the British and French military occupation of the Occupied Enemy Territory Administration (OETA) prior to the League of Nations endorsement of British rule and the beginning of the British Mandate. The Arab leaders petitioned the League of Nations for democracy and independence. They maintained that the Arab community held a sufficient number of educated and talented people to establish a stable representative democracy. [1896]

Sir Samuel established an investigative commission, the Commission of Inquiry, under the direction of the Chief Justice of the Supreme Court in Palestine, Sir Thomas Haycraft. Its report, *Palestine: Disturbances in May 1921*, published in October 1921, blamed the Arabs for the disturbances but said that, "Zionists were not doing enough to mitigate the Arabs' apprehensions." Further the report stated, "The fundamental cause of the violence and the subsequent acts of violence was a feeling among the Arabs of discontent with, and hostility to, the Jews, due to political and economic causes, and connected with Jewish immigration." [1897]

The report said that the clash between the socialists or Bolsheviks and the authorized Jewish Labour Party triggered the Arab violence against the Jews.

A summarization of Arab's grievances follows:

1) The British in Palestine, now led by a Zionist, had adopted "a policy mainly directed toward the establishment of a National Home for the Jews, and not to the equal benefit of all Palestinians.
2) An official advisory body to the government in Palestine, the Zionist Commission, placed the interests of the Jews above all others.
3) There was an undue proportion of Jews in the government.
4) Part of the Zionist program was to flood the country with people who possessed "greater commercial and organizing

[1896] Ibid. 173-190
[1897] Mark A. Tessler, A History of the Israeli-Palestinian Conflict, Indiana University Press, Bloomington, Indiana, 1994, pp. 171-172

ability" which would eventually lead to their gaining the upper hand over the rest of the population.

5) The immigrants were an "economic danger" to the country because of their competition, and because they were favored in this competition.

6) Immigrants offended the Arabs "by their arrogance and by their contempt of Arab social prejudices."

7) Owing to insufficient precautions, authorities allowed Bolshevik immigrants into the country leading to social and economic unrest in Palestine. [1898]

Some Jews argued with the Commission and claimed that a small group of Arabs who supported the Ottoman Empire with their propaganda caused the conflict. Apparently, these Arabs favored the old regime. The British "had put an end to privileges and opportunities of profit formerly enjoyed by them." Yet, the Commission took the Arab's accusations against the Jews seriously as it was "too genuine, too widespread, and too intense to be accounted for in the above superficial level." The Arab's resentment toward the British was a result of their involvement with Zionist's policies. [1899]

The report clarified the fact that the Arabs started the conflict and that the "Arab majority, who were generally the aggressors, inflicted most of the casualties." A majority of the Muslim and Christian communities tolerated the riots, but "they did not encourage violence." The Arabs attacked five Jewish agricultural colonies and "in these raids there were few Jewish and many Arab casualties, chiefly on account of the intervention of the military." The commission stated, "We have been assured, and we believe, that had there been no Jewish question, the Government would have had no political difficulty of any importance to deal with so far as its domestic affairs were concerned." The authorities did not believe that the Jews planned the riots in Jaffa. I am skeptical about that, given the Jewish predisposition for provoking terrorism. The Arabs realized that the Jews had a "preponderating

---

[1898] D. Edward Knox, The making of a new Eastern Question: British Palestine policy and the origins of Israel, 1917-1925, Catholic University of America Press, Washington, DC, 1981, pp. 135-136

[1899] Ibid. 135-136

influence over the Government," which they resented. However, this minor provocation by a small group of socialist Jews ignited rage against all Jews. [1900]

The report said, "Muslims, Orthodox Christians, Catholics, Maronites and other Uniates, Anglicans have been represented by witnesses, who included priests of the above Christian bodies and it has been impossible to avoid the conclusions that practically the whole of the non-Jewish population was united in hostility to Jews" [1901] Dr. David Eder, a British psychoanalyst, physician, and Zionist and writer, helped advance psychoanalytic studies in Britain. He was a socialist and was involved in the Fabian Society. He was the Zionist Executive in Palestine (1921-1927) and later became president of the British Zionist Federation (BZF). He headed the local Zionist Commission for Palestine, overseen by Dr. Chaim Weizmann, president of the BZF. Eder addressed the committee and stated that the authorities should only allow Jews to bear arms, and that "there can only be one National Home in Palestine, and that a Jewish one, and no equality in the partnership between Jews and Arabs, but a Jewish preponderance as soon as the numbers of the race are sufficiently increased." [1902]

On June 13, 1921, Pope Benedict XV criticized Zionism during a meeting of cardinals. He said that the Jews would "take away the sacred character of the Holy Places." He died of pneumonia on January 22, 1922, and Pope Pius XI replaced him on February 6. On April 2, 1922, Dr. Weizmann met Secretary of State Cardinal Gasparri, who continued to object to the Mandate over Palestine and the recognition of the Jewish Agency. Weizmann discovered that the Vatican planned to officially oppose the Mandate in a memorandum to the League of Nations. [1903]

[1900] D. Edward Knox, The making of a new Eastern Question: British Palestine policy and the origins of Israel, 1917-1925, Catholic University of America Press, Washington, DC, 1981, pp. 135-136

[1901] Ibid. 135-136

[1902] Ibid. 135-136

[1903] The Vatican and Zionism, http://www.jewishvirtuallibrary.org/jsource/judaica/ejud_0002_0020_0_20338.html As of May 2012

On May 15, 1922, Cardinal Gasparri officially notified the League of Nations that it opposed the British Mandate and that the Holy See could not consent to "the Jews being given a privileged and preponderant position in Palestine vis-à-vis the Catholics" or to "the religious rights of the Christians being inadequately safeguarded." The Pope opposed Jewish immigration and naturalization. On July 22, 1922, despite this opposition, the League of Nations authorized the British Mandate, including the Balfour Declaration. Finally, the Vatican acknowledged the British Mandate regardless of the fact that Vatican officials believed that the irreligious Zionists would ostracize the Palestinian Christians, and alter the Christian nature of the nation. The Vatican claimed that the Jews were responsible for the various life-style and moral values in the local population. [1904]

The Tanaka Memorial, a Plan for Aggression

On February 13, 1919, Japanese officials had submitted the Racial Equality Proposal at the Paris Peace Conference, as they demanded equal status and wanted their racial equality clause included in the League of Nations Covenant. In their Article 21, they wanted "equal and just treatment in every respect making no distinction, either in law or in fact, on account of their race or nationality." [1905] The Western Powers, not about to relinquish their coveted status, had been especially successful in subjugating non-white populations. Japan's proposal received a majority vote. Makino Nobuaki, former Foreign Minister, said, "We are not too proud to fight but we are too proud to accept a place of admitted inferiority in dealing with one or more of the associated nations. We want nothing but simple justice." [1906]

On April 11, 1919, the Covenant commission had its last meeting. Baron Makino reiterated Japan's petition for racial equality. Robert Cecil, the Assistant Secretary of State for Foreign Affairs of

---

[1904] Ibid

[1905] Paris Peace Conference, 1919: Reference, http://www.thefullwiki.org/Paris_Peace_Conference,_1919 as of May 2012

[1906] Ibid.

Britain it. [1907] Italy, France, Czechoslovakia, Brazil, China, Greece, and Serbia all accepted it. The British Empire, the United States, Portugal, Romania and Belgium were either absent or did not vote. President Woodrow Wilson, the Delegation Chairman, reversed the vote despite its strong support. Initially, he initially it but Colonel House persuaded him to support Britain. [1908] Though the British and the Americans often mouth equality and justice, they were not ready to dispense it. The British had colonies, like Australia, which had a White Australian Policy to distinguish them from the indigenous population. America's record, regarding its non-white population, counters all rhetoric regarding equality in the founding documents. This attitude apparently alienated the Japanese who, ironically, are prejudiced against the Chinese.

On February 6, 1922, England, France, and Italy signed the Nine Power Treaty, initiated by the United States, at the Washington Conference. Charles E. Hughes, Henry Cabot Lodge, Oscar W. Underwood, and Elihu Root ratified it. Japan justifiably viewed this treaty as commercial rivalry against them by Britain, and the United States regarding China. Regarding China, Article One stipulated respect for its sovereignty, its independence, and territorial and administrative integrity. It also granted China the opportunity to develop and maintain an effective, stable government. The treaty allowed equal opportunity for commerce and industry by all nations within China. [1909] Article Three of the treaty prohibited monopolies and "any arrangement which might establish superiority of rights with respect to commercial or economic development in any designated region of China." [1910]

Under-developed China was Japan's principle customer and the treaty, which they largely ignored, put Japan at a disadvantage and greatly restricted the development of the resources they had previously won

---

[1907] Naoko Shimazu, Japan, Race, and Equality: the Racial Equality Proposal of 1919, Routledge, New York, 1998, p. 28

[1908] Ibid. 32

[1909] The Nine Point Treaty, Treaty Series No. 723, http://www.ibiblio.org/pha/policy/pre-war/9_power.html as of May 2012

[1910] Ibid

from Russia. It limited their movements in Manchuria and Mongolia and allowed unlimited Chinese immigration into the area. Therefore, Baron Tanaka Giichi, head of the pro-military party, devised the *Tanaka Memorial*, which he presented to Emperor Hirohito, as a guideline for aggressive war and expansion. Baron Tanaka prepared it during an eleven-day conference in Mukden, Manchuria, from June 27 to July 7, 1927, attended by civil and military officials from Manchuria and Mongolia to discuss Japanese foreign policy in those two areas. Japanese officials have repeatedly discredited and/or denied the existence of the document. Yet, Fusanosuka Kuhura, then the Communications Minister, legitimized its validity in a magazine article. [1911]

Moreover, Japanese-born Tsai Chih-Kan claims to have personally copied the documents from the Imperial Library on the night of June 20, 1928, assisted by several influential pre-war politicians and officers. In as much as Baron Tanaka was Japan's Prime Minister (1927-1929), during the Shōwa financial panic of 1927, it would have been appropriate for him to hold a conference and then submit an official report and proposals to the Emperor afterward. He was simultaneously the Prime Minister and the Foreign Affairs Minister.

Many of the attendees at the meeting had Chinese servants and clerks, making it conceivable for a copy of the proceedings to fall into Chinese hands. Author Carl Crow argues that people should judge the report's credibility, despite denials, on the significant events following that conference. The report, according to Crow, was compatible to Tanaka's well-publicized ideas and policies and the group of militarists under his direction. Japan's policies and actions regarding China since about 1931 appear to have followed the document's suggestions. Whether Tanaka wrote it or not, it seems to have been the basis for all subsequent Japanese policy. [1912]

[1911] Carl Crow, Japan's Dream of World Empire, the Tanaka Memorial, Harper and Brothers, New York, 1942, pp. 19-22
[1912] Ibid. 19-22

The *Tanaka Memorial* maintains that Manchuria and Mongolia, with an area of 74,000 square miles, with a population of 28,000,000 people, is over three times as large as Japan, but has only one-third as many people. The area's wealth is in forestry, minerals and agricultural products. Tanaka wrote, "In order to exploit these resources for the perpetuation of our national glory, we created especially the South Manchuria Railway Company." The Japanese government and the people had joint ownership of the railroad. However, the government naturally controlled all railroad operations and selectively dispensed or retained the profits. The South Manchuria Railway company officials were empowered "to undertake diplomatic, police, and ordinary administrative functions" in order to "carry out our imperialistic policies," with the same powers as the Governor-General. [1913]

Tanaka felt that if Japan wanted to control China, then they would first have to defeat the United States just as they had beat Russia in the Russo-Japanese War. First, they would conquer Manchuria and Mongolia to use as a base to conquer China. He felt that if Japan could conquer China, the remainder of the Asiatic countries and the South Sea countries would surrender in fear. Then others would understand that Eastern Asia belonged to Japan and would relinquish interests in the area. [1914]

The *Tanaka Memorial* mandated fourteen rights within Manchuria and Mongolia. They wanted travel rights, the exploitation of the natural resources, a priority in the construction of infrastructure, an increase in Japanese political, financial and military advisers, and the exclusive right to sell special products, partnership rights in launching central banks in the Three Eastern Provinces, unlimited shipping business to Europe and America among other considerations. [1915] Author Mamoru Shigemitsu notes, "The subsequent course of events in East Asia and the incidental behaviour of Japan produced conditions just as though the *Tanaka Memorial* had been taken as a text-book, so that it is now difficult to wipe out foreign suspicions

---

[1913] Ibid. 23-25

[1914] Ibid. 29

[1915] Carl Crow, Japan's Dream of World Empire, the Tanaka Memorial, Harper and Brothers, New York, 1942, pp. 36-38

as to the document." [1916] Some people discredit the *Protocols of the Learned Elders of Zion* as a forgery. Yet, since its publication, it has provided an accurate prologue for the future.

Many regard the *Protocols* as an anti-Judaic document. However, the ideas are evidently not a hoax, given a practical consideration of the events in the world which gives abundant substantiation of their application. The *Protocols* appear to be the mandate for the Neo-conservative movement culminating in the Bush administration. Obama, though he promised change during his campaign, adopted the same methodology and administrative mentality with only a few cosmetic alterations. He filled his cabinet and a burgeoning bureaucratic system with people who apparently are moving the Protocol's objectives forward, especially the financial goals. From a critical reading of the *Protocols*, one might conclude that an elite clique used the precepts in it to write a contemporary document, the *Project for a New American Century.* [1917]

Communist Infiltration in China

In addition to infiltrating America, the Bolsheviks quickly established a presence in almost every country—England, France, Germany, Belgium, Sweden, Denmark, Switzerland, Austria, Romania, Czechoslovakia, Bulgaria, Greece, and in Asia.

In February 1834, Yale-educated Peter Parker, a physician and a Presbyterian minister, went to China, sponsored by the American Board of Commissioners for Foreign Missions, as the first full-time medical missionary and the first American surgeon to practice in China. On November 4, 1835, he founded the Guangzhou Boji Hospital. He became the president of the Medical Missionary Society of China, established in Canton, by Dr. Thomas R. Colledge, the first

---

[1916] Japan and Her Destiny: My Struggle for Peace by Mamoru Shigemitsu, edited by F. S. G. Piggott, translated by Oswald White, Dutton, New York, 1958, p. 46

[1917] Andrew M. Lobaczewski, Political Ponerology, a Science on the Nature of Evil Adjusted for Political Purposes, Red Pill Press, Fitchburg, Massachusetts, 1998, p. 186

part-time medical missionary, who was associated with the East India Company at Guangzhou and Parker's mentor. In 1844, Parker was Caleb Cushing's interpreter during the negotiations of the Treaty of Wàngxià. In 1886, Sun Yat-Sen became a student at the hospital.

Reverend Ho Tsun Shin, from a wealthy merchant family, had worked for the London Missionary Society, and had inherited several properties. In 1872, he sent his fourth son, Ho Kai, born in Hong Kong (1857), to England to study at Palmer House School, and, in 1875 to the University of Aberdeen to study medicine. He graduated in 1879, the first Chinese student. In 1881, Scottish-born Dr. William Young, a graduate of McGill University, established a successful Western-style dispensary at Tai Ping Shan, a crowded Chinese township on the northern side of Hong Kong. The London Missionary Society, founded in 1795, by evangelical Anglicans and Nonconformists, and a local committee directed by H. W. Davis, assisted him in this endeavor. The dispensary flourished despite the feelings of the local population who preferred traditional herbal methods. [1918]

Ho Kai returned to Hong Kong in 1882, where he financed the construction of a hospital, named after his first wife, the Alice Memorial Hospital, founded in 1887. Davis financed another hospital and early in the century, Dr. Ho Kai provided the money for a separate maternity hospital. The Alice Memorial Hospital staff included Drs. Gerlach, Jordan, Noble, Francis Clark, James Cantlie, and Patrick Manson. Soon, Dr. Ho Kai, Dr. Manson and Dr. Cantlie enthusiastically discussed the idea of creating a Hong Kong medical college for Chinese students. Dr. Ho Kai provided the money, Dr. Manson the organizational ability, and Dr. Cantlie the dedication. Six months later, by August 1887, they founded a College of Medicine in Hong Kong to train doctors for service in China and elsewhere in East Asia. [1919] In 1888, Dr. Cantlie, a Fellow of the Royal College of Surgeons and an Assistant Surgeon at Charing Cross Hospital, became the Dean of the Hong Kong College of Medicine where he taught the future Chinese leader Sun Yat-Sen (1866-1925).

[1918] Dr. James Kyle, The Hong Kong College of Hong Kong, British Medical Journal, June 2, 1979, pp. 1474-1476
[1919] Ibid. 1474-1476

Dr. Sun Yat-sen, revered as the Father of modern China and founder of the Nationalist Party (NP), was born in Guangdong province. While living with an older brother in Hawaii, he embraced the lofty concept of, government of the people, by the people, for the people. In 1883, he returned to China where he embraced Christianity and accepted baptism. Continuing British colonialism and the exploitation of resources troubled Dr. Sun so he abandoned his medical practice to participate in the reform movement of 1895, an attempt to establish a democracy. [1920] It failed miserably and the government summarily executed several reformers. However, he escaped the fate of his compatriots.

On October 11, 1896, while exiled in London, an agent reportedly induced Dr. Sun to go to the Chinese Legation, China's first foreign embassy, established in 1877. Minister Gong Zhao Yuan, the head of the legation, prompted this unexpected invitation, with the help of the legation's British Secretary, Sir Halliday Macartney who was completely loyal to the mandarins who hired him. The gracious invitation was nothing but a ploy as they planned to return him to China to face punishment. They incarcerated him in the legation, until he convinced a steward to deliver a message to his English host who managed his release on October 23, 1896. [1921]

In 1897, Dr. James Cantlie returned to London. Dr. Sun, after his release, stayed in London for another eight months, until July 1897. He spent most of his time at the British Museum reading books on politics, law, diplomacy and military issues. He told a new friend that it might take thirty years to transform China's government. Sun regularly visited Dr. Cantlie, and on October 25, 1896, at a dinner at the Cantlies, he listened to a Mr. Weay who had just returned from South Africa. Mr. Weay described how Sir Cecil Rhodes and the British South Africa Company had waged war against the Boers, and then annexed rich territories belonging to local sovereigns. He described the fall of Bulawayo in 1893 and Dr. Leander S. Jameson's raid in the

---

[1920] Archibald R. Colquhoun, China in Transformation, Harper & Brothers, New York, 1912, p. 106

[1921] Marie-Claire Bergere and Janet Lloyd, Sun Yat-sen, Translated by Janet Lloyd, Stanford University Press, Stanford, California, 2000, pp. 61-63

Transvaal in 1895. Dr. Sun recalled these tragic stories over a decade later when he struggled with the challenge of nationalism. [1922]

Sun spent time in numerous countries, including Japan where he changed his name to Dr. Nakayama, under which he established relationships with various political circles. The Meiji modernizers inspired him and contributed to his aspirations of reform. His Japanese friends, who he told about his London ordeal, wanted to organize "pan-Asian solidarity" against the omnipresent Westerners. [1923] It was the same in his country; the corrupt government was impervious and even complicit with the foreign powers who dominated the country. On October 10, 1911, after years of planning their offense against the Qing government, the Chinese Revolutionary Alliance began their revolution with the Wuchang Uprising over the handling of foreign railway construction, a catalyst to the Xinhai Revolution.

Following the Boxer Rebellion, foreign investors exploited China and many countries wanted to build railways in areas where they had influence despite the protests of the Qing government. Germany began constructing lines in Shandong, the British in Yangtze Valley, French in Kunming, Russians in Heilongjiang and the Japanese owned the Southern Manchuria Railway Company. During the Xinhai Revolution, the Manchu Qing Dynasty toppled. On December 29, 1911, the revolutionaries proclaimed Dr. Sun as the Provisional President of the new Republic of China. On February 12, 1912, Emperor Puyi abdicated. Dr. Sun hoped to establish peace, freedom, and equality in the country. [1924] Yet, uncooperative warlords, who ruled their territories with an iron fist, ran most of northern China.

Meanwhile, another individual, Chiang Kai-Shek, who would play a major part in the ultimate collapse of China, became an active member of the Green Gang in 1908. He participated in gang activities as a Chinese Army officer prior to the 1911 revolution. His police record in Shanghai's British International Settlement

---

[1922] Ibid. 64-65

[1923] Ibid. 69

[1924] Archibald R. Colquhoun, China in Transformation, Harper & Brothers, New York, 1912, pp. 283-84

included murder, extortion, and armed robbery. [1925] In 1916, William J. Keswick collaborated with Sam and Abe Bronfman to found the Pure Drug Company to illegally distribute whiskey into Canada. Keswick directed China's opium policy through Soong Tse-ven, as a Director, carried out the day-to-day business operations for Jardine Matheson. He was closely associated with the management of the Hong Kong and Shanghai Bank, founded by James Mackay, Lord Inchcape. Mackay was the first Chairman of the Shanghai Municipal Council (1865-66), Governor of the Hudson's Bay Company, Director of the Bank of England, Vice-Chairman of Alliance Assurance and a Director of British Petroleum. [1926]

Edward I. Ezra (1882-1921) born in Shanghai, to a wealthy Jewish family, was the first Chinese-born member of the Shanghai Municipal Council. He amassed a vast fortune, perhaps twenty to thirty million dollars, through the importation of opium. He also invested heavily into real estate in Shanghai in the early twentieth century. He was the largest stockholder and the managing director and major financier of Shanghai Hotels Limited and controlled the Astor House Hotel in Shanghai.

When the government banned opium imports in 1917, drug dealers went underground and the Shanghai traffickers set up their own refineries. The Green Gang, operating from the French Concession, was a criminal cabal and the most powerful secret society which merged into the corporate system after 1932. Thereafter, they dominated the domestic drug distribution, under the direction of Tu Yue-sheng, head of the Chung Wai Bank, and board chairman of the Commercial Bank of China, making it easy to finance his drug enterprise. [1927]

[1925] Alfredo Schulte-Bockholt, The Politics of Organized Crime and the Organized Crime of Politics: A Study in Criminal Power, Lexington Books, 2006, pp. 78-82

[1926] US Labor Party Investigating Team, Dope Inc. Britain's Opium War Against the US, New York, 1978, pp. 279-280

[1927] Post Japanese, the Opium Files, http://www.takaoclub.com/opium/postjapan. htm as of May 2012

Arnold Rothstein then sent Yasha Katzenberg, his employee, to Shanghai to confirm the opium pact. Rothstein, whose mother was Esther Rothschild, headed the infamous Jewish mafia. He had connections to the Seligman, Wannamaker, and Gimbel families. Rothstein, Meyer Lansky, and Lucky Luciano distributed liquor for the Bronfman cabal during US prohibition. Bronfman, after prohibition ended, sent his cohorts to Shanghai and Hong Kong to develop a drug network to export to America. Britain's criminal element, working with notable Chinese drug traders, sought to create an opium cartel. Keswick managed China's opium policy in coordination with Soong Tse-ven and directed heroin exportation into the United States Sir Eric Drake, a Keswick cohort, was a board member of Canadian Pacific, which transported massive amounts of drugs through Canada into the United States [1928] Rothstein and Meyer Lansky would send agents to China to purchase heroin in the 1920s. [1929]

On October 25, 1915, while exiled in Japan, Dr. Sun married, despite the opposition of her parents, Soong Ch'ing-ling, a very attractive American-educated young woman. She was one of the Soong sisters. Their incredibly wealthy father, Charles J. Soong, also educated in America, became Christian and participated in the revolutionary movement. [1930] Her sisters, Ai-ling and Mei-ling, were preoccupied with power and greed. Ch'ing-ling, apparently an anomaly within her elite family, unselfishly cared about the Chinese people. The mainland Chinese remarked of the three sisters, "One loved power, one loved money, and one loved China."

Dr. Sun had two brothers-in-law; Soong Tse-ven who attended Harvard, then received a Ph.D. from Columbia University, and then returned to China to become the head of the Sassoon-controlled Bank of China. He was the governor of the Central Bank of China and later Minister of Finance (1928-1931, 1932-1933). The other was financier K'ung Hsiang-his, known simply as H.H. Kung who received his

---

[1928] US Labor Party Investigating Team, Dope Inc. Britain's Opium War Against the US, New York, 1978, pp. 278-279

[1929] Ibid. 44

[1930] Lyon Sharman, Sun Yat-Sen His Life and Its Meaning: A Critical Biography, Stanford University Press, Stanford, California, 1968, p. 38

education at Oberlin College and Yale University. He was a YMCA secretary, and while exiled in Tokyo worked among Chinese students. [1931] Kung was Minister of Finance (1933-1944), succeeding Soong Tse-ven. He married Soong Ai-ling. The family, using Rothschild and Sassoon money, controlled the government and carved up the country into drug regions, which the warlords dominated. [1932]

By 1920, Shanghai, the focus of western economic interest, contained the majority of the country's industrial workers and the biggest base of communist support in China. The Chinese Communist Party (CCP), founded in July 1921, dominated Shanghai's municipal government. The NP and the CCP were officially still allies. [1933] In 1921, in an attempt to unify China, Dr. Sun, president and generalissimo, met with Henk Sneevliet, of the Comintern, with the objective of establishing a military government in the Guangzhou, Guangdong Province in southern China. To hasten the conquest of the warlords in northern China, he accepted Soviet help and cooperated with local communists after the western powers rejected his requests.

The Soviets and the Comintern supervised and, to an extent, financed the Chinese revolutionary movement. In March 1923, the Soviet leaders concluded that they would assist Sun Yat-sen with at least three million rubles channeled through Mikhail Borodin (born Mikhail Gruzenberg), a freemason, another Bolshevik agent in China (1923-1927), to provide the initial funding and operating expenses of the Whampoa Military Academy, according to Louis Fischer, a Borodin confidante. Bliukher's diary indicates that the monthly subsidy totaled 100,000 rubles in November 1924. Additionally, the Soviets sent a valuable shipment of arms, aboard the *Vorovsky*, in October 1924 for which they charged the Canton government. [1934]

[1931] Ibid. 179

[1932] US Labor Party Investigating Team, Dope Inc. Britain's Opium War Against the US, New York, 1978, pp. 277-278

[1933] Alfredo Schulte-Bockholt, The Politics of Organized Crime and the Organized Crime of Politics: A Study in Criminal Power, Lexington Books, 2006, pp. 78-82

[1934] John King Fairbank, The Cambridge History of China: Republican China 1912-1949, Part 1, The Press Syndicate, Cambridge University Press,

Borodin persuaded Dr. Sun Yat-Sen to allow communists in the Kuomintang, the nationalist party founded by Song Jiaoren and Sun Yat-Sen shortly after the Revolution of 1911.

In January 1924, the NP devised an anti-imperialist policy with an emphasis on workers and peasants. At the same time, technical and financial assistance arrived from the Soviet Union. This linked the Chinese NP to the Communist Party. [1935] The NP and the Communist Parties, encouraged and financed by Moscow, worked together in the Kwangtung province, until mid-1926, to create a national revolution. The Soviet Union also assisted Feng Yū-hsiang in building a large military organization in North China beginning in the spring of 1925. The Kuomintang and the Communist Party also collaborated and participated in labor movements among the students in numerous cities such as Shanghai, Hankow, Peking and others. All of these factions joined in the Northern Expedition, which they initiated in July 1926. [1936]

Investigators, during a raid of the Hoover Institute at Stanford University, found a document in the papers of Jay C. Huston, a US Foreign Service Officer in Peking and Canton in the 1920s. In September 1925, General Vasily K. Bliukher, using the pseudonym "Galen" wrote a report and military plan later discovered in the Central Archives of the Party, Institute of Marxism and Leninism of the Central Committee of the Communist Party of the Soviet Union. [1937]

Bliukher was a Soviet military adviser in China (1924-1927), using the name Galen, while he worked at Chiang Kai-Shek's military headquarters where he facilitated the military planning of the

Cambridge, United Kingdom, 1983, pp. 566-569

[1935] David A. Wilson, Principles and Profits: Standard Oil Responds to Chinese Nationalism, 1925-1927, The Pacific Historical Review, Vol. 46, No. 4 (Nov., 1977), pp. 625-647

[1936] Clarence Martin Wilbur, Missionaries of revolution: Soviet advisers and Nationalist China, 1920-1927, Julie Lien-ying How, Harvard University Press, 1989, pp. 3-4

[1937] Ibid. 3-4

Northern Expedition. This inaugurated the Kuomintang unification of China. Chiang permitted Bliukher to "escape" following his anti-communist purge beginning on April 12, 1927. Bliukher taught Lin Biao, pivotal in the communist victory in the Chinese Civil War and later a key figure in the Chinese People's Liberation Army. The intermittent Chinese Civil War, 1927-1936, 1941-1945, 1946-1950, was between the Kuomintang (KMT) or Chinese Nationalist Party, the governing party of the Republic of China, and the Communist Party of China (CPC) over the control of China. This war culminated with the division of the nation into the Republic of China (ROC) and People's Republic of China (PRC). The war began in April 1927, with the Northern Expedition, ending in 1949-1950.

On June 16, 1924, Dr. Sun officially established the Whampoa Military Academy, to train soldiers for the revolution, with Chiang Kai-shek as its commandant, under the Kuomintang. Borodin helped train students at the academy. Russian military advisors supplied, financed and staffed the academy. Sun Yat-sen's principle military advisor, General Bliukher, Commander of Soviet volunteer forces, helped found the academy. In the 1930s, Bliukher was a victim of Stalin's purges. At least 700 cadets were from the Green Gang. [1938] Perhaps never actually a freemason, Dr. Sun was active in a society referred to as Chinese freemasonry. [1939] He died of liver cancer on March 12, 1925, at age 58, at Rockefeller's Peking Union Medical College Hospital, a facility that the Rockefeller Fund funded by 1915. [1940]

In 1925, they founded the Institute of Pacific Relations (IPR) in ten Asian countries. The Rockefeller and Carnegie Foundations

[1938] Alfredo Schulte-Bockholt, The Politics of Organized Crime and the Organized Crime of Politics: A Study in Criminal Power, Lexington Books, 2006 pp. 78-82
[1939] Dr. Sun Yat-sen, Grand Lodge of British Columbia and the Yukon, http://freemasonry.bcy.ca/biography/sun_y/sun_y.html as of May 2012
[1940] Rockefeller Fund Tells China Plans; Medical Board Will Operate Union College, Peking, on Most Modern Lines. Commission To Scan Field Scholarships Provided for Training in America—Women of Far East to be Taught, The New York Times, June 16, 1915

financed it while an alliance of Morgan and Rockefeller interests on Wall Street controlled it. Other financing came from Standard Oil, IT&T, Vacuum Oil, Shell Oil, International Business Machines, International General Electric, *Time Magazine*, J. P. Morgan, National City Bank and Chase National Bank, as well as individuals with Wall Street connections. [1941]

At Sun Yat-sen's death, Chiang Kai-shek, one of several contenders for China's leadership, was the most popular. [1942] Dr. Sun's death split the NP, and rightwing Chiang Kai-shek took over the National Revolutionary Army and leftwing Wang Jingwei seized the national government, the perfect scenario for civil war. General Borodin's Soviet troops and Chiang looted the vaults of the Rothschild, Sassoon, and Soong bank in Shanghai, the nation's banking center. Understandably, this infuriated them. However, given Chiang's popularity, Soong Tse-ven offered him $3 million in cash, marriage to his power-seeking sister, Soong Mei-Ling and China's presidency for life if he would switch loyalties. He accepted and immediately ordered the Russians out of China. [1943]

They were about to leave anyway. The Soviets working in China, despite the growth of the Chinese Communist Party and the Socialist Youth Corps, grew frustrated with the progress of the overall movement. The Party did organize some successful strikes in late 1925 among workers in Hong Kong and Kwangtung farmers. On March 13, 1926, the Executive Committee of the Comintern (ECCI) issued a stern directive ordering an alliance between the Kuomintang and the communists. The Committee criticized the lack of membership growth and the "slowness in organizational development," apparently due to the "narrow sectarian views" of an insufficient number of

---

[1941] Carroll Quigley, Tragedy and Hope, a History of the world in Our Time, The Macmillan Company, New York, 1966, p. 947

[1942] Jonathan D. Spence, Recognized by Chinese everywhere as their country's modern founder, the physician-turned-nationalist failed in his dream of unification, Time-Asia, http://www.time.com/time/asia/asia/magazine/1999/990823/sun_yat_sen1.html as of May 2012

[1943] Des Griffin, Descent into Slavery, Emissary Publications, Clackamas, Oregon, 2001, pp. 190-199

local leaders and their criteria and what the ECCI referred to as the peasant problem. [1944]

On April 12, 1927, William J. Keswick, a Director of Jardine Matheson and Company (drug smugglers during the Opium Wars), and a principle of the Extraterritorial International Settlements ordered the Green Gang and Chiang, head of the Nationalist Army, to begin a reign of terror. They purged the leftists and labor activists from Shanghai in what people call the Shanghai Massacre. [1945] They quickly executed 5,000 to 6,000 captives and drove the CCP underground. [1946] Within six months they halted the Chinese communist movement. As many as 25,000 people perished in Shanghai, Nanking, Wusih, Soochow, Changchow, Hangchow, and Canton. [1947] In the 1920s, Chiang, a professional soldier, used the Kuomintang, or NP, a paramilitary organization to implement the Northern Expedition which forcefully integrated southern and central China and created an alliance with the bankers of Shanghai. [1948]

On December 1, 1927, Chiang Kai-shek married Soong Mei-Ling although her mother vehemently objected because he was a Buddhist and her American-educated daughter was Christian. Therefore, Chiang converted. Mei-Ling was the daughter of China's wealthiest family and the sister of a Rothschild agent, Soong Tse-ven. On October 10, 1928, the bankers installed Chiang as president of China.

[1944] John King Fairbank, The Cambridge History of China: Republican China 1912-1949, Part 1, The Press Syndicate, Cambridge University Press, Cambridge, United Kingdom, 1983, pp. 566-569

[1945] US Labor Party Investigating Team, Dope Inc. Britain's Opium War Against the US, New York, 1978, pp. 278-279

[1946] Exploring Chinese History, Rebellion and Revolution—Nationalist Movement, http://www.ibiblio.org/chinesehistory/contents/03pol/c03s06.html as of May 2012

[1947] Alfredo Schulte-Bockholt, The Politics of Organized Crime and the Organized Crime of Politics: A Study in Criminal Power, Lexington Books, 2006, pp. 78-82

[1948] Robert Smith Thompson, Empires on the Pacific: World War II and the Struggle for the Mastery of Asia, Basic Books, 2001, p. 18

[1949] After the marriage, Soong presented his sister with his personal mansion. [1950] Chiang would very subtly reveal his new alliances when he inexplicably abandoned Nanking, then the capital of the Republic of China, leaving its vulnerable citizens to endure six weeks of savagery by the invading Japanese in December 1937.

Soong Tse-ven had resigned as Finance Minister (1928-1931, 1932-1933) after failing to raise sufficient money to fight Communism. However, in early June 1932, he agreed to return only if China's government, now desperate, would resort to putting even more effort to growing opium, a profitable cash crop that became the backbone of the Chinese economy, which might resolve China's financial crisis. Consequently, they removed millions of acres from food production. China, short of food, was already struggling to feed its people. Choosing opium over food production caused a genocidal famine that led to the deaths of at least 6,000,000 peasants in four provinces, killing a third of the population in the Shaanxl Province between 1928 and 1933. [1951]

The Crash of 1929 and Continuing Economic Warfare

On November 8, 2002, Federal Reserve Chairman Ben Bernanke said, "Let me end my talk by abusing slightly my status as an official representative of the Federal Reserve. I would like to say to Milton and Anna, Regarding the Great Depression. You're right; we did it. We're very sorry. But thanks to you, we won't do it again." [1952] He was referring to Milton Freidman and Anna J. Schwartz who wrote *Monetary History of the United States 1867-1960* in 1971. He told the truth. Rather than a stock market crash followed by a

---

[1949] Des Griffin, Descent into Slavery, Emissary Publications, Clackamas, Oregon, 2001, pp. 190-199

[1950] Derek Sandhaus, Party Like it's 1929, August 22, 2008 http://www.cityweekend.com.cn/shanghai/articles/mag-sh/cover-story/party-its-1929/ as of May 2012

[1951] US Labor Party Investigating Team, Dope Inc. Britain's Opium War Against the US, New York, pp. 278-279

[1952] Remarks by Governor Ben S. Bernanke At the Conference to Honor Milton Friedman, University of Chicago, Chicago, Illinois, November 8, 2002

depression, they switched tactics. Starting at the end of the second Bush regime, members of Congress, the bank's accomplices, initiated bank bailouts, and did not conceal this huge resource transfer behind a contrived crash. Every economic crisis requires the same careful planning and preparations as the 1929 crash, executed by officials at the highest level of two governments—Britain and America.

Winston Churchill and Cecil Rhodes, intimate friends, shared the same Anglo-American beliefs of returning the United States to British rule. On June 2, 1899, Churchill and Rhodes had breakfast at London's Burlington Hotel and planned South Africa's war, which began on October 11, 1899. Rhodes, on behalf of the bankers, believed that he had found his "man of action" for returning America to British domination using economic warfare. Following America's financial obligations due to its costly participation in World War I, Churchill concocted an elaborate scheme, wherein he collaborated with US officials and media magnates, to launch an economic offensive against American citizens. He, with dozens of people, constructed a financial terrorist network to eventually facilitate the 1929 stock market crash that reverberated around the world to affect economics for decades. [1953]

Despite the deliberate New York Panic (1920-21), America remained resilient and industrially strong. Independent farms provided adequate food. American infrastructure and transportation systems were modern, efficient, and technologically advanced compared to the rest of the world. In 1921, per capita income was $522. Churchill joined forces with Treasury Secretary Andrew Mellon, New York Federal Reserve Chairman Benjamin Strong, and Montagu Norman to provide easy money for speculation. It was possible for investors to purchase $1,000 worth of stock for $100. On April 28, 1925, Churchill, then Chancellor of the Exchequer, returned England to the gold standard, adjusted the British pound to $4.86, limiting industry and the quantity of British goods and decreasing the amount of affordable goods for export, also a disaster for English consumers.

[1953] Pat Riott, The Greatest Story Never Told, Winston Churchill and the Crash of 1929, Nanoman Press, Oak Brook, Illinois, 1994, pp. 3, 57, 72-73

Simultaneously, hundreds of millions of dollars in gold flowed to the United States from Europe. The New York Federal Reserve gave the Bank of England a $200 million credit and J. P. Morgan gave the British Treasury a $100 million credit. Churchill and his accomplices invested heavily into the United States stock market. From 1923 to 1929, the Federal Reserve's printing press created a 62 percent inflation rate, and then abruptly stopped. [1954]

After World War I, America was Britain's principle competitor. On July 1, 1927, bankers, Montagu Norman of the Bank of England, and Hjalmar Schacht of the German Reichsbank arrived in New York aboard *The Mauretania*. They met with Benjamin Strong and Charles Rist, the Deputy Governor of the Banque de France. They laid the final plans to bankrupt America in order to rescue England's economy after Churchill's maneuvers. Strong planned to deliberately create inflation, by increasing domestic prices, making American goods less desirable and affordable. Importation of cheaper goods would shift the gold to the Bank of England. [1955] Treasury Secretary Andrew Mellon agreed to lower interest rates. By 1928, bankers transferred about $500 million in gold to Europe, especially to Germany, under the guise of post-war aid. [1956] This activity did not affect the elite. For Christmas 1928, J. P. Morgan Company gave all of the partners $1 million.

Mellon, from one of the wealthiest banking families, was Treasury Secretary under presidents Warren G. Harding, Calvin Coolidge, and Herbert Hoover. Between 1928 and 1933, while the economy forced the closure of thousands of smaller banks, another feature of the diabolical economic plan, Mellon's bank thrived. Ultimately, his financial interests included Gulf Oil, Alcoa, and numerous other

---

[1954] Ibid. 34, 86

[1955] G. Edward Griffin, The Creature From Jekyll Island, a Second Look at the Federal Reserve, American Media, Westlake Village, California, 1995, p. 425

[1956] David Allen Rivera, Final Warning: A History Of The New World Order, Conspiracy Books, Oakland, California, 2004, p. 168

corporations. His associates sat on their boards. [1957] President Coolidge appointed Ogden L. Mills as Undersecretary of the Treasury (1927-1932). In 1932, Mills became Treasury Secretary under Hoover, when Mellon left to become US Ambassador to the Court of St. James, the Britain's Sovereign's official residence. In 1932, Bernard Baruch gave Mills a partnership in his lucrative Alaska gold mining operation, obviously a huge conflict of interest. [1958]

Secretary Mills, a Pilgrims Society member, was son of the wealthy industrialist Ogden Mills, also a Pilgrims Society member. Mills' grandfather was Darius Mills, a financier of the Southern Pacific Railroad, and owner of the Virginia and Truckee Railroad, the only link from the Comstock Lode to the Union Pacific Railroad. He made a fortune in silver mining in Nevada, owned D.O. Mills & Company, a gold bank in Sacramento at the start of the California gold rush. On July 4, 1864, Mills founded the Bank of California, which became a principal center of exchange between the European, Japanese and Chinese money markets. [1959] In 1880, the London Rothschilds replaced their own California agency with the Bank of California. [1960] The Paris and Vienna Rothschilds used the services of the Bank of California as a correspondent bank. [1961] Darius Mills' daughter married Whitelaw Reid, a Pilgrims Society member and an editor at *The New York Tribune*. These families, through the generations, intermarried with other elite Pilgrim families associated with politics, steel and publishing. [1962] Reid was a close friend of avid socialist, Horace Greeley, who established *The New York Tribune* in 1841,

[1957] Pat Riott, The Greatest Story Never Told, Winston Churchill and the Crash of 1929, Nanoman Press, Oak Brook, Illinois, 1994, pp. 45-46

[1958] Ibid. 100

[1959] Charles Savoie, Pilgrims, Silver Investor, May 2005, www.silver-investor. com/charlessavoie/cs_may05_pilgrims.htm as of May 2012

[1960] Rondo E. Cameron, International banking, 1870-1914, Valeriĭ Ivanovich Bovykin, B. V. Anan'ich, Oxford University Press, New York, 1991, pp. 244, 581

[1961] Astronomical Society of the Pacific, Publications of the Astronomical Society of the Pacific, Volumes 11-12, San Francisco, California, 1900, pp. 8, 215

[1962] Charles Savoie, Pilgrims, Silver Investor, May 2005, www.silver-investor. com/charlessavoie/cs_may05_pilgrims.htm as of May 2012

the man that Hjalmar Horace Greeley Schacht's parents honored in naming their son.

In what people refer to as the *roaring twenties*, a time of wealth, optimism and excess, numerous newspaper and magazine articles promoted stock market speculation, claiming that one could make a veritable fortune in a short time for minimum monthly investments. However, there were also special speculators who owned dozens of accounts in various names, which they could trade in enormous blocks. Small investors, never in any position to actually manipulate the market, suffered the consequences, and received the blame for the 1929 crash, just as homebuyers received the blame for the real estate bubble and the financial crisis of 2007-2010. In 1929, Wall Street brokers reported that there were 1.6 million active stock market accounts and 600,000 margin accounts. Those margin accounts belonged to Churchill and his co-conspirators. [1963]

On October 14, 1929, President Herbert Hoover (1929-1933), said, "Secretary (Thomas W.) Lamont and officials at the Commerce Department today denied rumors that a severe depression in business and industrial activity was impending, which had been based on a mistaken interpretation of a review of industrial and credit conditions issued earlier in the day by the Federal Reserve Board." [1964]

Churchill, his younger brother John "Jack," his 20-year old nephew Johnny, and his 18-year old son, Randolph, toured America for fifty-four days prior to the crash. On October 4, 1939, Randolph would marry Pamela Beryl Digby, who people have described as a courtesan due to her numerous affairs with powerful millionaires including Baron Elie de Rothschild, William S. Paley, and others. On March 19, 1971, she contacted W. Averell Harriman the day after her husband, successful Hollywood producer Leland Hayward died. She married Harriman on September 27, 1971. She financially backed Bill Clinton

---

[1963] Pat Riott, The Greatest Story Never Told, Winston Churchill and the Crash of 1929, Nanoman Press, Oak Brook, Illinois, 1994, p. 35

[1964] The New York Times, October 14, 1929

who, after his election, rewarded her with an ambassadorship to England. [1965] [1966]

Bernard Baruch, Winston's favorite American, persuaded Charles M. Schwab to allow the British visitors the use of his luxurious private railway car. Schwab had worked for Andrew Carnegie, and participated in the 1901 deal with J. Pierpont Morgan to merge Carnegie Steel with US Steel, with Schwab as its first president. In 1903, Schwab became president of Bethlehem Steel, a company that, in 1914, built twenty submarines for Britain, in only six months, all assembled in Montreal, to avoid the neutrality issue. Bethlehem Steel produced as much as all of Britain combined. Jack Churchill was partners with Horace C. Vickers in a huge stock market firm in London, Vickers da Costa. It had a key role, second to Baruch, in the economic storm that the Churchill brothers were brewing. [1967]

Baruch introduced Churchill to William Crocker, head of the wealthy California banking family. The Churchill party spent the night of September 12, 1929, at the Crocker estate before visiting publisher William Randolph Hearst, another Baruch crony. They arrived at the $30 million San Simeon Castle on September 13, 1929, where they spent several days while Hearst and Churchill discussed the world's future. In 1951, Hoover, Baruch, Douglas MacArthur, Roy Howard, Arthur Sulzberger, Robert McCormick, and Earl Warren were Hearst's honorary pallbearers. [1968]

On September 23, 1929, Winston and Jack Churchill had dinner with William G. McAdoo, former Treasury Secretary (1913-1918) under

---

[1965] Harriman Fighting Step kids' Lawsuit By George Rush And Joanna Molloy With Jack Begg, Daily News, October 4, 1995, https://nydailynews.com/archives/news/1995/10/04/1995-10-04_harriman_fighting_stepkids__.html as of May 2012

[1966] 'Widow Of Opportunity' Faces Undiplomatic Mess—Pamela Harriman Fights Charges Of Squandering Money[By] Kiley Armstrong, Seattle Times, October 30, 1994, http://community.seattletimes.nwsource.com/archive/?date=19941030&slug=1938731 as of May 2012

[1967] Pat Riott, The Greatest Story Never Told, Winston Churchill and the Crash of 1929, Nanoman Press, Oak Brook, Illinois, 1994, pp. 49-52, 98

[1968] Ibid. 63-64

Wilson. No doubt, this lifetime Morgan agent knew exactly what was going to occur within a month, and he could supply Churchill with an understanding of Treasury operations. In the mid-1920s, Baruch bought a seat on the Chicago Board of Trade for his brother, Sailing. On October 2, 1929, Baruch, with cozy relationships in Chicago, met Churchill, and his party when they arrived in Chicago. Churchill met with several prominent Chicago businessmen, and they devised a test to see how their plot would play out in New York in just three weeks. In the final hour of trading on October 3, they flooded the market with 1,500,000 shares, forcing Schwab's competitor, US Steel to drop $10 a share. [1969]

On October 4, 1929, Churchill addressed the Commercial Club, whose members were the CEOs of some of Chicago's leading firms. He promoted an American and British naval agreement, allegedly for the continuation of peace. On that same day, Manhattan officials accorded James Ramsay MacDonald, at the time, the only sitting Prime Minister to visit America with a ticker-tape parade upon his arrival, purportedly a trip to discuss military naval agreements with President Hoover, and other politicians over a two-week period. On October 10, MacDonald had dinner with Thomas W. Lamont, senior partner at J. Pierpont Morgan. [1970]

On October 18, 1929, Churchill, accompanied by Charles Duncombe, Third Earl of Feversham and Ronald I. Campbell, visited Republican President Hoover who certainly knew the names of the plungers. At the top of the list were Baruch and John J. Raskob, a DuPont and General Motors executive, and the builder of the Empire State Building. Raskob was also the chairman of the Democratic National Committee (1928-1932). Obviously, party affiliations were and are totally irrelevant. On October 25, 1929, Hoover, with foreknowledge of the imminent financial catastrophe, about to destroy so many people, would proclaim, "The fundamental business of the country that is production and distribution of commodities, is on a sound and prosperous basis." [1971]

[1969] Ibid. 78, 82-84
[1970] Ibid. 84-85, 90
[1971] Ibid. 120

Churchill's grandfather, Leonard Jerome, had a seat on the New York Stock Exchange and was chummy with the Rockefellers and the Vanderbilts. During the final week before the crash, Churchill stayed with Percy A. Rockefeller (S&B), who arranged a special work area for him in his Manhattan office apartment. Percy's father, William Rockefeller, had been a close friend of Jerome, a Wall Street speculator and manipulator. [1972] Jerome and another friend, William K. Vanderbilt, helped found the American Jockey Club. Jerome, a shareholder in *The New York Times*, and another friend, August Belmont built the Jerome Park Racetrack where they held the first Belmont Stakes in 1867.

On October 24, 1929, Black Thursday, Baruch maintained close contact with his brothers at Hentz & Company brokerage firm, where he kept a secret account, known only as number 19. At the opening of the market, huge transactions began taking place, 12.9 million shares that day, in blocks of 15,000 to 20,000 shares, held in some of the biggest companies. The final assault was scheduled to take place the following Tuesday. Churchill met with Baruch at Rockefeller's office then visited the Stock Exchange at 10:45. [1973] On the day of the initial crash, referred to as Black Thursday, Churchill, perhaps like other saboteurs, apparently wanted to observe some of his handiwork. He was also present for the calamitous finale on October 29, 1929, when investors traded about 16 million shares. He witnessed the devastating panic caused by his machinations in conjunction with those of his cronies, just before leaving America, much worse off than when he arrived. [1974]

On the evening of October 29, Black Tuesday, Baruch threw a lavish party at his Fifth Avenue mansion where forty guests, Wall Street's leading bankers and financiers, held a jubilant celebration that lasted well past midnight. While regular Americans commiserated over their devastating losses, the participants in the plunge partied. MacDonald joined the festivities. There were many suicides, either immediately after the crash or within a few years. On October 30, the Churchills

[1972] Ibid. 3, 57, 72-73, 90, 113
[1973] Ibid. 116, 119
[1974] Ibid. 44-52

left on *The Berengaria*. Winston Churchill wrote, "No one who has fazed on such a scene could doubt that this financial disaster, huge as it is, cruel as it is to thousands, is only a passing episode in the march of a valiant and *serviceable people* who by fierce experiment are hewing new paths for man, and showing to all nations much that they should attempt and much that they should avoid." The so-called *serviceable people* of America fought in World War I, where at least 115,000 *serviceable* Americans perished, and 206,000 suffered serious wounds. In World War II, 294,000 *serviceable* Americans perished, and 671,000 suffered wounds; the total number of *serviceable* Americans who perished in both wars equal 409,000 and the total wounded was 877,000. [1975]

In 1929, Baruch had made repeated trips to Germany, England, and France. In September and October 1929, collaborators appropriated over $100 billion from Wall Street and other American markets. On December 6, 1929, Baruch accompanied $10 million in gold (16 tons) that bankers shipped to Lazard Frères, Guaranty Trust Company, Irving Trust, and Heidelbach Ickelheimer. Within five weeks after the crash, the bankers shipped $30 million (1929 prices) to France. After the crash, gold exports exceeded $111 million in gold, all shipped to Europe. In December 1929, $68 million went to England and France. [1976]

In 1929-1930, like 2008-2009, the banks, purportedly short on resources, refused to make loans to small companies or individuals. Yet, J. P. Morgan, First National Bank of New York, and First National Bank of Chicago sent massive amounts of money to the Bank of International Settlements (BIS) in Geneva, which ultimately helped countries prepare Europe for another war. Then the bankers systematically reduced the money supply to prolong the crises into the great depression. The middle class unavoidably defaulted on loans and the banks repossessed farms, homes and business properties. The worldwide crash and the subsequent depression functioned to

---

[1975] Pat Riott, The Greatest Story Never Told, Winston Churchill and the Crash of 1929, Nanoman Press, Oak Brook, Illinois, 1994, pp. 127, 132-133
[1976] Ibid. 136, 143-144

shift assets upwards. It caused joblessness, hunger, disintegration of production and national bankruptcies.

At the same time that banks were crunching credit and devaluing the money in circulation, they were creating the massive build-up of the military in the Soviet Union. In May 1929, during Hoover's administration, before Roosevelt officially recognized the Soviet Union, the Ford Motor Company contracted with Stalin to oversee the construction of a production facility. The Soviets agreed to order 72,000 unassembled Fords over the next decade. In February 1930, Albert E. Kahn, Inc. of Detroit, Michigan, founded by a German-born Jew who immigrated in 1880, signed an agreement with the Soviets to clone the Ford River Rouge of Detroit as part of a mega industrial complex at Gorky, which soon became a Soviet Detroit. Kahn, a brilliant industrial architect founded Albert Kahn Associates in 1895, and had designed buildings for General Motors, Packard, General Electric, Ford Motor Company's Highland Park and River Rouge plants and dozens of other American-based corporations. [1977]

On March 7, 1930, Hoover, apparently lying to alleviate the people's fears, said, "All the evidence indicates that the worst effects of the Crash upon unemployment will have passed during the next sixty days." He then signed the Smoot-Hawley Tariff Act against the advice of the thousand economists that Wall Street manipulators hired. They were concerned about the repayment of their foreign loans. Meanwhile, the Rockefeller family and others were buying huge amounts of stock. On September 16, 1930, Hoover appointed Eugene I. Meyer, Baruch's partner in his Alaska gold mining operation, as the Chairman of the Federal Reserve Board, a position he held until May 10, 1933. In 1946, he would become president of the World Bank. His father was a partner at Lazard Frères, in France. Baruch and Meyer raised the discount rate two points in two weeks. Within six weeks, United States production fell by twenty-six percent, shrinking the money base by $90 million while the bankers consolidated their

---

[1977] Antony C. Sutton, National Suicide, Military Aid to the Soviet Union, Arlington House, New Rochelle, New York, 1973, p. 70

assets and waited for the Democratic administration of Baruch-backed Franklin D. Roosevelt. [1978]

In September 1930, Baruch, after returning from visiting Churchill, sent a cable affirming his friend's views about British world supremacy. He wrote, "I better understand England and her people and her traditions and hope that new prosperity and happiness will come to her in order that she may continue for the world what she has done for so long. I trust that our country may join with yours in the great responsibility that lies before us." On December 11, 1930, New York's fourth largest bank, the Bank of the United States, failed. Its 450,000 depositors had no recourse and there was no FDIC insurance. Another 1,000 banks had already failed in 1930. [1979] In 1930, bankers exported at least $52 million from the Federal Reserve to Guaranty Trust, a company that Morgan and Lazard Frères later gobbled up. [1980]

In January 1932, Hoover, going through the appropriate motions, told Richard Whitney, the New York Stock Exchange President that he was going to convene an investigation into the crash. Thomas W. Lamont, who spoke for other bankers, told him to forget about it. He persevered, and by the third quarter of 1932, another banking crisis developed. The public did not re-elect Hoover. The bankers would now bring in Roosevelt and his New Deal. By March 8, 1932, the Dow Jones Index was down to $41.22, the bankers had wiped out nearly 90 percent of its value. Those with cash paid two cents on the dollar for equipment, farmland, and real estate—at the expense of those who had worked generations to acquire their land and assets. Meanwhile the plungers continued to strengthen their holdings. [1981] With every economic crisis, huge multinational corporations who care little about the land or the animals consume private farms and ranches. Government regulations routinely restrain the few remaining

[1978] Ibid. 151-153

[1979] Ibid. 148-151

[1980] Pat Riott, The Greatest Story Never Told, Winston Churchill and the Crash of 1929, Nanoman Press, Oak Brook, Illinois, 1994, pp. 136, 143-144

[1981] Antony C. Sutton, National Suicide, Military Aid to the Soviet Union, Arlington House, New Rochelle, New York, 1973, 1994, pp. 151-153

independent farmers and ranchers affecting their control over their own property.

Churchill toured the United States again (December 1931-March 11, 1932) to arrange support for American involvement in another war. On February 9, 1932, he delivered a speech to the New York Economic Club. His old friends sat on the podium—Baruch, Schwab, Rockefeller, Kahn, Henry Morgenthau, Samuel Seabury, Merlin H. Aylesworth, James Speyer, William C. Osborn, Nathan Miller, Raymond B. Fosdick and Karl Bickel. He thanked the United States for pouring billions of dollars into European countries since the end of World War I, and then warned about the crisis of Communism. He gave the same speech at Carnegie Hall and Constitution Hall. On February 13, 1932, he visited President Hoover and the House of Representatives. [1982] He had a strategy meeting with Carter Glass, a longtime Baruch associate who co-authored the Glass-Owen bill in 1913 with Robert L. Owen, which had led to the enactment of the Federal Reserve Act.

Meyer, Baruch, Strong, and Mellon instructed the New York Federal Reserve Board to purchase $1,100,000,000 of US Treasuries over an eleven-week period then abruptly stopped in June 1932, which halted the economic recovery to prime the people to get rid of Hoover. Hope disappeared when another 5,000 banks closed which eliminated the banker's competition. The American citizens blamed Hoover and the Republicans. The citizens readily elected Roosevelt and the Democrats controlled the country for the next two decades. [1983]

On February 27, 1933, the Dow Jones bottomed out. Baruch's candidate, Roosevelt, inaugurated on March 4, 1933, immediately closed the banks until March 15, 1933. By then, there were 15,000,000 unemployed Americans. By 1937, there would still be 11,000,000 without jobs. In 1933, fiat money replaced gold. The contrived

---

[1982] Ibid. 187-192
[1983] Ibid. 155-158

contraction of the economy was the result of the bankers shipping the gold out of the country. [1984]

Roosevelt, a thirty-second degree freemason, ordered the printing of the Illuminati seal on one dollar bills in 1933, a seal that symbolizes its claim to control of America, regardless who occupies the White House. [1985] On March 9, 1933, Roosevelt issued Executive Orders 6073, 6102, 6111, and 6260, which declared that America was bankrupt. He announced, "All the property of this country now belongs to the state and will be used for the good of the state." That evening, a joint session of Congress passed the Emergency Banking Act, amid an atmosphere of chaos and uncertainty, in less than an hour, allowing only Federal Reserve-approved banks to operate. Only Congressman Harry B. Steagall had a copy of the bill.

The Emergency Banking Act legitimized, after the fact, any regulations that the President and Treasury Secretary had issued since March 4, 1933. It allows the President to declare a national emergency and seize control of national finances. It authorized the Treasury Secretary to confiscate gold from individuals or organizations. It prohibited a bank from conducting business during a national emergency without the president's approval. It allows the Comptroller of the Currency to seize control of bank operations. It allows the FR banks to convert any US debt into cash at par value and allows Federal Reserve banks to make unsecured loans to any member bank.

Representative Carter Glass worked with Representative Henry B. Steagall to pass the Glass-Steagall Act, which Roosevelt signed on June 16, 1933, taking effect June 16, 1934. The Banking Act of 1933, conceived by the bankers, legislated and enacted by their longtime minions, separated bank types according to their activities— commercial or investment banking. In addition, the act introduced the Federal Deposit Insurance Corporation (FDIC).

[1984] Pat Riott, The Greatest Story Never Told, Winston Churchill and the Crash of 1929, Nanoman Press, Oak Brook, Illinois, 1994, pp. 159-163
[1985] Jüri Lina, Under the Sign of the Scorpion: The Rise and Fall of the Soviet Empire, Referent Publishing, Stockholm, Sweden, 2002, pp. 61-62

Republican Senators, true to the dialectical mentality, thought that Roosevelt should have done more to grant the government total control over banking. The act, they said, only provided temporary solutions to the problem. The Act divided the banks into three categories—class A banks were solvent, class B banks were marginal and mandated closure for class C banks. This act, which allowed only Federal Reserve-approved banks to operate, eliminated further competition in the industry. The public trusted Roosevelt and did not make panic runs on the banks when they reopened on March 13. His first fireside chat, written by several media-skilled people, restored a measure of confidence in the government. [1986]

On April 5, 1933, because of the stipulations in the Emergency Banking Act, Roosevelt made it illegal for citizens to own gold. He ordered people to turn in all gold coins, gold bullion, and gold certificates to the FR banks by May 1 (Illuminati was created on May 1, 1776). Baruch, the single greatest holder of gold bricks, retained possession of his gold. People faced imprisonment and fines if they failed to surrender their gold. On June 5, 1933, Congress enacted a joint resolution outlawing all gold clauses in contracts. Now the FR was free to print unlimited amounts. While the FR augmented the war in Europe, Roosevelt's activities really energized it.

Churchill and Norman had removed the English pound from the gold standard in 1931which altered world trade. In September 1931, Britain defaulted on their gold payments, intensifying the depression. Rothschild's Bank of England calculated this move to trigger another war. [1987] Roosevelt took the United States off the domestic gold standard with The Gold Reserve Act of 1934, as requested by Baruch in his meeting with the Finance Committee and the Foreign Relations Committee.

Roosevelt, with his communistic New Deal, strengthened the FR and introduced the practice of deficit spending, the brainchild of Britain's

---

[1986] Ronnie J. Phillips, The Chicago Plan & New Deal Banking Reform, M. E. Sharpe, Armonk, New York, 1995, p. 42

[1987] Charles Merlin Umpenhour, Freedom, a Fading Illusion, BookMakers Ink, West Virginia, 2005, pp. 134-136

John Maynard Keynes. In 1910, Lenin had said, "The surest way to overthrow an established social order is to debauch its currency." Keynes said, "The process engages all the hidden forces of economic law on the side of creeping socio-economic destruction, and does it in manner which not one man in a million is able to diagnose." [1988]

[1988] Peter Cook, Capitalism, Bane to Freedom & Security, M.Sc., C.M.E., New York Times of June 11, 1939; Monetary Realist, September 1991; Time Magazine March, 29, 1993

INDEX

A

Abdülhamid 25, 28-31, 36-7, 41, 43,
45, 306, 373-4, 476-7, 480-1, 486,
489-93, 496, 498, 500
abolitionists 13, 106
abortion 94, 109, 112
Abraham, Larry 243, 336, 562, 572,
582
Acre 6, 83, 166, 268, 332, 507, 515,
561, 632
Adams, John Quincy 156, 167
addiction 297-8, 302, 313
Adler, Cyrus 6, 46, 55
Admiralty 309-10, 439-40, 461, 621
Africa 8, 47, 69, 167, 230-1, 306-7,
321-7, 331-3, 377-8, 385, 422-3,
619-21, 625, 651-2, 715
Aguinaldo, Emilio 179, 183, 201, 205
Aharonson, Aharon 524-5
Alaska 560, 563, 726, 732
Albania 500, 506
Alder, Cyrus 19, 657
Aldrich Bill 282-4, 286
Aldrich, Nelson W. 122, 134, 216,
278, 633
Aleppo 297, 374, 379, 483, 508, 529,
536, 539, 542, 550
Alexander, Czar 9, 32, 369, 389, 391,
395, 397
Ali, Sherif Hussein bin 508-9
Allen, Gary 69, 336, 562, 572, 578,
582, 656
Allenby, Edmund 653, 704

Alliance Israélite Universelle 18-22,
82-3, 363, 371, 378, 399, 492, 657
Alsace-Lorraine 660, 678
American Bar Association 107, 643
American Board of Commissioners
482, 713
American Eugenics Society 109, 112
American Historical Association ix,
77, 523, 637
American Jewish Committee 14, 55-
6, 274, 339, 629, 631
American Psychological Association
(APA) 72, 75, 255, 638
American Relief 463, 637
American Sugar Refining 125-7, 131-
2, 153-4
Amery, Leopold M. 408, 652
Amsterdam 27, 293, 387, 413
Anatolia 43, 374-5, 478-81, 483-4,
494, 506, 541, 543, 548, 554
Anatolian Railway 375-6, 379, 500
Anglo-Jewish 21, 38, 401, 410, 651
Anglo-Palestine Bank 51-2
Anglo-Saxon 175, 227, 659
annexation 139-44, 146-8, 151, 168-
9, 174, 180-1, 184, 346, 351, 359,
429, 433, 502, 616, 676
Ankara 478, 537-8, 544, 549, 553
anti-Semitism 1, 19, 24-5, 34-5, 44,
53, 55, 85, 87, 94, 99, 395-6, 411,
592, 611-12
Antwerp 27, 193
Arab 47-8, 305, 377, 500-1, 505, 508-
9, 529, 624-5, 655, 701, 704-7

Dilling, Elizabeth 23, 74, 583
Dillon, Douglas C. 232-3
Disraeli, Benjamin 18, 304, 390, 459, 507
Dodge, Cleveland H. 416, 418, 425, 441
Dominican Republic 167-70
Donghak 343, 345
Dugdale, Blanche 627, 652
Dulles, John Foster 143, 667, 672, 687, 689
DuPont 229, 261, 264, 362, 402, 442, 559, 729

E

East India Company 19, 296-7, 307, 713
Eastern Europe 2, 32, 56, 58, 80-1, 83-5, 96, 99, 113, 117, 120, 265, 501, 505, 630-1
Ebert, Friedrich 517, 603, 609, 612, 671, 675, 684
Economic Warfare 237, 670, 723-4
Educational Alliance 83-4
Egypt 28, 304-7, 429, 484, 489, 505, 508, 511, 545, 704
Einstein, Albert 46, 104
Eisner, Kurt 608, 611-12, 616
Elihu Root 74, 123, 125, 136-7, 164, 181, 190, 205, 219, 233, 359, 385, 417, 464, 581
Eliot, Charles W. 70, 254
Elkus, Abram I. 57, 421, 524
emancipation 8-9, 19, 21, 24-5, 106, 120, 307, 364, 369, 371, 389-91, 406
embargo 318-19, 425

Emergency Banking Act 735-6
emigration 25, 31, 78, 81, 83, 382-3, 398
Engdahl, F. William 312, 691
Engels, Friedrich 23, 116, 306, 487
England xii, 6-8, 12-14, 228-9, 233-4, 263-4, 280, 333-5, 371-3, 389-90, 410, 462-6, 650-4, 657-8, 725
enlightenment 4, 6, 19, 398
Enver, Ismail 497, 499-502, 518, 525-6, 545, 549
epidemic 193-4, 555
equal rights 222, 431, 479, 490
Equitable Life 134, 238
Eretz Israel 29, 32, 34
Erzberger, Matthias 604-5, 609, 644, 664
Estonia 89, 597, 648
Etting, Solomon 17, 19
Europe 12-14, 55-6, 79-81, 83-5, 374-5, 380-2, 430, 472-3, 583-5, 595-6, 618, 630-2, 638-9, 659, 662-4
Executive Committee 54-7, 68, 119, 171, 226, 238, 257-8, 393, 591, 595, 631-2, 695, 722
expansionism 145, 148, 157, 180, 239, 540
extermination xii, 108, 158-9, 208-10, 523, 525, 527, 542-5, 557, 599, 601

F

Freedman, Benjamin H. 2, 5, 47
Fabian 63, 66, 73, 231, 408-9, 415, 661, 707
Federal Council of Churches 61, 64, 66

G

H

Harrison, Benjamin   124, 141, 199, 279

Harrison, George L.   690-1

Harrison, William H.   141, 235, 300

Hart-Celler   99-100

Harvard   63, 72, 76, 106, 108, 135, 144, 180, 186-7, 192, 232-3, 254, 284, 354, 718-19

Harvey, George W.   416, 420

Haskalah   4-5, 33-4

Havana   148, 155-6, 159-60, 182

Havemeyer   122-9, 131-2, 154

Havemeyer, Henry O.   122-3, 127-8

Havemeyer, Theodore A.   127-8

hawaii   128, 137-48, 151, 174, 176-7, 180, 184, 192, 235, 359, 714

Hay, John   137, 163, 165, 170, 175, 234, 243, 349

Hazard Circular   240, 288

Hearst, William Randolph   160, 728

Hebron   5, 51

Hechler, William H.   25, 29

Hegelian   24, 70

hemp   166, 201, 203-4, 206, 219, 221, 290, 381, 468

heroin   123, 221, 717

Herter, Christian A.   336, 637

Herzl, Theodor   23-4, 30, 35-6, 47-8, 53, 95, 505, 618, 650, 702

Hess, Moses   5, 23

Hibbat Zion   32-4

Hill, James J.   133, 240, 558

Hindenburg, Paul von   610, 615, 648

Hirohito   339, 357, 710

Hirohito, Emperor   357, 710

Hitler, Adolf   93, 432, 612, 688

Holland   7, 18, 79, 312, 322, 368, 378, 389, 454, 467, 630, 692

Holocaust   x-xi, xiv, 1, 47, 103, 450, 546, 551, 553, 556, 628-9, 631, 633-5, 642

Holocaust Memorial Museum   xi, 553, 634

Holy Land   6, 8, 12-13, 45, 389-90, 532, 700

homeland   5, 9, 23, 30, 32, 55, 58, 95, 449, 484, 498, 505, 508, 692, 694-5

Homeopathy   249, 252

Homestead Strike   246, 271

Honduras   166, 359, 437, 670

Hong Kong   179, 181-3, 198, 205, 223, 227, 254, 297-9, 301-2, 319, 332, 692-3, 713-14, 716-17, 722

Honolulu   142, 182, 184

Hoover, Herbert   xv, 120, 260, 326, 329-30, 333-4, 337, 447, 462, 464, 474, 564, 566, 637-8, 640

Hopkins, Johns   72-4, 227, 250, 252, 257-8, 261, 415, 658

House, Edward M.   68, 226, 335, 416, 419, 428, 430, 461, 469, 512, 569, 622, 625-6, 655, 660

House Judiciary Committee   100, 457

House of Representatives   84, 128, 144, 218, 265, 285-6, 291-2, 531, 534-5, 541, 553-7, 564, 568, 696, 734

Hovevei   33-4

Hudson's Bay Company   90, 716

Hull, Cordell   100, 568

Hungary   32, 82, 257, 315, 366, 372, 375, 389, 429, 431-2, 436, 596-600, 612-13, 644-8, 677-8

hyperinflation   684, 687

I

J

M

O

P

Z